FEARLESS WOMAN

FEARLESS WOMAN

HANNA SHEEHY SKEFFINGTON, FEMINISM AND THE IRISH REVOLUTION

Margaret Ward

UNIVERSITY COLLEGE DUBLIN PRESS
PREAS CHOLÁISTE OLLSCOILE BHAILE ÁTHA CLIATH
2019

First published 2019
by University College Dublin Press
UCD Humanities Institute, Room H103,
Belfield,
Dublin 4
www.ucdpress.ie

ISBN 978-1-910820-40-7 pb

CIP data available from the British Library

1 3 5 7 9 10 8 6 4 2

Text design by Lyn Davies

Printed in Spain on acid-free paper by GraphyCems

Contents

Illustrations between pages 160 and 161, and between pages 320 and 321

To Rory and Finn

Acknowledgements

When the first edition of my biography of Hanna Sheehy Skeffington was published in 1997 the late Róisín Conroy of Attic Press was a source of huge encouragement to me. I wish to acknowledge her legacy as a publisher, feminist activist, trade unionist and archivist of the women's movement. Ailbhe Smyth, in her former capacity as Director of the Women's Education, Research and Resource Centre at UCD, invited me as guest speaker in sufficient time to ensure I could access the necessary archives in Dublin. I will always be grateful to her.

The presence of Andrée Sheehy Skeffington in the early years of my research was a privilege and a continual reminder of the enduring links between past and present in the history of Irish feminism. Her daughter Micheline has been a generous and unfailing source of support. Her dedication to upholding the Sheehy Skeffington tradition has ensured that Dublin Castle has a plaque testifying to suffrage militancy and the work of her grandmother. The role of Irish suffragettes in fighting for women's equality can now never be forgotten. The late David Sheehy and Ronan O'Casey provided me with memories of their aunt Hanna and the Sheehy Skeffington family have been extremely generous with their time, both in providing information for the family tree and in supplying family photographs.

Mary McCoy, great granddaughter of Hanna's uncle, Patrick McCoy, is also a custodian of family history and I am most appreciative of her interest and her invaluable information on the McCoy family.

The family of Eva Stephenson Wilkins – Caroline Byrne, granddaughter of Roddy Wilkins and Paula Smith, granddaughter of Patricia Wilkins (with Malcolm Smith as conduit) – provided vital material regarding their grandmother.

I thank Keith Munro, great-nephew of Margaret Cousins, for his generosity in sharing information on Margaret Cousins and for his photo of Margaret and James Cousins.

Micheál Casey generously shared his knowledge of Meg Connery.

As a former Visiting Research Fellow and now Honorary Senior Lecturer with the School of History, Anthropology, Politics and Philosophy at Queen's University, I am deeply grateful to the support from Yvonne Galligan and Alister Miskimmon in facilitating this position, which has provided me with library access and enabled me to take part in aspects of academic life with colleagues Marie Coleman, Fearghal McGarry, Darragh Gannon and Peter Gray.

Over the years it has been my pleasure to meet a new generation of scholars of women's history while also appreciating the contributions of some veterans: Lauren Arrington, Catriona Beaumont, Grainne Blair, John Borgonovo, Rosemary Cullen Owens, James Curry, Brenda Collins, Linda Connolly, Donna Gilligan, Karen Fitzgerald, Myrtle Hill, Lucy Keaveney, Leeann Lane, Sinéad McCoole, Margaret MacCurtain, Mary McAuliffe, Lucy McDiarmid, Clare McGing, Eve Morrison, William Murphy, Senia Paŝeta, Nell Regan, Louise Ryan, Rosemary Raughter, Sonja Tiernan, and Helga Woggon.

For the first and this edition, I am indebted to the help given to me by many librarians and archivists: Mary Broderick, James Harte, Colette O'Flaherty, Berni Metcalfe of the National Library of Ireland and Barbara Bonini of the National Photographic Archive, NLI; Catriona Crowe, formerly of National Archives of Ireland; staff at the University College Dublin archives; National Museum of Ireland; Susan Schreibman and the Letters 1916 project; Queen's University of Belfast; the Public Record Office of Northern Ireland; Fianna Fáil Party archives; Haddo House Estate; the Women's Library, London; the Hoover Institution, Stanford, California; US National Archives, Washington DC; Richard Dabb, picture researcher at the Museum of London.

The anonymous readers at UCD Press provided comments that have improved the book in many ways. Noelle Moran of UCD Press has been a scrupulous copy editor and supportive presence, whose attention to detail is greatly appreciated. I would also like to thank Conor Graham and Ruth Hallinan of UCD Press for their assistance.

Friends can never be thanked enough: Marie Abbott, Lynn Carvill, Martina Devlin, Ann Dullaghan, Mike and Orla Farrell, Maggie Feeley, Ann Hope, Ann Hegarty, Marilyn Hyndman, Roisín McDonough, Marie-Thérèse McGivern, Joanna McMinn, Monica McWilliams, Paul Nolan, John O'Neill, Bill Rolston, Mike Tomlinson, and Margy Washbrook.

I am ever grateful to my husband Paddy Hillyard for his love, forbearance and support, and to the rest of the family – Medbh, Gavin, Rachael and, of course, Rory and Finn – thank you.

Margaret Ward, May 2019

List of Illustrations

Family Tree of Hanna Sheehy Skeffington

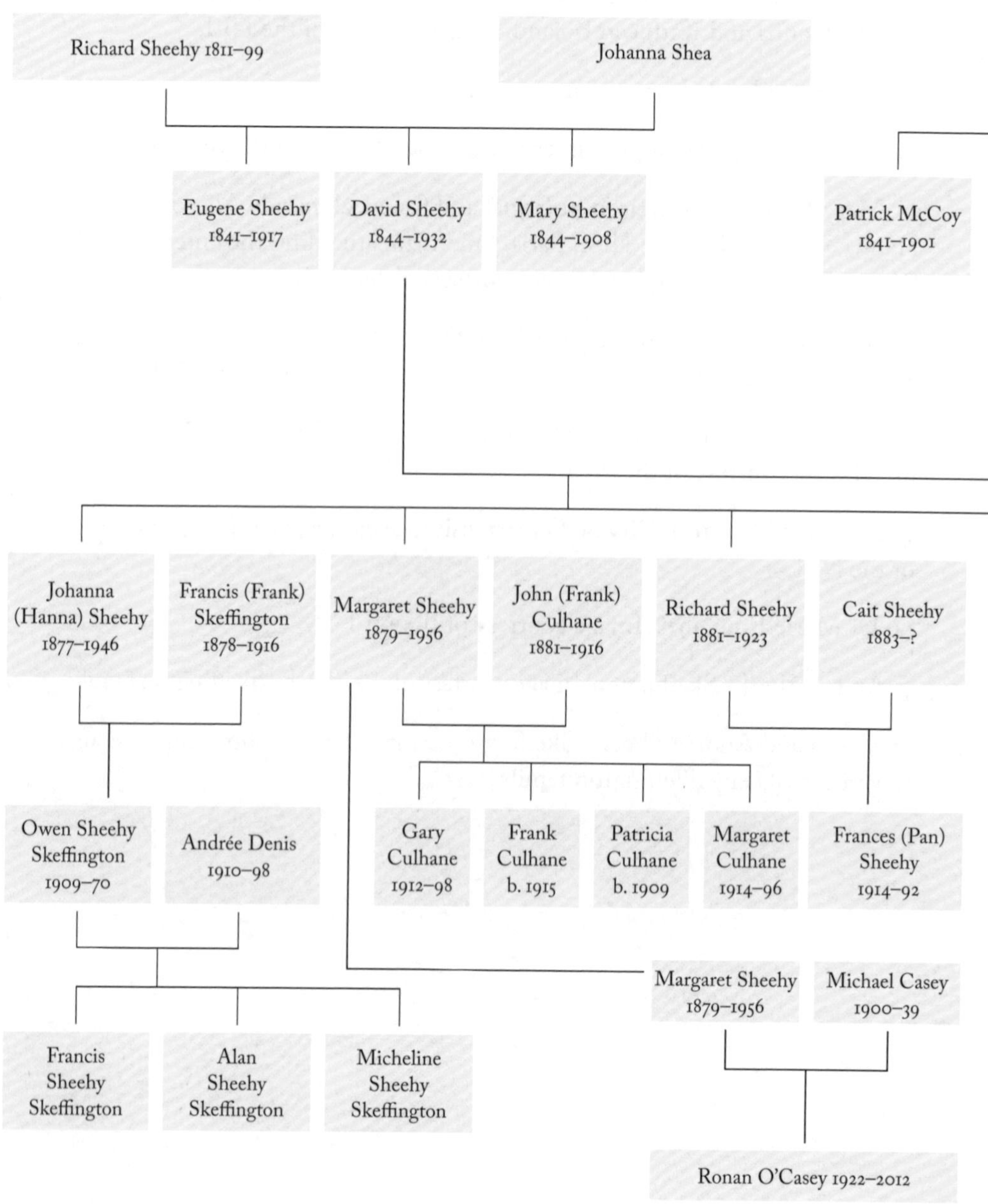

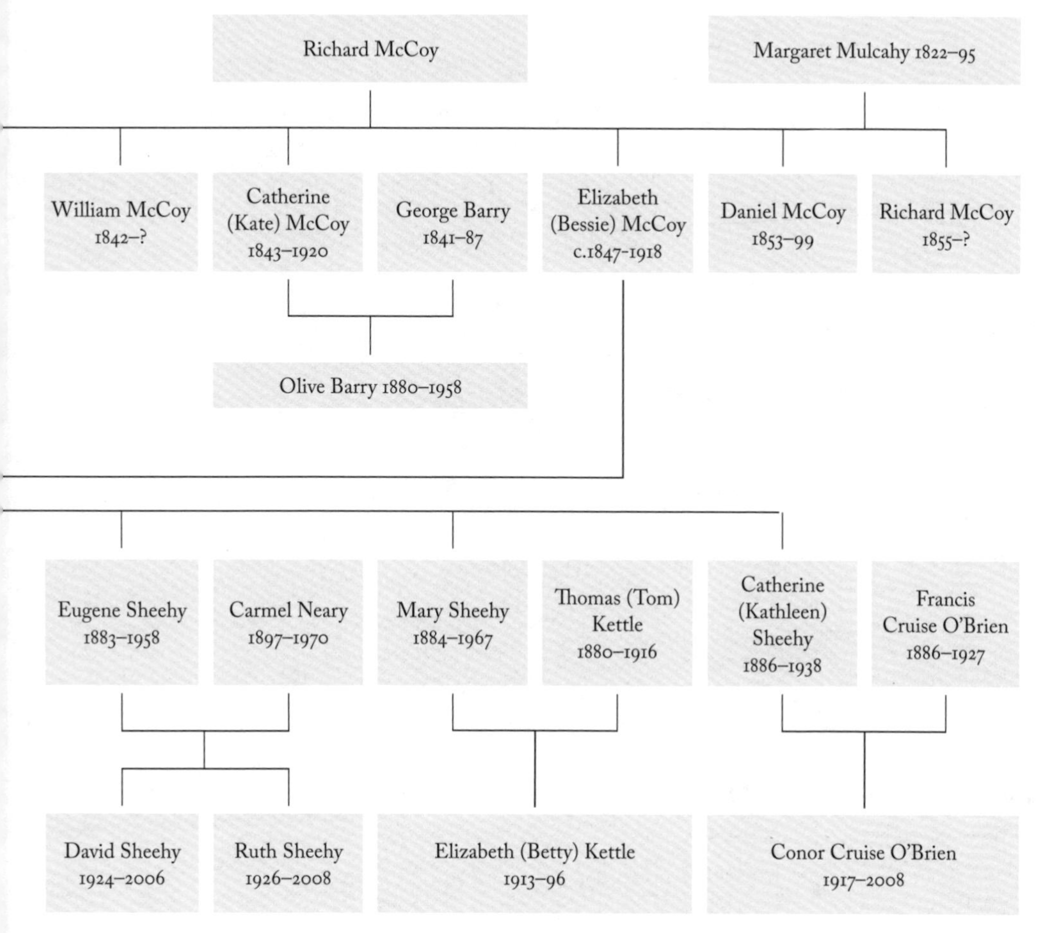

* A special thank you to Paddy Hillyard, Mary McCoy and Micheline Sheehy Skeffington for assistance on the creation of the Family Tree.

Hanna Sheehy Skeffington's Life and Times

1877

Birth of Hanna Sheehy, 24 May, Kanturk, County Cork, to David and Bessie (née McCoy) Sheehy.

1879

The wettest year on record affects harvest, creating rural distress. The Royal University, a new examining body with university status, is established. The Irish National Land League is founded by Charles Stewart Parnell and Michael Davitt. Margaret Sheehy born.

1880

The land war intensifies. First meeting of the Ladies' Land League, founded by Fanny Parnell, in New York, starts to collect funds.

1881

Ladies' Land League launched in Ireland with Anna Parnell as organising secretary. Land League proclaimed an illegal organisation and prisoners include Fr Eugene Sheehy. Birth of Richard (Dick) Sheehy.

1882

Parnell, Davitt and other Land League leaders released. Ladies' Land League dissolved. Death of Fanny Parnell. Birth of Eugene Sheehy.

1884

Nine women become the first to receive degrees from the Royal University of Ireland. Mary Sheehy born.

1885

Dominicans begin teaching university classes for women in Eccles Street. Royal College of Surgeons admits women.

1886

Gladstone introduces the First Home Rule bill. Isabella Tod, founder of first Irish suffrage group in 1872 in Belfast, organises protests against Home Rule. David Sheehy amongst those arrested and charged with criminal conspiracy when supporting tenant farmers in Plan of Campaign. Birth of Kathleen Sheehy, youngest of Sheehy children.

1887

Municipal franchise granted to women ratepayers in Belfast. Sheehy family move to Dublin.

1890

Irish Parliamentary Party splits over the issue of Parnell's relationship with Katherine O'Shea. David Sheehy opposes Parnell.

1893

Gaelic League formed. Gladstone introduces Second Home Rule bill.

1896

Women Poor Law Guardians (Ireland) Act passed. The *Shan Van Vocht*, published in Belfast by Alice Milligan and Anna Johnston first appears, continuing until 1899.

1898

Local Government (Ireland) Act allows women to become rural district and urban district councillors.

1899

First issue of the *United Irishman*, edited by Arthur Griffith and funded by Maud Gonne, appears in March, runs until 1906. Hanna receives B.A. degree in Modern Languages. Meets Francis (Frank) Skeffington.

1900

Irish Parliamentary Party reunites and John Redmond is elected leader. United Irish League becomes constituency organisation of the party. Queen Victoria visits Ireland and women organise Patriotic Children's Treat in protest. Inghinidhe na hÉireann subsequently formed as first woman-only nationalist organisation. Hanna spends time in Paris as an au pair to Pannier family. Travels also in Germany.

1902

Hanna receives M.A. degree with First Class Honours. Petition for woman suffrage organised by Esther Roper and signed by women graduates, including Hanna, presented to House of Commons in May. Women Graduates' and

Candidates' Association formed. Hanna becomes member of the Women's Suffrage and Local Government Association, publishes 'Women and the university question' and starts work as part-time language teacher. Frank Skeffington appointed lay registrar for University College Dublin.

1903

Hanna marries Frank Skeffington on 27 June. They take the joint surname 'Sheehy Skeffington'. The Pankhursts form the Women's Social and Political Union as militant suffrage organisation. David Sheehy defeats John Howard Parnell in Meath South by-election. Report of the Robertson Commission recommends restructuring Royal University.

1904

Women admitted to Trinity College, Dublin. Frank Sheehy Skeffington resigns post of registrar as protest against unequal status of women. Young Ireland Branch (YIBs) of the Irish Parliamentary Party formed. James Joyce meets his future wife, Nora Barnacle.

1905

Hanna, Mary and Kathleen Sheehy join the YIBs. First Convention of Sinn Féin held.

1906

Hanna and Jennie Wyse Power resign from committee of Irish Women's Suffrage and Local Government Association (IWSLGA).

1907

Margaret Sheehy marries John F. (Frank) Culhane.

1908

Inghinidhe na hÉireann launch their journal *Bean na hÉireann*. Irish Universities Act abolishes the Royal University and leads to formation of National University of Ireland with colleges in Dublin, Cork, Galway and Belfast. It gives equal status (but not resources) to women in higher education. Hanna and Mary Hayden publish 'Women in universities: A reply'. Irish Women's Franchise League (IWFL) formed in Dublin in November with Hanna and Margaret (Gretta) Cousins as founding members. Frank Skeffington ill with diptheria. Hanna and Frank move to Grosvernor Place, Rathmines.

1909

Owen Sheehy Skeffington born on 19 May. Hanna delivers lecture on 'Women and the National Movement' and her article 'Sinn Féin and Irishwomen' is published in *Bean na hÉireann.* Hanna is part of IWFL delegation meeting with John Redmond, Irish Party leader. Irish Women's Suffrage Society is formed in Belfast and Irish branch of the Conservative and Unionist Women's Suffrage Association formed in Dublin. Fianna Éireann formed by Constance Markievicz and Bulmer Hobson. Mary Sheehy marries Tom Kettle. Rose Skeffington dies.

1910

Hanna is part of Irish suffrage delegation when Conciliation bill is before House of Commons in June. Irish Parliamentary Party hold balance of power as Prime Minister Asquith leads minority Liberal government. Hanna is one of the speakers on Irish Platform at Hyde Park suffrage demonstration and part of deputation to see Redmond. Hanna and Hilda Webb heckle Chief Secretary Birrell in Greystones, the first act of militancy. Hanna and others in IWFL heckle Edward Carson at Rathmines meeting. Mrs Pankhurst tours Ireland in the autumn. Six IWFL members imprisoned in Holloway Jail after taking part in 'Black Friday' petition to House of Commons.

1911

Hanna sees Constance Markievicz, for the first time, acting in *Eleanor's Enterprise* at Gaiety Theatre. The Local Government (Ireland) Act enables Irish women to become members of county and borough councils. Suffragists evade 'census night' in April. Helena Molony of Inghinidhe na hÉireann arrested after protesting against King's visit to Dublin. Hanna, Delia Larkin and Constance Markievicz speak at inaugural meeting of Irish Women Workers' Union. Five more IWFL members imprisoned in Holloway Jail. Dublin Corporation, Cork, Limerick, Pembroke, Galway, Bray, Portrush and Newry councils pass resolutions in favour of women's suffrage. Irish Women's Suffrage Federation formed to link together non-militant groups. Ulster Women's Unionist Council founded. Death of Anna Parnell. Dr J. B. Skeffington re-marries. Kathleen Sheehy marries Francis Cruise O'Brien.

1912

Hanna and Meg Connery join Belfast suffragists in heckling Winston Churchill. Irish Party votes kill another Conciliation bill. Asquith introduces third Home Rule bill. IWFL members attacked by the Ancient Order of Hibernians (AOH) on 'Home Rule Day'. Hanna resigns from Young Ireland Branch. Sarah Cecilia Harrison elected to Dublin Corporation and Dr Mary Strangman to Waterford Council. First edition of *Irish Citizen* published 25 May. Mass meeting of women calls for Home Rule for Irishwomen. 13 June first act of militancy by 8 eight members of IWFL. Hanna imprisoned for window smashing, hunger strikes and is dismissed from teaching at Rathmines College of Commerce. Three English WSPU members imprisoned in Dublin for attacking Asquith and Redmond. Hanna's article 'Irish secondary teachers' published in the *Irish Review* in October. IWFL and Inghinidhe na hÉireann collaborate on School Meals campaign until School Meals (Ireland) Act passed in 1914. In November Snowden amendment to Home Rule bill to include women defeated by vote of Irish Party.

1913

In January three IWFL members sent to Tullamore Prison for one month and begin hunger strike. In May three further IWFL prisoners given six-month sentences and sent to Tullamore, released under 'Cat and Mouse Act' but not re-arrested. Margaret and James Cousins leave Ireland. Hanna and Frank speak in Ormeau Park, Belfast. In autumn Dublin Lock Out begins; soup kitchen organised in Liberty Hall supported by suffragists. Irish Citizen Army founded. IWFL moves to premises in Westmoreland Street. Hanna arrested and receives seven-day prison sentence in Mountjoy Jail for leafletting Bonar Law and Sir Edward Carson. Released after hunger strike. Irish Volunteers formed as nationalist response to Ulster Volunteer Force.

1914

Hanna and Meg Connery tour Longford, Leitrim and Roscommon. Daffodil fête includes 'Great Women of the Past' tableaux, with Constance Markievicz as Joan of Arc and staging of Frank's suffrage play *The Prodigal Daughter*. Cumann na mBan formed as women's auxiliary to Irish Volunteers. Home Rule bill passed in House of Commons. WSPU militancy begins in north as war declared on Ulster Unionists with Ulster Centre of WSPU established in Belfast. Kathleen Houston last IWFL prisoner, given six-week sentence. Joint Irish suffrage delegation to Westminster with Hanna, Margaret McCoubrey from Belfast and Dora Mellone from Warrenpoint. First World War begins in August. *Irish Citizen* headlines 'Votes for Women Now – Damn Your War!' IWFL sets up 'Ulster Centre' in Belfast after WSPU pull out of Ireland. Hanna thrown out of Redmond meeting in Wexford. Hanna and Meg Connery briefly arrested when leafletting Asquith recruitment meeting in Dublin. Home Rule Act suspended for duration of the war.

1915

Women's International Peace Congress held in The Hague and Women's International League for Peace formed. Hanna, Margaret McCoubrey, Lilian Metge and Louie Bennett all refused permission to travel to the Congress. IWFL organise protest meeting in Dublin, with support from Patrick Pearse and Thomas MacDonagh of Irish Volunteers. Frank Skeffington is given prison sentence for his anti-recruitment speeches and released under 'Cat and

Mouse Act' after hunger and thirst strike. Goes to America until December. Hanna takes over editorship of *Irish Citizen*. She attends funeral of Fenian O'Donovan Rossa. Irish Catholic Women's Association established in Dublin. David Sheehy declared bankrupt and he and Bessie leave Belvedere Place.

1916

Frank Skeffington debates with Constance Markievicz 'Do We Want Peace Now?' Easter Rising begins 24 April and ends with unconditional surrender on 29 April. Hanna brings supplies and messages to GPO and College of Surgeons on second day of rising while Frank attempts to set up citizen's militia to prevent looting. After his arrest by military he is executed on order of Captain Bowen-Colthurst who is found guilty but insane at court-martial. Hanna meets Prime Minister Asquith and urges full inquiry into murder. Royal Commission conducted by Sir John Simon convened in August. John Culhane, husband of sister Margaret, dies. Tom Kettle killed at Somme. Hanna and son Owen leave for America in December.

1917

Hanna's first public meeting held in Carnegie Hall, New York on 6 January. She speaks at 250 meetings in 21 states. After America enters the war in April Hanna is kept under surveillance by Department of Justice and War Department and some meetings banned. Her pamphlet *British Militarism as I Have Known It*, is published. League of Women Delegates formed by republican women, becomes Cumann na dTeachtaire. All remaining 120 Irish political prisoners, including Constance Markievicz, released. At Sinn Féin Convention four women are elected onto executive. Father Eugene Sheehy dies in July.

1918

Hanna attends debate in Congress on 9th Amendment to Constitution, which removes sex disabilities in federal voting. She meets President Wilson and presents him with Cumann na mBan Memorial on Irish Freedom. In the British parliament the Representation of the People Act enfranchises all men over 21 and grants the vote to women in Britain and Ireland over 30, with property qualifications. Hanna gives her last speech in America at 'Irish Peace Convention', Madison Square Garden on 4 May. Anti-conscription protest organised throughout Ireland in April with women's organisations uniting on 1 June for Lá na mBan. One hundred republicans arrested in so-called 'German Plot' arrests, including Kathleen Clarke, Maud Gonne MacBride and Constance Markievicz. Hanna leaves United States with Owen, Margaret Skinnider and Nora Connolly on 27 June, is detained in Liverpool on arrival and refused permission to travel to Ireland. In August smuggles herself back to Dublin, is arrested, sent to Holloway Jail and released after hunger-strike. IWFL hosts a welcome home reception. Hanna applies for membership of Sinn Féin and is elected onto executive. Hands money collected in America to Michael Collins. Moves into new home on Belgrave Road. Great War ends 11 November. IWFL and Cumann na mBan campaign for imprisoned Countess Markievicz in General Election. Hanna refuses to stand for unwinnable seat in North Antrim. Sinn Féin win 73 out of 105 seats. Markievicz is first woman elected to parliament. Winifred Carney in Belfast, only other female candidate, is defeated. Death of Bessie Sheehy.

1919

Dáil Éireann meets for first time on 21 January. War of Independence begins. Hanna refused passport to attend Congress of Women's International League for Peace in Zurich, which is attended by Louie Bennett. She speaks at meetings throughout Ireland and in Scotland and England. Co-edits *Irish Citizen* with Louie Bennett. Dáil Éireann declared illegal in September and ministers, including Countess Markievicz, on the run. Hanna clubbed by police at meeting in Kilbeggan, suffering head injury. Hanna and other women appointed judges in underground 'republican courts'. Dr Kathleen Lynn opens St Ultan's children's hospital in Dublin. Death of Dr J. B. Skeffington.

1920

Forty-two women elected to local government; Hanna elected to Dublin Corporation and Mary Sheehy Kettle elected to Rathmines Council. Hanna becomes Director of Organisation for Sinn Féin. Black and Tans arrive in Ireland as reinforcements for the police. Hanna's house is raided by military and police. Hanna publicises atrocities suffered by women from Crown forces. Last issue of *Irish Citizen* appears in September before raid by Black and Tans smashes typeface. Government of Ireland Act partitions Ireland, setting up six-county Parliament in the north.

1921

Funds received from American Committee for Relief in Ireland results in establishment of the Irish White Cross. Sinn Féin members elected to Second Dáil Éireann include six women. Parliament of Northern Ireland meets, attended by Unionists only. Hanna and Meg Connery travel to London as members of Irish Women's Deputation to the Dominion Premiers. In July a Truce between British and Sinn Féin called. Prisoners, including Markievicz, released. Negotiations with British government begin. Articles of Agreement between Ireland and Great Britain signed in London. Dáil Éireann meets to debate the Treaty, adjourning for Christmas.

1922

Dáil Éireann accepts the Treaty by 64 votes to 57. Éamon de Valera resigns as President and Arthur Griffith elected new President. Cumann na mBan votes against Treaty and pro-Treaty women form Cumann na Saoirse. Hanna part of delegation of suffragists leafletting Dáil as Deputy Kate O'Callaghan introduces unsuccessful motion for women over 21 to have franchise before Treaty voted upon. Shelling of Four Courts on 28 June signals start of Civil War. Hanna amongst group of women who meet, unsuccessfully, to speak to leaders. Free State Constitution published in June gives all adults over the age of 21 the vote. Women's Prisoners' Defence League formed. Hanna speaks at protest meetings in Derry and Belfast. Hanna, Kathleen Boland and Linda Kearns travel to America as 'Irish Women's Mission', raising $123,000 for prisoners and their families. James Joyce publishes *Ulysses* in Paris. Arthur Griffith dies of brain haemorrhage and Michael Collins is shot in ambush. Margaret Sheehy Culhane re-marries and she and husband emigrate to Canada.

1923

Civil War ends in May. Hanna leaves the United States. She is given a contract by the American paper, the *Irish World*, as 'special correspondent'. Sinn Féin re-organises. In June Hanna is dismissed from post of examiner for Intermediate Board because of political views and opposition to Oath of Allegiance. In November sent by de Valera to Paris to protest Irish Free State application to League of Nations but is unsuccessful. Dick Sheehy dies of TB.

1924

Hanna speaks for Sinn Féin around countryside and campaigns against Free State candidate in Limerick by-election. All prisoners released in July. Juries Act starts process of removing women from juries. Dublin Corporation dissolved. National Council of Women in Ireland formed to promote cooperation amongst women interested in social welfare.

1925

Hanna elected to Dublin County Council. *An Phoblacht* begins publication as organ for republicans. Civil Service Regulation Act gives government power to exclude women from civil service exams. Matrimonial Act outlaws divorce.

1926

Sinn Féin splits over question of abstention from Free State institutions. Fianna Fáil formed with Hanna one of six women appointed to its executive. She takes leading role in protests against Seán O'Casey's *The Plough and the Stars*. She attends International Women's Suffrage Congress in Paris and visits James Joyce. In July Women's International League for Peace and Freedom has congress in Dublin with 150 delegates. Hanna gives report on situation in Ireland. She is served with Order barring her from entering Northern Ireland.

1927

Fianna Fáil poll three seats less than Cumann na nGaedheal in June election. Women protest against Juries bill effectively removing women from jury service. Minister for Justice Kevin O'Higgins assassinated. Constance Markievicz dies, and Hanna is appointed executor of her estate. Fianna Fáil enters Dáil and Hanna resigns from the executive and from the party. Owen becomes a language student in Trinity College Dublin. Francis Cruise O'Brien dies of a heart attack.

1928

Hanna campaigns against the prospect of a censorship act being introduced. Act abolishes the right to referendum under the Free State Constitution. Owen spends the summer with the family of Germaine Fontaine in France. While in London Hanna meets with George Bernard Shaw (who was awarded Nobel Prize for Literature in 1926) and attends the trial of Radclyffe Hall's *Well of Loneliness*.

1929

Censorship of Publications Act passed in July. Hanna stops writing for the *Irish World* and starts to write for *An Phoblacht*. Juries Protection Act passed. Hanna and Rosamond Jacob attend Sixth Congress of Women's International League for Peace and Freedom, held in Prague. Hanna speaks in Dresden on theme of 'A world without war' and she becomes Secretary of the Friends of Soviet Russia.

1930

Hanna travels to Russia as part of six-member Irish delegation of Friends of Soviet Russia that includes Charlotte Despard. Later she gives several speeches on Russia to groups in Dublin. Speaks in Dublin on International Women's Day, 8 March.

1931

Hanna speaks in Paris and London for St Patrick's Day celebrations. Martial law in existence with Public Safety Act. Hanna working with Women's Prisoners' Defence Committee to support prisoners and to challenge Free State. *An Phoblacht* suppressed and Frank Ryan, editor, arrested. Hanna is editor of new paper, *Republican File*. First National Aid Association formed to support republicans forced out of employment. Maud Gonne MacBride is chair and Hanna and Charlotte Despard made treasurers.

1932

Hanna continues editorship of republican papers until prisoners released in March. Women's Prisoners' Defence Committee hold weekly protest meetings until election. Fianna Fáil wins general election and de Valera forms first Fianna Fáil government as Seventh Dáil assembles. Military tribunals suspended and Oath of Allegiance removed. Marriage bar for married women teachers introduced and extended to all women in the civil service. Mary Sheehy Kettle honoured by women for her long public service. Armistice Day protests by republicans led by Frank Ryan. Death of Mrs Pearse. Hanna challenges de Valera's portrayal of Markievicz as a philanthropist rather than revolutionary. Death of David Sheehy.

1933

Hanna travels to Newry to speak on behalf of imprisoned Cumann na mBan members and is arrested for defying Banning Order. After 15 day's detention she is sentenced to 1 month in Armagh Jail, returning to civic receptions in Drogheda and Dundalk and public meeting in Dublin. IWFL hold supper party on her behalf. Hanna and Frank Ryan resign from *An Phoblacht*. Communist Party of Ireland re-established. Connolly House and Charlotte Despard's house in Eccles Street attacked by the right. Despard moves to Belfast. Owen Sheehy Skeffington appointed lecturer in French at TCD.

1934

Hanna wins libel action against *Catholic Herald* who had stated she received a pension from the British government. Travels to America and Canada for a third lecture tour, returning January 1935. Criminal Law Amendment Act bans importation of contraceptives.

1935

Wedding of Owen Sheehy Skeffington and Andrée Denis in France. Hanna speaks at meeting at Minerva Club while travelling through London. Conditions of Employment bill passed, with Section 16 restricting numbers of women in industrial employment. Joint Committee of Women's Societies and Social Workers formed (chaired by Mary Kettle). Hanna speaks at women's protest meeting in Mansion House. Criminal Law Amendment Act forbids the importation of contraceptives and raises the age of consent to 17. De Valera declares IRA an illegal organisation and *An Phoblacht* suppressed.

1936

Spanish Civil War begins. Eoin O'Duffy leads Blueshirt followers to Spain and Frank Ryan leads republicans to fight in the International Brigade in support of the republican government. Irish Friends of the Spanish Republic formed. Hanna chairs Women's Aid Committee. Fourth reprint of *British Militarism as I Have Known It*. Her article 'Women in the Free State: A stocktaking' reveals low numbers of women in public life. Hanna and Miss Montgomery attend launch of International Peace Campaign in Brussels as Irish delegates for Women's International League. De Valera abolishes Irish senate. Joint Committee of Women's Societies begin their lobbying campaign.

1937

De Valera meets Joint Committee on 29 January but no outcome. Hanna gives talk on Irish Women Writers at Minerva Club, London. Hanna and Linda Kearns record two radio programmes on women voters and women police. 21st anniversary of murder of Frank. Hanna is given half brick from wall in Portobello barracks where Frank was shot. De Valera publishes draft constitution and all women's organisations lobby against. Passed by Dáil and by referendum it comes into force in December. Women's Social and Progressive League formed in November; committee members include Mary Hayden, Mary Kettle and Hanna.

1938

Owen Sheehy Skeffington treated for TB in Switzerland. Hanna goes to America and Canada for last lecture tour. Women's Social and Progressive League circulate 'Open letter to women voters' for 1938 General Election. Three women returned to Dáil; none of them feminists. Kathleen Sheehy Cruise O'Brien dies following a stroke. Michael Casey dies, and Margaret Sheehy Casey returns to Ireland.

1939

Hanna returns in May from Canada and is in Paris in August, watching preparations for war. Owen, cured of TB, returns to Ireland. Hanna becomes member of Dublin Anti-War Committee and resumes part-time teaching in technical colleges. Kathleen Clarke elected first female Lord Mayor of Dublin. Second World War begins. De Valera announces 'Éire' would be neutral.

1940

Hanna takes her first plane trip, a day excursion to the west of Ireland. Frank Ryan, captured in Spain, is sent back to Germany while attempting to reach Ireland. Hanna publishes tributes to her friends, former British Labour MP George Lansbury and the anarchist Emma Goldman, following their deaths in May and August. First issue of *The Bell* is published, edited first by Seán O'Faolain and then by Peadar O'Donnell.

1941

Death of nationalist-feminist Jennie Wyse Power in January and artist and former Dublin Councillor Sarah Celia Harrison in August. Hanna's lengthy obituaries are published in the *Irish Press*. Death of James Joyce. *The Land of Spices* by Kate O'Brien is banned in Éire.

1942

Irish Housewives Association formed, founded by Hilda Tweedy and Andrée Sheehy Skeffington with support from Hanna.

1943

Hanna stands in general election, one of four women standing as independents, but receives only 917 votes. She writes lengthy article in *The Bell*, analysing women's experiences in the election.

1944

Hanna writes eulogy for Dorothy Evans, former WSPU organiser in Belfast, for the British feminist Six Point Group. Begins to write her memoirs. Death of Frank Ryan in Germany.

1945

In April Hanna attends fourth 1916–21 Annual Commemoration Dinner with many other republican women. VE Day ends war in Europe. Hanna is confined to bed for four months with heart problems and friends organise a testimonial to relieve her financial problems. Her first grand-child, Francis, is born. She is interviewed about her life for RTÉ in November. She assesses British women MPs in the post-war Labour government for *Workers' Review*.

1946

Hanna's letter to the *Irish Press* in support of national school teachers' pay strike is published on 6 March. She writes an article for first issue of the *Irish Housewife*, which is published posthumously. Hanna dies on 20 April and is buried in Glasnevin cemetery with her husband.

Suffrage Friends and Colleagues of Hanna Sheehy Skeffington

Louie Bennett (1870–1956)

Born into a wealthy Protestant Unionist family in Dublin, her mother Susan Boulger came from an army background with high social status and her father James ran the family business of fine art auctioneers. She was one of nine surviving children. She went to school in England but did not take any exams. She then acted as housekeeper for one of her brothers and after her father's death in 1918, as the only unmarried daughter, she was responsible for her mother and aunt and, later, for an invalid brother. She was a member of the IWSLGA in 1909 and 1910 and in 1911 she and Helen Chenevix (one of the first women graduates from Trinity College Dublin) became joint honorary secretaries of the Irish Women's Suffrage Federation, formed to coordinate the work of the numerous small suffrage organisations emerging throughout the country at this time. Chenevix would become her lifelong friend and companion. They also formed the Irish Women's Reform League in 1911, non-party and non-militant, as a Dublin branch of the Federation, intended to highlight issues facing working class women. During the Lockout Louie volunteered in the Liberty Hall soup kitchen along with other suffragists but refused Connolly's request to help reorganise the Irish Women Workers' Union as she disagreed with his support for armed rebellion. When the First World War began, she and Frank Sheehy Skeffington were both vocal in their insistence that violence should not be used to achieve political ends. She was devastated by his murder and attended the courtmartial of his killer, Captain Bowen-Colthurst. She admitted that the execution of the leaders of the Rising had awoken 'dormant nationalist feeling' in her, and she did much to support the *Irish Citizen* and Hanna Sheehy Skeffington, taking over as editor while Hanna was in the United States. After 1918 they worked on the paper together but disagreed on whether to change it from a feminist suffrage paper to a feminist trade union paper. Helena Molony, imprisoned after the Rising, asked Louie to help revive the Women's Union and in August 1916 Louie, with Helen Chenevix, attended the Trade Union Congress in Sligo. From later 1916 she, Chenevix and Molony would work together in the IWWU, with Louie and Chenevix its honorary secretaries. Louie was a key figure in mobilising women's opposition to conscription and the Labour Party wanted her to be a candidate in the 1918 elections, but she refused. Labour then withdrew in order to allow Sinn Féin to run unchallenged. As a pacifist, Louie was included in both women's delegations to present peace proposals to pro- and anti-Treaty leaders in the days before the start of the Civil War and she was a key figure in Ireland's representation on the Women's International League, which had been formed at The Hague in 1915. She and Hanna often clashed over differing policies when both were members of the Irish section of the WIL, with Louie refusing to accept the notion of 'justifiable warfare'. She toured the United States in 1920 and gave evidence to the American Commission on Conditions in Ireland on the brutalities perpetrated by the Black and Tans. In 1932 she was elected the first woman president of the Irish Congress of Trade Unions, serving a second term in 1947. Louie was a formidable public presence and a leading figure in the campaign against the 1936 Conditions of Employment Act which legalised restrictions on women's employment. She supported the landmark 1945 laundry worker's strike in aid of a fortnight's paid holiday, retiring from the IWWU in 1955, the year before her death.

Elizabeth Bloxham (1877–1962)

Born into a large Church of Ireland family in Claremorris, County Mayo, the daughter of John Bloxham and Brigid McGreal. Her father was a member of the Royal Irish Constabulary and the family were not sympathetic to nationalism, although later supported Elizabeth's right to be politically active. Elizabeth became friendly with neighbours who gave her a copy of the *United Irishman* newspaper. She soon began contributing articles to the paper, and over time wrote for *Sinn Féin*, the *Irish Review* and the *Irish Volunteer*. In January 1911 she began work in Newtownards as a domestic economy instructor. Thereafter she would spend her Easter and summer holidays in Dublin. During the summer of 1912, when the IWFL was under attack by Hibernian opponents, she was a regular speaker on their behalf at outdoor events in the Phoenix Park, but her position in the north made it impossible for her to devote more time to suffrage. She was a founding member of Cumann na mBan, stating that this was first discussed in 1914 with Jennie Wyse Power during her Easter holiday in Dublin. Her suffrage experience led to her becoming an organiser for Cumann na mBan, but when speeches she made were reported in the Newtownards press, her position in the north became increasingly difficult. She remained friends with Hanna and wrote an account of the two of them walking together to Glasnevin Cemetery in August 1915 for the O'Donovan Rossa funeral. In June 1916 she was dismissed from her post as domestic economy instructor, a consequence of her nationalist sympathies and her employer's disgust at news of the Easter Rising. After a short time in county Meath she settled in Wexford, continuing to teach and remaining a Cumann na mBan activist. While in Wexford she followed the activities of feminist protestors against government policy and in 1945 wrote with great warmth to Hanna after hearing of her illness. She retired from teaching in 1944 and later moved to Dublin. Elizabeth is buried in St Andrews Cemetery, Malahide.

Mary Bourke-Dowling (?–1944)

Mary was a strong supporter of the IWFL, an Irish nationalist and a firm believer in militancy as a tactic. She spoke for the IWFL in open-air venues like the Phoenix Park and also wrote for the *Irish Citizen*. In November 1911 she took part in a WSPU protest in London, smashing windows in the War Office and receiving a five-day prison sentence in Holloway. She worked in the office of the *Irish Citizen* during the period Frank was imprisoned for anti-war activities, writing articles on O'Donovan Rossa and on the Pankhursts. She also worked with Louie Bennett in editing the *Citizen* after Frank's murder in 1916. In January 1916 she was listed as treasurer for the IWFL and she remained a member of the organisation in the 1917-18 period. She also joined Cumann na mBan and took the anti-Treaty side in the Civil War, serving six months in Kilmainham and North Dublin Union in 1923. She remained a friend of Hanna's, working with her on republican-feminist issues in the 1920's. In 1926 she was in Dumfrieshire for a time, teaching sunday school, having lost her job in the civil service. In 1928 she was living in Termonfeckin, County Louth, where Hanna and Cahalan visited her. In 1932, after a long campaign, she won reinstatement in the civil service. She married William Lewers in 1933 and, because of the marriage bar, had to leave her job. She died at home in Clontarf in 1944.

Cissie Cahalan (1876–1948)

Always known as 'Cahalan' to her friends, she was the daughter of a school-teacher, born either in Tipperary or Cork. She was a shop assistant in Arnotts in Dublin and a member of the Irish Draper Assistant's Association. She was an early member of the Irish Women's Franchise League and an executive member in 1917-18. She was an IWFL delegate seeking Dublin Trades Council support for women's suffrage and was one of the IWFL members to give strong support to Hanna and to the continuance of the *Irish Citizen* following the murder of Frank Skeffington. She lost her job in Arnott's in 1916, apparently because of her suffrage campaigning, winning reinstatement in 1917. She supported inclusive trade unions for women and men, disagreeing strongly with the position of Louie Bennett and the Irish Women Workers' Union. In 1918 she headed a strike at Arnott's that won a 30 per cent pay increase. She was president of the Irish Drapers' Assistants Association from 1922-1924, winning a minimum wage and ending the 'living-in' system. In 1932 she married the northerner John Burns, who had been a strong supporter of the suffrage movement, at one time disrupting a service at St Anne's Cathedral in Belfast in protest against the imprisonment of Belfast suffragettes. Cahalan spoke on behalf of Mary Sheehy Kettle and Hanna at events in 1932 and 1933, when they were being honoured for their services to women. John Burns died in 1936, and she went to live with Kathleen Sheehy O'Brien. She was a keen member of the walking group 'the Pilgrims', which gave continued friendship to many, including Hanna and Meg Connery. After Kathleen's death Cahalan lodged for a time with Hanna and worked part-time at St Ultan's hospital.

Winifred Carney (1887–1943)

Maria Winifred Carney was born in Bangor, County Down, the youngest of six children, to Sarah Cassidy, a Catholic, and Alfred Carney, a Protestant commercial traveller. When her parents' marriage broke up, she lived with her mother and brother in Carlisle Circus, north Belfast. She qualified as a secretary and for a time worked as a clerk in a solicitor's office. In her early 20s she became involved in the Gaelic League and in suffrage and socialist activities in Belfast. In 1912 she became secretary to the Irish Textile Workers' Union, set up by James Connolly in 1911 as the women's section of the Belfast Transport and General Workers Union. As a committed nationalist Winifred also became an active member of the Belfast branch of Cumann na mBan. During the Easter Rising she was the first woman to enter the GPO, as a member of the Irish Citizen Army and aide-de-camp to James Connolly. She surrendered together with the republican leadership and was imprisoned in England for a time afterwards. She stood unsuccessfully for Sinn Féin on a Workers' Republic platform in east Belfast in the 1918 election. She continued to work for the Transport Union while also remaining an active republican, in the confidence of the IRA leadership in the north. She was secretary of the Irish Republican Prisoners' Dependents' Fund 1920–22 and her home in Carlisle Circus was frequently raided. She was imprisoned in Armagh jail in 1922, being released on the grounds of ill-health. With the formation of the state of Northern Ireland, political repression and increased sectarianism, republicanism in the north was forced to retreat. She retained her commitment to socialism and in 1920 became a member of the Socialist Party of Ireland, also attending the convention of the Independent Labour Party in Glasgow. In 1924 she joined the Court Ward Branch of the Northern Ireland Labour Party where she became friendly with George McBride, a working-class Protestant from the Shankill Road, who had fought for the British during the Great War. They shared a commitment to socialism, although McBride disagreed with her nationalist views and her continued defence of the Easter Rising. Despite objections from family, the couple married in North Wales in 1928. After their marriage they lived in Whitewell Parade, Whitehouse, where they also supported Winifred's elderly mother. Winifred suffered from bad health in the last years of her life and she died on 21 November 1943. She is buried in Milltown cemetery, Belfast.

Margaret (Meg) Connery (1887–1955)
Born in Westport, County Mayo, to John Knight and Bridget Kelly, the third of nine children. Her father had a farm, a pub and a post office franchise. John Knight was involved in the Land League in 1880 and later in land protests with the United Irish League. The family emigrated to New York in 1894, returning to Ireland a few years later. Meg then learned shorthand and typing and moved to Dublin where she worked with a printing firm. In 1909 she married John (Con) Connery, a civil servant. She joined the IWFL in early 1909 and was soon a member of its executive, a lively public speaker and a leading militant. In November 1911 she served a month's prison sentence in Holloway Jail after taking part in a WSPU window breaking protest. She and Hanna were amongst the hecklers of Winston Churchill in Belfast in 1912. In November 1912 Meg and Kathleen Emerson were arrested for window breaking and imprisoned in Mountjoy, released after two days when their fines were paid anonymously. She was imprisoned again in 1913, after breaking windows in the Custom House, and imprisoned in Tullamore, along with Margaret Cousins, and Barbara Hoskins (and joined later by Mabel Purser), where they were known as the 'Tullamore Mice' as they had been arrested after the introduction of the Cat and Mouse Act. In November 1913 she and

Hanna attempted to give leaflets to Sir Edward Carson and Bonar Law, Meg wearing a placard stating: 'Questions for Bonar Law'. Hanna was arrested and charged with assaulting a police officer and given a seven-day jail sentence. In 1914 she and Hanna embarked on a suffrage tour of the west, holding meetings in Longford, Carrick-on-Shannon and Boyle. Meg suffered a miscarriage in 1914 and after that experienced periods of debilitating ill-health. She returned to work with the IWFL in 1915, was a speaker at a meeting in support of Frank Sheehy Skeffington after his return from America, and chaired a protest meeting following the government refusal to allow Irish and British feminists to attend the Women's Peace Congress at The Hague. She was a loyal friend of Hanna, giving much emotional and practical support both to her and to the continuation of the *Irish Citizen* after the murder of Frank. Her articles for the *Citizen* reveal strong support for working class women and the labour movement. She was active during the War of Independence in highlighting the attacks by the Crown forces on the population, particularly women and children. In June 1921 she and Hanna were part of the Irish Women's Deputation to the Dominion Premiers, attempting to persuade the premiers to visit Ireland in order to see the devastation that had been created. In 1924 she went to London to lobby the Labour Party on behalf of the Irish prisoners and in 1931 she and Rosamond Jacob travelled to the USSR as members of the Friends of Soviet Russia. In 1938 Meg spoke at a meeting of the Women's Social and Progressive League urging women to organise politically to use their vote, arguing that the 1916 Proclamation showed republicans were those who supported women's equality. This appears to have been one of the last times she spoke at a public meeting. Con Connery died in 1950 and Meg's last years were spent in a series of nursing homes. There is no record of where she is buried.

Margaret (Gretta) Cousins (1878–1954)

Born Margaret Gillespie in Boyle, County Roscommon, to a middle-class Methodist family. Her father Joseph was a clerk in the Boyle courthouse. She won a scholarship to Victoria High School Derry, and later studied music at the Royal Irish Academy of Music, receiving a degree in music from the Royal University in 1902. She married the Belfast-born James Cousins in 1903. He was a poet and playwright and shared her commitment to theosophy and vegetarianism. Both were part of Dublin's literary circles. Following attendance at a women's suffrage meeting in Manchester, Margaret joined the IWSLGA in 1905. In 1908, with Hanna Sheehy Skeffington, she founded the Irish Women's Franchise League as a militant, specifically Irish-centred organisation. She was its treasurer and one of its most effective speakers and organisers. In 1910 she organised an Irish tour for Emmeline Pankhurst and was one of the Irish delegates invited by Pankhurst to attend the Parliament of Women in Caxton Hall in London. Margaret was one of six Irish women arrested following the protests that followed, serving a one-month sentence in Holloway Jail. In 1912 James Cousins became co-editor (with Frank Sheehy Skeffington) of the suffrage paper the *Irish Citizen*. Margaret received another one-month sentence in January 1913, for breaking government windows following the failure of the Snowden Amendment to the Home Rule bill. She and the other two IWFL prisoners were sent to Tullamore Jail, 60 miles from Dublin and went on hunger strike in protest at being denied first-class status. In May 1913 the Cousins left Ireland, hoping to move shortly to India, to work for the theosophist Annie Besant. However, they lived in Liverpool for two years, and Margaret was a frequent visitor to Ireland, continuing to support the IWFL. They emigrated to Madras in 1915 and Margaret started the National Girls' School in Mangamore. In 1917 she helped to establish the Women's Indian Association. In 1923 she became the first woman magistrate in India and in 1926 helped to establish the All-India Women's Conference as a women's rights movement. In 1932 she served a year in prison for supporting Gandhi's free speech campaign. She suffered a stroke in 1943 after a two-mile walk to a mother and child welfare centre. James cared for her until her death in Adyar, Tamil Nadu, in 1954.

Charlotte Despard (1844–1939)

Born in Kent, England, to former naval commander John William French and Margaret Eccles. One of five girls and one boy – the future Lord John French, military commander and Lord Lieutenant of Ireland during the War of Independence. The French family were of Irish descent, originally from Frenchpark, County Roscommon. In 1870 she married Maximilian Despard, a wealthy Irish businessman who had made his fortune in the Far East. She visited Ireland for the first time on their honeymoon but most of their married life was spent abroad. Encouraged by her husband she wrote novels and poetry. His death in 1890 precipitated a breakdown and when she recovered she moved to the Nine Elms district of the east end of London where she joined the Independent Labour Party, became a Poor Law Guardian and set up a working man's club, child care centre and health clinic. She also converted to Catholicism. Charlotte became increasingly radical, a friend of Eleanor Marx, member of the Second Socialist International, and a militant suffragette who was twice imprisoned in Holloway. In 1907, disagreeing with the autocracy of the WSPU, she helped to co-found the Women's Freedom League and under this banner visited Ireland several times, making links with Irish suffragettes. She remained president of the Women's Freedom League until her death. It was an organisation for which Hanna felt much sympathy, visiting its premises each time she was in London. Charlotte supported the workers during the Dublin Lockout and in 1918 she stood, unsuccessfully, in Battersea for the Labour Party in the general election. In 1920, during the War of Independence, she came to Ireland as part of a Labour Party Commission of Inquiry, collecting evidence of atrocities by Crown forces. She and Maud Gonne MacBride toured Cork and Kerry, with Charlotte using the fact that she was the Viceroy's sister as a means of gaining publicity. In 1921 she settled in Dublin, buying Roebuck House with Maud. They worked together in the Women's Prisoners' Defence League during the Civil War. In 1930 she and Hanna were part of an Irish delegation to Russia, and afterwards Charlotte joined the Communist Party. She left Roebuck House, bought a house in Eccles Street and supported the setting up of a workers' college. After these were attacked by right-wing mobs she felt she had no place in Dublin. Hanna advised her to go to Belfast, where workers from Catholic and Protestant backgrounds were uniting over class issues. However, after sectarian rioting in 1935 she moved out of the city to Whitehead. She died there at the age of 95 and her remains were given an escort to Dublin, where Maud gave the oration at her funeral in Glasnevin cemetery.

Kathleen Emerson (1885–1970)

Born into a Protestant family, her father William Holmes was a stationmaster with the Great Southern and Western Railways. In 1910 Kathleen married the Revd George Emerson but he died in 1911. As a widow Kathleen moved back to her family home, her parents and three siblings having moved to the Rathgar area of Dublin. Her mother Robina was already a member of the IWFL and Kathleen joined the organisation, becoming its secretary, combining this role with a paid post as an office worker with the British Vacuum Cleaner Company. She was an excellent organiser but had little confidence as a public speaker. In February 1912 she joined the WSPU in London in smashing shop windows in central London, receiving a sentence of two month's hard labour in Holloway Prison. During the Home Rule controversy of 1912, when the Ancient Order of Hibernians mounted a campaign against the suffragettes, Kathleen narrowly missed bring thrown into the Liffey while feminists were organising protests at O'Connell Bridge. In November 1912 she and Meg Connery smashed windows of Dublin's Custom House and were sentenced to 14 day's imprisonment in

Mountjoy Jail. Their fines were paid anonymously and they were released after two days. She resigned as IWFL secretary in the summer of 1914 and concentrated upon writing poetry and short stories, some of which were published in the *Irish Citizen*. In October 1918 she married Harry Nicholls, an engineer from Derry, who was a member of the Irish Volunteers and who had been active during the Easter Rising. After many years of ill-health Kathleen died in 1970. Her husband died five years later.

Marie Equi (1872–1952)

Born to working class parents in New Bedford, Massachusetts, her father John was Italian and a stone mason and her mother, Sarah Mullins, was Irish. Three of her siblings died of childhood diseases and she was influenced by her mother's life of pregnancy, childbirth, and childcare. Marie dropped out of high school to support the family by working in the textile industry and later went to Italy to pick olives on an uncle's farm. Her school friend Bessie Bell Holcomb, who attended Wellesley College, had moved to an Oregon homestead in 1891 and the following year Marie joined her there. They lived openly in a lesbian relationship and in 1897 moved to San Francisco where Marie enrolled as a first-year medical student. In 1903 she obtained her medical degree from the University of Oregon, later establishing a general practice, primarily treating working class women and children and providing abortions to both poor and wealthy women - the fees from the wealthy paying the costs of free abortions for the poor. In 1907 she began a 15-year relationship with heiress Harriet Frances Speckart, and the pair adopted an infant girl, Mary. Marie campaigned for women's suffrage and many progressive social reforms, but by 1913 she considered herself an anarchist and supporter of the Industrial Workers of the World, following her experience of violent clashes between police and workers during a strike by canning workers. She opposed the First World War and was arrested when Margaret Sanger came to Portland in 1916 as the two women actively promoted birth control. She welcomed Hanna to Portland when Hanna was speaking during her first tour, and she also welcomed the Irish Women's Mission in 1922, as a strong supporter of the Irish republican cause. In 1918 Marie was charged with sedition for her anti-war speeches, serving ten months in San Quentin Prison. After her release she lived with Elizabeth Gurley Flynn for a decade. She suffered bad health as a result of her prison experiences and gave up her medical practice in 1930. She died in Portland, cared for by her daughter Mary and is buried beside Harrier Speckart.

Sarah Cecilia Harrison (1863–1941)

Born in Holywood, County Down, to Letititia and Henry Harrison JP, a great grand-niece of Mary Ann and Henry Joy McCracken, the latter the executed United Irishman leader. She attended the Slade School of Art in London and returned to Ireland in her mid-20s, making Dublin her home. Her paintings were regularly exhibited with the Royal Hibernian Academy and the Royal Ulster Academy, her portraits including Henry Joy McCracken, Frank Sheehy Skeffington and Anna and Thomas Haslam. In 1912 she was the first woman to be elected to Dublin City Council, where she campaigned on issues of public health, housing for the poor and extension of school meals. She was defeated in the 1915 election when 'Big Business' put a nominee against her. She was a member of the IWSLGA and, briefly, a supporter of the Irish Women's Franchise League when it first began, before deciding that she could not support militancy. In the 1918 election she was one of those in the suffrage victory procession escorting Anna Haslam to vote. She was a close friend of Sir Hugh Lane, director of the National Gallery, and after his death campaigned strongly (although unsuccessfully) to have his 39 paintings returned to Dublin. In 1924 she was secretary of the Anna and Thomas Haslam Memorial Committee, designing the memorial as well as organising the raising of funds, bringing together women from a variety of different political backgrounds to support the memorial. Her paintings are included in the collections of the Ulster Museum, the National Gallery of Ireland and the Hugh Lane Municipal Gallery, Dublin.

Anna Haslam (1829–1922)

Born in Youghal, County Cork. Her parents Jane and Abraham Fisher were Quaker merchants. Anna was an assistant teacher in Yorkshire when she met Thomas Haslam, a Quaker from Mountmellick. They married in Cork in 1854, moving to Rathmines, Dublin in 1858. Anna established a stationery and toy business at their home. Both Haslams were active in campaigning for married women's property reform, equal rights for women in education and employment, repeal of the Contagious Diseases Acts and women's franchise. In 1876 Anna and Thomas founded the Dublin Women's Suffrage Association, which became the Irish Women's Suffrage and Local Government Association in 1898, following the introduction of the Local Government Act. Women were now encouraged to become involved in local politics. The IWSLGA was a non-militant organisation, concentrating on raising public awareness and organising Irish signatures when petitions to the House of Commons on women's franchise were presented. Most of the membership supported the union with Britain. Nevertheless, many active suffragists began their involvement with the IWSLGA and appreciated the commitment of Anna, who continued as secretary to the organisation until 1913. During the First World War the IWSLGA sponsored a hospital bed for wounded soldiers in the Red Cross Hospital in Dublin Castle and Anna was instrumental in the formation of the Women's Patrols, formed as a precursor of the women's police service during the war as a means of safeguarding women from the increased presence of soldiers on the streets. Thomas died in 1917, the year before women gained the right to vote. On election day Anna was presented with a bouquet of flowers by leading suffrage campaigners, as tribute to her work for suffrage. She voted for the Unionist candidate, Sir Maurice Dockrell, who was a member of the IWSLGA. St Stephen's Green has a stone seat dedicated to Anna and Thomas Haslam.

Mary Hayden (1862–1942)

Born in Dublin, daughter of Dr Thomas Hayden and Mary Anne Ryan. Her father was a doctor and a professor in the Catholic University School of Medicine. Her mother died when she was eleven and her father when she was 19. Mary was educated at the Dominican College, Eccles Street and studied for her degree at Alexandra College. She was one of the earliest women graduates from the Royal University, with a BA in 1885 and MA in 1887. She was one of the first women to win a Junior Fellowship of the University in 1895, a campaigner for equality for women within higher education and a founder of the Irish Association of Women Graduates and Candidate Graduates, in which she worked with women such as Hanna in campaigning for better employment prospects for women graduates. From 1909 to 1924, after the abolition of the Royal University system, she was the first woman to serve on the senate of the National University of Ireland. In 1911 she was made first female professor of Modern Irish History in University College Dublin, retaining that position until her retirement in 1938. She was a friend of Anna Haslam and joined the IWSLGA, disagreeing with militancy. During the Home Rule controversy she argued that home rule had to come before women's suffrage, but she also chaired the mass meeting of women of 1 June 1912, which called for the inclusion of women's suffrage into the Home Rule bill. She also spoke at a public meeting protesting against the introduction of the Cat and Mouse Act. She was a member of the Gaelic League and a friend of Pearse but did not support the militarism of the Irish Volunteers. In 1915 she founded the Catholic Women's Suffrage Association with Mary Gwynn, the wife of Nationalist MP Stephen Gwynn, as a means of encouraging Catholic women into the movement. In 1921 she and George Moonan published the text book *A Short History of the Irish People*. During the feminist campaign against the proposed 1937 Constitution she was actively involved, as part of the Irish Association of Women Graduates and Candidate Graduates, in opposing the threat to women's participation in public life. She then became a founding member of the Women's Social and Progressive League. She retired from UCD in 1938, devoting her time to improving the conditions of Dublin children through a social club she had formed, which had Joan of Arc as its patron saint.

Rosamond (Rose) Jacob (1888–1960)

Born in Waterford to Louis Jacob and Henrietta Harvey, the youngest of three children. Her father, although agnostic, came from a Quaker background, and her mother was interested in the radical issues of the day, attending a House of Commons debate on women's suffrage in 1884, where she sat alongside Isabella Tod (Ulster-Scots founder of the first suffrage society in Ireland) in the Ladies' Gallery. Rosamond considered herself a separatist and joined the Gaelic League and, with her brother Tom, founding a Waterford branch of Sinn Féin in 1906. Agreeing with much of the philosophy of Inghinidhe na hÉireann, she sold copies of their journal *Bean na hÉireann* in Waterford. Although sympathetic to the suffrage cause, as a separatist she did not join any suffrage organisation. After the outbreak of war in 1914 she began to sell the *Irish Citizen*, agreeing with its anti-war stance. She did not join Cumannn na mBan, agreeing with Hanna that women were too subordinate within the overall Volunteer movement. She was a Waterford delegate to the Sinn Féin Convention of 1917, one of the few women delegates, where she played an important role in getting Sinn Féin to accept the principle of women's equality within the organisation. After the death of her mother, whom she had cared for since her father's death, Rosamond moved to Dublin in 1919, where she at first lodged with Hanna and her son Owen. At the start of the Civil War she was one of the delegations of women who met with both sides in a fruitless effort to prevent fighting. While Hanna was in America in 1923 Rosamond allowed the publicity department of Sinn Féin to use the house. When it was raided she was imprisoned in Mountjoy, where she shared a cell with Dorothy Macardle. She was secretary of the Irishwomen's International League, the Irish branch of the Women's International League for Peace and Freedom, between 1920 and 1927, and was delegate to a congress in Vienna in 1921 and to Prague in 1929, the latter of which was also attended by Hanna. Rosamond also helped to organise the League's congress in Dublin in 1926.

In April 1926 she resigned from Sinn Féin, and later joined Fianna Fáil, along with several of her women friends. Like many feminists she became increasingly disillusioned with the emerging Irish state and she became close to radical republicans like Frank Ryan, with whom she had a long-lasting affair. In 1931, as Irish delegates for the Friends of the Soviet Union, she and Meg Connery travelled to the USSR, later reporting favourably on conditions there. Her first novel, *Callaghan*, was published in 1920, when it appeared under the pseudonym 'F. Winthrop'. It dealt with the relationship between a protestant suffragist and a catholic nationalist, Other books included a novel, *The Troubled House* (1938), a children's story and *The Rebel's Wife* (1957), based on the life of Wolfe Tone's wife Matilda. She was vegetarian, a great animal lover and a member of the Anti-Vivisection Society. She remained politically active until her death in October 1960 after being knocked down by a car. She is buried in the family plot of Lucy Kingston, suffragist and member of the Women's International League.

Helen Laird (1874–1957)
Born into a Church of Ireland family in Limerick, the daughter of John Laird and Marion Seymour. Her father was a pharmacist. She joined the Gaelic League and Inghinidhe na hÉireann and through her activities with the Inghinidhe, became increasingly involved in theatre, using the stage name of 'Honor Lavelle'. She was with the Abbey theatre at its foundation but left with others in 1905 in protest against the theatre becoming less involved with the national movement. She then helped to form the Theatre of Ireland, which performed Irish language versions of plays by Yeats, Lady Gregory and George Russell. She also worked as a science teacher in Alexandra College, Dublin. She was a theosophist and her friendships crossed many different groups. At one time she shared a flat with Susan Mitchell, journalist and poet, who worked with George Russell as his assistant editor and with whom Helen worked on set design and costumes for the theatre. As secretary of the School Dinners Committee, Helen worked with both Maud Gonne and Hanna, and in 1912 she became a member of the IWFL executive. In this capacity she went to London to lobby Irish MPs to support the Snowden amendment to the Home Rule bill. She was also a member of the committee set up to support Hanna after she was dismissed from her teaching post in the Rathmines School of Commerce. She married Con Curran in December 1913. He was a lawyer and art critic, a close friend of Tom Kettle, James Joyce and Frank Skeffington. For a time after her marriage Helen continued to act, mainly in Irish language plays. She was on the committee that organised Lá na mBan,

the women's day of protest against conscription in 1918, but she had little other active political involvement. The Curran 'At Homes' in Rathgar were occasions for many artists and writers to congregate. Helen was a member of the Save the Children Fund from the late 1920s until her death. She had one daughter, the art critic Elizabeth Curran. Her funeral was attended by the president, Sean T. O'Kelly. She is buried in Deansgrange Cemetery.

Dr Kathleen Lynn (1874–1955)

Born near Cong, County Mayo, to a Church of Ireland clergyman, Robert, and his wife Katherine Wynne, she was the middle of three daughters. She attended Alexandra College and studied also in England and Germany, receiving her medical degree from the Royal University in 1899. She was on the staff of Sir Patrick Dun's Hospital and worked also at the Rotunda before starting her own practice at her house in Belgrave Road, Rathmines in 1904, a home she shared with her partner Madeleine ffrench-Mullen. In 1909 she was made a Fellow of the Royal College of Surgeons. She supported the suffrage movement, joining both the IWSLGA and the WSPU, and became medical attendant to the imprisoned Dublin suffragettes. She presented the Dean of St Patrick's cathedral with a petition signed by over 1,300 members of the Church of Ireland to ask for church support for women's suffrage, but this was denied. She supported the Irish Women Workers' Union and during the Lockout of 1913 she gave her medical services to help the families of the locked-out workers who came to the soup kitchen in Liberty Hall. She joined the Irish Citizen Army at Connolly's invitation and began to teach first aid and ambulance work to its members. She was appointed Chief Medical Officer of the Citizen Army and during the Easter Rising, with the position of Captain, was Chief Medical Officer for the insurgents, responsible for medical planning and supplies. While she was at the City Hall garrison its commander, Sean Connolly, was killed and Kathleen remained at the outpost, giving the surrender to the British. She was imprisoned in Kilmainham and Mountjoy jails and then deported for a while to Bath in England. At the Sinn Féin Convention of 1917 Kathleen was one of four women elected to its 24-person executive. She was also involved in the republican women's group Cumann na dTeachtaire, intended to promote the position of women in political and public life. After the flu pandemic of 1918 she and Madeleine ffrench-Mullen (who had served in the St Stephen's Green garrison during the rising) bought a house in Charlemont Street and opened it in 1919 as a children's hospital, named St Ultan's. With few resources, many republican women volunteered their services as cleaners and helpers. In 1923 she was elected to the Dáil as a Sinn Féin member but as an abstentionist did not take her seat. She pioneered the use of BCG vaccinations and promoted the work of Maria Montessori in St Ultan's. She was still working in St Ultan's until a few months before her death and remained GP to a number of feminist and republican friends. At her funeral the Irish Citizen Army formed a guard of honour.

Dorothy Macardle (1889–1958)
Born in Dundalk, to Thomas Macardle and Minnie Ross, the eldest of five children. Her family were owners of Macardle Breweries and her father was later knighted. Her mother was an English Anglican who converted to Catholicism on marriage but retained unionist politics while her father was a Home Ruler. Dorothy attended Alexandra College and continued her studies in Alexandra's collegiate department, graduating in 1912 with a first-class honours BA in English language and literature. She came third in Ireland in English literature and won a scholarship to the Dublin University School of Education, where she qualified as a teacher in 1914. She worked in England between 1914–16 and two of her brothers fought in the Great War (one was killed), but Dorothy, who moved back to Ireland in early 1917, gradually came to sympathise with the nationalist cause. She became a teacher at Alexandra College and wrote plays, one of which was staged by the Abbey in 1918. She met Maud Gonne MacBride and Constance Markievicz and, by early 1919, had become a member of Cumann na mBan and a publicist for Sinn Féin. She took the republican side during the Civil War and was an active member of the Women's Prisoners' Defence League. She was imprisoned twice, the second time in 1922, when she was interned in Mountjoy, Kilmainham and the North Dublin Union, where she became friendly with Rosamond Jacob. She went on a hunger strike for seven days, along with other prisoners, and was eventually released in May 1923, in poor health. The experience led her to abandon her Catholic faith. Alexandra College had dismissed her on her arrest and she now worked for the Sinn Féin publicity department, as well as writing plays and novels. She and Rosamond Jacob shared a house at this time. She was a founder member of Fianna Fáil, along with Hanna and other women, but left over the question of taking the oath in order to enter the Dáil. However, she remained on close terms with de Valera, and was godmother to his youngest son, born in 1922. She opposed the 1935 Conditions of Employment bill, which allowed the government to exclude women from certain industries, and joined the feminist opposition to the 1937 Constitution, objecting to its emphasis on women's domestic

role. In 1935 she was appointed vice-chairwoman of a committee formed by the National Council of Women in Ireland to examine legislation affecting women. During the Second World War she lived in London and worked on behalf of refugee children. Her book *Children of Europe* (1949) examined the position of children in Nazi-occupied Europe and the aftermath. Her best-known work is *The Irish Republic* (1937), a history of Ireland from an anti-Treaty point of view. She wrote several novels in a gothic style, one of which was made into a film *The Uninvited.* She also wrote plays for children. She returned to Ireland after the war, serving as vice-president and president of the Irish Association of Civil Liberties (1949–57). She died of colon cancer in Our Lady of Lourdes Hospital, Drogheda and was buried in St Fintan's cemetery in Howth, near to her home.

Maud Gonne MacBride (1866–1953)

Born in Surrey, England, the eldest daughter of Captain Thomas Gonne of the 17th Lancers and his wife, Edith Frith Cook. The Gonnes were wealthy wine importers and the Cooks were prosperous London drapers. She had a younger sister, Kathleen. After their mother died in childbirth the family returned to Ireland, settling in Howth, where the girls were looked after by a nurse. Maud was 6 when they went to live in London and 16 before she returned to Ireland, with her father now assistant adjutant-general at Dublin Castle. By 1886 she had become a nationalist, having witnessed evictions and great suffering in the countryside. Her father died in 1886, and on her 21st birthday she inherited a fortune and was free to live an independent life. She had already begun an affair with Lucien Millevoye, a married journalist with right-wing politics, forming a passionate alliance against the British Empire. When she returned to Dublin she soon became involved in nationalist circles, supporting the land movement in Donegal and Mayo and campaigning for prisoner release. She was unable to join any organisation because of her sex, but in 1900, with other nationalist women, founded and became president of Inghinidhe na hÉireann. In 1903 she married Major John MacBride, whom she had met when campaigning for the Boers. After their separation she remained mostly in France with their son Sean and Iseult (her daughter by Millevoye), although she spent time in Ireland during 1910–11, campaigning for school meals in collaboration with women from Inghinidhe and the IWFL. During the First World War she and Iseult nursed the wounded in France. She returned to Dublin in 1917 as 'Maud Gonne MacBride', was arrested in connection with the 'German Plot' and interned in Holloway Prison for six months, with Constance Markievicz and Kathleen Clarke (and, briefly, with Hanna). During the War of Independence Maud worked for the Irish White Cross. She was one of the group of women who tried to intercede at the start of the Civil War, becoming strongly anti-Treaty and serving two periods in jail in 1923. She was a key figure in the Women's Prisoners' Defence League, working closely with Hanna and with Helena Molony. At Roebuck House, Clonskeagh, which she and Charlotte Despard bought in 1922, they set up cottage industries to provide employment for republicans in need. Her journal *Prison Bars* publicised the plight of republican prisoners. Maud lived at Roebuck House till her death, with her son, daughter-in-law Catalina ('Kid') Bulfin and grandchildren. In 1938 she published an autobiography, *A Servant of the Queen*. She is buried in the republican plot, Glasnevin cemetery.

Margaret McCoubrey (1880–1955)

Margaret Mearns Morrisson was born on 5th January 1880 in Eldersley, near Glasgow. At the age of twelve she began working in a men's outfitter shop, but qualified as a shorthand typist at the age of 16. She became a private secretary before moving on to teach at Skerries Business Training College, where at the age of 24 she was appointed deputy head mistress. She married John Taylor McCoubrey, an electrical engineer at Harland and Wolff on the Clyde, in 1905. The couple had two children. After the family moved to Belfast Margaret joined the suffrage movement in 1910, becoming an active militant, a member of the Irish Women's Suffrage Society and then the Women's Social and Political Union. She wrote frequently for the *Irish Citizen*, and regularly spoke at open-air meetings. During the most militant period of suffrage activity in Belfast in 1914 the McCoubrey household was kept under police surveillance. On the outbreak of war Margaret supported the pacifist stance of the IWFL and worked with Hanna in setting up a Belfast branch of the IWFL. While supported by some in the labour movement, it found it difficult to attract members in the political circumstances of the time. She had been a delegate in the deputation to meet Asquith and Redmond in London just prior to the outbreak of war, and she was also one of a delegation of women chosen to represent Ireland at the Women's Peace Congress in The Hague in May 1915, although unable to attend when the government refused to issue passports to the women and closed North Sea shipping lanes. As a pacifist she was actively involved in the Glasgow-based Women's Peace Crusade, speaking and writing on the impact of war on women, and attempting to hold a peace meeting in Bangor, County Down, where she was met with some hostility. She served as the first woman on the Management Board of Belfast Co-Operative Society (1914-26) and was active in the Women's Guild and in the educational department where she taught for many years. She attended and spoke at meetings of the International Women's Co-Operative Guild and arranged educational tours for cooperative members. She was local editor of *Belfast Wheatsheaf* (later *Home Magazine*) and the Irish correspondent for *Co-Operative News and Scottish Co-Operator*. She was also an active member of the north Belfast branch of the Northern Ireland Labour party, representing the central branch of the Women's Advisory Council. She was elected to Belfast Corporation as a Labour councillor for the Dock Ward in 1920. In 1933 she moved to Carnlough, County Antrim, where she ran Drumalla House as a non-profit-making base for members of the Belfast Girls' Club Union to come on holiday. After the deaths of her husband and, later, her son, in 1938 she went to live with her daughter's family in Belfast. She died in hospital aged 76 on 11 April 1956 following gallstone surgery.

Constance Markievicz (1868–1927)

Born in London, daughter of Sir Henry Gore-Booth of Lissadell, County Sligo and Georgina Hill. Constance, her sisters Eva and Mabel and brothers Josslyn and Mordaunt grew up in Lissadell, where their father was a progressive landlord. In 1896 the sisters formed the Sligo branch of the Irishwomen's Suffrage and Local Government Association. Constance studied art at the Slade School in London and also in Paris, where she met Count Casimir Markievicz, whom she married in 1900. Their daughter Maeve was born in 1901 and reared in Lissadell. Constance and Casimir settled in Dublin, moving in bohemian circles, writing and acting in plays. In 1908 she joined Sinn Féin and helped to found *Bean na hÉireann*, the paper of Inghinidhe na hÉireann. With Bulmer Hobson she co-founded Fianna Éireann in 1909 as the youth movement of republicanism. By 1911 she had a high profile within nationalist circles, as executive member of Sinn Féin and the Inghinidhe. While she refused to join the IWFL, believing that women's priority had to be the fight for national freedom, she supported the suffragettes when they came under attack from the Ancient Order of Hibernians and a speech to the IWFL, published in the *Irish Citizen* in October 1915, revealed a similar view to Hanna's regarding the subordinate role of women within the Volunteer movement. She became increasingly concerned with issues of social justice, speaking at the launch of the Irish Women Workers Union, organising a soup kitchen in Liberty Hall during the Lockout, and becoming Hon. Treasurer of the Irish Citizen Army in 1913. While she helped Inghinidhe become a branch of Cumann na mBan in 1914, she remained an activist with the Citizen Army, and took part in the Easter Rising as a member of the St Stephen's Green/

College of Surgeons garrison. Her death sentence was commuted to penal servitude for life because of her sex. She was the last prisoner to be released, in June 1917. That year she converted to Catholicism, became president of Cumann na mBan and was elected onto the executive of Sinn Féin. She was interned with Maud Gonne MacBride and Kathleen Clarke in Holloway Jail in 1918 as part of the 'German Plot' arrests and while still in prison was elected for Sinn Féin to the St Patrick's constituency in Dublin. She refused to take her seat at Westminster and became Minister of Labour in Dáil Éireann. She spent the War of Independence 'on the run', being imprisoned twice during that time. She opposed the Treaty, believing it served the interests of the capitalist class, and during the Civil War took part in the fighting in Dublin. She then toured America to enlist support for the republican cause. She was a Sinn Féin abstentionist TD 1923-26, joining Fianna Fáil in 1926 and was elected to the Dáil in 1927. However, she died in July of that year, before the party took the decision to enter the Dáil. Her funeral was witnessed by thousands of Dubliners, who lined the streets in tribute. She is buried in the republican plot of Glasnevin cemetery.

Helena Molony (1883–1967)
Born off Henry St., Dublin, daughter of Michael Moloney, a grocer, and Catherine McGrath, she had an unhappy childhood and was orphaned when young. She and her brother Frank ran away from their alcoholic stepmother when he was 21 and Helena was 16. Despite her father's spelling of the family surname, she always insisted on 'Molony'. In 1903, hearing Maud Gonne speak outside the Custom House against the royal visit of Edward VII, she joined Inghinidhe na hÉireann, adopting the pseudonym 'Emer' for Inghinidhe work. She would be called by that name by republican women for the rest of her life. She edited the journal *Bean na hÉireann*, from 1908-11 and also wrote its 'Labour notes'. She was responsible for introducing Constance Markievicz to the Inghinidhe when she invited her to an editorial meeting to set up the journal. This work was unpaid, Helena surviving on a bequest of £30 a year from her mother's estate. She was sympathetic to the suffrage cause and invited Hanna to contribute articles to *Bean*, but as an Irish republican refused to ask for votes from a British parliament. In July 1911 she became the first woman to be arrested for a political offence since the days of the Ladies' Land League when she protested against the visit of King George V, throwing a stone at his portrait. She served only a few days of a one-month sentence because her fine was paid by Anna Parnell, who wanted her free to continue the work of editing her manuscript of the history of the Ladies'

Land League. Helena also began acting professionally in 1911 and became a regular with the Abbey Theatre. On the recommendation of James Connolly, she was appointed secretary of the Irish Women Workers' Union in 1915 and secretary of Irish Citizen Army women's group. During the Easter Rising she was part of the City Hall garrison and one of five women subsequently interned in Aylesbury jail. On her release she returned to the Abbey stage and, for a while, became a member of the Sinn Féin executive. In 1918 she was replaced as IWWU general secretary by Louie Bennett, but she remained an official with the organisation, although often in disagreement with the more moderate views of Louie Bennett and Helen Chenevix. One area of work she concentrated on was the organisation of domestic servants, and Hanna was a speaker she often called upon. Helena retired from the stage in 1922 and was active in that period supporting the anti-Treaty forces. She was an activist, with Maud Gonne MacBride, Charlotte Despard, Hanna and others, in the Women's Prisoners' Defence League and the People's Rights Association, opposing the Cumann na hGaedheal government and fighting on behalf of the republican prisoners. Like Hanna, she was a member of the Friends of Soviet Russia, visiting the USSR in 1929 (the year before Hanna) as a delegate from the Dublin Trades Council. Helena and the IWWU took a leading role in opposing the 1935 Conditions of Employment bill and in 1936 she was elected President of the Irish Trade Union Congress. Becoming increasingly disillusioned with the conservativism of Irish society and the growing attacks on women in public life, she suffered from bouts of depression and alcoholism. She retired on health grounds in 1941. She lived with Dr Eveleen O'Brien of Grangegorman Hospital who cared for her and they lived together until Helena's death. She was buried in the republican plot at Glasnevin cemetery.

Lilian Metge (1871–1954)

Her father, Richard Grubb, was from Tipperary and her mother was Harriet Richardson, daughter of Jonathan, who had been an MP for the Lisburn constituency in the 1850s and senior partner in the Quaker firm Richardson, Sons and Owden. In 1892 she married Captain Robert Metge, who had been an MP for County Meath but who had resigned his seat in 1883. He died in 1900 and Lilian and her two daughters moved to Lisburn, where she established the Lisburn Suffrage Society. She was also treasurer for the northern committee of the Irish Women's Suffrage Federation and represented the Federation at the International Women's Congress in Budapest. She was captain of the Lisburn Ladies' Golf Club. This respectability ended in 1914 after she took part in a suffrage demonstration in London and witnessed the brutal treatment of women by the police when 200 women tried to petition King George when he entered Buckingham Palace. She now described herself as a suffrage militant, joining the Ulster Centre of the Women's Suffrage and Political Union. She became a close friend of its chief organiser, Dorothy Evans. She horsewhipped the editors of two Belfast newspapers for their unsympathetic coverage of the suffrage campaign and smashed windows in Belfast courthouse during the trial of Dorothy Evans. She, Dorothy Evans, Joan Wickham and Dorothy Carson were sent for trial after attempting to blow up Lisburn Cathedral on 31st July 1914. While in Crumlin Road Jail they began a hunger strike and were released on 12th August. A decision not to prosecute their case was made following the outbreak of war. Lilian remained close to Hanna. She opposed the Great War and was one of the IWFL delegates chosen to attend the Women's Peace Congress at The Hague in 1915. She moved to Shrewsbury before eventually settling in Dublin. Her youngest daughter Gwendoline committed suicide in 1920 and she seems to have stopped all political activity by that time. She is buried in Deansgrange cemetery, Dublin. Her hunger strike medal, awarded by the WSPU, is on display at the Irish Linen Centre and Lisburn Museum.

Agnes O'Farrelly (1874–1951)

Born at Raffony, County Cavan, to Peter Farrelly and Ann Sheridan, she came from a large farming family of five daughters and three sons. After boarding school she attended St Mary's University College, Dublin and gained a B.A in 1899 and an M.A. in 1900. She became a lecturer in Alexandra and Loreto Colleges before being appointed lecturer in Modern Irish at University College Dublin in 1909. With Mary Hayden she was co-founder of the Irish Association of Women Graduates and Candidate Graduates. She was a member of Sinn Féin in its early years, agreeing with Griffith's philosophy of self-reliance and later becoming president of the Irish Industrial Association and Homespun Society. She was an executive member of the Gaelic League and a strong supporter of women within the League. As a writer she produced two novellas in Irish and two books of poetry. Her standing within the nationalist movement was reflected in the decision to ask her to chair and give the inaugural address at the founding of Cumann na mBan in 1914. However, her emphasis on the organisation's role as an extension of women's duty to protect the home did not win the support of many younger women and she resigned from Cumann na mBan when the organisation split over whether or not to support John Redmond when he pledged nationalist Ireland would provide Britain with soldiers following the outbreak of the Great War. She did not take part in the Rising or the War of Independence, becoming an advocate for peace when she was chosen to participate in the women's delegation to the two opposing sides at the start of the Civil War. In 1932 she was appointed Professor of Modern Irish Poetry at UCD, holding the position until her retirement in 1947. In 1937 she was actively involved, as a member of the Irish Association of Women Graduates and Candidate Graduates, in opposing the clauses in the constitution relating to women. She was president of the Irish Federation of University Women from 1937–9 and of the Women Graduates' Association from 1943–7. As well as devoting much time to encouraging the revival of Irish, particularly through the development of summer schools, she was a strong supporter of women playing Gaelic games, through founding a camogie club in UCD and eventually becoming president of the Camogie Association. The President and Taoiseach attended her funeral. She is buried in Deansgrange cemetery. Her brother Alphonsus, who was Professor of Science at UCD, was a witness at the wedding of Hanna and Frank.

Marguerite Bannister Palmer (1886–?)
Born Marguerite Bannister in Moneyrea, outside Belfast, from a Unitarian background. She became a founder member of the IWFL and one of its most militant members. In 1910 she married R. J. Weldon Palmer, from a Church of Ireland background, a clerk for a wholesale rubber company, who was also a strong supporter of the suffrage cause, joining Frank Sheehy Skeffington in heckling Asquith when he visited Dublin in 1912 (while their wives were in jail), and being badly beaten by the stewards as a result. Marguerite boycotted the 1911 Census but her husband and his older brother, both living with their mother Eliza, described their religion as 'Theosophist' on the census return and Eliza, the head of the household, wrote 'disenfranchised' in the column relating to disabilities. Marguerite, Hanna and Meg Connery were in London in 1911 when a Conciliation bill was being debated in the Commons. She served one week in Holloway Jail in November of that year, having taken part in a WSPU protest in Parliament Square. She was one of the first IWFL prisoners when she, with Hanna and six others, was imprisoned for window smashing in protest at women's exclusion from the Home Rule bill. In June 1913 she was imprisoned again, this time with Dora Ryan and Annie Walsh, having smashed the windows of the United Irish League. They were released under the terms of the Cat and Mouse Act, having been on hunger strike for five days, but were not rearrested. She was also part of deputations to politicians and notable for having heckled prominent politicians like Chief

Secretary Birrell and Edward Carson. In January 1913 she and Margaret McCoubrey took part in the Derry by-election, when Irish suffragists organised an unsuccessful campaign against the Liberal candidate. Marguerite was an executive member of the IWFL from its inception in 1908 until 1910, returning to the executive in 1912-13 and becoming secretary in 1914. She had a baby in August 1914 and withdrew from activity for a while, but returned to support the IFWL in 1915, agreeing with its anti-war stance. From comments in letters she appears to have suffered from illness and there are no records of her involvement after that period.

Alice Locke Park (1861–1961)

Born Alice Locke in Boston, Massachusetts, she married Dean Park in 1884 and moved to Palo Alto, California, where she lived for the rest of her life. The couple had a number of children. It is not known what her husband did, or how long he lived, but Alice appears to have been able to lead an independent life. She was wealthy and devoted her life to the causes of suffrage, socialism, and pacifism. In 1894 she picketed the White House as a member of the International Feminist Movement and she founded the Votes for Women Club in Palo Alto. During 1911 she was one of a number of women activists who campaigned for the legalisation of women's suffrage in California and she helped a number of other states to have suffrage bills passed. In 1913 she attended the International Women's Suffrage Alliance Congress in Budapest and visited Ireland on her journey back to America, where she came into contact with the IWFL and formed a lasting friendship with Hanna. As a pacifist she had great admiration for Frank Skeffington. She was a delegate to the International Women's Peace Congress at the Hague in 1915 and that year she founded the Palo Alto Women's Peace Party. Her other campaigns included birth control, sex education for schools, anti-child labour laws and a six-hour working day. In 1918 she was working with Congressman Edward Raker, who was chair of the Woman Suffrage Committee. In this capacity she enabled Hanna to meet a variety of politicians in Washington during the campaign for the 19th Amendment. When in Palo Alto she hosted Hanna on her various lecture tours of America and the two women maintained an extensive correspondence until Hanna's death.

Margaret Skinnider (1893–1971)

Born in Glasgow, Scotland, to immigrant parents from County Monaghan, she became a teacher in Glasgow's Hillhead district. She was a member of the WSPU and an active suffragist before joining the Glasgow branch of

Cumann na mBan. At the outbreak of the Great War she joined a women's rifle club, becoming an expert shot. On her first visit to Ireland, in December 1915, she smuggled detonators concealed in her hat, which she and Constance Markievicz then tested in the Dublin mountains. She became a friend of Markievicz and a close friend of Nora Connolly, joining the Irish Citizen Army. Markievicz alerted her to plans for a rising and she returned to Dublin at the start of the Easter school holidays. During Easter Week she served in the St Stephen's Green contingent, acting as both scout and sniper, arguing with Michael Mallin, her commanding officer, that the Proclamation gave women the same right to risk their lives as men. She was badly wounded while leading a group to cut off the retreat of British snipers and held in hospital for seven weeks before being released. She was able to obtain a travel permit to Glasgow by using her Scottish accent. In 1917 she travelled to America and was one of the first to meet Hanna on her arrival in New York. While in America she wrote *Doing My Bit for Ireland*, to promote the Irish cause. She, Hanna and Owen and Nora Connolly all travelled back to Ireland on the same boat in 1918. Margaret was active with Cumann na mBan through the War of Independence. She opposed the Treaty and acted as IRA paymaster general during the Civil War, until her arrest. She was then imprisoned in Mountjoy jail and North Dublin Union alongside women like Dorothy Macardle. On release she obtained a teaching position in a primary school run by the Irish Sisters of Charity national school, Kings Inns St., Dublin, which she held until her retirement in 1961. She became an activist in the Irish National Teachers Organisation and a member of its executive for many years, campaigning for equal pay and status for women teachers. During the 1946 teachers' strike (which Hanna supported through letters to the press in the last weeks of her life) she served on the strike executive committee, and on the salaries and arbitration committee established in the aftermath. On her retirement from teaching she served on the Irish Congress of Trade Unions executive council (1961–3). She was buried beside Countess Markievicz in the republican plot of Glasnevin cemetery.

Hilda Webb (1874–?)

Born into a Church of Ireland family, her father Randolph Webb had been an Army doctor but by 1901 he was retired, a widower, and living in Rathmines with his children. He, Hilda and her older sister Mabel were all born in England while her younger brother George had been born in Gibralter, presumably while the family was stationed there with the British garrison. While Mabel received an M.A. from the Royal University and became a teacher, and George studied at Trinity College, Hilda did not study at university level and there is no record of any employment. She was one of the first militants in the IWFL when she and Hanna accosted the Chief Secretary at Greystones Pier in October 1910. The following month she took part in suffrage militancy in London, serving a two-month prison sentence in Holloway, together with Kathleen Houston and Eva Stephenson. She became an executive member of the IWFL in 1909 and in the 1911-1912 period served as treasurer for the organisation. Hilda was also one of eight IWFL members who first undertook window smashing in Ireland on 13th June 1912. She, Kathleen Houston, Marjorie Hasler and Maud Lloyd received six-month sentences in Mountjoy, joining Hanna, Marguerite Palmer, and the Murphy sisters, who were serving two-month sentences. In the 1911 census Mabel is listed as head of the family, and still living in the family home. Hilda is not listed in the census and there is no record of any involvement with the IWFL after 1912.

Eva (Stephenson) Wilkins (1881–*c.*1973)

Born in Dublin to Mathew Stephenson and Selina Moore, who came from Drogheda. Eva had an older sister and four brothers. The family were Church of Ireland. Eva was christened 'Jean Evelyn' but appears not to have used that name. After her father's death her mother re-married a Mr Percival and the couple had a daughter. In 1901 Selina Percival was listed in the census as a widow, earning a living as a spirit grocer, and the head of a household of seven children ranging in age from 24 to eight. Eva moved to London in 1902 and worked as a clerk with the British Postal Service. While living there she took part in the first protests mounted by Irish women in London, serving a two-month prison sentence in Holloway Jail between November 1910 and January 1911. She had already met Maurice Wilkins, exchanging letters with him while in prison, and he visited her while she was in Holloway. Eva returned to Ireland after her release, finding clerical work in a village near Greystones, County Wicklow. Maurice also came from a Church of Ireland background. His father, who greatly disapproved of Eva's suffrage militancy, was headmaster of the High School, Dublin. Maurice was a gold medallist at Trinity College before becoming a school teacher. The couple married in July 1911. Maurice moved to several schools in the ensuing period, which made it difficult for both himself and Eva to devote as much time to the suffrage campaign as they might have wished. Eva was treasurer for the IWFL in the 1912–1914 period, resigning in 1915 as she had a young daughter, born in 1913, and she struggled to cope with domestic and suffrage responsibilities. Maurice was a close friend of Frank Sheehy Skeffington and helped with the editing of the *Irish Citizen* in 1915, while Frank was in America. Hanna appointed him a co-executor of her will in 1916, together with her sisters Mary and Kathleen, believing that his values would provide her son Owen with a strong mentor. Eva and Maurice had four children and in 1923 Maurice was appointed headmaster of Bangor Grammar School. After that time the couple were absorbed with the running of the school, with Eva as headmaster's wife looking after the school boarders. They remained in Bangor for 24 years before retiring to County Dublin. Eva died aged 92 and Maurice lived until 1980.

Jennie Wyse Power (1858–1941)

Born Jane O'Toole to Edward O'Toole and Mary Norton in Baltinglass, County Wicklow, where her father had a shop. She was one of seven children. They moved to Dublin when Jennie was two. Her family home was strongly nationalist and supported the Fenian movement. One of her brothers was an active Fenian. Both O'Toole parents had died by the time Jennie was 20 and it is not known where she lived or if she was working after that time, but records show that by 1881 she had become a member of the Ladies' Land League, set up that January in order to support the Land League in its campaign to support tenant farmers. By August 1881 Jennie was an executive member of the Ladies' Land League and a strong supporter of its organising secretary, Anna Parnell. She supported families when they were being evicted and she also organised a library of books that were sent to the imprisoned members of the League. In 1883 Jennie married John Wyse Power, a journalist, and they had four children. In 1885 they moved to Dublin where John joined the staff of the paper *Freeman's Journal*. Both were strong supporters of Parnell during the divorce controversy and after Parnell's death Jennie became treasurer of the group of women who looked after his grave. She joined the Dublin Women's Suffrage Society and in 1899 set up a shop and restaurant in Henry Street which became a meeting place for nationalists. In 1900 Jennie joined the group of women who formed a committee to provide a treat for children who had not supported the visit of Queen Victoria to Ireland. This led to the formation of Inghinidhe na hÉireann, and Jennie was elected one of the four vice-presidents. Jennie and John Wyse Power joined the Gaelic League and their children became fluent Irish speakers. Jennie became a poor law guardian in 1903, serving for eight years, and when Sinn Féin was formed she was a prominent member. She joined Cumann na mBan in 1914, becoming its first President. Her daughter Nancy, who had been the Irish language correspondent for the Irish Women's Franchise League, also joined. Before the Easter

Rising the leadership met at her house in Henry Street and the Proclamation was signed there. Her daughter Maire died of TB in July 1916. Jennie and Nancy Wyse Power remained active Cumann na mBan members, supporting the election of Constance Markievicz and working with Sinn Féin. In 1920 she was elected to Dublin Corporation. Jennie was amongst the minority of women in Cumann na mBan who supported the Treaty, becoming an executive member of a new organisation, Cumann na Saoirse, which campaigned for the Treaty. She was appointed to the Senate of the Free State and in 1924 was appointed one of three commissioners to run the city after Dublin Corporation was dissolved by the government. In 1925 Jennie left Cumann na nGaedheal, remaining on the Senate as an independent, feeling free to champion women's rights. Her husband John died in 1926. The Senate was abolished by de Valera in 1936, and Jennie's 55 years of public service came to an end, the last few years as a Fianna Fáil supporter. Her funeral in 1941 was attended by government and opposition members, and a large contingent from old Cumann na mBan.

Ann (Nancy) Wyse Power (1889–1963)

Daughter of Jennie and John Wyse Power, Nancy became a member of the Gaelic League in 1901 and was active in Sinn Féin. As Aine de Paor she became the Irish language correspondent for the *Irish Citizen* and an active member of the IWFL. She graduated from UCD with a first class honours BA in Celtic Studies in 1912 and then began to study for a Ph.D. at the University of Bonn but had to return to Ireland in 1915 after the start of the Great War. She gave a number of talks on the position of women in Germany, and the strength of the women's movement that she had observed while living there. She joined Cumann na mBan in 1915 and acted as a courier in the days before the rising. On Easter Tuesday she joined the garrison in the GPO. In autumn 1917 she was appointed one of two honorary secretaries of Cumann na nBan and spent some time in Belfast, where she helped to reorganise and restructure the branch, as well as working for the organisation, which by 1920 numbered over 500 branches throughout the country. She was chief organiser for Cumann na mBan during the campaign to support the election of Constance Markievicz in 1918 and she remained an active member of Cumann na mBan during the War of Independence. She was recruited to Dáil Éireann's fledgling foreign service and in April 1921 travelled to Berlin, where she set up the offices of the Irish political mission. On her return to Ireland in 1923 she joined the Department of Industry and Commerce. She later worked for Sean T. O'Kelly and was one of the first women to rise to the position of principal officer in the Irish Free State civil service, where she was an advocate of equality for women in the service. She retired from the Department of Local Government as principal officer in 1954. Nancy was appointed one of the governors of the Dublin Institute for Advanced Studies from 1940 until her death. She was president of the UCD Women Graduates' Association 1959–62.

ONE

EARLY YEARS, 1877–1900

For an impatient young Irish woman 'in a hurry with reform' and contemplating the possibilities offered by the dawning of the twentieth century, Dublin was becoming an interesting place. While Hanna Sheehy was growing into busy adulthood, the city of her childhood was slowly emerging from that state of 'paralysis' so famously detested by her friend, James Joyce. Independence was coming. A native middle-class was developing. Its pretensions were scorned by Joyce, who escaped as soon as he could, but the Sheehy family were proud to be members. A Catholic bourgeoisie waited eagerly for the era of self-government to arrive. The Irish Parliament had voted itself out of existence with the 1800 Act of Union. Parliament House had been sold to the Bank of Ireland and Irish members of parliament had instead taken their seats in Westminster. Many Irish MPs were now determined to play an important role in the new Ireland. There were some who felt that the family of David Sheehy, Member of Parliament for South Meath, embodied the qualities that would be needed in the future state.

David Sheehy, son of Richard Sheehy and Johanna Shea, had been born into a moderately prosperous family at Broadford, near Drumcollogher, County Limerick in 1844. He had an older brother, Eugene, and a sister, Mary. Their father, a devout Catholic, owned a mill and apparently dreamed of both his boys becoming priests. Richard was strongly nationalist in outlook, refusing to allow his sons to enter Maynooth, the Irish seminary established by the British. As Hanna, his equally anti-British granddaughter later remarked, to escape the compulsory Oath of Allegiance to British rule 'young clerical students of rebel hearts' were sent to European colleges, where no such restriction was imposed'.[1]

Instead of Maynooth, David and Eugene went to the Irish College in Paris. Only Eugene became a priest. A religious life was not necessarily their choice: Eugene would have preferred law or politics, while David once told his daughter that he would have liked to be an artist.[2] A cholera epidemic in Paris led to his return to Ireland. He began to develop an interest in politics and joined the Irish Republican Brotherhood, the 'Fenians', a conspiratorial organisation that hoped to win independence for Ireland through force of arms. However, after taking part in a raid on Mallow barracks, David was forced to escape arrest by going to America. The Fenian Rising of 1867 failed and although politics continued to dominate his life, David Sheehy soon moved into the mainstream of constitutional nationalism.[3] On returning from America he became friendly with Jim O'Brien, the elder brother of William, who was a member of parliament for the Irish Party and close associate of the man who was soon to become its inspirational leader – Charles Stewart Parnell. David began to settle down. Eugene, now a curate in Limerick, introduced his brother to Elizabeth (Bessie), the second daughter of Richard McCoy and Margaret Mulcahy of Curraghmore, Loughill, County Limerick, 'hoping they would like each other, but saying nothing.'[4] The McCoys and Mulcahys were also of strong nationalist stock: some involved in the MP Daniel O'Connell's movement to repeal the Act of Union, others sympathising with the physical force Fenians. Bessie, born around 1847, was the fourth of six children. Her widowed mother, running two or three farms with the help of her older sons, was unusual in more ways than one: it was said that Bessie and her older sister Catherine, (known as 'Kate'), were sent to convent boarding school in Limerick rather than being kept home to help with domestic chores.[5] Bessie was a strong-minded woman, intelligent and ambitious, who 'had the fighter in her too', as Hanna was proud to recall. When her brothers Dan and Pat were arrested as Fenians, and lodged in Mountjoy jail, Bessie defied the hostility of the local priest, managing to obtain the keys to the parish church where she led the evening Rosary 'to a packed congregation', her mother and the priest remaining 'wisely silent'. Hanna was full of admiration: 'How she managed to get the keys I never learned, but enter she did, and said the rosary to a packed congregation.'[6] Uncle Dan was a powerful man with an awesome reputation for having swam three miles across the River Shannon.[7] He died in 1899 (due to complications following a hernia operation) while Pat died in 1901. Their mother Margaret, living in Dublin at the time of her death in 1895, was brought home by train for burial. Hanna, the oldest 'Miss Sheehy', aged

18, was listed as one of the chief mourners, travelling with her mother Bessie and aunt Kate.

Bessie McCoy and David Sheehy married in July 1876. The Rev. Eugene Sheehy officiated at the ceremony, assisted by the Rev. Daniel Fitzgerald and the Rev. James McCoy, both from the McCoy side of the family. David now returned to the life of his childhood, becoming a millowner like his father. Johanna, their first child, was born a year after the marriage, on 24 May 1877, in the millhouse in Kanturk, County Cork. She was christened 'Johanna', as her parents followed the old Irish naming system of naming the first son after the paternal grandfather and the first daughter after the paternal grandmother, before then naming children from the maternal line. Hanna loathed the name and appears never to have used it. Family and friends often addressed her as 'Joan'; she was always 'dearest Joan' in letters from her sisters, using the appellation herself with close friends, but for a time in early adulthood took pains to minimise even this inoffensive nickname. In her diary of 1894–5 she refers to herself as 'Hanna Sheehy' and the family census return for 1901 also lists her as 'Hanna'.[8] The following year her first article, on 'the woman question', appeared under the name of 'Hannah Sheehy'. By the time the young woman graduated from university she had become 'Hanna' (not the 'Hannah' that is often spelled as her name). It was her creation, part of the development of her own identity.

Kate McCoy had married George Barry in 1861. The couple lived in Limerick City, running a hotel, where their daughter Margaret was born, dying in infancy. Olive Mary, their only other child, was born in 1880. The Barrys then moved to Dublin, where Kate opened Barry's Hotel in 1888, a year after the death of her husband. She was the obvious choice of godmother to the first-born Sheehy daughter. As a very small child enjoying the rare treat of a visit to the capital, it was her Aunt Kate's hand that Hanna remembered holding while the two stood on O'Connell Bridge and admired the view of Dublin's streets full of intriguing shops and busy people, the pungent River Liffey meandering under their feet. Hanna wondered if this was really Ireland, so different was it from the countryside of her home and the little girl was worried she might have 'gone outside my own country to the land of the Sassenach'. Relieved, she agreed it was lovely, although the country-bred child took some time to adjust to the confinement of city life.[9] In maturity, she loved Dublin, a city that could be admired 'at all hours and seasons'.[10] A special empathy between aunt and niece developed from those early times. As a penniless student Hanna valued the birthday present of the summer dress that Kate always bought her. By the time she was 24 she confessed to feeling a 'little humiliated', to be still in that position, while admitting it was a 'relief' because money was 'very tight' at home.[11] In the years to come Aunt Kate Barry, proprietor of Barry's Hotel in Great Denmark Street (a few streets away from the Sheehy home), would provide unfaltering support for her highly principled and outspoken goddaughter.

When Hanna was three the family moved to the site of another mill, at Loughmore, County Tipperary, where the other Sheehy children were born in rapid succession. In 1911 Bessie, while filling out the Sheehy census form as head of the household (David not being home), wrote that she had had 'seven children born alive, six still living', the only occasion when such a loss was ever mentioned.[12] Three more daughters and two sons did reach adulthood. Margaret was born two years after Hanna, followed by Richard (known as Dick) in 1881 and Eugene in 1882. Mary was born in 1884 and Kathleen, the youngest, in 1886. Hanna had warm memories of those peaceful early years, surrounded by 'the sound of the millwheel and of the waters of the Suir, the smell of fresh bread from the adjoining bakery'.[13] While locals later remembered a well behaved girl sitting on the benches at the national school, the children were a politicised little group, their favourite game that of 'Evictions and Emergency men'. No one wanted to take the part of 'bailiff or peeler' because all wanted to be 'the evicted family guarding the home (it was an outhouse in the mill) against the crowbar, and fortified with water, hayforks and other means of defence.'[14]

The children's game mirrored life in Ireland. By 1880 the Land War between Irish farmers and the British government was reaching its climax. Pat McCoy, the eldest of the McCoy brothers, set up a branch of the Land League in Loughill and he became the Land League representative for County Limerick. Hundreds of ordinary people were being imprisoned for their part in resisting landlordism and this power of coercion was extended to many people, including the Rev. Eugene Sheehy. Unlike his brother David, Eugene was still a convinced Fenian. His first curacy, in Kilmallock, County Limerick, was to a place where 'the embers were still burning' from the Fenian Rising of 1867.[15] It suited him very well. Father Eugene became the President of the local branch of the Land League. He was not only a radical on the land issue, but, more unusually, also a fervent supporter of the women's organisation, the Ladies' Land League, headed by Parnell's sister Anna. This had been formed in January 1881 (and disbanded in August 1882) to provide a means of continuing the agitation after the Land League had been declared an illegal organisation and its members imprisoned. Not all men favoured such a move and the women often found themselves struggling to organise public meetings in the face of unruly men jostling the platform and enjoying the sport of heckling. In contrast — and in defiance of the church hierarchy — Eugene shared a platform with Anna Parnell, encouraging the women present to join the Ladies' Land League themselves. His title of 'the Land League Priest' was well earned.[16]

From May until September 1881 Eugene shared cells in Kilmainham Jail with other prominent members of the Land League, including Parnell himself. Hanna was intensely proud of her warm-hearted, generous-spirited uncle. One of her earliest memories was as 'a chit of four' going with her Aunt Kate, who was a member of the Ladies' Land League, to visit him in Kilmainham and, escaping under the counter where the lunch baskets provided by the Ladies' Land League were being unpacked, 'running across the huge reception hall to acclaim my uncle, walking soberly at exercise with tall John Dillon'.[17] Before their marriage she told Frank of her godfather, 'in early times I preferred him to everyone else in the world and often told him so.'[18] A family friend said of the priest that he was 'full of fun and malicious wit'.[19] Hanna, a witty woman herself, loved clever word play and games. It was Eugene who encouraged his intelligent and independent-minded niece, offering his support even when she shocked almost everyone with her stone-throwing activities during the suffrage years.

Eugene remained an active Fenian all his life, a senior member of the secret IRB and close friend of John Devoy, the exiled Fenian who devoted the rest of his life to ensuring that Irish Americans channeled their hatred of Britain into funds for revolutionaries back home. Much of his activities remained a mystery to the family, who at one time knew only from newspaper reports that he was out of the country and giving lectures. Sometimes he would arrive, unannounced, at the Sheehy home, ignoring his parish responsibilities, before disappearing mysteriously once again. Hanna felt the bishop was 'rather glad to be free of him'. In trying to explain the absent Eugene to Frank, to prepare him for their eventual meeting, all Hanna could conclude was that his life was a 'sad story and strange'. When he had told her he would have preferred the law or to be an MP to the priesthood, he was also providing some explanation for what would become a debilitating problem: alcoholism.[20] Eugene twice travelled to Rome, to argue before the Pope after being suspended by his parish priest. To Hanna he wrote cryptically from New York, as an inveterate conspirator: 'a letter care of my friend J -D--- or to this hotel will find me', before travelling to Italy to engage lawyers for his case. He disliked the ostentation of the Vatican, adding with contempt 'I dare not write my thoughts over the Maynooth grovel' to Rome.[21] A year later he was able to boast, that he fought 'the battle of my life – my victory was complete, I refused to accept less.'[22] When he became parish priest in the small town of Bruree, County Limerick, he made a lasting impact upon one of his parishioners, Eamon de Valera - although Eugene's enlightened views on the right of women to participate in political affairs were not shared by that parishioner. They were, however, to have a profound impact on his niece, who understood that Irish women had been very active in the days of the Land League and who, gradually, came to realise why the disenfranchised women of the Ladies' Land League had been powerless to protest when the men insisted that they disband. When Eugene discovered that Hanna intended to research the history of women's involvement in political movements in Ireland, he wrote to extend a cordial invitation to his niece, to work on her notes on 'the illustrious ladies of this land' in the peace of the parochial house.[23]

David was a less forceful personality than either his brother or his wife, increasingly aware of his status in life and inclined to pomposity. He also suffered terms of imprisonment because of his political commitments. Given the nature of British rule over Ireland, it was difficult for anyone who opposed that rule to escape the penalty of jail at some time in their lives. He had become a nationalist member of parliament for South Galway in 1885, taking part in the Plan of Campaign, another Irish Party initiative to force landlords to lower their rent demands. In consequence he served a four-month jail sentence in 1887, protesting strongly for the right to be treated as a political prisoner. Altogether, David was to be imprisoned on six occasions.[24] Another early memory of Hanna's was visiting her father in jail, 'dashing across the prison yard, as other children dash across the playground.'[25] She was always conscious of the family tradition of non-conforming prisoners. Although Hanna would claim her family home was 'strongly political', and that both her parents had been Fenians, there is no evidence that Bessie was ever an actual member. She would have been absorbed by pregnancy and babies during the short months of life of the Ladies' Land League, but the family story of her courage as a young woman defying the parish priest was a clear demonstration of her commitment to the cause. Hanna was at pains to stress that there were other female relatives in previous generations who shared that deep commitment. A paternal great-great-grandmother had known Lord Edward Fitzgerald, who had been one of the most illustrious of the United Irishmen who organised the Rising of 1798: 'I saw her when I was about four, about a year before she died. She lived to be 106. She was tall and spare and wore a stiff white cap with strings, and had a stick, though her hair was still reddish.'[26] Hanna found it extraordinary to realise that she had 'actually touched the withered hand that had clasped his.'[27] That family tradition of rebellion would take many forms in her life, but its roots were there from the start in the refusal by the Sheehys to accept British domination over Ireland.

In 1887 the family moved to Dublin so that David would have easier access to the boat. An MP's life meant constant travel between London and home. Their first Dublin home was a fairly modest redbrick affair at 126 Hollybank, Drumcondra, in the north side of the city. Hanna remembered her father's first letter from London, in which he promised 'Home Rule before the next Christmas turkey'. It was not to be. In 1890 the parliamentary party split into bitter factions following the disclosure of Parnell's affair with the married Katharine O'Shea. Prominent amongst those who turned against their leader was David Sheehy, possibly because his Catholicism overrode other considerations, or perhaps because he felt betrayed by Parnell's duplicity. No one was ever quite sure where the truth lay. David's grandson (Kathleen's son), Conor Cruise O'Brien, in trying to recreate a sense of the time, imagined Bessie urging her husband to forget about any sense of loyalty, reminding him that 'he had been losing his hearing in that cold cell in Tullamore jail while Parnell was in Brighton with that woman. It was up to him…to keep that respected place, for his family's sake, and for the country.'[28] In Conor Cruise O'Brien's eyes, his grandmother was a formidable figure. Donald Akenson, O'Brien's biographer, develops this image of Bessie so that she becomes 'the primary keeper of the family mythology and the person who intended to fashion the Sheehys' past into the Sheehys' future.'[29] In reality, however, it was not Bessie who stressed the family's Fenian past, it was Hanna - the one member of the family who did not reject that tradition. Many people have invested the personality of Bessie with attitudes that may not have been her own. Not only does she become a cipher for attempts to understand what exactly motivated that clever, ambitious and diverse set of personalities, she also – unwittingly – symbolises the gendered nature of our responses to women who occupy a central position in the heart of a large family whose members' activities extend beyond the domestic setting. In *Stephen Hero* Joyce describes visiting the Daniel family: a home of 'liberal patriotism and orthodox study' with 'several marriageable daughters'. The daughters were 'studious', but also delighted in playing games that were often organised by 'the young feminist McCann', who possessed a 'Cavalier beard' and a 'Northern accent' (a barely disguised Frank Skeffington, at this time one of Joyce's closest friends). Mr Daniels, a chess player and reciter of 'national pieces', enjoyed taking part in these entertainments, but Mrs Daniels is absent.[30] Despite an abundance of domestic servants in Dublin (still the largest source of employment for Irish women), the Sheehy family could afford to employ only one. Consequently, their social life was achieved through the hidden labours of that imposing matriarchal figure.

In 1893 the Sheehys moved nearer the city centre, to 2 Belvedere Place, an impressively tall house, four stories plus basement, 13 windows in front, with high granite steps leading to a majestic pillared door topped by a fanlight. A moody teenaged Hanna wrote in her diary, 'No one will ever climb up here to see me – to wonder at my loneliness, to take me "a rambling".'[31] T. D. Sullivan, author of the ballad 'God Save Ireland', lived at number 1, together with his four unmarried daughters and a son. He had been an MP and had just finished a term of office as Lord Mayor of Dublin. An old Fenian with just the right degree of social respectability was the ideal kind of neighbour and Belvedere Place was the neighbourhood Bessie had dreamed of. It was on the corner of fashionable Mountjoy Square while Belvedere College, the best day school for boys, was just down the road and its female counterpart, the Dominican College in Eccles Street, a few streets away. The house was big, but there were plenty of people to fill the rooms. As well as parents and children there was often a boarder, adding much-needed income to the household finances. In addition, there was usually a visiting relative or someone else up from the country who needed a base for a few days. Politicians *en route* to London also found the Sheehy household a convenient stage on the journey. Pressure for space was such that Frank Skeffington, when staying overnight, had to share a bed with one of the Sheehy boys.

Women who visited Belvedere Place could see clearly that the never-ending task of running a busy household on so many floors left Bessie, by the end of the day, utterly worn out. One visitor testified: 'Mrs Sheehy, so sweet and so active, who in spite of her painful feet never stopped attending to household tasks all day long.'[32] Another friend of Hanna's, who came to know Bessie a decade after this period in the family's life, said she was 'a woman of gentle and retiring nature', devoting herself to the family and giving those who came to her home, 'a genuine welcome and warm smile'.[33] It was a self-effacing role, but of course there was more to Bessie than the archetypal martyred mother. She might have felt compelled to insist that 'James-Disgusting-Joyce' (a name coined by Dick) accept a clean shirt from her hot press when that young man's impecunious lifestyle became too overwhelming for polite society, but Joyce did not depict her in a maternal role. In *Ulysses* Bessie is depicted as a social-climbing matriarch: 'the wife of Mr David Sheehy, MP looking so well ... the jet beads of her mantilla inkshining in the sun.'[34] It was too cruel, but it had the ring of truth. The wife of Mr

David Sheehy did want her family to do well. It was an ambition she did not hide. The activities of the Sheehy family in the years before the First World War were to become part of international literary heritage. Like it or not, they were members of 'Joyceland'; none of the Sheehys ever wrote anything that contradicted Joyce. Only two members of the Sheehy children wrote any form of memoir and in these neither Hanna the rebel nor Eugene the conformist said anything about intimate Sheehy family life in Belvedere Place.

The mother who appears in Hanna's letters is loving, often conflicted in loyalties between husband and daughter, and much less inclined than her husband to stand on the moral high ground, 'Mother always has a peculiar "air of mystery" with a secret and anyone that knows her well will find it all out' was how Hanna visualised her mother's response to the news of her engagement and the need to keep it a secret for the time being.[35] Her letters to Frank were full of details of a conventional middle-class family, with everyone joining in the evening routine of 'supper, rosary and bed'. If Bessie believed herself to be presiding over the birth of a new ruling class – those who would run the country when Home Rule was won – then her mission in life was to ensure that each member of the family would be ready to play their part when that glorious moment finally arrived.[36] As there was no directly political role the voteless women of that time could fulfil, knowledgeable women with very definite views on public affairs had little choice but to direct their energies into nurturing others. Unusually, Bessie wanted her daughters to do more with their lives than simply make a good marriage. Her endless domestic labours were partly a reflection of the fact that she did not expect her daughters to help her around the house. Hanna's lack of interest in housework extended to giving a small sum of money – even though she was almost penniless – to a French servant to tidy her room, while she was in Paris as an au pair. Marriage would come into Bessie's plans in time – and her insistence that her daughters met the right sort of man would cause more than one family crisis – but culture and education were prized for their own worth, rather than a means to a particular end.

The Sheehy parents wanted the best possible education for all their children – girls as well as boys – and fortunately, by the time Hanna had come of school age, enough progress had been made to enable her to compete on an almost equal footing with her male contemporaries. Boarding-school fees were out of the question. MPs had no salary and the Irish Party could afford to pay its representatives only a modest stipend. The Intermediate Education Act of 1878 had established an examination system of junior, middle and senior grades with schools paid by results. Prizes were awarded to the best pupils and well-timed lobbying by a few dedicated reformers ensured girls were eligible. The prospect of attracting money was a lifeline for impoverished schools catering for girls. In 1883, the Dominican nuns set up their Eccles Street school, a rival to the Protestant establishment of Alexandra College. It had not been an easy task. The first Prioress, Mother Antonina Hanley, had to make a forceful case to Archbishop Walsh of Dublin before permission was granted. Her successor, and the driving force behind the convent's expansion, was Mother Patrick Shiel, who held unusually advanced views, insisting that her girls were entitled to an academic education that would enhance their employment opportunities.[37] Education held the key to a future filled with possibilities unknown to previous generations. Clever girls from less well-off families could finance themselves by winning prizes in examinations and all the Sheehy sisters succeeded in winning exhibitions. The awards, ranging from £20 to £50, were substantial additions to the household expenses. Hanna Sheehy was a model student, winning prizes at each of the three levels in secondary education, a feat which bettered that of the much-lauded Joyce, five years younger.

Her determination to do well shines out from each photo of her school days. A picture from infant class, the children dressed up in costume for 'Arabian Nights', reveals a solemn little girl on the far right of the group, slightly apart from the others. Not someone who would willingly indulge in imaginative or frivolous play. A family portrait, taken when Hanna was in early adolescence, portrays a serious looking young person. A grave, self-possessed figure, leaning over brother Eugene's chair, looks directly at the camera without affectation. The dark hair, deep-set eyes, strong jaw and firm mouth are attractive but not beautiful, unlike Mary, a mass of blond curls and Margaret, whose jawline was softer, cheekbones more defined. Kathleen, the youngest, sits on the floor, another strong face, less feminine in appearance than Mary. Father Eugene, every inch the patriarch, took his seat in the middle of the picture, while David and Bessie, proud parents, stood behind. The addition of the two brothers, Eugene and Dick, wearing sailor suits, rounds off a typically Victorian family scene. Hanna's best feature – blue eyes which were appreciated by many – are lost in those black and white images. Shyness prevented disclosure of her real self. She confided to her diary 'I now realise fully how ugly I am. Eh bien!'[38] She was a slight young woman, conscientiously recording her statistics when doing daily Sandow exercises while in Paris: a 25 1/2 inch waist reduced to 24 1/4 and a 30 inch chest when expanded reduced to 29 3/4.[39] When she was 17 a friend read her character by studying her face. Hanna recorded the results: 'Determined, <u>very</u>, even to obstinacy (heavy brows, closed lip). Sensitive. A good hater. A good lover too, when I did love. Fearinspiring to men! Ah! Ah!' Her diary revealed a self-critical young person, 'It will not be egotism to give a glimpse of myself – from my earliest years I have been a sensitive and even morbid being, fond of weighing the slightest words and giving undue importance to the most trifling accidents. Pride, obstinacy and ambition are my characteristics. Later on I got a tinge of sarcasm.'[40] Only with the supreme indifference that is one of the few gifts of old age could she let the defences drop, and then the whole woman, in all her warmth and humour, can be glimpsed in photographs.

As a school-girl Hanna was given a small antique desk, its intricate mother-of-pearl inlay and tantalising hidden compartments and drawers just the thing to gladden the heart of any young scholar. Father Eugene gave it to his god-daughter with the intention of encouraging her studies.[41] It was obviously a successful ploy, if such was needed. After one of her prizes Eugene treated Hanna to a trip to London, where they visited her father's place of work, the House of Commons. The adolescent girl heard Gladstone, one of the last of the great nineteenth-century parliamentarians, speak on Home Rule.[42] On the summer of her Intermediate exam results Eugene interrupted her family holiday in Rockhill to take her to Cork and Limerick. The river Lee was Cork's only beauty she thought, as the city was 'dimmed with smoke, much disfigured with worldliness' while the introspective adolescent, despite catching up with cousins in Limerick, concluded 'on the whole I did not enjoy my visit to Limerick', resenting her uncle's 'abrupt refusal' to let her go to Laurel Hill (a convent school in Limerick) and muttering that he would be 'hoist with his own petard'. This period seems to have been a difficult time for Hanna, who was full of doubts, convinced she was underachieving academically. She berated herself for lacking purpose, ambition: 'I have no encouragement, no one cares and I am weary of it all!' She hoped her 'old courage' would soon return. On her exam results all she could write was 'I will only relate all when all grief is over. At present, no.'[43]

In common with many convent girls, religion, not politics, was Hanna's preoccupation. She had a strong religious sense and was not in any way critical of religious dogma or of church institutions. Ireland at the turn of the century had few openings for women and one of the most significant of all influences were the women with whom she came into daily contact, the nuns who taught her. The female religious she encountered were strong-minded and well-educated women who appeared – to outsiders at least – to have great independence of action. For a young woman trying to decide what her future path should be, there were obvious attractions in the life of a teaching order like the Dominicans. Bazzie Hughes, her best friend in college, entered the order after graduating in classics, her degree substituting for the dowry her family could not afford.[44] She became 'Sister Peter', but was always 'Bazzie' to the Sheehy women. She and Hanna remained friends for life. Hanna's nephew believed that, for a while, she too intended becoming a nun. If that had been the case, surely she would have become 'a great reforming Mother Superior'.[45] There were several she could have modelled herself upon. In those early years of struggling for women's access to education, nuns like Mother Patrick and her Loreto counterpart, Mother Eucharia, were formidable women who had to overcome many obstacles in their efforts to improve educational facilities for Catholic girls. They were well-known characters, remembered with deep affection by all who encountered them.

Improvements in access to education were not confined to secondary schools. A small élite of Irish women was to benefit from the reform of higher education which arose through the passing of the Royal University of Ireland Act of 1879. This was intended as an examining body only, without any facilities for teaching subjects, and it was introduced primarily as a means of providing Catholics with access to degrees. It was up to the students themselves to study at any college they chose, then enrol for the exam papers set by the Royal. The handful of women involved in campaigning for improvements in girls' education seized the opportunity they had been waiting for: parliament was lobbied, and MPs agreed that women could be awarded degrees by this new body. At first, the provision of higher education for women was confined to the Protestant sector, but not for long. The Dominican nuns succeeded in convincing Dr Walsh that if the nuns were unable to provide a university education for their senior pupils there was a danger that these girls would defect to Protestantism. Apostasy had to be prevented; the bishop gave in. In 1885 university classes began in Eccles Street. Five years later, one of Mother Peter's students, Catherine Murphy, took first place in Ireland in the BA degree in Modern Languages [46] In 1893 there was further recognition of the enhanced status of women students with the setting up of St Mary's University College at 28 Merrion Square. It was a constituent part of the Royal system, administered by the Dominicans. The prospectus announced that 'St Mary's University and High School has been founded for the purpose of affording Catholic ladies complete facilities for Higher Education in all its branches.' Church approval was made public the following year, when Archbishop Walsh donated £500 to the college, to be given out in prize money.

Ill-health appears to account for the morbid thoughts Hanna expressed in her adolescent diary. She didn't realise this, writing furiously when Uncle

Eugene, on a family visit, questioned her too closely on how she was, 'I wish he weren't so demonstrative – asking me was I well in every way? Now what's the meaning of that. I am not sick. I am not deranged. It implies both.'[47] However, as her health grew worse, Bessie wrote to Eugene to say they hoped, if finance could be arranged, to send Hanna to Germany. He immediately, out of his private funds, sent £50, thereafter writing to Hanna while she was abroad what she described as 'letter after letter…of passionate tenderness and affection'.[48] In later years she confirmed that incipient tuberculosis sent her 'roving to the Rhineland' for a short time at the end of the school year.[49]

Recovered, Hanna enrolled in St Mary's as a first-year student of modern languages. Mlle Lydie Ducondon was a teacher for whom she had a strong affection. Although she later moved to New York, they kept in touch. In 1916, one of Hanna's first acts in arriving in that city was to contact her old teacher, 'hearing with joy the well-known voice over the phone of my former professor of French and pouring into her eager ears all the news of many of her old friends and pupils'. She visited again in 1922, pleased then to discover that Mlle Ducondon shared her hostility to the Treaty.[50] Hanna remained loyal to the Dominicans, but when the Loreto order of nuns set up their own university classes in St Stephen's Green, Mary and Kathleen Sheehy decided to go there for their BA studies. These developments meant that the girls were able to benefit from an education that differed very little from that of their brothers, although they complained, with justification, that because of their sex they were denied attendance at University College lectures. They were also a tiny minority amongst the students. In 1911 there were still only 280 female students, compared with over 3,000 males. Hanna's later reservations concerning the influence of religion upon the development of Irish society never extended to the female religious of her youth. In 1904, reviewing a morality play staged as part of the Sion Hill Convent's Jubilee festivities, with many past pupils taking part, she declared 'such a performance is to justify fully the reputation as educators which the Dominican sisters have already won'.[51] In 1918, in the midst of a hectic schedule of meetings in New York, she took the time to write to her old friends in Eccles Street, just to let them know that she was surviving, despite everything that had happened.[52] They cared for her and wanted to know of her well-being. Not long before her death, all religious beliefs firmly relegated to the past, Hanna was still able to acknowledge the fact that the nuns who taught her had given her 'great independence of thought and action'.[53] She could not have bestowed any greater praise.

The most privileged group of students were the men from Trinity College; most were members of the Anglo-Irish élite, enjoying the finest of educations. Their female counterparts in Alexandra College at least benefited from having some of the same lectures, as staff repeated their lectures to the women. In contrast, none of the colleges, male or female, comprising the Catholic Royal system possessed the facilities so essential to student life. There were no purpose-built dining halls, libraries or athletic fields. The one slight gain from this situation was the use of the reading room of the National Library, a substitute for the non-existent college libraries. As the library was only around the corner from the women's colleges it served several generations of students, its spacious entrance hall an informal meeting place which, in a small way, helped to break down the enforced segregation of the sexes. Students came and went freely, a clicking turnstile the only marker on their movements. There was a room set aside for women, but this was so little used that the library eventually took it over for much-needed storage space. The table arrangements were different in those days, the desks were four-square instead of individual, encouraging talk and mild flirtation, or, in Hanna's case, enabling discreet notes to be dropped, arranging later rendezvous.

Women and men took the same exams and all were judged on their merits. This could sometimes give the men a salutary lesson concerning the intellectual merits of female scholars. There were undeniable weaknesses in an under-resourced convent education, particularly given the lack of higher training of many of the staff, but they had strengths in several areas, in classics and in 'Mental and Moral Science' as well as in the more usual disciplines of English and languages. Many of the orders had strong links with Europe and this meant that female students posed a strong challenge to the men when it came to examinations in modern languages. The men were distinctly uncomfortable at this unheard-of competition. In *Stephen Hero*, Joyce, a language student himself, described a scene outside the examination hall, where 'The girl students were not the subject of the usual sniggers and jokes but were regarded with some aversion as sly enemies.'[54] Mary Macken, a Loreto student and one of the first female professors, was encouraged by Sister Eucharia to go abroad for language study. As Macken remembered, the nuns had excellent contacts and were experts in finding suitable centres for their students in Germany, France and Italy. Hanna loved Europe, declaring it to be 'a mighty good thing to travel when young'.[55] In her case, it established a curiosity about other places and other lives that remained with her always. She was an inveterate traveller.

This recognition of a life beyond the narrow confines of Ireland was shared by the Sheehy sisters. It was the outcome of the efforts of three remarkable women, who shared a dedication to furthering the cause of women's education and who preferred to bypass Britain in so doing. Sophie Raffalovitch was the daughter of a Paris-based Russian Jewish banker (married to the same William O'Brien who had been a friend of David Sheehy since his youth). Her friend Blanche Gabrielle Merten was headmistress of a girls' school in Amiens and Mother Peter, head of the Dominican school in Eccles Street, completed the trio.[56] This chain of contacts meant that from 1904 onwards, a succession of pupils from the Eccles Street school was able to spend a year at the Amiens Ecole Primaire Superieure de Fines. Mary Sheehy was first, to be followed the next year by Kathleen. Hanna had left school before this exchange scheme began, but she was to benefit from the development of a strong and enduring friendship between her family and the Fontaines of Amiens. Germaine Fontaine, who came to know the family very well, spent the Christmas of 1904 at Belvedere Place. Her reminiscences contain telling little sketches of each family member. All were attractive personalities, but in Germaine's eyes Hanna appears to have combined the most appealing of the different Sheehy character traits:

> Margaret, majestic and beautiful in a rather haughty way … Mary, whom I knew and liked very much, gentle and lovely; Kathleen, very jolly and dynamic, about the same age as me … Dick whom I admired greatly because he seemed to be a well of knowledge … Eugene, very amusing with his deadpan humour, skinny and bony but full of vitality. I soon got to know the oldest daughter Hanna … She too was very attractive because she knew how to incorporate more subtly all the qualities of the others.[57]

As the Sheehy children matured and developed their own friendships, their house became a notable venue for people from many different walks of life. Friendships between the sexes were not frowned upon at 2 Belvedere Place, where Sheehy 'At Homes' were held on the second Sunday of each month. Their hospitality was valued and eagerly sought. One of the young visitors recalled the 'genuine homeliness' of 'Old David and Mrs Sheehy (who) were open-hearted and had an old-style Irish welcome for everybody, young and old, rich and less rich.'[58] Entertainment was not on a lavish scale – refreshments were limited to tea and sandwiches – but attributes of wit and quick-thinking were highly-prized. Germaine Fontaine, used to the formality of the French, found herself astounded by the 'heaps' of people who found seats where they could, from the basement to the staircase. One habitué fondly remembered the Sheehy back parlour: 'I think all the so-called modern games originated there, "information please", "question time", and all the rest. In those days we invented our own amusements and there was no lack of imagination.'[59] In her later years Hanna recalled those days with great affection:

'Yes, Jim Joyce and many of the UCD and old "Royal" students came to our Sundays in Belvedere Place … Joyce was then gay and boyish, flinging himself into topical charades. He loved to 'dress up' and produce plays and parodies, and to sing old folk ballads in his sweet tenor.'[60] She remembered her parents being very hospitable to their children's friends. The possession of two brothers was a great asset in obtaining extra male company. Dick and Eugene both attended Belvedere College. Dick, described by Stanislaus Joyce as 'a big, stalwart, good-natured fellow whose jokes were sometimes on the heavy side',[61] later became a professor in law at University College, Galway while Eugene rose to the heights of circuit court judge. Unlike their sisters, they were destined to become pillars of the establishment.

All the Sheehy sisters, in their different ways, retained a capacity to impress acquaintances that age did little to diminish, as Patricia Hutchins discovered when researching Joyce's Dublin: 'Later on I met one of the daughters of this family. They had all been handsome, vivacious, sharing that pleasant-sounding, half-humorous intonation, the accent of the Ireland-educated gentlemen and gentlewomen of another generation.'[62] Margaret (always known as Maggie to her family), less intellectual than her sisters, was the instigator of many of their plays and charades. When she persuaded Joyce to write a paper on Ibsen for her literary group, Hanna commented wryly 'Power of the smile!'[63] Margaret enjoyed clothes and drama and the gossip of everyday life, impatient with those who preferred boring conversations on politics. She and Hanna cooperated in writing a play called *Cupid's Confidante* with Joyce playing the part of the villain, Geoffrey Fortescue, at a public performance at the XL Café on Grafton Street.[64] Mary was the one with the looks. 'She is very handsome and wears an immense plait of soft black hair', wrote Stanislaus Joyce in his diary.[65] Many agreed, but she was more than merely a pretty face. James Joyce, who knew the family better than his brother, confided that in his opinion Mary Sheehy seemed to have 'a great contempt for many of the people she knew'.[66] Men coming to the Sheehy household knew better than to presume that they could have interesting flirtations with the sisters of Eugene and Dick. Hanna was quieter than her sisters but was possessed of a cutting wit, which she learned to put to good use. Her intelligence was immediately apparent; her seriousness enough to deter the idle.

Suspicions of those who were trying to promote the Irish language was a common trait amongst many of Ireland's educated middle-class at this period. It was part of their identification with progress, with sympathy for the radical and anti-clerical elements in European political life, combined with a fear that the revival of ancient traditions would hold back progress rather than stimulate it. Kathleen (Kay to the family), the sister Hanna was closest to in later years, was the only one to join the Irish language movement, the Gaelic League. Although in her youth it was fashionable for members of the student debating society to walk around with copies of O'Growney's *Simple Lessons* in Irish peeping from their jacket pockets, Hanna's attitude was similar to Tom Kettle's quip: 'Here we are, learning Irish on the threshold of becoming accomplished speakers of English.'[67] On her return from Paris, meeting up with her school friend Agnes O'Farrelly and hearing all about the Gaelic League bored Hanna greatly, 'she spoke of Irish nearly all the time and really I was tired when she went!'[68] Hanna was a proficient speaker of both German and French. Throughout her life her letters contained French and German words used in the unselfconscious manner of someone steeped in a language that was almost her own. She was an internationalist, enjoying conferences abroad, where she revelled in her ability to communicate. A typical occasion occurred after an International Women's Suffrage Congress, held in Paris, where she had a long meeting with the leader of the Egyptian delegation. Hoda Shaarawi had very little English, so they spoke in French.[69] The only period when promoters of the Irish language had her public support was in the very different circumstances of post-Treaty Ireland, when the issue became a convenient one with which to berate the Free State government.

In these early years of women's entry into higher education there was a marked contrast between the casual life of the typical male student and the restricted existence of the women. The latter were barred from entering the male dominion of University College, Dublin and both those who lived in hostels and those who lived at home were subject to restrictions on where they could go and at what time they could return. Unregulated interaction between the sexes was regarded with horror and every precaution was taken to ensure that this would not occur. Mary Maguire, another pupil of Loreto College, remarked that 'male and female students at the university in those days paid little attention to one another, as such relations were frowned on by the authorities'.[70] Mary Macken, less interested in meeting members of the opposite sex, considered the worst aspect of this segregation was not the restricted freedoms but the lack of any common centre of student life, a place to encourage a meeting of minds and 'interplay of energies and ideas'.[71] One could arrange to meet on the steps of the National Library, but this was too public for those who valued their privacy.

The men of University College had the ramshackle, candle-lit Old Physics Theatre of 86 St Stephens Green, venue for the famous debates of the Literary and Historical Society, but the women were barred from attendance. Even the innocuous suggestion that the women be admitted for one debate each year (to be held in the Aula Maxima rather than the notorious surroundings of No. 86), was defeated. The only concession to the 'unfairly-treated' sex (as Hanna's brother Eugene recalled with loyal indignation) was permission for them to attend the yearly inaugurals. Other than that, 'Mr Barrett of Wimpole Street' was still in control.[72] Father Delany, President of University College, was the Irish equivalent of Mr Barrett. He was a staunch opponent of co-education, advancing several arguments against the presence of women students at the L & H. The ladies would have the great danger of being out late at night and having to cross the city on their return home; furthermore, they might jeopardise the morality of the male students, not to mention the possibility of undesirable or unhappy marriages that might result. In 1907 he used his powers to nullify an interpretation of the rules that would have admitted women, and only in 1910 (a sign of the changing times), was a vote allowing women into the Society finally taken.[73] But they were still subject to the curfew imposed by the residential hostels, which resulted in the ritual of the 9 p.m. 'simultaneous swish of the skirts' as the female section of the audience was forced to exit.

Female students did their best to create some form of intellectual life for themselves, despite their meagre resources. In 1889 young women at St Mary's had set up their own debating society: St Mary's Literary Academy. Much less attention was paid to the outcome of their debates, but in terms of topics chosen for discussion, there was little discernible difference between the sexes. Amongst those listed for St Mary's are: 'Nationality versus Cosmopolitanism in Literature', 'Young Ireland' and (one topic chosen by Hanna) 'Some Moral Aspects of the Drama'. They also chose issues that had a more specific relevance for women: 'What women can do for the city poor' and The Last Four Generations of Women'.[74] Conventions were slowly changing. Hanna remembered when a woman was first seen riding a bicycle on the Quays 'she was set upon by the mob and narrowly escaped ducking in the Liffey by the shocked male hooligans of the day', but the bicycle had come to stay and 'it helped more than any single factor to emancipate the 20th century girl.'[75]

Formal interaction between male and female students occurred in the columns of *St Stephen's*, the student magazine of University College. Here the women could write – by invitation only – in a column called 'Girl Graduates Chat'. Several of the men recalled Mary Olivia Kennedy, sister of Hugh, the first editor, 'tartly and smartly' writing her page.[76] Being relegated to trivia of this kind infuriated many. William Dawson claimed that 'in times of stress' it was written by the men, which might explain the quality of some of those pages.[77] Mary Kennedy later moved to London, to become a staff member of *The Times*, so her desire to write was probably greater than any scruples about the type of publication requiring her contribution. As the women had no journal of their own (the Dominicans only began to produce *The Lanthorn*, their college yearbook, in 1913), frustratingly, we have very little information on the views that young female students might have wanted to express.

As the nineteenth century drew to a close, important changes began to improve the status of Irish women. In 1896 the Poor Law Guardians Act allowed women to vote for and to become poor law guardians, while the Local Government Act of 1898 allowed Irish women to vote for and to be elected as members of district councils. All this was 30 years behind women in Britain, yet it did seem, finally, that women in Ireland were entering a more modern age. Another small advance was made in the 1899 elections when 85 women were elected as poor law guardians, another 35 women becoming councillors.[78] A Dublin Women's Suffrage Association had been formed as early as 1876 by the Quaker couple, Anna and Thomas Haslam. This held few public meetings, concentrating most of its activities in the drawing-rooms of the influential. Such a genteel plea for the franchise held little attraction for many female students, particularly as they were too young to vote, but the Haslam group would be an important first stage for many young militants. It served an invaluable function in providing a forum where like-minded people could meet. In 1901 the organisation changed its name to the Irish Women's Suffrage and Local Government Association, a reflection of its emphasis in supporting women who wanted a role in local government or as poor law guardians.

Hanna graduated in 1899, receiving a BA with second class honours in modern languages. By this stage she had met Frank Skeffington, but as far as her family was concerned, he was no more significant than any of her other friends. Their growing love for each other was kept quiet as Frank was completing his studies and his future prospects were extremely vague. David Sheehy was out of parliament between 1900 and 1903 and family finances, never robust, were precarious until the Irish Party appointed him as secretary to the United Irish League. When Hanna went to Paris in October 1900 her room was let out to an Englishman, who paid £1, receiving breakfast and tea in return. It was a huge relief, 'I am not a burden … my room is contributing to the fund,' she wrote to Frank.[79] As eldest in a close-knit family, she often worried about her siblings. Maggie, Mary, Kathleen, mother, Minnie (the maid) and Aunt Kate were all 'in floods of tears' as she left for Paris (with

Frank waving frantically to her from a distance, unable to reveal his presence).[80] She felt guilty at leaving Mary and Kathleen, now aged 16 and 14, feeling very involved with their education and development as young women.

Being a companion to the invalid Madame Pannier (who died in May 1901) and her daughter Gabrielle was a pleasant interlude, although Hanna was surprised that they didn't attend Mass, causing her considerable consternation in missing Mass on her first Sunday in Paris. After that she was dutiful in attendance, also going to Benediction on occasion. There was an unvarying routine of an early morning chat with Madame, then translation with Mademoiselle, followed by lunch at 11.30 am. After resting, reading and writing she was able to go out from 3 until 5-30, with dinner at 6.30 pm. This was followed by reading French to Madame Pannier (*Cyrano de Bergerac* was greatly enjoyed) before socialising with Gabrielle in the salon and retiring at 10 pm. Gabrielle played piano and tried to teach chess to an unenthusiastic Hanna. Père Lachaise cemetery was a favourite location for walks and the two young women made several visits to the Exposition, a world's fair that took place in Paris between April and November that year, showcasing Art Nouveau. The food at the Panniers was 'splendid' with white wine and black coffee and plenty of fruit. She later confessed to a teetotal Frank that she had decided she didn't care for champagne as it made her hot and 'inclined to headache'.[81]

While in Paris Hanna continued to plan for her future. She began to attend lectures in the Sorbonne and was determined to study for a studentship, urging Frank 'you must win me that studentship', wishing he could sit the English part while she concentrated upon the languages. She thought (wrongly as it turned out, as the pair fought over the priority to be given to their different intellectual interests) that she would be a 'docile' student and, full of confidence for the future, declared 'we ought to be a formidable alliance'.[82] Frank completed his degree with brilliant results, 'I laughed at your account of the orals. My dear old "cheeky" Frank!'[83] and was teaching, most unhappily, in Kilkenny, lonely and overburdened with marking. Hanna expected him to make some decision regarding his future, and to have a firm plan on how to achieve his goal. She was a stern critic of what she felt was his 'hopeless drifting', not wanting to continue teaching, trying unsuccessfully to write a novel, being urged by her to decide upon the civil service, the Bar or literature so that they could fix the date of their marriage.[84]

Once back in Dublin Hanna resumed her studies and enjoyed taking part in the student life. The realisation that more than half of her friends had entered the convent to become nuns astounded her: 'extraordinary the amount of fine girls that enter every day.'[85] She enjoyed the debates and reported to Frank that Mary Hayden's paper on European literature 'showed deep wide reading and keen, good humoured powers of criticism. Sentimentalism she attacked strongly'. Hanna was a harsh critic – Miss Ryan – (presumably Mary Kate) speaking at the same event, was dismissed as being 'no good. Nervous in delivery and commonplace generally.'[86] There may have been some element of prejudice in this assessment, as Mary Kate Ryan would go on to have a distinguished academic career, becoming Professor of Romance Languages in University College Cork in 1910. However, the Loreto-educated, country-born Ryan sisters felt 'looked down upon by the *haute bourgeois* Sheehys'. As a possible complication, Mary Kate was also involved with Tom Kettle who, in 1909, would marry Mary Sheehy.[87] When the nuns asked Hanna to prepare a paper on Mrs Humphrey Ward for their next debate it was a task she took seriously, although she felt that Mrs Ward would be attacked by the priests 'and probably Miss Hayden will be my only supporter'. Mrs Ward's stress on the importance of social concerns rather than theology in religion would undoubtedly have been unpopular with the Catholic clergy, but championing this position provides a clue on the continuing development of Hanna's views. She was grateful to Frank's help on delivery (he had won a silver medal for oratory from the Literary & Historical Society), 'you'll make me an orator yet Frank! I am very apt to get too indignant and I think in speaking that would be very bad!'[88] It is an irony of history that Mrs Humphrey Ward later became a leading figure in the anti-suffrage movement in Britain.

In 1902 Hanna obtained an MA with first class honours and a special prize of £25. Her achievements, as one of her professors testified, were 'much above the level attainable by a brilliant student' because of her 'steady persistent application' as well as her 'superior mental equipment',[89] but there were other outstanding female graduates, all of them conscious of their role as pioneers. Some of Hanna's contemporaries from Eccles Street later distinguished themselves as scholars and teachers. Mary Hayden, slightly older, founder of their Past Pupil's Union, became the first female professor of history at University College, Dublin, while Louise Gavan Duffy, who later went on to found the Irish-speaking school *Scoil Bhride*, taught in Patrick Pearse's school and was writing her dissertation for her MA degree when the Easter Rising began. That task was abandoned, temporarily, when she decided to offer her services to the rebels in their GPO headquarters. Agnes O'Farrelly became the first Celtic teacher in Alexandra College, the leading Protestant school for girls. It is significant that the best of the intellects ended up in the teaching profession. What other openings were there for intelligent, highly qualified women? Office work and the civil service were new areas of employment for women, but graduates were over-qualified for the work on offer. It was not easy for young Catholic women to secure teaching work as the nuns enjoyed a monopoly in that field. When they did employ outsiders, it was as cheap labour, filling in until a qualified nun took her place.

Through her friendship with the Dominicans, Hanna secured some part-time teaching of literature. Degree-level teaching had transferred back to Eccles Street and she was able, from her home in Belvedere Place, to come and go with ease. At this stage in her life she was a dutiful daughter, living at home, earning a modest living in teaching, somewhat of a 'bluestocking' with her serious attitudes and fondness for intellectual pleasures. She was still a committed member of the Roman Catholic faith. True, women occupied a notably subordinate place in the Catholic hierarchy, but the female-centred world created by the nuns was the reality she experienced in her daily life. What irked Hanna was the fact that her sex and her religion were insurmountable obstacles on the ladder of career advancement. Catholic lay women had no possibility of achieving high status in the teaching profession. In beginning to question the rationale for this situation she was to find herself becoming estranged from the political and religious institutions she held responsible. In a few short years she would develop a burning resentment at the undemocratic and unaccountable nature of church power in Ireland. As a campaigner, the goal of achieving equality for women teachers was one that stayed with her throughout her life. Before long, she would start to see connections between women's lack of economic power and their political disenfranchisement. She was unusual in having the influence of her family's involvement with the Ladies' Land League as a reminder that women had played a role in past struggles and as a warning that their male colleagues had not appreciated that contribution. Hanna's intellectual journey towards a lifetime of fighting for a society free from the authoritarianism of both the church and the British state was rooted in a growing understanding that the feminist aspiration for political, social and economic equality had to be a part of all movements for social change. As her views continued to develop, she was fortunate to have a companion who was equally principled and single-minded.

NOTES

1 Hanna Sheehy Skeffington, 'Memories of Father Sheehy of Kilmallock', in *Irish Press*, 18 July 1932. With thanks to Roisin Sheehy Culhane.

2 Hanna Sheehy to Frank Skeffington (hereafter Hanna to Frank), 26 Oct. 1900, Sheehy Skeffington MS (hereafter SS MS) 40,464/2.

3 Obituary of David Sheehy, 'David Sheehy (S. H. C. 1861–4)', *S. H. C.*, 1933. Journal of Sacred Heart College, Limerick. The school was known as St Munchin's College at the time of David and Eugene Sheehy. With thanks to Roisin Sheehy Culhane for this reference.

4 Hanna to Frank, 14 Nov. 1900, SS MS 40,464/2.

5 I am indebted to Mary McCoy, great grand-daughter of Hanna's uncle, Patrick McCoy, for information in this chapter regarding the McCoy family.

6 Hanna Sheehy Skeffington, 'Unpublished memoirs', in Margaret Ward (ed.) *Hanna Sheehy Skeffington: Suffragette and Sinn Féiner: Her Memoirs and Political Writings* (Dublin, 2017), p. 4.

7 Eugene Sheehy, *May It Please The Court*, (Dublin: C. J. Fallon, 1951), p. 124.

8 Hanna Sheehy, diary 1894–5, SS MS 41,183/2.

9 Hanna Sheehy Skeffington 'Unpublished memoirs', in Ward, *Hanna Sheehy Skeffington*, pp 8–9.

10 Hanna Sheehy Skeffington, 'Looking backward', in *The Distributive Worker*, Dec. 1941.

11 Hanna to Frank, 27 May 1901, SS MS 40,464/7.

12 Dublin Street Census, 1911, Belvedere Place, 44/5, National Archives, Dublin. This was the first time when the census asked specific questions concerning fertility, hence Bessie's entry.

13 Quoted in Leah Levenson and Jerry Natterstad, *Hanna Sheehy Skeffington: Irish Feminist* (Syracuse, 1986), p. 5.

14 Hanna Sheehy Skeffington 'Unpublished memoirs', in Ward, *Hanna Sheehy Skeffington*, p. 9.

15 *Irish Press*, 18 July 1938.

16 Jane Côté, *Fanny and Anna Parnell: Ireland's Patriot Sisters* (Dublin, 1991), p. 174. Hanna referred to her uncle's appellation in her article 'The Land League Priest: memories of Father Sheehy of Kilmallock', *Irish Press*, 18 July 1938.

17 *Irish Press*, 18 July 1938.

18 Hanna to Frank, 14 Nov. 1900, SS MS 40,464/2.

19 Germaine Fontaine, *Unpublished Reminiscences 1903–4*, courtesy of Andrée Sheehy Skeffington.

20 Hanna to Frank, 14 Nov. 1900, SS MS 40,464/2.

21 Fr Eugene Sheehy to Hanna Sheehy, 23 Apr. 1903 from New York and 1, 17 Aug. 1903 from Rome, SS MS 41,176/18.

22 Fr Eugene Sheehy to John Devoy, 14 Dec. 1904, in William O'Brien and Desmond Ryan (eds) *Devoy's Post Bag 1871–1925* (Dublin, 1948, reprinted Dublin, 1979), p. 353.

23 Fr Eugene Sheehy to Hanna Sheehy Skeffington, 12 July 1904, SS MS 22,662.

24 Obituary of David Sheehy, *S. H. C.*, 1933.

25 R. M. Fox, *Rebel Irishwomen* (Dublin, 1935), p. 73.

26 Hanna Sheehy Skeffington 'Unpublished memoirs', in Ward, *Hanna Sheehy Skeffington* p. 3.
27 RTE radio interview with Dr Dixon, interviewer, 1945, incomplete transcript, SS MS 24,164.
28 Conor Cruise O'Brien, *States of Ireland*, (St Albans, 1974), p. 34.
29 Donald Akenson, *Conor Cruise O'Brien* (Montreal, 1994), p. 11.
30 James Joyce, *Stephen Hero* (St Albans, Triad/Panther Books, 1977), p. 45.
31 Hanna Sheehy, diary 1894–5, SS MS 41,183/2.
32 Germaine Fontaine, *Unpublished Reminiscences 1903–4*.
33 Obituary of Bessie Sheehy, in *Irish Citizen*, Jan. 1918.
34 James Joyce, *Ulysses* (London, Penguin Books, 1969), p. 219.
35 Hanna to Frank, 29 Oct. 1900, SS MS 40,464/1.
36 Cruise O'Brien, *States of Ireland*, p. 62.
37 For more on the education of girls in Ireland, see Mary Cullen (ed.), *Girls Don't Do Honours: Irish Women in Education in the Nineteenth and Twentieth Centuries* (Dublin, 1987); Judith Harford, 'The admission of women to the National University of Ireland', in *Education Research and Perspectives*, 35:2, 2006, pp 44–54.
38 Hanna Sheehy, diary 1894–5, SS MS 41,183/2.
39 Itemised measurements, copied for Frank, in SS MS 40,464/5.
40 Hanna Sheehy, diary 1894–5, SS MS 41,183/2.
41 Andrée Sheehy Skeffington, interview with author, Nov. 1993.
42 Hanna Sheehy Skeffington, RTE radio interview, 1945, SS MS 24,164.
43 Hanna Sheehy, diary 1894–5, SS MS 41,183/2
44 Margaret MacCurtain, 'Women of Eccles Street', in *The Lanthorn*, yearbook of the Dominican College, Eccles street, centenary year 1982, p. 56. With many thanks to Margaret MacCurtain for the gift of this copy, and for sharing her knowledge of the Dominicans with me.
45 Cruise O'Brien, *States of Ireland*, p. 81.
46 Sister M. Enda O.P., '*Jubilate Deo*, the Story of Dominican College Eccles Street', *The Lanthorn*, 1982, p. 21.
47 Hanna Sheehy, diary 1894–5, SS MS 41,183/2.
48 Hanna to Frank, 14 Nov. 1900, SS MS 40,464/2.
49 Hanna Sheehy Skeffington, RTE radio interview, 1945.
50 *Irish World*, 31 Jan. 1925.
51 Sion Hill Jubilee Festivities, 22 Dec. 1904, SS MS 24,146.
52 Margaret MacCurtain, 'Women of Eccles Street', *The Lanthorn*, 1982, p. 56.
53 Hanna Sheehy Skeffington, RTE radio interview, 1945.
54 Joyce, *Stephen Hero*, p. 119.
55 RTE radio interview with Dr Dixon, interviewer, 1945, incomplete transcript, SS MS 24,164.
56 Andrée Sheehy Skeffington, *Skeff: A Life of Owen Sheehy Skeffington* (Dublin, 1991), p. 53.
57 Germaine Fontaine, *Unpublished Reminiscences 1903–4*.
58 Patricia Hutchins, *James Joyce's Dublin* (London, 1950), p. 72.
59 Ibid.

60 Hanna Sheehy Skeffington, RTE radio interview, 1945.
61 Stanislaus Joyce, *My Brother's Keeper* (London, 1958), p. 123.
62 Hutchins, *James Joyce's Dublin*, p. 72.
63 Hanna to Frank, 14 Oct. 1900, SS MS 40,464/1.
64 Joseph Holloway diaries, MS 23,247, National Library of Ireland (hereafter NLI). Richard Ellman claims that Margaret wrote the play (see Richard Ellman, *James Joyce* (Oxford, 1982), p. 93); however, Andrée Sheehy Skeffington states that the play was written by Hanna and produced by Margaret, see Andrée Sheehy Skeffington, *Skeff*, p. 10. In conversation, Andrée Sheehy Skeffington stated her belief that Margaret would not have been capable of writing the play.
65 J.B. Lyons, *The Enigma of Tom Kettle: Irish Patriot, Essayist, Poet, British Soldier, 1880–1916* (Dublin, 1983), p. 43.
66 Quoted in Bonnie Kime Scott, 'Emma Clery in *Stephen Hero:* A young woman walking proudly through the decayed city', in Suzette Henke and Elaine Unkeless (eds), *Women in Joyce* (Hertfordshire, 1982), n33, p. 62.
67 James Meenan (ed.), *Centenary History of the Literary and Historical Society of University College Dublin 1855–1955* (Tralee, 1957), p. 96.
68 Hanna to Frank, 19 Apr. 1901, SS MS 40,464/5.
69 *Irish World*, 3 July 1926. Hoda Shaarawi founded the Egyptian Feminist Union in 1923. Pacha was the name of her husband, who died that year.
70 Quoted in Kime Scott, 'Emma Clery in *Stephen Hero*', p. 62.
71 Michael Tierney (ed.), *Struggle with Fortune: A Miscellany for the Centenary of the Catholic University of Ireland 1854–1954* (Dublin, 1954), p. 157.
72 James Meenan, *Centenary History*, p. 79.
73 Ibid., p. 140.
74 Bonnie Kime Scott, *Joyce and Feminism* (Hertfordshire, 1984), p. 42.
75 Hanna Sheehy Skeffington 'Unpublished memoirs', in Ward, *Hanna Sheehy Skeffington*, p. 12.
76 C. P. Curran, *Under the Receding Wave* (Dublin, 1970), p. 118.
77 James Meenan, *Centenary History*, p. 46.
78 Rosemary Cullen Owens, *Smashing Times: A History of the Irish Women's Suffrage Movement 1889–1922* (Dublin, 1984), p. 30.
79 Hanna to Frank, 11 Dec. 1900, SS MS 40,464/2.
80 Ibid., 7 Oct. 1900, SS MS 40,464/1.
81 Ibid., 15 Dec. 1900, SS MS 40,464/3.
82 Ibid., 18 Dec. 1900, SS MS 40,464/3.
83 Ibid., 10 Oct. 1900, SS MS 40,464/1.
84 Ibid., 15 Dec. 1900, SS MS 40,464/3.
85 Ibid., 28 Apr. 1901, SS MS 40,464/5.
86 Ibid., 25 Apr. 1901, SS MS 40,464/5.
87 Roy Foster, *Vivid Faces: The Revolutionary Generation in Ireland 1890–1923* (London, 2014), pp 66–7.
88 Hanna to Frank, 3 June 1901, SS MS 40,464/8.
89 William Magennis, advisory examiner in English to intermediate board, University College Dublin, 12 Dec. 1903, SS MS 22,662.

TWO

THE MAKING OF A FEMINIST, 1900–03

'Skeffy', the man Joyce dubbed 'hairy jaysus', had become an important figure in Hanna's life soon after they met in 1899. By 24 May the following year – the date of Hanna's birthday – they had decided they wanted to marry, keeping this secret until Frank had established himself in a profession. Francis Skeffington was five months younger than Hanna and still an undergraduate, so the engagement was lengthy, causing much emotional and sexual anguish to both. As a young woman studying for her degree and irritated by the second-class status of university women, Hanna had warmed to that opinionated young man, his distinctive appearance impossible to overlook on the steps of the National Library, his high-pitched voice equally difficult to ignore. The fact that one of the issues he felt so strongly about was women's rights, made him all the more interesting. He was very different from those who surrounded him. One victim remembered 'Skeffington's arguments, in his crisp Ulster accent, came in sharp telling bursts, suggestive of machine-gun fire, and with the same shattering effect on the views of his opponents.'[1] In Roger McHugh's opinion, 'If you were a carefree student you would not have liked Skeffington particularly.' He was too apt to take casual remarks seriously, expecting you to have the courage of your convictions and to speak up for them at a public meeting arranged by himself, walking briskly away and leaving the unfortunate 'with a totally unwanted sense of responsibility.'[2]

No one could deflect Frank from doing whatever he had decided to do. His physical appearance alone made it plain that here was an espouser of causes. Sporting a ginger beard (he had never shaved, a protest against the tyranny of having to do so), he always wore tweed knickerbockers, long socks and boots. When he commissioned a suit for himself, discussing the issue endlessly in letters, Hanna replied, with the enthusiasm of early love, 'I would be very interested in your taste … you know without being told that I am absolutely indifferent as to opinion on this style or that, so I begin my education free from prejudice!'[3] She was less enthusiastic on hearing details, 'a grey and green that is khaki' … Well, I shall see.'),[4] trying later to persuade him that the purchase of another suit might be necessary. He wore the suit for his graduation, ignoring the disapproval of his mother. Only five feet four and a half inches in height (according to Dublin Castle prison records), he was a cartoonist's dream. He was against smoking and drinking, an anti-vivisectionist, a convinced pacifist. Once the suffrage movement began Frank always wore a badge in his lapel declaring 'Votes for Women'. As an Ulsterman, his directness was in some contrast to the easy-going Dubliners, who never failed to be amused by his expectation that meetings would start on time. His father, Dr Joseph Bartholomew Skeffington (known as Dr J. B.), a graduate of the Royal College of Science and, by profession, an inspector of schools, 'knew more about education than most people' and therefore refused to send his only son to school, teaching him at their home in Downpatrick. Father and son were men with strong views on all manner of subjects, although seldom in agreement with each other. It was a difficult household. Hanna, contrasting this with her own busy family life, was often outraged on her lover's behalf, 'tortured … in your own home … Every detail of your home life surprises me – even though I know the state of affairs from you already, Frank. What a life dear!'[5] The solitary nature of his upbringing, lacking brothers or sisters with whom to quarrel and possessing a mother (married to a man eighteen years her junior), who was forty-nine years old in 1878 when she gave birth to her only child, contributed towards the development of character traits that accentuated his natural inclination to individualism. Con Curran felt he behaved as if his decisions were 'regulated in accordance with long-settled opinions privately arrived at'.[6] As he said of the 'restless propagandist' who had collared him as a likely recruit for the Literary & Historical Society: 'His every opinion was a principle for which he was ready to die.'[7]

In the early years of his relationship with Hanna, Frank had to work hard to curb character traits of argumentativeness and aggression. He now had a companion who confronted him when she felt he was in the wrong: 'There was that old tyrannical air about you several times tonight and it doesn't please me at all.'[8] Frank was always full of contrition, 'My own beloved darling, I had no right to try to bully you into a course you objected to. With all my theories of equality, I find I am again and again trying to exercise an altogether undue control over your actions and wishes ... '[9] 'I ought to have conquered that burst of ill-temper in the hall last night ... try for the hundredth time to pardon your weak, hasty, repentant Frank.'[10] 'How sorry I am, my own true, loyal Hanna, for vexing you and crushing your fond heart so coarsely. These outbreaks of brutality and violence in myself sadden me, beloved ...'[11] Theirs was a tempestuous courtship, with many rows and tearful reconciliations. On Frank's own admission, he was hot tempered; a characteristic he later felt was also part of his son's temperament.

It was, on both sides, a deeply felt passion. The young Hanna, in Paris for eighty days (she counted each day they were apart), poured out her feelings: 'Ah my love, my love, my Frank, my heart yearns for you – for your fond caresses, your tender claspings, your loving passionate glances, my dear betrothed',[12] which were fully reciprocated, 'I love you darling, & I want you. Good-night my sweet, pure love, my darling, angelic, stainless Hanna, my own beloved betrothed wife, your own Frank.'[13] Much of their courtship was spent in contriving excuses to have time alone together. Friendships between young women and men were conducted according to well-defined codes of conduct. Not being alone with a member of the opposite sex was the most important rule. Reputation was all, hence the popularity of group rambles which did allow courting couples some freedom to detach themselves from the group. Before Frank visited Hanna in Paris, having somewhere private ('Ah Frank, you are really terrible!') was a preoccupation of several letters, with Hanna suggesting that a visit to 'the Bois' would enable them to 'get in a fairly satisfactory amount of kissing'.[14] Planning for a picnic in Dublin took weeks, as they needed people who would turn a blind eye to their absence, 'suppose anyone around there, seeing me so demure, were to get a glimpse of us on our "mossy bank"! And I have the grace to blush – and brace up!', said a defiant and somewhat frustrated Hanna.[15] While they did not altogether abide by convention, neither was unconventional enough to avoid blushes when caught out. An extract from Frank's diary recalls an incident while he and Hanna were out cycling unchaperoned: 'Rain, shelter under tree – Mary, riding with Molly and Tom! Mutual embarrassment!'[16]

They had decided, before Hanna left for Paris, that as soon as Frank had completed his degree he would ask David Sheehy for permission to marry his daughter. For both, the approval of parents was very important. Hanna urged Frank to give her every detail of the interview, including the mood and any disagreeable note, 'so that I can have as clear an idea as if I were there myself!' She was ecstatic that at last 'the interview' had been achieved and 'cordial consent (which) satisfies me completely' given, as 'father's consent means mother's too and we don't mind outsiders.'[17] Frank had managed to get an opportunity to speak to David Sheehy while both were at the Bective rugby football ground at Ballsbridge. He provided Hanna with every detail, as requested:

> I decided to plunge at once. I was very nervous – physically. But it passed into my legs, which trembled violently under me (it was a cold day!); and I managed to keep both my voice and my face cool. Now that I have the opportunity of speaking to you alone,' said I, 'I want to speak to you about something of a private nature, but I must ask you to keep it entirely between ourselves.' All right,' said he, with a dawning light already in his eyes. We were both manoeuvering a little with our feet now, each trying to get the setting sun full in the other's face and neither quite succeeding. I went on, very steadily and coolly. 'I want to ask you if you would consent to an engagement between Hanna and myself?' Without showing any surprise, he answered gravely, 'I assure you, Skeffington, I'd be very happy.' Well, I said something like 'then, that's all,' and we shook hands. He went on, 'I don't know any young man that I'd sooner have for my son-in-law than you. I believe you have such qualities as will make her happy; and her happiness is the only question with me.' Then I went back and watched the match.[18]

Hanna's sisters were not informed. The engagement had to remain a secret until the couple were in a financial position to marry. That did not prevent an emotional Hanna from wearing her engagement ring while safely away in Paris, enjoying the excitement of telling all to the Panniers. When she returned to Belvedere Place Frank had to use the poste restante services of the GPO for his letters, a ruse to prevent inquisitive sisters from wondering why Hanna was getting daily letters from her friend. She also doubted whether her mother would approve of letters arriving so frequently. When Frank was home in Ranelagh with his parents for Christmas Hanna could not write to his home address, as the Skeffington parents did not approve of the engagement. Dr J. B. did not reply to his son's letter informing him of the betrothal and stopped speaking to Frank for some time. He had apparently felt his son was too immature for marriage.[19] Frank's mother was equally unenthusiastic. Hanna, reading one of her letters, was shocked by the harsh tone. Six months later, there was no change in attitude, 'I feel very sorry for your mother, dear, and regret very much that she'll be so prejudiced against me.'[20] Almost a year after Frank's 'interview' with David Sheehy, Dr J.B. wrote a letter to Hanna's father, which Frank described as 'one of his usual violent and offensive rigmaroles'. His only consolation was that, after 'bitter argument' and 'hot interchanges', his mother had submitted to 'the inevitable'. She had 'nothing against' Hanna and thought her a 'sensible girl enough'.[21] It is impossible to see what attribute was lacking in this middle class, educated and Catholic young woman. But just as no school was good enough for the son of Dr J. B. Skeffington, it was likely that no woman would ever be good enough either. In retaliation Frank decided that the engagement had to be known publicly and he suggested that Hanna let her sisters into the secret before they left for school– 'tell Mary and Kathleen and show them the ring in your room … that would be sufficient, I think, to ensure publicity!'[22] This did not happen. The engagement would continue for another eighteen months and in that time they both continued to develop their political views and began to establish their professional lives.

They maintained their copious correspondence after Hanna returned from Paris, as Frank was only able to return to Dublin for occasional weekends. In April 1901 Hanna calculated that she had received 251 letters - a figure which provides us with a sense of the scale of their communications while also indicating Frank's tendency to excess when enthused. At times she attempted to impose some discipline on the letter writing, arguing as they needed to devote themselves to work, they should give up daily writing. Hanna's suggestion that he wrote on Saturday and she replied on Sunday (threatening she might have to give up her studentship otherwise) ended up like all her other attempts: 'I won't stop writing every day until I have your consent and approval.'[23]

Despite his serious-mindedness, Frank could be fun. On Sunday evenings at the Sheehy household he was more than willing to take his turn in charades or in any play that might be rehearsed for an evening's entertainment. He was one of the first to recognise Joyce's genius and, in return, Joyce considered Skeffington to be the second cleverest man in University College, after himself of course. Joyce and Skeffington, two non-conformists, agreed on very little apart from a refusal to conform to the narrow orthodoxies of conventional Dublin society. That was enough to cement their friendship. On leaving the Sheehy's at midnight one Sunday, Frank wrote to Hanna that, as usual, he had kept Joyce 'in fits of laughter by the simplest of remarks'. The pair protested against censorship by publishing, at their own expense, a pink covered pamphlet containing 'Day of the Rabblement', Joyce's views on the debasement of Irish drama and Skeffington's 'Forgotten Aspect of the University Question', in which he argued forcefully that co-education was essential as a means of fostering comradeship between the sexes. The college magazine had refused to publish the articles, so they sold the 2d pamphlet themselves, at the college gates, in shops and through family and friends. When Joyce became famous it turned out to be the most valuable article Skeffington ever wrote.[24]

Their friendship was affected by Frank's disapproval of Joyce leaving Ireland with his lover Nora Barnacle, without Nora having the security of marriage. Joyce never forgave Frank's refusal of a loan and his chilly reference to the possible fate of the 'companion'. In several letters to his brother he referred to Nora as 'the companion' and on one occasion, wondering what Nora really thought about her new life, he suggested sarcastically: 'Ask hairy Jaysus what am I to do? He ought to know.'[25] Frank's response must have been motivated by doubts for the future well-being of Nora, an unmarried woman in a foreign country with no income and with none of the status that marriage would have conferred. Joyce's determination to outshine his old friend Skeffington in some way was well recognised by their mutual friend Vincent Cosgrave, whose letter of congratulation on the birth of Giorgio Joyce made mischievous reference to the continued rivalry: 'Mrs Skeffington's anteroposterior diameter is unaltered. I regret not having been the first to communicate the joyful intelligence of Nora's delivery to Skeffington.'[26]

Frank's article on women and education was published one year before Hanna wrote her own condemnation of women's inferior position within higher education. At this stage he had developed his philosophical ideas rather more than she had. Her views were an emotional response to her own experience of university life and to the growing lobby for co-education. Hanna always insisted that her feminism, as an intellectual understanding of the extent of women's unequal position within society, developed as a result of meeting the man who would become her husband. She was able to be present on the occasion he read his paper 'The Progress of Women' to the L & H[27], taking, she confessed, the opportunity to admire him 'furtively, nearly all the time', also noticing that his father sitting in the audience, seemed 'very proud' of his son.[28] By now the couple were arranging regular meetings at Bewley's café, the first branch of which had opened in 1894, its discreet booths a boon to young Dubliners. Occasionally, wanting total privacy, they ate at the vegetarian restaurant, confident 'their set' would not be there. They were kindred spirits, sharing a conviction that a fully human society could never be achieved unless there was a true equality of the sexes that went far beyond mere legalistic reforms.

Reading Lecky's *Democracy and Liberty*, as she wanted to read about women's suffrage (while Lecky was conservative on many issues, he was a strong supporter of votes for women), she enthused: 'It's a fine book. I read all about the woman question, he is very calm & logical & though he sometimes mentions difficulties he is altogether with the movement all the same & thinks it will eventually work out only for good.'[29] She and Frank were continuing to develop their ideas through a mutual process of reading and discussion. Forty years later, on being interviewed by R.M. Fox, she insisted again that her interest in feminism had been stimulated by her husband:

> Far more than any academic knowledge which she gained was the influence which came into her life when she met Francis Skeffington ... He it was who first interested her in feminism and gave her that enduring interest in the women's movement to which she has given conspicuous service. He talked to her of John Stuart Mill, whom he made the subject of his Inaugural Address at the University.[30]

There was, however, despite this idealism, tension when it came to plans for their future. Hanna was impatient at Frank's apparent delay in settling for a profession, as he continued to write articles and fiction, trying to make a name as a writer. Her tone could be extremely stern, '... never mind about the projects - we are not a bit enlightened as to your future path. Teaching and literature haven't worked well obviously ... something more definite must be agreed on.'[31] The towering DBC café, with its distinctive Chinese pagoda, was a constant source of temptation for the passing chess addict. Frank was reputed to have the ability to play blindfolded two or three simultaneous games - the only occasion when Con Curran saw that restless figure sit still.[32] In his wanders around Dublin Frank found it hard to resist challenges to matches, confessing how an afternoon could occasionally slip away. It was a hobby Hanna failed to share, criticising him for 'not planning ... not writing, reading in a desultory way, playing chess, strolling around ... ', her feeling exacerbated by the fact that her father often 'persecuted' Frank to have a game with him when he called round to Belvedere Place, thereby denying her the pleasure of her beloved's company. When Frank admitted to feeling' occasional chess-impulses', to be dealt with by calling early at the Sheehy's to have 'a game or two before tea', he added, half in jest, 'unless I get a wire from you forbidding any such frivolous waste of time!'[33] While he promised to lead a more productive life, Hanna was realistic enough to recognise he was unlikely to change completely, 'I am glad you are getting sensible and that I may hope for obedience. Sometimes of course I see the spirit of rebellion all the time under the shadow of submission.'[34] As their lives became closer, arguments that reflected their different personalities continued. While it is impossible to calculate, from the scraps of evidence in their letters, the degree of physicality involved in what Frank termed his 'outbreaks', there would be a serious altercation in the early years of their marriage which would lead Hanna to threaten to leave her husband. Despite the personal cost, she refused to be intimidated by her husband. However, the tempestuous nature of their relationship continued until the milestone of the birth of their son.[35]

On the intellectual question of women's emancipation, they were in full agreement. 'My sweet betrothed indispensable to me in every direction', Frank confided to his diary.[36] Pressure to change the unsatisfactory system of higher education was continuing and women took the opportunity to argue for changes that would also benefit them. Agnes O'Farrelly and Mary Hayden both applied to the Royal for Fellowships in 1900, only to be told that they were disqualified because the statutes excluded women.[37] The government appointed the Robertson Commission in 1901, with the brief of examining the workings of the Royal University. When women took put their case to the Commission it was the first occasion in which they were able to state publicly their own views. Strong differences of opinion emerged between those who wanted women-only colleges and those who wanted co-education. The *New Ireland Review* published a series of articles on the controversial issue of university education for women, and, in May 1902, one of the first contributions to that controversy was an article by 'Hannah Sheehy BA'. Her contribution was a reply to a previous one by Lilian Daly favouring separate spheres for the sexes. Her tone was earnest, the language formal and the style more than a little awkward, yet a slight hint of the ironic form of humour she often displayed as a more seasoned polemicist can be faintly discerned:

> Woman is surprisingly like man in most of her feelings, tastes, desires and antipathies and the evil has ever been that the differences have hitherto been far too much accentuated by education and convention, thereby producing the highly undesirable idiosyncracies known as 'feminine' and 'masculine' weaknesses.

In arguing that 'everything human' is also woman's province, Hanna called upon women to organise in order to pursue their demands, recognising that mutual support was important in developing solidarity of purpose: 'An organised public opinion, as well as a bond of sympathy between individual workers … would do much to help and fortify single effort.'[38] Her article contained several references to J. S. Mill (whom she accused her antagonist, Lilian Daly, of misinterpreting), substantiating her memory of Frank having developed her initial interest in the philosopher. Despite this, the arguments presented by Hanna and Frank contain significant differences in emphasis. As a woman impatient to abolish male privilege she was at pains to stress the fact that men would not 'stand aside to allow woman her free choice as to whether or not she will enter upon their ground', whereas Frank's paper had emphasised the desirability of a future in which the sexes could co-exist in harmonious friendship. His portrayal of the life of the ideal college as a 'large family circle of brothers and sisters' was a utopian piece of wishful thinking from someone who had been denied that experience in childhood. Hanna was more concerned with the means by which equality could be achieved. Her strategic sense as a political activist was developing. Those who, like herself, rejected the idea of women's colleges, decided to mobilise their forces by forming a new organisation. The Irish Association of Women Graduates and Candidate Graduates (IAWG) was inaugurated at a meeting held in March 1902. Alice Oldham, from Alexandra College, one of the first women to enter the Royal College of Science when it opened its doors to women in the 1870s, became the first president and Mary Hayden, one of the first graduates of St Mary's, was elected vice-president.[39]

A statement by Hanna called for the creation of a movement that would not be confined to women in the educational world: 'A permanent organisation is greatly needed and should be open not only to men and women graduates and Candidate BAs but to any persons interested in the question of women's education.'[40] She joined up, despite these reservations on woman-only organisations. Its aims were straightforward: To provide a means of communication and mutual action in matters concerning the interests of university women in Ireland; to promote women's interests in any scheme of university education and to ensure that educational opportunities were available on an equal basis to women; to form a register of members seeking appointments and to supply potential employers with information regarding members' qualifications. Two hundred women affiliated almost immediately.[41] For many of that original band of pioneers, membership of the organisation would be revived during the battle for women's economic and political rights in the Irish Free State. Although Hanna was vocal in discussion at the first AGM of the organisation, she was not elected a committee member. By 1908, however, she was secretary of the Association.[42]

In England, women's access to higher education was an important factor in helping to revitalise the campaign for women's suffrage. Esther Roper, one of the first women to graduate from Manchester University, had spent years organising massive women-only petitions for the vote. None were successful and newspapers gave them little attention. One of the last of these petitions had been aimed at women graduates.[43] It met the fate of the others when it was presented to the House of Commons in March 1902, but Roper was able to use the names that had been gathered as the basis for recruitment into the suffrage movement. Relevant names were forwarded to the only suffrage organisation that existed in Ireland, and Hanna, as one of the signatories, found herself written to by Anna Haslam:

> It is exceedingly important that we should have as many educated women as possible amongst our published list of supporters. Your name has been forwarded to me by Miss Roper, BA, Manchester, as one of those who signed the Women Graduates Petition in March.[44]

In a later reference to this occasion, Hanna dated her political awareness to the experience of signing the petition:

> I was then an undergraduate and was amazed and disgusted to learn that I was classed among criminals, infants and lunatics – in fact, that my status as a woman was worse than any of these. Naturally, I signed, and became a conscious suffragist from that hour on. Later, or perhaps that same year … my education was continued by Mill's 'Subjection of Women', to which I was introduced by Francis J. Skeffington, who made it the subject of a College paper.[45]

This account of events is extracted from her unpublished 'Memoirs of a Suffragette', its conversational tone conjuring up a vivid picture of the woman and her times, written long after the events occurred. The Skeffington influence was a crucial factor before the petition and all the published evidence shows that the pair, from the outset, operated as a unit when it came to political campaigns.

The next step was to become a member of the Irish Women's Suffrage and Local Government Association. Its annual report for 1902 acknowledged 'Miss H. Sheehy MA' as having contributed one shilling to their funds, while 'F. J. Skeffington MA' contributed two shillings and sixpence. They were slightly more prominent the following year. Frank was one of the speakers at a suffrage meeting in the Mansion House which had been presided over by the Lord Mayor and Hanna, by then Mrs Sheehy Skeffington, a member of the committee, was busily engaged in recruiting as many of her family as could be prevailed upon to join.[46] Her three sisters paid their shilling subscriptions that year and would do so for the next three years. Dick Sheehy's name appeared on the subscription list for two years and, for 1904, the 'Rev E. Sheehy of County Limerick' contributed a generous five-shilling subscription. Her brother Eugene was politically fairly conservative. The Sheehy parents were not persuaded of the cause. David had said to Hanna in 1901 that he had voted for women's franchise bills, but 'half-heartedly, as it worked out badly, even in limited spheres as the danger of corruption was great'. The exclamation '!' was Hanna's comment, in reporting this to Frank.[47]

In a somewhat surprising move, given the unconventionality of his views, in 1902 Frank was appointed first lay registrar of University College, Dublin. He had been awarded his M.A. that year, making him a more attractive proposition regarding academic employment. The authorities must have known what they were taking on when they appointed him; his application bluntly stated, 'I will spare you the fatuity of testimonials.'[48] They knew better than to ask him to wear something other than the tweed suit. He had had some success with writing for newspapers and periodicals, but the financial rewards were uncertain. Finally, he and Hanna could contemplate marriage.

While a married woman was still regarded as the property of her husband, Hanna did not see herself becoming 'Mrs Francis Skeffington'. Soon after their engagement she had written 'a fond kiss too for the name I shall one day share with you, my love – Skeffington. (I mean, dear, to keep the initial S. before that name, just for the sake of an old theory of mine against absolute change of name.)[49] They had many discussions regarding the impact of marriage on the lives of women. Hanna's idealism and unwavering optimism for the future was based on a conviction that her future husband's commitment to equality of the sexes would never be compromised by the everyday realities of marriage:

> Certainly, home is the crowning of manhood just as much as of womanhood -one must complete the other to make Home at all possible. And to come to our own ideals in the future, dearest, that Home for me, that crowning is not four walls, you know, but – you, just as for you is it I, my love, is it not so! What I was thinking of chiefly though, was the theory that woman lowers herself by being bound down to Home, that she should be independent, having no domestic ties and is complete in herself. I admit that many women are infinitely better unmarried & working for themselves but when a woman can marry without giving up her ideals, it is only then her existence is complete & capable of highest development. And of course, the same is true of man. But of course, all this we know & agree to always, Frank. And thank you darling, for watching carefully over Woman's Rights and reminding me when I omit direct mention. Of course, darling, when the time comes we shall settle all those things perfectly & am only delighted beyond expression, darling, to share all cares & management with you …[50]

Her ambivalence was expressed in oblique fashion in 'Life's Choosing', a prize-winning short story written in the early days of her engagement. It recounted the sorry plight of a young woman, Lucy Molloy, whose early marriage enabled her to lead a hectic social life until it all ended in tears. Financial ruin forced her home to mother, the marriage in tatters. In contrast, Lucy's schoolfriend Madge rejected a marriage proposal to devote herself to the intellectually satisfying career of journalism and literary criticism.[51] The moral could not have been plainer, but Hanna had been full of optimism for the future since her first encounters with Frank:

> I hope when I join you the work will be arduous, if different, and we can fight together, Frank, just as we climbed those rocks and crossed those streams and fought the wind and rain so often together, all adding only to our delicious sense

> of progress, of proximity, of even mutual help. That was how I grew to love you Frank, in spite of myself – that exquisite charm that lay in your ever-ready help, in your surmounting obstacles, your enthusiasm for struggle, your unfailing brightness, your genial warmth of heart.'[52]

She was no longer emotionally lonely or intellectually isolated. She had found happiness and delighted in writing to her godfather to tell him. She hoped that Frank and Eugene would get on, telling Frank that 'he will either like you passionately or not at all! But we ought to be able to convert him, you and I.'[53] Eugene, in New York, and absent from Ireland for so long that his family had almost given up seeing him, sent back effusive greetings, immediately planning his departure to be home for the wedding:

> I send you lavishly of all my warmest wishes/prayers, benedictions for all you can hope for of happiness and good from your projected marriage. You tell me you are 'happy', and I grandly say that I wish to share in it. I am satisfied that your choice – Mr Skeffington – is all that we all should wish … be assured I shall have the greatest possible pleasure in meeting him … I suppose I had better begin and call him Frank …[54]

NOTES

1 Thomas Bacon in James Meenan (ed.), *Centenary History of the Literary and Historical Society of University College Dublin 1855–1955* (Tralee, 1957), p. 69.

2 Roger McHugh, 'Thomas Kettle and Francis Sheehy Skeffington', in Conor Cruise O'Brien (ed.), *The Shaping of Modern Ireland* (London, 1960), p. 126.

3 Hanna Sheehy to Frank Skeffington (hereafter Hanna to Frank), 2 Nov. 1900, Sheehy Skeffington MS (hereafter SS MS) 40,464/2.

4 Ibid., 11 Dec. 1900.

5 Hanna to Frank, 26 Dec. 1900, SS MS 40,464/3.

6 C. P. Curran, *Under the Receding Wave* (Dublin, 1970), p. 112.

7 Ibid., p. 113.

8 Hanna to Frank, 27 Dec. 1901, SS MS 40,464/11.

9 Frank Skeffington to Hanna Sheehy (hereafter Frank to Hanna),16 Jan. 1902, SS MS 40,461/1.

10 Frank to Hanna, Christmas night, midnight, 1900, SS MS 40,460/4. Hanna and Frank wrote to each other every day during their three-year courtship, only some of these letters remain. Andrée Sheehy Skeffington wrote that her son Owen, following her instructions, burnt 5 envelopes of about 140 letters in each, but he did not have the heart to destroy a few remaining bundles, see Andrée Sheehy Skeffington, *Skeff: A Life of Owen Sheehy Skeffington* (Dublin, 1991), p. 125. These were amongst the letters subsequently deposited in the National Library of Ireland (hereafter NLI) and used for this biography. While they deal with deeply personal, private matters, they also reveal much

about women's lives in this period, particularly their lack of knowledge of sexual matters, and are invaluable as an historical record, but are fragmentary in terms of disclosure of the most intimate details of their relationship.

11 Frank to Hanna, 13 Aug. 1902, SS MS 40,461/3.

12 Hanna to Frank, 19 Oct. 1900, SS MS 40,464/1.

13 Hanna to Frank, 15 Oct. 1901, SS MS 40,460/10.

14 Hanna to Frank, 15 Dec. 1900, SS MS 40,464/2.

15 Hanna to Frank, 4 June 1901, SS MS 40,464/8.

16 J. B. Lyons, *The Enigma of Tom Kettle: Irish Patriot, Essayist, Poet, British Soldier, 1880–1916* (Dublin, 1983), p. 17.

17 Hanna to Frank, 23 Oct. 1900 and 27 Oct. 1900, SS MS 40,464/1.

18 Andrée Sheehy Skeffington, *Skeff*, pp 10–11.

19 Micheline Sheehy Skeffington has recollections of seeing a 12-point memo from Dr J. B. Skeffington summarising the reasons why Frank should not get married – including general unreliability, lack of money and his personal hygiene. The memo is not in the NLI catalogue.

20 Hanna to Frank, 7 May 1901, SS MS 40,464/4.

21 Frank to Hanna 15 Oct. 1901, SS MS 40,460/10.

22 Ibid.

23 Hanna to Frank, 1 May 1901 and 2–5 May 1901, SS MS 40,464/4.

24 Francis Sheehy Skeffington and James A. Joyce, *Two Essays* (Dublin, 1901).

25 Bonnie Kime Scott, *Joyce and Feminism* (Hertfordshire, 1984), p. 36.

26 Richard Ellman, *James Joyce* (Oxford, 1982), p. 205

27 Mentioned by Hanna in a letter to Frank, 8 May 1901. She was about to attend the university debate, recalling that 'it will bring back last year when…' SS MS 40,464/5.

28 Ibid.

29 Hanna to Frank, 11 May 1901, SS MS 40,464/5.

30 R. M. Fox, *Rebel Irishwomen* (Dublin, 1935), p. 74.

31 Hanna to Frank, 4 June 1901, SS MS 40,464/8.

32 Curran, *Under the Receding Wave*, p. 112.

33 Frank to Hanna, 16 June 1902, SS MS 40,411/4.

34 Hanna to Frank, 17 Oct. 1900, SS MS 40,464/3.

35 See Chapter 3 for further information on Frank's violence and Hanna's response.

36 Leah Levenson, *With Wooden Sword: A Portrait of Francis Sheehy-Skeffington, Militant Pacifist* (Dublin, 1983), p. 37.

37 Ríona Nic Chongail, 'Gaelic Ireland and the female dream: Agnes O'Farrelly's cultural nationalism', in Sarah O'Connor and Christopher C. Shepard (eds), *Ireland: Dissenting Voices?* (Cambridge, 2009), pp 51–66.

38 Hanna Sheehy Skeffington, 'Women and the university question', in *New Ireland Review*, xvii, May 1902.

39 Eibhlin Breathnach, 'Charting new waters: Women's experience in higher education, 1879–1908', in Mary Cullen (ed.), *Girls Don't Do Honours: Irish Women in Education in the Nineteenth and Twentieth Centuries* (Dublin, 1987), p. 70.

40 Leah Levenson and Jerry Natterstad, *Hanna Sheehy Skeffington: Irish Feminist* (New York, 1983), p. 13.

41 Fathers of Society of Jesus, *A Page of Irish History: The Story of University College Dublin, 1883–1909* (Dublin, 1930), pp 463–4.

42 *Irish Times*, 'Irish Association of Women Graduates and Candidate Graduates', 9 Feb. 1903.

43 Gifford Lewis, *Eva Gore-Booth and Esther Roper: A Biography* (London, 1988), p. 88.

44 Levenson and Natterstad, *Hanna Sheehy Skeffington*, p. 14.

45 Hanna Sheehy Skeffington, '*Reminiscences of an Irish Suffragette*', in Margaret Ward (ed.) *Hanna Sheehy Skeffington: Suffragette and Sinn Féiner: Her Memoirs and Political Writings* (Dublin, 2017), p. 69.

46 Irish Women's Suffrage and Local Government Association, *Annual Report*, 1903. The meeting took place on 14 Jan. 1903.

47 Hanna to Frank, 8 May 1901, SS MS 40,464/5.

48 Levenson, *With Wooden Sword*, p. 37.

49 Hanna to Frank, 21 Dec. 1900, SS MS 40,464/3.

50 Ibid.

51 Levenson and Natterstad, *Hanna Sheehy Skeffington*, p. 12.

52 Hanna to Frank, 20 Nov. 1900, SS MS 40,464/2.

53 Ibid., 17 Nov. 1900.

54 Eugene Sheehy to Hanna Sheehy, 23 Apr. 1903, SS MS 41,176/18.

THREE

PARTNERSHIP, 1903–08

On 27 June 1903, Hanna Sheehy and Francis Skeffington were married in the university chapel at St Stephen's Green. She was 26, her husband 25. A typical Irish summer's day, it poured with rain. The groom no longer believed in Catholicism, but the bride did, so it was a Catholic ceremony, without any elaborate trimmings. A cousin, remarking on a photo Frank had sent to Downpatrick some time earlier, said people had wondered if he would wear his 'knickers' at his wedding. Frank was dismissive, 'very characteristic of Downpatrick gossip!'[1] and, oblivious to ridicule, wore his usual tweed costume, complete with knickerbockers. Hanna had finally met her prospective mother-in-law nine days before the ceremony, Frank acting as go-between for the women: 'Mother will meet you as arranged tomorrow – 10.15 at the GPO. She is most indignant with me for being so "reticent" and has expressed her intention of asking you all sorts of things, expecting to find you more communicative than I am!' He would have preferred a smaller ceremony, wondering if they could tell people that the wedding was an hour later than it was, in a vain effort to ensure privacy, but in one important respect, the wedding was conducted on their terms.[2] As proof of their absolute commitment to the equality of the sexes, Hanna and her husband took each other's name. They were now the 'Sheehy Skeffingtons'. The Sheehys made no comment on the new name. Their daughter was retaining her family identification rather than losing it, but Dr J. B. never reconciled himself to what he felt was a betrayal of the Skeffington name. In many ways he was right; his son was explicitly rejecting the patriarchal values with which he had been brought up. He had developed his own identity, just as his wife had. They were Frank and Hanna Sheehy Skeffington.

Contrary to outward appearances, Frank was extremely aware of his sexuality. He had shocked Hanna by confessing to having masturbated for the past 14 years, a habit she exhorted him to give up. During their long engagement she had come to realise how little sex knowledge she possessed: 'women should be warned and that is the fatality in our education that we are kept from knowledge until accident reveals the reality in its horrors'.[3] They had both been strong adherents of 'Sandow' exercises while she was in Paris, understanding that these were intended to curb sexual desire as well as encourage physical fitness. (Mary Sheehy thought it would do Tom Kettle, a heavy drinker, good to take them up.) Six months before their wedding Hanna wrote that her 'passionate, thrilling longing would not be satisfied until I can rest in your dear breast forever! ... I worship you my dear betrothed – oh, my husband help me to be all yours, help me to banish my perversity & to trust all to your devoted love! ... my body is thrilling at the memory of your touch tonight & at the thought of all the fond caresses of last year, in anticipation of ... when we may indulge in all loves paradise of delight without a regretful thought.'[4] Reading two "Sex" books, as she described them, wanting to improve her understanding of 'sex passion', Hanna was relieved to find Frank's sanity and the health of their children would not be affected by his past actions. Her tone was much softer, as she felt 'great tenderness' for him in his struggles, 'you know I am apt to be "down" on men - & that will remain in general matters – but, dearie, as regards sex passion I see what a terrible power it has over all men & how noble these must be that can be master of themselves...' Above all, she was glad that they had a 'perfect confidence' between themselves 'for having opened our hearts always to each other in our difficulties & I am so happy to have known all those doubts and troubles of yours, love & to have been able to discuss them & my own with you'[5] She worried whether she had the 'sex-passion' and Frank tried to reassure her:

> If you are still at all disturbed, my pure angel, about the existence in yourself of the sex-passion, think of the mystery of parenthood, of the awful sacredness of this mighty passion – think how it alone makes possible the whole of this great world, this glorious life. But I need not tell you, my Hanna; I know you will be wise, & not wrong.
>
> Ah, dear, I wish, I wish, I had you always by me![6]

For his part, six days before their wedding, Frank wrote of his belief that the wedding would be 'an ideally happy one, united as we are in heart and soul, eager for the same work and seeking the same rewards. Nor will the attraction of body to body be lacking, my own, my passionate virgin-wife.'[7] Frank habitually used words like 'angelic' and 'stainless' to describe his betrothed; it was a distinction he must have been making with what he regarded as his sinful self, eternally struggling to resist vice.

Their honeymoon symbolised a determination to live a simple life while allowing each other the greatest possible freedom. They combined a bicycling trip around the south of Ireland with a climb to the top of Carrauntuathail, Ireland's highest mountain, staying in hotels in Bray, Glengarriff, Valencia, Cork and Killarney. Hotel receipts, dry cleaning bills and the flowers from the wedding were all preserved, as were Frank's notes of the mileage achieved each day.[8] Both loved hill walking and had taken many trips out to the Wicklow Mountains during their courtship. The advent of the bicycle had heralded an enormous liberatory change for women all over the world, giving them a mobility and opportunity to develop an entirely separate existence. Frank saw great symbolism in their hill walking: 'emblems of what our life shall be; always making onward towards some highest point, always exultant even when struggling'.[9] During their honeymoon they visited an uncle (undoubtedly Father Eugene) who had been warned off whiskey by his doctor. Frank, with his characteristic forthrightness, discovered a full bottle of whiskey which he promptly poured down the sink, remarking to Hanna that he would do everything possible to prevent her uncle's death. The punchline was that the uncle carried this 'preventive logic' a stage further by showing them both out.[10] Hanna often recounted the story, her amusement partly a reflection of the fact that she did not share Frank's absolute commitment to teetotalism. She had enjoyed wine when in Paris and during their courtship teased Frank 'you must prepare to convert me to Temperance Frank, really – in principle I mean!'[11] An admirer of the culture of many European countries, she combined some of their customs with her more frugal Irish lifestyle.

The young couple were away from Dublin for a month, returning then to their first home, a small but elegant house at 8 Airfield Road, Rathgar. This was a move away from the north side where Hanna had grown up, to the suburbs of the 'pro-British' (a euphemism for 'Protestant') south. Electric trams had arrived on Dublin streets at the turn of the century and people began to venture further afield, but there was no direct tram linking north and south of the city. Sydney Gifford, another non-conformist, who came from a well-off Unionist family, recalled how insular the area was: 'we who lived on the south side knew as little about any point north of the Pillar as if it had been a foreign country.'[12] Although the majority of their neighbours probably resembled the 'lifelike but inanimate models of distinguished English people' so detested by Sydney, the Sheehy Skeffingtons were not the only rebels to have made their home in this 'stronghold of British Imperialism'. As a radical middle-class migrated to the south side of Dublin, many of their closest friends took up residence in the attractive village-like surrounds of Rathmines and Rathgar. George Russell, better known as 'AE', the poet, artist and mystic, lived in Rathgar. His Sunday evenings were famous in artistic and political circles. Maud Gonne, for a time, lived next door. Others nearby included the venerable Quaker, Deborah Webb, in Rathgar, suffrage militant Hilda Webb in Rathgar and Eva and Maurice Wilkins in Rathmines. Gradually, civic amenities essential to intellectual life were built. Rathmines Public Library, made possible through Carnegie funding, opened in October 1913, the same date as the Rathmines Technical Institute opened its doors.

Frank might be the most complete feminist that Hanna had encountered in the male sex, yet he was hardly free of double standards in some of his attitudes. At this time manufacturers had begun to market small, scented cigarettes called 'My Darling's Cigarettes', obviously aimed at young women.[13] Mary Sheehy was one of those who took up the habit. Hanna commented in her diary of 'the curious prejudice of even the best intentioned men', a reference to Frank's vociferous objections to Mary smoking, despite his acceptance of his male friends doing exactly the same, although never in his own house.[14] Her feminist principles would not have made a distinction between the sexes when it came to the question of a woman choosing to smoke. Mary, who as a schoolgirl Hanna laughed at for writing a letter 'brimful of slang as usual' was now a 21-year-old graduate of the Royal, recently returned from her year in Amiens and beginning to make her own choices in life.

The Sheehy Skeffingtons instituted their own 'At Homes' on Wednesdays. They were, of course, conducted according to the principles by which Frank was determined to live. Con Curran remembered a party, not long after the wedding: 'from which at a certain moment we were all thrown out of his house and given a quarter of an hour to smoke in the garden before plunging back to our talk indoors.'[15] Frank was gregarious, Hanna shyer and somewhat reserved on first acquaintance. She found the role of hostess a strain, 'most of them a bore & a bother', although some were enjoyable. They were becoming an established fixture and she resolved to 'work them up better'.[16] As she relaxed and discovered who she wanted to be friends with, life became easier. Not many of their friends had yet married, so the freedom to attend the Sheehy Skeffington events was welcomed, not least by the unmarried Sheehy sisters. Mary Maguire did not marry the poet Padraic Colum until 1912. She echoed the thoughts of many in her appreciation of Dublin's sociability, generated by an educated élite who valued intellect over materialism: 'Nobody I knew had any interest in money, and nobody would have thought of spending any considerable portion of his life trying to make it. We had a great many friends and we all saw one another almost every day, owing to the Dublin custom of having evening reunions.'[17]

The Sheehy Skeffington household, with its plethora of books and newspapers, was not run on lines that conventional people would have recognised. Hanna argued, somewhat disingenuously, that women's possession of a university education was no threat to family life: 'How the sentiments of a woman with a mind and heart disciplined and elevated by years of serious study and the literary culture of a university, can militate against the "unity of the home", is not obvious to moralists, or even to ordinary people.'[18] However, she had no intention of living in a manner that 'ordinary people' would necessarily understand or sympathise with. Frank's theories of housekeeping had made her laugh before her marriage, but she agreed with him that 'order & system' were important.[19] Their idea of order was not immediately apparent, as Rosamond (known as Rose) Jacob, a young woman from an unusually free-thinking background in Waterford (agnostic parents who had both broken away from their families' Quaker tradition) wrote in some amazement to her cousin Deborah, 'It is one mass of books and papers all over the ground floor, and I believe there is another room full upstairs.'[20]

Others in their circle were of similar mind. Contemplating the prospect of her future life Mary Maguire (who had many men interested in her company) had concluded: 'I supposed I would eventually marry somebody, though I certainly did not covet the role of some of the dreary married women I knew, with the monotonous domesticity, the dreary commonplaces and often loneliness of their lives.' She was 'deep in the woman's suffrage movement' and a teacher in St Ita's, the school for girls set up by Patrick Pearse, which soon folded for lack of funds. Mary, determined not to exchange 'the independent and interesting life I was living for pottering around a kitchen' left the suffrage movement to become an unpaid volunteer in the offices of Cumann na mBan during the turbulent months of 1914. The preoccupations of the housewife were never her concern.[21] Hanna too had a life-long dislike of housework, as she testified humorously, 'Like the lilies I dust not, neither do I darn, and wash-up only in acute domestic crisis, when I have worked through all the ware in the pantry and piled it perilously in the kitchen.'[22] There was no way that she was prepared to suffer this tyranny, regardless of income. Frank's salary as registrar was £100 a year, not a great amount, but enough to pay the going rate of £8 for a live-in servant. Modem sensibilities make people uncomfortable with the notion that a woman who proclaimed herself a feminist would employ a low-waged domestic servant to relieve her of the tedium of housework. For Hanna, and for many of her contemporaries, refusal to become immersed in domesticity (although gained only because of the existence of the vast reserve army of female labour), was a sign of liberation from the confines of the home. It was an assertion of personal independence. She had not been brought up to emulate her mother's sacrifice. Margaret McCoubrey, a suffragist friend from Belfast, unable to afford help in the home, envied this freedom: 'the eternal dishwashing goes on – which, even though it is reduced to a minimum takes so much valuable time'. When McCoubrey succeeded in obtaining work with the Women's Co-operative Guild her first thought was that the 'slight remuneration will enable me to have some help in the house and it will not therefore prevent me from managing suffrage work'.[23] Other suffragists had similar attitudes. One, waiting to give birth, wrote that training a new girl had taken all her energy but it was worth it, 'I am beginning to feel myself free again from household drudgery'.[24] This is not to say that they agreed with low wages or exploiting their staff. In 1920 Meg Connery, another hater of housework, would call for 'communal house-keeping' with 'modern equipment and well-paid workers' when the *Irish Citizen* published an article on women's work in the home.[25] As a middle-aged woman Hanna was asked to help the Irish Women Workers' Union in their attempts to organise domestic servants into the union. Although Sunday was the only day when servants had a day off she readily gave up her own free time on several occasions to speak at meetings. Her friend Margaret Cousins, in reflecting on those times remarked that she and her husband James 'were very Irish about money', possessing little and with no prospect of accumulating any because they attached more importance to other things in life. Many shared this philosophy. Social life became more adventurous. Dublin could boast a vegetarian restaurant, even if some were less than enamoured of the mix of 'moral principles with dietetic statistics on their depressing menu cards'[26], while the numerous cafés dotted around the streets offered all sorts of possibilities for animated conversation. Literary societies blossomed and new theatres provided venues for plays beginning to redefine notions of Irish identity during this 'glorious Copper Age of Ireland', when 'six little brown pennies' would get you into any theatre, provided you didn't mind being in the cheapest seats. Sydney Gifford and her sisters, like so many others, hardly spent one night at home in those heady days:

> work and pleasure were blended to a point where you could hardly say where one began and the other ended. You met so many interesting people everywhere,

> and the talk was so stimulating, that you found it hard to decide which you had enjoyed most: the entertainment or the people you met during the intervals.[27]

Hanna was another enthusiastic drama lover. She was happy to go off, often in the company of her sisters, to sit in the gods or, later, in the cheapest cinema seats. She never showed the slightest ambition to be able to afford anything different.

Louie Bennett, who was to become a close but not uncritical collaborator in the suffrage movement, was full of admiration for the unworldly nature of the Sheehy Skeffington union. She herself came from a wealthy background and was able throughout her life to work without salary for both the women's and the trade union movements, while managing to afford stylish clothes and the donation of a holiday home to the Irish Women Workers' Union. It was hardly surprising that the inhabitant of the exclusive neighbourhood of Temple Hill would view the lifestyle of the Sheehy Skeffingtons with some wonder:

> It was a sort of revelation and an admonition to find two people, who seemed to live literally in the spirit of the text, 'Take no heed for the morrow', surrendering personal aims and ambitions, and giving themselves with almost reckless selflessness to the service of humanitarian causes. But there was a joyousness in their manner of living which the more worldly and more outwardly comfortable people entirely miss.[28]

Lack of interest in material goods was combined with a belief in the value of the individual and the right of each to pursue their own interests, separately if need be. Bennett described the Sheehy Skeffingtons as able to retain 'complete individual independence…yet (working) together for the same objects'. They shared a wide circle of friends, but marriage gave them the freedom to meet their friends singly or together. Hanna was no longer troubled about the vexed issue of chaperones and she cycled long distances around Dublin, maintaining contact with family and friends as well as continuing the daily round of work and meetings. However, while this egalitarianism might have appeared easily achieved, true individual independence within the Sheehy Skeffington marriage was not obtained without difficulty. There would be a considerable period of adjustment before an equilibrium was found.

The volatility in Hanna and Frank's relationship continued after marriage, despite the fact they were now finally enjoying the longed-for intimacy they had craved for so long. She had been candid about her difficulties, with physical pain and emotional turbulence attending her monthly cycle (her 'usual trouble'). The severity of her premenstrual syndrome was often debilitating, enough for her to comment each month on how she fared, 'my illness threatens today but I've hardly any pain … I take a slug of one of the old bottles every now & then!'[29] and Frank was always solicitous about Hanna's health and mental wellbeing, with advice on iron supplements and other remedies. However, the arguments they had had in the courtship days continued, becoming heated and even violent on occasion. Only a short while after their first wedding anniversary the couple had a disagreement that was so serious it led Hanna to believe they had made a mistake in ever getting married. After several day's reflection, she wrote to Frank late in the night, telling him exactly how she was feeling and ending with an ultimatum that she felt was the only way to save the marriage:

> I am not afraid of you – I should despise myself to the uttermost if I were, but I have to recognize that the physically stronger may have the best of it sometimes & though your physical violence was not great it did inflict a bodily hurt & a bodily shock of a sickening kind that was bitterly degrading. The sense of horrible humiliation in the whole scene comes up vividly every time I see you & I wonder I am alive! … I recognize that our marriage has been a failure & that there is only one consolation – that there are no nearer ties between us. Looking back now I feel that neither of us should have married at all & that the fact of each marrying the other only made things worse. But it is too late to think of that & the fact that we are married does make a difference. We can never be the same again besides we have entered into a contract. I am prepared to keep to that contract if I can, on one condition. I shall regard myself as released from all claims if, on any pretext whatsoever, you lay a violent hand upon my person. I regard my right over my own person as sacred & inviolable & I will fight to the death to defend it. I don't care what the plea & I don't care whether the violence is small or great it is the principle itself that I intend to maintain. Of course I got your letter – I suppose the sealed one contains some solemn pledge- but I must say that I feel no confidence in your promises. Your last action has shaken the foundations my faith in you – even the fine binding compact I must tell you I do not regard as sacred any longer. I suppose you wonder why then I consent to live with you at all. It is because if you violate your faith I can always settle the matter finally for myself. Beyond that, I don't care. If you agree to my condition, do so in writing & remember that nothing will induce me to reconsider the question if you break faith again. Hanna[30]

It was an extraordinary communication from someone who was still newlywed. And still more exceptional given that it was addressed to a man who described himself as a feminist, a pacifist and a follower of John Stuart Mill. We do not know how Frank responded. What does exist is a letter, written two weeks later from Dijon, in which he apologised for his 'selfishness' in leaving Hanna 'without a loving word in such a time of trial'. According to Frank, she had been ill and melancholic (was this due to her premenstrual syndrome?) and he was glad to hear that she was going to Rockhill, to see her Uncle Eugene. His preoccupation was the progress he was making with his French and his plans to then move to Bonn to improve his German. Most of the letter was written in French. He asked for advice and urged Hanna to join him in Bonn. Frank's immaturity on several fronts was evident as he added if they did not have enough money, he would borrow some from his father, giving her a 'warning … not to wear her nightdress' so that he could feel her body, putting kisses on her breasts and thighs.[31]

In England, domestic violence and husband's rights over their wives were issues coming to public attention, from the 1878 Matrimonial Causes Act enabling wives to leave brutal husbands to an 1891 declaration by judges that husbands did not have the right to beat or confine their wives. However matrimonial issues in relation to Ireland – despite extensive reports of wife beating constantly reported in the Irish press – were regarded as separate by a Westminster parliament that failed to extend such legislation. [32] Hanna's response to her personal situation indicated a feminist understanding of women's rights as well as an intense awareness of her own bodily integrity. When the *Irish Citizen* appeared in 1912, giving feminists in Ireland a platform from which to voice their concerns, it published a range of articles concerning violence against women, calling for the need for equal marriage and equal divorce laws and for the rights of women to participate in the legal system as judges, barristers, jurors and police.[33] In all of this, she was a vocal advocate.

Their physical relationship evidently resumed because, in a poem written that December in celebration of Frank's birthday (describing hard work and omitting any reference to more contentious subjects), Hanna ended with a coy hint that she might, before the year was out, have new life in her body:

<u>To Frank</u>   23/12/4
Your birthday, dear, with Christmas comes again,
Another year has rolled away – a year
Of parting, task-work stern and worldly care,
Yet Love between, around, through all the days
And Love redeeming all!
Glad is my heart
Today – this happy day that gave me you.
No flowers are here to give you – verse is poor
And I have given my heart these many years
Keep you that till until it beats no more,
And take withal my wishes for the year –
Success, to crown long days of anxious work,

Love, ever keeping pace with fullest life –
Perhaps – e'en too – new pledge of love, the last,
Fruit of Love's blossom, ripening neath my heart
May quicken – ere December come again.[34]

The violence may have come to an end, yet some of the damaging pattern of behaviour was repeated in June of the following year, when Frank again left home abruptly. Not knowing where he had gone, Hanna wrote piteously, addressing her letter to post offices in London and Paris: 'come back to me, I throw myself at your feet, have pity on me, I can't live without you.'[35] He obviously returned, as the following month, again on a family holiday in Rockhill, she was writing to 'dearest Frank', now back home in Airfield Road.[36] After that, the volatility within the relationship appears to have subsided. By August 1907 Hanna believed that they had reached 'the last solemn stage, the consummation of all our love'. In 'longing for a child of our bodies', she hoped she was about to conceive and took the opportunity to reflect again upon their relationship. Her emphasis was upon their spiritual rather than physical union:

> There are pages in that history I fain would blot out, there are unkindnesses in word & deed. Forgive them, erase them all, my darling. Let our sweet new stage renew all the sweetness of the past & all its joys & let the flood of love wash out all stains.
>
> I think our souls are one & that you understand perhaps my very silence best. I shall try to convey what I have left unsaid in that supreme embrace & when the body's clamour is being satisfied I know that beneath all there will be a spiritual union true & deep that will abide when fleshly desire has passed away. Je t'attends. Je te désire!
>
> Your wife Hanna.[37]

She did not conceive, later describing this period of hopefulness as 'the perilious (& fateful!) month of August', adding 'I feel no stirrings of passion save at odd times in dreams & too when you are away sometimes.'[3] Losing herself to sexual desire was 'humiliating', she confessed. She believed it to be 'a very small piece of love':

> we have always managed so much better without it than most people who regard it as the essence of love. On my side I'm ashamed of sense-passion I must say & feel a bit humiliated by my senses when they do show themselves … so its very well for me that I'm not married to a sensualist whose exactions would drive me mad with disgust.

Years later, in conversation with her friend Rose Jacob, Hanna confided that she and Frank had occupied separate bedrooms, 'the most civilized way'.[39] In middle age, however, she revealed herself to be far from prudish, remembering an occasion when she and other women were first elected to Dublin Corporation in 1920. A colleague had found it impossible to refer, even indirectly, to venereal disease, although a grant to a city hospital treating VD was on the agenda. In her embarrassment the woman resorted to 'asking us to turn our downcast eyes to the fourth word of the second last line on page 21'. Hanna recalled the incident while reviewing Vera Brittain's book, *Halcyon, or the future of monogamy,* the contents of which included advocacy of sex-instruction for the young, understanding of companionate marriage and a general critique of the hypocrisies and taboos associated with conventional marriage. All of this she commended as 'challenging and provocative, and essentially sane and sound'.[40] Given her own struggles and early ignorance, this was a heart-felt commendation. As a tactful and understanding mother-in-law, she later gave her son and his bride books on family planning. Although no one felt able to discuss such issues openly, the young couple were made aware of Hanna's strong feelings that they should spend time getting to know each other before contemplating any additions to their family.[41]

If sexual differences contributed to the Sheehy Skeffington problems, the honesty of Margaret Gillespie on the issue conveys some of the reactions of a young woman coming from a life dominated by academic pursuits and having to adjust to the requirements of married life. Margaret (known as Gretta to her friends) was from a middle-class Protestant family in Boyle, County Roscommon. She was one year older than Hanna, an accomplished pianist with a Bachelor of Music degree from the Royal. She too was a friend of Joyce, a favourite of hers despite his 'bad boy' reputation, and when he stayed at her home she accompanied his 'lovely tenor voice' on her piano.[42] She and James Cousins, from a working-class Protestant Belfast background, married the same year as the Sheehy Skeffingtons. Their preparations made the Sheehy Skeffington union appear positively bohemian as Gretta 'had to retire to the bosom of (her) family to be taught how to cook, to collect a trousseau, and learn household management'.[43] The Cousins' duo-biography *We Two Together* contains an outspoken account of Gretta's attitude towards sex: 'I knew nothing of the technique of sex, but I had utter trust in his knowledge, his will and his integrity ... Jim and I had realised that our surest unity was in our similar aspirations to build purity and beauty into our lives and into the world.'[44] Her trust could not overcome her reservations and during their first year of married life she grew thin and white, finding that 'Every child I looked at called to my mind the shocking circumstance that brought about its existence ... I found myself looking on men and women as degraded by this demand of nature.'[45] When Annie Besant (who would shortly become a dominant influence in their lives), became a theosophist in 1891, she withdrew from publication her birth-control book on the grounds that it was 'incompatible ... with her new belief that the evolved soul occupies itself with higher things.'[46] Influenced by her own belief in theosophy, Gretta contended that she and her husband would not 'be satisfied, be purified and redeemed ... until the evolution of form has substituted some more artistic way of continuance of the race.'[47] The Cousins did not have children.

The revolution most dear to the Sheehy Skeffingtons remained women's struggle for emancipation. As women's fight for equality in higher education had not yet been won, it was the cause to which both devoted their energies in the early months of marriage. Frank, although registrar of University College, had no intention of being seduced into an easy life of undemanding meetings and conversation. He was still a 'crank' and would remind those who teased that 'a crank is a small instrument that makes revolutions'.[48] He drew up a petition calling for women to be admitted into University College on an equal basis with men. It was then circulated by Hanna and other members of the Irish University Women's Graduates Association, who approached everyone at all eligible to have a say on the issue. The Reverend Delany pointed out to his registrar that an officer of the institution had no right to challenge college policy. This official reprimand was to be expected. Frank had already felt constrained by being unable to sign his name to an open letter attacking the bishops at Maynooth for welcoming King Edward VII to Ireland. Before his marriage he had complained that his working life gave him no time for his writing; he wanted his days 'free for thought, for plans, for dreams of love!'[49] Wanting no more compromises in his life he resigned, with the explanation that he wished to be free to express his opinions in the future.

From now on, their financial position would always be precarious with Hanna's income the only guaranteed part of their family finances. In May 1906 Frank recorded in his diary 'Debts closing in, position becoming impossible', but his commitment to publicising his views on all the issues of the day meant that it was impossible to change his way of life.[50] He continued to be far less responsible than his wife when it came to financial affairs. While he was free to travel to England and Europe when the notion took him, she was tied to the demands of the scholastic year. In London, partly to meet those involved in the suffrage movement, he visited the headquarters of the Women's Social and Political Union. Hanna, having to live vicariously, urged him to return with lots of news and impressions. David Sheehy had returned to his life as an MP in London, so she added, 'love to the suffragettes, father (unholy blend!)'.[51] Enough of Frank's journalistic articles were appearing to ensure that his name was becoming known in certain liberal circles, but many were for short-lived radical publications, payments from which were either small or non-existent. The Reverend Eugene Sheehy, despite belonging to an older generation of revolutionaries, recognised the importance of this wave of radicals, as he responded to an edition of *New Ireland* sent to him by Hanna, 'such writing is sure to give a new direction, fresh impulse to Irish thought.'[52] Over time Frank's journalistic reputation grew and he became Irish correspondent for a number of established papers, including the *Manchester Guardian*, the French Socialist paper *L'Humanité* and the London *Daily Herald*. His most difficult task was trying to interest editors of publications which could pay to invest in articles concerning subjects dear to his heart. The Sheehy Skeffington papers are full of editors' rejection slips, usually softened by the request that he continue to submit work for consideration. On occasion he wrote leaders for the moderate nationalist paper *Freeman's Journal*, where his views were not always appreciated. One famous story has W. H. Brayden, the editor, complaining that he could not print Skeffington's leader on 'Rat Week' because it 'spoke of the rats as if they were an oppressed nationality'.[53]

Hanna loved teaching and had a natural gift for communicating with students. Her methods as a language teacher were modern, a great deal of her classes devoted to conversation rather than dreary rote learning yet pursuing a career as a Catholic lay teacher was not easy. A testimonial accompanying her application for the position of Assistant Examiner in English had referred to her abilities in glowing terms, but even this was no guarantee of employment:

> In the Intermediate examinations and in those of the Royal University, Miss Sheehy uniformly won high distinctions; but these only inadequately indicate the full measure of her ability and scholarship and in recent years she has had no little success as a teacher.[54]

Understandably, she resented the privileged position of those belonging to religious orders. While a Protestant woman graduate had some chance of a career and promotion, the fact that only nuns could be in positions of authority when it came to the education of Catholic girls meant that university graduates like herself were given yearly tenures and often displaced by cheaper teachers. Her total salary for 1904 was the not-insignificant sum of £70, but she felt it to be hard-won, taking up much of her time and using up too much of her energies.[55] She was bitter that those with MAs were often not picked because they were too expensive so, in desperation, highly qualified graduates like herself were forced to accept ludicrously small salaries.

A pamphlet entitled *Open Doors for Irishwomen: A Guide to the Professions Open to Educated Women in Ireland*, issued in 1907 by the Irish Central Bureau for the Employment of Women, drew a sorry picture for women teachers in Hanna's position:

> The prospects for teachers in Ireland are not very good. There are not many large Protestant schools, and as the education of Roman Catholic girls is almost entirely in the hands of the religious orders, the number of openings for highly-qualified women teachers is small.

Such was the sectarian nature of the educational divide that crossing over to the 'other side' was unthinkable. Alexandra College did educate Catholic girls before Catholic colleges were set up, but faculty staff were drawn from the appropriate sections of the community. These were Protestant. In 1905 Hanna succeeded in being appointed an examiner, chairing the National Examination Sub-Committee during the year and in 1910 she achieved success in having her name selected for the list of examiners of German, with an enthusiastic endorsement from Arthur Williamson, Principal of Rathmines College of Commerce:

> Apart from her ability as a teacher, Mrs Sheehy-Skeffington is deeply and widely read in the literature of England, France, and Germany. She is consequently an examiner of much discrimination and fairness, and is able to put herself at the point of view of the youngest and least mature of her students equally with that of the most advanced.[56]

When her political activities limited her teaching career to evening classes paid on an hourly basis, she often had to struggle to ensure that she was kept on when the authorities were looking for opportunities to dispense with her services.

At the beginning of 1907 Uncle Eugene became seriously ill and Hanna rushed to be with him, even though it meant missing the start of the new teaching term in Eccles Street. The consideration shown to her by everyone was clear indication that they knew how dearly she loved her godfather. Letters sent on to her at Bruree included one from Aunt Kate, hoping that Eugene was getting better and looking forward to seeing Hanna on her return to Dublin; from Sister Patrick, who had asked Frank to reassure Hanna that she was 'not to trouble', even if she could not return to teach the week after, and hoping 'the poor uncle' would pull through; Kitty Murphy (later, Kate O'Callaghan, T.D.), a former pupil of Hanna's, wrote to say that 'the BAs told me to say to you that they hoped your uncle was better'. They were postponing their opening meeting until Hanna could be with them.[57] Eugene was suffering from alcohol-induced jaundice and neglecting his parish duties. Hanna and her father were with him not only to help with nursing, but to prevent him relapsing. He was a difficult patient, 'the more he improves, the more unmanageable as to diet, temper, etc does he become – looks on us as "watch dogs"', wrote an exasperated Hanna. After ten days with her uncle she was writing to Frank 'I never value my little home so much as when I'm away from it and never appreciate my husband so well as when forced to be away from him!'[58] Eugene was soon living full-time in Belvedere Place, when he was not off on his travels, having retired from duties as parish priest.

Both Hanna and Frank were nationalists, wanting political independence, but the Irish-Ireland route was not the path they chose to take. Inghinidhe na hÉireann, formed by Maud Gonne and a group of like-minded women in 1900, was going from strength to strength, but the excitement of belonging to Ireland's first nationalist-feminist organisation did not appeal to Hanna. Many Inghinidhe members were outspoken advocates of physical force as a method of winning independence. For Frank, that was unacceptable. Can we say the same for Hanna? Although she argued against the subordinate role played by women in nationalist organisations, she did not take issue with the different strategies used to fight for the goal of national independence. Indeed, she often lauded the 'stone thrower' and those who used direct action against landlords and other agents of repression. Her father and uncle had been amongst those who had chosen that route. However, in this first decade of the century, her political life centred around constitutional organisations. She had grown up in an atmosphere in which the achievement of Catholic emancipation in 1829, despite a severe property qualification, was still a notable victory. The vote was the cornerstone of democracy, possession of it a vital part of citizenship and she urged her family to join her in membership of the IWSLGA. The prospect of a separation from Britain being achieved peacefully, by means of an act of parliament, was regarded as a real prospect once a Liberal government was returned to power. There was therefore little point in urging armed rebellion. Even Patrick Pearse was a 'Home Ruler' until 1912. Only after 1914, when Ulster Unionist opposition made this an unlikely prospect and British involvement in a world war altered the odds on a successful uprising, did some decide upon the path of insurrection. As Hanna made her personal journey from respectable graduate to uncompromising militant, she made it clear, privately, that unlike her husband she held no doctrinal adherence to the creed of pacifism.

An early joint endeavour in the political field (and one that included most of the Sheehy family and many of their friends) was the Young Ireland Branch, commonly known as the YIBs. New blood was badly needed by the parliamentary party, so in 1904 a Young Ireland branch of the United Irish League (which was the constituency organisation of the Irish Parliamentary Party) was formed with the specific aim of winning over some of this generation. Tom Kettle was elected president while membership of the committee included Frank, Hanna and her brother Eugene. Dick Sheehy also joined, as did Francis Cruise O'Brien, soon to become involved with Kathleen Sheehy. The secretary, a young solicitor called Frank Culhane, married Margaret in 1907. Mary and Kathleen were also listed as members of what the *Irish Times* later described as 'one of the most brilliant of Dublin's coteries before the war'.[59] So many of those connected with the Sheehy family were involved that the prospect of a new dynasty emerging was more than fanciful thought. Amongst the audience in Dublin's Mansion House on 14 December 1905 were David and Bessie Sheehy, listening to the presidential speech of Tom Kettle, their daughter's fiancé.[60]

The Irish Party, delighted with this influx of bright young talent, provided the Young Irelanders with keys to their offices and greeted them with enthusiasm. The honeymoon did not last long. The main problem was the fact that the warm welcome given to the men had not been extended to the young women who also wanted to join, and some of the men flouted party discipline in their support for their friends. As soon as the women expressed a desire to join the Young Ireland Branch, doubts about their eligibility were raised. An official of the United Irish League advised them to form a 'ladies branch', obviously intended for social purposes only, relegating them to the usual role of tea-makers. It was Hanna's first battle with the male world. A 'rumour' went around that there was nothing in the constitution of the United Irish League to exclude women from joining the ordinary branches. The women made their next move:

> Several of us students determined to put the matter to the test and invaded the League offices on the occasion of the second meeting, planked down our entrance fees to an amazed official, who though visibly reluctant and embarrassed did not openly refuse us, murmuring something of course about a 'ladies' branch', which we ignored. Once formally enrolled as members our position was firmer; still we had a struggle (supported by many … of the men) before our state was assured.[61]

It was a victory, of sorts, but the experience left her sceptical of the Irish Party ever taking up the cause of female suffrage. The YIBs were essentially the 'youth movement' of the Irish Party and some of the more ambitious graduates' enthusiasm for membership rested on the belief that, with Home Rule in sight, this was an avenue to a future place in government. They were not prepared to jeopardise their future by supporting the women's cause.

Women were still excluded, even as visitors, from conventions of the United Irish League, so their acceptance into the Young Ireland section was little more than a device to quell further dissent and a calculated move to retain the allegiance of key members like Frank Skeffington and Tom Kettle. Many of the most militant of the Irish suffragists began their political lives as members of the YIBs, an experience that ensured their future disbelief in the good intentions of most politicians. When nineteenth-century women who had fought to free slaves found themselves excluded from anti-slavery conventions they responded by forming suffrage societies so that they could free themselves. And that was not so long ago. Deborah Webb's Quaker parents had attended the World's Anti-Slavery Convention in London in 1840, an experience which had stimulated their interest in feminism, an interest passed down to their daughter.[62] In Hanna's eyes this was a significant precedent, and one she was beginning to consider.

There were other venues where women were permitted entrance only as a privilege rather than as a right. The long-established and exclusive Contemporary Club, a notable debating society famous for being the scene of Maud Gonne's debut into the world of politics, had opened their doors to women for a monthly 'ladies night'. Frank was a member of the Contemporary Club; Hanna was entitled to no more than temporary visitor status. That she went at all was probably a reflection of the limited number of venues suitable for a young courting couple desperate to meet as much as possible but restricted by the conventions of the period. A diary entry for the start of 1902 commented upon the fact that the inequalities of the female sex remained taboo as a subject suitable for discussion. Hanna had had a 'most interesting evg. though woman's question was shunted by Chairman'.[63] Mary Macken, another woman irritated by the fact that the 'exclusive males' debarred her from membership, was also a regular visitor at this period. She said she 'went gladly', but such insistence upon maintaining masculine superiority was becoming intolerable to many.[64]

The Gaelic League accepted women as members: its existence a welcome catalyst in the breaking down of barriers between the sexes. Hundreds of young men and women flocked to join the various clubs and societies that were springing up and a new Irish-Ireland identity was forged by a generation that had lost faith in conventional politics. Sinn Féin held its first Convention in 1905 and women were elected to positions on its executive. Despite these outward signs of commitment to women's equality, Hanna was suspicious, believing it to be no more than a tactical manoeuvre by a movement in its infancy in need of all the support it could get. If Sinn Féin gained in strength it was more than likely, she commented sardonically, that with a new line-up of (male) members: 'woman falls naturally out of step and is duly left behind'.[65] Uninterested in the language revival, nothing would alter her conviction that without the vote women would never be taken seriously by any of the political organisations. She had not yet lost hope that a revitalised Irish Party could be pressurised into taking up the issue. Her father had a position of some importance as a long-standing member of parliament and in 1906 Tom Kettle, having demonstrated his mettle with the YIBs, was elected Member of Parliament for East Tyrone.

The campaign for women's right to an equal education was also continuing to gain ground, although there were still those who favoured the separate education of men and women. In the transition from the shelter of college to the rougher world of political life, the battle for women's equality in education was an important rite of passage. An article by Norah Meade (yet another Eccles Street graduate) in the January 1907 issue of *New Ireland Review* had argued that because there were essential differences in the modes of thought of men and women, women's best interests would be served in having separate colleges. This provoked a joint reply from Hanna and Mary Hayden, whose heated and deeply-felt response was a powerful argument against sexual segregation:

> if women will not consent to eat at a common table provided for men and women alike, it will, we fear, be their fate to go hungry or to be obliged to content themselves with a few crumbs and husks flung to them in half contemptuous charity.[66]

That view finally won the day. The unsatisfactory 'Royal' was abolished and co-education was instituted. The Universities Act of 1908 established two universities: Queen's University in Belfast and the National University with its three constituent colleges in Dublin, Cork and Galway. The women's colleges were dissolved, the buildings becoming residential hostels. Women were finally granted equality with regards to teaching, awarding of degrees, staff appointments and appointment to university authorities. The outcome had by no means been a foregone conclusion, but it was in many respects a Pyrrhic victory. Co-education did not mean that women were equal partners in academic institutions. The appointment of Mary Hayden and Agnes O'Farrelly to the governing body of the Dublin college was not followed by new staff appointments of women. Academic life still held few opportunities for the female sex.

The realisation that such small gains were little more than markers of what had to be achieved before true emancipation was won, led many women with academic backgrounds into taking up the suffrage cause. Few were militant (Mary Hayden became a founding member of the Irish Catholic Women's Suffrage Society) but they shared a recognition that possession of the vote was a common goal. Her friend Agnes O'Farrelly, immersed in the Gaelic League and academia, in talking of Maud Gonne had declared, to Hanna's great surprise, that 'woman's place was not on the public platform'.[67] Hanna was still a member of the Irish Women's Suffrage and Local Government Association, continuing her yearly subscription until 1909, although having resigned from the committee in January 1906. Her resignation was prompted by the defeat of her suggested amendment to the annual report, where she proposed, seconded by Jennie Wyse Power, that 'British' be substituted for 'our own' in the phrase 'our own enterprising colonies'. Both Hanna and Jennie Wyse Power resigned. While the IWSLGA was 'non-party', its ethos was predominantly unionist.[68] Her increasing impatience with the organisation was evident in her report of a meeting held in the salubrious setting of Montpelier House, Phoenix Park, the following year. James Crozier presided and Thomas Haslam read his paper on 'Women's suffrage, objections considered' before the group went on to discuss women and the poor law. Mrs Sheehy Skeffington was listed as having talked about 'changes in public opinion and the progress made in other countries and the anomaly of women, though voteless, being elected in England as county councillors and mayors'.[69]

Her exasperation with the slow pace of change in Ireland is almost tangible. While acknowledging women's achievements in the local government field, she was much less convinced than other IWSLGA members of the wisdom of concentrating upon this area. In her opinion it was 'ameliorative and limited … having to do with children, poor law, and the like – the kind of things that men generally 'really have not time for'. She was also discovering an inequality in social status between herself and many of the IWSLGA members. She wickedly over-emphasised the difference: 'one of the favourite arguments used for suffrage by them was, "My gardener and my butler have the vote. Why shouldn't I?"[70] She would not be content with that political circle for much longer. Changes were in the air. Across the water, the formation of the Women's Social and Political Union in 1903 had introduced an exciting new dimension to the increasingly stale world of well-heeled, sedate campaigners. News of the Pankhursts and their associates intrigued many young women. For Hanna, it 'stirred a responsive chord in some Irish feminist breasts'. In a few years Irish women would begin to 'start a fire on (their) own'.[71]

The different paths taken by the Sheehy sisters reflected some of the options open to middle-class Catholic women of the time. Mary, who was always feminist in outlook, critical of all institutions for their male bias, had little sympathy for the aims of the new generation of revolutionary nationalists. She had finally married Tom Kettle in a smart society wedding in 1908, in this way linking herself to the Irish Party, but she and her husband, as parliamentarians and as feminists, were also associated with the early years of the Irish Women's Franchise League. However, once the League came into conflict with the Irish Party both were less visible as League supporters. Margaret, although a nominal IWSLGA member, had little interest in politics. After her marriage she had four children in quick succession. Kathleen remained unmarried until 1911. She worked in the Franchise League offices when they were set up and was a strong, if less militant, supporter of the suffrage cause. Her great passion was the revival of the Irish language, spending time on the Aran islands in order to improve her ability to speak it, becoming a teacher of Irish and eventually writing the textbook *Irish Grammar*, for many years the only one in existence. Although Frank was no cultural nationalist, his inquisitive and generous nature, incessantly interested in different causes, led to Kathleen teaching him the rudiments of the language. Dr J. B. was a fluent speaker of Irish, another point of conflict for father and son. Mischievously, Frank once carried out a heated newspaper correspondence against his father on the subject of the Irish language revival. He wrote under a *nom-de-plume* and never owned up to having been the author who had so enraged Dr Skeffington.[72]

Religion was an even greater cause of conflict between Hanna, Frank, and their parents. In his student days Joyce had taunted Frank on the contradiction of a rationalist continuing to be a Catholic and Frank, rather lamely, had promised that he would take a year off to study the religious question.[73] It was not something that could be dismissed lightly. Shaking off the burden of one's religious upbringing was not an easy process. It took both Frank and Hanna several years before they could define themselves as atheists. Their son claimed later that his parents practised their religion for some years after marriage, but two or three years before his birth 'had thought themselves out of it – not drifted out – and became convinced rationalists and humanists'.[74] Hanna was still going to Mass in 1908 but a year later had stopped practicing her religion. Once the intellectual decision had been made, Frank would never compromise. He became a vehemently committed atheist. Hanna found renunciation more difficult and, the first time she found herself in a hostile environment, clung shamefacedly to the comfort of old habits. While about to embark on hunger strike during her first prison sentence, she almost succumbed to the reassurance of the confessional. Frank was appalled and totally unsympathetic: 'Let them associate suffragism with atheism if they like – they will be right! This is one of the things on which I am drastic and can't understand compromise! … I think you ought to give up even formally calling yourself a Catholic, it's absurd after Owen's non-baptism; and it takes in nobody.'[75] There is no evidence that she ever weakened again. David Sheehy was deeply religious. In his old age he went to mass six times a day; it was assumed that each was dedicated to one of his six children. His gradual estrangement from Hanna began with her rejection of religion, making her continued closeness to her Uncle Eugene the more notable.

The realisation of what life would be like without Frank was brought home to Hanna in the worst way when he became dangerously ill with diptheria in May 1908. As it was a contagious illness (and vaccinations would not begin until the 1920s), Hanna's family 'the Belvederians' kept his illness 'dark', although her father, writing from the House of Commons, wrote of his relief that the 'throat trouble was no longer dangerous', offering the masses he attended for Frank's recovery.[76] In her diary Hanna commented 'Frank's illness a great change in many ways.'[77] She sent him some sweet pea on the eve of their wedding anniversary 'for the day's sake', reflecting 'this long illness and subsequent parting is a long widowhood, but I think … it draws us closer together in spirit dearie.'[78] She would not forget 'how near I was to losing you.'[79] He had a lengthy convalescence, staying at the Green Park Hotel in Youghal with some expenses covered by Dr J. B. who exhorted him not to bathe too much 'a wash once a week in tepid water or in summer fairly cool water may be useful for cleansing. But as a stimulant it is bad – bad for the heart especially.'[80] The benevolent father was a less than generous husband to Rose. Frank was also receiving letters of bitter complaint from his mother: 'very stingy with me, just gave me a pound going away. As I said before he thinks little should do me but I do not intend to do myself an injustice.'[81] This disregard for the women of the family would go a long way in explaining Hanna's antipathy towards her father-in-law. Her references to Rose and Dr J. B. in letters written during Frank's convalescence are ungraceful, 'Give my love to your mother and father if you like and any news of me as well – I'll not bother writing to either' but they also reflect her hurt that his mother never wrote to her.[82]

Over-work and worry may have been a contributing factor in Frank's illness. Although his journalistic efforts continued, his dream of establishing his own paper as a vehicle to expound his own distinctive philosophy remained fraught with problems. The *Nationist* – a vehicle for the YIBs that Tom Kettle and Frank had collaborated on – lasted a bare six months, its continued weekly publication impossible without an influx of capital. That pattern was to repeat itself. At the beginning of 1907, together with the socialist Fred Ryan, a new friend, Frank began production of the *National Democrat*. The two editors found that a hectic round of political meetings left little time for the duties of editor, while the need to earn money from writing meant that time also had to be found to write for other publications. Frank's admiring biography of Michael Davitt, founder of the Land League, published to good reviews shortly before his illness, had too small a print run to make any money. The situation did not improve. Forced to refuse his friend John Byrne's request for a loan, he bemoaned that the 'inability to oblige one's best friends, is, I think, quite the worst consequence of poverty'.[83]

There were several reasons why Hanna had not joined her husband in his convalescence. While he recovered his strength in Youghal, she was busy supervising a move from their small house in Rathgar to a much larger Victorian terraced house at 11 Grosvenor Place, Rathmines. The move took place in pouring rain on 11 June. She was conscious of the responsibility placed upon her, particularly as Frank was fanatical about detail. He was reassured to be told 'all papers housed in perfect order', but Hanna admitted feeling melancholic at uprooting herself from their first home: 'I do hate pulling up my roots even for a beneficial transplanting … I fear I'll be even sorry to die!' She was pleased to have been given helpful hints about the garden from the 'gardener's man' and enclosed some elderblossom for Frank as 'adieu' from their old house. He was urged not to think of returning until his strength had returned, 'don't overdo walking dearie, especially in bad weather'.[84] 'Deadly friendly' English people lived on one side of them while the other side 'swarms with kids' who were all over the front and back of the garden until shoed away by Hanna.[85] The letters give a fascinating, if disconcerting, glimpse into the domestic relationships of the household. The attitudes are those of a middle-class woman who takes the existence of servants for granted. Minnie, their maid, was efficient, but Hanna had nothing but complaints about Johnny, an occasional handyman, who was 'slovenly and impudent', leaving work early to get drunk. She put a brave face on their financial plight, sending £7 with reassurances that payment of 300 marks for a German article had arrived; she had just received £1 10s payment from Eccles Street and had other cheques yet uncashed in reserve, 'I'm just paying nothing save milk or bread & the ordinary calls … notice people for some weird reason never press you if you only go on buying.' Busy with book arranging and gardening she insisted that she was in 'capital form'. She had been unwell during the days of the move but it was 'nothing to speak of – my old complaint, with *mal de mer* as well – I think stopping tea jogged my old liver a bit'.[86]

Gynaecological matters were the reason why Dr Elizabeth Tennant was consulted at this time. In her letter 'On the eve of conception' letter she had written lyrically of her hopes for a child:

> I shall do my best to shape it well, when it shall lie beneath my heart & I hope I shall transmit nothing that is base in me. I hope that a blossom will spring of our sowing – for the image that pleases me best is a garden – that the seed implanted will ripen in the darkness & earth like mystery of my womb to a goodly fruit.[87]

Now, one year later, she sought medical advice. Because Frank was not in Dublin he wrote separately to the doctor, wanting to know exactly what she had told Hanna. The reply confirms the impression that much of her ill health stemmed from difficulties with her reproductive organs. It was nothing serious, but treatment would be required for a short time, and 'during treatment it will be advisable to abstain from marital relations – but you both may feel quite at rest & content that there is nothing to prevent her in due course having a family'.[88]

Hanna kept busy, continuing to put the new house in order, marking the Intermediate exam papers (a chore that only those desperate for money would have undertaken), and keeping up with her political interests. She wrote to Frank of a suffrage meeting at the Haslams she had attended. By mid-July he was home for a few days before travelling to London, staying in a hotel in Fleet Street and working hard to extend his range of journalistic contacts. In June she had said 'I'd hardly be able to get to London were I ever so rich as I've too much to do yet … I hope you are not disappointed dearie?'[89] but now she was frantically finishing her chore of marking so that she could join him. In a postcard sent just after she had handed in her papers she complained of being 'awfully limp, so can't write more – but was determined to get it done today'. She assured Frank that she would be all right 'when fatigue passes' and hoped to be able to travel over by the Saturday, despite a host of domestic details to be attended to. She wondered whether she really needed to leave word at the police station while she was away, as Mrs Donovan, their landlady had suggested.[90] Mrs Donovan, a most unsympathetic landlady, was no doubt concerned because her new tenants were planning to be away for a considerable length of time. They spent most of August touring Normandy, spending time in Paris at the Hotel de Bresagne.[91] It was an important holiday, allowing them both time to relax (their son was conceived at this time), and to regain their energies before the start of the next phase of their lives together.

NOTES

1 Frank Skeffington to Hanna Sheehy (hereafter Frank to Hanna), 9 Feb. 1903, Sheehy Skeffington MS (hereafter SS MS) 40,461/4.

2 Frank to Hanna, 21 June 1903, SS MS 40,461/5. Witnesses to the marriage were Alphonsus Farrelly (brother of Agnes and a UCD contemporary of Frank), and Mary Sheehy.

3 Hanna Sheehy to Frank Skeffington (hereafter Hanna to Frank), 19 Nov. 1900 SS MS 40,464/2.

4 Hanna to Frank, 2 Jan. 1903, SS MS 40,465/1.

5 Hanna to Frank, 23 Feb. 1902, SS MS 40,465/1.

6 Frank to Hanna, Sheehy Skeffington 16 June 1902, MS 40,411/4.

7 Frank to Hanna, 21 June 1903, SS MS 40,461/5.

8 Memorabilia from wedding and honeymoon, contained in SS MS 41,207/1.

9 Andrée Sheehy Skeffington, *Skeff: A Life of Owen Sheehy Skeffington* (Dublin, 1991), p. 12.

10 Roger McHugh, 'Thomas Kettle and Francis Sheehy Skeffington', in Conor Cruise O'Brien (ed.), *The Shaping of Modern Ireland* (London, 1960), pp 13–23.

11 Hanna to Frank, 7 May 1901, SS MS 40,464/5.

12 Sydney Gifford Czira, *The Years Flew By* (Dublin, 1974), pp 4–5.

13 Owen Sheehy Skeffington, 'Francis Sheehy Skeffington', in Owen Dudley-Edwards and Fergus Pyle (eds), *1916: The Easter Rising* (London, 1968), p. 137.

14 Leah Levenson and Jerry Natterstad, *Hanna Sheehy Skeffington: Irish Feminist* (New York, 1983), p. 17.

15 C. P. Curran, *Under the Receding Wave* (Dublin, 1970), p. 113.

16 Levenson and Natterstad, *Hanna Sheehy Skeffington*, p. 18.

17 Mary Colum, *Life and the Dream* ((Dublin, 1947), p. 185.

18 Hanna Sheehy Skeffington, 'Women and the university question', in *New Ireland Review*, xvii, May 1902.

19 Hanna to Frank, 11 Dec. 1900, SS MS 40,464/2.

20 Rose Jacob to 'Cousin Deborah', 27 May 1914, SS MS 41,177/27.

21 Colum, *Life and the Dream*, p. 174.

22 Hanna Sheehy Skeffington, 'Random reflections on housewives: Their ways and works', in *Irish Housewife*, Issue 1, 1946, pp 20–2.

23 Margaret McCoubrey to Hanna Sheehy Skeffington, n. d., (1915), SS MS 24,133.

24 Marguerite Palmer to Hanna Sheehy Skeffington, 11 Aug. 1914, SS MS 22,666.

25 *Irish Citizen*, July/Aug. 1920.

26 C. P. Curran, *Under the Receding Wave*, p. 113.

27 Gifford Czira, *The Years Flew By*, p. 33.

28 *Irish Citizen*, July 1916.

29 Hanna to Frank, 26 July 1908, SS MS 40,466 /2.

30 Hanna to Frank, 2 July 1904, SS MS 40,464/5.

31 Frank to Hanna, 26 July 1904, SS MS 40,461/6.

32 Elizabeth Steiner-Scott, 'To bounce a boot off her now & then…': Domestic violence in post-famine Ireland, in Maryann Gialanella Valiulis & Mary O'Dowd (eds), *Women & Irish History* (Dublin, 1997), pp 125–43.

33 Louise Ryan, 'Women, morality and the law', in *Winning the Vote for Women: The Irish Citizen Newspaper and the Suffrage Movement in Ireland*, (Dublin, 2018).
34 Hanna to Frank, 'To Frank', 23 Dec. 1904, MS 40,461/6.
35 Hanna to Frank, 26 June 1905, SS MS 40,465/1.
36 Hanna to Frank, 20 July 1905, SS MS 40,465/1.
37 Hanna to Frank, 'On the eve of conception', 18 Aug. 1907, SS MS 40,466/1.
38 Hanna to Frank, 28 June 1908, SS MS 40,466/1.
39 Rose Jacob, diary entry for 9 Nov. 1919, quoted in Carmel Quinlan, *Genteel Revolutionaries: Anna and Thomas Haslam and the Irish Women's Movement* (Cork, 2002), p. 17.
40 *The Vote*, 25 Oct. 1929.
41 Andrée Sheehy Skeffington, interview with author, Nov. 1993.
42 James and Margaret Cousins, *We Two Together* (Madras, 1950), p. 105.
43 Ibid., p. 88.
44 Ibid., pp 54–5.
45 Ibid., pp 108–9.
46 Rosemary Dinnage, *Annie Besant* (Middlesex, 1986), p. 81.
47 Ibid., p. 109.
48 Owen Sheehy Skeffington, 'Francis Sheehy Skeffington', in Dudley-Edwards and Pyle, *1916: The Easter Rising*, p. 137.
49 Frank to Hanna, 21 June 1903, SS MS 40,461/5.
50 Leah Levenson, *With Wooden Sword: A Portrait of Francis Sheehy-Skeffington, Militant Pacifist* (Dublin, 1983), p. 71.
51 Hanna to Frank, 17 Feb. 1907 and 19 Feb. 1907, SS MS 40,466/11.
52 Eugene Sheehy to Hanna Sheehy Skeffington, 17 Aug. 1903, SS MS 41,176/18.
53 Owen Sheehy Skeffington, 'Francis Sheehy Skeffington', in Dudley-Edwards and Pyle, *1916: The Easter Rising*, p. 139.
54 William Magennis, Advisory examiner in English, to intermediate board, University College Dublin, 12-12-03, SS MS 22,662.
55 Levenson and Natterstad, *Hanna Sheehy Skeffington*, n. 14, p. 191.
56 Arthur Williamson, Principal Rathmines School of Commerce, 6 Dec. 1910, with statement of renewal Jan. 1912, SS MS 33,603/16.
57 Letters to Hanna while in Bruree, courtesy of Andrée Sheehy Skeffington.
58 Hanna to Frank, 31 Jan. 1907, SS MS 40,466 /1.
59 Obituary of Francis Cruise O'Brien, in *Irish Times*, 28 Dec. 1927.
60 *Freeman's Journal*, 15 Dec. 1905.
61 Typescript of 'Women and the national movement', SS MS 22,226, published in *Irish Nation*, 6, 13, 20 Mar. 1909. Reprinted in Margaret Ward (ed.), *Hanna Sheehy Skeffington: Suffragette and Sinn Féiner: Her Memoirs and Political Writings* (Dublin, 2017), pp 48–58.
62 *Votes for Women*, 21 June 1909.
63 Levenson and Natterstad, *Hanna Sheehy Skeffington*, p. 11.
64 Mary Macken, 'Yeats, O'Leary and the contemporary club, in *Studies*, viii, 1939, p. 137.
65 Hanna Sheehy Skeffington, 'Women and the national movement'.

66 Mary Hayden and Hanna Sheehy Skeffington, 'Women in university: A reply', in *New Ireland Review*, i:5, Feb. 1908.
67 Hanna to Frank, 8 May 1901, SS MS 40,464/5.
68 Quinlan, *Genteel Revolutionaries*, p. 161.
69 Report of IWSLGA meeting, Montpelier House, 6 Dec. 1907, SS MS 22,258.
70 Hanna Sheehy Skeffington, 'Memories of the suffrage campaign in Ireland', in *The Vote*, 30 Aug. 1929.
71 Hanna Sheehy Skeffington, *Reminiscences*, p. 12.
72 Andrée Sheehy Skeffington, *Skeff*, p. 243.
73 Richard Ellman, *James Joyce* (Oxford, 1982), p. 62.
74 Owen Sheehy Skeffington, 'Francis Sheehy Skeffington', p. 139
75 Francis Sheehy Skeffington to Hanna Sheehy Skeffington, 30 July 1912, courtesy of Andrée Sheehy Skeffington.
76 Levenson, *With Wooden Sword*, p. 75.
77 Hanna Sheehy Skeffington diary, 1908–9, SS MS 41,183/2.
78 Hanna to Frank, 26 June 1909, SS MS 40,466/1/.
79 Levenson and Natterstad, *Hanna Sheehy Skeffington*, p. 22.
80 Levenson, *With Wooden Sword*, p. 75.
81 Rose Skeffington to Frank Sheehy Skeffington, n. d., SS MS 21,631.
82 Hanna to Frank, 14 June 1908, SS MS 22,263.
83 Levenson, *With Wooden Sword*, p. 72.
84 Hanna to Frank, 14 June 1908, SS MS 22,263.
85 Hanna to Frank, 12 June 1908, SS MS 40,466/1.
86 Ibid.
87 Hanna to Frank, 'On the eve of conception', 18 Aug. 1907, SS MS 40,466/1.
88 Quoted in Levenson, *With Wooden Sword*, pp 75–6.
89 Hanna to Frank, 19 June 1908, SS MS 40,466 /1.
90 Hanna to Frank, 28 July 1908, SS MS 24,098.
91 Hanna Sheehy Skeffington, visa application, 1915, gives details of past foreign trips, SS MS 22,688.

FOUR

A FEMINIST MOTHER, 1908–10

On first impressions, Gretta and James Cousins appeared highly unlikely allies for the rationalist and agnostic Sheehy Skeffingtons. Gretta was a practising medium, her ability to commune with dead friends an attribute she took entirely for granted and to which she often casually referred. She and James were deeply interested in eastern philosophies, joining the Theosophical Society in 1908, a commitment which was, eventually, to lead to James working for Annie Besant's theosophical journal *New India* and teaching at the Madanapalle Theosophical College in India. Gretta's acceptance of a spiritual undercurrent influencing world events was the antithesis of the Sheehy Skeffington insistence on men and women taking responsibility for all human change. Frank was totally lacking in 'otherworldliness'. Con Curran testified to his friend possessing 'little or no sense of the supernatural, no interest in philosophy or metaphysics and he was as deaf to music as he was blind to the visual arts'.[1] When spotted in the Louvre during a French holiday it turned out that Frank had ignored the paintings, being too busy walking through the galleries to see if it would take the two hours mentioned in Baedeker! Hanna loved theatre and books, sharing her husband's indifference to music, joking she knew two tunes, 'one was the national anthem, the other wasn't'. She scoffed at what she described as Gretta's insistence 'that we were all in the cosmic procession or some such guff with cosmic in it'.[2] Despite all this, the four had much in common. Gretta was a fierce fighter for many causes and she and her husband shared the deeply felt political commitments of their friends, rejecting worldly advancement while recognising that imprisonment – or worse – might wait for them. Joyce sneered at Gretta as the epitome of the educated middle-class young woman, but her devotion to the cause of women's emancipation never faltered. Her work earned her the accolade of becoming India's first woman magistrate and, in 1932, imprisonment for protesting against draconian legal measures being incorporated into the Indian penal code. Gretta and Hanna shared much: the same age, both graduates, both angry at the injustice of women's inferior status. Frank and James: northerners, writers, free thinkers. They complemented each other to perfection.

Gretta's interest in feminism had begun before she met the Skeffingtons. For her, the turning point came when she attended a vegetarian conference in Manchester. That city was at the heart of the renewed suffrage movement, having given birth to all sorts of organisations, including Esther Roper and Eva Gore-Booth's North of England Women's Suffrage Society and the Pankhursts' Women's Social and Political Union. It was therefore not surprising that the vegetarian conference should coincide with a meeting of the National Council of Women, a gathering Gretta decided to visit. Her 'insular life in Ireland' had not prepared her for the experience. It was the first large gathering of women she had ever seen and what they were saying opened her eyes to 'the injustices and grievances which were taken for granted as the natural fate of my sex'.[3] As soon as she returned to Dublin she ensured that she was introduced to that 'remarkable old pair', Thomas and Anna Haslam, and she joined their association. The IWSLGA Annual Report for 1905 includes Mrs Cousins in their list of subscribers for the first time. She found it a novel experience. The Cousins had recently moved to a larger home on the Strand Road at Sandymount and in January 1907 Gretta proudly hosted her own suffrage meeting, presided over by Lady Dockrell, with Anna and Thomas Haslam as speakers. She became a committee member of the association in 1908, but soon began to share Hanna's impatience with the slow pace of this genteel approach to political change, particularly when, in late 1907, Emmeline and Frederick Pethick-Lawrence began to publish *Votes for Women*, a vehicle for publicising the daring actions of the WSPU militants.

Votes for Women was immensely important in introducing ideas of the militant suffrage movement to an audience far removed from British centres of activity. Gretta asked a publisher friend, Ernest Bell, to send her each copy when it came out. James also took an interest in this new vehicle for women's emancipation. The March 1908 issue published one of his poems, a sonnet entitled 'To the Suffragettes', which ended with the stirring refrain 'The new great age that brings new hope to all.' Another 'sonnet on suffrage' was published the following month. While James had a new outlet for his poetry,

Gretta was discovering that she was – vicariously and enviously – following the progress of the English women's campaigns. When she and James attended a Skeffington 'At Home' they discovered another couple interested in the possibility of forming a militant suffrage organisation on Irish lines.

According to Gretta, on 4 November 1908, following refreshments and when everyone else had left, the four sat around discussing the problems involved in setting up an organisation which, by calling for the right of Irish women to have the vote without insisting that it must be for an independent Irish parliament, would almost certainly have criticism heaped upon it by every nationalist in Ireland. And, of course, politicians of the Irish Party – including Hanna's father – would undoubtedly be sensitive to criticisms that they had not done enough to support women's petitions to Westminster. They agreed that their demand would be for the vote to be granted to women 'on the same terms as it is, or may be, granted to men'. This was a repetition of the countless petitions presented to parliament by women since the Second Reform Act of 1867 had doubled the male electorate in England and Wales. Although it could be regarded as restricting the vote to people of property because it did not demand abolition of the property qualification, it was essentially a plea for equal treatment of both sexes. There was still a property qualification for male voters, albeit substantially reduced since 1867. Removal of the sex disqualification had to be the priority. The demand for adult suffrage was often made by those who opposed women's suffrage and who used this tactic as a means of frightening off potential supporters of the women. The new organisation would argue, along with the labour movement, that the local government register should be the basis for the parliamentary vote before adult suffrage was achieved. One of their priorities was to persuade every Irish member of parliament (numerous enough to make a crucial difference), to vote for all woman suffrage bills that might be introduced into the House of Commons. This would be for the benefit of both British and Irish women. However, they made it clear that they were not unionist in political orientation because they also wanted to ensure that votes for women would be included in any bill for Irish self-government that might in the future be introduced into parliament. As Gretta put it, they were 'as keen as men on the freedom of Ireland', but the men showed 'no recognition of the existence of women as fellow citizens'.[4] Not every recruit to their ranks would be a nationalist, but all would have to be in agreement that, whatever the constitutional change, women had to be included within its provisions.

The four greatly admired the energy and commitment of the WSPU but they had no intention of simply forming an Irish branch of that organisation. They would follow the lead of the WSPU by using militancy as a weapon if it should prove necessary, but they were perfectly competent to lead themselves. The decision was made. Two days later a small group visited Anna Haslam to explain that they intended to start a new suffrage movement, to be conducted on militant lines. The 'dear old leader' regretted what she felt to be a duplication of effort, but, in Gretta's inimitable phrase: 'she sensed the Time Spirit, and we parted as friends, agreeing to differ on means, though united in aim and ideals'.[5] This was a romanticised description of events as, in reality, Haslam lamented the loss of IWSLGA members to militancy, considering the IWFL as a 'more militant – nationalist – R.C. association.'[6] Carmel Quinlan, biographer of the Haslams, considered the IWSLGA leadership as 'part of the dying fall of southern unionism, while the IWFL was lifted by the buoyant vibrancy of self-confident nationalism.'[7]

Events moved quickly. On 11 November a new society, the Irish Women's Franchise League, was announced. There were some surprising names in the initial provisional committee, as Hanna and Gretta must have made efforts to enlist women whose names were prominent in political and public circles. Kathë Oldham, German-born artist wife of National University professor Charles Oldham (and by one of history's coincidences, the man who had introduced Maud Gonne to the Contemporary Club), while declaring she wished to remain on the committee of the IWSLGA, was listed as a committee member, offering her Rathgar house for meetings as her dining room held 30 or 40 'quite nicely'. While the younger women hoped Mrs Oldham would preside at the first committee meeting, one of Hanna's colleagues reported Käthe had said to her, 'as we have a definite programme to get through it would be better if one of our lot took the chair & left her free just to make people welcome. She advises us to definitely state that we are not a branch of any organisation from outside this country.'[8]

It was obvious that some needed persuading that the new group was not linked with the WSPU in Britain. The artist Sarah Cecilia Harrison (who would, in 1911, be the first woman elected to Dublin Corporation) was initially an enthusiastic member of the committee, writing to Hanna before a meeting 'How angelic of you to offer to come & help me. If you could spare an hour before 1 o'clock tomorrow…'[9] She was a northerner from County Down and a great grandniece of Mary Ann McCracken (social reformer and supporter of Mary Wollstonecraft's views on women's subordination) and of Henry Joy McCracken, the executed leader of the United Irishmen. While Harrison's house was used for all the early committee meetings she was, however, unsure of whether she could support all the aims of the organisation and within a few weeks was sounding much less certain of her role, 'I hope you will ask as many people as you can to come here next Monday evening. I find I know no one who would consent to come over, except two friends and one is abroad! Have you heard from Miss Hayden? Mrs Oldham proposes to bring Miss O'Farrelly.'[10] In her reckoning of the gains and losses in 1909 Hanna put 'Miss Harrison' down as 'lost'.[11] Jennie Wyse Power, after some thought, did not join the committee. While approachable as a speaker for events, she was not an active member. Her daughter Nancy did join, becoming an active promoter of all things Gaelic within the IWFL. Their stress on 'suffrage first' was a problem for many nationalists, while the commitment to adopting militant methods if necessary was anathema to others. Apart from Hanna and Gretta, the other members of the provisional committee who remained committed members were Kathleen Shannon BA, a graduate of the Royal and an active member of the YIBs, and Marguerite Bannister, who married Weldon Palmer in 1910. Like the WSPU it was a woman-only organisation, but men could be associate members. Some would prove to be invaluable supporters.[12]

Starting with just five members, the IWFL would reach a peak of over 1,000 in 1912, male associates numbering around 160.[13] Their offices and their resources were modest: a room at 34 Wicklow Street, not far from Trinity College, too small for anything but routine business and committee meetings.[14] For holding public meetings they were dependent on the support of friends. A large room at the Contemporary Club was one venue, arranged on their behalf by Charles Oldham. The other venue was Barry's Hotel, where Aunt Kate proved a loyal supporter of the League. The Sheehy family and friends provided a significant proportion of the early League membership. Mary Sheehy joined the committee and she and Kathleen were prominent figures at meetings and deputations. At Mrs Barry's on 26 January 1909 Kathleen Sheehy was reported to have made a 'brilliant debut' as a speaker, the other speaker on that occasion being Tom Kettle, who was becoming well-known in feminist circles as one of the few MPs to support suffrage delegations to Westminster.[15] The saturnine Kettle was a superb orator and his combination – uniquely Irish – of nationalist fervour and romantic feminism made him a firm favourite as speaker at WSPU events in London. Who could resist such sentiments as the following, uttered at one of the WSPU 'At Homes': 'If Ireland was a nation deprived of its liberty, womanhood disenfranchised was the greatest nation of the earth deprived of its liberty.'[16] Much less flamboyantly, Francis Cruise O'Brien, anxious for any opportunity to see Kathleen, was also a frequent attender at League events.

The new generation of suffragists were pioneers, women attempting to discover their own individuality despite the fact that the society in which they lived was deeply conservative. It was, wrote Hanna with excitement, 'big and varied work and full of interest.'[17] That pride in their womanhood led to young women insisting upon asserting their identity even in settings as traditional and conformist as the wedding ceremony. A report of the marriage of Mary Sheehy and Tom Kettle, written for *Votes for Women* (and surely penned by Frank), provides us with a glimpse of an event 'full of suffrage atmosphere'. The bride wore a 'Votes for Women' badge pinned to her white gown and another mounted in her floral wreath. Many of the guests also wore badges. John Redmond, leader of the Irish Party and many other Irish Party politicians were wedding guests, as befitting the marriage of one of their most brilliant MPs to the daughter of one of the most senior of the older generation of MPs. It was an ideal opportunity for those engaged in the fight against old masculine traditions, and allusions to suffrage were made in several of the congratulatory speeches. There must have been a few stony faces seated around that wedding breakfast table.[18] John Dillon was later to inform Hanna that in his opinion women's franchise would lead to the downfall of western civilisation, while Redmond would prove himself to be an implacable foe of feminism. The Irish Parliamentary Party gave the Kettles that most traditional of presents, a silver plate. The Sheehy Skeffingtons gave two presents that symbolised their idea of the ideal partnership: a writing desk and a set of George Meredith's novels.[19]

Hanna was now only a spasmodic attender at her other interest groups – secretary for a while for the Women's Graduate Association but finding the Legion Française held her 'objectionable propaganda' against her.[20] She was more than satisfied with what the IWFL was achieving, realising that the movement gave:

> a liberal education for all those who took part in it; it developed a new camaraderie among women, it lifted social barriers, it gave its devotees a new ideal … it helped women to self-expression through service … for the first time in history, not for a man's cause but their own.[21]

Gretta was in complete agreement. For her part, becoming a suffrage campaigner demanded all kinds of sacrifice, forcing them to do things for which they had no training, bringing them ridicule, scorn and misrepresentation, but also:

> a sense of great blessing, an expansion of capacities, the happiness of great friendships, a widening of contacts … an enlarged experience of the inequalities of opportunity imposed on women, an increasing sense of protest against the injustices under which women lived, most of all the women of the working classes.[22]

The formation of the IWFL, even if no more than a handful of women at first, was a sign of the mood of the times. Women's lives became transformed through their commitment to the suffrage cause, a new element of friendship developing out of their experiences. They taught themselves to speak in the open air and they travelled around Ireland, camping in fields, braving hostility, determined to preach the cause in every county. After the 1910 elections, followed the next year by the curbing of the House of Lords veto over legislation, it appeared that prospects for national freedom were only around the corner. The Irish Party, supporting a minority Liberal government, now had the power to insist that the government introduce a Home Rule bill. Outside parliamentary politics Sinn Féin, the Gaelic League, Inghinidhe na hÉireann and other organisations launched by this new generation of Irish nationalists were contributing to that ferment of talk and argument and hope. Journals were being launched to continue discussion of these ideas and to provide a vehicle for publicising the activities of the different groups. Before long the IWFL would find itself a controversial part of this whirlwind of propaganda and argument, its demand for immediate enfranchisement received with some sympathy by a few but (for all sorts of different reasons), rejected by the majority.

Disagreements between the Inghinidhe and the suffragists were brought out into the open at a meeting at the Abbey Theatre in February 1909. English suffragist Theresa Billington-Greig was guest speaker, along with Tom Kettle, Professor Mary Hayden, Sarah Harrison and – the IWFL principal speaker at this time – Gretta Cousins. The Inghinidhe women were a lively group who had been very successful in establishing themselves as a political force to be reckoned with. They had formed in 1900 after organising an ambitious 'treat' for 25,000 children who opposed the visit to Ireland of Queen Victoria and since then had mobilised riotous opposition to another royal visit and had staged highly effective theatrical productions, most notably Lady Gregory and W. B. Yeats's play *Cathleen ni Houlihan*, with Maud Gonne in the title role as the old woman who regains her 'walk of a queen' when she persuades young men to fight for the cause of Ireland. It was understandable that they should object to English women coming over to instruct Irish women on how to organise. Activities like deputations to Westminster could not be reconciled with Sinn Féin 'ourselves alone' principles. In nationalist eyes, this was an 'English agitation', because in asking for the vote, the women were not also demanding an Irish parliament. Some of the IWFL women retorted that they were 'running their principles to death', but Constance Markievicz of the Inghinidhe replied to this charge by declaring that Irish suffragists were 'so blinded by the light of the new half truth that dazzles their visions, that they fail to see the glorious figure of Freedom that stands so near them'.[23] As the feminists struggled to hold their own, Jennie Wyse Power and Arthur Griffith, the two most senior figures in Sinn Féin, came to their rescue, refuting the suggestion that their demand for the vote was necessarily acceptance of Westminster rule.

Reading between the lines regarding comments made at that meeting, it would appear people belonging to Sinn Féin were more confident of their position than were the IWFL members. It was early days still, membership was small, and many of those who had joined the IWFL were unused to public speaking, particularly when the occasion was formal and the audience in combative mood. There is another important factor. Hanna, one of their most capable members, was not in evidence in those early months when the women of the Irish Women's Franchise League struggled to find their public voice. The reason was simple. By the time the IWFL was formed, she was three months pregnant and by the time of the Billington-Greig meeting she was seven months into what had become a difficult pregnancy. Her diary entry for the week of 26 April commented 'Suff business – out of it now though still behind the scenes busy.'[24]

Not only did Hanna and Frank have the worries of pregnancy to contend with, just when the organisation they had such high hopes for was establishing itself, but Frank's mother Rose had become seriously ill at the start of 1909. The Skeffington parents had moved a few years previously to the Dublin suburb of Ranelagh, but Dr J. B. was still travelling around, attending to his duties as school inspector. Given the various resentments Rose continued to feel about her husband, she was more than happy to let him continue his work while Frank visited almost daily, helping to nurse his mother, keeping relatives informed of her progress and eventually, ten days before her death on 16 April 1909, calling his father back to the deathbed. For a long time after that, Frank and Hanna had to contend with a widower who was unexpectedly devastated by his wife's death and who found the task of coping with the petty details of daily life to be almost beyond him. They had other family difficulties to deal with. Hanna's diary entry for February 1909 included a reference to the problems faced by her sister Kathleen in wanting to marry Francis Cruise O'Brien: 'Cruise O'Brien affair starts – fierce henceforth.' On 17 March she noted 'coolness in Belvedere still'. Her mother and sister Margaret visited her on 24 April, an unusual enough event to have it recorded. She was six months pregnant and she and Frank were enjoying the 'lovely weather' in the garden.[25] During the next year family disagreements would increase in intensity.

On 19 May at 9.45 pm, after a very difficult labour in which it was feared that Hanna would not pull through, their son Owen Lancelot was born. Revealing the true nature of Hanna's emotional ties, the name Owen was chosen as the Irish equivalent for Eugene while Lancelot, more fancifully, was for the Arthurian Lancelot du Lac.[26] Gretta wrote almost immediately, shocked to hear 'how near we all were to losing our dear Mrs Skeff'. Frank did not need any emphasis of the feminist message regarding the dangers of childbirth, but Gretta's horror was a spontaneous outburst: 'the absurdity of saying women can't fight when every day many of them are going into the "valley of the shadow" willingly for the future of the race & country & that without all the excitement of war but almost as one might say in cold blood.'[27] Hanna was more earthy in her blunt reactions. The text she had relied on, *Maternity Without Suffering*, she described as 'all about nature and god, maternity higher than toothache etc. It makes me wild to think of it even yet and shows great self-restraint when I tell you I never burnt it.'[28]

Before giving birth, realising the dreadful eventuality that might befall, she had sought to reassure Frank rather than condemn him for inflicting this upon his wife. Her statement reveals her as a woman of integrity, ready to take responsibility for her actions. She assured her husband that she had taken up motherhood of her own 'absolute free will and pleasure' and was happy about this, despite everything. If she was to die, she wanted 'no religious trappings ... only real friends', particularly women, at her funeral.[29] She made no bones of the fact that she had longed for a daughter. Writing two months later to her French friend Germaine, newly married, she sent a postcard of Christabel Pankhurst's portrait with the message 'This is a symbolic card, for I am very sorry Owen isn't a girl! I'd have liked the woman warrior type – *Tant pis*!'[30] But, as Owen's wife Andrée (who was, with perfect symmetry, the daughter born later to Germaine) has testified, Owen never suffered from this disappointment and over the years mother and son developed an exceptionally close and loving relationship. Hanna's stay in the Lower Leeson Street nursing home was a long one, a not unusual practice for first-time mothers. When IWFL member Lucy Kingston had her first baby in 1918 she remained in the nursing home for two weeks, despite a straightforward delivery.[31] However, Dr Tennant was still paying twice weekly visits to Hanna in June, which probably indicates that the complications following the birth were slow in healing. There was a price to be paid for this kind of care and the expenses continued to mount until the proud grandfather, J. B. Skeffington, came to the rescue.

Despite her joy at Owen's birth and her satisfaction with the progress being made by the Franchise League, it was a time of mixed emotions. Hanna and Frank's insistence on living according to their own principles included a refusal to have their son baptised. The infant would be free to make his own choices in life. For Catholic grandparents, horrified by the prospect of their unbaptised grandson ending up in 'limbo', denied entry into heaven, that decision was a shocking rejection of their beliefs. The rift over the issue was deep and the repercussions were not confined to the family circle. The profoundly Catholic nature of Irish society led to those who chose not to conform being treated as outsiders. Teaching in convent schools was no longer a possibility for Hanna. She was too human not to suffer from the anger and hurt that had been expressed. Her diary entry at the end of 1909 contained a bleak summary of the past months:

> One of the most eventful and on the whole most painful of my life. Sickness, death and estrangement. On the other hand, humanizing process and deepening and widening of responsibility, the discipline of acute mental and physical agony … the breach between family widens ever – nearly all ties gone. Same of Frank's family since death of Mrs S., breaking up of home etc. First Xmas at home, left much to ourselves. Changes in household – many nurses and domestic upheavals … Gradual slackening of ties to Mary and all the rest. New ménage not friendly, definite religious departure re Owen. Teaching ceased so far as convents go. Restart Rathmines School of Commerce.

Mary invited them to tea on 23 December and Uncle Eugene, Kathleen and Cruise O'Brien came to visit them on Christmas Eve. On Christmas Day Hanna and Frank went alone on a long walk.[32] There was no merry Christmas at the Sheehy family home and disapproval from the newly married Mary and Tom (the 'new ménage'), whose commitment to feminism did not negate their strong Catholic beliefs, although Mary's love for her sister remained strong. As a grown man, Owen was able to write with pride of his parents' determination that their son should be brought up with a free mind and without formal religious instruction'. It was a decision, he said, 'for which I never cease to be grateful to them'. When a friend asked the young boy whether he was Protestant or Catholic Owen didn't know what answer to give, so he asked his father. He was told to answer, 'I am an Irish boy'. While not 'theologically satisfactory' to his friend, it seemed all right to Owen.[33] Despite the difficulties involved in her new status as a mother, Hanna was not the type to recline quietly at home. Gaelic League enthusiast and IWFL member Evelyn Nicolls, writing to a friend, had commented with wonderment 'a little Skeffington is expected in May. Somehow, it is hard to imagine a kiddie there, isn't it?'[34] With six years of marriage and increasingly intense political involvement, she would not be the only one to wonder if the Sheehy Skeffingtons would be able to incorporate a child into their busy lives. The *Sinn Féin* paper of 5 June recorded Hanna's attendance at a franchise meeting, presided over by Gretta. Hanna's contribution was to announce that the Franchise League hoped to continue its work during the summer, through the holding of open-air meetings. Arguing their case to passing strangers in the park or on the street was a novel, nerve-wracking, departure for Irish women. The presence of their male associates was very welcome. James Cousins captured the tentative mood of that first meeting in Dublin's famous Phoenix Park:

> Frank Sheehy Skeffington carried a banner wrapped around two poles. Someone carried a chair borrowed from the gate lodge. At the meeting-place a group of well-dressed ladies, obviously with a purpose, drew the familiar crowd of unemployed and curious. The banner was unrolled flat on the grass. The raising of it as the signal of a new era was given to an Englishwoman and myself, one at each pole. When the title 'IRISH WOMEN'S FRANCHISE LEAGUE' went up against the background of elms, Skeffy led an applauding clap. This drew the scattered and tentative watchers closer and encouraged others. By the time the first speaker, standing on the chair in front of the banner, now in other hands, had got into the whys and wherefores of the occasion, a large crowd was eagerly listening.[35]

A jubilant report declared that the experimental meeting in the Phoenix Park was so successful that a second was already being planned. The Irish women were full of optimism, contrasting the success of their first public outing with the 'painful experiences of English suffragists' when they had first presented their case to the general public. Because this report was given in *Sinn Féin,* which never lost an opportunity to make flattering comparisons on Ireland's behalf, the meeting was apparent proof of the 'innate chivalry, sympathetic respect and high moral tone existing between the sexes in Ireland'.[36] The speakers on that occasion had been Mrs Isabella Richardson (an IWFL committee member 1909–10), Gretta Cousins and a Mr O'Hara, the policy being to have two women and one man on the platform each time. Gretta practised strengthening her voice in a field at the back of her house, with only a bemused donkey for company. Later, Dora Ryan's husband made them a portable wooden platform, invaluable for venues which lacked some means of raising oneself above the crowd. It was in Hanna's house at her death; a hall-stand so laden with coats and hats that her daughter-in-law had never seen the slogan 'Votes for Women' emblazoned across its top, nor realised what was buried beneath all the clothes.[37] It was historic, and Hanna had known that, despite its prosaic function in later years.

No false sentiment would ever have turned it into a relic during her lifetime. The fledgling organisation felt itself riding high, but although Sinn Féin, largely due to the presence of Jennie Wyse Power, was sympathetic towards its efforts, there were many who did not hesitate to voice their criticisms, and these included women that the suffragists considered to be their friends. Hanna voiced the feelings of many IWFL members when she said that the political sympathies of 'such good rebels' as Constance Markievicz and Helena Molony should have been with them and against the English politicians. Only when the prison gates opened to Irish suffragists did some of the more militant of the nationalist women give any support to those who were insisting on their right to demand the vote from an English government.[38] As Hanna was well aware, their main opponents in the 'rough road' they had chosen were not the advanced nationalists but 'the powerful Irish Party and its machine, backed by such organisations as the sectarian Ancient Order of Hibernians … To these we were a pestilential red herring across the trail of Home Rule.'[39] The AOH (always described by Frank as 'the Ancient Order of Hooligans') was a counterpart to the Protestant Orange Order, a Catholic version of freemasonry in its secretive manipulations. Sectarian and highly reactionary, it did all it could to ensure the continued supremacy of the Irish Party, a bulwark against the radical new groups that were beginning to challenge the party's hegemony. Prominent in that party machine was, of course, her father, David Sheehy, an elder statesman distinguished for his many years of service, if for little else. In her sarcastic comments on the hostility of so many of the Irish Party to the feminists, Hanna made oblique reference to her father's personal history of political involvement:

> Here were good Irish rebels, many of them broken into national revolt, with all the slogans of Irish revolution and its arsenal of weapons – Boycott, Plan of Campaign, Land for the People, and so forth, the creators of obstruction in Parliament – yet at the whisper of Votes for Women many changed to extreme Tories or time-servers who urged us women to wait till freedom for men was won.[40]

She spent the month of August on holiday in the sea-side resort of Malahide together with Frank and Owen. By the autumn, employing a nursemaid to help with the care of their baby, they were both busy again, attending meetings of the IWFL and the Socialist Party of Ireland, although Hanna admitted she was not 'actually interested' in the SPI. That was more Frank's territory. She still retained her ability to be overly self-critical, chastising herself at the end of the year as: 'not disciplined, over-worry still. Middle aged feeling grows.'[41] It was far too harsh. The evidence is that she threw herself into campaigning and writing. What worries she had were understandable, given their precarious finances and the deteriorating family relations.

Hanna and Frank were not the only troublesome members of the family. Kathleen was having great problems trying to convince her parents that the agnostic and penniless Francis Cruise O'Brien was the man she wanted to marry and the start of 1910 saw matters becoming extremely heated. The Sheehys divided on predictable lines. Some, particularly Mary and the parents, were strongly Catholic, Margaret and Eugene more easy-going in their views, while Hanna, Frank and Cruise O'Brien represented, in the eyes of the family at least, the extreme of godless radicalism. Dick Sheehy also took his parents' side in the long-running saga of whether Kathleen could marry Cruise O'Brien without breaking her parents' hearts. One famous family anecdote concerning the dispute provides a telling snapshot of Frank, whose ability to sustain an argument was guaranteed to infuriate the opposition:

> At the height of the long debate, an argument between my grandfather and Frank Skeffington grew so hot that Dick Sheehy threw Frank Skeffington bodily out of the front door and down the steps of 2 Belvedere Place. Frank simply got up, knocked on the door, said 'Force solves nothing, Dick' and resumed his argument with grandfather.[42]

There was an irrevocable breach after David Sheehy wrote a terse note to Hanna, ordering her not to come again to the house, 'I know it is the intention of yourself and your husband to come here this evening. I don't want him to my house. It pains me to have to say this to you, but I do so to avoid greater pain.'[43] Hanna's response was to be so hurt and furious that she had to compose several drafts of a letter before she calmed down. Her first effort included: 'I have just received your extraordinary note closing the door in Frank's face. It follows of course that you close it in mine also … It is a matter for regret for me as a daughter to have such evidence of intolerance and petty spite shown by a parent whose years and grey hairs ought to have brought him a little sweet reasonableness and ripeness of judgment…' Her final response was more measured:

> Personally, I am sorry I cannot congratulate you on your new role of household Pasha. I choose p.c. form of reply so that the other members of the family may be acquainted with our correspondence – in case you have kept them ignorant – what precisely is the meaning of this ebullition. I am quite at a loss to know. HSS[44]

The days of charades and friendly banter were over. Attitudes were hardening. Despite the fact that he was a priest, Uncle Eugene does not seem to have taken a stand on the question of his niece's religious faith. As a rebel himself, he was more tolerant of other people's rebellions than his more conventional brother. During 1910 Eugene was in America, representing the

Supreme Council of the IRB at the annual Clan-na-Gael Convention. The atmosphere in Belvedere Place was getting him down, as Frank mentioned in a letter to his friend John Byrne, *en route* to America himself: 'Do you know that Father Eugene Sheehy is going to America?… He has been very restless in Belvedere Place, and the family rows have made things disagreeable for him. The American lecturing life will suit him far better.'[45] It is likely that the Sheehy-Cruise O'Brien marriage would never have come about, were it not for the efforts of Frank and Hanna, whose arguments eventually helped to win the day. As Conor, the child of that marriage, later wrote: 'Grandmother was afraid of Hanna: a force of will and intelligence equivalent to her own, and a moral force which she had it in her to respect … Grandmother began to back away. A simple exercise in parental authority could not stand against the spirit of the age, incarnate in the Skeffingtons.'[46]

Slowly, some of the wounds healed. Although Mary had been furious with Hanna's defiance of their mother in insisting on her support for Cruise O'Brien, there was no permanent difference between the sisters. For as long as they lived, they gave each other unstinting support through the worst of times and were, as Hanna said, 'truly a precious boon'.[47] One doubts if there was ever a real reconciliation with David Sheehy, other than that designed to allow contact between grandson and grandfather, as visits to 2 Belvedere Place did not resume until 1 January 1911, when Owen was eventually introduced to his grandfather. From America Eugene was anxious to hear of 'Owen's first call on his relatives at no 2'. He loved the 'gossipy letters … so spicy and satisfying' that he believed only women could write and wanted every detail from Hanna, 'the little comedy, especially stage fitting, dramatis personae and how they did their several parts.' His attitude towards his brother was very similar to his niece's, highly contemptuous of the 'empire building not nation building' of the Irish Party politicians. Eugene was on another secret mission, convinced Home Rule was now 'visible and assumed', and dismissed the views of David Sheehy: 'Father sneers at it. I sneer back.'[48] Once the ice was broken, either parent felt free to bring their little son across town, by tram, to Nelson's Pillar, the marker for the north side of the city. From there it was only a short walk to the Sheehy residence. But as David made no effort to support his daughter when she was imprisoned, it is reasonable to assume that his disapproval ran deep, and the barriers remained.

Frank's rejection of the policies of groups he had been associated with before the formation of the League was also embroiling him in further controversies with the Sheehy clan. He and Cruise O'Brien, at this stage the still unacceptable suitor of Kathleen's, were amongst a group of YIBs howled down at a convention of the United Irish League in February 1909. Cruise O'Brien's motion called for a return to the old Parnellite policy of vigorous opposition to any British government that refused to grant Home Rule. Under Parnell's leadership the Irish Party had excelled in tactics that obstructed the business of the House of Commons. The younger generation felt that present-day politicians were ineffectual, doing little more than waiting patiently for some measure of reform to be handed out. The motion was viewed as a disloyal challenge by the party's leaders and all their considerable muscle was used to ensure that it was defeated. Another resolution, placed last upon the agenda, was also defeated. This was a call for women's suffrage to be given support by the Irish Party. It was presented by the Young Ireland Branch, following a request by women from the Franchise League, and of course, three members of the League happened to be Sheehy sisters. It was women's first shot across the bows of the parliamentarians, and some of the men were only too happy to take up the challenge on their behalf. Frank had volunteered to introduce the motion while Tom Kettle was to second it. At the last moment however, Kettle refused, party loyalty winning out. Frank remarked bitterly of his brother-in-law that this was 'Mr Kettle's first breach of faith with the women's suffrage party'.[49] Tom Kettle resigned his parliamentary seat at the end of 1910, to concentrate upon his other role in life, that of Professor of Economics at University College. He was still prominent on suffrage platforms, but there would be further occasions when party loyalty took precedence. Mary was an important part of many suffrage delegations; her personal knowledge of the politicians was an indispensable asset during the few years when the politicians could be persuaded to talk to the women. Her approach was more conciliatory than that of her elder sister. However, differing loyalties towards the Irish Party would cause more rifts between the Kettles and the Sheehy Skeffingtons.

That difference of opinion was made public in one of the most important of Hanna's early writings, an analysis of the relationship of women and the national movement. It was the text of a speech she had given to the YIBs, a topic she had been researching for some time and a project she had finally concluded during the last long weeks of pregnancy. It was serialised during March 1909, in three editions of the *Irish Nation.* As well as detailing the humiliations of the women attempting to join the YIBs, Hanna also described the dilemma of women in families like her own: 'whose father or uncle went to prison in the days of the Land League, whose mother or aunt centred about Fanny Parnell ... such a girl will have her enthusiasm stirred by family sagas but how can her enthusiasm be utilized ere it be atrophied or is alienated?' She devoted a great deal of her analysis to the shameful treatment of the Ladies' Land League, rejected by Parnell and the other parliamentarians. As a result, Irish women had lost touch with parliamentarianism and there seemed to be little prospect of regaining that contact. It was a cry from the heart. In calling for women to be enfranchised, 'even by an alien and grudging Parliament' she asked the question: 'Will the Irish Party be bold enough to make this act of faith and help the citizenship of women?'[50] She might as well have been putting that question directly to her father.

During the time when Hanna's immediate concern had been whether she would survive childbirth, the propaganda battle between nationalists and suffragists had developed in intensity. A speech by Constance Markievicz, presented to the Students' National Literary Society, on the topic of 'Irishwomen's Duty at the Present Time' was considered so important that, mindful of the curfew suffered by women students, they put the time of the meeting forward to 7 p.m. in order that 'all the ladies might be present for all the discussion'. This was Inghinidhe na hÉireann's response to the growing success of the IWFL, a continuation of the arguments raised at the Billington-Greig meeting. The opening statement took the form of a condescending reference to the IWFL, whose members would have been enraged to read that the Countess had described their organisation as 'a very vague organisation', before concluding, with all the hauteur of one born into the Ascendency class, 'we see no reason why, when its members have gained a little experience, it would not become something definite, and something useful to Irishwomen and *par consequence* useful to Ireland'. In a back-handed way, this was an indication that the new organisation was being treated seriously by those who, sharing a similar constituency, were concerned to prevent young Irish women from being seduced by the arguments of those promoting the cause of women's suffrage. The heart of the Markievicz objection to an organisation whose propaganda bore 'the hallmark of an English agitation' was that Irish suffragists were simply copying their programme from the 'English societies'. It was therefore not enough to demand the vote on the same terms as it was granted to men, without adding an additional proviso 'and a parliament to be represented in'. She also poured scorn on those 'law abiding' people who thought that possession of the vote was so important. As Ireland's history was one where 'felons and convicts' who had challenged the right of England to rule were heroes, and who lacked the vote just as much as women did, she called on Irish women to glory in not having the right of British citizenship and to join with 'men who believe in Liberty in making Ireland ungovernable'.[51] It was a resounding assertion of nationalist faith.

Kathleen Shannon, as secretary of the IWFL, wrote to *Sinn Féin* with the IWFL response. Writing under her Gaelic name, as Caitlín Maire ní Sionnan, she gave a vehemently nationalistic interpretation of the IWFL position: 'We adopt a Sinn Féin policy of agitation in Ireland by Irish women for Irishwomen and we refuse to be drawn off on other issues.' The League had been formed to remove sex disability and not to make any declaration about parliament, a topic on which they were not all in agreement. She herself welcomed the revival of an Irish society modelled on the old Brehon system that had existed in Gaelic Ireland before the advent of British rule, although she admitted that there were differing views on that too. Some would welcome the return of the old native Irish parliament which had existed before the Act of Union had been imposed in 1801. This all-Protestant assembly had not been an institution noted for its democratic views, confirmation that the IWFL, in its early years at least, contained women holding a variety of opinions and religious traditions.[52]

Hostilities between Inghinidhe na hÉireann and the Franchise League were particularly prominent at this time because of the appearance of *Bean na hÉireann*, the new journal produced by the Inghinidhe to promote their own style of nationalist feminism. In reply to a paper read by Kathleen Shannon to the Central Branch of Sinn Féin, a Mary McLarren wrote in to denounce those women who 'in their endeavours to get a foot on each side of the Channel will be in a constant state of unstable equilibrium'. As far as she, and the rest of the Inghinidhe were concerned, 'The women of Irish Ireland have the franchise, and it would only be humiliating themselves and their country to appeal or even demand the endorsement of a hostile Parliament.' The woman who wrote in to challenge that view was not a member of the IWFL but Mary MacSwiney, a teacher from Cork, who joined the non-militant Munster Women's Franchise League when it was set up in 1911. Although she would later become one of the most vocal of all republicans, at this time she too was of the opinion women would not be taken seriously until they possessed the vote.[53] Hanna was following this debate with great interest. She resumed teaching, starting on 9 November 1909 at Rathmines School of Commerce, the same month that her article, 'Sinn Féin and Irishwomen' was published in *Bean na hÉireann*. This was a lengthy dissertation on the extent of the social, economic and political disabilities suffered by Irishwomen, coupled with a thoughtful analysis of the role occupied by women within the various nationalist groupings. It was an important step in the development of an Irish feminist discourse. Her researches and earlier writings were coming to fruition in works which display a degree of knowledge and a maturity of insight that signal a polemicist of the highest rank.

Before moving to the heart of her argument Hanna declared her fundamental belief that 'until the women of Ireland are free, the men will not achieve emancipation'. This unequivocal statement is one of the cornerstones underlying Irish feminism, an article of faith that she sustained throughout her life. Her analysis is acute and practical, lacking any trace of sentimentality or romanticism. As far as she was concerned, women's prominent status within the Sinn Féin organisation was not due to a reversion to older Irish ideals but was simply a function of the type of work involved. In a caustic reference to individuals within Sinn Féin (and there were worse than the dour figure of Griffith), she commented that such individuals were 'as narrow as (their) presumably less enlightened brother'. Women within the Gaelic League and Sinn Féin were lauded in their capacity as mothers and housekeepers, not as aspirant citizens. One prominent member of Sinn Féin had founded university scholarships from which women were expressly excluded, demonstrating that 'in spite of theoretical equality, some Sinn Féiners have not yet rounded Cape Turk where women are concerned'. No organisation escaped from this impassioned denunciation, the culmination of several years' experience of Irish political life and humiliations suffered as a result of male hostility to the presence of women in the public sphere:

> Irishwomen may be excused therefore if they distrust all parties in Ireland, for what I have said of the Sinn Féin organisation applies with far greater force to the Parliamentarian movement which, since the extinction of the Ladies' Land League in the '80s has steadily ignored Irishwomen, hitherto indeed with impunity. It is for Irishwomen of every political party to adopt the principle of Sinn Féin in the true sense of the word and to refuse any longer to be the camp-followers and parasites of public life, dependent on caprice and expediency for recognition. It is for Irishwomen to set about working out their own political salvation. Until the Parliamentarian and the Sinn Féin woman alike possess the vote, the keystone of citizenship, she will count but little with either party, for it is through the medium of the vote alone that either party can achieve any measure of success. This is a fact which we Parliamentarians have long been aware of to our cost, but which Sinn Féin women have yet to learn.[54]

A reply the following month from 'A Sinn Féiner' scathingly described 'Mrs Skeffington' as part of 'that section of Irish who do not desire separation, but who merely wish to see Ireland growing more prosperous, quiet and resigned under British rule'. That could be a jibe at some members of the Irish Party, but it would never be a description of Hanna Sheehy Skeffington. She was part of a new generation of determined women who would not accept anything less than total emancipation. She hit back immediately, declaring 'the time for patience and resignation is over'. The double standards were those of the nationalists, but Irish women would no longer accept their arguments: 'Irishwomen, because they suffer a two-fold and therefore a doubly unbearable wrong are told to submit in patience because the wrong is inflicted by an alien government.'[55]

It seems impossible to imagine that those on opposite sides of these camps would ever place themselves voluntarily in each other's company, but some of the most prominent of antagonists developed a liking and respect for each other, despite the harshness of their public pronouncements. Hanna had first encountered Constance de Markievicz, the rebel from the Anglo-Irish Gore-Booth family who had married a Polish Count, when Constance was floating around the bohemian literary world with her husband Casimir. Constance was acting the part of Eleanor in George Birmingham's comedy *Eleanor's Enterprise* – a Casimir Markievicz production – and Hanna was part of the Gaiety Theatre audience. Her critical faculties were unaffected by the fact that she and Constance became friends: 'As an actress her high-pitched voice and English accent and short sight were disabilities. But her temperament suited rebel and heroic parts and these she shone in.'[56] By 1911, Constance now deeply immersed in her new life of committed nationalism, had left her previous circles far behind her and had moved to Surrey House in Leinster Road, Rathmines, just around the corner from the Skeffingtons in Grosvenor Place. The irrepressible Constance, delighting in opportunities for discussion and conviviality, would rush through the front door and announce breathlessly: 'Come along tonight; I want you to meet so-and-so. The gas is cut off and the carpets are up – but you won't mind. Tell Frank to come along' – and they would talk for hours around a big fire, sitting on her large divan in the big bow window, the light coming from innumerable candles stuck around the room. Hanna, although considering Markievicz 'not a feminist ever and only a mild suffragist' appreciated her relish for 'direct action of any sort against authority' and her genuine interest in people.[57] During all their arguments and exchanges of opinion, for Constance it was Ireland first, while Hanna could never conceive of an issue that did not have women in the forefront. However, the IWFL soon learned that Constance 'had a knack of being on the spot when there was trouble',[58] so there was enough to agree upon, to offset some of the more public disagreements. Hanna had strong recollections of the Rag Day when Trinity College students poured into their premises, throwing out of the windows anything they could get hold of and seizing the IWFL banner, 'our dearest treasure'. It was Markievicz who called a halt to the rampage, seizing the pole, crying 'Come boys, not that! That's our best flag. Be sports! You can have the bunting and ribbons but leave us our flag.'[59]

Hanna was now firmly back in the public sphere. A nursemaid had been hired so that she could resume her public life. The IWFL was gathering strength and by the end of its first season of open-air meetings had gained enough recruits and additional income to move to offices in the Antient Concert Rooms in Great Brunswick Street (now Pearse Street), at the tail end of Trinity College, where they proudly hung out their green and gold banner, made by the women of Dun Emer, embroidered on one side with 'Irish Women's Franchise League' and on the other its Gaelic equivalent 'Cumannacht is Coir Comhthruime na mBan'.[60] The newly inaugurated Independent Labour Party of Ireland also had rooms there, and Frank was in the thick of that too, so there was a constant flow of radicals in and out of the building. One advantage of the new rooms was that they now had a hall large enough to hold meetings and a new winter programme of weekly Tuesday night sessions was immediately begun. Annie Besant and Charlotte Despard came over from England to speak in October and November. Fred Ryan lectured to both the IWFL and the SPI on different dates. Life was now so busy that Hanna decided they had to drop their Wednesday 'At Homes'. She presided over the first winter meeting, proposing a resolution that made it clear where her commitments would lead:

> The IWFL at this, the first meeting of its second session, desire to express warm admiration for and sympathy with, brave English suffragettes, who are struggling so nobly to achieve the emancipation of women and to protest against barbaric methods employed by the English Liberal Government against these heroic women.[61]

Despite their differing views, Hanna maintained links with Anna Haslam. When a Cabinet Committee on Home Rule was established in Westminster, she was happy to share her knowledge, writing a warm letter, apologising for not being able to call in person earlier as she had been kept busy with teaching and care for a sick husband and a sick mother (the latter she had visited every day for the last week). While providing information, Hanna made it plain that arrangements for deputations were already being made by the militants:

> I was too late on Tuesday when I got home & tonight after school your window was dark. The name is Cabinet Committee on Home Rule, sitting weekly. Asquith, Birrell, Grey & Hobhouse are for it – six in all & it meets on Tuesday. We have asked our London society & Belfast to ask also for deputation – former will be received by Redmond this week in London.[62]

The suffragists were forced into concentrating a great deal upon events in Westminster, not because they necessarily accepted the right of Westminster to rule Ireland, but because of the simple fact that it was the forum where bills on women's suffrage were being debated – and, soon, where proposals for Home Rule would be put forward. The IWFL wanted Home Rule for Irish women as well as Irish men, while many of the IWSLGA members, as unionists, hoped that the constitutional status quo would be maintained. The WSPU, recognising the strategic importance of the Irish Party in terms of votes for women, sent the Pankhursts and other prominent members to Ireland in order to rally people around the need to persuade their MPs to vote in favour of bills for women's suffrage. The issues of Home Rule and votes for women were inseparable.

In December 1909 Hanna was part of an IWFL delegation that finally managed to meet Redmond. It was very unsatisfactory. He asserted that he could not commit the Irish Party into supporting suffrage bills as it was a matter for each individual MP. His own personal views, the delegation reported, were 'somewhat vague' on the question. Neither would he use the political influence of the Irish Party to have the suffrage prisoners in English jails treated as political.[63] In Irish eyes, this was very damning, running counter as it did to every tradition in Irish political life. Optimism that the Irish Parliamentary Party would give a positive lead to members of other political parties was rapidly fading, although there was still hope that those Irish MPs who supported the suffragists would exert some pressure on the government.

The focus of all hopes was Westminster, where an all-party Conciliation bill was due to be discussed by the House. Irish women who were prepared to lobby Irish MPs and who could organise to demonstrate the determination of Irish women to fight as hard as their British counterparts were a new element in suffrage history. The WSPU wanted to convert to the cause as many women in Ireland as they possibly could. Equally, the Irish militants welcomed the undoubted spur that the appearance of high-profile campaigners like the Pankhursts would give them. In March 1910 Christabel Pankhurst spoke at an IWFL-sponsored meeting at the Rotunda, where she declared that the WSPU, following the tactics of Parnell, had decided to canvass against the Liberals at the next general election in protest at their refusal to support women's suffrage. Forestalling Irish protests that this tactic would damage their chance of achieving Home Rule, she declared her surprise that nationalists believed Prime Minister Asquith's pronouncements on Home Rule – suffragettes were not fooled so easily.[64] Frank Skeffington had already anticipated this new strategy. Writing in the *New Age* six months previously, he had remarked that 'Nothing in connection with the suffrage campaign has been more striking than the utter blindness of the Irish Party to the essential similarities between suffrage tactics and the Irish Party in Parnell's time.' He was in complete agreement with suffrage militancy:

> Every successive step of the militants, from the first interruption of Sir Edward Grey to the axes and bricks of Newcastle, has had my enthusiastic approval ... That is why I am eagerly awaiting the General Election – to learn from them what is the proper policy for a cause in the position of suffrage or Home Rule.[65]

This unqualified endorsement of the WSPU programme became part of the policy of the Irish militants – until the issue of Home Rule added a layer of complexity to the relationship between British and Irish suffragists. In their private discussions with the visiting speakers from England Irish women had opportunities of learning more about the techniques of agitation from those who were pioneers in the new strategies of direct action and they attempted, with limited resources, to emulate the WSPU. The IWFL announced, in developing a strategy for Irish circumstances, that they would establish branches of the IWFL in the constituencies of those who opposed women's suffrage. Given the realities of support for suffrage, this was an overly ambitious promise. Sinn Féin was stung to comment that Irishwomen should be enabled to vote and sit in an Irish Parliament, but Ireland would 'never be roused to enthusiasm or even interest by a demand that Irish women should have votes for an English Parliament'. [66] As the daughter of a long-serving parliamentarian, Hanna had no patience with this view. If parliament could be used to achieve the basic right of citizenship then it would be, and those who complained that feminists were signalling their acceptance of rule by Westminster were quite clearly hostile to women's interests.

Suffrage activism gave Hanna opportunities as well as giving her more prominence within the Sheehy Skeffington partnership. She and Frank gave each other the freedom to travel independently and, as the suffrage movement developed, so too did Hanna's self-confidence. The summer holidays were a busy time for her, and excitement spilled out of her letters home. In June 1910 she and her sister Mary travelled over to London with a small group of women, including some from Belfast, as part of a united campaign to support a Conciliation bill for suffrage going through parliament. Their instructions, coordinated by Cork-born Geraldine Lennox, now a leading WSPU militant, were to meet at Cleopatra's Needle on the Embankment at 5.30 p.m. sharp, dressed in green and headed by the Irish flag. Daniel O'Connell's granddaughters sent a message of support, hoping to join them there. The two-mile long procession, with 10,000 women and 700 banners in its ranks, swamped the small group of Irish women but their presence did lead to a London branch of the IWFL being formed. At the second demonstration, in Hyde Park on 23 July, the Irish contingent was more visible. Mary Carson had written to Hanna to ask if she could travel over with anyone going on the London demonstration.

Interest and enthusiasm were mounting while hopes were rising – as Mary Carson wrote excitedly – this demonstration, 'if strong in numbers might help to get the Conciliation bill before a Committee of the whole house before the end of this session'.[67] The Irish women made a strong presence, 'a blaze of orange and green ushers in the Irishwomen with their national pipers', was the description in *Votes for Women*. They were allocated Platform 6, chaired by Kathleen Shannon, with Hanna and Agnes Kelly as the other speakers.[68] Hanna reported 'Miss Hoey and her sister were got up as "Irish Colleens" – a WSPU touch … we didn't care much about', but the band, composed of pipers was 'grand' and a dozen men, including Charles Oldham, walked at the back of their group. She reassured Frank that they were only spending money on bus fares as they were being treated to lunches and were being put up in a 'palatial flat.' They went to the House of Commons, met with a few MPs and visited the WSPU – 'a colossal organisation' – but Hanna confessed to 'a personal feeling of disappointment & chill as regards the individual suffragette. They are exceedingly English & the mixture of a certain stock gush with English coolness leaves one rather paralysed.' She liked Mrs Pankhurst best of the leaders. The Women's Freedom League, with whom Hanna would remain in close contact for decades, was also visited and a 'collection tea' which raised £5 was organised for the Irish group. In adding 'I miss you and Owen – but you'll look after each other' Hanna was being truthful, but the experience of being regarded as an independent figure was one, she relished.[69]

During these weeks the IWFL had been busily canvassing all the Irish MPs, urging their attendance at the debate on the second reading of the bill and writing personal letters to individual MPs, impressing upon them how keenly Irishwomen were looking out for their names on the voting lists. The bill passed its reading, but no further parliamentary time was granted to it. When the voting lists were published, David Sheehy's name was listed as having been absent, unpaired. The result was the same as a vote against. All the efforts of the IWFL and his daughter's eloquence in Hyde Park had failed to persuade him.

Remaining faithful to the promise of equality within their marriage, in August, without Frank, Hanna and Owen (and their servant, Minnie who helped with the 15-month-old Owen) went north, to Belfast, Downpatrick and Bangor, visiting Skeffington relatives. On a day when it didn't rain, they managed a trip to Ardglass. Hanna reported, happily, that she had 'astounded' one relative with her 'Votes for Women' badge.[70]

In these few years before the outbreak of war the Sheehy Skeffington name crops up in endless reports of meetings, demonstrations, petitions, protests. If it wasn't Hanna, it was Frank and often it was the two of them together. Frank, as a member of the Socialist Party of Ireland, had spoken at a public meeting to welcome Helena Molony and James McArdle after their arrest in protest against the King and Queen's visit in July 1911. He had declined to be elected President of the YIBs, while remaining an active member; and, of course, was writing and spreading his views on every conceivable subject in a whole variety of publications, often without payment. For her part, Hanna continued to organise the IWFL and to speak on women's suffrage at every opportunity. She joined Constance Markievicz at a meeting in the Antient Concert Rooms which was to launch a trade union for working women. Constance, more concerned to encourage women's active involvement than debating whether women should organise separately, said a union would make men out of them, helping them to obtain better wages and the vote. Hanna urged the trade union movement to work together for the benefit of both sexes (she did not support women-only unions), before devoting the rest of her speech to the question of women's franchise which, said the *Irish Worker*, 'seemed to have the support of all present'.[71] Although not involved in the Irish Women Workers' Union, she was sympathetic to their existence and was always counted as a supporter. During the bleak months of the 1913 Lockout, when the Transport Union needed all the help that was offered, the IWFL women offered their services in the soup kitchens of Liberty Hall. That gesture had nothing to do with charity and everything to do with the expression of solidarity in the class struggle between workers and employers. The experience did much to cement ties between militant feminists and others who would concentrate their energies on forming links between nationalists and the labour movement.

The campaign to persuade the municipal authorities to provide school meals for children also helped to smooth relations between the suffragists and their nationalist counterparts. Dublin had the highest infant mortality rates in Europe; the levels of poverty in its reeking tenements made people justifiably liken the place to Calcutta. A Schools Meals Act, enabling local authorities to provide a lunch for schoolchildren, had been passed in Britain in 1906, but not extended to Ireland. The same political compromises necessary in campaigning for women's suffrage were involved in campaigning for amending legislation which would allow Irish authorities to strike their own rate to pay for school meals. Some members of Inghinidhe na hÉireann had the same misgivings about that demand as they had about suffrage. It was Maud Gonne, then living in semi-exile in Paris, who first decided to do something on behalf of the starving children. She used the pages of *Bean na hÉireann* to advertise the fact, despite the doubts of its editor, Helena Molony. Maud Gonne and James Connolly, who was recently returned from America and was now, vainly, attempting to turn the unruly Socialist Party of Ireland into a disciplined body, headed a deputation to the weekly meeting of the IWFL to persuade suffragists to join the campaign. Agreement reached and a bargain struck, it was announced that 'Madame Gonne' would speak on suffrage at the next IWFL meeting.[72] It took two years before legislation was passed and during that time, to prove the desperation of the need and to alleviate the worst of the deprivation, a small group of women – the Ladies School Dinners Committee – each day voluntarily fed children from two of the poorest of Dublin's schools. The bulk of the committee was drawn from the ranks of Inghinidhe na hÉireann, under the inspiration of Gonne, their revered president. Helen Laird (later to marry Con Curran, old student colleague of Frank's) was a very active member of the IWFL and secretary of the School Dinners Committee. She was also a friend of Gonne, thereby bridging the gulf between the groups. Other members of the IWFL, apart from Hanna, do not appear to have been involved.

The suffrage campaign was gathering momentum, some members were about to go to prison in England, and altogether their preoccupations were very different. Gonne's motivation was rooted in her nationalism: 'If we are to get free and keep free we must keep up the strength of the race'[73] while Hanna, very differently, shared the philosophy of Connolly, a belief in municipal socialism – the community taking responsibility for its people. Frank and Hanna were to become close friends of Connolly's, whose support for feminism was unwavering and whose influence upon Irish radicalism was immeasurable. Hanna's contribution to the school meals campaign was directed towards the legal process of achieving change, not doling out Irish stew in freezing cold playgrounds. Her knowledge of the parliamentary process and her educational background enabled her to draft an appropriate addition to the school meals legislation, which Maud then took over to Westminster, to Stephen Gwynn MP, a suffrage supporter and friend of both women. Finally, in 1914, the School Meals Act (Ireland) was passed. Significantly, when Helen Laird spoke at an IWFL meeting in Phoenix Park in the summer of 1912, on the subject of feeding schoolchildren, her talk was described by the *Irish Citizen* as a 'domestic aspect of women's suffrage'.[74] Feminists did not intend the public to think they were concentrating upon children and home, those traditional areas of women's lives from which they were struggling hard to escape. The message was that when women possessed the vote, they could influence the content of legislation. No one pointed out the anomaly that some, at least, of the nationalist women were prepared, on this occasion, to approach Westminster, that stronghold of imperialist rule.

Three out of the four Sheehy sisters were fully engaged in the çause of women's suffrage. Margaret, who had never had much interest in politics, had been a nominal member of the IWSLGA but was hostile to the militants. While visiting Margaret after the birth of her daughter Patricia, Hanna bent over the baby and pinned on to her clothes the ribbon of the IWFL. According to Patricia, this was snatched off as soon as Hanna left. Had Margaret hesitated to remove it while Hanna was still present? She was still in some awe of her highly principled eldest sister. Kathleen Sheehy had achieved the rare accolade of election to the vice-presidency of the YIBs in 1910.[75] She was also a regular volunteer in the offices of the Franchise League, preferring the routine of the back room to the public platform. She did, however, speak at many open-air meetings, particularly at times when Hanna was in jail. Mary led one of the early deputations of the League, to Chief Secretary Birrell in Dublin Castle, to persuade him to back the Conciliation bill.[76] Hanna described her sister as 'wife and daughter of MPs and an able exponent', adding that Birrell had advised the deputation to 'keep on hammering', a phrase so ambiguous she wondered if it was meant purposely.[77]

To everyone's great surprise, Dr Skeffington got married again at the end of 1911. The re-marriage was difficult for Frank to accept, as his description of a typical visit from his father indicated: 'He was most genial; asked how was everybody and made no allusion to his wife, nor did I.'[78] There appeared to be little contact between the two families. Bessie bumped into Frank's father and his new bride 'Anna Maria' in Gardiner Street one day, reporting back that 'she was a quiet person and Dr S. was gone about Owen!'[79] Although reassuring Frank that he would still help him out financially because he was 'so extravagantly good natured' as a father, Dr J. B. remained furious that his son appeared to favour the Sheehys over the Skeffingtons: 'having practically given me up and ranged yourself as a Sheehy – under which name (and not Skeffington) you appear in Thom's Directory. Therefore, it is the Sheehys you should in reason look to.' His disapproval of the irreligious manner in which his grandson was being brought up was very plain: 'He is not to blame, poor child – and indeed I feel greatly grieved at the way he is being brought up – as a mere animal – without any development of the spiritual which is an essential element of humanity as distinguished from animality.'[80] Dr J. B. made it clear that it was Hanna, not Frank, whom he blamed for this. Frank's adoption of the Sheehy name was proof of her power over his son and, as a mother, it was her responsibility to ensure that her child was educated properly. Relations with his daughter-in-law were non-existent. While Hanna was in jail, he took advantage of her absence to make numerous visits to the house, indulging Owen with chocolate and biscuits. Frank did not help matters by telling Hanna that his father's only allusion to her welfare was the one comment 'Hope all well'.[81] Discretion might have been a better option.

Frank's earnings for some of the months of 1911 would have driven his father to apoplexy if he had seen his accounts: five shillings for March and two pounds for both July and October. To put this into some context, Tom Kettle's income from writing for 1915 was £40 – a similar amount to that of Frank's – but with an additional £500 derived from his salary as university professor. In 1912 the Teacher's Guild had recommended pay scales for secondary teachers (and been roundly condemned by the *Irish Citizen* for their acceptance of differential male and female rates), which ranged from a lowly female rate of £80 to a more reasonable £250.[82] Hanna's salary was vital in keeping the small household struggling on the edge of survival.

Frank might have found it hard to admit, but in some respects he and his father were very similar. Hanna had no daughter to cherish into a realisation of her potential, but she was tolerant enough for her son to develop into a non-conformist whose views often challenged her own. In Frank Skeffington's case, what he and J. B. shared was a conviction that the potentiality of childhood required the active intervention of parents to make the most of all opportunities. All the little things that make up infant life were to be used to develop a child's capabilities. From the time Owen was two months old until he reached two years and eight months, Frank kept a diary of progress: 'a biography as well as an educational narrative'. He was an exacting critic of both himself and his son, considering Owen 'cowardly and cautious in physical matters, bold and aggressive in temper – just like myself'. But he was proud that his son, at two and a half, had more knowledge of colours and numbers and more power of concentration and control than his cousin Patricia.[83] Hanna too kept an account of the progress of Owen, detailing the coming of each tooth, his sleeping and eating habits, when he began to grab, crawl and other baby milestones. Her attention was focused more on the physical: 'Modification of dress gradually introduced. Supervision necessary now (eight months), a restless period…' He had two dolls to play with and liked the zoo, the museum and visiting the ducks in Stephen's Green. 'Face is cross' was one of his terms of reproach to his parents.[84] Frank was a proud father, enjoying writing to an imprisoned Hanna that when he and Owen were in the offices of the conservative *Telegraph* newspaper 'even the *Telegraph* people had to admit he was a credit to his suffragette mother!'[85] He told the

American suffragist Alice Park that when friends called at the house before they set off to visit Hanna in jail, they asked Owen what message they should take. 'Tell her "Votes for Women"' was the boy's precocious response.[86]

Both parents were determined to bring up a son who would be able to think for himself but, being products of the Victorian age themselves, they were strict disciplinarians and wanted an obedient child. Frank thought corporal punishment was acceptable up until the age of seven; after that time children reached the age of reason and were no longer akin to small animals. Despite his pacifism, Frank had no objection to the use of physical violence when it came to children. It greatly upset Hanna, who disliked the idea of any smacking, just as she had objected to Frank's 'brutality' against her. She preferred the sanction of sending the child to bed, which he considered degrading. These disagreements were expressed in letters written while Frank was in America. When Hanna reported that Owen was in 'dire disgrace' because he had struck some children for no apparent reason, admitted to the offence, and had been sent to bed after dinner, she added 'I hate beating'.[87] Frank's reaction was swift and stern: 'I disapprove of sending Owen to bed, it's in many ways a more objectionable punishment than beating; but as you are clearly unable to manage him you must just do the best you can till I take a hand again!'[88] For Frank, even childish inquisitiveness could be incorporated into the learning process: 'Putting pepper in the butter doesn't sound very bad! It is merely misdirected zeal for chemical experiment! The punishment I would suggest is to make him eat it!'[89] Easy to say – when one is over on the other side of the Atlantic – might have been Hanna's muttered comment.

Owen was fully part of their lives. One of his first memories of attending a public function with his parents was the League's Christmas Fair in 1912. Hanna's correspondence contains many letters inviting her to have tea with old friends, often containing the addition 'and do bring Owen'. And life went on, a small boy growing up, realising that his parents were very busy people, but not too busy to make time for him. He might have to wait patiently for a story, but he knew that eventually it would be read. It would not be long before Owen would find himself becoming more aware of the scope of his parents' activities.

NOTES

1 C. P. Curran, *Under the Receding Wave* (Dublin, 1970), p. 115.

2 Hanna Sheehy to Frank Skeffington (hereafter Hanna to Frank), Mountjoy Jail, 10 Aug. 1912, Sheehy Skeffington MS (hereafter SS MS) 40,466/5.

3 James and Margaret Cousins, *We Two Together* (Madras, 1950), p. 128.

4 Ibid., p. 85.

5 Ibid., p. 164.

6 Anna Haslam to English suffragist Ray Strachey, quoted in Carmel Quinlan, *Genteel Revolutionaries, Anna and Thomas Haslam and the Irish Women's Movement* (Cork, 2002), p. 164.

7 Ibid. p. 189.

8 Unknown (name not legible), 29 Eccles Street to Hanna, 12 Nov. 1908, SS MS 41,180/1. A Maria Shaw is listed as living in this address, but no one with this surname is known to have involvement in suffrage.

9 S. C. Harrison to Hanna Sheehy Skeffington, Nov. 1908, SS MS 41,180/1.

10 Ibid., 23 Nov. 1908.

11 Hanna Sheehy Skeffington diary, 1908–9, SS MS 41,183/5.

12 IWFL Annual Reports 1908–1913, IF423, NLI.

13 *Irish Citizen*, 25 May 1912.

14 *Votes for Women*, 26 Nov. 1908.

15 Ibid., 18 Feb. 1909.

16 Ibid., 14 May 1909.

17 Hanna Sheehy Skeffington diary, 1908–9, SS MS 41,183/5.

18 *Votes for Women*, 17 Sept. 1909.

19 J. B. Lyons, *The Enigma of Tom Kettle: Irish Patriot, Essayist, Poet, British Soldier, 1880–1916* (Dublin, 1983), p. 158.

20 Ibid.

21 Hanna Sheehy Skeffington, *Reminiscences*, p. 71.

22 Cousins, *We Two Together*, p. 166.

23 *Sinn Féin*, 27 Mar. 1909.

24 Hanna Sheehy Skeffington diary, 1908–9, SS MS 41,183/5.

25 Ibid.

26 Andrée Sheehy Skeffington, *Skeff: A Life of Owen Sheehy Skeffington* (Dublin, 1991), p. 4.

27 Leah Levenson, *With Wooden Sword: A Portrait of Francis Sheehy Skeffington, Militant Pacifist* (Dublin, 1983), p. 82.

28 Hanna Sheehy Skeffington to 'Dear doctor', n. d., courtesy of Andrée Sheehy Skeffington.

29 Andrée Sheehy Skeffington, *Skeff*, p. 4.

30 Ibid.

31 Daisy Lawrenson Swanton, *Emerging from the Shadow* (Dublin, 1994), p. 79.

32 Hanna Sheehy Skeffington diary, 1908–9, SS MS 41,183/5; also quoted in Andrée Sheehy Skeffington, *Skeff*, n. 2, p. 243.

33 Owen Sheehy Skeffington, 'Francis Sheehy Skeffington', in Owen Dudley-Edwards and Fergus Pyle (eds), *1916: The Easter Rising* (London, 1968), p. 139.

34 Eibhlín ní Niocaill to 'Frances', 8 Apr. 1909, MS 49,445, National Library of Ireland (hereafter NLI). With many thanks to Mary Broderick, Assistant Keeper II, Social Collections and Manuscripts, NLI for bringing this to my attention.
35 James and Margaret Cousins, *We Two Together*, p. 196.
36 *Sinn Féin*, 3 July 1909.
37 Andrée Sheehy Skeffington, personal interview with author, Nov. 1993.
38 Hanna Sheehy Skeffington, *Reminiscences*, p. 75.
39 Ibid., p. 70.
40 Ibid., p. 69.
41 Hanna Sheehy Skeffington diary, 1908–9, SS MS 41,183/5.
42 Conor Cruise O'Brien, *States of Ireland* (St Albans, 1974), pp 80–1.
43 David Sheehy to Hanna Sheehy Skeffington, 8 Feb. 1910, SS MS 41,176/5.
44 Hanna Sheehy Skeffington to David Sheehy, n. d. SS MS 41,176/5.
45 J. F. Byrne, *Silent Years: An Autobiography* (New York, 1953), p. 91.
46 Cruise O'Brien, *States of Ireland*, p. 81.
47 RTE radio interview, 1945, fragment of transcript, SS MS 24,164.
48 Eugene Sheehy to Hanna Sheehy Skeffington 25 Jan. 1911, SS MS 41,176/18.
49 *Irish Citizen*, 3 Aug. 1912.
50 Hanna Sheehy Skeffington, 'Women and the national movement', in SS MS 22,266, reprinted in Margaret Ward, *Hanna Sheehy Skeffington: Suffragette and Sinn Féiner: Her Memoirs and Political Writings* (Dublin, 2017), pp 48–58.
51 *Sinn Féin*, 27 Mar. 1909.
52 Ibid., 3 Apr. 1909.
53 *Bean na hÉireann*, May 1909.
54 Hanna Sheehy Skeffington, 'Sinn Féin and Irishwomen', in *Bean na hÉireann*, Nov. 1909.
55 Hanna Sheehy Skeffington, 'A reply to some critics', in *Bean na hÉireann*, Feb. 1910.
56 Hanna Sheehy Skeffington, 'Memories of Constance Markievicz', reprinted in Margaret Ward, *Hanna Sheehy Skeffington: Suffragette and Sinn Féiner: Her Memoirs and Political Writings*, p. 289.
57 Ibid.
58 Hanna Sheehy Skeffington, '"The countess": some memories', in *Irish Press*, 4 Feb. 1936, reprinted in Margaret Ward, *Hanna Sheehy Skeffington: Suffragette and Sinn Féiner: Her Memoirs and Political Writings*, p. 304. That Rag Day was in June 1914. Nine students were brought to court.
59 Ibid.
60 Andrée Sheehy Skeffington, *Skeff*, p. 4.
61 *Votes for Women*, 15 Oct. 1909.
62 Hanna Sheehy Skeffington to Anna Haslam n. d. (1909/10), (Winston Churchill joined the committee in 1911 so it was before that date), SS MS 41,180/1.
63 *Votes for Women*, 24 Dec. 1909.
64 *Sinn Féin*, 19 Mar. 1910.
65 *Votes for Women*, 29 Oct. 1909.
66 *Sinn Féin* 23 July 1910.
67 Mary Carson to Hanna Sheehy Skeffington, 17 July 1910, SS MS 41,180/1.

68 *Votes for Women*, 22 July 1910.
69 Hanna to Frank, 24 July 1910 and 26 July 1910, SS MS 40,466/4.
70 Hanna to Frank, 25 Aug. 1910, SS MS 40,466/4.
71 *Irish Worker*, 9 Sept. 1911.
72 *Votes for Women*, 18 Oct. 1910.
73 Quoted in Margaret Ward, *Maud Gonne: A Life* (London, 1990), p. 99.
74 *Irish Citizen*, 1 June 1912.
75 Leah Levenson, *With Wooden Sword*, p. 109.
76 *Freeman's Journal*, 29 Oct. 1910.
77 Hanna Sheehy Skeffington, *Reminiscences*, p. 14.
78 Frank Skeffington to Hanna Sheehy (hereafter Frank to Hanna), 14 July 1912, courtesy of Andrée Sheehy Skeffington.
79 Hanna to Frank, 25 July 1912, SS MS 40,466/5.
80 Leah Levenson, *With Wooden Sword*, p. 110.
81 Frank to Hanna, 11 July 1912, courtesy of Andrée Sheehy Skeffington.
82 *Irish Citizen*, 1 June 1912.
83 Andrée Sheehy Skeffington, *Skeff*, p. 12.
84 Hanna Sheehy Skeffington, small notebook, n. d. SS MS 41,183/6.
85 Frank to Hanna, 14 July 1912, courtesy of Andrée Sheehy Skeffington.
86 Alice Park, notes n. d., Alice Park Collection, Hoover Institution Archives.
87 Hanna to Frank, 12 Oct. 1915, SS MS 40,466/10.
88 Frank to Hanna, 23 Oct. 1915, SS MS 21,636.
89 Frank to Hanna, 15 Oct. 1915, SS MS 21,636.

FIVE

THE STONE AND THE SHILLELAGH, 1910–12

Opponents of the suffragists were masters of the most devious of manipulations. The IWFL redoubled its attempt to pin down exactly what the attitude of the Irish Party was on the thorny issue of votes for women. Augustine Birrell, the politician who, as Chief Secretary for Ireland, was responsible for implementing British government decisions regarding Ireland was candid when he wrote to John Dillon: 'the wire pullers are satisfied that … both the Conciliation bill and the wider amendment will be lost, the one because it doesn't go far enough and the other because it goes too far. This might plainly be called trickery.'[1] Birrell was pro-suffrage, voting in favour of the Conciliation bill, yet he too was reluctant to speak to the women. When the IWFL attempted to meet him, he protested that pressure of work made that impossible. That led to the first militant action of the League.

On 25 October 1910 Hanna and Hilda Webb successfully heckled the Chief Secretary while he was on an official inspection of the dilapidated Greystones pier. The *Irish Times* reported the incident as an 'amusing scene', adding that one of the women was heard to retort: 'you would not hear our views, and so you have left us no alternative but to approach you in this way, and we shall do so every time you appear in public.' When Sir James Dougherty, the Under-Secretary, tried to intervene, protesting that the question of the pier had nothing to do with votes for women, it was Hanna who argued back: 'We pay rates for piers, and we are entitled to be heard'. When an onlooker shouted: 'You are a disgrace to your sex', she replied immediately:

'You are a disgrace to humanity'. Eventually, after Willie Redmond had intervened with the promise that Birrell would receive a suffrage deputation within days, the militant duo walked away, highly satisfied with what they had accomplished.[2] Frank wrote proudly of that victory, proof that the militant path was the right one.[3] It was no accident that Hanna had been the initiator. She was longing to give a public demonstration of Irish women's commitment to the cause, and Birrell was an appropriate figure with which to begin. It was Mary Kettle, the path cleared by her outspoken sister, who then presented a dignified front to the officials of Dublin Castle, that forbidding complex of military and legal bureaucracy housing the administrative centre of British rule. Birrell was important because he was Chief Secretary, and because he was also more approachable than the leading figures of the Irish Party, as Hanna was able to testify on encountering him again, two years later:

> I collared (him) once when selling the *Irish Citizen* at the corner of Grafton Street. He walked with his plain-clothes officers in attendance. A Press man gave me the word, and I dashed after him, poster in hand. He stopped and asked: 'How much?' I said: 'Anything you like to give, Mr Birrell. It's a penny.' He plunged his hand into his pocket, pulled out a handful of miscellaneous coin and extracted a threepenny bit.[4]

That hour of newspaper-selling netted two doctors, a professor, a Transport Union 'striker', a member of the 'G' Division, a Land Commissioner, an Insurance Inspector, a messenger boy and several 'mere women', as well as the Chief Secretary.[5]

Hanna, Meg Connery and others heckled Sir Edward Carson at Rathmines Town Hall that December, an occasion Hanna 'vividly and joyfully' remembered.[6] Marion Duggan, a law graduate and more sympathetic than Hanna to Carson, later claimed that his 'unpleasant memories' of the occasion when he was 'terribly put out', led to him agreeing to 'appease' Mrs Sheehy Skeffington by meeting her. There would be a time in late 1913 when that arch anti-suffragist appeared to be agreeing to votes for women in an independent Ulster outside of Home Rule and the columns of the *Irish Citizen* then were full of reminiscences by those who wondered who had been responsible for landing the Ulster Chief. While Marion Duggan tried to single out the IWFL, Hanna herself preferred to list a number of organisations and individuals who had devoted their energies into 'securing the slippery haul'. Of course, to stay with the fishing metaphor, with the benefit of hindsight we can add that the catch proved elusive and got away in the end as the Unionists reneged on that promise.

On more than one occasion Hanna pursued Redmond to Limerick, once managing to get herself onto the platform ('Limerick being my home town in a sense'), where the organisers, thinking she was a friend of Mrs Redmond's, recognised her too late to throw her off. Having succeeded in making her protest she was then pinioned and hustled down the steps, a threatening mob in pursuit. A Sheehy cousin, 'an infuriated male relative' felt obliged to accompany her as she was being marched off – 'his cousinship struggling visibly with his Party feelings' was Hanna's barbed comment. At the gate women tore her hat from her head, an old man spat in her face and she found her hands being held with such 'cousinly firmness' that she was unable to protect herself. At that point the police offered to escort her to the police station. A great many would have been grateful for this opportunity for escape, but Hanna's recollection of her response has an undeniable ring of authenticity:

> Being a strong disliker of police by nature, distrustful of protection, I declined with an inspiration: 'I will not go to the Police Station. I want no police protection from a Limerick crowd,' I answered. It worked like magic, and I was allowed to go my way in peace, and to clean the spit from my face. Crowds are queer things.[7]

Her family background and her own understanding of the oppressive nature of the forces of 'law and order' provided the impetus for her quick-witted reaction. The cousin remains anonymous, but his attitude was a smaller-scale reflection of David Sheehy's own. We can see how, within the family setting, affections were being visibly strained by these conflicting allegiances.

Irish women, excluded from the closed male circles of power, did their best to discover the truth through paying assiduous attention to every statement made by a politician. The best way to do this was by organising deputations which would be free to put questions in as unambiguous a manner as possible, hoping for replies which would be equally straightforward. For this, two obstacles had to be overcome. The first hurdle was getting the politicians to agree to see them, the second was getting them to make some significant comment. Gradually, the policy of closely following important politicians and listening to their speeches (and of course heckling them to make their own point), built up an impressive picture of the extent of political chicanery within the Irish Party. It developed into an intense battle between two camps. Suffragists – militant and non-militant – were determined to extract meaningful statements out of politicians whose careers had been forged on the ability to speak without saying anything definite. They, on the other hand, were determined to ensure that suffragists would be in no position to make any political capital from their meetings.

In July 1910 Hanna had taken part in another fruitless deputation to see John Redmond. He had privately told her that he feared clerical domination if women, reckoned to favour conservatism, had the chance to vote. He asked her not to quote him on this, possibly proving that he did fear those forces.[8] As he failed to provide any reassurance that he would have favoured women getting the vote if circumstances were different, his argument failed to impress.

Ireland was small enough to ensure that busy suffragists were able to make their presence felt on each occasion a politician attempted to hold a public meeting. A small branch of the IWFL was started in Limerick, another in Sligo, and other branches, not always long-lived, began in the wake of meetings addressed by leading figures of the IWFL. A branch in Cork developed into the non-militant and separate organisation of the Munster Women's Franchise League when the members disassociated themselves with the IWFL insistence on arguing for votes for women in the tense period when the Home Rule bill was going through parliament. In February 1912 Winston Churchill spoke in Belfast and Hanna and her equally outspoken friend, Meg Connery, went up to join five Belfast suffragists in their well-planned chorus of heckling. Meg, born Margaret Knight, came from a relatively prosperous family that ran the local post office as well as owning a small farm and pub in Westport, County Mayo. Her father John had been involved in the Land League and he was still involved in agrarian protests on behalf of the local small farmers.[9] In 1909 she married John (Con) Connery, the couple settling in the coastal village of Portmarnock, just north of Dublin city. Small, pretty and inclined to the dramatic, she was one of the most courageous – and outspoken – of the militants and a strong supporter of the labour movement. Leaflets calling for 'Votes for Women in the Home Rule bill' were distributed before the meeting, during which each woman shouted 'Votes for Women' in a pre-organised numerical sequence. The hall was fitted with wires to carry the sound of the speakers' voices, so that every time a woman was ejected the sounds of her protests reverberated around the hall, adding to the general mayhem.[10] Hanna was number three, by which time male tempers were breaking. Her Dublin accent was 'extra offence' to a northern crowd. Once again, she proved her ability to keep her nerve:

> I was seized and hustled to the top of a rough flight of steps leading to the soggy field. Two rough and angry stewards held me. One said 'Let's throw her down the steps', and made a grabbing gesture. I turned and caught the lapels of his coat with each hand firmly, saying 'All right, but you'll come along too!' I wasn't thrown down.[11]

She was proud of her ability to provoke a reaction. In meetings her wit could disarm hecklers, on other occasions her quick-thinking prevented physical abuse. The determination never to let anyone escape hearing the suffrage cry eventually led to the Irish Party barring women from their meetings, but this was more difficult to achieve at open-air meetings in the country.

Until the summer of 1912, the centre of suffrage activity continued to be focused upon Britain. There was still the hope that the government might give time to another Conciliation bill and, of course, the Home Rule bill was still to be voted upon. Emmeline Pankhurst toured all the major towns of Ireland in the autumn of 1910, explaining the importance of Irish women supporting a forthcoming delegation to parliament which was to plead for government backing for the Conciliation bill. Gretta Cousins escorted Mrs Pankhurst to her venues around Ireland. Hanna presided over her Dublin meeting at a packed hall in the Palace Skating Rink in Rathmines. Amongst a crowded platform of people eager to share the stage with the most famous woman in England was the deputy Lord Mayor of Dublin and one MP, Tom Kettle. It was the most important meeting to be organised by the League and they had gone to great efforts to decorate the hall with their orange and green colours, using Celtic artwork to mark out that this was Ireland, not England. Hanna's speech also emphasised the difference: their League was independent of English organisations but the members associated themselves with the militant policy of the advanced English suffragists.[12] At the end of her tour Mrs Pankhurst returned to Dublin and held a private meeting with IWFL members. Several volunteered for what they described as 'danger service': the next WSPU deputation to the House of Commons.[13]

Frank wrote that it was the first time a body of Irish women would cross the Irish Sea to represent their nation in the forefront of the fight. The volunteers were almost sanctified in advance: 'The devotion that makes this sacrifice is the crown of all the previous labours of the League.'[14] Hanna, despite her previous participation in London events over the summer, was not among the small band of martyrs. On the most practical of levels, it was taking place in the middle of the autumn term and she and Frank could ill-afford the loss of her earnings. But it was also apparent that the women were going over to court imprisonment, as proof of Irish women's equal commitment to the struggle. Gretta, on her way to Holloway Jail, was in a tearful mood, realising the full consequences of her action, 'I was troubled by the length of the sentence. I had not expected to be away from home for more than a fortnight.'[15] Hanna did not travel over with any of these contingents. She had Owen to consider and the cause could be furthered as profitably by her continued – and increasingly vocal – presence at home.

Six members of the IWFL served jail sentences of one and two months, not as a result of what came to be known as the 'Black Friday' attempt to petition parliament on 8 November 1910, but in consequence of their later stone-throwing, when angry and frustrated women marched to Downing Street and to the homes of the most influential politicians they could find. Irish women broke the windows of Birrell's house, the most direct connection between suffrage and Ireland that they could make, refusing to allow anyone but Irish women into their group.[16] Back in Dublin, Hanna presided over their usual weekly meeting, where the suffragists listened intently to Tom Kettle's description of those violent scenes outside Westminster. Kettle had been one of the few MPs to come to the women's support, hurriedly returning from London so that he could tell the League in person what had happened. While he was still speaking, a telegram arrived with the news that four members of the contingent had been arrested. People were delighted to hear that their colleagues had struck back and the meeting erupted with enthusiastic speculation as to what would happen now. They were all sure that a turning point in the history of the movement had been reached. Using his parliamentary position to the utmost, Kettle telegrammed Churchill on the women's behalf, demanding that they be treated as political prisoners.[17] But he was in a decided minority. The majority of Irish MPs had no qualms concerning the jailing of their countrywomen.

The excitement of Irish women sacrificing themselves for their cause by serving time in an English jail was a tremendous boost for the IWFL. It gave the existing members the confidence to redouble their own efforts, while the welcome publicity helped them to recruit 80 new members in the following weeks. When the first prisoners – Gretta Cousins, Miss Allan and Mrs Anna Garvey-Kelly (whose husband Andrew, a former surgeon to the British forces, had died in 1907) returned home on Christmas Eve there were emotional scenes at Westland Row station. The IWFL had formed a reception committee and members in their sashes of orange and green, headed by a band marshall, paraded through the city from the offices of the League, their male supporters carrying torches. Gretta found herself in an open horse-drawn carriage, travelling through the dimly lit drizzling streets of Dublin, torchlight illuminating the way ahead.[18] At the Antient Concert Rooms Hanna, who had coordinated the preparations for their welcome, presided over a jubilant meeting.

The torchlight procession in February 1911 for Kathleen Houston, Eva Stephenson and Hilda Webb, all of whom had served two-month sentences, was even more elaborate. A band led the way in front of banner-carrying women who were flanked on each side by male associates carrying flaming torches. The men were also positioned to act as bodyguards, if any hostility occurred, but Hanna and the other senior League members who acted as marshalls ensured that the triumphant marchers maintained an orderly line along Dublin's busy streets. Kathleen Emerson and Hanna had organised medals for the prisoners, and at the crowded reception which followed Mary Kettle presented all the ex-prisoners with medals decorated with interwoven bayleaves and shamrock, inscribed 'from Prison to Citizenship'.[19]

Other delegations in 1911 and 1912 also ended in terms of imprisonment for those who took part. Marguerite Palmer wrote in excitement from London in November 1911 that 'Everyone was in best of spirits & ready for anything that may come ... We intend to be well to the front tonight.'[20] She, Meg Connery, Maud Lloyd (a landscape painter who had exhibited in the Royal Hibernian Academy), Mary Bourke-Dowling and Hilda Baker all received one-week sentences.[21] Altogether, 18 Irish suffragists, including Dr Elizabeth Bell and Margaret Robinson from the northern Irish Women's Suffrage Society, were to serve time in British jails.

Kathleen and Francis Cruise O'Brien finally married on 7 October 1911. Cruise O'Brien was scraping a living as a journalist – he was for a short time in an editorial position in Wexford after the marriage – but earlier in the year he and Hanna had disagreed in print on the suffrage issue. She sent the cuttings to Uncle Eugene, who did not take her side. He felt Hanna had been 'very hard' and cautioned her that pushing matters too far did not help the cause. His letter struck a most uncharacteristic note for a fond uncle who normally indulged his 'dearest one', 'You owe him an apology. I <u>know you won't</u> make one. But please don't fight with Cruise.'[22]

Some protests were more fun than others. Resistance to the 1911 Census was one, although open defiance, given the small numbers of suffragists, was more difficult in Ireland than in Britain. The Irish census enumerators were all policemen and they possessed powers their civilian British counterparts lacked: they could ask any questions they wanted with failure to give a full answer incurring a stiff £5 fine. James Cousins wrote on his form that he was 'unable to give a true enumeration of my household as its female members were absent in protest against being officially classed with children, criminals, lunatics and such like'.[23] Most evaded the census rather than resisted, spending the night with friends, where they were also joined by women from the country, who had come up to the relative anonymity of Dublin.[24] Constance Markievicz lent her cottage in the Wicklow Hills for registration night and the women 'led the police a dance, camping on the hills or in empty houses, scattered far and wide'.[25] Meanwhile, back home, Frank had diligently filled out the census return for himself, Owen, their servant Philomena Josephine Morrissey (Minnie) and nurse Mary Butler, but had left blank the space for the absent Hanna. She would have been amused to read that the inventive enumerator had decided that she was 'Emily Sheehy Skeffington, age 28, born Dublin City'. His powers of invention gave up on the question of religion. As Frank had insisted that he would not fill in anything on religion, that remained blank.[26] Hanna declared the census protest to have been 'an unqualified success'.[27] although she later admitted that the numbers abstaining 'did not greatly throw out the census figures'.[28]

Historian William Murphy, with the benefit of the digitisation of census records, has discovered 47 women involved in absolute refusal, although others used the form as an opportunity to make a suffrage protest, for example giving their religion as 'militant suffragette'. There were others, such as Mary MacSwiney and Rose Jacob, who took the opportunity to fill out their forms in Irish, giving priority to their nationalist sympathies.[29] Although the IWSLGA officially opposed the census boycott, scrutiny of the returns reveals a much less clear-cut situation, with some women on the non-militant side participating and some well-known militants filling in their forms. In fact, the Irish response mirrors that of Britain, where there were more evaders than resisters, but the numbers were equally small, despite newspaper headlines of census resistance parties. The census had added a new dimension to its questions, centred on women's fertility, asking how many children were born in the marriage, sub-divided into children living and dead. Significant numbers therefore appeared to believe that a future prospect of welfare reform, based on the information contained in the census returns, was more important than census evasion.[30]

This period was a good one for suffragists, providing a number of opportunities to publicise the cause. On the following Monday they met up at City Hall where they thronged the gallery during the corporation's debate on whether the Lord Mayor should bear a petition to the Bar of the House of Commons to plead for a bill for women's suffrage. It was a noisy occasion, the gallery erupting with groans any time a nationalist argued that it was an irrelevant 'West British' affair which could be decided when Ireland had its own parliament. There was general euphoria in suffrage ranks in both Ireland and Britain when the motion was passed by 22 votes to nine. Credit was given to the Irish suffragists, who had unearthed the existence of the archaic and unused right of Dublin Council to petition the House of Commons.[31] In

May, the Lord Mayor, his wife and entourage travelled over to London, to be treated as honoured guests by the British suffrage movement.[32]

There were other advances in the constitutional sphere that year: resolutions in support of women's suffrage were passed not only by Dublin Corporation but also by Cork, Limerick, Pembroke, Galway, Bray, Portrush and Newry councils. At the end of 1911 the Local Authorities Ireland (Qualification of Women) bill passed into law, which meant that four years after the same reform had been introduced in Britain, Irish women were eligible for election to county and borough councils. Again, militant and non-militant organisations united to canvass on behalf of female candidates. Sarah Cecilia Harrison was elected in Dublin and Dr Mary Strangman in Waterford.

From all the evidence, there was a considerable amount of sympathy for the women's cause. A concerted violent opposition would come from the Ancient Order of Hibernians, but the organised anti-suffrage movement, the Irish branch of the National League for Opposing Women's Suffrage (the 'Antis'), was confined to the highest levels of Anglo-Irish society. Unfortunately, where support for the women's cause was lacking was where it was most needed – in parliament. On 28 March 1912, the votes of the Irish Party killed off another Conciliation bill, one which would have given the vote to women occupying property with a rateable value of more than £10. No member of the Party voted in favour. Their justification – that if the Conciliation bill had passed, it would have eaten into the time available for discussion on the Home Rule bill – was not well received. As the *Irish Times* put it: 'Redmond gained a week of parliamentary time and alienated the sympathies of every woman suffragist in Ireland. Many agreed with the admonition of the O'Brienite *Cork Free Press*: 'it never pays in politics to do evil that good may come.'[33] However, the deed was done. The Home Rule bill was soon to be published and many nationalists preferred to forget what had happened to women's hopes as they looked forward to the passing of the bill. A unity of forces was the greatest service that could be done for the Irish cause, it was argued, and that meant remaining quiet. As the women insisted on voicing their anger thereby disrupting the celebrations of the politicians, sympathy for their cause rapidly disappeared. Hanna explained, 'not only were we enemies of Home Rule, but rebels as women.'[34] And their political opponents were able to use this to their own advantage.

The IWFL were in a bitter mood. They had two members serving two-month sentences with hard labour in an English jail and after the Commons vote on the Conciliation bill they immediately issued a statement accusing the Irish Party of committing 'a distinct act of treachery' which they would 'neither forget nor forgive'. They understood the reaction of Englishwomen, who had declared war on the Irish Party, and warned that 'whether the party will have to encounter the hostility of organised Irish women as well depends on your answer to us today'.[35] In this, they were referring to a request for a meeting with Redmond that had been made by the League. More was to happen before that meeting finally took place. Just when emotions were running at their highest, salt was rubbed into the women's wounds by the staging of 'Home Rule Day' two days after the defeat of the Conciliation bill. The two causes were now so inextricably intertwined that whatever happened in the world of politics had repercussions for suffrage hopes.

'Home Rule Day' was Ireland's opportunity to show the world how dearly it valued the coming prospect of independence. Feminists decided that they needed to remind the celebratory crowds that, so far, Irish women had little to celebrate. Their defiant reminder of 'Votes for Women' appeared on all the walls and hoardings around Sackville Street, where the culminating rally was to take place, and at 12.30p.m., a small group of 20 women draped with sandwich boards marched through the streets, accompanied by three other women handing out leaflets and selling the WSPU paper *Votes for Women*. There was general good nature from the crowds milling by, until the women approached the Mansion House, when stewards belonging to the Irish Party suddenly set upon them. It was a vicious assault. Meg Connery's militant slogan 'Remember the women of Limerick' (written in Irish) was torn off her shoulders by a man wearing the costume of the Irish National Foresters.[36] That organisation and the Ancient Order of Hibernians was prominent in orchestrating attacks on the suffragists. The women fought back. As Hanna said: 'Irishwomen were not passive resisters, and … when she was struck by a steward or official she was inclined to hit back.'[37] During the struggle to keep her placard her glasses were knocked off and broken. She had the wit to remark that it was to 'blind her to the defects of the party', but inwardly she was furious at what had happened.[38] One of the participants, Maud Lloyd (at 40, the oldest of the suffrage prisoners), who had been imprisoned in England a few months previously, was quite clear that 'the treatment of the poster paraders by the official Nationalist stewards was in itself proof positive that the Irish Party had taken the field against our cause'.[39] She believed people like Tom Kettle – who had assured a meeting addressed by Christabel Pankhurst that he intended being an MP in the Home Rule Parliament and that he was quite certain he would be elected by women as well as men – were dangerous allies. Their words had 'lulled' Party women into the comfortable belief that women's suffrage would be included in Home Rule. And now they knew differently. Hanna's anger was fuelled by her sense of personal betrayal. Her last shreds of belief in constitutionalism had disintegrated along with her roughly torn poster.

The attitude of the politicians was not helping to prevent the plunge into full-scale militancy. One of the final disillusionments was a prearranged meeting with John Redmond, scheduled to take place the day following the ill-fated poster parade. A grim-faced delegation of Hanna, Gretta Cousins, Deborah Webb and Meta Louisa Tatlow met him in the plush surroundings of the Gresham Hotel. There was no satisfaction from that quarter. Redmond insisted that whatever he said had to remain confidential.[40] Gretta's memory of the occasion is revealing in its depiction of Hanna as the recognised political power behind the Franchise League:

> After we were seated, Mr Redmond at the head of the table, Miss Webb next to him, and as our memorandum was about to be read, Mr Redmond said, 'I am not prepared to allow these proceedings to be published in the press.' Miss Webb hastily consulted with Mrs Skeffington, who knew that such stricture was contrary to usual procedure. I can still visualise the dignity with which Miss Webb rose from her seat, stated that under such conditions the deputation would be a farce and serve no useful purpose, and left the room, followed by the rest of us.[41]

Hanna was not a Quaker. Her reaction was more combative as she attempted to argue with Redmond, protesting that the IWFL was not a secret society and that they would never have agreed to an interview under such conditions. All she could do was to put on record her protest at this unheard-of interpretation of 'private interview'. Against their will, they found themselves unable to make any public announcement on what had taken place. As Marguerite Palmer, chairing the next meeting of the IWFL said, the deputation to Redmond was 'shrouded in mystery' for all who had not been present.[42]

Redmond had 'peremptorily refused' to allow the deputation to publish a 'brief statement' after the meeting. In response, the IWFL sent a confidential statement to its members and associates, explaining the situation and asking them to respect the conditions imposed regarding secrecy.[43] When the *Freeman's Journal*, organ of the Irish Party, later published the circular as a way of proving the untrustworthy nature of the militants, Frank Skeffington accused Tom Kettle of knowing how this had happened.[44] At that time Kettle was still an associate member of the IWFL (his letter of resignation not yet accepted by the committee), and he therefore had received a copy of the circular. People said that Tom Kettle was most at home on a public platform while Frank would speak from a street corner, a statue or a lamp-post, wherever he could find an audience. That gulf between politician and agitator had become impassable. Frank accused his brother-in-law of 'double hypocrisy', 'betrayal' and 'trickery'. His condemnation included both Tom Kettle and David Sheehy: 'It is the failure of men, who have the power, to do their utmost to assist them, that makes it necessary for women to fight their own battle with whatever weapons come to hand.'[45] Women who now contemplated militancy were totally justified because they had no other weapon left.

The IWFL meeting following the abortive deputation to Redmond was a turning point in the Irish campaign. Hanna announced – to loud applause – that they were done with the Irish Party. She had sent in her resignation to the Young Ireland Branch and she urged all women to leave every organisation connected with the Party. She threatened that the women of Ireland would 'break the power of the Party'.[46] They were about to enter a new phase, but it was not one that everyone welcomed. Isabella Richardson, also a member of the IWFL and the YIBs, was unhappy at the direction Hanna was now calling the League to take. Trying to forestall this, she wrote an open letter to the *Irish Times*, describing the 'almost painful degree of intensity' which was felt by all at the meeting as Hanna stood in front of them, urging them to recognise that the time for militant action had arrived.[47] Mrs Richardson sympathised with the emotion but pleaded publicly for militancy not to be adopted. In a letter to Hanna she somewhat naively wondered why a non-militant like Louie Bennett should then have accused her article of providing the mob with an incitement for further maltreatment of the women, when all she had wanted to do was to prevent the IWFL from adopting methods which would ruin the women's cause in Ireland.[48]

However, it was highly debatable as to whether militancy would 'ruin' a cause which was struggling to stay alive while Irish politicians were busily trying to bury it amongst the growing pile of items to be attended to at some future date. Newspaper debate continued.

What made certain male politicians even more culpable in feminist eyes was the fact that the third Home Rule bill had now been introduced into parliament. There was no earthly reason why the defence of jeopardising Home Rule could have any more credence. What people were now concerned with was the actual content of the bill: the powers of the Irish parliament; the rights of religious minorities; the relationship of the unionist north to the rest of the country; the system of voting; the question of women's enfranchisement. All these issues, and many more, were topics of discussion. It was up to each interest group to fight its own corner. Ulster unionists, who did not want to be part of Home Rule Ireland, were beginning to organise a militant resistance, so why could women not take the same militant path?

A National Convention to discuss the content of the Home Rule bill was to be held at the Mansion House on 23 April 1912. This stage-managed event was billed as the people's opportunity to approve what was being put forward in their name. And once again the IWFL attempted to remind people that this was a question that Irish women also found to be of great importance. It was becoming more difficult to maintain a 'suffrage first' position, as some suffrage supporters worried that disunity in the ranks could jeopardise Home Rule. The Limerick branch of the IWFL considered a suffrage delegation 'unreasonable, ill-timed and likely to do harm to the cause ... in present circumstances'.[49] Agnes O'Farrelly wrote a letter to the *Freeman's Journal* arguing that, with a cabinet divided on the issue of women's suffrage, it would be 'extremely dangerous' to insist on its inclusion within the bill for Home Rule while Mary Hayden wrote an open letter to the *Freeman's Journal*, imploring suffragists not to take any action as 'nothing is now so important as the speedy passing of the Home Rule bill.' In her eyes women's franchise was bound to come in a 'few years' and would be 'as good as if it came tomorrow', but the country, without self-government was 'bleeding to death'.[50] Further divisions were occurring within the Sheehy family circle, as Kathleen wrote to Frank to argue that there was no sense in a demonstration that would only serve to 'give the Nationalist party an excuse to say suffragists are opposed to Home Rule.'[51]

Tom Kettle, rather bravely considering the reception he was obviously expecting, called round to talk to Hanna before the convention. She was out. The note he left for her made it clear that his priority remained supportive of for the Home Rule bill: 'Dear Hanna, I called to let you abuse me. I am of course going to move a motion but also to make it clear even if no amendment whatever to any clause can be carried I think that the Bill ought to be accepted.'[52] No motion for women's suffrage was put forward – the reason for this giving rise to more contentious debate in the Sheehy family circle – but Kettle later gave Hanna a verbal promise that, instead, he would make a strong plea during his speech for women to have the vote.[53] This he failed to do. The strong differences of opinion between Hanna and her brother-in-law became public following a letter from Kettle to the effect that the League was becoming little more than an imitation of the WSPU, its insistence upon organising a deputation to the convention a hostile act because its only effect would be to create further controversy.[54] Hanna was enraged by this attempt to minimise the importance of the women's demand through discrediting the Franchise League. She rejected the charge that they were blindly following the lead of the English suffragettes: their tactics had been inspired by the example of Parnell, an 'origin (which) ought to be sufficiently home-bred to appeal to Professor Kettle'.[55]

The only women allowed into the event, claimed the IWFL, were acquiescent 'party women' who could be guaranteed not to speak out of turn – an unfair criticism with regards Sarah Cecilia Harrison, one of those received into the Mansion House – but it was the case that women who had been elected as accredited delegates, such as Patricia Hoey of the London Branch of the United Irish League (and a member of the London IWFL), were refused admittance if they were known to have suffragist sympathies.[56] Tickets were so strictly controlled that it was out of the question for suffragists to resort to their old heckling routine. They could not get near the convention and the police outside the Mansion House ensured that their presence was as insignificant as possible, coralling the women to one side and refusing to allow them the freedom to plead with delegates entering the building. It was the most carefully controlled event that anyone had experienced. IWFL members formed themselves into a deputation to ask permission to put their case to the convention. They were refused.

The only way that the IWFL could establish their presence was through the creation of a visible group directly outside the venue. Hanna, Gretta and about 30 others arrived early at the Mansion House, waiting for the delegates to arrive. Mrs Sheehy Skeffington and Mrs Cousins, said a *Freeman's Journal* reporter, 'walked boldly up the steps of the Mansion House, in spite of remonstrances from the Inspector and knocked at the hall door' which was 'shut abruptly in their faces'. They then walked back and continued to distribute literature 'as if nothing had happened'.[57] The police cordoned off Dawson Street to prevent further groups of women from joining them, so the small band found themselves in the midst of their opponents. A rival group handed out leaflets which claimed that Irish women wanted Home Rule and not the vote. Kettle's accusation that the feminists were unduly influenced by the British had been taken up by the protestors, who concocted the following slogan: 'Irish women condemn the masculine conduct of Sheehy Skeffington and Cousins. Beware the English Pankhursts and their Irish Cousins.'[58] The heavy-handed attempt at wit was lost on the suffragists, who seethed at the infuriating treatment they found themselves subjected to. Maud Lloyd said they 'were surrounded by phalanxes of police and herded together into a corner as if they were sheep, the only occasion on which they could move being when they were now and again suddenly set upon by the police and chivied from one spot to another.'[59]

The long wait was frustrating and in vain. Police prevented Hanna and Gretta from speaking to Redmond when he emerged at the end of the day.

The Lord Mayor refused Frank's request that the women be allowed to hold an informal meeting in the Mansion House. When Hanna then stood up on a chair smuggled out of the Round Room and tried to speak, the police lifted her down and forcibly took the chair away from Frank, who had rushed to hold on to it. He was then, said the *Freeman's Journal* reporter, turned 'practically upside down by a couple of policemen, one of them holding him by the head and the other by the heels'.[60] After this scuffle the crowd broke up and were escorted towards Grafton Street. Students from nearby Trinity College, hostile both to Home Rule and to female suffrage, decided to join in the fun by throwing bags of flour at the women. The fracas made the evening paper, where Isabella Richardson read that Hanna had fainted but returned 'to the fray'. Mrs Richardson somewhat tactlessly repeated her assertion that the recent methods of the IWFL were 'ruining the women's cause in Ireland' but she wanted her friendship with Hanna to continue: 'For your great courage I shall always have an admiration, no matter to what deeds it may lead you to.'[61] Surprisingly, particularly considering how caustic she could be with those with whom she disagreed, and the extent to which she had been criticised recently by those with whom she had been close, Hanna replied almost immediately to say she considered their private friendship to be intact.[62] It was a 'kind' letter, but as Mrs Richardson had also argued at the Young Ireland Branch that people 'should not be instructed against their consciences to vote for suffrage', the friendship had worn pretty thin. The IWFL lost members as a result of their decision to challenge the Irish Party – 'the usual "up-to-this" friends that shook off the tree each time anything fresh was done' – as Hanna commented sardonically,[63] but there would be new recruits from those who welcomed the challenge that militancy brought.

Those hectic weeks in March and April provided the growing movement with a great deal of newspaper coverage. The suffragists considered the provincial press to be generally more sympathetic than the party-political press in Dublin which had very partisan views, but none of the reports really dealt with the overall aims of the movement, nor reflected the distinct differences between the militants and the non-militants. By 1911 the non-militant section of the Irish movement had rapidly gained in numbers and influence, particularly after Louie Bennett had formed the Irish Women's Suffrage Federation as an umbrella group to provide coordination for the small groups scattered around the country. The assumption that there was no difference between the British and Irish movements was having a detrimental effect. Suffragists needed to have some forum which would emphasise the distinct nature of the Irish movement. It was becoming urgent, particularly as

Christabel Pankhurst continued to declare that the WSPU would ensure that there would be no Home Rule for Ireland unless British women won the vote. This, of course, was very different from those Irish women who were arguing simply for women's inclusion within the terms of the Act. *Bean na hÉireann*, the only woman's journal in Ireland, had folded in February 1911. There was now no publication which would willingly accept lengthy articles arguing in favour of the feminist position. Even Sinn Féin, which had been moderately sympathetic to the suffragists, was now defending the Irish Party's action in voting against the Conciliation bill. Arthur Griffith maintained that 'half the population can't stop the country getting Home Rule just because the English didn't pass the suffrage bill first', an attitude which drew a dignified and effective rebuke from Jennie Wyse Power: 'we women who have worked for the interest of Sinn Féin must feel somewhat disappointed at the want of consideration of us you display…I do not think that the government of half the population by the other half is self-government. It is a new theory that the women of Ireland form no part of the Irish population.'[64]

Frank Skeffington, walking about the Dublin streets 'with the pockets of his overcoat and knee breeches stuffed with newspapers, and his brain, above his brown virgin beard, trained in the technique of magazine production'[65] knew better than anyone how vital a propaganda tool a journal could be. Bumping into James Cousins at the front of Trinity College, he discovered that both agreed on the necessity of having a paper which would 'keep the British and Irish suffrage movements distinct and carry on propaganda along our own lines'. Frank's calculation was that they needed sufficient funds to allow them to lose five pounds a week for a year. After that time, a weekly paper should be firmly established.[66]

Funds for the venture came from Emmeline and Frederick Pethick-Lawrence, treasurers of the WSPU. Both the Sheehy Skeffingtons and the Cousins knew their English counterparts well. They had encountered each other many times in London and shared a commitment also to socialist and pacifist causes. A sum of £260 was quickly smuggled over to Gretta by an anonymous messenger. Cloak-and-dagger activities like this were necessary because the Pethick-Lawrences and Emmeline Pankhurst were about to be tried for conspiracy. The outcome of that trial was the seizing of their personal assets in retaliation for their refusal to pay the cost of the prosecution. Frank's calculation on how long a subsidy would be needed was fairly accurate: after six months the editors were exhorting the readership to increase sales and attract new advertisers or else face the consequence of the paper folding within the month. There was an immediate and very impressive response to this. No one wanted to lose what had become an invaluable means of communication, a standard bearer for militant and non-militant alike and a forum for the expression of ideas which had no other outlet.

The first issue of the eight-page journal of the Irish suffrage movement appeared on 25 May 1912, the day after Hanna's birthday. Getting it ready for publication was a process that absorbed the energies of more than just the two editors. Kathleen sent her sister a birthday card, 'accept my fond love and many happy returns of your birthday. I expect you are far too busy to call and see me.'[67] It was called the *Irish Citizen*, printed 'in Ireland on Irish paper' and its motto made it plain that in terms of the struggle for emancipation, the sexes were engaged in a joint venture – 'For men and women equally the rights of citizenship. From men and women equally the duties of citizenship.' Frank Skeffington and James Cousins were joint editors, although their names never appeared in this capacity. Frank, who wrote the editorial matter under the heading 'Current Comment', lost no time in conveying the feminist attitude towards the Home Rule crisis:

> The Irish Party killed the Conciliation Bill. No justification for the action has been vouchsafed ... Unionist women have had their traditional opposition to the Nationalist Party intensified and embittered. Militants ... immediate work is not, as was lately alleged, the breaking of the Irish Party or the defeat of Home Rule, but the obtaining of votes for women in the Home Rule bill. No matter how their Unionist members regard the Bill, they hold that it will be a lesser evil if women have a say in the future of Ireland. To their nationalist members, Home Rule will not be Home Rule unless it includes the mothers, sisters, wives and daughters of Irishmen.[68]

In the week following the launch of the *Citizen*, one final appeal to the consciences of the politicians was made. Women from all over the country (many with no desire for Home Rule, but with a common purpose in demonstrating their conviction that no constitutional settlement of the Irish question would ever be possible if the existence of half the population was ignored) came together in the most important mass meeting yet organised by Irish women. The first issue of the *Irish Citizen* played an invaluable role in publicising the forthcoming meeting and succeeding issues gave every possible prominence to that historic event. Women gave up their Whit bank holiday to take part in poster parades and to chalk pavements to advertise the meeting. At the usual open-air meetings held in the different towns, it was widely discussed. In Belfast, just as in Dublin, women protested the insult of their exclusion from the Home Rule bill. A triumphant front cover was prepared for the 15 June edition. With a heading 'UNITED IRISHWOMEN – NATIONALIST

AND UNIONIST, MILITANT AND NON-MILITANT', seven women were ranged across a Dublin street, proudly displaying their sandwich boards advertising the 'Votes for Women' mass meeting, while above them were photographs of seven of the most prominent participants: Mary Strangman from Waterford, Mrs Gibson from Limerick, Hanna Sheehy Skeffington, Mary Hayden, Gretta Cousins from Dublin, Geraldine Lennox from London, Mrs Chambers from Belfast. The range of opinions represented at that meeting and the determination to maintain a united front over that one issue remains unique in Irish feminist history. Other issues regarding women's right to equality would receive support, but this was the only occasion when women put aside contentious political differences in their determination to ensure that women would be heard. Historian Senia Paseta, in her discussion of this 'huge meeting', noted the 'exceptionally high level of co-operation' on display that evening.[69]

As Hanna sat on the platform at the Antient Concert Rooms she reveled in what she and her colleagues had achieved: 'Women possess the genius for organisation, for skilled manipulation of effect. Attention to detail gives their meetings an element of the picturesque.' Levenson and Natterstad described her as displaying 'strong female chauvinism' in this enthusiastic celebration of women's capabilities,[70] but such an accusation is made without any acknowledgement of the circumstances leading up to the meeting. The disillusionment and hurt experienced by the IWFL members who had battled so hard and so unsuccessfully over the previous weeks in their struggle to get men to listen to them undoubtedly influenced their reactions. This mass meeting was not only an historic opportunity for women from each part of Ireland to come together in a united voice. It was also an affirmation – after all the harsh words, physical assaults and bags of flour – that women could indeed speak and were capable of creating a setting which evoked the kind of colourful and creative environment that feminists believed could only be achieved in the wider society when women won the right to participate in the body politic. Hanna's description celebrated women's creativity, but its aim also was to show the men what they were missing by their refusal to grant citizenship to women:

> Those 20 shields of black and white lettering, bearing names of the provincial centres represented at the meeting, those banners and pennants of orange and green, azure and silver, dark blue and gold that lined the hall, adding a further emphasis to their exclusively feminine platform, representative of so many varying feminine activities, from medicine and the law to artistic needlework and craftsmanship.

She couldn't resist a final dig, just to rub home her point: 'I am almost sorry for the politicians at their party play, those little legislators blindly making little laws for those who make the legislators.'[71] Nineteen organisations sent representatives to that meeting, chaired by Professor Mary Hayden because her academic reputation and her non-militant suffragism were credentials acceptable to all. There had been frantic behind-the-scenes negotiations before that had been agreed. Inghinidhe na hÉireann, the Irish Women Workers' Union, the Irish Drapers' Assistants' Association, Sinn Féin, suffrage groups throughout the country and the Irish League for Women's Suffrage in London came together, in Professor Hayden's words, 'to ask in a perfectly constitutional manner for the redress of a great wrong ... We have joined on this one issue without sacrificing our individual political opinions, and we ask the members of all parties in the British Parliament to help us to obtain this measure of justice to women.'[72] They wanted the Local Government Register to become the basis for voting in the new Irish parliament. It would not be full adult franchise as there was still a property qualification, but it was the most democratic demand deemed acceptable at the time. Hanna's speech – dramatically headlined by the *Irish Citizen* as 'The Voice of Leinster. The Last Constitutional Chance' – dealt with the implications of a rejection of their resolution. She began in conciliatory style, exempting from blame individual members of parliament and placing all responsibility on the Liberal government, which had introduced the Home Rule bill and which was the only body with the power to ensure that the women's amendment would be added to the bill. But at the heart of her speech was an unmistakeable warning:

> We want to go in by the front door, and if this constitutional meeting does not force its way, no doubt women will find other ways. Do not be mistaken. If the Liberal Government refuses to respond to our resolutions, there is no further chance for constitutional agitation.

Ireland was imagined as a home, with women wanting the freedom to enter that house by the front door. If that door was barred to them, however, then they would have no hesitation in breaking down the barriers. She continued to use similar imagery in her conclusion. Women as well as men were actively involved in local government, thereby helping to prove to the British government that the Irish could rule themselves: 'We have helped to build up the house out of which we are now to be shut.'[73] Consciously or unconsciously, her words refuted the claim that the militants were men in disguise. Her ideal, bolstered by a marriage in which she and her husband attempted to render gender-based differences unimportant, was for harmony in a home to which the sexes contributed equally. The struggle would be more intense and the sacrifice greater, but she was ready.

Copies of the resolution from the meeting were sent to all Irish MPs and to each member of the Cabinet. There was no response. Hanna had warned that 'breaking point' had been reached, all that was left was 'the historic and well-tried argument of the stone'.[74] For the past month she had been urging for this step to be taken and now they could claim with justification that the limits of constitutionalism had been reached. On 13 June, at 5 a.m., eight members of the IWFL marched off to their pre-arranged targets: the windows of the GPO, the Custom House and Dublin Castle. While planning the attack Hanna had asked for Dublin Castle, potent symbol of British rule over Ireland, to be hers, avenging 'the treasured wrongs of fifty years'.[75] The small and dirty window panes near the Castle Gate proved difficult to break, and the garrison was close enough to arrest her before she had done too much damage. The policeman who grabbed her arm assumed she was right handed and the left-handed Hanna, still clutching her cherrystick, quickly got in 'a few more panes' before the Castle military arrived and she and her companion, Margaret Murphy, were led off to Chancery Lane police station.

Hanna complained that the station sergeant refused to deliver her message to Frank, but she was not allowed to bring this up when the case came to court because of (as the 'special representative' – Frank – writing in the *Irish Citizen* took pains to explain) 'the absurd law that husband and wife cannot be examined in each other's favour'. It was afternoon before the women could leave the station. Frank had appeared, as he was to do with increasing regularity when suffragists needed someone to put up bail for them. He also gave them superb publicity. The front page of the 22 June issue was particularly dramatic, its banner headline 'Prisoners for Liberty: members of Irish Women's Franchise League on trial for breaking Government windows', complete with details of the four militants. Hanna was described as 'eldest daughter of David Sheehy MP. Six times imprisoned for political offences in connection with agrarian and Home Rule agitations. Uncle Father Eugene Sheehy first priest imprisoned by Forster.' There was also the following quotation from Frank's hero, Michael Davitt, who had written of the part played by women in the Ladies' Land League:

> No better allies than women could be found for such a task. They are, in certain emergencies, more dangerous to despotism than men. They have more courage, through having less scruples, when and where their better instincts are appealed to by a militant and just cause in a fight against a mean foe.

For some men, those references to the past were uncomfortable reminders they would prefer not to think about. For David Sheehy, there was no comparison between his actions and those of his daughter, no matter how much she and that husband of hers might insist that there was.

That Saturday, Hanna explained herself to a 'friendly gathering' at the usual Phoenix Park venue. Presumably, in speaking at open-air meetings, the technique was to pitch one's argument at the audience's weak spot. In which case, one can understand her exaggerated rhetoric:

> If Wolfe Tone, Emmet and Davitt had not stood in the dock and suffered death and imprisonment, those at the meeting might not be present that day but very likely would be in the colonies ... If she had to go to Mountjoy Gaol she was exceedingly proud, for her father had been in Mountjoy Gaol before her, and her uncle was the first priest who was sent to Mountjoy Gaol in the Land League days for Irish freedom.[76]

People unsympathetic to the militants might criticise and say that the mention of her father and uncle was a piece of opportunism. Others might defend her and understand her desperation to convince the public of the validity of her cause, and to convince politicians like her father that the struggle for citizenship took many forms and included both sexes within its ranks. It might also be concluded, in following the progression of her political evolution, that sympathy with militant Irish nationalism was always part of her political make-up.

In the week before her trial Hanna had given considerable thought to the new stage of development within feminism now arrived at as a result of the militant's actions. They were 'scattered thoughts', penned in anticipation of her knock on the prison door, unequivocal in their celebration of militancy:

> Now that the first stone has been thrown by suffragists in Ireland, light is being admitted into more than mere Government quarters and the cobwebs are being cleared away from more than one male intellect.

Very deliberately, no reference was made to the British suffrage experience. Her argument was for the intrinsically Irish nature of her act: 'the stone and the shillelagh need no apologia; they have an honoured place in the armoury of argument.' She was part of the tradition that had seen women hurling stones upon the Williamites during the Siege of Limerick and defying landlords in Land League times. What, of course, was different now was that women had resorted to violence 'on their own behalf' rather than in furtherance of 'male liberties.' This element of 'unwomanly selfishness' was 'repellent to the average man' who only 'applaud the stone-thrower as long as the missile is flung for them and not at them'. This double standard of accepting violence when it was adopted for political or economic ends, but not when used by women for their own needs, intensified the bitterness towards Irish politicians, whose stance militants felt was inexcusably hypocritical. The lessons of Irish history added an extra dimension of estrangement between parliamentarians and feminists.

As Hanna continued her analysis, her tone lost its scornful note and became more impassioned. The militants were fighting to end 'the injustices and abuses suffered by so many women, ranging from the sweatshops of Belfast, the prostitution on Dublin streets and the sordid institution of the bargain marriage', contracted to keep farms together and which banished love from the Irish countryside. Ireland was almost 'oriental' in its disregard of women. They were excluded from public occasions, there was a 'scarcely veiled contempt' of wifehood and the term 'old woman' was synonymous with imbecility. It was a sweeping condemnation of the economic and social oppression endured by women, one which went far beyond purely legalistic reform. Women had tried meetings, petitions, campaigns, deputations, processions, resolutions, heckling; they had, in other words, 'run the gamut of constitutionalism'. For all those reasons, the women 'of a younger generation (were) somewhat in a hurry with reform', and which, 'if it falls asleep at its post, we shall wake ... with a stick.' The chapter of constitutionalism - which 'might have been a serial' but for the militants – was now closed. Hanna had taken her stick to the windows of Dublin Castle. Although she had called this her 'scattered thoughts' on what Irish suffragists hoped to achieve through their adoption of militancy, she was too modest. It is a crucial article in terms of arriving at an understanding of where militant Irish feminism can be located within the Irish political panoply. For Constance Markievicz and other nationalists, the needs of the nation were the priority and suffrage would come after. For Hanna, the needs of women were the priority as she believed there could be no meaningful change until women had equal citizenship. She regarded militant feminism in Ireland as part of an historical tradition of resistance, the object, however, centering on women's emancipation rather than 'male liberties'. Furthermore, it was made explicit that the vote was only one stage in a feminist revolution aimed at bringing to an end the social and economic subordination of Irish women. The interests of the exploited and the marginal were central to her conception of feminism. She might, she thought, have 'more to add' when she came out of prison.[77] She would indeed.

When the case of the first four of the eight militants (Hanna, Marguerite Palmer and the sisters Margaret and Jane Murphy) came to court on 20 June, their trial received enormous and very welcome publicity. The report of the *Daily Express* could have been taken from its theatre rather than court correspondent:

> The suffragettes were early in attendance and they took up as far as possible positions in the gallery and in the well of the court ... the waiting period was obviously happily spent in the stuffy court by the women and their male friends. The women in the gallery laughed and joked amongst one another and with friends in other parts of the court. They were all attired in fashionable costumes and prominent amongst them were Miss Hilda Webb, Miss Maud Lloyd, Miss Margery Hasler and Miss Kathleen Houston, all of whom are awaiting trial for somewhat similar offences. Mr Francis Sheehy Skeffington and other male supporters of the 'votes cause' were also prominent ... Mrs Sheehy Skeffington who carried two large bouquets of flowers, occupied a seat at the solicitor's table. Her husband was in the same part of the court.[78]

Marguerite Palmer came from a Unitarian family from Moneyrea in Belfast. At 26 she was nine years younger than Hanna, whom she admired with a fervour bordering on hero-worship. The public ordeal of the dock was uncomfortable, but Marguerite was 'supremely happy and at home ... ensconced in the dock with my able leader beside me'.[79] Margaret and Jane Murphy were the pseudonyms of Leila and Rosie Garcias de Cadiz. They had been born in India, orphaned at an early age and brought up in England by relatives. They were members of both the IWFL and the WSPU and – despite their membership of the IWFL – not sympathetic to Irish nationalism.[80] Hanna and Margaret Murphy had been charged with 'wilful damage' to 19 panes of glass, property of the War Department, while the other pair had smashed glass in the office of the Irish Land Commission. The Murphys had solicitors to represent them, while Hanna and Marguerite represented themselves, taking the opportunity to deliver lengthy speeches from the dock in explanation for their actions. In her conclusion Hanna was reported as saying:

> They were out on a very serious mission and to make in their strongest possible way a protest against a state of affairs that had become iniquitous. They wanted to arouse the public to their demands and she personally would like to go to Mountjoy Prison because she wanted to see how political prisoners were treated there and she would insist on her rights in that respect.[81]

The *Irish Citizen* claimed 200 supporters attended the trial, and it criticised other papers for not giving greater prominence to the women's eloquent defence. Although that particular reporter was perhaps too emotionally a part of events to be able to take a detached view, it is true that papers omitted an important part of the judge's speech. Justice Swifte had been patently nonplussed at the spectacle of these 'ladies of considerable ability' appearing in his dock and felt some difficulty in deciding what course to adopt. According to the *Irish Citizen*, he then added that if he had the power, he would make them first-class misdemeanants.[82] Newspapers omitted all this, only publishing the last part of his remark, when in reply to Hanna asking what division they would go into, he stated that it was a matter for the Prison Board. The full text of the judge's remarks was used incessantly by the prisoners and their supporters when campaigning for an improvement in conditions for themselves and for those who came after them.[83]

After refusing to pay fines or to give bail, the women were given one month's imprisonment with a further month for refusing to pay a fine. They left the court in defiant mood. Marguerite Palmer turned around to the gallery, shouting 'keep the flag flying' while Hanna reminded the crowd that militancy was to continue: 'you are out, and remember that Mr Asquith is coming here in July'. The thunderous applause greeting all this led to the clearing of the galleries and general confusion, with Hanna continuing to protest that earlier that day a wife beater had received a lighter sentence than they had. Irish militants were euphoric that at long last women had taken the initiative and had struck out for the cause. Marguerite Palmer's last impressions of the courtroom summed up the general feeling of optimism that had been created after all the frustrations of the past weeks:

> The defiant words of Mrs Skeffington, that by going to prison we had achieved the utter breakdown of the law', the evident sympathy and understanding of both the public in the court and the magistrate – all combined to make me feel that a good day's work had been done. I knew that that day's proceedings had marked the beginning of the end – the struggle for the vote had entered upon its final stage.[84]

Hanna was conveyed to Mountjoy still clutching her bag, bouquet and the cherrystick, which had been pressed into her hand by a policeman in the courtroom. It was a novel experience and she noted with interest all the bureaucratic procedures that attend the admission of people to prison. After her personal details were entered into a 'ponderous volume' she was cheered to see that the name and address of some 'friend' was also entered into the book, 'It looked quite human, as if the officials meant to dispatch daily bulletins to my anxious relatives, but I learned later that the friend was expected to fetch my body from the Government in case death cut my sentence short of the time laid down by Mr Swifte.'[85]

Those who had experienced the harshness of Holloway Jail were pleasantly surprised by the regime they now encountered in Ireland. Marguerite's heart had sunk on hearing the prison gates close behind them, but she said their spirits rose as a 'sweet-faced matron' came to meet them. She was smiling and so too were other prison officials, unlike their grim English counterparts. Their physical environment too was very different from Holloway. Here, the prison grounds were 'artistically laid out' and the green grass, shrubs and flowers helped to lend a 'touch of beauty to the otherwise cold, bare place'. Her memories were of the women ingeniously contriving to furnish their cells from nothing, receiving well-wisher's donations of carpets, vases and tablecloths. Once, out on exercise, they managed to divide and eat a melon without cutlery or plates, a messy situation she found embarrassing, but the melon disappeared. Those who thought that such exotica only arrived in Ireland with the advent of foreign travel might be surprised to learn of such small details, evidence of greater sophistication than is often realised.[86]

Hanna was less concerned to give domestic details in her account. Even in later years she remembered the books she had read and the reviews she had written while imprisoned, despite Frank's complaints that he couldn't get any articles for the *Citizen* out of her 'and we have needed them badly the last two weeks'. What she remembered and detested was the fact that Mountjoy was run on military lines. The wardresses, dressed in 'hideous garb' – half nurse, half military – had to give the military salute and were paraded which, in Hanna's eyes, made them 'as much prisoners as we were'. A man was governor and her feminist instincts resented the 'male limitations and the male delight in red tape' that occurred in consequence.[87] Like Marguerite, she too found the female staff sympathetic towards the women, 'sometimes a kindly wardress would leave a mug of coffee or soup, with strict injunctions to hide same should any colleague come along ... Once, when a prison chaplain came I had to hide away two separate mugs.'[88]

The women received a modified first-class misdemeanant status, their only restrictions being the withholding of the privileges of being able to talk at exercise time, to follow their own trade in prison or to have visits and letters more often than once a fortnight. Full first-class misdemeanant status meant that prisoners could wear their own clothes, order food from outside, pay a prisoner to clean their cell, and with few restrictions on visitors and letters. It was the restriction on visitors and letters that they protested about, refusing to take any exercise. Support from the outside was immediately mobilised. Gretta provided wonderful back-up: writing to Lord Aberdeen, arranging an immediate visit to find out the prisoners' own views and then preparing a memorial to Aberdeen, which had to be rushed to him with the first 80 signatures when word came that the Lord Lieutenant was about to leave Ireland.[89] Dublin Castle officials were so confounded by these female political prisoners and their energetic supporters that Birrell sent a query to the General Prisons Board to ask about the treatment given to Helena Molony, who had been arrested for her part in the protest over the King's visit the year before. That was the only occasion since the Ladies' Land League when Irish women activists had been imprisoned. The vice-chairman of the board replied that the case of Miss Molony 'was one for throwing stones in connection with the socialists and not with the female suffrage movement'.[90] There was no precedent they could call on, so the officials had to decide for themselves how to treat their prisoners. Within ten days, all the privileges of first class status had been given to the women. They could have two visits daily and as many letters as they liked. Hanna felt that they were often given liberties 'on the quiet' as the authorities realised that it was better not to look for trouble, but they also had the advantage of being the first of the Irish suffragist prisoners, and the attitude of the Irish prison authorities had not yet hardened.[91]

As privileged prisoners they could not, they realised, 'dig deep' into prison life, although they did their best to observe everything, conscious that the treatment of women in prison would be an item on the agenda once women were in a position to influence the legislators. Apart from attendance at chapel, they saw little of the other prisoners, but Hanna was intrigued by the sight of the faces she caught glimpses of, many with little toddlers 'exercising' with their mothers. According to the reports in the *Irish Citizen*, which gave detailed updates on the women's treatment, they were in an enviable position. Their demand to be attended by a female doctor had been granted. They had three hours exercise per day together and a further hour's associated work in a special room every afternoon, when they did their needlework and made 'Votes for Women' bags. These artifacts became sought-after items at fund-raising events. The women got up at 6.30, half an hour later than the other prisoners, and special gas burners were put into their cells, which they were allowed to keep on until 10.00 each night. The menial work of cell cleaning was done for them and the glaring white-washed walls were painted over so that they would be less 'trying' on their eyes. They were deluged with presents from well-wishers; Jennie Wyse Power's restaurant sent in a daily meal, and there were so many people queuing to visit them that a rota had to be kept in the IWFL offices.

Frank was desperate for occasions when he and Hanna could be alone during a visit: 'As you're booked up on Monday I'll try to keep Tuesday for ourselves – My dodge is simply to put myself down for an early hour ten or 11, and then no one else comes. The visitors are rather a bore, but it can't be helped; they mean well!' Uncle Eugene, worried and 'at least a little amazed' at his niece's behaviour, was on his way back from Germany – 'and after that you'll have another daily visitor, though how he'll reconcile himself to the 15 minutes I can't imagine! he'll only just have begun to settle down when he has to leave!'[92] Hanna remembered Father Eugene's support with great fondness, 'one of those dear comfortable relations who condone anything in a favourite'.[93]

Owen was also an occasional visitor, sometimes accompanying Uncle Eugene as well as Frank. Hanna wrote to her Belfast friend, Elfreda Baker, that he was at first 'greatly afraid he'd get locked in with his mammie' but, as a typical three year old, he didn't miss her a bit.[94] He achieved the unheard-of concession of being brought to his mother's cell to eat chocolates after having fallen on the stone floor of the reception room 'and raised such a howl that the Superintendent said it would never do for him to go out roaring, as it might get into the Press!'[95] The prison chaplain reminded Hanna that he had been there when her father had been imprisoned in Mountjoy, 'a stubborn man' he drily commented. That stubborn man did not return to visit his equally stubborn daughter. As a loyal party member he disapproved of her actions. Hanna described their differences very circumspectly: 'He was a stoic father and I responded and respected, though I officially disapproved of his attitude as much as he of mine.' Bessie came, 'disapproving but fond', and so did Aunt Kate and the sisters.[96] Kate proved to be the backbone of family support for Frank at this time, constantly urging him to take his meals with her. She and her unmarried daughter Olive, an elocutionist, always had a steady stream of McCoy relatives amongst the numbers of boarders at Barry's, a fact which guaranteed that members of the Sheehy clan would also drop in on a regular basis. Owen was full of having met another 'uncle Gene' (Hanna's brother Eugene, who did not visit his sister), and a cousin Jim when eating apple-pie there, brought over by his nurse Mary one Sunday afternoon so that Frank could have a break. Frank and his brother-in-law Tom encountered each other there at one Sunday dinner. In the absence of Mary, whom Frank found difficult, Kettle was 'comparatively genial' and they 'sparred, but good-humouredly'.[97]

There was no mention of invitations to Sundays in the Sheehy residence. When in court observing the fate of other suffrage prisoners Frank bumped into brothers Dick and Eugene, there in their professional capacities, and had a 'passing word' with Dick. No message for the imprisoned sister was forthcoming. The shaky signature of T. D. Sullivan, Hanna's old neighbour in Belvedere Place, was prominent on various memorials to Lord Aberdeen, the Lord Lieutenant, ceremonial representative of the British government, in support of suffrage prisoners. If it was possible to get Sullivan in the hectic rush before Gretta Cousins had to present the petition on behalf of Hanna and her sister prisoners, it would surely have been as easy to get hold of David and Bessie Sheehy. That their names did not appear must be considered persuasive evidence for their disapproval?

Frank's father, in the process of moving house with his new wife, was a daily visitor for Owen, taking advantage of Hanna's absence to indulge his grandson with sweets, biscuits and toys. Owen became so spoilt by this attention that he complained when he wasn't brought anything, and he began to demand items like boxes of chocolates. It might be argued that David Sheehy was in London, still attending sessions of parliament. He was there at the beginning of July, when a heated vote was taken on the question of support for a continuance of government policy on forcible feeding of hunger striking prisoners. Thirty eight Irish MPs voted in favour of forcible feeding, an act which the *Irish Citizen* considered to be a 'gratuitous demonstration of hostility to women's rights as political prisoners'. Readers were urged to 'cut out this list and keep it for future reference'.[98] One name on that blacklist was David Sheehy. For Frank, rushing around Dublin, between jail, the League offices, home for Owen, writing, producing the *Citizen*, still turning up at the various public rallies, life was hectic, but some of it was self-induced, to cover the gap that his wife's absence had left. She was his 'darling Hanna' and he missed her every day she was apart from him:

> Just a line, on this our anniversary (just as wet as the original day!) to tell you that I love you with all my heart and soul and that I am very proud of you and your sacrifice. We may treat it lightly, but it is no light thing to sacrifice liberty as you have done for the sake of a great cause. I miss you, dearie, and I'll value you more, I think, when you come back to me than I have done! I've been very peevish and cross with you often, dearest, and I'm sorry –I didn't mean to![99]

Unable to relax, he threw himself into a spate of gardening, 'hope to keep it up. Poppies are glorious and nasturtiums just coming out.' He felt more 'widowed' than he had done when she was away attending language courses in Germany and, sitting alone at home on a wet Sunday evening (it was an appalling summer that year), with Owen chattering away in his cot, and no-one else around, he fantasised about having a more conventional family life in the future: 'I don't think I'll let you spend yourself so much on suffrage work in future – after all your first duty is to your husband and family!!! In other words darling, I can't do without you! (Owen can – he's quite calm in your absence.)'[100] Hanna's response was amazed incredulity, but Frank still felt the same way a few days later: 'yes, I mean that about suffrage work! I'm afraid I've been inclined to forget the human needs of ourselves in our work for humanity. Not that I'm not glad and proud of all you've done dearest; but in future I think I'll keep you a bit more to myself!' Was there some underlying resentment on Frank's part that he had been relegated to a domestic, supportive role while his wife took centre stage in the struggle for women's rights? This was a pivotal moment in their marriage. Public recognition of Hanna's significance would enable her to have greater agency within the marital relationship. The struggle was too intense and the outcome too important for the indulgence of Frank's daydreams. He might have wanted his wife to spend more time at home in the future but, while she was incarcerated, he supported her in every way possible. As Hanna said: 'he enjoyed the experience vicariously and urged us on even to the hunger strike. He was never amenable to the Governor's suggestion to advise his wife to be "sensible".'[101]

The prisoners were determined to convey how well they were treated because they wanted to emphasise that they were political prisoners, not criminals, and were being dealt with as such. Hanna was clear on this, as she wrote to Gretta, 'We came here determined to wrest political rights at any cost after a stipulated week's truce, should they be denied', and she was 'adhering absolutely' to that policy.[102] However it was not that easy. Four hours association obscures the fact that for 20 hours a day they were in 'unmitigated solitude' and yet had to suffer from a total lack of privacy. She found this hard to take: 'the very decencies are broken down. You never quit the sight or surveillance of an official for a single moment. You are escorted to your bath, which has but a scanty half-door.'[103] Supporters on the outside had the exhausting time of maintaining awareness of the prisoner's existence and keeping up the programme of summer open-air meetings. The women of the League appeared to want to organise that part themselves. Frank offered his services, but nothing came of it. He said he didn't mind 'so long as their speeches are sound on militancy which they are; if they weren't, I'd insist on speaking!'[104]

In addition to all this, the suffrage message still had to be spread to parts of Ireland which had not yet seen a suffragist in the flesh. Summer, even a wet one, was the best time in which to do it. Gretta and three other members of the Franchise League (together with assorted grown-up children) borrowed a side car and spent a week camping in various fields in Sligo and Donegal, speaking at impromptu meetings in whatever venue they could find. Kathleen Emerson and Mary Earl successfully dogged Churchill's footsteps in Cork, heckling him wherever he went. The prisoners wrote to declare that they were 'watching with admiration all the suffrage activities in the outside world'.[105]

The necessity for all this activity from the IWFL was partly in response to the disapproving reaction from non-militant suffragists. Anna Haslam wrote to express her 'strong disapproval of the breaking of windows as a means of advancing our cause'[106] and the Suffrage Federation too was at pains to disassociate itself from the window breakers. A letter to Hanna from Ellen Duncan, campaigning at a by-election in Yorkshire, summed up the views of many: 'Foolish tactics – and doubly foolish now. However, I can only hope ... that they will treat you decently. The news has even penetrated the local papers here!'[107] Of course, those natural rebels, Constance Markievicz and Helena Molony, took great delight in visiting someone who had decided that the time for the 'stone and the shillelagh' had arrived in Irish politics. Anna Haslam came too, although not in an official capacity. They had been friends for a long time, and she found it impossible to turn her back: 'Don't think I approve – but here's a pot of verbena I brought you ... here's some loganberry jam, I made it myself.'[108] Knowing that their actions had internationalised the Irish women's cause was wonderfully satisfying. Isa Lawlor, who was in Germany at the time, wrote to let Hanna know that there was even mention of their actions in the *Freiburger Zeitung*, 'very small but still an advert'.[109] Lawlor was soon back in Ireland, to be arrested for throwing stones at windows during Asquith's visit.

On 12 July the prisoners were joined by Kathleen Houston, Marjorie Hasler, Hilda Webb and Maud Lloyd who, having managed to break more glass, had received a punitive six months each. Hanna and Marguerite observed their new companions prison behavior with amusement:

> We have two 'grandes passions' here – Lloyd-Webb, Hasler-Houston. They are interesting to watch, like engaged couples, the first in each group being the wife, the second the oak! They bill & coo all day, do each other's mending, embrace in bed when cells are thrown open each morning & drink out of same cup! ... Mrs P. and I though chums are more like married folk – I suppose having husbands we don't waste our sweetness.[110]

Hanna's jocular portrayal provides a vivid picture of a small group of women who challenged the assumption that women without men were incomplete. However, possibly conscious that she was writing to her husband, her final comment 'we don't waste our sweetness', minimised that challenge to heterosexuality, reinstating the primacy of female/male relationships. In later years, as a widow she would develop strong friendships with women like Eva Gore-Booth and Esther Roper, who advocated 'female same-sex life unions ... as a superior alternative to heterosexual marriage'[111] and she would become a close friend of the American radical Dr Marie Equi, an outspoken advocate of lesbianism. Her neighbour in Belgrave Road, Kathleen Lynn, lived with her life partner and lover Madeleine ffrench-Mullen. Other friends like Louie Bennett also shared their lives with female partners. By that time Hanna's life – and those of her sisters – was very different. With the loss of their husbands, they created a female world of emotional and physical support.

The Murphy sisters, irritating Hanna more each day, were not on speaking terms with any of the other women, or with the prison matrons, favouring only the governor, 'to whom they lend improving books of suffrage tendency.' Their prison sheets had the warning 'neurotic tendencies' emblazoned over the top and in this assessment the prison authorities and Hanna were in agreement. There were now eight women of the Franchise League in Mountjoy, during one of the most hectic of suffrage summers. Hanna's exhortation from the dock, to remember that Asquith was coming, was partly a reflection of the fact that the IWFL had not received a favourable response to their request for a meeting: 'We would ask you to take this opportunity of hearing Irish women, in the capital of their own land, put their special claim before you with regard to their inclusion in the Home Rule bill.'[112]

Asquith arrived in Ireland on 18 July. Every effort was made to ensure that he was shielded from witnessing the anger of Irish women, but they were enterprising in their efforts to make their voices heard. The IWFL took a yacht out from Kingstown harbour to meet his steamer as it was nearing shore, endlessly shouting 'Votes for Irishwomen' through a megaphone. Poster parades were organised through the Dublin streets and Greta managed to hire a room in a top storey of a house in Nassau Street, ideal location to hang flags to make their point while the Prime Minister was conveyed through the streets. Frank too was busy making his presence felt. He had spent days attempting to get tickets for the Asquith meeting for Weldon Palmer and himself, husbands of the prisoners. His friend, the actor Dudley Digges, was helping him with a disguise which was put through a rehearsal at Constance Markievicz's house before Frank was let loose. He was confident that his meek little clergyman would succeed. He had, he reassured Hanna, a 'grand set of pads' to protect himself from the type of injuries he had received from Irish Party stewards the last time he had protested.[113] Such kicks were the only ones he feared.

All these ingenious ploys were deliberate efforts to make a non-violent protest. There were to be no smashed windows to inflame public opinion during the visit of the Prime Minister. The suffragists had been warned of the consequences if they did so. During the last few days the nationalist press had orchestrated a 'venomous' campaign against them, calling for such violent reprisals as horsewhipping and ducking in the Liffey for those 'who might venture to disturb Mr Asquith's serenity'[114] An *Evening Telegraph* editorial warned 'Mr Sheehy Skeffington and the little band who share his views' to keep their hands off Mr Asquith. It was a tense period, but none of this was of any concern to the English women of the WSPU, who seized upon Asquith's public visibility in Dublin as an ideal opportunity to continue their campaign against the government. Mary Leigh, Gladys Evans and Jennie Baines (in Ireland under the assumed name of Lizzie Baker), the three women who crossed over to Ireland in pursuit of Asquith, had had years of WSPU service, and in England the levels to which militancy had reached were far more serious. A symbolic hatchet was thrown at the carriage conveying Asquith and Redmond through the Dublin streets (grazing Redmond's ear) and that evening they attempted to burn down the Theatre Royal, the venue for the Asquith meeting the following day.

It was the last thing the Irish militants wanted. They had been careful not to take their protests too far, yet they were to find public hysteria unleashed, as the Hibernians took advantage of the outcry against the WSPU actions. They now had the pretext they wanted. The IWFL members holding a protest rally at Beresford Place were attacked and Kathleen Emerson narrowly missed being thrown into the Liffey. Constance Markievicz and Jennie Wyse Power, who were supporting the IWFL's rally, also suffered from the attentions of the mob. It was said that no woman walking around the Dublin streets was safe from assault. The novelist Katharine Tynan reported that the women were 'hunted like rats in the city'[115] and the Irish press carried reports of the brutality that was witnessed by many. Bessie wrote to her daughter, thanking 'providence' that she was 'safe' in jail.[116]

At the Asquith meeting, the two husbands courageously carried out their planned heckling, despite the heightened atmosphere. Hanna's 'smoked glasses' had been slipped to Frank on the last visit, to help his disguise on entering the building. His defiant cry for women's suffrage was quickly delivered before he was hurriedly thrown out onto the street. He was unhurt, but Weldon Palmer, in the Dress Circle where stewards had congregated in case the women had managed to infiltrate, was badly beaten up by the over-zealous guards. Frank was delighted at his coup: 'Everyone is vastly amused and I'm sure the "machine" is very mad! General testimony that I would have been murdered if I had been at Beresford Place!'[117]Only the most confident spoke at open-air meetings during this time. Gretta Cousins and Helen Laird joined Frank in speaking at Beresford Place, near Liberty Hall.[118] Elizabeth Bloxham, later to be a founder member of Cumann na mBan, volunteered as a speaker in the more challenging arena of Phoenix Park, where her spirited rejoinders – 'The men had no self-respect or self-control or self-restraint in regard to those who differed with them' – struggled to be heard over the shouts of the crowd.[119] Fred Ryan was another who gave support as a speaker, despite his reluctance to support militancy. Frank had a great deal of barracking to contend with at his next appearance in Phoenix Park. Dr J. B., standing at the rear of the crowd, was appalled to hear the remarks being made about his son. It had less effect upon the irrepressible Frank who, at the end of the meeting was escorted to the main road by the police, where he mounted his bicycle and rode off, teasingly 'waving his cap to those who had rushed after him.'[120] Hanna wrote, admiringly, 'that Park meeting seems to have gone splendidly and you were in your element.'[121] Some of those who threw objects were brought to court, leading the *Irish Times* to comment that when Mrs Richards, Miss Bloxham and Mr Sheehy Skeffington spoke in Phoenix Park later in August, the 'peacefulness' of the meeting was a consequence of the recent prosecution of the persecutors.[122]

The IWFL regretted that the Englishwomen had not left protests against Asquith to their Irish counterparts. Gretta immediately issued a statement to disclaim any IWFL participation in their actions. Hanna's rueful comment was that 'even the best-meaning English have blind spots where the Sister Isle is concerned', but she was anxious for their actions not to be repudiated by the IWFL members organising the office in her absence. A solidarity of forces between militants was essential. Frank reassured her that the organisation was not wavering in her absence, 'You needn't be afraid that there is any "repudiation" in the air … the popular feeling is one of rage at the IWFL for refusing to condemn the Englishwomen, a refusal which is regarded as identification with them and endorsement.' He warned her that 'public opinion in Ireland since the hatchet incident would positively welcome forcible feeding.'[123] The damage to the suffrage cause was seized upon with glee by groups like the Ancient Order of Hibernians, who took the opportunity to orchestrate further attacks upon all the women's public meetings. No firm would now rent them a lorry, so at some meetings a chair was the only platform, while out in Phoenix Park a bench could be used. It was this experience which prompted the making of their portable platform. James Connolly, now Transport Union organiser in Belfast, came down to Dublin to show solidarity with the women. His conclusion, after attempting to speak to a howling mob with the aid of police protection, was that it would be wise to drop meetings for a while. Frank of course disagreed, arguing that the 'moral effect' of holding them was important. On that Sunday he, Connolly, Fred

Ryan and Miss Evans were forced to retreat to the nearby zoo, where, said Frank, they 'had tea quietly' until the mob dispersed.[124]

By the time Gladys Evans and Mary Leigh were sentenced to five years each and Jennie Baines to seven months hard labour, some of those in Mountjoy who were nearing the end of their imprisonment decided that they had to mobilise opinion to prevent the women being forcibly fed. The English women were determined to pursue their own path, regardless of any other consideration, and Jessie Kenny, the WSPU organiser sent over from England, admitted in heated discussion at the prison gates, that they had no control over the women's actions. Frank felt hunger striking was the wrong tactic, fearing that forcible feeding would set a terrible precedent in Ireland. The pace of events was forced by the determination of the English women, and the Irish prisoners had to consider their options very carefully. Letters on the subject were smuggled in and out of Mountjoy, a gift to anyone intent on discrediting the movement. Frank was concerned at this possibility – 'I suppose there's no chance of these notes ever falling into anybody's hands? Will your baggage be searched as you leave the prison?' – but it was important that those on the inside understood what was happening.[125] They were unable to communicate with the English prisoners, who were kept isolated in the prison hospital, so their only source of information was clandestine communications; no one could speak on such subjects during visits overheard by prison officials. Hanna and Frank agreed that they could create an impression that the Irish prisoners would hunger strike in sympathy with the English women and that this might be enough to defuse the situation, winning an early release for both groups. The Irish prisoners presented a petition to the Lord Lieutenant on behalf of the English women, citing, on Hanna's suggestion, the precedent of 'Mr David Sheehy, sentenced to hard labour but transferred to the First Division in a vain attempt at persuasion.'[126]

Hanna had written in confidence to Gretta, 'Personal, this is for yourself alone', making it plain that protests on behalf of the WSPU women had to be effective. It was not only a question of sisterly solidarity; this was vital for the future of the Irish movement. The introduction of the principle of force feeding for prisoners would be a disaster: 'Once the horrors of forcible feeding begin here, the precedent is set up for all and the information that the Irish section of prisoners will resist and protest will influence Irish opinion which might otherwise acquiesce in their being practiced on the English.'[127] It was a delicate situation. The IWFL committee was divided over the issue of hunger striking, eventually passing a resolution against its adoption and, to Hanna's huge annoyance, Gretta wrote a long letter to Marguerite Palmer (who of course immediately showed it to Hanna), advising her 'not to be guided by "Mr S." (or Mrs S. I couldn't be sure which) – clear all League and WSPU against us on this! Lovely advice to go through official hands … In the end she said whatever happened it didn't matter, that we were all in the cosmic procession or some such guff with cosmic in it … I am depressed & distracted by the many difficulties outside and inside – but I'll be all right & 'twill soon be over anyhow.'[128]

With the WSPU women refusing food and the threat of forcible feeding hanging over them, Hanna, Marguerite Palmer and the Murphys now decided that they would have to embark on a sympathetic hunger strike to force the authorities to release them all. The other four prisoners had longer time still to serve and, amongst that group, Maud Lloyd and Hilda Webb were vehemently against such a decision. Kathleen Houston and Marjorie Hasler were not in good health, and it was agreed that a longer period of hunger strike in their cases would be unwise.[129] Frank was supportive as ever, hating the idea of his wife suffering, but still convinced that the power of the will was the most potent weapon of all: 'I am quite satisfied that you are right on that, though I naturally shrink from the notion of your being forcibly fed, my darling. If you have to hunger strike, remember that the most important thing is not to fear. Regard the fast as medicinal and beneficial and it will be!'[130] Hanna was combative in her reaction 'it won't be so hard to fast here. As to forcible feeding I'll give them hell if they touch me … I'll resist the process even if they tie me down – but I don't feel 'twill come to that with us Irish.' She was having her period and not feeling too well, 'old complaint plus neuralgia', but her resolve was strong. She had written her article for the *Citizen*, urging Frank to hold on to it because if there was hunger strike it would require 'much re-editing.' Hanna had drawn sketches of the prison layout so that Frank knew exactly where their cells were. White handkerchiefs would be tied outside their cell windows to signal the start of the strike.[131]

A week without food was, Hanna admitted, 'a step in the dark, a plunge into the unknown' and it was the first time that Irish prisoners had undertaken such an act. The Governor, exasperated, reported to the Chairman of the General Prisons Board, 'this appears to be the result of a concerted plan arranged among themselves and fostered and encouraged by the suffragette press.' He recommended that their privileges be withdrawn.[132] Hanna observed with caustic humour that in her experience, no-one in prison ever felt it in their power to grant privileges, but everyone always felt competent enough to withdraw those privileges.[133] The authorities were at a loss as to what to do, dreading the public furore if Irish women were known to be undergoing forcible feeding. Hanna thought the doctors were 'puzzled and scared', and no wonder. They were faced with an entirely new phenomenon. Frank warned her not to expect early release as a result, advising the women that in the present climate of opinion they should be prepared for anything, even forcible feeding, 'you know how the authorities are sensitive to atmosphere.' Relatives were allowed in, to plead with the women not to go through with their threat. Bessie and Aunt Kate visited: 'mother tearful over H.S. of course! I had to take some plums from her to stop a scene but told her not "to repeat offence". Mother is very indiscreet and doesn't understand red tape.' Now the decision had been made, Hanna wanted to start, desperate to do something rather than 'eat grapes' in her cell when other suffragettes were 'on the plank'.[134] Wardresses too tried to persuade them against and each, alone in their cell, was told that the others had given in. None of these tactics met with success. Hanna reassured Frank she no longer felt hunger, adding an emotional description of hearing Mary Leigh's whistle in the jail, a reminder of why they had undertaken this course of action:

> We hear Leigh's whistle (a specially beautiful one) every morning and every night. It goes through the whole prison: an Australia coo-ey call & the Marseillaise. Its specially moving – a wonderful pure clear note like a lark.[135]

Senses sharpened through hunger, they heard footsteps far away, dreading the prospect of doctors and forcible feeding, braced for an ordeal that did not come. Recollections of those days were forever etched in the memory:

> One hears one's heart pound, and it awakes one tossing in the night. Water applied to one's head evaporates as if a sponge were put on an oven; one gets slightly light-headed. The sense of smell becomes acute – I had never smelt tea before. A dying woman craved for a rasher, and it was fried somewhere nearby (perhaps to tempt us?). That was tantalizing. One instinctively skips in books the descriptions of food; I never realised before how much both Scott and Dickens gloat, and how abstemious are the Brontës and Jane Austen.[136]

Hanna was able to sleep; her companions were not. Time passed, and odd scraps of prison news concerning the state of the WSPU women filtered through to them. After five days their sentence came to an end and it was over. On 19 August they were released, together with Jennie Baines. Hanna had lost over a stone, others more. While the Irish women were on hunger strike, the prison authorities delayed the start of forcible feeding of the English women. They could not justify differential treatment, yet they dared not treat the Irish in the same way. The authorities now immediately began to force feed Evans and Leigh.

NOTES

1 Rosemary Cullen-Owens, *Smashing Times: A History of the Irish Women's Suffrage Movement 1889–1922* (Dublin, 1984), p. 47.

2 Rosemary Raughter, 'The suffragettes and the Chief Secretary: An "amusing scene" on Greystones pier, in *Greystones Archeological and Historical Society*, 2018, accessed on-line www.countywicklowheritage.org, Dec. 2018.

3 *Votes for Women*, 11 Nov. 1910.

4 Hanna Sheehy Skeffington, *Reminiscences*, p. 14.

5 *Irish Citizen*, 4 Oct. 1913. The 'G' Division were detectives in the Dublin Metropolitan Police.

6 Ibid., 11 Oct. 1913.

7 Hanna Sheehy Skeffington, *Reminiscences*, p. 16.

8 Ibid., p. 18.

9 I am indebted to Micheál Casey for sharing his biographical researches on the life of Meg Connery.

10 *Votes for Women*, 16 Feb. 1912.

11 Hanna Sheehy Skeffington, *Reminiscences*, p. 17.

12 *Votes for Women*, 7 Oct. 1910; 14 Oct. 1910.

13 Ibid., 14 Oct. 1910.

14 Ibid., 11 Nov. 1910.

15 James and Margaret Cousins, *We Two Together* (Madras, 1950), pp 179–80.

16 *Votes for Women* 25 Nov. 1910; Cousins, *We Two Together*, pp 176–180. The first Holloway prisoners were Margaret Cousins, Kathleen Houston, Eva Stephenson, Hilda Webb, Mrs Garvey-Kelly and Miss Allan.

17 *Votes for Women*, 2 Dec. 1910.

18 Ibid., 16 Dec. 1910; Cousins, *We Two Together*, p. 182.

19 *Votes for Women*, 10 Feb. 1911.

20 Marguerite Bannister Palmer, Chelsea, to Hanna Sheehy Skeffington, 11 Nov. 1911, Sheehy Skeffington MS (hereafter SS MS) 41,180/1.

21 *Irish Citizen*, 25 May 1912.

22 Eugene Sheehy to Hanna Sheehy Skeffington, from *Gaelic American* office, New York, 7 Mar. 1911, SS MS 41,176/18.

23 Cousins, *We Two Together*, p. 202.

24 Therese Moriarty, 'No vote, no information', in *Irish Times*, 3 Apr. 1981.

25 Hanna Sheehy Skeffington, *Reminiscences*, p. 26.

26 *Dublin Street Census 1911*, return for Grosvenor Place, Index 61/86, National Archives, Dublin.

27 *Votes for Women*, 21 Apr. 1911.

28 Hanna Sheehy Skeffington, *Reminiscences*, p. 25.

29 William Murphy, '"Voteless Alas": Suffragist protest and the census of Ireland in 1911', in Diarmuid Ferriter and Susannah Riordan (eds), *Years of Turbulence: The Irish Revolution and its Aftermath* (Dublin, 2015), pp 25–43.

30 Jill Liddington and Elizabeth Crawford, '"Women do not count, neither shall they be counted": Suffrage, citizenship and the battle for the 1911 census', in *History Workshop Journal* 71, 1:1, Mar. 2011, pp 98–127.

31 *Votes for Women*, 14 Apr. 1911.

32 Sylvia Pankhurst, *The Suffragette Movement* (London, 1931, reprinted, 1977), p. 352.

33 *Votes for Women* carried reports from a number of Irish papers regarding the actions of the Irish Party, 31 Mar. 1912.

34 Hanna Sheehy Skeffington, *Reminiscences*, p. 74.

35 Irish Women's Franchise League (hereafter IWFL) to Redmond, n. d., typewritten statement, SS MS 21,639.

36 *Irish Citizen*, 16 Nov. 1912; *Votes for Women*, 31 Mar. 1912.

37 *Votes for Women*, 12 Apr. 1912.

38 Ibid.

39 Maud Lloyd, 'What led to militancy: A brief retrospect', in *Irish Citizen*, 20 July 1912.

40 *Irish Citizen*, 20 July 1912.

41 Cousins, *We Two Together*, p. 168.

42 *Votes for Women*, 12 Apr. 1912.

43 Letter from Hanna Sheehy Skeffington, *Freeman's Journal*, 20 Apr. 1912.

44 'Professor Kettle and the suffrage cause', in *Irish Citizen*, 3 Aug. 1912.

45 Ibid.

46 *Votes for Women*,12 Apr. 1912.

47 Leah Levenson, *With Wooden Sword: A Portrait of Francis Sheehy-Skeffington, Militant Pacifist* (Dublin, 1983), p. 121.

48 Letter from Isabella Richardson to Hanna Sheehy Skeffington, 24 Apr. 1912, SS MS 22,663.

49 *Freeman's Journal*, 23 Apr. 1912.

50 *Freeman's Journal*, 22 Apr. and 28 Apr. 1912.

51 Senia Pašeta, *Irish Nationalist Women 1900–1918* (Cambridge, 2013), p. 83.

52 Tom Kettle to Hanna Sheehy Skeffington, n. d., (1912), SS MS 22,663.

53 *Irish Citizen*, 1 June 1912.

54 Mentioned by Frank Sheehy Skeffington, in *Irish Citizen*, 3 Aug. 1912.

55 J. B. Lyons, *The Enigma of Tom Kettle: Irish Patriot, Essayist, Poet, British Soldier, 1880–1916* (Dublin, 1983), p. 210.

56 *Irish Citizen*, 1 June 1912.

57 *Freeman's Journal*, 24 Apr. 1912.

58 Ibid.

59 Maud Lloyd, 'What led to militancy', 20 July 1912.

60 *Freeman's Journal*, 24 Apr. 1912.

61 Isabella Richardson to Hanna Sheehy Skeffington, 24 Apr. 1912, SS MS 22,663.

62 Ibid., 27 Apr. 1912.

63 Hanna Sheehy Skeffington, *Reminiscences*, p. 76.

64 *Sinn Féin*, 13 Apr. 1912.

65 Cousins, *We Two Together*, pp 204–5.

66 Ibid., p. 230.

67 Kathleen Sheehy to Hanna Sheehy Skeffington, 23 May 1912, SS MS 22,663.

68 *Irish Citizen*, 25 May 1912.

69 Pašeta, *Irish Nationalist Women*, p. 84.

70 Leah Levenson and Jerry Natterstad, *Hanna Sheehy-Skeffington, Irish Feminist* (Syracuse, 1986), p. 36.
71 Hanna Sheehy Skeffington, 'Mass meeting of Irish Women: An impression from the platform', in *Irish Citizen*, 8 June 1912.
72 Ibid.
73 Ibid.
74 *Irish Citizen*, 22 June 1912.
75 Hanna Sheehy Skeffington, *Reminiscences*, p. 74.
76 *Votes for Women*, 21 June 1912.
77 Hanna Sheehy Skeffington, 'The women's movement – Ireland', in *Irish Review*, July 1912, pp 225–7.
78 *Daily Express*, 21 June 1912.
79 Marguerite Palmer, 'Mountjoy jottings', in *Irish Citizen*, 7 Sept. 1912.
80 Information on the Cadiz sisters courtesy of Richard Collins, St John's House, a cousin of the Cadiz sisters. Based on an article by Frank McNally published in the *Irish Times* in 2008.
81 *Daily Express*, 21 June 1912.
82 *Irish Citizen*, 29 June 1912.
83 Details of their petitions and treatment in prison contained in General Prisons Board Suffragette Box 2, National Archives, Dublin.
84 *Irish Citizen*, 7 Sept. 1912.
85 Hanna Sheehy Skeffington, 'In Mountjoy: My prison experiences', in *Irish Independent*, 20 Aug. 1912.
86 *Irish Citizen*, 7 Sept. 1912.
87 Hanna Sheehy Skeffington, *Reminiscences*, p. 76.
88 Ibid., p. 21.
89 Gretta Cousins to Francis Sheehy Skeffington, 15 June 1912, SS MS 21,623.
90 Vice-Chairman, General Prisons Board to Chief Secretary's Office, 27 June 1912, Suffragette Box 2, National Archives, Dublin.
91 Hanna Sheehy Skeffington, *Reminiscences*, p. 75.
92 Francis Sheehy Skeffington to Hanna Sheehy Skeffington, 7 July 1912. A series of 21 letters of varying length written by Frank to Hanna while she was in jail, folded into tiny squares and stored in a long manila envelope, was discovered by Andrée Sheehy Skeffington and shown to me while I was writing the first edition of this biography.
93 Hanna Sheehy Skeffington, *Reminiscences*, p. 75.
94 Included in Rosemary Cullen-Owens, *Did Your Granny Have A Hammer?* (Dublin, 1985).
95 Hanna Sheehy Skeffington, *Reminiscences*, p. 76.
96 Ibid.
97 Frank Skeffington to Hanna Sheehy (hereafter Frank to Hanna), 19 July 1912, courtesy of Andrée Sheehy Skeffington.
98 *Irish Citizen*, 6 July 1912.
99 Frank to Hanna, 27 June 1912, courtesy of Andrée Sheehy Skeffington.
100 Frank to Hanna, 27 June 1912; 7 July 1912.
101 Hanna Sheehy Skeffington, *Reminiscences*, p. 75.

102 Hanna Sheehy Skeffington to Gretta Cousins, 27 July 1912, courtesy of Andrée Sheehy Skeffington.
103 Hanna Sheehy Skeffington, 'In Mountjoy: My prison experiences', in Margaret Ward *Hanna Sheehy Skeffington: Suffragette and Sinn Feiner*, p.359.
104 Frank to Hanna, 7 July 1912, courtesy of Andrée Sheehy Skeffington.
105 *Irish Citizen*, 13 July 1912.
106 Ibid., 6 July 1912.
107 Ellen Duncan to Hanna Sheehy Skeffington, 17 June 1912, SS MS 22,663.
108 Hanna Sheehy Skeffington, *Reminiscences*, p. 75.
109 Isa Lawlor to Hanna Sheehy Skeffington, 16 June 1912, SS MS 22,663.
110 Hanna Sheehy to Frank Skeffington (hereafter Hanna to Frank), 25 July 1912, SS MS 40,466/5. In the close 'female world of homosocial networks' that developed in the Victorian and Edwardian women's movement, women who deliberately defined themselves as 'spinsters' became a significant political force. Carroll Smith-Rosenberg, 'The female world of love and ritual: Relations between women in nineteenth-century America', in *Signs*, 1:1, autumn 1975, pp 1–29. The Irish novelist and suffragist Edith Somerville, whose romantic friendship with Violet Martin ended only with her death, had observed that there was a 'profound friendship' among women 'who live by their brains'. Lillian Faderman, *Surpassing the Love of Men*, (London, 1980), p. 205. Such expressions of female love – emotional, possibly physical also – could be described as lesbian, but many historians urge caution regarding the complexities of defining lesbianism in different historical contexts. The experience could be romantic and passionate; it did not have to be explicitly sexual. In Margaret Jackson's discussion, if one includes sexual and political considerations, then lesbians can be defined as women 'who make their love for women central to their existence and refuse to organise their lives around men as patriarchy demands.' Margaret Jackson, *The Real Facts of Life: Feminism and the Politics of Sexuality c1850–1940* (London, 1994), p. 87.
111 Sonja Tiernan, *Eva Gore-Booth: An Image of Such Politics* (Manchester, 2012), p. 228.
112 *Irish Citizen*, 15 June 1912.
113 Frank to Hanna, 14 July 1912, courtesy of Andrée Sheehy Skeffington.
114 *Irish Citizen*, 4 Jan. 1913.
115 Cullen-Owens, *Smashing Times*, p. 60.
116 Hanna Sheehy Skeffington, *Reminiscences*, pp 22–3.
117 Frank to Hanna, n. d., courtesy of Andrée Sheehy Skeffington.
118 Frank to Hanna, 27 July 1912, courtesy of Andrée Sheehy Skeffington.
119 *Irish Times*, 12 Aug. 1912.
120 *Cork Free Press*, 5 Aug. 1912.
121 Hanna to Frank, 25 July 1912, SS MS 40,466/5.
122 *Irish Times*, 24 Aug. 1912.
123 Frank to Hanna, n. d., courtesy of Andrée Sheehy Skeffington.
124 Frank to Hanna, 28 July 1912, courtesy of Andrée Sheehy Skeffington.
125 Ibid., 23 July 1912.
126 Details in General Prisons Board Suffragette Box 1, National Archives, Dublin.
127 Hanna Sheehy Skeffington to Gretta Cousins, 27 July 1912, courtesy of Andrée Sheehy Skeffington.

128 Hanna to Frank, 11 Aug. 1912, SS MS 40,466/5.
129 William Murphy, *Political Imprisonment and The Irish, 1912–1921* (Oxford, 1914), pp 16–20.
130 Frank to Hanna, n. d., courtesy of Andrée Sheehy Skeffington
131 Hanna to Frank, 25 July 1912, SS MS 40,466/5.
132 Major Owen-Lewis, Governor of Mountjoy to Chair of General Prisons Board, 15 Aug. 1912, Suffragette Box 1, National Archives, Dublin.
133 Hanna Sheehy Skeffington, 'In Mountjoy: My prison experiences' in Margaret Ward *Hanna Sheehy Skeffington: Suffragette and Sinn Feiner*, p.360.
134 Hanna to Frank, 10 Aug. 1912, SS MS 40,466/5.
135 Ibid., 11 Aug. 1912.
136 Hanna Sheehy Skeffington, *Reminiscences*, p. 77.

SIX

OUTLAWS, 1912–14

Uncle Eugene and Frank went together to greet Hanna on her release from Mountjoy. A photo of the event reveals a drawn face, eyes not directly confronting the camera, unlike the stalwart figure of the top-hatted Eugene and the spritely presence of Frank. She was weak but wasted little time in recuperation. The problem of the Murphys made her hesitate about agreeing to a formal reception of welcome – she was worried what they might blurt out – but it was finally agreed that the League would hold a party that Saturday. Attendance was good enough to ensure the sale of 80 copies of the *Irish Citizen*.[1] An executive meeting of the organisation dealt with the sisters' refusal to accept League policy by expelling them. Hanna had argued that it was 'for the sake of the future as they breed such mischief' while Marguerite Palmer threatened to resign if the women were allowed to remain as members.[2] The sisters refused to accept expulsion and began a tiresome and unprecedented process of appealing to the law courts. League business continued, although prominent members like Kathleen Emerson reported that detectives were again watching her house.[3]

Frank made arrangements for their summer holiday to be spent in Malahide, the attractive little sea-side resort to the north of Dublin where they had first gone in the summer following Owen's birth. He rented rooms for August and the first week of September. He and Owen had been there for a while already (the small boy proved hard to amuse in the wet Dublin summer and had caught a cold), his father hoping fervently for fine days to come. Frank struggled to meet the exacting demands of the landlady of their boarding house, worrying how he was to transport cutlery and linen as well as all their clothes and other luggage and finding little sympathy from Hanna. Not only did she not appreciate her husband's labours, she decided that she wanted to go somewhere else on her release. In a wet summer, the one possible dry spot would be the far south east. Frank had to be conciliatory:

> Dearest – sorry you're not satisfied about Malahide. I thought – and still think – it was the best thing to do. You see, you had warned me not to be too late about engaging rooms, and indeed as regards August only just in time to secure Mrs Hall's rooms. As regards September, I think it will be much better for you to be at Malahide and come into your class three times a week than any other holiday. Wexford would be no good at all … dearie, I hope you'll make up your mind to accept the position and to enjoy yourself at Malahide during the beautiful September which is going to wind up this wet summer.[4]

Owen had been equally uncooperative at his first sight of the resort, declaring 'this isn't Malahide, there's no sea' and threatening to walk home. Feverish sandcastle building by his father helped to change his mind. His imprisoned mother had little alternative either. All three eventually managed, as a family, to have some quiet time together in Malahide. But not for too long.

Three weeks after her release, Hanna was one of the speakers at the last of the 1912 season of open-air meetings in the Phoenix Park. The organised groups of disrupters who had been such a problem earlier in the summer, having been dealt with in the law courts, had lost interest in the sport of 'suff baiting', so meetings had resumed their usual format. They were pleased to be able to sell 100 copies of the *Citizen* to the crowds milling around the platform. Hanna spoke of the unfair press reporting of the suffragists and of the 'government funk' in releasing Leigh and Evans, both of whom had been discharged 'on licence' by an administration reluctant to continue the forcible feeding ordeal.[5] She and Marguerite were also the first speakers at the IWFL 'At Home' later in the week, launching their winter programme. Gretta presided as they spoke of their prison experiences. The publicity had attracted recruits to the ranks and a very welcome 12 new members were enrolled at the meeting.[6]

Although it was now the beginning of the school year, Hanna had no reason to commute from Malahide to the classroom, as Frank had planned. Waiting for her on her release had been a letter of dismissal from Rathmines College of Commerce, where she had been teaching part-time for the past three years. The letter referred blandly to a falling off in numbers in the weeks before the end of the summer term as justification for not re-employing her. The real reason for their eagerness to get rid of this notable ex-convict was transparent to all, and she fought hard to ensure that everyone was aware of this attempt to silence and censor those who chose the militant path. In a lengthy account of her grievances she itemised the irregular way in which she had been treated by the college authorities and gave a convincing rebuttal of the aspersions cast on her teaching abilities: the dismissal notice had been sent to her only one week before the beginning of term when it was impossible to obtain another position; the drop in attendance had taken place in all institutions providing evening classes attended on a voluntary basis; the number of her students obtaining certificates of merit was greater than it had been the previous year; the inspector's report indicated increased efficiency since she had been teaching and for three years she had made every effort to maintain a high teaching standard, keeping herself abreast of the latest teaching methods by taking special courses abroad at her own expense.[7] Many who spoke on her behalf were all the more credible as supporters because of their public rejection of militancy. Mary Hayden was one who came to her defence, while making it plain that her testimony did not imply approval of window breaking. She was protesting against a 'flagrant piece of injustice' and was surprised to note that 'in this country where sympathy has always been accorded to the men who suffer for their political principles and political action … a woman who has shown a courage equal to theirs should be deprived of her means of livelihood without a voice being raised in her defence.'[8] Catherine Mahon, President of the Irish National Teachers' Organisation, also wrote on her behalf, although she too preferred the non-militant approach to women's suffrage.[9] The *Irish Citizen* and Hanna's friends and colleagues rallied round to launch a vigorous campaign in support of the right to free speech. It became another cause in the fight for women's right to citizenship. By November it had been announced that a committee was gathering signatures to the following protest:

> In the interests of education and to protect the security of tenure of teachers and their rights as citizens, protest against the summary dismissal, without sufficient reason, of Mrs Sheehy Skeffington from her post in the Rathmines School of Commerce.[10]

Mary Hayden, Maud Joynt, Dr Katherine Maguire (who had attended Marguerite Palmer in Mountjoy), Kathleen Shannon, Kathë Oldham, Jennie Wyse Power and Helen Laird were the committee members. Helen Laird, the committee's secretary, was particularly active on the issue. By January 1913 the protest had been endorsed by practically everyone connected with the teaching profession in Limerick (no doubt some of those cousins had come up trumps this time) and, of course, all the IWFL members and husbands had rallied to their friend. Many of the nationalists who signed, Thomas MacDonagh, for example, were themselves teachers as well as personal friends. Those lists, totalling 160 names, provide much insight for a biographer attempting to discover who were the friends of her subject. Amongst the prominent, who included the Lord Mayor of Dublin, was Maud Gonne, who admired Hanna's defiance of the law. Muriel Gifford, married to Thomas MacDonagh and her sister Sydney (known in nationalist circles as the journalist 'John Brennan'), who was a member of Inghinidhe na hÉireann, also signed. John Brennan had also spoken on the subject of 'Inconsistencies in Irish education' at an IWFL meeting the previous year. A 'Catherine Cruise O'Brien' was there, which was either a misprint for Kathleen or an attempt to disguise the close relationship that existed between signator and subject. And Bessie McCoy also put her name to the list, surely the first time that Hanna's mother had used her maiden name since her marriage?[11] But no David Sheehy was to be found, hidden or disguised. Perhaps he was stoutly maintaining that his headstrong eldest daughter had brought it all upon herself by her hot-headedness.

This victimisation was referred to many times in the pages of the *Irish Citizen*. WSPU member Mabel Small, jailed in Belfast in March 1914, kept her teaching post because she had given an undertaking to the Belfast Technical Committee that any militancy would take place during the holiday period. She resumed teaching immediately on release, having engaged a substitute for the only class she had been unable to attend. The *Citizen* commented that Mrs Sheehy Skeffington had been willing to give a similar undertaking and her protest had occurred entirely during the summer vacation. The lesson was that 'Belfast has set Rathmines a much-needed example on liberty of conscience'. Belfast was unique in this liberalism. Another Dublin teacher, Georgina Manning, was forced by her school governors to resign from the school she taught in after daubing a statue of John Redmond with green paint. This was despite the fact she had paid her fine rather than go to jail as her sister had died while she was waiting for her case to go to court.[12]

Rathmines College lost a conscientious and innovative teacher. A warm-hearted and humorous woman, who enjoyed the company of young people, who was a fluent French and German speaker and who had put a great deal of thought into ensuring that her classes were interesting, and her pupils motivated. Frank and Hanna lost an income they could not afford to lose, but the women's movement in Ireland was rendered much stronger now that one of its most important influences was free to devote her time to the cause. Catherine Mahon had ended her letter with the hope that 'something a thousand times better may open up for her'. Apart from the fact that the 'something' was unpaid, that hope became reality. From now on, Hanna's name appears constantly, not only at meetings and demonstrations, but also as the author of book reviews and articles for the *Citizen*. Her contribution is not always obvious, as the *Citizen* liked to give the impression of a vast network of correspondents; sometimes the initials 'HS' might be used, sometimes her old name of 'Joan' appears, while at other times, when wanting her report attributed, she used the official 'HSS'. But whatever the subject, the authorship was unmistakable. A book review on the Penal Reform League's report on *Prostitution: Its Nature and Cure* is characteristic in its unmoralistic recounting of the main points: the circumstances forcing women into prostitution; the need for living wage levels so that women would not need to earn their living by selling themselves; measures that could help women who were prostitutes, such as special woman-only courts and meaningful rehabilitation. Her tone throughout was practical, modern and woman-centred.[13] Her abiding love of the theatre and the thrill of first nights is also evident in reviews for the *Irish Review* (edited until July 1913 by Padraic Colum and then by James Plunkett and Thomas MacDonagh) and, as 'Joan', in frequent reviews for the *Citizen*.

Freed, at least for the foreseeable future, from the constraints imposed by employment as a teacher, she was able to give vent to some of her feelings regarding the conditions suffered by teachers. In an article for the *Irish Review* she analysed Birrell's proposals for improving the position of secondary teachers. Birrell's reforms were 'revolutionary in character' because for the first time some standards would be laid down for the education provided by the Catholic church. She, however, wanted reform to go much further. Gold medallists like herself had suffered the ignominy of having 'to accept salaries a competent cook would have scorned' because of the monopoly of the convents. Nuns needed no training, other than a vocation for the religious life, and she wanted that brought to an end. Tests for religious teachers and an employment register for teachers were essential measures. Equal pay for women teachers, who were still receiving half the rate of their male colleagues and pension rights for all, were other vital issues. She concluded that Birrell's scheme was 'the first brave attempt to ameliorate the condition of the most harassed and exploited class in the country – the secondary teacher.'[14] Other efforts to improve the position of women within education were also continuing. Agnes O'Farrelly wrote to ask for her and Frank's support when standing for election to the UCD governing body. Mary Hayden was also going forward but Agnes was not hopeful as there was 'a semi-official ticket' with six men standing. On this issue, even Agnes was militant: 'If there is any other woman standing who has a fair chance of getting in I would gladly let her take my place – an independent woman, not one who can be worked by any clique.'[15]

It was a good time to be free to devote oneself to the cause of women's emancipation. Hopes that women would get the vote in Home Rule Ireland were not entirely dead, at least not in the minds of the most determined of the suffragists. Frank was now urging the Irish Party to admit that, tactically speaking, it had had to vote against the enfranchisement of English women, but this did not mean that they were against the vote being given to Irish women. They could still vote for an amendment to the Home Rule bill which would not antagonise Asquith, jeopardise Home Rule or do anything objectionable. It would please nationalist women and could possibly persuade unionist women that Home Rule would not be too intolerable if it meant that women would have a say. The IWFL resumed lobbying the politicians, sending over Helen Laird to persuade Irish MPs to vote in favour of Philip Snowden's forthcoming amendment to Clause 9 of the Home Rule bill, which called for the local government register to be the basis for elections to the Home Rule parliament. Not all women would be enfranchised by this, but 100,000 had the necessary property qualifications, many of them widows managing their own farms.[16] There was a brief attempt, instigated by British feminist Millicent Fawcett of the non-militant National Union of Women Suffrage Societies (and a supporter of the unionist cause), to have Snowden's amendment dropped if Redmond would promise to use his influence to have a women's amendment attached to the Manhood Suffrage bill. Knowing only too well the extent of Redmond's hostility to women's suffrage, Hanna was appalled, declaring 'Any deal with these notorious promise-breakers is unthinkable.'[17] All 16 suffrage groups in Ireland did their utmost to demonstrate the strength of feeling concerning the issue, although nobody had any illusions about the prospects of an amendment without government backing getting through. Helen Laird, disillusioned after her experience in London, warned that the party whips would be put on Irish MPs, who would use that as an excuse for their failure to show support. Nevertheless, the size of the majority against was a blow. When the vote on the Snowden amendment was taken on 5 November 1912, only 141 voted in its favour. Eleven Irish MPs did vote for it – but 72 voted against. Irish women would be disenfranchised when the new state came into being and would remain so for at least three years because another clause in the Home Rule bill stipulated that constitutional changes could not be made in the first three years of the state's existence.

Even if Irish politicians had every good intention of rectifying this injustice after independence – a forlorn hope – their hands were tied. They would be 'free' to make what they would of their new-found independence, but without any contribution from the female half of the population.

The WSPU lost no time in making their response in London. Windows were smashed in exclusive Bond Street. The papers commented that the lack of any similar militancy in Ireland must mean that Irish women felt less strongly on the question. It was an incitement to violence. Belfast women smashed windows in the Donegall Place Post office, attacked letter boxes and cut telegraph wires. The IWFL, on receiving a telegrammed copy of those comments, decided they too had to make a protest.[18] Meg Connery and Kathleen Emerson went off to break a token amount of windows in the Custom House. They were arrested, refused bail and removed to the squalor of the Bridewell, a fate they fought hard to resist. Their ill-treatment reinforced their commitment to the militant path more effectively than the adverse vote had done. Unwell after an uncomfortable night, Kathleen Emerson was able to say only a few words in court in her defence. Meg was different, with spirit enough to hector the judge with a long and defiant lecture. Like Hanna, she saw the demand for the suffrage in much wider terms than simply admitting middle-class women to the political realm. When she thought of the 'White Slave Traffic and the sweated women of Belfast and Dublin':

> it nerved her to break every window in Dublin, including his worships. She did not break the law because she liked it, but because she had been driven to adopt these methods to draw public attention to the intolerable grievances under which women had to live. She was an outlaw; she was not a person.[19]

Their fines were paid anonymously, so they avoided prison on that occasion.

Kathleen Emerson had said that the vote on the Snowden amendment was a 'deliberate insult' to the women of Ireland. The Irish Party had again voted to get rid of any obstacle that might hold up the progress of the Home Rule bill. In reaction, the militants of the IWFL felt themselves compelled to protest at every opportunity. Hanna made no effort to moderate her language. The House of Commons was 'a den of thieves' and they had this time 'overreached themselves in their chicanery towards the women's cause'.[20] If the law would not recognise them as people they were indeed 'outlaws'. Their contempt for parliamentarians was outspoken. A bitterly sarcastic article on the front page of one edition of the *Citizen*, entitled 'Masculine Militancy', described an unruly meeting at Wrexham, addressed by David Sheehy, who 'tried to play the Redmond trick of double-shuffle to an English audience'.

The article made the point that the male interrupters were not indecently assaulted, did not have their hair pulled from their head and were not kicked or thrown out, all of which was now commonplace treatment for women hecklers: 'it may be that such methods are reserved for the women of England by those gentlemen of England whose virtuous souls are aggrieved at a political partisan's ancient clap-trap'.[21] It was an odd story to use for the front page, but it may have been the only vehicle through which Hanna could ridicule a father who, in 1901, had 'said some tough things about England' but who, eleven years later, was not prepared to stand up for the cause his daughter had gone to prison for. Father and daughter were now so far apart that he could be mocked for peddling 'ancient clap-trap'.

Everything in the patriarchal state reinforced her conviction that women's inferior status was entrenched so deeply within the collective consciousness that feminists needed to make their protests heard at every conceivable opportunity. The *Freeman's Journal* published a list of graduates nominated for election to the governing body of University College Dublin, adding in a footnote: 'It may be necessary to explain that "Johanna M. Sheehy", which appears on the graduate's register, is the maiden name of Mrs Sheehy Skeffington.' The *Citizen* carried an enraged small piece on this 'stupid and insulting piece of red-tapeism on the part of the university authorities'. Any male graduate was free to change his name to whatever he wished, by simply informing the university, but they refused to change a married woman's name unless she produced her marriage certificate. As Hanna and like-minded women refused to submit to different conditions from their male counterparts they had the additional annoyance of seeing their names remain in their original form on the register.

Life was not all insult and rage. Sometimes, small occasions for celebration would occur. Feminists welcomed the 'wind of feminism' blowing through newspaper birth notices, rejecting the standard format of 'The wife of John Brown, of a son' (which, as the *Citizen* rightly remarked, read like 'a disavowal of paternity') in favour of the 'feminist form': 'to Mr and Mrs Brown, a son'. The newspapers, as an everyday form of communication, were responsive to the undoubted modernising forces which were slowly forcing the pace of change. Irish feminists were not that numerous, but in terms of the total population they existed in similar proportions to their British counterparts. These small changes reflected that influence.

Frank, as far back as 1907, had commended the British militants for their courage. Hanna had been the first to urge Irish women to adopt the weapon of militancy. In the public mind, they were associated with support for window smashing rather than for peaceful action. Not until the outbreak of war would the Sheehy Skeffington name be synonymous with pacifism but there was another year of frenzied activism before then. By 1913 Irish women had succeeded in persuading a significant section of public opinion and local authorities of the justice of their cause, yet the politicians remained unmoved. What else could they do? In Britain, a new stage of militancy had been reached, whereby the public was now to be inconvenienced. Instead of breaking government glass, suffragists concentrated on interfering with government services – the post-office and the telephone – through cutting wires and putting chemical substances in the letter boxes. The new stage of 'militant militancy' was applauded by Hanna. Society was 'rotten at the core' because a 'corrupt bureaucracy' denied the rights of half the community. She therefore had no qualms about that society being forced to change. The lessons of history, from Catholic Emancipation to the Reform Act, demonstrated that politicians would yield only under pressure. For her at least, there would be no more of the 'resolution-passing, petition-presenting, lobbying and wire-pulling' that the 'constitutionals' insisted upon. She wanted militant militancy. The 'reasonable militancy' used up to now was ineffective because the public dismissed it as mere play:

> Desperate diseases need desperate remedies and if the vote is wrested from Government by methods of terrorism when five and forty years of sweet and quiet reason produced only seven talked-out or tricked-out suffrage bills, why, who can say it wasn't worth a mutilated letter, a cut wire, a Premier's racked nerves?[22]

Her response to protests that letter-box militancy 'savours of anarchy and the final dissolution of society' was to agree. It was. And it was what she wanted. Her commitment to the militant path was total. It led old friends like Fred Ryan (who had expressed his reservations in print) to enquire anxiously after Hanna's release from prison: 'Delighted Hanna is alright again. Give her my very kind regards. I hope she is not on the warpath for my blood because of what I said in the *Irish Review* article.'[23]

Family life must have been a hectic affair. Mindful of Owen's need for companionship, Hanna and Frank decided to enrol him at Rathgar Kindergarten, a few minutes' walk from home. He started there in January 1913, aged three and a half, staying for mornings only. It was a Quaker nursery, a pioneer of Froebel education in Ireland, founded by Gertrude Webb, and now run by a Miss Isabella Tuckey. The Webbs were political colleagues and close friends. Childless themselves, their affection for Owen was strong and long-lasting. The experience of warmth from many of his parents' friends, while never substituting for the love of two parents, would be an important element in Owen's emotional life in the times to come. Hanna described her son at this stage as 'easy wounded. Hates being set right in any point and always tries to save his face somehow.'[24] They wanted a boy who could play with his peers and not be pushed too early into academic pursuits. Miss Tuckey was warned by Frank that he would take the child away if he showed signs of learning anything. She understood.[25] He did of course learn as he grew, with his report for the summer of 1916 giving marks achieved in reading, spelling, natural science, arithmetic, art and a number of other subjects. His conduct was 'very good' and he was 5th in class.[26]

In the early weeks of 1913 Hanna was particularly busy organising support for a new batch of IWFL prisoners. On 28 January, Meg, together with Gretta Cousins and Barbara Hoskins (a relatively new member of the League who had just returned with Gretta from one of her 'tours of the west'), were given one-month sentences for window breaking. This time they were dispatched not to Mountjoy but to Tullamore Jail, 60 miles from Dublin. Unlike the previous groups of prisoners, they were not given first-class status. The authorities obviously hoped to isolate the prisoners from the support they could command in Dublin, and it was feared that a new policy on the treatment of Irish suffrage prisoners was being implemented. It was vital that the IWFL fought as hard as they could on the women's behalf. Emmeline Pethick-Lawrence and the Labour MP George Lansbury had addressed a large public meeting in Dublin on the day the women had smashed the windows of Dublin Castle yard. Hanna had chaired that meeting and declared in her speech: 'The time had come when the only place for a self-respecting woman was the prison.' She also informed the audience that the prisoners' message to them was: 'they would resist to the death any attempt to treat them as other than political prisoners … if full political rights were not conceded by Saturday, they would hunger strike.'[27] Hanna and Kathleen Emerson then travelled down to Tullamore. It was announced that the IWFL would keep a representative in the town for as long as the prisoners were there. Three days later, Hanna was replaced by Eva Wilkins (formerly Eva Stephenson, now married to Maurice Wilkins), so that she could speak at a private IWFL reception being held in honour of Emmeline Pethick-Lawrence.

It was a busy few weeks. The three Tullamore prisoners, as announced, began their hunger strike on Sunday 2 February. They were joined by Mabel Purser, grand-daughter of the famous Young Irelander William Smith O'Brien who, in 1848, had fought in an unsuccessful revolt against the British. Mabel made a point of selling her copies of the *Citizen* from a chosen pitch beside the statue of her famous ancestor. She was 39, married to a doctor and with a young daughter. Her window smashing action had been a solo action. She too hunger-struck.

The IWFL annual general meeting was held on 4 February but, in the circumstances, it was little more than a token event. Members were balloted on the voting for the new committee and the names elected later published in rank order of votes cast. Hanna topped the list, followed by Gretta Cousins, Marguerite Palmer, Helen Laird and Meg Connery. She was the 'chairman' of the IWFL, a position she was to retain for as long as the organisation existed.[28]

On 5 February, Tullamore Urban District Council unanimously passed a resolution demanding full political prisoner treatment for the prisoners. That weekend, Hanna was back in the town and on the Saturday morning experimented with a megaphone from a field outside the prison, shouting messages to her imprisoned colleagues. Barbara Hoskins was released that afternoon, the authorities frightened by her collapse from the effects of hunger strike on a weak heart. She delighted the women outside by letting them know that the megaphone had managed to penetrate the fortress-like jail.[29] The IWFL were now in a strong position to mobilise public concern for the women's well-being. The next day, Hanna and a new committee member, a Mrs Evans, were the speakers at an 'enthusiastic and crowded meeting', from which apparently hundreds had to be turned away. It was presided over by Mr Lumley, chair of Tullamore Urban District Council. The small town was having more excitement than it had had since the townspeople had escorted the heroines of the Ladies' Land League to prison. The move from Mountjoy had not had the desired effect and later that day the prison authorities gave in, promising full political status if the women gave up their hunger strike. It was to take another period of petitioning on the part of the League before all the privileges of first-class prisoners were granted, but they were euphoric at their victory. At least one thousand signatures in support of the women had been gathered, a great boost to the cause, and they had won without the women being forcibly fed.[30]

The experience of dealing with the authorities hardened Hanna's attitudes towards officialdom. She and Mrs Evans had wanted to take charge of Barbara Hoskins on her release, only to be confronted with a wardress who insisted that her orders were to bring the woman to a friend's house in Dublin. Hanna wrote a letter concerning this incident which was published widely: 'The idiocy of this proceeding becomes manifest when I add that the friend to whose house she was brought was Mrs Evans, who was actually in Tullamore for the purpose of meeting her ... If the authorities adopt the same barbarous method of dealing with the other prisoners, they will hear more of it, both in Parliament and elsewhere.' As far as she was concerned, it was more than simply bureaucratic ineptitude, it was a deliberate attempt to 'torture prisoners'.[31] She managed to telegram Frank so that when Barbara Hoskins arrived in Dublin, her condition of total collapse confirmed by the correspondents of various papers, she was met by a trio of Frank, Meg Connery's husband Con, and Aine de Power, the *Citizen's* Irish-language contributor, (better known in nationalist circles as Nancy Wyse Power, daughter of Jennie). Hanna's confidence that the prison authorities would be censured in parliament was misplaced.

When Meg Connery and Gretta Cousins were released at the end of their sentence, they saw the Sheehy Skeffingtons standing at the head of the crowd at the Kingsbridge terminus. The irrepressible Meg waved the umbrella which James Cousins had obligingly wrapped with strips of lead, a most effective weapon for window smashing.[32] A great deal of newspaper attention had been given to the women's prison struggles, all of which helped to maintain a momentum of interest for their return to Dublin. A large attendance was reported for their reception of welcome at the IWFL offices and a surprisingly sympathetic account was written up by the reporter for the *Freeman's Journal*, even though the paper represented the views of the Irish Party. There was a 'very pleasant social character' during the first hour, when tea was served: 'Prominent suffragists proved themselves gracious and admirable hostesses and dispensed their hospitality lavishly.' There was nothing warlike in the atmosphere – even the two detectives present were offered tea, which they uncomfortably refused. As the reporter joked, maybe they wanted something stronger.[33] It is rare to find mainstream journalism describing a scene in this way, providing an impression of suffrage militants which attempted to go beyond the usual stereotype.

Another pleasant social occasion for suffrage supporters occurred a couple of weeks later. It was not a public event, but it was reported widely in the nationalist and suffragist press. Friends of Hanna had formed themselves into a small committee to make some presentation to her in recognition of the shameful way she had been treated by the college authorities in Rathmines. The original plan had been to organise a public appeal for a testimonial which would have helped the seriously depleted finances of the Sheehy Skeffington household. Hanna was desperately embarrassed at the prospect and pleaded that they should do no such thing. It was agreed that she would accept a small presentation – from her friends only – to be made at her home rather than at any more formal venue. Kathleen Shannon, Helen Laird, Cissie Cahalan and Gretta Cousins were all part of the committee and each paid warm tribute to the woman with whom they had been associated for the past few years, but Agnes O'Farrelly and Jennie Wyse Power were also prominent. They were all, to a greater or lesser extent, drawn from the nationalist side of the political spectrum. Cissie Cahalan (known simply as 'Cahalan' to her friends), was a shop worker in Arnott's, the large department store. Her involvement in the Irish Drapery Assistants' Association had led her to the cause of women's suffrage.

None of the non-militant suffragists were there. Their disapproval of Hanna's window smashing made it morally impossible to join those gathered in condemnation of the Rathmines action. And, possibly, Hanna had made it very plain to the committee exactly who she considered to be her friends at this time. It was appropriate that the oldest of Ireland's nationalist-feminists, Jennie Wyse Power, should make the presentation of the silver tea service and cup, of Irish design and manufacture. She and Hanna disagreed on some things, but not on the fundamental issue of campaigning in their different ways for the emancipation of women in an Ireland free of the British presence. Jennie declared that the tribute was a small indication of the esteem in which Hanna was held, and the admiration felt for her. Agnes O'Farrelly described herself as one of Hanna's oldest friends. As an educationalist, she felt the treatment of Hanna to be as unjust as her suffrage friends did. All spoke of the distinctive qualities possessed by this fearless campaigner, whom they were proud to claim as a friend and colleague. Gretta summed up the general feeling: 'They were all proud of her and felt that Ireland was the richer because such a woman was in it.' Hanna's emotions were evident in her response. She valued her presentation most especially because it was the gift of personal friends who had been associated with her in suffrage work and in educational and other fields. But she was overwhelmed and embarrassed by the kind things that had been said about her and could not adequately express her thankfulness to all her friends. The fighting spirit was much in evidence as she concluded by stating firmly that this kindness 'would hearten her to continued endeavour, and their gift would remain, she hoped, in more peaceful times, as a reminder of her first visit to Mountjoy and its sequel'.[34] The hint that the Mountjoy sojourn might only be the first of many was characteristic. The fight was continuing.

The defeat of the Snowden amendment and the defeat of all the Conciliation bills sponsored by individual MPs had led the suffrage movement in both Britain and Ireland to take stock. On each of the seven occasions in which suffrage bills had passed a second reading they were unable to go any further because the government had not allocated space in the parliamentary timetable. It had become obvious that only a government measure could succeed in enfranchising women and the working class. That much was plain, and a symposium in Ireland to discuss the question led to militants and non-militants agreeing to call for a government bill. However, the IWFL militants wanted much more. Hanna argued that there should be a definite anti-government policy until the government agreed to put forward such a bill. If the government refused, then the suffrage movement should 'weaken and lower its prestige … to make its continued existence impossible.' The fact that she also argued diplomatically that if the government did decide to back female suffrage then every suffragist would support the government and work to keep it in power until its pledge was redeemed was not enough to convince those who shrank from breaking the law.

The gap between the two groups widened but the militants' argument was strengthened in May, when 55 Irish Party MPs (including David Sheehy) voted against the Dickinson bill which had proposed giving the vote to women over 25 years of age. Hanna hadn't liked the age discrepancy between men and women that this would have opened up but felt 'twould serve'.[35] Even that was too much for some: only seven Irish MPs had supported Dickinson. An immediate response came from the IWFL. On 16 May, Marguerite Palmer, Annie Walsh and Dora Ryan smashed the glass in the fanlight of the United Irish League. They were given six-month sentences and dispatched to Tullamore, where they eventually went on hunger strike because they were not given first-class status. The battle on their behalf was complicated by the introduction of a new law, the Prisoners' (Temporary Discharge for Ill-Health) Act, introduced in March and immediately dubbed the 'Cat and Mouse Act', whereby hunger striking prisoners could be released but rearrested once they had recovered their strength. This was supposed to do away with the need for forcible feeding, which had proved to be such a liability for the government.[36]

The hunger strike began on Friday, 13 June. In an interview in the *Evening Herald* Hanna declared that they would fight the Cat and Mouse Act 'to the bitter end'.[37] That Sunday, a meeting to mobilise public opinion was held at 4 p.m. in Foster Place; the following day Hanna was in Tullamore. Dr Flinn, the medical officer for the Prison Board, came down by the same train and he and Hanna, old adversaries by now, were soon engaged in a battle of wits. Hanna had the advantage of getting first to Dr Kennedy, the medical officer for the prison. She saw him waiting on the station platform, presumably to greet Flinn, and immediately approached him. She then went to Colton's Hotel where, as the correspondent for the *King's County Independent* put it, Flinn 'was not found, at least by Mrs Skeffington, who was most anxious to secure an interview with him as to the condition of the prisoners'.[38] Wisely, that afternoon the prison governor did allow her to see her friends, one by one, in a small reception room, carefully supervised by the prison wardresses.[39] There was no need this time to stay in town to mobilise opinion on the women's behalf. They had enlisted sympathisers who would undertake that task and who would continue to visit the prisoners. What was important was to organise a political campaign against the Cat and Mouse Act. So far, the Act had not been applied in Ireland and a determined campaign was necessary to ensure that the government realised the strength of opposition. That was the new objective of the League.

Hanna returned to Dublin after receiving from the prisoners a pledge not to observe the terms of their licence if they were released. She was back in Tullamore on the Wednesday, this time accompanied by Helen Laird, to take charge of the prisoners who were in the process of being released. They had served three weeks of their sentence and were out for 14 days under the conditions of the Cat and Mouse Act. They were under police surveillance, could not change address without notification, could not leave their homes for more than 12 hours at a time and were to present themselves to the authorities in Tullamore on 2 July, when they would be expected to complete their sentences. It was draconian and the 'mice', according to a sympathetic reporter who had gone to Tullamore station to see them depart for Dublin, 'presented a rather woe-begone appearance' as they walked with difficulty to their carriage. In contrast, Hanna was relaxed enough to remark humorously when asked for an interview, 'I suppose this means I am going back to prison.' Her charges were weak and forbidden to speak in public, and the contrast between them and the commanding presence of their leader was dramatic. As the women struggled onto the train, Hanna's parting shot was to assure the onlookers that they were as determined as ever to fight on for the cause.[40]

The Irish campaign against the Act was an effective show of unity. A packed meeting in the Mansion House on 28 June represented a tremendous variety of intellectual, religious and political opinion. It was a triumph for the militants. Councillor Sarah Cecilia Harrison chaired the meeting and Tom Kettle moved the resolution:

> That this meeting of Dublin citizens regards the Cat and Mouse Act as a dangerous weapon of political oppression in the hands of any Government; declares that the Act has been shown to be useless for its avowed purpose, the suppression of suffragist militancy, and therefore demands its immediate repeal.

Hanna was secretary to the meeting, instrumental in contacting prominent supporters and obtaining letters of apology from those unable to attend.

These she read out at the meeting, as well as delivering a short speech of her own. She echoed the feelings of many who also stressed the Irish tradition of political protest and the English history of repression, although none were quite as dramatic as she was: 'The only precedent for (the Act) in Ireland was the half-hanging of the rebels in '98, who were strung up, let down to recover, and then strung up again repeatedly.[41]

The three 'mice' sent their own message, to say that they would not be abiding by the Act. They did not present themselves at the prison gates but although not re-arrested they had the constant anxiety of that prospect hanging over them. The suffragists demanded that the rest of their sentence be remitted, and the IWFL made Lord and Lady Aberdeen's lives a misery by their determination to confront the Lord Lieutenant over the issue. There were seven occasions in the first two weeks of July when one or other of the Aberdeens was approached by some member of the IWFL. Hanna was the most prominent of the hecklers, and the only one to be named as such by the *Irish Citizen*, so presumably the others wished to remain anonymous. It could, of course, also be the case that she was even more ubiquitous than usual, and the *Citizen* did not want to draw attention to the fact that only a few members had the temerity to gate-crash the Vice-Regal grounds and other exclusive venues.

One unexpected benefit of the Act was the amount of sympathy for suffragists that it generated. Constance Markievicz became a regular speaker at the IWFL open-air meetings at their new pitch in Foster Place, close to the Transport Union headquarters of Liberty Hall. She specialised in delivering 'vigorous and spirited condemnations' of the Act, as the IWFL reports commented.[42] Tom Kettle's public stance against the Cat and Mouse Act was a welcome reminder of his previous commitment to the suffrage cause. But the Kettles had moved away from their earlier association with the Franchise League. Tom would soon be promoting the Volunteer movement along with party leader John Redmond, and Mary was busy with their baby daughter Betty, born 31 January 1913. Hanna asked her to join one of the last deputations to Redmond, only to receive a rather miserable reply from her 'fond sister' who apologised for not going on the deputation but added that it would make no difference 'as the name is not of as much importance at present as it used to be'.[43]

The Irish militants were so immersed in pursuing their campaign and in ensuring that full support was given to their imprisoned colleagues that international concerns had to be ignored. The Seventh Congress of the International Suffrage Alliance took place in Budapest over 15–21 June 1913.

Louie Bennett represented the IWSF and Lady Dockrell the IWSLGA. Both were listed as delegates from 'Britain'. Ireland had no separate representation, as a subject country within the United Kingdom. Perhaps that explains the IWFL indifference? The cost of attendance might also have been a factor. Katherine Gatty, a WSPU militant with a Fermanagh background on her mother's side, wrote to Hanna bemoaning the fact that Kathleen Shannon was not present 'to settle Lady Dockrell', whom she described as a 'jovial Unionist who hopes Ulster will fight because it is "right" and thinks Miss Davison's death an "impertinence" to His Majesty's horse! and that women who fight are using "unethical methods of barbarism"'. She was also spending a great deal of time telling 'these benighted foreigners Ireland *doesn't* want Home Rule.'[44] It was an interesting glimpse into the growing distinction between the views of IWFL and IWSLGA members.

That busy summer of protest and of new alliances between the League and the labour movement went on without one of the most stalwart of the IWFL members. Gretta and James Cousins left Ireland in May, hoping to spend as little time in England as possible before heading off to their eventual destination in India. Gretta realised their departure 'surprised and disappointed some of our friends, seeing that we were leaving the scene of our work just when Home Rule and Votes for Women seemed on the point of becoming law in Ireland.'[45] It was not a spur of the moment decision and the actual leaving of Dublin took several months. Long before their eventual departure, a Cousins Presentation Committee had been formed, its members coming from suffrage, vegetarian, theosophical and dramatic groups, in all of which the couple had been so vital a part.

The farewell ceremony at the Hardwicke Hall was an emotional occasion, beginning with the re-staging of two of James' best plays: 'The Racing Lug' and 'The Sleep of the King', both starring former Inghinidhe member, Maire nic Shiubhlaigh, now a well-established actress, and ending with speeches and tributes from friends. Hanna's contribution was the shortest, and the most heartfelt. She had already said a great deal about her friend Gretta at a special IWFL reception and now all she wanted to say was that she was there 'with a feeling of heartache at the great loss the women's movement was sustaining in the departure of their dear friend and comrade ... With all her heart she wished them God Speed and "Come Back to Erin".' Frank's tribute was warm but typically Frank. He valued 'the journalistic ability, the high conception of duties and possibilities of journalism, the inexhaustible fertility in ideas, that he had learnt to respect in Mr Cousins in collaborating with him on the *Irish Citizen*'. However, he went on to say, 'He disagreed with Mr

Cousins on many things, because they were both alive and therefore different.' An illuminated address was presented, along with a bag containing £1,200 worth of sovereigns. As Gretta said, it meant that 'the future was happily seen to'.[46] The IWFL contributed £200. The Sheehy Skeffingtons were the prime movers in organising the presentation. James was an undischarged bankrupt, the pair had no assets to speak of, and Frank and Hanna, struggling themselves, knew only too well the importance, not only of having some income, but also of having public tribute paid to the sacrifices entailed by years of political involvement.[47]

Hanna and Gretta were in constant communication over the two years the Cousins remained in Liverpool while waiting for their promised position in India to materialise. Gretta found it impossible to relinquish her part in the League and she returned to Ireland several times to carry out activities that she felt unable to delegate to anyone else. Her letters provide an indiscreet window into the internal workings of the suffragists, revealing the extent to which Hanna was indispensable to the existence of the militants. There were many fine women within that organisation, but they were young women with the usual life circumstances of their age –pregnancy, miscarriage, sick children – all of which affected their ability to contribute.

With the departure of the Cousins, the *Irish Citizen* lost a valuable editor. Hanna undertook some editorial duties, but Frank's perfectionism and his years of journalistic experience meant that she steered clear of the production process, concentrating upon writing and commissioning articles. James Cousins had remarked with truthful humour that 'Skeffy' had put their editorial board at the top for efficiency and pleasure: the ideal board 'consisting of two persons in complete agreement, with one of them mostly absent'.[48] Hanna enjoyed writing reviews of plays that interested her: Strindberg was commended, and W. B. Yeats's play *The King's Threshold*, an exploration of the hunger strike in Celtic times, she found 'a glowing and radiant glorification of the Hunger-Strike … eternal in its nature and appeal as is poetry'. She felt the plea for poetry within the play 'might be the plea for outlawed womanhood, or for anything oppressed and defiant unto death'.[49] For her, art and politics were closely interwoven. Her decision to leave Frank to his own devices was a sensible one, as his reaction to the IWFL Report of 1912 makes very plain. He was infuriated by its misprints and inaccuracies and did not hesitate to use the pages of the *Citizen* to criticise: 'It is our duty to point out to suffragist organisations that efficiency, even in small matters, has in itself a great propaganda value and that, in a movement such as this, slovenliness is a crime.'[50] His partner managed to avoid the ordeal of the printers until

October 1914, when Frank was forced to ask their friend Maurice Wilkins to stand in as editor during his absence: 'As she has no experience of the technical part, could you possibly assist her by going to the printing works for a couple of hours on Wednesday? Of course, you will not have to do any writing, or to undertake any worrying responsibility; just to help her in putting the pieces of the puzzle together.'[51]

Frank's hope of future domestic bliss after Hanna's release from jail was never more than a dream. The kind of harmony the pair achieved was not found in the comfort of the home. The Wednesday evening 'At Homes' of their early married life had been transformed into the IWFL Tuesday evening 'At Homes', where the tradition of discussion and tea continued, but in a public setting. Private life was limited to the early evening hours before Owen's bedtime and the night's round of meetings. They shared many platforms during the season of outdoor meetings and in the summer of 1913 took a brief working holiday at the end of July, when they visited Skeffington relations in Downpatrick. Elfreda Baker, a member of the Irish Women's Suffrage Society, who lived in Knock, just outside Belfast, not knowing their address but wanting to arrange a meeting with Hanna, sent a postcard to 'Hanna Sheehy Skeffington, Downpatrick, County Down'[52] It found her easily. Arrangements were being made by the IWSS, a society containing both militants and non-militants, to have Hanna and Frank as guest speakers at their open-air meeting in Belfast's Ormeau Park. Belfast City Council gave permission for the IWSS to hold one meeting a year in the Park, and they were determined to have the most prominent of Ireland's suffrage militants at the venue. Mrs Baker hoped Hanna (and Owen too) would spend the Friday night of the week before the meeting with her, so that they could plan the event and spend some time together. It was probably a welcome break from the Skeffington relatives.

The Belfast meeting was a lively affair as the crowd reacted to Hanna's Dublin accent. Standing in the middle of a lorry in the unaccustomed setting of a Belfast park, Hanna showed her skill in disarming the hostile onlookers, introducing herself as 'only a voteless woman and as such, standing by no political party, and not there to discuss with them whether any good comes out of Dublin – some of them seemed sceptical on that point for she was of the opinion that outside of Hell something good comes out of any place.' Sectarian differences neatly set aside; she then developed her message on the need for women to have the vote so that they could have an influence on changing the social evils that existed. Frank, as a northerner and as a male, did not have to establish his credentials in this manner. His contribution was an attempt to persuade the audience to look beyond sectarian divisions by recognising women's enfranchisement as a basic civil liberty. He also tried to convince the Ulster unionists in the audience that the methods advocated by suffrage militants were the same as those put forward by Carson and the other leaders who were organising opposition to Home Rule. They made few converts, but 81 copies of the *Citizen* were sold and, in the circumstances of Belfast, that in itself was some kind of success.[53]

Frank and Hanna shared a less contentious platform at the last Phoenix Park meeting of the season. By then, the IWFL was concentrating its energies on the labour movement, with more meetings being held around Liberty Hall. James Connolly had always given the IWFL unstinting support, and he was a regular speaker at its meetings when in Dublin. He declared that he took an interest in the suffragettes 'because they were rebels and would continue to do so as long as they continued in revolt … he had never yet heard of a militant action which he was not prepared fully and heartily to endorse.'[54] The IWFL praised him as the 'soundest and most thorough-going feminist amongst all the Irish labour men'.[55] Hanna was particularly fond of Connolly and always counted him as a friend who never failed to show support: 'one of those all too rare revolutionaries whose doctrines of freedom apply all round.'[56] Transport Union members signed the petition against the Cat and Mouse Act and gave visible and very welcome support to the IWFL open-air meetings in Beresford Place. The burly figures of the dockers deterred many a heckler. Connolly was also instrumental in fostering closer links between socialist republicans and militant feminists. He had wanted Kathleen Shannon to act as secretary to the Socialist Party of Ireland, in preference to his unpredictable friend Skeffington, and he was an important influence upon Constance Markievicz, moving her towards recognising that national independence had to include the freedom of the working class. Hanna, Meg Connery and Cissie Cahalan were leading League members who saw it as part of their feminism to encourage working-class women to demand the vote. When, in the autumn of 1913, the Lockout of members of the Transport Union by their employers began, members of the IWFL, green and orange suffrage badge prominent, were to be seen in the soup kitchens of Liberty Hall, together with Delia Larkin, Markievicz, Molony and some of the other women who would soon join Connolly's Irish Citizen Army. This had been formed in November 1913, to defend workers from police attack and provide militant opposition to hostile employers. Years later Meg Connery, reminiscing sadly on the death of Markievicz, wrote how it 'brought back to me all the old memories of Liberty Hall and Connolly and the strike – all the friends and work and enthusiasm of the past.'[57]

Louie Bennett and the constitutionalists were also sympathetic to the struggles of the Dublin workers. The Irish Women's Reform League devoted much of its time to investigating and publicising the conditions suffered by working women, but its members saw their role in a strictly non-political sense. Their function during the Lockout was to help alleviate distress through working with the Relief Fund set up by the Lady Mayoress, distributing food and clothing to families in need. In contrast, the philosophy of the IWFL was closer to that of the socialist Sylvia Pankhurst. Sylvia, admiring Frank as a 'citizen of the world, a comradely man with broad views and a quick intelligence' had met him at the offices of the *Citizen*. He had made a vivid impression: 'a small man in knee-breeches, jumping about as though on springs, with a red beard covering the greater part of his face.'[58] Frank was a member of the Independent Labour Party, and, in turn, party members like Walter Carpenter were frequent speakers at IWFL platforms. By the time the open-air meetings of the 1913 season came to an end the IWFL – referring to their meetings around Liberty Hall – were reporting their 'veritable joy' at having spoken to audiences 'whose sympathy, interest and enthusiasm for a cause has been so wholehearted and complete.'[59] Those who had diligently continued the heckling of politicians around the country also commented on the fact that they had received great support from the crowds in places like Navan and Limerick. It was all very different from the Hibernian-orchestrated violence of the year before.

Suffragists felt themselves in strong form to commence their winter round of activities. The non-militants were planning a big suffrage week for November, while the IWFL was immersed in plans to move to new, much bigger premises in Westmoreland Street, right in the centre of the city. Those who enjoyed homemaking put their skills to use in the new premises, hanging green and orange curtains with cross blinds and sashes, supervising the lettering of 'Irish Women's Franchise League' across the windows, laying 'pretty green matting' on the floor, begging donations of tables, chairs, pictures and bookcases. They were planning an extensive tearoom and lending library, an oasis of feminism in the heart of Dublin. Not all were so domestic. Hanna donated a picture and some cutlery, but beyond that had no interest in extending her limited domestic skills. Fund-raising events ranged from jumble sales to a fancy dress party that must have been great fun, given the reports of a muscular associate dressed as a 'great big beautiful doll'; '5 ft 2 in of femininity' appearing as a very masculine Apache, and a 'Water Carrier from the East' in suffrage colours. The inversion of gender roles was interesting – daring for pre-war Dublin. A repeat event the following year must have gone even further, to judge from the scandalised letter one member wrote to Hanna, refusing to have any more to do with fancy dress dances because of the 'indecent costumes indulged in by some of our members – Mrs Connery and Mrs Browne in particular'.[60]

Some suffragists were attempting to extend feminist influence in other directions, through the fostering of links with various churches. The IWFL activists were a mixed lot of Quakers, Unitarians, Church of Ireland, Methodists and Roman Catholics as well as non-believers. At a joint meeting of constitutional and militant suffragists, called to discuss the question of suffragists also joining a suffrage society of their particular church, there was a very definite division of opinion. Hanna had to chair the meeting, substituting for Eva Wilkins who was ill, and therefore gaining an unexpected opportunity to influence the course of events. While some speakers emphasised the 'spiritual' side of the suffrage movement, the chair's summing up was blunt: she deprecated any suggestion that women should join 'sectarian leagues' in addition to other suffrage societies, on the grounds that such action would lead to the setting up of new barriers. She wanted no suggestion of any link between suffrage and religion.[61] Meg Connery was vocal in her support. Now that Gretta was no longer there it was Meg, mercurial, witty and a great platform performer, who was her closest companion. The two were often paired together, as in the celebrated heckling of Churchill in Belfast and, more recently, both had followed Redmond to Limerick.

In November, Bonar Law, leader of the Conservative and Unionist Party came to Dublin. He had refused all requests for a deputation, so suffragists from different groups arranged for extensive leafletting at all likely venues. Hanna and Meg were allocated the prime location of Lord Iveagh's house in Stephen's Green, where both Bonar Law and Edward Carson were staying. After a 'gay sallying forth from League Headquarters', armed with the customary sheaf of leaflets and an *Irish Citizen* placard with its appropriate legend 'Questions for Bonar Law', the two women took their stand. As the men posed on the steps for the press photographers, Meg seized the moment, rushing forward with her leaflets. The photo that appeared in the *Irish Independent* captured the incident well. (The League was delighted with the prominence given to the *Irish Citizen* poster.) Meg was removed by a policeman, but not arrested, just as Hanna attempted to approach the politicians from the other side. To her great surprise, the treatment meted out to her was very different. Police Sergeant Thomas seized her violently, pulled her arms across her chest, shook her like a 'terrier shaking a kitten' and when the cameras turned to capture the scene, arrested her and charged her with assault.[62]

That evening, while Bonar Law spoke in the Theatre Royal, an unusual looking gentleman in long overcoat and large bowler hat, vivid red complexion and white whiskers and moustache ('a somewhat violent colour scheme' in the opinion of the reporter for the *Freeman's Journal*), interrupted the speaker by shouting 'What about the women's conflict? Why don't you support the women?' before being thrown out, to join members of the IWFL and the IRL handing out leaflets on the pavement outside. It was of course Frank, who explained seriously to a reporter that he had succeeded in getting in because he was 'disguised as a gentleman'.[63]

The trumped-up nature of the case against Hanna was evident to the 200 who flocked to hear the evidence in court. The *Irish Times* reported the sergeant as testifying 'Mrs Skeffington rushed at him, struck him deliberately on the chest with her elbow, and punched him several times on the arm.' For additional emphasis he added that he could still feel the pain. Laughter swept the court as the audience looked at the vast figure of the policeman whose belt, as Hanna said, came to her forehead. She was refused leave to press a counter-charge and so was denied any opportunity of entering the witness box on her own behalf. Meg Connery's evidence that the police sergeant had grabbed Hanna violently, only letting her go when she shouted to the photographers to take a photo of the assault, was ignored. Justice was summary: find bail to be of good behaviour or go to jail for seven days. Frank was incensed by Mr Swifte the magistrate declaring that he would willingly accept Mr Sheehy Skeffington's bail: 'I won't take part in this farce. My wife does not wish to have anyone go bail and I won't take any part. If you don't hear the counter-charge it is a farce.' Hanna immediately began to shout her agreement, 'I don't wish any bail given for me and protest against this. I wish to have the whole matter investigated. I will take no food in prison until I am released. It is a travesty of justice Mr Swifte and I am surprised at you taking such a one-sided view of the case.'[64]

It was 'dark November'; she was in prison again, an experience 'like having a second tooth out. The novelty is over, and one knows exactly how much it hurts.' She was on hunger strike and well aware of how awful the experience would be.[65] Non-militant suffragists had no qualms of conscience in joining in the protests on her behalf. After all, she had been engaged on an entirely peaceful mission when arrested. There had been no militancy in Ireland for months, and none had been planned for Bonar Law's visit. The day after her removal to Mountjoy, the IWFL began their protests outside the prison, Frank in the thick of it all. The police were still heavy-handed, banning the proposed meeting, cordoning off Royce Road (an inoffensive cul-de-sac

1. The Sheehy family 1895–6. Left to right standing: Hanna, Richard, David, Margaret, Eugene, Mary; seated: Fr Eugene, Kathleen, Bessie. Image courtesy of the NLI.

2. Hanna in the Dominican College, Eccles Street play of *Comedy of Errors*, 1893. She is far right, playing 'Angelo, a goldsmith'. Image courtesy of the NLI.

3. Hanna and her sisters. Left to right: Hanna, Mary, Kathleen, Margaret. Image courtesy of the Sheehy Skeffington family.

4. Dr J. B. Skeffington, Frank's father, wearing a black armband. Possibly after the death of his wife Rose in 1909. Image courtesy of the NLI.

5. Rose Skeffington, née Magorian, Frank's mother. Image courtesy of the NLI.

6. Hanna and Frank in graduation gowns 1903, just after their marriage. Image courtesy of the NLI.

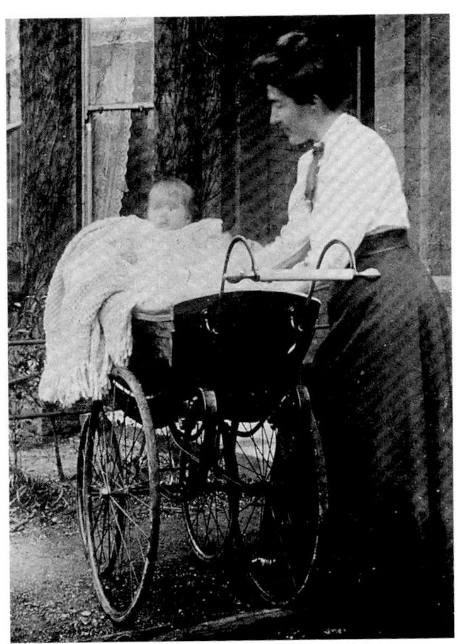

7. Hanna and Owen in pram outside their Grosvenor Place home. Image courtesy of the NLI.

8. Hanna, Fr Eugene Sheehy and Frank outside their Grosvenor Place home, June 1910 (photo taken by Francis Cruise O'Brien). Image courtesy of the NLI.

9. Meg Connery. Image courtesy of the NLI.

10. Marguerite Palmer. Image courtesy of the NLI.

11. Kathleen Emerson. Image courtesy of the NLI.

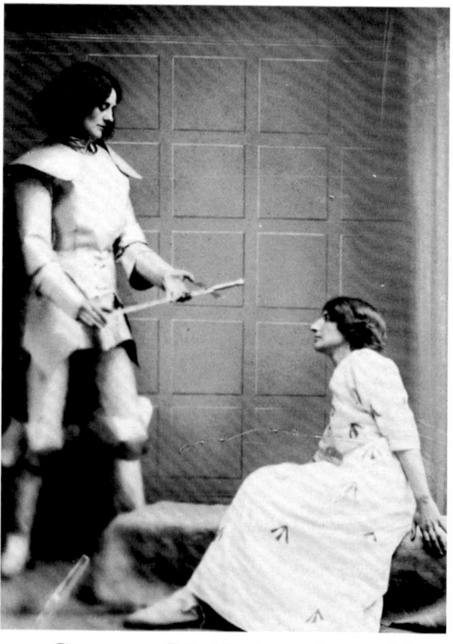

12. Constance Markievicz as Joan of Arc appearing to Kathleen Houston, Irish Women's Franchise League Daffodil Fête, 1914. Image courtesy of the NLI.

13. **Irish women at Platform 6, Hyde Park, London, July 1910.** Hanna in centre with mortar board; Kathleen Shannon in mortar board beside her; Mary Sheehy Kettle in mortar board at far right; Geraldine Lennox, wearing banner captain sash; Patricia Hoey and sister on top, in 'colleen' costume. IWFL banner has its Irish wording to the fore of the photo. **Image courtesy of Museum of London.**

14. IWFL activists 1912/3. Seated, from left: Eva Wilkins, Hanna, Marguerite Palmer; standing, from left: Margaret Cousins, Cissie Cahalan, Maud Lloyd, unknown, Meg Connery. Image courtesy of the Wilkins family.

15. Margaret and James Cousins, 1913.
Image courtesy of Keith Munro.

16. Suffrage meeting in Phoenix Park. Meg Connery speaking and Margaret Cousins seated behind her. Image courtesy of the NLI.

17. Meg Connery at Lord Iveagh's house in Stephen's Green, leafletting Edward Carson and Bonar Law at the time of Hanna's arrest, 1913. Image courtesy of the NLI.

REBELLION THROUGH A MEGAPHONE: HOW A SUFFRAGETTE "MOUSE" WAS CHEERED IN HER PRISON CELL.

Mrs. Sheehy-Skeffington addressing a protest meeting under the prison walls.

A message of encouragement to the prisoner.

... the imprisonment under the "Cat and Mouse" Act of Miss Kathleen Houston, who broke the Post Office windows on College Green, the suffragettes held

18. Hanna protesting outside Mountjoy prison, 1914 featured in *Daily Sketch*. Image courtesy of © RTÉ Stills Library.

19. Silver medal given to Hanna by the IWFL following her release from Mountjoy jail in August 1912. Image courtesy of the National Museum of Ireland.

20. Travelling speaker's platform made for the IWFL. Image courtesy of the National Museum of Ireland.

between the canal and the prison where the suffragists were attempting to gather), removing Frank to the edge of the crowd and generally forcing everyone to keep moving until they dispersed. Many continued at intervals to mount their biscuit box in order to make short calls for women's suffrage – to a crowd that by then consisted of unsympathetic football supporters coming home from the nearby park.

On the following day the IWFL members, armed with a megaphone, were back at the same spot. This time they had not informed the police of their plans and at least 40 (according to the *Irish Times* which had no interest in inflating the figures), succeeded in holding the meeting, speeches being made by all the usual stalwarts. There was more fighting with the police, Kathleen Emerson being carted off and charged with assault, despite the fact several women had visible signs of injury. Tension was mounting, but great excitement was felt when Hanna's hanky was seen waving from her cell window to show that she had heard their shouted messages of support. Emotionally, she felt the moment was 'an unforgettable experience, a joy that helped to clear away the mists of pain and brought messages of cheer and hope, penetrating through the megaphone across the prison bars like a ray of sunshine in that wintry place of shadows'.[66] The governor of Mountjoy was visibly embarrassed by reports of this event appearing, of all places, in the paper of the élite.[67] A memo was immediately dispatched to the Chairman of the General Prisons Board, assuring him that Mrs Sheehy Skeffington did not reply by waving her handkerchief: 'she was not in her cell but at exercise and for the short time she was in her cell she was under observation and made no attempt to do anything of the sort.'[68] Given the fact that large numbers of people testified otherwise, and that they were well aware which cell was occupied by Hanna (which was why they insisted on Royce Road as the venue), it might be said that the man protested too much and not too convincingly.

While Hanna remained on hunger strike and public meetings, petitions and poster parades on her behalf continued, the IWFL also held its long-awaited 'Open House Warming' in their new premises. Marguerite Palmer, chairing the meeting, said: 'With our leader in prison, many would have wished to postpone the first social function in our new rooms until she could have been present.' Their feelings that Hanna would not have wanted this were confirmed by a message from Mountjoy, wishing them every success, which was read out 'with a tumult of applause.'[69]

By the third day of hunger strike, Hanna's health had begun to deteriorate. On 2 December, Governor Munro reported that her brief visit from her friends was held in the boardroom of the prison, instead of the usual meeting place, because the prisoner had stated she didn't feel equal to walking over to the building.[70] Hanna retorted that it was a protest on her part against receiving visitors in a draughty shed in the prison yard. However, the following day her doctor, Dr Elizabeth Tennant, found her weak and with a bad headache and she advised the authorities that her patient's health could be permanently damaged if she was not released.[71] At 4 p.m. that afternoon, finding Hanna 'very depressed and in a low state of health' the doctor telephoned Dublin Castle. She managed to speak in person to a sympathetic Lady Aberdeen who promised to talk to her husband. As a result of this intervention Hanna was removed to the prison hospital that evening.[72] Despite this, release did not come about until after 7.30 a.m. the next morning, the fifth day of hunger strike. Controversy raged over the discrepancy in time between Lord Aberdeen's instructions for Hanna to be released and when she was actually allowed to leave. Neither she nor Frank was informed of the order until the following morning. The IWFL made much of it, the prison governor justifying himself at great length to Max Green, Chairman of the Prisons Board, but his main excuse was to fall back on bureaucratic inflexibility. The prisoners were in bed and the night staff on duty: 'I must say that it is not customary when orders are received overnight for the release of a prisoner the next morning to then and there acquaint the prisoner of the fact unless there are special directions to do so.'[73] It was mean and vindictive behaviour. As Frank pointed out with scorn, the suggestion was 'preposterous' because Mrs Pankhurst was released at ten at night and James Connolly released at an even later hour.[74] The governor had no convincing explanation for his failure to alleviate Hanna's anxiety and to allow her to take some nourishment by informing her that she had won the battle and would be released the next day, two days early.

The inexperience of Dr Tennant, who all too easily accepted the prison official's reasoning that release in the coldness of the night might be injurious to health, led to a breach between Hanna and the woman who had been her doctor for many years. The doctor's 'lack of knowledge of the ways of officials' had made her 'an easy prey to their unscrupulous misrepresentations', was how Kathleen Emerson explained the situation to the public.[75] The gullibility might have been forgiven, but the initial error of judgement was compounded by Dr Tennant's further attempts to clear the bureaucracy of Dublin Castle from responsibility for having imprisoned the hunger striker for an unnecessary additional 15 hours. Frank's editorial in the *Citizen* was outspoken on the issue; Dr Tennant had to take some blame in not insisting on her patient's immediate release. Sharing a common belief in the suffrage cause was not enough; their attitudes on the oppressive nature of the patriarchal state were too different.[76]

The report of the Mountjoy Medical Officer on Hanna's condition on release indirectly confirmed her assertion that it was she who had been injured during the fracas with Police Sergeant Thomas. Six days after the event Dr Dowdell still found 'three small discoloured marks on the left upper arm, which would have been caused by a hand grasping the arm, but little force was used … The injuries were trivial.'[77] The IWFL issued a very different statement: Mrs Sheehy Skeffington was released in a state of extreme exhaustion, having been unable to sleep for the past three nights and having suffered repeated vomiting attacks after drinking water. She had lost a stone in weight and the bruises were still clearly visible on her arm.[78] A notice in the *Irish Citizen* gave the information that she was now under the care of Dr Kathleen Lynn. Hanna was faithful to those in whom she had confidence. Dr Lynn would be her doctor until the day she died.

Why had so much fuss been made over the attempt by two women to gain the attention of two politicians? Hanna believed she had been treated unjustly because a police officer had lost his temper and had saved himself from censure by inventing the charge of assault.[79] This would explain the actual incident, but not the reason why the police were so concerned to prevent an innocuous attempt to hand out leaflets. The establishment had closed ranks in its anxiety to ensure that Bonar Law's stay in Dublin was accompanied by none of the protests that had marred Asquith's visit. They over-reacted at the time, and then felt that putting one notorious female militant behind bars would convey a clear message to her colleagues. It was unjust, but justice was not a consideration. After her release her anger was apparent. It stayed with her, a constant reminder of the reason why she had taken the militant road:

> I hope that I shall never again have to suffer imprisonment for an offence of which I am innocent. Such a sentence makes every turn of the jailer's key an outrage, and burns into the victim's soul a searing hatred of the whole infamy of our prison system, whose victims cry to heaven for vengeance.[80]

It was a heartfelt wish. Her later memoirs echo those sentiments, softened by a dryness developed through time: 'I promised myself that never again would I go to prison without doing something to justify detention, if I had to throw a stone at the judge's head.'[81] When free she did not forget the women who remained imprisoned. On 17 December she wrote to Lady Aberdeen to ask her to repeat her 'great act of kindness' of some years previously by ordering a special dinner be supplied to the prisoners on Christmas day, thereby relieving 'the terrible loneliness and dreary monotony' that 'one who has lately been herself a prisoner in Mountjoy' had experienced.[82]

NOTES

1 *Votes for Women*, 20 Oct. 1912.

2 Hanna Sheehy to Frank Skeffington (hereafter Hanna to Frank), 31 July 1912, Sheehy Skeffington MS (hereafter SS MS) 40,466/5.

3 Kathleen Emerson to Hanna Sheehy Skeffington, n. d. SS MS 33,603/16.

4 Frank Skeffington to Hanna Sheehy (hereafter Frank to Hanna), 28 July 1912, courtesy of Andrée Sheehy Skeffington.

5 *Irish Citizen*, 12 Oct. 1912.

6 Ibid.

7 Leah Levenson and Jerry Natterstad, *Hanna Sheehy Skeffington: Irish Feminist* (New York, 1983), p. 43.

8 *Irish Citizen*, 5 Oct. 1912.

9 Ibid., 9 Nov. 1912.

10 Ibid., 16 Nov. 1912.

11 Ibid., 18 Jan. 1912.

12 Ibid., 17 May 1913; 7 June 1913.

13 Ibid., 12 Feb. 1912.

14 Hanna Sheehy Skeffington, 'Irish secondary teachers', in *Irish Review*, Oct. 1912, pp 393–8.

15 Agnes O'Farrelly to Hanna Sheehy Skeffington, 13 Nov. 1912, SS MS 33,603/17.

16 *Irish Citizen*, 2 Nov. 1912.

17 Cliona Murphy, *The Women's Suffrage Movement and Irish Society in the Early Twentieth Century* (Hertfordshire, 1989), p. 191.

18 *Irish Citizen*, 16 Nov. 1911.

19 Ibid.

20 Ibid., 1 Feb. 1912.

21 Ibid., 30 Nov. 1912.

22 Hanna Sheehy Skeffington, 'Militant militancy', in *Irish Citizen*, 4 Jan. 1913.

23 Fred Ryan to Francis Sheehy Skeffington, 26 Sept. 1912, SS MS 21,623. See Frederick Ryan, 'The suffrage tangle', in *The Irish Review* 2:19, Sept. 1912, pp 346–5. While sympathetic to the suffrage cause, Ryan argued for victory won by 'persuasion rather than fear'.

24 Hanna Sheehy Skeffington, small notebook concerning Owen's early development, n. d. MS 41,183/6.

25 Andrée Sheehy Skeffington, *Skeff: A Life of Owen Sheehy Skeffington* (Dublin, 1991), p. 14.

26 Report from Rathgar kindergarten, summer exam, 1916, SS MS 41,207/2. Given the trauma of losing his father, having his home raided by the British army and having to move house following the Easter Rising, it is extraordinary to learn that Owen was only late on 21 days and absent on 13.

27 *Irish Citizen*, 1 Feb. 1913.

28 Ibid., 22 Feb. 1913.

29 *Irish Independent*, 10 Feb. 1913.

30 For full details of the Tullamore imprisonment and campaign by the Irish Women's Franchise League (hereafter IWFL), see General Prisons Board Suffragette Box 2, National Archives, Dublin.

31 *Freeman's Journal*, 10 Feb. 1913.
32 *Evening Herald*, 27 Feb. 1913.
33 *Freeman's Journal*, 5 Mar. 1913.
34 *Irish Citizen*, 22 Mar. 1913; *Sinn Féin* 22 Mar. 1913.
35 Murphy, *The Women's Suffrage Movement*, p. 192.
36 Details of their imprisonment in General Prisons Board Suffragette Boxes 2 and 3, National Archives, Dublin.
37 *Evening Herald*, 19 June 1913.
38 *King's County Independent*, 21 June 1913.
39 Memo, J. Boland, Governor of Tullamore, to Chair of General Prisons Board, Dublin Castle, 16 June 1913, Suffragette Box 3, National Archives, Dublin.
40 *King's County Independent*, 21 June 1913.
41 *Irish Citizen*, 5 July 1913.
42 See Ibid., 12 July 1913; 19 July 1913.
43 Mary Kettle to Hanna Sheehy Skeffington, n. d., (1914), SS MS 22,670.
44 Katherine Gatty to Hanna Sheehy Skeffington, 15 June 1913, SS MS 33,603/17.
45 James and Margaret Cousins, *We Two Together* (Madras, 1950), p. 194.
46 Ibid., p. 215.
47 For details of Presentation Committee, see SS MS 21,648.
48 Cousins, *We Two Together*, p. 205.
49 *Irish Citizen*, 25 Oct. 1913.
50 Ibid., 31 May 1913.
51 Levenson and Natterstad, *Hanna Sheehy Skeffington*, pp 46–7.
52 Mrs Baker to Hanna Sheehy Skeffington, 30 July 1913, SS MS 22,664.
53 *Irish Citizen*, 16 Aug. 1913.
54 Ibid., 13 Nov. 1913.
55 Ibid., 6 Sept. 1913.
56 Hanna Sheehy Skeffington, 'Memories of the suffrage campaign in Ireland', in *The Vote*, 30 Aug. 1929.
57 Meg Connery to Hanna Sheehy Skeffington, 20 July 1927, SS MS 41,177/10.
58 Sylvia Pankhurst, *The Suffragette Movement* (London, 1931; reprinted London, 1977), p. 382.
59 *Irish Citizen*, 1 Nov. 1913.
60 Mary Burke Dowling to Hanna Sheehy Skeffington, 18 Nov. 1914, SS MS 22,668.
61 *Irish Citizen*, 8 Nov. 1913.
62 Ibid., 6 Dec. 1913.
63 *Freeman's Journal*, 29 Nov. 1913; 1 Dec. 1913.
64 *Irish Times*, 29 Nov. 1913.
65 Hanna Sheehy Skeffington, 'Mountjoy revisited', in *Irish Citizen*, 3 Jan. 1914.
66 Ibid.
67 *Irish Times*, 1 Dec. 1913.
68 Governor Munro, Mountjoy, to Chair of General Prisons Board, 1 Dec. 1913, Suffragette Box 3, National Archives, Dublin.
69 *Irish Citizen*, 6 Dec. 1913.
70 Governor's Report, Mountjoy, 2 Dec. 1913, Suffragette Box 3, National Archives, Dublin.

71 Dr Tennant to Chair of General Prisons Board, 2 Dec. 1913, Suffragette Box 3, National Archives, Dublin.

72 Statements made by Dr Tennant, in *Irish Times*, 4 Dec. 1913; 5 Dec. 1913.

73 Governor Munro, Mountjoy, to Chair of General Prisons Board, 11 Dec. 1913, Suffragette Box 3, National Archives, Dublin.

74 *Irish Citizen*, 13 Dec. 1913.

75 Kathleen Emerson, letter to the editor, in *Irish Independent*, 6 Dec. 1913.

76 *Irish Citizen*, 13 Dec. 1913.

77 Report of Medical Officer Dowdall, Mountjoy, 3 Dec. 1913, Suffragette Box 3, National Archives, Dublin.

78 *Freeman's Journal*, 4 Dec. 1913.

79 Hanna Sheehy Skeffington, 'Mountjoy revisited', 3 Jan. 1914.

80 Ibid.

81 Hanna Sheehy Skeffington, *Reminiscences*, p. 24.

82 Hanna Sheehy Skeffington to Lady Aberdeen, 17 Dec. 1913, in Margaret Ward, *Hanna Sheehy Skeffington: Suffragette and Sinn Féiner: Her Memoirs and Political Writings* (Dublin, 2017), p. 365.

SEVEN

'ROLLING UP THE MAP OF SUFFRAGE', 1914–16

A short Christmas break was all the time that could be spared for recuperation from the ordeal of hunger strike. Then it was business as usual. The League's new season of campaigns was opened by Hanna on 6 January, her first public appearance since coming out of prison. Gretta, spending the holiday season with family and friends, was there to share the platform. The two were their usual effective combination. Hanna's address explained the political importance of knowing the views of the leader of the Conservative Party on the question of women's suffrage, while Gretta concentrated on praising the women of the League for their dedication to the cause. She was very emotional, outspoken in her hatred for the city of her exile. It was 'ugly and hateful' and her work for suffrage, amongst the reserved and sober English, so much less enjoyable than it had been when she was at home in Ireland. The serious mood was diffused by the irrepressible Meg, who presented Hanna with her prison medal, joking that but for the accident of her position outside Lord Iveagh's house, she might have been the recipient instead. The following day saw Hanna presiding at an 'At Home' for Gretta, held in the League rooms rather than at anyone's house. It might be nearer the truth to say that those premises had become their home. Gretta was impressed with this new venue, its very centrality proof that suffrage was no longer confined to drawing rooms or back streets. The occasion included a musical event, in which Francis Cruise O'Brien took part. He and Kathleen were still involved with the League and still on close terms with Hanna and Frank, despite some differences of opinion.[1]

The treachery of the Irish Party was a subject that Hanna returned to time and again in her addresses as chair of the League. Devising an appropriate political strategy was her preoccupation and her greatest talent. She was the political brain of the movement, its preeminent strategist, and this was the area upon which she concentrated her energies. Others were offering their services to candidates in local government elections, or raising money through whist drives, making goods for stalls, or rehearsing parts for the programme of *tableaux vivants* to be staged during the Daffodil Fête on 24 April. There were many different tasks for the suffragist who was nervous of public speaking and who shied away from actions that might result in a prison sentence. Hanna was not one of those. Her latest prison experience had intensified her insistence that the League maintain its pressure upon the Irish Party. Her language was excoriating: the party had degenerated into the 'appendage of corrupt Liberalism and … only responded to the crack of Mr Asquith's whip'.[2]

Most of the League's discussion nights were open to men as well as women, in keeping with their policy of wanting a society where women and men would contribute equally. But there were subjects that were difficult to talk about in mixed sex groups, particularly for the younger, single women of the group, who were shy about speaking out on most topics. To encourage greater participation, and to provide an arena for controversial topics like venereal disease and prostitution to be discussed openly, women's nights became a regular feature. Women who were not League members also came, so those occasions helped to build bridges between different groups. Single women, regardless of age, were constrained by the conventions of the period; they were not supposed to have intimate knowledge of sexual matters. Hanna, respectably married, had no reservations about leading off discussions on delicate subjects. With great relish she volunteered to read a paper criticising a book by a young German philosopher, whose reactionary views on women had been causing a stir amongst those who had borrowed his book from the League lending library. Otto Weininger's *Sex and Character* (1903) characterised women as 'mere creatures of sex', divided into lover-type and mother-type. This pseudo-scientific rationalisation for women's exclusion from every form of activity ranging from science to the arts had a certain following during this period: James Joyce was convinced that Nora was living proof of Weininger's theory.[3] Irish feminists had very different opinions and a lively debate followed Hanna's exposition of this absurd exercise in wishful thinking. It was a good way to learn the art of public speaking.[4] Violet Jameson, when asked to speak, replied that it was 'awfully kind … really have no right to attempt it as I've no experience', but she had the courage to suggest giving a talk on 'the relation of the suffrage to and its importance as regards what is politely known as "The Social Evil".[5] In this way the movement provided young women with invaluable opportunities not only to speak, but to develop their thinking on key social issues of the time.

In early March, as soon as the worst of the winter was over, the energetic team of Hanna and Meg came together again, this time for a speaking tour of those few counties that had yet to see a suffragist. Longford, Leitrim and Roscommon were 'a disfiguring blot' on the suffrage map, so into the west to wipe out that stain the pair went. The groundwork had been undertaken by Meg, who had visited the towns decided upon, talked to all the necessary 'magnates' and booked the required halls. When they returned, however, it was to discover the combined forces of the church and the Irish Party doing all they could to prevent the suffrage message from contaminating the women of their town. Only in Longford did all go according to plan. In Carrick, both Protestant and Catholic clerics had put pressure on the locals to ensure that no halls were available. There, the women encountered 'a howling, raging mob, led by a drunken virago' who proceeded to create pandemonium for over two hours, until the sight of two policemen dispersed them. 'So much for Carrick', Hanna wrote. Boyle was similarly exciting, with pressure from the local branch of the Ancient Order of Hibernians and the priests keeping away the crowds. Thanks to one friendly Protestant clergyman, they did get a hall and an audience. It was by no means a peaceful evening. A stone shattering one of the windows, together with fights between rival factions, ensured that the meeting received publicity in several papers: 'five baton charges, yards of shattered glass – what journalist could resist these appeals to "copy"?' The stone that smashed the window was later auctioned off as a relic. Everything could be used to further the cause. It was hardly surprising that only the veterans of the League ventured so far from home. Strong nerves and unyielding commitment were essential.[6]

After Boyle, Hanna was back in Dublin, ready to preside over the next evening meeting. The thrust of her talk this time concerned the situation in Ulster. This was becoming very interesting, now that Sir Edward Carson had reneged on a promise made by the Ulster Unionist Council to give women the vote if Ulster formed an independent provisional government outside of Home Rule Ireland. To prevent an Ulster breakaway, the Liberal government was proposing amendments to the Home Rule bill and the moral was plain. If the women of Ireland were not getting the concessions granted to Sir Edward Carson, it was only because they had not been militant enough.

Hanna appealed for women to join the militant ranks and to be ready for the next call.[7]

The double standard of the treatment of Ulster unionists and militant suffragists was galling to both British and Irish militants. Asquith was prepared to amend the Home Rule bill on the unionists' behalf, but when the women had tried to have an amending clause attached to the Bill, they were told it was not possible. The League warned:

> We of the Irishwomen's Franchise League will not only urge these demands by every constitutional means, but will also, following the example of Mr Redmond in the past, and of Sir Edward Carson in the present, take steps to render the government of Ireland impossible by any Party that denies Irish women a share in the election of their rulers.[8]

Gretta travelled down to London to lobby MPs, with the help of some of the London-Irish women. It was dispiriting. Something big was needed to bring Irish women to popular attention. A joint deputation from Ireland of militants and non-militants to see Asquith and Redmond was decided upon. Organising the various disparate groups into a united force was to require considerable diplomacy.

The long-awaited Daffodil Fête in Molesworth Hall in April– successful beyond expectation – was an event that in retrospect seemed part of a brief golden age. So many of those who contributed their time and their talents would not be there when independence was finally won. A women's orchestra played for both afternoons; there were stalls, sideshows, fortune telling, competitions, all with a specifically suffrage flavour. By now this was commonplace in Britain, but not for Irish women, whose smaller resources made an undertaking on this scale a rare event. The highlight of the two days was an ambitious and wide-ranging series of *tableaux* of great women of the past. The dramatic scenes worked best, and greatest praise went to Muriel MacDonagh for her portrayal of Queen Maeve of Connaught; her sister 'John Brennan' as a tortured Anne Devlin; Kathleen Houston about to be burnt at the stake as the martyred Joan of Arc and Constance Markievicz in full armour as 'an astonishingly realistic' Joan of Arc leading her troops into battle. The latter contribution became one of the most powerful images to be associated with Irish feminism. Her posed photograph was a popular addition to the fund-raising souvenirs sold by the movement. Hanna praised her efforts at authenticity: 'What fine fifteenth century pieces she contrived out of cardboard silvered over … And how she toiled over old pictures of the time to get it just right … She flung herself with her usual zest into the part, making a magnificent Joan.'[9] As a finale to the tableaux, the militant Joan of Arc led on the women who had been imprisoned for the cause. They joined together in singing the Women's Marseillaise. Political and strategic differences were put to one side, but it was not an event for someone with unionist sympathies.[10]

Frank's play, *The Prodigal Daughter*, written for the occasion, was staged just before the start of the *tableaux*. This was the tale of a young militant suffragist returning to her small-town home after serving a prison sentence, her determination to lead an independent life challenging the views of her conservative, shop-owning family. The 'entirely suffragist production' was considered 'very good propaganda', by the *Citizen's* critic, who was less happy with the playwright's device of presenting the argument in 'Shavian' terms: the weak characters' objections were 'successively bowled over like ninepins by the strong character, who shares the outlook of the author'.[11] It was a diplomatic response. The main character was much like the argumentative author, always challenging conventional thinking, always prepared to voice what others would hesitate to articulate. That play, while without any literary pretensions, makes an interesting comparison with that of *Cathleen ni Houlihan*, in which Maud Gonne had acted the title role 12 years previously. Then, in the part of the old woman who is transformed into a young girl when men fight for her honour, she influenced a generation of young nationalists. Lily Considine, the heroine of Frank's play was very different. She was not asking any man to act on her behalf: 'I'm not going to settle down to my old, idle, useless life ever again … I'm going to raise the flag of the women's movement in Ballymission and Malmoy!' Those sentiments could not have been expressed in 1902. Dublin Suffrage Week, organised by the non-militant Irish Women's Suffrage Federation the previous December, had introduced Ibsen to an Irish audience through the staging of his play *Rosmersholm*. While not explicitly about suffrage, it 'echoed concerns voiced by the Irish suffragists about the importance of integrating the masculine public sphere and the feminine private sphere.'[12] These cultural events were strong indications of the extent to which the feminist message had penetrated Irish society, in Dublin at least.

Militancy had erupted in the north, where the WSPU had decided (to the great annoyance of the militants of the IWFL) to concentrate its energies. An 'Ulster Centre' was established in Belfast, with Dorothy Evans, a long-serving member, sent over as paid organiser along with two colleagues from Scotland, and local women from the IWSS recruited into the new organisation. Hanna made her displeasure very plain in correspondence with Christabel Pankhurst: 'Under the circumstances it would have been wiser to have tried to cooperate with the local militant society, as you have always hitherto done most helpfully than to scatter militant forces and dissipate militant energies by the introduction of the English militant organisation.[13] Militancy was in danger of making a difficult situation in Ulster a great deal worse. In the circumstances it was an embarrassment for the League to have the Murphy sisters continue to fight against their expulsion from the organisation. When they took their case against the IWFL to court, evidence was given that the executive committee of the League had expelled the women because they were working wholly for the WSPU, whose campaign the Irish women considered 'ill-judged, misdirected and ineffective'. Then, an appalled judge had declared that 'one party was bringing an action against another party arising out of a criminal conspiracy in which they were engaged' and had dismissed the case. Now, in January 1914, an appeal against that decision was heard in court. The Lord Chancellor dismissed the appeal.[14] There was, in any case, little more that militancy could accomplish in Ireland. Hanna believed that the resolution passed by many local councils for the inclusion of women in the amending Home Rule bill and the strong support by the Trades Union Congress for women's enfranchisement, was evidence that public opinion was being won over.[15] In addition, the spectacle of Irish women suffering imprisonment for their beliefs had revived Irish feelings of solidarity with political prisoners; many of the nationalist women they had been at odds with in the past were rallying to their right to protest, despite the perennial issue of suffrage versus nation remaining unresolved. The Home Rule bill was working its way through parliament. It was now all down to Westminster.

There was one last IWFL prisoner. The support she received was yet another indication of the change in attitudes towards the militants. At the end of April Kathleen Houston received a six-week sentence for breaking the windows of the Post Office in College Green. It was a gesture of solidarity with Belfast suffragist Mabel Small, who had been released from Belfast Jail, but only under the terms of the Cat and Mouse Act. Kathleen went on immediate hunger strike to test whether the Act would be put into practice in the south. Two photographs of Hanna outside the jail made the front page of the *Daily Sketch*, its headlines declaring: 'Rebellion through a megaphone: how a suffragette "mouse" was cheered in her prison cell.' Release came after five days. As Kathleen was not required to give any undertakings the *Citizen* boasted that she had 'given the Cat and Mouse Act its quietus in Ireland'.[16]

The League began to attract support from new quarters. The Dublin Trades Council passed a resolution condemning the Cat and Mouse Act;

Jennie Wyse Power and other nationalist women began attending League meetings; Jack White, the maverick ex-British hero who was now drilling the Citizen Army and transforming it from a workers' defence force into something quite different, was a regular speaker for the League. When Emmeline Pethick-Lawrence spoke to a packed meeting at Sackville Hall on 14 May, the contrast with the raucous reception of her last visit was very apparent. Then hecklers from the Irish Party had interrupted the proceedings; now all was harmony. The resolution proposed by Hanna – protesting against the Cat and Mouse Act and demanding a women's suffrage amendment to the Home Rule bill – was passed unanimously.[17] When Barbara Hoskins went to heckle members of the Irish Party in Blackrock, she and her companion discovered an 'unexpected feature of the meeting was the extremely friendly spirit evinced towards the two suffragists'. Not only that, the women got a response to their interjections. The speakers stopped referring exclusively to 'fellow countrymen' and began to refer to 'men and women' or 'people', while some of the participants went as far as declaring themselves in favour of women's suffrage.[18]

The fortunes of the IWFL appeared, to the public eye, to be in very good shape. They had a significant body of members dedicated to the cause and they were certainly having an impact upon public opinion, even if party leaders remained unmoved. Behind the scenes, however, signs of strain were visible. After six years of intense campaigning, the pace of events was beginning to tell. Not all were confident in their abilities to undertake the type of public role that the leaders had shouldered for so long. Their paid office worker, Kathleen Houston, although competent in a supportive role, was too nervous to speak at large public meetings. She resigned in December, after long service to the cause. Another stalwart, Kathleen Emerson, agreed to speak only after being begged to by a desperate Hanna: 'shall go to the Park as promised but dread it and feel horribly nervous – seem to get worse and worse'.[19] The vicissitudes common to any woman's organisation also had a detrimental effect upon their ability to maintain the momentum. As Hanna had discovered when she was expecting Owen, the social conventions surrounding the conduct of pregnant women were an infuriating hindrance to those committed to fighting for a cause. Marguerite Palmer, who gave birth in August, found this particularly difficult, wishing 'this wretched waiting period was over'. That June, Meg Connery had either a miscarriage or an operation that led to a miscarriage. She was to suffer intermittent ill health (attacks of 'lassitude and mental exhaustion … when this trouble descends on me can't do anything') constantly in the decades to come.[20] Some indication of the pressures this put

Hanna under can be seen in this letter from Gretta, who was fretting over her inability to ease the burden of her friend:

> I was troubled to hear that you have had to shoulder all the office work. I did hope Mrs Palmer would have stuck it till June … and to think Miss Houston too is so far from fit! I'm glad to hear Mrs Connery is not in hospital. Poor you, you must be feeling in a tired, strained condition. I wish I could be with you to help … Good that Miss Maxwell has come in so strong. She should be pillars of strength to you.[21]

Everyone realised that the organisation could not survive without Hanna. While Gretta soothingly agreed with her friend's complaints about the treasurer's shortcomings, she made it plain that she believed the problem to be more far-reaching than simply one individuals' inefficiency, 'agree it's hard not to have a more active treasurer than Mrs Wilkins. yet who would be really any better of our present members?'[22] Marguerite Palmer was also explicit in her recognition that the other League members were far less competent than their chairwoman:

> Thank you dear Hanna Sheehy Skeffington for your thoughtful offer of help – to know that you are at the helm again is all I need – I never know an easy moment when your hand is off the ropes. Don't worry over me – I'm as fit as a fiddle and shall be back at work in no time … if you see me wavering, don't show me any quarter![23]

She was too optimistic. Ill-health after childbirth meant that, although she continued to visit her friends in the IWFL rooms, it was mid-1915 before she was truly able to return to 'active service'. A reception (premature, as it turned out) to welcome Marguerite and Meg's 'return to the firing line', acknowledged the gap that their absence had created. All present agreed that at least a dozen workers were needed to fill the place of each.[24]

Other members had to juggle political commitments with their family concerns. Eva Wilkins, the League treasurer, whose husband Maurice helped occasionally with the *Citizen*, struggled to cope with a husband who was desperately searching for teaching posts in England and the north of Ireland, a baby with whooping cough, no domestic help, and the exacting demands of the League. She finally gave up the struggle in May 1915 and resigned the treasurership.[25] Hanna, although sympathetic to those she considered to be doing their best to remain active, had little sympathy for those whom she thought were not pulling their weight. After all, she also had to cope with domestic responsibilities and she also had a husband who was often away from home. Everyone was needed in this last phase of the struggle. She was, however, fortunate to have some domestic help and an important network of female relatives. She also had a sublime indifference to domestic concerns. So long as there was time for Owen, now a sturdy five-year-old, the house could muddle along as best as it could.

The final effort to persuade Redmond and Asquith to amend the Home Rule bill on women's behalf was a joint effort by all the Irish suffrage groups. Cooperation was only gained after much delicate negotiation: no militancy, no talk of militancy, no suggestion that participation in the delegation was indicative of a nationalist or unionist persuasion. Hanna was chief negotiator/persuader for the League, responsible for a flurry of correspondence hurtling around Ireland and Britain, as women were entreated to take part. Many of the Irish women felt that there was little point in meeting their arch enemies again. More than a few had reservations about taking part in a joint platform with militants, particularly militants whose political views could be regarded as distinctly nationalist.[26] On the other hand, support from women in Britain was encouraging. Emmeline Pethick-Lawrence, expelled from the WSPU and now part of the 'United Suffragists', was particularly helpful. She would put Hanna up in her flat in central London and she did all she could to ensure that the delegation would have some impact, regardless of whether the politicians took notice of them. If the women were refused an audience, then the United Suffragists would sponsor an 'indignation meeting' at Essex Hall so the Irish women would have an opportunity to vent their feelings.[27]

On 11 June Hanna, Margaret McCoubrey from Belfast and Dora Mellone from Warrenpoint, assembled at St Stephen's Hall, armed with copies of the *Irish Citizen* and wearing orange and green badges. Sympathetic MPs, briefed by Emmeline Pethick-Lawrence, delivered their messages, and the women waited for some reply. They had decided in advance that they would wait for two hours before making any protest, so they whiled away the time by intercepting Irish and Labour MPs, asking for their views. Hanna's account of the afternoon was written with her customary shafts of wit. Most MPs were too busy 'escorting parties of fashionably-dressed ladies to the inner sanctuary of the House (no woman can pass nowadays without a member, who vouches for her "good conduct"), where strawberries and cream awaited them on the terrace'. It was not an occasion for anger – the nonappearance of the politicians had been anticipated – so instead of impassioned denunciations the article was very much a reflection of the woman as she was in everyday life. Encountering a 'party woman' ('despised species for all suffragists') 'doing the drudgery for the politicians', who was also waiting for a politician to turn up and complaining that too often MPs signed petitions without reading the contents, Hanna's response was the cynical comment 'that would be the only way of getting them to sign anything worth signing'. Another party hack gave 'harrowing details as to the physical and mental degeneracy of the militants which make me thankful I had hitherto escaped committal as a criminal lunatic'. Her most constructive conversation was to be asked, by a female German journalist, to explain the difference between suffragist and suffragette. It felt good to be able to use her proficiency in languages once again.[28]

At five o'clock, weary of the pointless wait, the Irish women held their protest meeting in the lobby. Margaret McCoubrey, representing northern militants, shouted 'they only mind the militants who have guns' while another cried out 'Had we been men, they would have heard us.' The women were finally escorted off the premises by the police, but at least it was without the violence that had been a feature of previous demonstrations. Later, Hanna and other women returned to the House of Commons. On their way they saw mounted police brutally breaking up a demonstration of working-class women from Sylvia Pankhurst's organisation, the East End Federation. Sylvia herself was rearrested and then the women watched in horror as the police rode their horses 'upon the pavements, on to the steps even of private houses, flinging the crowd, men, women and little children, pell-mell before them, penning them frightened into corners, crushing them together in masses and closing in on them'. It was an indication of how much more bitter the suffrage campaign was in Britain. The women from Ireland, even at the height of the controversy during Asquith's visit, had not experienced those kinds of scenes.[29] That evening the United Suffragists hosted an indignation meeting in Essex Hall for the Irish delegates, attended mainly by Irish women in London, at which all three delegates insisted that Irishwomen of all shades of political opinion were united in the demand for recognition as citizens.[30]

The deputation to Britain was the last of the big events to take place before the First World War broke out, which altered every calculation. By August, Britain and Germany were at war and pacifists everywhere despaired. The *Irish Citizen* immediately printed a poster with the slogan 'Votes For Women Now – Damn Your War!', which Frank insisted on sticking to the gatepost of their house. Grosvenor Place was largely inhabited by retired professionals belonging to various Protestant denominations. They were staunchly pro-British. The poster was torn down. Frank put up another. Owen was told to stand guard and warn his father if any neighbour attacked it. The little boy remembered being 'rather frightened'. A retired colonel from over the road, armed with golf club, came out and pushed him aside, ripping the poster with slashes of the club. Owen gave his warning too late. There was no one there when Frank dashed out, hoping for an opportunity to argue over the issue.[31] Some of the women selling the *Citizen* were afraid to display the poster, in case they were mobbed. The braver souls reported 'no unpleasantness', but it was a contentious issue in suffrage circles. Some objected to the issue of the vote being linked to the war. The Irish Women's Reform League announced in haughty tones that it was suspending selling the *Irish Citizen* for the next three months.[32] Hanna's immediate response was to write an impassioned article for the *Citizen*, calling on women to stand firm in their determination to keep the feminist cause alive:

> attempts will be made to induce women to abandon propaganda, to roll up the map of suffrage with the map of Europe, to forget their own pressing economic and political grievances (now more acute than ever) because of the 'national crisis'.
>
> ... If male statesmanship after all these centuries has nothing better to offer by way of adjusting differences than a universal shambles, then in heaven's name let men allow women to lend a hand, not at mopping up the blood and purifying the stench of the abattoir, but at clearing away the whole rotten system. Until then it is our duty to press on with unabated energy to increase our activities at this crisis, to preach peace, sanity and suffrage.
>
> ... War must not devastate our ranks: this at least is in our power to prevent. Our guns must be directed, not against the Germans (from whom, by the way, we have much to learn) but against our common enemy - the war-mongering politicians, the pledge-breaking government, now so sentimental over the wrongs of oppressed nationalities, while it continues to sweat and bully with impunity the women of the land. These are the enemy; it is these upon whom we wage war until they offer terms[33]

Many women did not share these views. Hanna's friend Violet Jameson, now Violet Crichton, married and living outside London, wrote to protest that the wounded had to be tended. Hanna's insistence that 'it is not for us to mitigate by one iota the horrors of war' was, Violet argued, an 'inhumane stand'.[34] A year later, her irritation at Hanna's opposition to the military census led her to write an 'Open Letter' to the *Citizen*. Hanna's reply insisted that her opposition was based upon strict suffrage principles. It was not she who had deviated from the feminist cause.[35]In Britain, the WSPU became violently patriotic. Suffrage work was called off and women pledged their services to the war effort. The WSPU Belfast office was shut down, leaving some of its members bemused and wondering what to do. The *Citizen's* editor made a strong riposte to the jingoist British: 'We have all along steadily opposed the establishment of WSPU branches in Ireland, on the ground that this organisation could not take root in Ireland and was liable to be diverted from its Irish work at any time, without regard to the welfare of its Irish members or the actualities of the Irish situation.'[36] Gretta, still in England and meeting suffrage workers who had been told to cease activities, shared the outrage felt at the WSPU closing down their local offices: 'I can well imagine you and Mr Skeffington feeling sick at the pro-English sentiments current in Ireland now.' She too felt that the IWFL was the only 'bright spot on suffrage work'.[37]

Margaret McCoubrey wrote to ask Hanna for her help in establishing a branch of the IWFL to replace the WSPU. She felt it was important to have one militant group in the north, but many refused to have anything to do with a group based in the nationalist part of the country. Margaret, a plain-speaking Scot married to a trade unionist, was a forceful and determined character, desperate to ensure that the feminist cause remained alive in Belfast. She and Hanna corresponded over many months in their efforts to establish the League in Belfast. As so many women had testified before, Hanna's political acumen was recognised and urgently needed: 'You have accumulated much wisdom over the years.' Hanna's steady encouragement and her patience in maintaining the correspondence gives the lie to those who would see her as too hasty or impatient in expressing her opinions. Her understanding of the difficulties in establishing progressive politics in the sectarian atmosphere of Belfast led her to counsel caution. While there in November to meet with Margaret McCoubrey and Lilian Metge (and finding the time to visit Frank's Aunt Bella), she thought the place 'very war-mad' and felt a few weeks would be needed to enable acrimony between members to die down before anything constructive could be suggested.[38] McCoubrey acknowledged her support with gratitude, 'I can't express how much your letter cheered me and gave me courage to go on … note all the things you say – we must just go slowly – if only we may have the glory of "going on" I shall be exceedingly pleased.'[39] As chair of the IWFL, Hanna did everything in her power to keep its 'Ulster Centre' alive by speaking at Belfast meetings, insisting that the Ulster branch was represented at League events and reporting all its meetings in the *Citizen*. It was represented as being greater than it really was, an exaggeration pardonable in the cause of maintaining an all-Ireland dimension to suffragism, but it was supported by Marie Johnson, Winifred Carney and others in the labour movement, as well as by Lilian Metge and a few other northern militants.

There was even more reason to challenge Redmond at every conceivable opportunity, now that the militants in Britain had given up the fight. In October, Hanna pursued Redmond as he toured the country on a recruiting mission. She kept a press photo of Redmond's platform amongst her papers, adding her own pencilled inscription: 'I was there – and thrown out.'[40] That short inscription does not tell the whole story. Maire Moran, a young Cumann na mBan activist, later recalled meeting Hanna at that Redmondite meeting in Wexford. The Irish Volunteers were handing out leaflets and getting 'a very rough handling from the crowd' while Hanna 'got so badly beaten that she had to be attended by a doctor.'[41] Sean T. O'Kelly (writing his witness account in the 1940s when President of Ireland) was even more explicit in his account of Hanna's intervention. To the surprise of the Irish Volunteers, who were preparing to heckle, a woman stood on a box right in front of the platform, 'calling on people to repudiate Redmond and his recruiting policy.' When she threw back her veil they saw the woman was Mrs Skeffington, who was then very roughly handled by men, 'tearing her clothes' and carrying her towards the harbour, 'After she had been carried a considerable distance from the meeting, the police and some of the crowd intervened and much battered and torn and, I am sure, very much bruised, Mrs Skeffington was rescued.'[42] Divisions between the Irish Party and advanced nationalists over the war had made political rallies even more contentious than before.

Hanna tried to persuade Rose Jacob to heckle Redmond when his entourage arrived in Waterford. Rose was quite capable of writing effective polemical pieces for the *Citizen*, but this was different: 'I know Redmond should be heckled at next Sunday and told what decent people think of him, but the plain fact is, I haven't the courage to do it. The idea makes me feel sick with terror.' She would be prepared to distribute more anti-enlisting leaflets but felt that the one produced by Hanna was 'rather too strong for them; they would not understand it'.[43] Women abroad were impressed by the stance of the IWFL. Alice Park had stopped off in Ireland on her way home from the Budapest conference, and she and Hanna began a friendship which continued until Hanna's death. This American connection provided an invaluable outlet for propaganda. Alice ensured that Hanna's article against the war was circulated as a small pamphlet by the international suffrage organisations.[44] It was reprinted several times in many different forms, a fervent advocacy of the causes of feminism, pacifism and socialism. Within Ireland, some who had not been on good terms with the League now found themselves in agreement with its current stand. Louie Bennett, who had been such an opponent of the militant policy, was terribly depressed about the war and the fact that all the women's organisations had 'gone to pieces', except for the IWFL, whose stability she admired.[45] The non-militant Mary Hayden agreed to speak at a forthcoming League meeting. The changed circumstances of war and the difficulty in maintaining momentum on the suffrage issue enabled alliances to be made between different groups and individuals which helped to break down some of the barriers.

Hanna's single-mindedness was not always shared by some of her less politically minded colleagues. Florence Ball, a committee member, resigned in indignation after being accused by her of disloyalty. She was uncompromising with those who did not follow policy absolutely. The League was a political organisation and as such, demanded discipline from its members. Meg Connery, often the most outspoken of them all, stepped in as mediator. Hanna agreed to withdraw the 'disloyal' charge, but not unconditionally, insisting that Mrs Ball gave a 'written assurance she will work cordially for the IWFL in future and support its policy unreservedly'.[46] Florence Ball's interests had always been on the social and fund-raising side - invaluable on occasions like the Daffodil Fête – but people like her began to slip away in the harder times now coming. At least Meg was back at work, her writings in the *Citizen* applauded by Frank as a 'reawakening'.[47]

The undaunted duo of Meg Connery and Hanna Sheehy Skeffington were together again in September, busy leafletting 'friendly, if puzzled' crowds while Asquith visited Ireland on an army recruiting mission. Tight security surrounded the visit and all streets leading to the Mansion House were blocked off. Asquith was guarded by the Volunteers, while a labour meeting, spoken to by Larkin and Connolly, was guarded by members of the Citizen Army, who occasionally discharged their rifles into the air during the meeting. Hanna felt as though the streets 'bristled with armed men'. Their leaflets handed out, she and Meg were arrested as they tried to make speeches from the fountain at the top of Dawson Street. One 'hero' attacked them – a postman in uniform struck Meg between the shoulders and then the face, while she was immobilised by the police holding her hands – but they felt the crowds were sympathetic, not hostile. As they were marched down Grafton Street to the College Street police station friends joined the procession in their wake. To Hanna's amusement, there was great confusion in the police station. Looking around her, she remarked on the difficulty in sorting out the sheep from the goats. At midnight, after being held for two hours, they were released without charge.[48] Some progress had been made. When Bonar Law had come to Ireland, Hanna had served a week in jail. This time, she had only a short detention and found no hostility from the Dublin crowds. Significantly, the women concluded that the police had not interfered with the labour meeting because they were afraid of the Citizen Army bodyguard. It was a 'striking' contrast to the treatment of the women.[49] The gun was increasingly visible in political life. Not everyone thought this was always to be deplored. Passive resistance could take some very militant forms.

As war fever and censorship increased, the pages of the *Citizen* were one of the few places where opposition could still be expressed. It gave space to many letters rejected by the ordinary press because of their anti-war stance. Frank's voice was a desperate attempt to instill some sense of the reality of war's consequences:

> War can breed nothing but a fresh crop of wars. By accepting this war, in any degree whatsoever, we are helping to perpetuate war. If we want to stop war, we must begin by stopping this war. The only way we can do that is to hamper as far as possible the conduct of it. The best way to do that is to stop recruiting.[50]

He would continue to make that argument, Sunday after Sunday, in Beresford Place. But it was no longer the Franchise League holding weekly meetings at that spot, it was the Socialist Party of Ireland. Frank and Hanna were still members of that organisation, as were several other IWFL members, Meg included. James Connolly, the driving force behind the socialists, had moved from Belfast to Dublin to take over as chief organiser for the Transport Union while Jim Larkin was in America. Connolly had supported the suffragists in their struggle and now the most active of the suffragists were to prove themselves sympathetic to the socialist message.

There were other controversies too. In 1913 nationalists had formed the Irish Volunteers as an armed body in response to the Ulster Volunteer Force. Soon after, the Volunteers had been taken over and tamed by the politicians of the Irish Party. When, in a final affront to nationalist sensitivities, Redmond had insisted in offering the services of the Volunteers to the British war effort, the organisation split into two very different sections. Tom Kettle was one who followed Redmond's lead. The small group of advanced nationalists who refused to follow Redmond included Thomas MacDonagh. Now that the hated incubus of the Irish Party had been thrown off, Frank found himself tempted to join, but there were a number of issues he first wanted answers to. Times had changed and he expected nationalists to understand that. Skeffington wanted 'to see the age-long fight against injustice clothe itself in new forms, suited to a new age'. His 'Open Letter' to his old friend Thomas MacDonagh, printed in the *Citizen* and later republished as a pamphlet, eloquently described the vision that motivated him:

> Can you not conceive an organisation, a body of men and women banded together to secure and maintain the rights and liberties of the people of Ireland, a body animated with a high purpose, united by a bond of comradeship, trained and

> disciplined in the ways of self-sacrifice and true patriotism, armed and equipped with the weapons of intellect and of will that are irresistible?[51]

It would be, he hoped, very different from the militaristic, masculine fighting force that had traditionally taken up the gun for Irish freedom. The other important issue to be settled was the type of future society envisaged by the Volunteers. The Volunteers' silence on women's suffrage made him hesitate. Having experienced six years of intense struggle around that issue, women's right to citizenship had to be included within the aims of the organisation. Would they support the liberties of the people of Ireland 'without distinction of sex, class, or creed', he asked? They remained silent. Irish women did not have the vote, but the Volunteers refused to alienate any potential supporters by insisting that such a commitment be included within their policies. Although MacDonagh claimed, awkwardly, that he himself included women in his conception of 'the nation', it continued to be an all-male organisation that said nothing about women.

In March 1914 nationalist women launched their separate organisation – Cumann na mBan – as an auxiliary to the men. Inghinidhe na hÉireann became a branch of Cumann na mBan, but in reality, the most radical of the Inghinidhe women were involved in working with the labour movement in Liberty Hall, and the egalitarian Citizen Army was much more to their liking. The subordinate status of Cumann na mBan, exemplified in their lack of representation on the Volunteer executive, was a constant source of irritation to the women of the Franchise League. Old friends and former colleagues like Jennie Wyse Power, as president of the new organisation, Elizabeth Bloxham, who had provided invaluable support as a suffrage speaker during the difficult months in the summer of 1912, and Mary Colum, now threw their energies into this new group. Hanna hated the idea that women were not equal within nationalist ranks. She made her views plain on every possible occasion, an uncomfortable and isolated presence at many nationalist meetings. Her heckling at the inaugural meeting of Cumann na mBan in Wynn's Hotel produced uproar and cries for the 'insolent one' to be put out. As Hanna surveyed the scene, she summed up her feelings with some bitterness. Men were unable to buy a rifle unless women collected the money: 'women the ministering angel of the ambulance class, who provides the pyjamas and the lint, but who sinks below the human the moment she asks for a vote!'[52] Those who had served prison sentences as a consequence of their fight for women's right to equality were in no mood to accept explanations or reassurances and her language became steadily more accusatory, to the point where she dismissed Cumann na mBan women as nothing more than 'animated collecting boxes' for the men.

The old antagonism between those who put the 'nation' before the women's cause had flared up once more. And women were the losers. In public, Constance Markievicz shared the indignation of nationalist women, who bitterly resented these slights upon their status. In private, however, she tended to agree with feminist criticisms. When the League invited Constance to address one of their meetings, she was exceptionally explicit:

> Today the women attached to national movements are there chiefly to collect funds for the men to spend. These Ladies' Auxiliaries demoralise women, set them up in separate camps and deprive them of all initiative and independence.[53]

It was vindication of all Hanna's angry reproaches. The pity was that a united feminist voice could not be put to the Volunteers, forcing them to declare themselves committed to women's liberation as well as the liberation of the nation. On principle, no matter how much circumstances or policies changed over the years, Cumann na mBan was the one organisation that Hanna would never join.

In retrospect, the years of campaigning and imprisonment prior to the war would seem like halcyon times. War changed everything. The anti-war stand of the *Citizen* was seriously damaging its finances, as many who had supported it would do so no longer. Frank wrote to Margaret McCoubrey, asking her advice on whether he could approach the wealthy Miss Lindsay to act as guarantor for a £100 loan on the *Irish Citizen* after one of its guarantors had pulled out in protest against the *Citizen*'s opposition to conscription.[54] For him, as a freelance journalist, the situation caused by war and press censorship was a disaster. His income plummeted. Fortunately, Hanna was able to find some work with the Dublin Technical Institute, again teaching languages. Aunt Kate was one of several to write of her pleasure in hearing of the new job. Although Kate was always generous with loans of money when times were bad, they were reluctant to get into further debt. And now other members of the Sheehy clan were in worse straits. In March 1915 David Sheehy was declared bankrupt with unsecured debts of £683 and assets valued at £65. Belvedere Place, the scene of so much good companionship, was left empty as they went to live with their daughter Margaret and the Culhane family.[55] Their neighbour, T. D. Sullivan, had died the year before, his house listed baldly as 'tenements' by Thom's Directory. The Sheehy home became part of the war effort, as Trinity College's V. A. D. Belgian Hostel. David and Bessie went over to England. In March, Gretta, on a speaking tour for the

Freedom League, met them with Mary Kettle in Bath.[56] Why they were there she didn't say. Bessie's arthritis had worsened, so possibly they were there for medicinal reasons, to take the waters. Uncle Eugene too was in England, writing to Hanna with his new London address and sending money.[57]

A Women's International Peace Congress was planned for the Hague in May 1915, and seven delegates were chosen to represent Ireland. Numerous tense meetings took place as they attempted to agree upon some common policy. Lucy Kingston, a member of the Irish Women's Reform League, noted in her diary that during these hot debates: 'Mrs Sheehy Skeffington good and non-party.'[58] Louie Bennett was insistent that 'all controversial topics in connection with war – pro-Germanism, recruiting, etc' be ruled out of order before she would agree to speak at the weekly League meeting. She did not want to be 'unreasonable', but she refused to be drawn into what she termed 'futile arguments'.[59] Markedly unsympathetic to Irish nationalism, she believed the cause of international peace was the only valid issue for the Congress. All personal opinions should be suppressed. Hanna's attitude was in striking contrast, as she made plain in private correspondence with Louie. Many in Ireland were pro-German and anti-British and would be happy to see their traditional enemy defeated. They had to be made to feel, as Hanna explained, that the peace cause could be of some benefit to Ireland: 'Peace propaganda in Ireland must be different from England – need to stir up feeling against this particular war by stirring up Irish sentiment. That is why a protest meeting succeeds where a purely peace meeting would not.'[60] None of this was voiced publicly. The compromise solution to what was an intractable division of opinion was that the Franchise League should have a separate delegation comprising of Hanna, Margaret McCoubrey and (a last-minute addition) Lilian Metge from Lisburn, also from the old Ulster WSPU. Hanna was jubilant:

> For the first time Ireland has a separate entity and Irish delegates take their place as representatives of their own country. It is the hour of small nationalities. Long live the small nationalities of the earth![61]

Peace would be achieved when justice and liberty were won. The twin causes of feminism and national self-determination could not be separated. As well as agreeing to resolutions on such matters as economic boycotts as an alternative means of settling disputes between nations, the Franchise League had its own, quite separate resolution to put to the congress. Hanna's hand was evident in its wording:

> This International Congress of Women, recognising that Peace, to be permanent, must be founded on Justice and Liberty, and that the government of one nation

> by another is a frequent cause of war, urges that Subject Nationalities should be offered a path to freedom not involving war or war-like preparations and that to this end international machinery should be provided under the auspices of a world-wide International Council, whereby all subject people shall have the power, by plebiscite of their men and women effectively to declare whether they are contented with their lot or would prefer a change of government.[62]

There was no way the authorities would have facilitated such a platform. The Irish delegates went over to London to meet their British counterparts and then discovered that Reginald McKenna, the Home Secretary, had decided that none of the militant suffragists – British or Irish – would be given permits to travel. She spent a fruitless week 'besieging' the House of Commons and the Home Office: 'I tried to buck up Harrison again & goaded Devlin but he shows no sign of life'. Her general impression was 'votes is dead in England – everywhere ... and I am more disgusted with all women than I can say.' Of the Irish delegates, only Louie Bennett was considered acceptable in government eyes. Her permit proved utterly useless, as the government closed the North Sea to all ships so, in the end, only one solitary British woman succeeded in reaching the Hague – Emmeline Pethick-Lawrence – who sailed from the U.S. with the American contingent. All the women were furious. Hanna was outspoken in her anger, 'Really the boats dodge is the best yet.'[63] Despite this disappointment, 1,000 delegates from 12 countries did manage to get to the Hague. They formed the Women's International League for Peace, an organisation which would have close future links with Ireland.

At a public meeting in the Dublin Trades Hall, organised to show solidarity with the suppressed peace delegation, Hanna insisted that they would have been delighted if Louie Bennett had succeeded in getting through to represent Ireland. She could not, however, resist making a dig at her colleague: 'The selected twenty included Miss Bennett, who was discreet, she (the speaker) notoriously was not (laughter).' They had called the meeting so that they could send Asquith and McKenna a message that 'Ireland was still alive; and apt to kick them now and then'. Militancy was the keynote of the evening. The event, well attended by nationalists as well as by feminists, was notable for an ill-considered message of support from Patrick Pearse, who hoped that the 'present incident will do good if it ranges more of the women definitely with the national forces'. Meg Connery, a most interventionist chair, felt compelled to protest at what she condemned as this 'very masculine inversion'. There was loud applause for her feminist re-reading: 'The incident ought to have the effect of ranging the national forces on the side of women', and an embarrassed Thomas MacDonagh, on the platform to second the resolution of protest, was forced to accept her criticism. He added that as a Volunteer he hoped he would have a better opportunity than voting to show that by 'people' he meant the women as well as men of Ireland. His graphic and gruesome description of bayonet practice left his audience in no doubt as to his future hopes. Meg again used the privilege of the chair to intervene. She had considerable sympathy with the Irish Volunteers, but she objected intensely to bloodshed. In her eyes, it was a 'finer patriotism to live and fight for your country than to die for it'. The aspirations of the militant nationalists were well understood by many.[64] To the IWFL members Hanna continued to argue that war needed to be fought by 'active as well as by passive methods'. Resolutions were not enough. In this, she and Frank were in complete agreement. After making 40 speeches against the war he was eventually arrested, charged with making statements likely to cause disaffection to the King and likely to prejudice recruiting for His Majesty's forces.

Frank was taken to Mountjoy, to await trial on 9 June. Dr Skeffington was furious, blaming his daughter-in-law for having influenced his son through the example of her own prison sentences: 'he courted all this and even said he rather liked a while in gaol, probably to rival your heroic deeds for you are no wiser than he is, in action at least, and I am afraid set him a bad example, instead of being a restraining influence and when the house is on fire at both ends, it is as bad as candle burning at both ends.'[65] However apoplectic Frank's father became, Owen would not suffer - £10 was still enclosed in the letter. In their different ways, people rallied round. Louie Bennett was 'very sorry', although not at all surprised to learn of Frank's arrest and immediately offered to help with bringing out the *Citizen* during his absence. [66] Charles Oldham, fearing that Hanna would now be 'in temporary financial difficulties' as he tactfully phrased it, immediately sent a cheque for £4-19 and offered to pay the rent while Frank was in jail.[67] Another gift of money came from Deborah Webb, a 'little legacy' which she wished would be used by Hanna and Frank.[68] Their financial situation was so precarious that Hanna even tried, while Frank was in jail, to persuade their landlady to release them from the rest of their lease on the house.[69] Hanna now had her husband to campaign for, her son to look after and the *Irish Citizen* to keep going. In letters to Frank she maintained a positive, breezy tone which she could not have been feeling 'inundated with callers and inquirers – you needn't worry about me – I'll be all right, so will Owen's sums! He is quite delighted telling everyone Dada is in jail! And wants to go to see you.'[70] She sent parcels of almonds, cheese, jam and a whole host of food, along with books and newspapers, assuring him that the Wilkins, the Oldhams, the Houstons and Louie Bennett had all offered to help with any work required.[71] Frank was a demanding prisoner. Sir Matthew Nathan, the new Under Secretary for State for Ireland, contacted Hanna to inform her she could see him in some other room 'than that to which you referred as objectionable in your conversation … this morning.'[72]

As a political propagandist Frank had absolute confidence in the integrity of his position. He was a militantly passive resister but an Irish nationalist also. To those who could not understand, he would argue to his last breath. He concluded his speech from the dock with the words: 'any sentence you may pass on me is a sentence upon British rule in Ireland'. When the magistrate imposed six month's hard labour and six additional months in default of bail – the maximum penalty possible – Frank went on immediate hunger strike, vowing that 'long before the expiration of the sentence I shall be out of prison, alive or dead!'[73] After six days he also began a thirst strike, and family and friends were frantic in their efforts to win his release. Dr J. B. wired everyone, pathetically anxious about his boy, as in this telegram to the prison doctor: 'please see that my son is not done to death in prison'.[74] He wired Hanna constantly, wanting the latest news, but he never asked about her or about how she was coping under this intolerable strain.

Hanna was of course fighting hard, writing to anyone with influence. George Bernard Shaw sent her back a splendidly defiant letter. He was full of anti-British sentiments but not prepared to act as Frank had done. The Defence of the Realm Act and the suspension of normal democratic safeguards that had accompanied the advent of war allowed the state to do what it would. In Shaw's opinion, Frank had 'made a very grave mistake in putting his head into the lion's mouth'.[75] When Hanna wondered if she could make his letter public, his wire replied grandly, 'Certainly, I wrote it for publication at your discretion.'

The IWFL petitioned the Chief Secretary on behalf of Frank and Seán Milroy and Seán MacDermott, who were imprisoned with him – MacDermott, a key figure in the IRB, would be one of the leaders of the Easter Rising. As a suffrage group, with no other mandate, they had to be careful how they phrased their protests. While 'in no way associating ourselves with their views or propaganda' they felt that 'in the interests of humanity and justice this man should not be allowed to die'.[76] Hanna's presence at the IWFL platform in Phoenix Park was 'very sympathetically received by the crowd', but she was no grieving wife – certainly not in public. Defiantly she argued that 'no one got anything from government without asking, and when necessary, pressing for it.'[77]

In private, her closest friends knew how hard it was for her to endure the thought of Frank on hunger and thirst strike. Gretta understood that it was 'more trying' to have her husband in prison than to be in prison herself.[78] Her bleak experiences of hunger strike haunted her. She was distraught enough to wire London to ask her father for help, something she would never have countenanced on her own behalf. As he and Bessie sat in the Gower Hotel, waiting helplessly for news, Bessie wrote to Hanna that David declared that he felt so desperate he was prepared to take Frank's place in prison.[79] That might have been Bessie's way of reconciling daughter and husband rather than a truthful depiction of reality, as in private correspondence with British officials David Sheehy took a much less sympathetic line. Birrell, as Chief Secretary, told his Lord Lieutenant, Sir Matthew Nathan, that David Sheehy 'was most anxious that his son-in-law should be left in prison but hard labour for him is really impossible'.[80] A few days later, realising how weak Frank was, David admitted to Nathan he was 'apprehensive' and promised that he and Hanna ('yea, even she') would use their influence to prevent him from making further anti-recruitment speeches.[81] Even at this most difficult of times, David Sheehy's antagonism towards his daughter and son-in-law remained evident.

Apart from the ambivalence of David Sheehy, the prospect of losing Frank served to unite the family. Mary Kettle, on holiday in Wales, wrote immediately of her admiration for the 'splendid courage to support your ideas' which both Frank and Hanna so obviously possessed. Mindful of their past arguments over religion, she worded her goodbye with care: 'and – if you let me say – God help you, your loving sister'. As her husband had joined the Dublin Fusiliers and was a prime speaker at recruiting meetings around Ireland, Mary's position was delicate. Tom Kettle's new cause was in direct opposition to that of his friend and brother-in-law. Germany, not Britain, was his enemy and a good Irishman was one who would enlist in the British army. In these circumstances, her feelings for Frank, difficult to put into words, were also those of a woman caught in an impossible situation: 'though we do not quite agree on politics – still you both fight splendidly. It is dreadful to think what you have both gone through. I have been very anxious and worried, but Kathleen was good and wrote every day. Really I did not know how fond I was of Frank till this – but I am almost a pro-German now!'[82] Their brother Eugene had also enlisted in the Dublin Fusiliers and David Sheehy, as a loyal follower of Redmond, backed the Irish Party's support for Britain. As Hanna admitted, she and Frank 'were in a small minority' in the family.[83] Kathleen and Cruise were the only other members to continue supporting the League. In these circumstances, expressions of support for Frank required a determined suppression of personal views. Kathleen, at home in Dublin, kept the various scattered members of the family informed of the latest developments, while Cruise O'Brien used all his contacts on behalf of his brother-in-law. On the seventh day of the hunger strike O'Brien had good news. He wrote confidentially of his intervention with Nathan - there would be no forcible feeding and Frank should be out that evening. The situation was very different from the days of suffrage protests and celebrations for released prisoners, as her brother-in-law made clear, 'But do Hanna try to get him away after this. They are apt to be savage. Kathleen will tell you more ... Cheer up. They are determined not to kill him this time.'[84]

A relieved Hanna dashed off a postcard to her Uncle Eugene: 'F. released tonight at 6.30. Am fetching him home. Very weak. Has been an awful time but is over!'[85] Owen remembered his father, 'a pale skeleton of his recent self', being slowly helped up the garden path on his return home. Even his voice was almost gone as he tried to greet me, "Hello laddie."'[86] It was not an unconditional release. Frank was a 'mouse' under the Cat and Mouse Act, expected to report back to prison two weeks later. Hanna was indignant, bombarding the press with letters to explain that this was the first non-suffragist offence to come under the operation of the Act. According to its terms, her husband was condemned to repeated hunger strikes, followed by permanent disablement or death.[87] She demanded that the rest of his sentence be remitted, and the government, aware of the strength of his support, made no move to re-arrest him.

Mary found a reasonably priced cottage near herself in the village of Penmaenmaur, where she and little Betty were continuing to holiday. Tom was drinking heavily, his role as recruiting officer totally unsuitable to his abilities and temperament – it was best to be away. As soon as Frank was well enough to travel, he, Hanna and Owen crossed the Irish Sea, slipping away from the threat of re-arrest. Suffragist friends sent delicacies to help him regain his strength. He decided to try a vegetarian diet, on the grounds that this would be the most healthy. Owen remembered that month in Wales very clearly. It was his last family summer.

Frank's concern for the future of the *Irish Citizen*, a crucial weapon in his non-violent armoury, had led him to take out a £500 life insurance policy.[88] If anything happened to him, the paper would be able to go on. At this time, its debts were close to £200, and although he continually urged supporters to get more advertisements to increase revenue, he was very choosy as to what kind of advertisement he would allow – tobacco and alcohol were definitely out. During the time he and Hanna were in Wales, two members of the IWFL, Marion Duggan and Mary Bourke-Dowling, helped Maurice Wilkins to produce the paper. Marion was a recent recruit, her antipathy fading as the campaign of militancy ended. The harassed temporary editor hoped that Hanna thought the first issue he produced 'was good enough'. While his female helpers were working 'like trojans' he worried about his abilities on the editorial side, 'not feeling quite au fait about things generally – don't think I want to spoil your holiday, but hints or criticisms will be gratefully received'.[89]

Frank could not make a living as a journalist while the Cat and Mouse threat hung over him. Nor was a return to Ireland particularly prudent. It was decided that a lecture tour of America might be financially and professionally rewarding. As soon as Frank sailed away at the end of July, Hanna and Owen returned home, she to take over the *Citizen*, to continue teaching, to look after League business and, of course, to take care of their son. Frank's first American article showed that he had recovered his old form: 'On the boat, coming across the Atlantic, I had many arguments and discussions on the question with my fellow passengers. Hardly any were opposed to the suffrage.'[90]

On 1 August nationalist Ireland united in tremendous strength to pay tribute to the veteran Fenian O'Donovan Rossa, who had died in exile in America. Constance Markievicz was in one of the mourning carriages, and Cumann na mBan members came from all over the country, including Belfast, to take part in the funeral procession. Elizabeth Bloxham, attending as a Cumann na mBan member, had clear recollections of marching beside Hanna, including in her account numerous small details that provide an air of veracity:

> We were tired for we had been lined up an hour or two before the march. We were also very thirsty and when there was a pause in the tempo of the march we happened to be beside "a standing" on which glasses of water stood invitingly. The addition of a little powder made the water fizz. We paid for our drinks but did not quite finish them and then we saw the vendor fill up the glasses for the next comers and we became aware that we had drunk the dregs left by previous consumers. Mrs. Skeffington asked me if I was afraid of germs. I said I wasn't and fortunately neither was she.

The pair do not appear to have been walking in formation with Cumann na mBan, as they caught up with the Volunteers when they reached the gates of Glasnevin. There they saw Thomas McDonagh, who 'so arranged matters that Mrs Skeffington and myself were beside the grave when Pearse delivered his oration.'[91] The comment from the *Irish Citizen*, undoubtedly written by Hanna, was to claim that the crowd presumed the large numbers of women taking part were suffragettes: 'all women who take part in public life in any way must be connected with the movement for votes for women.'[92] Was Frank's absence in America a significant factor in Hanna placing herself so publicly amongst the nationalists?

While there were plenty of women who gave all their available time to League work, only a few felt confident in dealing with the myriad political issues raised by the League. Predictably, these tended to be women with many other commitments in their lives. Cissie Cahalan, busy with her trade union activities, was to lose her job with Arnott's in 1916, apparently because of her suffrage campaigning (winning reinstatement in 1917); Kathleen Emerson, a young widow who had moved back home, worked in the offices of the British Vacuum Cleaner Company and had an elderly mother to care for; Kathleen Keevey, a tireless seller of the paper, was another working woman with limited spare time. After the resignation of Kathleen Houston, it was decided that they could no longer afford the annual £42-18 that her salary had cost. Despite all their efforts, the League was no longer making ends meet. Hanna had little money herself but contributed a steady amount of donations to the League: 10/- in December 1915; 12/- in January 1916 were listed, and there must have been many more.[93] She urged members to attend the annual general meeting, admitting that all their work for 1915 had been done by voluntary helpers and 'the strain entailed … is very great.'[94] They could only keep their offices open for three hours in the afternoon, so when Barbara Hoskins announced that she had decided to give up the *Citizen* 'absolutely' because she couldn't face 'continuous work' Hanna was beside herself with frustration and rage. A former close companion blessed with good health had decided to pull out while her colleagues struggled to stop the paper from going 'on the rocks'. It was betrayal.[95] In trying to keep the open-air meetings going in the atmosphere of 1915, when opposition to the war had lost the IWFL one group of supporters and the formation of Cumann na mBan had drained away another source of support, the League's resources were being stretched to their utmost. On the other hand, with an old friend like Meg, struggling with ill-health, she was tenderness itself, the last person to want Meg 'to overdo things':

> now I am in a fix for I have no one and I fear the meetings must be abandoned and that looks very slack … can't ask those who have been at nearly every meeting since the end of May to go on through September. Please don't think this is a reproach. I know quite well you need no reminders, my dear, and I do feel for you at present with all this illness. I think you ought to really make up your mind to see a specialist and not let it run on any longer. I'm driven to death between Citizen and other work but fortunately I'm fairly well just now.[96]

Committed, efficient, practical, yet warmly concerned. A woman who would make sure that niggling illnesses were treated, so that they could not interfere with one's ability to contribute to the cause. A woman who would not let the inessential things of life monopolise her time, as her friends had often commented. Margaret McCoubrey had sighed, 'I know you use up every minute in other ways. But it must be more satisfying than housework'.[97] Another friend, on moving to London at the start of the war and presumably finding domestic help more difficult to obtain than in Ireland, admitted she enjoyed the satisfaction of creating 'a clean house and a good dinner', adding 'I'm afraid you won't agree but please don't be scornful even if I am discovering myself to be the old fashioned woman'.[98] Hanna was less free from domestic concerns than her friends supposed. Owen had said 'no dada to torment me now … We'll be lonely for a little while.'[99] In his father's absence the little boy proved to be a handful, possibly, as children will, to reassure himself that his mother was there, and she had to pay attention to him or suffer the consequences. In print, Frank sounded very alarming and uncannily like Dr J. B., 'as you are clearly unable to manage him you must just do the best you can till I take a hand again!'[100] Only to her husband could she reveal the strain she was experiencing in keeping everything functioning during his absence. While he was glad to hear that the IWFL was 'going strong' he hoped she was getting someone to work besides herself. There is no doubt that she was far less confident of her abilities than the public image would allow. She suffered from bouts of depression and confessed to being 'cranky'. There were times when money worries exacerbated such moods, as her husband understood only too well:

> I'm sorry to hear of your being depressed again, Hanna sweetheart; I thought from your last that you were in good form again. For fear cash may have something to do with it, I am enclosing $20 (about £4) in the hope that it may help you to tick over! I agree it's better not to draw on K (*Kate Barry*) if possible, for though I'm doing quite satisfactorily here, there won't be much of a profit when all expenses are paid and its as well not to increase debts.

Her teaching commitments, on top of everything else, were certainly tiring, but the money was vital. It was a topic on which the two did not entirely agree. Frank felt she was being exploited as an hourly-paid teacher, 'I hope you're not letting yourself get sweated in that technical place; evidently it takes a lot out of you and you should at least insist on proper pay – not less than 5/– an hour.' As he complained in a later letter that Hanna had still not told him of her rate of pay, it was obvious that she was not getting the minimum he felt she should have insisted upon. It was September 1916 before the hourly rates for teachers were increased to 5/–. Their household accounts were increasingly precarious, with the grocers Leverett and Frye sending a stern request for payment. If they did not 'substantially reduce' the amount they owed on their

Rathmines account, the firm would 'ask you to let us have cash payments for further supplies of food.'[101]

For Hanna's efforts with the *Citizen*, Frank had nothing but praise. He hoped they could organise a joint editorship on his return:

> The paper continues to be very good, you are getting into writing editorials excellently, as I knew you would when you had to! … I love you sweetheart and I wish you were not so rushed! Try to take things a little less strenuously and in particular to get the IC into a routine; you need not think you're not doing it well because you are! So don't let it worry you, it can stand a lot of neglect yet!

Hanna was adamant that her editorship would be a temporary affair, 'I do find it a big pull & it's not a bit easier yet. It never gives me peace! … not all your palaver will make me continue after yr return.'[102] At the end of the year she calculated that the IWFL had held over 60 suffrage meetings; had intervened in two local government by-elections in Dublin, (where Sarah Harrison failed to be re-elected, despite the suffragists' efforts, victim of a backlash against women); had organised a series of meetings in Clare; were involved with temperance and peace campaigns; were monitoring court proceedings as part of a concerted feminist campaign to improve facilities for women and girls and, not least, were part of the movement to help with the betterment of the economic condition of women.[103] In some of these areas of work Hanna kept a low profile, encouraging others to undertake the less exacting work of election canvassing and court monitoring, but she was irreplaceable as speaker and as administrator. This litany of undertakings makes the suffragist life seem earnest and humourless, but it is only half the picture. There were occasions of fun and laughter as well, even in times of war. One newspaper went so far as to criticise them for 'unseemly fiddling' while Rome burnt. Hanna, in her more light-hearted persona of 'Joan', the zealous theatre lover, explained the importance of 'suffragette revels'. The suffrage life was a varied and eventful one, and dancing was enjoyed by many. Social functions helped to dispel the hoary old myths of ugly, men-hating women. Warming to the subject, she insisted of the suffragist:

> She is no prude: in fancy dress she frankly favours doublet and hose. Her chosen characters mirror her pet virtues – the Rosalinds, the Charlotte Cordays; but neither is she a philanderer. She enjoys herself whole-heartedly with the more zest because to her a ball is not a thing of everyday; in most cases she has been hard at work all day and her occupations will not allow her to indulge in a long sleep on the morrow.[104]

She was talking of herself as much as of her colleagues. That love of life's pleasures was an essential part of her character, although it can be missed if we concentrate too much on the public image. As a friend said fondly, Hanna was a woman who 'got great fun out of the minor pleasures of life'.[105]

Frank loved the freedom and the pace of America, loved the newness of it all. How simple the invention of the telephone made life! He could boast that he was able to understand Alexandra Kollantai speaking in German, even though he hadn't heard the language spoken for eleven years. He was having a hectic time travelling around the eastern states, attending an enormous variety of political meetings: New York Cumann na mBan, peace meetings with old acquaintances like the Pethick-Lawrences, trade union and socialist groups, friends from Ireland like Padraic and Mary Colum (who had moved to America in late 1914), J. F. Byrne and Jim Larkin. His father urged him to stay in America until the war was over. The Ford brothers offered him an editorial post on their paper, the highly regarded *Irish World*, but there was no question in his mind of not returning to Ireland. He was looking forward to Christmas at home, despite the war and the Cat and Mouse Act and possible re-arrest, and Hanna was given numerous instructions on what to do to prepare for his return. The *Irish Citizen* was not to take up their time – four pages for the fortnightly Christmas period would be enough – but he worried that she would be 'a wreck' by the time he came home. He was 'quite calm' about his prospects, aware that the likelihood of arrest was very strong.

In November David Sheehy approached the authorities in Dublin, to see if it was safe for his son-in-law to return. The reply was not encouraging: 'We think that his speeches in the United States have aggravated his original offence and that no assurance can be given him if he returns during the War.' Hanna sent Sir Matthew Nathan's reply to Frank, along with family news: her mother was 'better' but leaving soon for Bath, and Uncle Eugene was coming over sometime in December.[106] On 16 December, while still on board ship, Frank wrote a last letter as a precaution. If it reached Hanna before she heard from him, she would know that 'something has happened'. Otherwise, he added cheerily, he hoped to be home on Monday morning. Poignantly, in blue pencil, Hanna later added at the top: 'last letter F. wrote me'. She meant it was the very last one of all.

She was on edge, waiting for Frank's return, terrified that he would be arrested and the whole ghastly experience of hunger strike relived yet again. She went over to Liverpool – either to be there to greet him, or to be ready to mobilise support if the worst happened – and immediately issued a statement from the Bee Hotel: 'Mr Sheehy Skeffington arrived this Sunday morning on the St Louis from New York. He was removed from the boat before the other passengers, being taken into custody. His friends have so far been unable to ascertain his whereabouts. He is liable to re-arrest under the Cat and Mouse Act, licence having expired last June.'[107] Perhaps it was this determination to show the authorities that she was prepared for a fight that resulted in his release. Frank was allowed to leave the Bridewell four hours later, although his belongings were confiscated and many of them never returned, despite repeated protests. Later, Deborah Webb wrote to say she hoped Hanna had recovered from all she went through in Liverpool. A dear and thoughtful friend, as well as a Quaker, she recognised that the Sheehy Skeffingtons had developed to its utmost potential the art of militant pacifism. The cost to the individual was also appreciated.[108]

Frank was home in time for a family Christmas, made even more special by the exciting American presents he had brought back with him. Owen remembered a magic lantern. But the holiday season was short. While still in America he had emphasised that he wanted to speak out at the earliest opportunity, 'a public reception on arrival, regardless of Castle'. Meg Connery, with difficulty, had booked the Forresters Hall. She had not stated that the meeting was being organised on Frank's behalf as she felt Hanna would prefer that to be kept quiet, and Connery was annoyed to discover they were to be charged more than double the rate as the committee were afraid the hall would be wrecked. She declared she would like to wreck it herself.[109] The Forresters, as a conservative nationalist group, were probably trying to put off a group of troublesome women, but the meeting went ahead as a warm welcoming home, chaired by James Connolly, who praised his friend's moral courage. Connolly, desperate to make a stand against the British Empire while it was weakened by war, declared his conviction that 'It was those who had the strongest desire to secure social freedom who could best be trusted to fight for national freedom.'[110] Where the two men differed was in their conception of what kind of weapon it was legitimate to use against the forces of tyranny. Frank clashed with Constance Markievicz at the meeting. She objected to his urging the audience to support the Peace Crusade at the Hague. Constance did not want the war stopped until the British Empire was smashed.

Frank's position was subtle. He detested militarism and yet did not automatically condemn all those who took up the gun. Did the fact that he was also an Irishman have a bearing on this? Hanna, on the eve of her first imprisonment for window smashing had declared 'as to the method, no one has much to say in Ireland'. She justified the use of 'stone and shillelagh' as having 'an honoured place in the armoury of argument'. It was part of the Irish history of political struggle. Similarly, her husband, in writing on the ill-fated Fenian Rising of 1867, had concluded that they were not justified but 'morally bound' in attempting insurrection if they felt there was a chance of success. He had extended this reckoning from national to class issues when speaking in support of the workers' defence force, the Irish Citizen Army, soon after it was formed. Then he was reported to have said: 'When the Citizen Army was properly drilled and disciplined they would not be at the mercy of the superior discipline of the police and when that time came, and it would not be long, they would see about getting arms for the use of the men'.[111] Those who knew him were well aware of the nuances in Frank's espousal of pacifism. Con Curran disclaimed any form of ineffectual non-aggression on the part of his friend: 'Skeffington was not a pacifist in the Quaker or Tolstoyan sense … He was always mounting barricades … His physical courage, remarkable in a man who was not very robust, was as boundless as his moral courage.'[112] Another old friend agreed: 'I would call him a pacifist, but to do that would be to classify him, and you could not classify Skeffington.'[113] Could one classify Hanna? In her case, the description 'pacifist' requires even more qualification. Her reason for opposing the war then being fought by the imperialist powers was that war entailed 'the destruction of human life and the devitalising of the human race in the pursuit of property'.[114] She regarded a revolt by a small country against imperialist domination in a very different light. When she and Louie Bennett were arguing over their differing views regarding Irish attitudes towards the Hague Congress, Louie had made it plain that her conception of pacifism was of a philosophy that admitted no exceptions:

> I do not care for a pacifism which is not truly international, which is not tolerant towards all nations … I shall in future take no part in peace meetings which put Irish nationalism above international tolerance and which are embittered by anti-English feuds.[115]

In encountering this view Hanna continued to insist that a war for national freedom had to be evaluated by different criteria:

> There are pacifists who hold with Tolstoi that resistance to all violence is wrong – I quite see the extreme logic of the position and if you hold to that view of course all war is equally hateful to you. But there are other pacifists (and I am one of them) who hold that while war must be ended if civilisation is to reign supreme, nevertheless there may still be times when armed aggression ought to be met with armed defence.

Her definition of armed aggression included British rule over Ireland. Therefore, an armed uprising could legitimately be defined as 'armed defence'. She went further, placing herself on the same side as the Irish Volunteers and Cumann na mBan in support of an armed rising:

> If I saw a hope of Ireland being freed forever from British rule by a swift uprising, I would consider Irish men justified in resorting to arms in order that we might be free, and I should still be radically opposed to War and Militarism. This is of course my personal view and in no way represents the League. But I hold no such hopes.[116]

A public debate to discuss the issue of ending the war was organised for 15 February 1916. Frank Skeffington was billed to argue the question 'Do We Want Peace Now?' against Constance Markievicz. Louie Bennett, sitting in the large audience, calculated that the pacifists numbered a mere 26. To her ears, the Countess's supporters were speaking in a 'bitter and sinister vein' and she resented Connolly's last-minute intervention and insistence on extra time:

> As well as I can remember he spoke strongly in favour of seizing the moment to fight now against England. I gathered he regretted that more were not ready to do it. As always, one felt the tremendous force of the man, with his big, powerful body, and powerful face and head, and it came home to me that here, in this man, was the centre of danger at this time, and that he would be relentless in the carrying out of a purpose.[117]

Her hostility is a dramatic contrast to Hanna's memory of a debate conducted without rancour:

> After a warmly contested word-duel, just before the vote was taken, James Connolly, who had been a quiet on-looker, suddenly intervened, on Madame's side, swinging the meeting round. When Skeffington laughingly reproved him for throwing in his weight at the end, he replied, with twinkling eyes, 'I was afraid you might get the better of it, Skeffington. That would never do.'[118]

The audience had sat and listened to the arguments without any inkling that a date for insurrection had already been set. Connolly was a member of the military council which had taken that decision. Preparations for the event were becoming an 'open secret that was never betrayed to the authorities'.[119] Frank, a constant visitor to the Citizen Army's headquarters in Liberty Hall, now bustling with military-style preparations, was alarmed at the prospect of future bloodshed, but Hanna conveyed no sense of unease at the sentiments expressed by Connolly. She did not share Louie Bennett's hostility to the notion of armed uprising against Britain. On this issue she was closer to Connolly than to her husband.

NOTES

1 *Irish Citizen*, 10 Jan. 1914.
2 Ibid., 23 Jan. 1914.
3 James Fairhall, *James Joyce and the Question of History* (Cambridge, 1993), p. 239.
4 *Irish Citizen*, 28 Feb. 1914.
5 Violet Jameson to Hanna Sheehy Skeffington, 26 Oct. 1911, Sheehy Skeffington MS (hereafter SS MS) 41,180/1. Jameson was referring to prostitution.
6 Hanna Sheehy Skeffington, 'Votes for women in the west', in *Irish Citizen*, 14 Mar. 1914.
7 Ibid.
8 Manifesto of Irish Women's Franchise League (hereafter IWFL), acting on mandate of resolution passed at meeting of 17 Mar., in *Irish Citizen*, 28 Mar. 1914.
9 Hanna Sheehy Skeffington, '"The countess": Some memories', in *Irish Press*, 4 Feb. 1936.
10 *Irish Citizen*, 4 Apr. 1914.
11 Ibid., 2 May 1914.
12 Paige Reynolds, 'Staging Suffrage: The events of 1913 Dublin suffrage week', in Louise Ryan and Margaret Ward (eds), *Irish Women and the Vote: Becoming Citizens* (Dublin, 2007, reprinted 2018), pp 60–74.
13 Hanna Sheehy Skeffington to Christabel Pankhurst, n. d., SS MS 24,134.
14 *Belfast Newsletter*, 22 Jan. 1914.
15 Speech reported in 'London's welcome: Essex Hall meeting', in *Irish Citizen*, 20 June 1920.
16 Details of Kathleen Houston's arrest, Suffragette Box 3, National Archives, Dublin; *Irish Citizen*, 9 May 1914.
17 *Irish Citizen*, 23 May 1914.
18 Ibid., 6 June 1914.
19 Kathleen Emerson to Hanna Sheehy Skeffington, 24 Sept. 1915, SS MS 22,676.
20 Meg Connery to Hanna Sheehy Skeffington, May 1931, SS MS 41,177/10.
21 Gretta Cousins to Hanna Sheehy Skeffington, n. d., SS MS 22,665.
22 Gretta Cousins to Hanna Sheehy Skeffington, 29 Oct. 1914, SS MS 22,667.
23 Marguerite Palmer to Hanna Sheehy Skeffington, 11 Aug. 1914, SS MS 24,146.
24 *Irish Citizen*, 11 Oct. 1914; 17 Oct. 1914.
25 Eva Wilkins to Hanna Sheehy Skeffington, 8 Mar. 1915, 10 Mar. 1915, SS MS 22,672.
26 See, for example, Dora Mellone to Hanna Sheehy Skeffington, 4 June 1914; Helen Chenevix to Hanna Sheehy Skeffington, 8 June 1914, SS MS 22,665.
27 Emmeline Pethick-Lawrence to Hanna Sheehy Skeffington, 27 May 1914, SS MS 22,665.
28 Hanna Sheehy Skeffington, 'Two deputations', in *Irish Citizen*, 20 June 1914.
29 Ibid.
30 'London's welcome: Essex hall meeting', in *Irish Citizen*, 20 June 1914.
31 Andrée Sheehy Skeffington, *Skeff: A Life of Owen Sheehy Skeffington* (Dublin, 1991), p. 15.
32 *Irish Citizen*, 24 Oct. 1914.

33 'Duty of suffragettes', in *Irish Citizen*, 15 Aug. 1914.
34 Violet Crichton to Hanna Sheehy Skeffington, 21 Aug. 1914, SS MS 22,66.
35 Open Letter, in *Irish Citizen*, 24 July 1915; Hanna Sheehy Skeffington reply, *Irish Citizen*, 31 July 1915.
36 *Irish Citizen*, 22 Aug. 1914.
37 Gretta Cousins to Hanna Sheehy Skeffington, 17 Aug. 1914, SS MS 22,666.
38 Hanna Sheehy to Frank Skeffington (hereafter Hanna to Frank), Nov. 1914, SS MS 40,466/7.
39 Lengthy correspondence between Margaret McCoubrey and Hanna Sheehy Skeffington provides essential information on the state of feminist politics in Ulster during the period 1914 to 1915, SS MS 24,133.
40 *The People*, 4 Oct. 1914, in SS MS 22,667.
41 Maire Fitzpatrick, née Moran, Bureau of Military History, Witness Statement (hereafter BMH WS) 1,344 p. 4.
42 Seán T. O'Kelly, BMH WS 1,765, p. 9.
43 Rose Jacob to Hanna Sheehy Skeffington, 7 Oct. 1914, SS MS 22,648.
44 Alice Park to Hanna Sheehy Skeffington, 9 Sept. 1914, SS MS 22,667.
45 Louie Bennett to Hanna Sheehy Skeffington, 1 Oct. 1914, SS MS 22,666.
46 Hanna Sheehy Skeffington to Meg Connery 13 Nov. 1914, SS MS 22,666.
47 Frank Skeffington to Hanna Sheehy (hereafter Frank to Hanna), 23 Oct. 1915, SS MS 21,636.
48 *Irish Citizen*, 3 Oct. 1914.
49 Ibid.
50 *Irish Citizen*, 12 Sept. 1914.
51 Frank Sheehy Skeffington, 'Open Letter to Thomas MacDonagh', in *Irish Citizen*, 22 May 1915; reprinted in Owen Dudley-Edwards and Fergus Pyle (eds), *1916: The Easter Rising* (London, 1968), pp 149–152.
52 *Irish Citizen*, 9 May 1914.
53 *Irish Citizen*, 23 Oct. 1915.
54 Frank Sheehy Skeffington to Margaret McCoubrey, 10 Jan. 1916, SS MS 33,612/18.
55 J. B. Lyons, *The Enigma of Tom Kettle: Irish Patriot, Essayist, Poet, British Soldier, 1880–1916* (Dublin, 1983), p. 277. I have been unable to discover the reason for this, although one family member suspects that gambling on horses might have been a factor.
56 Gretta Cousins to Hanna Sheehy Skeffington, 18 Mar. 1915, SS MS 22,672.
57 Eugene Sheehy to Hanna Sheehy Skeffington, Oct. 1915, SS MS 22,676.
58 Daisy Lawrenson Swanton, *Emerging from the Shadow: The Lives of Sarah Anne Lawrenson and Lucy Olive Kingston, Based on Personal Diaries 1883–1969* (Dublin, 1994), p. 71.
59 Louie Bennett to Hanna Sheehy Skeffington, 17 Mar. 1915, SS MS 22,672.
60 Hanna Sheehy Skeffington to Louie Bennett (fragment of letter), n. d., (1915) SS MS 24,134.
61 *Irish Citizen*, 17 Apr. 1915.
62 Ibid., 24 Apr. 1915.
63 Hanna to Frank, Gower Hotel, n. d. SS MS 40,466/8.
64 *Irish Citizen*, 22 May 1915.

65 J. B. Skeffington, 5 June 1915, quoted in Leah Levenson, *With Wooden Sword: A Portrait of Francis Sheehy Skeffington, Militant Pacifist* (Dublin, 1983), p. 178.
66 Louie Bennett to Hanna Sheehy Skeffington, 31 May 1915, SS MS 22,648.
67 Charles Oldham to Hanna Sheehy Skeffington, 31 May 1915, SS MS 22,648.
68 Deborah Webb to Hanna Sheehy Skeffington, 16 June 1915, SS MS 22,648.
69 E. Donovan to Hanna Sheehy Skeffington, 4 June 1915. If she secured a 'satisfactory and solvent tenant' she could be released from her husband's agreement, SS MS 22,648.
70 Hanna to Frank n. d. SS MS 40,466/9.
71 Hanna to Frank, June 1915, SS MS 40,466/9.
72 Hanna to Frank, 2 June 1915, SS MS 40,466/9.
73 Speech from the dock published in full in Levenson, *With Wooden Sword*, pp 245–9. It was published as a pamphlet by the Irish Workers' Cooperative Society in 1915. Letter from Constance Markievicz to Hanna indicates that she and Connolly were the ones who arranged publication, SS MS 22,670.
74 Telegram from J. B. Skeffington to Dr Flynn, Prison Board, 15 June 1915, SS MS 22,648.
75 G. B. Shaw to Hanna Sheehy Skeffington, 14 June 1915, SS MS 22,648.
76 Mary Bourke to Chief Secretary Birrell, 15 June 1915, SS MS 22,648.
77 *Irish Citizen*, 19 May 1915.
78 Gretta Cousins to Hanna Sheehy Skeffington, July 1915, SS MS 22,676.
79 Bessie Sheehy to Hanna Sheehy Skeffington, 18 June 1915, SS MS 22,648.
80 William Murphy, *Political Imprisonment and the Irish, 1912–1921* (Oxford, 2014), p. 48.
81 Ibid., p. 49.
82 Mary Kettle to Hanna Sheehy Skeffington, n. d., SS MS 22,648.
83 Hayden Talbot, *Michael Collins' Own Story* (London, 1923), p. 97.
84 Cruise O'Brien to Hanna Sheehy Skeffington, n. d., SS MS 22,648.
85 Hanna Sheehy Skeffington to Eugene Sheehy, 16 June 1915, SS MS 22,648. Possibly still in her possession because she sent it to 448 instead of 224 Westbourne Grove, London and had it returned.
86 Owen Sheehy Skeffington, 'Francis Sheehy Skeffington' in Dudley-Edwards and Pyle *1916: The Easter Rising*, p. 143.
87 Suffragette Box 3, National Archives, Dublin, contains details of Frank's imprisonment, press cuttings and Hanna's letters to the authorities on her husband's behalf. Because of his hunger strike he was regarded by the prison authorities in similar light to the women prisoners.
88 Norwich Union Life Insurance Policy, SS MS 22,274.
89 Maurice Wilkins to Hanna Sheehy Skeffington, July 1915, SS MS 22,676.
90 Frank Sheehy Skeffington, 'Suffrage in the air', in *Irish Citizen*, 28 Aug. 1915.
91 Elizabeth Bloxham, BMH WS 632, p. 31.
92 *Irish Citizen* 7 Aug. 1915.
93 Receipts contained in SS MS 41,207/5.
94 Hanna Sheehy Skeffington to members of IWFL, giving details of AGM being held on 8 Feb. Letter dated Jan. 1916, Alice Park Collection, Hoover Institution Archives, Stanford, California.

95 Barbara Hoskins to Hanna Sheehy Skeffington, 1 Oct. 1915, SS MS 22,676. Hanna's angry comments are pencilled in the margin, their ferocity indicating that she was under great strain: 'she has health, knows all the ropes, no babies, and lots of time and is very fit for this kind of work – why should she lie about it?'.
96 Hanna Sheehy Skeffington to Meg Connery, n. d., SS MS 22,676.
97 Margaret McCoubrey to Hanna Sheehy Skeffington, n. d., SS MS 24,133.
98 Laura Ervine to Hanna Sheehy Skeffington, 15 Sept. 1914, SS MS 22,667.
99 Andrée Sheehy Skeffington, *Skeff*, p. 15.
100 Frank to Hanna, SS MS 21,636, a collection of letters from Frank to Hanna. Frank dated and numbered each letter, so we can tell that the first 21 are missing (presumably confiscated).
101 Letter from Leverett and Frye, 10 Jan. 1916, SS MS 41,207/5.
102 Hanna to Frank, 12 Oct. 1915, SS MS 40,466/10.
103 Hanna Sheehy Skeffington, letter to IWFL members, giving details of 1915 AGM, Jan. 1916, Alice Park Collection, Hoover Institution Archives, Stanford, California.
104 Joan, 'Suffragette revels', in *Irish Citizen*, 3 Dec. 1914.
105 Anna Kelly, 'Hanna Sheehy Skeffington: An appreciation', in *Irish Press* 27 Apr. 1946.
106 Hanna to Frank, n. d. SS MS 40,466/10.
107 Hanna Sheehy Skeffington, n. d., Bee Hotel, SS MS 22,648.
108 Deborah Webb to Hanna Sheehy Skeffington, 29 Dec. 1915, SS MS 22,676.
109 Meg Connery to Hanna Sheehy Skeffington, n. d., SS MS 22,676.
110 *Irish Citizen*, 8 Jan. 1916.
111 *Freeman's Journal*, 1 Dec. 1913.
112 C. P. Curran, *Under the Receding Wave* (Dublin, 1970), p. 117.
113 J. F. Byrne, *Silent Years: An Autobiography* (New York, 1953), p. 122.
114 *Jus Suffragii*, Apr. 1915.
115 Louie Bennett to Hanna Sheehy Skeffington, 12 May 1915, SS MS 22,675.
116 Hanna Sheehy Skeffington to Louie Bennett (fragment of letter), n. d., (1915), SS MS 24,134.
117 R. M. Fox, *Louie Bennett: Her Life and Times* (Dublin, 1958), p. 48.
118 Quoted in Jacqueline Van Voris, *Constance de Markievicz in the Cause of Ireland* (Amherst, 1967), p. 160.
119 Desmond Greaves, *The Life and Times of James Connolly* (London, 1972), p. 399.

EIGHT

DEATH OF A PACIFIST, 1916

In the early months of 1916 Hanna and Frank considered taking an Easter holiday. Money was still a problem, but they needed a break together, and the weather promised to be good. One possibility was the small seaside resort of Howth, where the Waverly Hotel was offering an Easter weekend rate of 13/- per day, everything provided except for soap and sugar. War-time restrictions meant that visitors brought their own supplies of these items.[1] During the week before Easter Frank took Owen north, to see his father and other Skeffington relatives in County Down. The increasing support for militarism that was pervading all political discussions and meetings in Dublin had made him uneasy, and he spoke of his fears to his father. Anything might happen in the next months, the situation was so volatile, but he had decided, as a militant pacifist, to put his energies into mobilising an anti-taxation movement as a safety valve for anti-government feelings.[2]

Hanna was in a very different frame of mind when she, at home in Dublin, encountered James Connolly. For once, that most direct of men spoke in cryptic tones: 'If you are interested in developments, I would not advise you to go away on holiday just now.' He also added that equal citizenship for women was included within the Proclamation of the Irish Republic – only one man had objected.[3] What did all this mean? A hint from Connolly was not to be ignored. The Sheehy Skeffingtons stayed in Dublin.

Imminent excitement was expected, but the audacity of what had been planned took almost everyone by surprise. At the time of the Women's Peace Congress Hanna had said she held 'no such hopes' of an Irish rising against

British rule and yet, only a few months later, a full-scale armed uprising had begun, led by some who were close friends of many in the Franchise League. Connolly, who had served in the British Army years before, had been openly advocating insurrection since the war had begun, but Thomas MacDonagh, teacher and poet, and others like him, it was unbelievable, yet it was happening. At noon on Easter Monday, 24 April, the combined forces of the Irish Volunteers and the Irish Citizen Army, united as the Irish Republican Army, marched onto the streets of Dublin to begin the fight for the Republic. Shortly before that time a small contingent of the Citizen Army (including Helena Molony) had headed off to capture Dublin Castle. They were unsuccessful, too few in number and with no real plan of how to go about it, but in the skirmish a British officer was mortally wounded. No one knows how Frank happened to be there, but he was. Despite the crossfire, he persuaded a chemist to dash over with him to the Castle gates, where the man lay bleeding to death. At home that evening, Frank told Hanna about the incident. It turned out, when they got there, that the officer's colleagues had managed to drag him back through the gates. Hanna was appalled at the risk he had taken, ignoring bullets coming from all directions, but he simply replied, 'I could not let anyone bleed to death while I could help.' That attitude summed up the man. When Hanna relived those moments she remembered, with transparent pride, her husband's 'simple heroism, cool courage and horror of bloodshed'.[4]

While the Sheehy Skeffingtons shared Connolly's commitment to the establishment of a workers' republic, Frank was outspoken in his belief that there could be another route to achieve that end. He had hovered anxiously around Liberty Hall on Easter Sunday when those in the know had read in the papers that Eoin MacNeill, nominal head of the Volunteers, had cancelled the mobilisation orders previously issued by Pearse.[5] For Frank, but not for those he spoke to, there was some hope that the Rising might be called off. Hanna's reactions are less easy to describe. She had been selected by the leadership to act as one of five members in a Civil Provisional Government, to be put into effect in the event of the insurrection managing to sustain itself for any significant length of time. William O'Brien of the Transport Union, a close friend, was one of the other members chosen. Connolly had informed him of the fact some time before Easter Week.[6] Connolly must have communicated this decision to Hanna when he advised her to stay in Dublin. Her appearance at events like the O'Donovan Rossa funeral would have indicated where her sympathies lay.

Hanna's views on the Rising became clear in the aftermath of those days, when she gave unstinting praise to the political leadership of Connolly 'who wrote into the proclamation of the Irish Republic … the enfranchisement of women … It is the only instance I know of in history where men fighting for freedom voluntarily included women'.[7] As a feminist who had endured prison and hunger strike because of her determination to achieve citizenship for Irish women, how could she not fail to thrill to the notion that Irish men had struck a most resounding blow for the rights of women – one that would go down in history, ensuring that women in Ireland need never return to that state of subjection they had fought so hard against? She had Connolly's promise that the Proclamation contained what she had fought for during the past decade. Pearse, from the front of the General Post Office, had read out its text to an uncomprehending assortment of passers-by. It included the words: 'The Republic guarantees … equal rights and equal opportunities to all its citizens' in a 'National Government … elected by the suffrages of all her men and women.' The Tuesday before, having come home in a state of elation, Tom Clarke, chosen by his comrades as the first signatory, told his wife Kathleen 'it represented the views of all except one, who thought equal opportunities should not be given to women'. Tantalisingly, Kathleen would not elaborate: 'Except to say that Tom was not that one, my lips are sealed.'[8] Women combatants were not slow to recognise the significance of this assurance. Margaret Skinnider, a Scottish member of Cumann na mBan and now a member of the Citizen Army garrison in Stephen's Green, argued successfully that this declaration of equality entitled her to undertake a military role. She attacked snipers on the roof of the Shelbourne Hotel as well as leading a squad of men trying to cut off the retreat of British soldiers. She was seriously injured during this manoeuvre.[9]

Neither Frank nor Hanna could remain as onlookers when support was needed. Frank hated the thought of lives being lost because the gun had taken over, but neither would he permit the Rising to be dishonoured because of the widespread looting being carried out by the Dublin crowds. Organising a citizen's militia so that order could be constructed out of chaos would, he decided, be his contribution. His intervention was totally consistent with his unshakeable faith in the pacifist approach. He would try to prevent mob rule, but he would not directly assist the insurgents. No-one would have dreamed of co-opting 'Skeffy' without his permission. They had his 'Open Letter to Thomas MacDonagh' to remind them of his strong objections to militarism. It was different with Hanna. On the Tuesday, the second day of the Rising, once she knew what was happening, she walked with her husband the two miles from Rathmines to the centre of Dublin. Armed only with a cane he was to spend that day pleading with individuals to stop looting the ruined shops and distributing circulars calling on civilians – men and women – to attend a meeting at the League's offices in Westmoreland Street at five o'clock. Hanna, looking at the actions of 'Dublin's slum on holiday' mused 'sadly on Connolly's sacrifice for the citizens of Dublin' and wondered if they were worth it. But she also understood what propelled the 'ragged smoke-grimed urchin' hugging a huge pineapple to his tattered breast, 'the first and probably last chance of getting his young teeth' into what was the 'preserve of the rich'.[10] She went straight to the General Post Office, headquarters of the insurgents, where Connolly and Pearse were busily organising their forces, to ask Connolly if there was anything she could do. His face, she recalled 'was radiant and he was in the midst of military activity and preparations.'[11] For her beloved Uncle Eugene this was the culmination of a lifetime's hopes. Once Hanna had made the decision to offer assistance to the insurgents, it seems entirely fitting that one of the first people she should meet in the GPO was that dearly loved relative – 75 years old, in bad health, but as steadfast as ever in his commitment. As he had been living in London, his good friend Tom Clarke must have whispered that it was time to come home. Father Eugene cried out 'My God, Hanna, what are you doing here?' and she, with some humour, retorted in similar vein. He said he was there to give spiritual consolation. She brought what she considered to be of more importance, physical sustenance, and was bringing Tom Clarke a cup of Bovril when the two met on an upstairs landing. It became a family tale, often recounted, even by those members who disapproved of the rebels.[12]

Eileen Walsh, a member of the garrison, testified that when Desmond Fitzgerald (in charge of food supplies) asked for volunteers to bring over a sack of food to the College of Surgeons, Hanna volunteered to go with herself and Bridie Mahon. They had some difficulty in getting into the College as they were not recognised by those on sentry duty, but they knew Countess Markievicz and so were able to enter.[13] Constance, in the thick of events, said she was amazed to recognise the voice of the person asking for Commandant Mallin. The woman 'staggering under the weight of a huge sack bulging out into queer shapes and completely concealing her' was none other than Hanna Sheehy Skeffington, leading a party of 'laden figures', members of the Franchise League, who had collected 'all manner of eatables from their friends' and who braved the bullet-swept streets to bring them in. Constance had fond memories of that experience. It was, in her eyes, yet another instance when the Sheehy Skeffingtons 'instinctively took the right side and were always ready to help'. The rebels had great fun unpacking the parcels and hearing who had contributed the various tins of soup, ham and salmon. They then sat down and 'had a glorious meal'.[14] That recollection was a deeply embellished account, noteworthy for her claim that the food was brought by Franchise League members rather than by Hanna accompanying members of Cumann na mBan. With the passage of time, it was the feminist contribution she remembered.

As the British sent reinforcements to attack the insurgents' garrisons and unpredictable bursts of gunfire cracked through the air, moving around the streets became more and more hazardous. One was liable to be stopped and searched, arrested or worse. Women who could use their 'respectability' as a cover were few, but their contribution to the Rising was considerable. Many Cumann na mBan members had joined the Rising and significant numbers of women were also involved in the Irish Citizen Army.[15] All Hanna's feminist instincts baulked at being given the traditionally female roles of cook or medical attendant, the two main tasks allocated to women. She would have been hopeless as a cook and was untrained in first aid. Cumann na mBan were a vital part of all the garrisons (apart from Boland's, where Commandant Eamon de Valera infamously told those who volunteered to return home), but it is obvious that Hanna could never have been in their ranks. The fact that they were auxiliaries to a military organisation, whose principles stood in opposition to those of the pacifist, was not the only obstacle. It would have been for Frank, but the situation was less clear-cut with her. She needed to be where she could make a contribution, not relegated to making the tea.

In late afternoon Frank and Hanna met briefly at the IWFL rooms, snatching time to compare notes before the expected meeting of the citizen's militia. Frank reported that some people had put on his armbands and begun to patrol the streets. It was difficult to resist his appeals, but he didn't know that when he left them, they made for home as quickly as they could.[16] Both were anxious about leaving Owen at home alone with the maid. As no trams were running Hanna decided she had better set off on the walk home. At 5.30 p.m. she started off for Rathmines while Frank said he would stay a while longer, to see if anyone would respond to his plea. He would follow her in an hour or so.[17] His family never saw him again. No-one turned up for his meeting, and Frank started for home. As he reached Portobello Bridge between 6.30 and 7.00 p.m. he was arrested, 'unarmed and unresisting', as witnesses later testified, and brought into Portobello Barracks.[18] His stand against the war had marked him out. In the barracks he was searched and questioned. He was asked if he was a 'Sinn Féiner' and he replied that he was in sympathy with the movement, but he was in favour of passive resistance and opposed to militarism. Not all the soldiers who gave testimony to having heard that exchange could understand what he meant by that.[19] Nothing incriminating was found, but he was to be detained overnight. Frank asked that his wife be informed of his whereabouts, but this request was refused. He was the perfect hostage for a raiding party organised by Captain Bowen-Colthurst, an officer in the barracks. Everyone knew what that most notable of non-conformists looked like – even at a distance his knee-breeches and red beard blazoned his identity.

The British could be certain that the rebels would not fire on them; no one would risk wounding that particular captive. It was a journey into hell. Before they left the barracks, Frank's hands were tied behind his back and he was ordered to say his prayers. He refused to do so. The raiders fired at houses along the Rathmines Road. When they encountered two boys near Rathmines Church, one of the lads, James Coade, who had turned to walk away rather than answer the patrol, was shot dead by Bowen-Colthurst. Frank's horrified protests received the response that he would probably be next. Afterwards, Bowen-Colthurst sacked a tobacconist shop and took prisoner the shopkeeper and two journalists sheltering there. Ironically, the journalists, Thomas Dickson and Patrick MacIntyre, were unionists and loyal supporters of the British state. The following morning the three men were marched out into the yard of Portobello Barracks. A firing party of seven was given the order by Bowen-Colthurst to shoot the men dead. Eyewitnesses testified that, without warning, they were then shot down in cold blood. Frank's leg was noticed later to be moving as he lay on the ground. When this was reported to Bowen-Colthurst, another firing squad was lined up to finish him off. It was an image that haunted Hanna. She was never able to find out how long Frank had lingered, or if the second volley had been more effective than the first. At 11.15 that night his body, tied up in a sack, was buried in secret in the barrack yard. His widow was never informed officially of her husband's arrest, of his murder, or of his unauthorised burial.[20]

Owen knew his father had not returned, but his worried mother struggled not to alarm the boy. Her frantic figure, scurrying around the Dublin streets, was seen by many people over the next few days. So many women were in agonies of not knowing what was happening to their menfolk. Hanna met Muriel MacDonagh, wheeling her babies in a pram to her mother's house. The MacDonagh home had been wrecked by soldiers in retaliation for Thomas's role in the Rising. The great city of Dublin had been transformed, as James Stephens, a bewildered onlooker, testified: 'our peaceful city is no longer peaceful; guns are sounding, or rolling and crackling from different directions, and, although rarely, the rattle of machine guns can be heard also.'[21] Stephens heard a rumour that Sheehy Skeffington had been killed. He hoped fervently that it was just another of the many rumours filling the air. To him, Skeffington was 'the most absurdly courageous man' he had ever met. When, later in the day, he met Hanna on the street, she was able to confirm the rumour that Frank had been arrested, but she had no other news of him. Stephens remembered the innate goodness of a man for whom 'a cause had only to be weak to gain his sympathy, and his sympathy never stayed at home', despite blows, indignities and ridicule.[22] When he knew the details of the murder his poetic gifts conjured up Frank's thoughts during those last terrible seconds:

> His tongue, his pen, his body, all that he had and hoped for were at the immediate service of whoever was bewildered or oppressed ... He who was a pacifist was compelled to revolt to his last breath, and on the instruments of his end he must have looked as on murderers. I am sure that to the end he railed against oppression, and that he fell marvelling that the world can truly be as it is. With his death there passed away a brave man and a clean soul.[23]

It was a perceptive imagining and a fine epitaph.

Cumann na mBan member Maeve McGarry (whose mother had been an active suffragist as well as founder member of Cumann na mBan) was at home in Rathmines during the Rising, as her mother had gone to Limerick and Maeve was needed to take care of the house. She wanted to join the College of Surgeons garrison but was conscious that there was a quantity of ammunition in the house that needed to be delivered. In her recollections Hanna arrived at her home on the Wednesday morning to collect the ammunition, placing it in her umbrella and 'in a pocket which she had specially made inside the tail of her skirt.' She came again in the afternoon, by which time they had heard that Frank had been arrested. According to Maeve, Mrs Skeffington:

> was in a very nervous condition although the average onlooker would not have noticed that. But I knew her so well and I could see she was terribly upset. She was so courageous that, even if she had any inkling of her husband's arrest, it would not stop her carrying out the task she had been given to do. Maurice (Danaher, a Volunteer) looked at me to see whether he should tell her. I bowed my head and he informed her. She replied in a low tone, 'I surmised something had happened to him. I must get on with the work'. She had been asked at the College of Surgeons to secure a doctor.[24]

Was Hanna at the College of Surgeons again on the Wednesday? She said of herself that she was unable to get into the city again after Tuesday as the south side was cut off by the Wednesday, with military posts on the bridges over the canal. While she said in interview in the 1930s that she went from the College of Surgeons to look for a doctor as a man in the garrison was bleeding to death, that had been on the previous day.[25] Nancy Wyse Power testified to seeing her near the Wyse Power home in Henry Street on the Wednesday, making inquiries about Frank. Jennie was able to tell her that she had given Frank something to eat (and he also went to the chemist for her, as her daughter Maire was very ill) before he started to walk for home, but that was all anyone knew. Nancy remembered Hanna going with her to the GPO, and afterwards volunteering to bring further supplies to the College of Surgeons.[26] With the passing of time details can obviously be mis-remembered, but what we are left with is a vivid impression of Hanna's anxiety for her husband, and her continued commitment to helping the insurgents. She still clung to the hope that, as a non-combatant, Frank would have been entitled to trial before a jury and that she would be notified. The rumours of his execution were too incredible to be believed. But the nightmare grew worse.

Hanna's neighbours in Grosvernor Place, deeply hostile to the rebels, tried to offer some comfort, but their sympathy must have been hard to take. On the Thursday Minnie Deale, from number 21, writing 'woman to woman', was sorry for her 'fresh trouble' and hoped Hanna had been able to communicate with her husband. She added 'we are all suffering over this calamity' perpetrated by 'poor misguided boys' whom she doubted would 'ever get sense'.[27] Mrs Deale, a Methodist, had four young boys and one wonders if they had been the boys that Owen had hit for no apparent reason while Frank was in America? It would seem a reasonable explanation for an action that had been so out of character. If so, it was a brave effort to defend a father against children parroting views overheard from their parents. And his refusal to offer any explanation a young boy's attempt to shield his mother from unpleasantness.

On the Friday, by which time 'horrible rumours' had reached her, Hanna tried to see a doctor connected to the barracks but found herself stopped by the police. She discovered that she herself was being watched. Her sisters, Mary and Margaret, then offered to enquire on her behalf. The police at Rathmines Police Station told them to go to Portobello. On arriving there, they first enquired for the whereabouts of their brother, Lieutenant Eugene Sheehy, who was garrisoned somewhere in the city. They received a courteous reply, until they then asked about their brother-in-law. The young officer, in some confusion, excused himself and went to consult his superiors. To their astonishment, they then found themselves under arrest, accused of having been seen 'talking to Sinn Féiners'. The only possible person they knew who could be described in such terms was their sister Hanna. An enquiry, 'a drumhead court-martial' Hanna called it, was held after the women were marched across the barrack square. Bowen-Colthurst informed them that no information concerning Skeffington was available and the sooner they left the premises the better. Not only were they marched off by an armed guard and escorted to the tramway line, but they were also forbidden to speak to each other on the way. Mary had a 'glimpse of hope' when told that there was no information about Frank. Then she saw the expression on Bowen-Colthurst's face, and all her suspicions were confirmed.[28] It was clear that something dreadful was being covered up. When Hanna found Mr Coade, the father of the boy who had been murdered near Rathmines Church, she knew the worst. He had seen Frank's body in the mortuary when he went for his son. The evidence led to only one conclusion, but Hanna could not let it rest there. She still had to try to find out for herself what had happened. No one would help. It was an injustice she felt keenly, as she was to make plain while giving evidence during the eventual inquiry: 'She would like to say that she never got any formal notice of the death of her husband, and that every scrap of information she had got was only as a result of endless research. She would like evidence as to whether a medical man saw her husband immediately after his death.'[29]

The painful process of investigation continued. Mr Coade suggested that she went to see Father O'Loughlin, the chaplain of the barracks, and the person who had informed him of his son's death. The priest did not think it was his responsibility to communicate any similar information to the widow of Sheehy Skeffington, although later he denied 'putting difficulties in the way of Mrs Skeffington seeing (him)'. When Hanna pleaded for information, he had to tell her: her husband was dead and already buried. The days of hideous searching for facts were over. Hanna tore out a page of her notebook and scribbled a broken-hearted note to her father-in-law:

> 3rd May 1916
>
> Dear Dr S.
>
> You may have got a card from me yesterday. We have the worst news – F. is I fear no more.[30]

It became clear to Bowen-Colthurst that in shooting Sheehy Skeffington he had chosen a victim who would be as troublesome in death as he had been in life. In order to concoct some evidence against Frank he led a raiding party to Grosvenor Place. On the evening of the same day that her sisters had visited the Barracks, Hanna was putting Owen to bed when the maid noticed soldiers lining up around the house. They then burst in, firing into the air and, panic-stricken, she ran out of the back door, carrying Owen with her,

Hanna in pursuit, trying to stop them in case they were shot for running away. Hanna's account of those days, given on many occasions, never varied in detail. It was all etched forever on her memory. Little Owen's account, given in an interview with an American paper eight months later, confirmed his mother's:

> After I was brought into the house by the maid, I heard a crack of glass and then saw the soldiers with fixed bayonets climbing in through the windows ... They told me to hold up my hands. They told the same thing to my mother and the maid. Then they rushed downstairs and broke my daddy's desk and took a lot of papers and other things.[31]

For three hours the house was ransacked, pictures torn from the walls, toys broken, papers pulled from shelves and drawers. Owen's childish drawings of planes and bombs were seized – evidence of German sympathies! Hanna and Frank's private papers were taken, many never returned. Most chillingly, Bowen-Colthurst had brought Frank's keys - stolen from his dead body – and used them to open the locked study door. Frank had always insisted on keeping that room locked, disliking the maid disturbing his papers. Other items, like his signet ring and the 'Votes for Women' badge he always wore on his lapel, had also been taken from the body, grisly souvenirs for the soldiers who kept them.[32]

The following Monday, 1 May, while Hanna was out, another raid was made on the house. The original maid had left, terrified by what had happened to her, and Margaret Farrelly, a young woman who worked for one of Hanna's sisters, and who had been sent over to help out at Grosvenor Place, now found herself under arrest. The only possible charge could be that she was in the Sheehy Skeffington household. At the Simon inquiry Sergeant Claxton was forced to admit that he had taken the terrified young woman, hiding underneath a table in the kitchen, because he had been told that 'two unknown persons' had been seen going into the Skeffington household. As Tim Healy so damningly concluded, 'And the Dublin Metropolitan Police employed three soldiers to effect the arrest of a maid servant in the house of a murdered man.'[33] It took until the Saturday before the Sheehy women finally succeeded in securing her release. This was surely the equal of any invention of Kafka. From being the widow of an innocent man murdered in cold blood by a British army officer, Hanna had become an unspecified suspect, contact with whom would lead to reprisals. The British authorities, from the highest level down, were determined to cover up what had happened. It would help if the widow could be vilified. If she was seen as a rebel, then her husband's murder could be more easily explained. Sir Francis Vane, the English officer who refused to go along with the cover-up, found bitter amusement in receiving a letter from the military authorities after he had accompanied Hanna to army headquarters, 'strongly advising' him not to be seen with Mrs Sheehy Skeffington. Vane replied, 'as we had killed her husband most certainly I should do everything in my power to help her, as it was in my opinion an Imperial duty'.[34] As the gentleman he was, Vane decided, in the name of the army, that he had to visit the widow to apologise for the wrong that had been done: 'Never was a more frightening task allotted to me, but it seemed that in honour it ought to be done.' He was fortunate to see Owen first. The childless Vane loved children (he was a doting uncle) and the two made friends. With Owen's hand in his, the British soldier then faced the widow. Extremely surprised, she received him coldly. When she heard of his attempts to alert Lord Kitchener and the war cabinet to the incident, she was generous in response, thanking him as she shook his hand.[35] He was the first member of the British establishment to have accepted the truth of Frank's murder. The knowledge that she had an ally in her struggle was a huge relief. Anna Vane, after learning from her husband of Frank's murder, was moved to write to say how much she felt for Hanna and her son. Her husband had described Hanna as 'a great and noble woman', and she was sure that he, a 'chivalrous' man, would be a great comfort.[36]

Vane was more than just a decent man. Commendations for his services during the Boer War had not prevented him from protesting to the authorities for their treatment of civilian internees in southern Africa. He was a Home Ruler, mildly left-wing in politics, a friend of many English feminists. A Chaucerian 'perfect knight' he, a retired officer, had immediately offered his services on the outbreak of war. That was why he had found himself stationed in Rathmines during the Rising. Vane soon heard rumours of the dark deeds in Portobello and investigated further. What he discovered shocked him to the core. He could not believe that the army he knew would sanction such actions, and he believed, as an honest person, that when the authorities knew the truth and justice would prevail. Justice proved very elusive, conspired against by those in power. His determination to right this wrong was to lead him to Mrs Sheehy Skeffington, and to the forging of a most unlikely, yet enduring, friendship. Without his support she would never have recovered some of the property stolen from Frank. Together, they went to Dublin Castle to demand the handing over of the dead man's possessions. Hanna received his ring. She also, horribly, received some blood-stained garments which were later discovered to have belonged to Patrick Pearse.[37]

Vane believed the Portobello murders to have been the work of one deranged officer. He thought at first that once the authorities knew the truth, they would act to have Bowen-Colthurst removed and would instigate a thorough inquiry to discover the facts. However, the interests of the British imperial state would not be served by such openness and what happened was very different. Vane, a senior officer with a distinguished career behind him, was ordered by his commanding officer to give up his post and to hand over responsibility to Bowen-Colthurst. The man who had been responsible for the murder of at least five civilians during those dark days was given promotion only six days later. It was this which prompted Vane's journey to London, in a desperate attempt to inform Kitchener of events. Kitchener did indeed order the arrest of Bowen-Colthurst, but that order was ignored by General Maxwell, who had been sent over to Ireland to deal with the rebels and to suppress any possibility of dissaffection continuing. Maxwell's secret report ensured that Vane was dismissed from the service, deprived of his rank, and refused a hearing at the court martial of Bowen-Colthurst.

Still in shock and struggling hard to keep her grief from overwhelming her, Hanna found that all the forces she and Frank most hated were united in conspiracy. The only way she could ever begin to come to terms with her loss was through fighting to have the truth made known throughout the world. James Connolly, badly injured during the Rising, was imprisoned in Dublin Castle and awaiting execution when she went to confront officials at the Castle. Ina, one of his daughters, met her there and, hearing of her confrontation with officialdom, thought she could never be as brave.[38] Connolly had asked his family to give all his writings to Frank Skeffington, the man he trusted above all to ensure that his ideals were kept alive. They now had to tell him the truth before he too went to his death. Nora Connolly left a touching letter for Hanna as bereaved women began to share their experiences and lend each other support:

> Dear Mrs Skeffington
>
> Could mama see you at any time. We went up to your house but you were out. Papa, before he died, sent out a message to Mr Skeffington, not knowing that he was dead. We were unable to tell him so until last night when we paid our last visit to him. Mama would like to see you.
>
> With deepest regards & sympathy
> I am most sincerely yours
> Nora Connolly[39]

Three days before Connolly's execution Hanna had published a lengthy statement, detailing the information she had managed to acquire concerning her husband's last hours and the harassment she and her family had experienced as they tried to discover the truth. She demanded 'the fullest enquiry into all the above circumstances' and, as her husband's next of kin, insisted upon the right to be legally represented at that inquiry. She added a touching postscript. 'Private sources' had provided information on how Frank had met his end. Was it out of kindness for her distress? It was the only consolation left:

> He refused to be blindfolded, and met death with a smile on his lips, saying before he died that the authorities would find out after his death what a mistake they made. He put his hand to his eyes, and the bullet passed through his hand to his brain.[40]

But the reality was brutal, sordid and hasty. The incomprehending victims were allowed no last words.

Without her knowledge – certainly she would not have given permission – while she was composing this statement Frank's body was being exhumed and reburied beside his mother in Glasnevin cemetery. His remains had been handed over to Dr J. B. Skeffington on condition that the funeral would be held in the early hours and that Hanna would not be notified. Dr J. B. gave his consent to these terms, although unwillingly. He had been assured by General Maxwell that compliance in this would result in the trial of the murderer. Hanna could never have agreed to such a wretched bargain. To have her beloved husband disposed of so unceremoniously, as though he was some criminal to be shunned by society, deprived of the presence of family and friends, she could never forgive her father-in-law.[41]

Eva Gore-Booth, on hearing that her sister's sentence of death had been commuted to life imprisonment, applied for permission to visit Constance in Mountjoy. She and Esther Roper crossed over to Dublin on the night of 11 May. After their 20 hurried minutes of conversation, in which they tried to give the prisoner all the information they possessed, listening to her worries over her friends, they promised to do all they could to find and help those in need. Constance could not understand why 'Skeffy' had been shot and neither could they, who had known him and had admired his pacifist commitment. They found Dublin to be 'a city of mourning and death' as they searched for the bereaved and grieving. They found Hanna at home, sitting in a room in which the window was still broken by the volley that had been fired into it by the soldiers. She showed them what had been sent from the barracks: 'the poor little parcel … containing a watch, a tie and a collar' and told them of what had happened. When they reflected on what they knew of Frank, that 'troublesome idealist', Eva understood why he had been shot:

> Hearing Mrs Skeffington talk, one realised that though her husband never had a weapon in his hand, militarism was wise in its generation, and in Sheehy Skeffington militarism had struck down its worst enemy – unarmed yet insurgent

> Idealism. It was not for nothing that the half-mad officer who carried out the murder was promoted a week afterwards.
>
> The authorities knew their business well [42]

John Dillon had been unable to move out of his home in North Great Georges Street during the Rising. He and Hanna did not agree on politics, but he could be a powerful force if he believed in a cause. She managed to get to see him, and, as she recounted the dreadful saga of events, 'never (saw) a man more moved'.[43] Dillon went over to London, taking Hanna's statement with him, to be included in an emotional speech to the House of Commons on the horrors being perpetrated by the British forces in the aftermath of the Rising's defeat. On her behalf he called for a public inquiry 'as a matter of elementary justice to this unhappy lady for this cruel injury which has been inflicted upon her'. Nothing less would be acceptable: 'To tell us that there will be a court martial, which, of course, will be secret, and that we may be sure justice will be done, is really an outrage upon every principle of fair play.'[44] Indignation had the effect of bringing Asquith over to Ireland, to see for himself. A Royal Commission was appointed to enquire into the causes of the rebellion, but there was still to be no inquiry into the atrocities committed by the British troops. What the government decided upon, in an obvious attempt to deflect criticism, was to allow the court martial of Bowen-Colthurst to be made open to the public.

It took place on Tuesday and Wednesday, the 6 and 7 June, at Richmond Barracks, Dublin, an event like no other court martial. Bowen-Colthurst and his family were free to stay in the smart Hibernian hotel in Dawson Street during the proceedings, admission to which was by ticket only. Seats were reserved for the relatives of the three deceased men, as approximately 100 civilians piled into the large square hall which was to serve as a courtroom.[45] The room was almost bare, its windows high and barred, a great skylight providing most of the illumination. Wooden chairs and benches were provided for the public who filled three sides of the room, facing an array of military figures, presided over by Major-General Lord Cheylesmere, on the opposite side of a large green baize table. Only the military were to be called to give evidence. Hanna had her close family and friends to give her much-needed support. Father Eugene described simply by Louie Bennett as a 'pale and spiritualised priest', sat beside her.[46] Tim Healy, Mr White and her brother Dick followed the case on her behalf, but were forbidden from making any intervention. Many of the women whose cause Frank Skeffington had championed with such vigour were present, all wanting to ensure that justice was done to his memory. Louie Bennett, one of that group, described Hanna as a 'mute presence', but a tremendously powerful one: 'pale, still, like a stone image of tragedy. She emitted extraordinarily the impression of tense, absorbed interest, every fibre of her being strung to one single point in life.'[47] The prisoner, Bowen-Colthurst, was described as a 'tall, well set-up young officer. He heard the charge read with composure, and in a firm voice pleaded "not guilty".'[48] Later in the trial he displayed some 'restlessness' as the evidence against him was presented and by the second day was reported to be 'more depressed and preoccupied'.[49] No matter how he appeared, he drew no interest from Hanna, who concentrated all her attention on listening to the details of her husband's murder.

Afterwards she was bitter about this 'wooden tribunal' where all the witnesses were 'drilled to tell a special tale'.[50] It was a stage-managed affair without any doubt. Uncomfortable facts, such as the incriminating material purporting to come from Sheehy Skeffington having in reality been planted on his dead body, which nearly emerged in court, were deliberately not pursued by any member of the military prosecuting team. The raids on the Sheehy Skeffington household were not mentioned. But despite the careful selection of evidence, a sickening tale of brutality and callous murder was dragged out of the reluctant military witnesses. With bated breath the court listened to Second Lieutenant William Dobbin as he was cross-examined over whether he had noticed a movement in the legs of Sheehy Skeffington. He did not know if it had been 'a twinge of a muscle', and he baulked at repeating the word 'living' when asked if he believed Skeffington was dead or still alive. He was dying, or dead, 'done for'. In telling of the order that he was to shoot again, he made it appear as if an animal needed putting out of his misery.[51] It was unendurable, and Hanna's self-control vanished. She cried out in horror. An officer from the medical corps asked Father Eugene if she would like to leave the court, but she managed to gather sufficient strength to make her own response: 'I will not leave this court except by force.'[52]

Bowen-Colthurst's counsel argued that the accused was a man of 'gentle disposition and deep religious convictions, who took the Bible for his guide'. He was an Irishman 'who was profoundly fond of his country and perfectly loyal to the King'. After spending Easter Monday fishing, he had returned to barracks to discover that his country was in rebellion, with armed rebels attacking the forces of the crown. The experience of this had the effect of destabilising a man badly affected by trench warfare in France. That was the defence. It was, in other words, all the fault of the Irish rebels. The lawless conduct of the Royal Dublin Fusiliers in terrorising Dublin civilians was not an issue.[53]

Towards the end, the proceedings were interrupted by a terrific shower of hail, battering on the roof and skylight with such force that all other sound was drowned out and the court-martial forcibly suspended for several minutes. They sat 'intense stillness'. That moment, when the heavens joined in the chorus of condemnation, felt like a final piece of evidence against Colthurst. June 1916 was one of the coldest on record; such contrast to the bright sunshine which had greeted the insurgents striding out to fight for the republic on that bright April morning six weeks earlier. When it was all over, Louie Bennett reeled out into the vast square of the bleak barracks, wondering if she was in the real world. Could her city of Dublin have been home to such cruelties and agonies?[54] Never again would she think favourably of the British imperial presence in Ireland. She, the dedicated campaigner for suffrage, no longer had the heart to work for the vote, 'every instinct in me rebels against asking for such an act of justice from such a government'.[55]

The verdict of 'guilty but insane', with Bowen-Colthurst sent only reluctantly to Broadmoor, drew a chorus of protest from around the world. Tim Healy, who did not think the man was shamming madness, still believed it to be the greatest travesty of justice since the trial of Christ.[56] Bowen-Colthurst's fate was, for the Sheehy family, a running sore that never healed. How could a man judged to be insane, convicted of the most heinous crimes, escape punishment? Three days after the court-martial he was placed on 'retired pay', which he continued to receive until his death in 1965.[57] The Ministry of Defence always refused to reveal how much they had paid the murderer of Sheehy Skeffington over the following 50 years. Less than 18 months later, in a remarkable recovery of sanity, he left Broadmoor and sailed off to a new life in Canada. When Margaret Sheehy later moved to Canada, she was tormented by the prospect of encountering the man responsible for the death of her brother-in-law. In 1926, sure she had spotted Colthurst's son in a hotel, she tried unsuccessfully to obtain more information from the emigration authorities. The conspiracy to protect him was still in operation.[58]

As news of events in Dublin during Easter 1916 began to filter through to the outside world, the international network of Irish and feminist sympathisers rallied in support. Women in Ireland, headed by Kathleen Clarke and Aine Ceannt, widows of two of the leaders of the Rising, were proving themselves efficient organisers of relief for those directly affected by the Rising. Women pooled what little resources they had, united by a common widowhood. From New York, a Mrs Shanahan sent over £310 to Hanna, a donation organised rapidly by a few women for the immediate necessities of the women and children 'deprived of their protectors'.[59] An Irish National Aid Association was formed, its temporary executive comprised mainly of women. They calculated that they needed at least £700 a week for relief payments and money began to trickle in – an expression of support for those suffering from the consequences of that brief stab for independence.[60]

Hanna paid the rent, the milk and the butcher, continuing the normal process of living, but the raids and the damage to the house were too much for her deeply hostile landlady. Mrs Donovan asked her to leave. Later, she was astounded to discover how quickly her former landlady had received compensation from the authorities for the damage.[61] Some civilians had no scruples in pressing claims against the military authorities. The only compensation Hanna ever wanted was the return of her possessions stolen by the military. She and Frank had very little that others would consider of value. An inventory of household items they had made the year before showed them to have possessed almost the barest minimum considered necessary for middle-class requirements. They could never have contemplated a dinner party with the paucity of crockery at their disposal.[62] By the end of May, Hanna and Owen had moved to rooms in 43 Moyne Road, on the other side of Rathmines, and Hanna continued with the only two causes that mattered: establishing the truth of what had happened in Portobello and ensuring that the *Irish Citizen* did not die along with its editor. Owen, who now knew that his daddy was never to fulfil his promise to take him to the museum for his Easter treat, went back to Rathgar Kindergarten after the Easter holidays. He needed the distraction of friends and play. Reality could be too heavy a burden for a small boy.[63]

Feminists of many different persuasions swiftly rallied in support of the *Irish Citizen*. A meeting was held on 30 May and a fund set up to ensure that the paper could continue. From Margaret McCoubrey in Belfast, Alice Park in Palo Alto, Vida Goldstein in Melbourne, Charlotte Shaw (the playwright's wife), and Emmeline Pethick-Lawrence in London, the response was immediate and generous: £132.0.6 had been donated by March 1917. Louie Bennett, in tribute to the editor whose pacifist views she had so much admired, became chair of the 'Irish Citizen Fund' committee. She remembered with fondness going to Manico's 'dark little printing offices in Temple Lane' where she acquired a respect for the 'meticulous care he gave to the lay-out … Skeffington's code did not permit of half measures and slip-shod methods even in minor matters.'[64] Over time, she and Hanna were forced to establish a fairly close working relationship. It was never without tension, but they managed to struggle along.

The July issue of the *Citizen*, the first to be produced since his death, was a four-page memorial to Frank. There was no shortage of tributes from friends and colleagues although many had to be excluded because of lack of space. Maurice Wilkins, recalling his time working with him at the printing press, paid tribute to his friend's patience: 'he raised us to the height of which we were capable by the spiritual force of his own example.' James Cousins sent a poem written specially for the occasion. Gretta was upset that no tribute from her had been included, but there were short pieces from some IWFL members. Meg Connery wrote: 'We have rallied from the shock and our only thought is to "carry on"', while Kathleen Emerson added: 'none more brave and none more truly selfless. Frank Sheehy Skeffington, it was a privilege to have known you.' Louie Bennett contributed an unsigned editorial: 'His optimism was never dashed, and he had an abiding faith in everything working out for the ultimate good, joined to a passionate, unquenchable love of life, every hour of which he enjoyed', adding also a warm and heartfelt tribute to Hanna:

> Those of us who have had the privilege of coming into contact with Mrs Skeffington during this period of such tragic experience as few men or women are called upon to endure, have been roused to amazed admiration of her courage, moderation and sense of justice … Mrs Sheehy Skeffington has no desire that life should be taken to pay for her husband's life.[65]

In the shocked aftermath of the rising and the execution of so many former friends, women were determined to maintain a sense of the importance of their fight for citizenship. The paper was a beacon of pacifist hope, now more needed than ever, for its insistence on values that had been all but extinguished in the bloody fields of war. It was difficult to keep one's bearings in these, the worst of all times, and although many tried, they still needed Hanna's unrivalled ability to assess a situation and to develop the appropriate response. Meg Connery was great for articles, but her temperament was too mercurial for sober leadership. Louie Bennett, apologising for planning to be absent for three weeks in August, felt that it would be useless to continue the *Citizen* in its attenuated form if Hanna too left Dublin, 'who would maintain its interest if you too are absent?' she asked.[66] Cissie Cahalan, despairing of her attempt to obtain permission from the police for IWFL meetings to be held while martial law continued, asked Hanna for advice: 'shall I write to the chief commissioner of police – perhaps you could send me word sometime tomorrow. I hate to worry you during this awful time but there is no one else to get sound advice from.'[67] They did not want to bother her, but no one could really do without her clear-headed presence. They all agreed that the work of the *Citizen* should not 'be imposed' on her, yet the paper was so identified with Hanna and Frank it did not seem as if it could live without the presence of one of them. Hanna 'in spite of overwhelming sorrow' edited the September issue, which was a tribute to those dead or imprisoned who had supported the suffrage cause. Her tone was defiant:

> The *Irish Citizen* will continue its work. Though badly wounded by recent losses, it is not dead: great causes go marching on, even though their pioneers be mouldering in their graves. The rally to our appeal has been prompt and generous; it justifies the faith which our dead editor reposed in the future of the paper; his work is not lost.[68]

As the July issue had been a 'phenomenal success', selling out within a few weeks, with one seller managing to dispose of over 400 in one day, they printed three thousand copies. It was only a four-page monthly, but they hoped 'for better days' to come. Hanna and Louie Bennett revived the Irish Committee of the League of Irish Women, formed in the wake of the Hague Congress and published an appeal to President Wilson, urging him as 'head of the great American Republic … to use your good offices on behalf of our small Nationality … to have Ireland included as a small nation in any international conference which may be formed on the conclusion of the war … Of all the subject nationalities none has suffered longer or more keenly than Ireland has under England's rule.' Hanna's pen was surely responsible for the uncompromising condemnation of British rule in Ireland contained within this open letter:

> rebellion after rebellion has been put down by martial law; Ireland has been wasted and depopulated, and England has added new Acts for the coercion or the better government of Ireland, while the unceasing struggle goes on with alternating hope or despair, ending for Ireland's sons, in exile or the felon's grave.[69]

Preoccupation with obtaining a public inquiry did not prevent her involvement with other political issues. But whatever she did, it was in the conscious knowledge that Frank would have done the same. For her, at this point, they were totally one. Pleading for the life of Sir Roger Casement, facing execution for treason, she wrote to the government:

> As the wife of one whose life was taken by the Military wrongfully, and without trial, during the recent rising, and as the victim of many wrongs yet unredressed, I feel that I have the right to approach you to ask you to prevent any further shedding of the blood of my countrymen by sparing the life of Sir Roger Casement, now under sentence of death … In expressing this wish I am conscious that I am speaking in the name of my murdered husband, who abhorred the taking of life under all circumstances, and that I am voicing the sentiments of the majority of the Irish people.[70]

Recovery from the first shock of bereavement was more difficult than her business correspondence would suggest. She had remarked, with no attempt at wit, that when she had heard that the military had regretted they had not shot her as well as her husband, her reaction had been that it would have saved her as well as them much trouble if they had.[71] She was at rock-bottom, with little will to go on. In the days of their engagement she had written to Frank, 'Isn't there a bond between us that will outlive our mortal bodies when our loving hearts are long still in death?'[72] One of those loving hearts had been brutally stilled, but she was determined their bond would continue. During this period of desperate loneliness and despair over the prospect of continuing life without the one who had shared her hopes and her battles, she attended some seance sessions with Thomas Webb, a cousin of her friend Deborah. Thomas had had unspecified communication with someone possessing the initials 'FSS' and they hoped this might be Frank trying to communicate.[73] That Hanna went back for repeated attempts, assuring Deborah she was not too discouraged when she failed to make any connection – an act so out of character for that sceptical rationalist – is testimony to her heartbreak and desolation. Delicately, Louie Bennett also tried to bring comfort by writing of contact she had made with a dead relative:

> I don't as you know pretend to believe in anything very particular … but I have a deep-lying sense that the dead are not so very far away from us. I thought I would like just to tell you this – though perhaps such impressions don't appeal to you at all – may even in a sense irritate you.[74]

Spiritualism was practised by many bereaved people at this time as women struggled to come to terms with the appalling loss of their loved ones in the mass slaughter of war, but Frank had never hesitated to voice his total rejection of any belief that there could be communication with the dead. He had even done so at the Cousins's farewell party, but now that he had been so cruelly wrenched from life, any prospect of re-establishing contact – if only to say a proper good-bye – had to be grasped. Hanna had scoffed at Gretta's 'cosmic guff', but now she listened to her communication with the occult world. Gretta was certain that Frank's spirit was still in existence; she had felt his presence beside her while she was 'walking on a quiet path from the sea'. He was 'still all alive & more acutely conscious than ever', still preaching peace, especially to the soldiers who had 'passed over' and he was very proud of Hanna, whom he was sure he would meet again.[75] Over the next year there were other messages from Frank via Gretta, praising Hanna's work, expressing confidence in the growth of the causes of feminism and pacifism.

Gretta declared her arm 'aching with the force Frank used in shoving the pencil from the left … he wants to do it his way!'[76] Maybe that helped to ease some of the horror surrounding his death, the suggestion that even death could not prevent Frank from having his say. There is a significant piece of evidence which shows very clearly that, for a time, Hanna did have some hope of another life with Frank. In America, lecturing in those first months of bereavement, she would tell her audience:

> I am not here just to harrow your hearts by a passing thrill, to feed you on horrors for sensation's sake. I want to continue my husband's work so that when I meet him some day in the Great Beyond, he will be pleased with my stewardship.[77]

That second sentence was left out of later editions of the pamphlet that reproduced her lecture. It had been a hope which flickered only briefly: a small crutch discarded as soon as a degree of emotional equilibrium was regained.

Other friends tried also to provide consolation through expressing their belief in Frank's continued presence in an after-life, but they tried as well to persuade Hanna to think of the future rather than concentrate on what seemed a fruitless and heartbreaking effort to obtain justice. Elfreda Baker's letter attempted to offer support. She had no difficulty in believing that Frank's spirit lived on, but she felt it to be more important for Hanna to concentrate on rebuilding her life. To someone still struggling to find out exactly what had happened to her husband, these kinds of sentiments must have felt like a betrayal of her husband's memory:

> I think you know me well enough to know that not for ever would I urge you to turn your attention and thoughts on the untrue. With you, it is that unless you are granted understanding, you can't rest on the faith side. I think of dear Mr Skeffington as so alive in a more congenial atmosphere, more able to grow – and so we cannot fret for him – his suffering over – I have simply boiled at it all – but I don't think, now, that your friends can help you by dwelling on that aspect. I want to know how you are; and whether you are able to make any plans for your daily life.[78]

Not everyone understood her determination to keep re-living the tragedy until justice had been achieved. Some shied away from the repetition of such pain, wanting the healing process to begin. Others admired her courage, while not fully understanding what was involved. Her insistence on being allowed full access to Portobello Barracks, where she could see for herself the yard which had been the last sight before her husband's eyes, and thereby understand precisely what was being referred to in any inquiry into those events, was certainly not a visit that many would have undertaken in the immediate aftermath of such tragedy.[79]

Thoughts on moving to America began to preoccupy her. Frank had been happy in that open, more tolerant society where many of their old friends had made new lives. She could tell his tale on a wider stage, one less compromised by British interests. Friends representing every political strand began to suggest useful contacts for when she crossed the Atlantic. Maybe she would stay there. Her sisters came upon her one day, sorting out her furniture to sell. They had to argue hard to prevent her from getting rid of it.[80] But she could not go yet. First of all, the British must be forced to confront what they, through their cult of militarism and their imperialist attitude towards the Irish, had allowed to happen.

The global network of suffrage proved particularly invaluable to Hanna as she continued her quest for a full inquiry. Muriel Matters, who had been in Ireland on a suffrage tour in 1914, wrote to invite her to London. She was convinced that only Hanna's presence could force some response from the government. The Australian-born Muriel, a member of the Women's Freedom League, had once hovered over London in a balloon dropping suffrage leaflets while the issue was being debated in Westminster. She had also chained herself to the railings of the 'ladies' gallery' in the House of Commons. Her readiness to take part in direct action was precisely what was needed at this time. She and Emmeline Pethick-Lawrence would do everything in their power to help, but they needed Hanna to come over. Muriel had a 'tiny quiet flat' in Kensington.[81] Hanna agreed. She brought Owen with her, but as the old suffrage round of interviewing people with influence began, it was clear that her stay would be prolonged. Owen returned to Dublin. Hanna tried hard to remain cheery when writing to him, but her heartbreak was evident:

> I hope you came home all right and that you, John and Alice have great games together. I know you will be a very good boy while I am away. Sir Francis is here. He is going to write to you soon … It rains a lot here now. Perhaps you will come to meet me to the train, like dada used to. Everyone over here is very sorry for dada and they are helping me to find out all about it. I'll bring you something nice from London. What would you like best?
>
> Mama[82]

Those who met Hanna during this period found themselves in awe of her determination to go on, no matter how long it might take. Asquith did not appreciate the resolve of the woman he invited to meet him. On 19 July, accompanied by Muriel Matters as witness (Hanna trusted no member of the British government), they met in the Cabinet Room in Downing Street. All her suffragist instincts were on the alert; she had experienced too many unsatisfactory meetings with politicians over the past decade. Her powers of observation were acute, her ability to assess character equally sharp. Asquith, 'mellow and hale, with rosy, chubby face and silver hair, a Father Christmas air about him', attempted to escape from the demand for an inquiry.[83] Military interests did not permit it: 'Nothing we can do can bring your husband back; you have a boy to educate; this is war-time and the prestige of the Army must be upheld.'[84] Asquith tried to bargain:

> Would I be satisfied with an inadequate inquiry, which was 'the best they could do'? I told him I would not be satisfied with any inquiry that he told me in advance would be unsatisfactory and inadequate, and that, while I must accept the best he could give – I would not be 'satisfied'. I said I would take further action if I wasn't – for even then I had in view a visit to America to tell an honest country what British militarism could do.

He pressed her to accept 'adequate and even generous compensation', of £10,000. That was the point of the interview, Hanna realised, as she watched the 'wily statesman' tapping his fingers on the green baize table, glancing sideways but never looking straight into the face of the determined Irish woman sitting at the end.[85] She rejected the suggestion of 'hush money' then, and would reject it always. She would work and bring up her son through her own efforts. No amount of blood money from the British government could soften the pain of her loss or compensate Owen for the lack of a father. The interview came to an end. Inwardly, Hanna scornfully concluded that those 'pitiful little traps and quibbles and his "hush money" suggestions were hardly worthy of a great statesman'. Dr Skeffington might try to get around this, but she was adamant. Frank's father did indeed attempt to have a sum of money paid separately to his grandson, as some insurance for him as he grew up. He did not tell Hanna that he had made an application to the Rebellion (Victims) Committee on the matter. Henry Lemass, her solicitor, wrote to inform her that he had received a letter from the secretary of that committee, advising of Dr Skeffington's claim and asking for a response. The response was prompt and unequivocal. Lemass was to send an immediate letter of rejection. The Committee must be told that the application made by Dr Skeffington was without his client's sanction and in direct opposition to her wishes.[86] It was a point of such honour to her that she could never let any suggestion to the contrary simply pass by. Twenty years later she won a bitterly fought and widely publicised libel action against the editor of the *Catholic Herald* for daring to suggest that she had ever accepted money from the British.[87]

The insurance company paid out Frank's life insurance of £550 without any quibble, an act for which she was forever grateful. She used it to pay off every debt she and Frank had incurred. Charles Oldham was astounded to receive back a cheque for £4-19, lent during Frank's hunger strike. His acceptance was reluctant, but he appreciated how much she wanted to pay her debts while she could. Although unnecessary, he understood it was worthwhile if it helped to 'make her independent in fact and in mind'.[88] She also paid off 14 guineas to her old landlady, terminating the tenancy of Grosvenor Place, even though she had been forced to move out weeks previously.[89] She was scrupulous in all her financial dealings. That September, in a macabre claim, the publishing house of Fisher Unwin sent Frank a peremptory demand to settle his account. His life of Michael Davitt had not sold well, and he owed £8-8-4.[90] There is no record of what must have been a wrathful reply from his widow.

Asquith granted the inquiry. Those who knew the circumstances behind this decision understood what a victory had been achieved. Muriel Matter's friend Jill, who had grown fond of Hanna during her stay in London, sent a small donation to help with her expenses, 'all my life the memory of your extraordinary courage and unselfishness will be an inspiration to me'.[91] Emmeline Pethick-Lawrence, veteran observer of the ways of politicians, congratulated Hanna on her 'great achievement' in forcing the government into giving such a promise. She, equally wary of politicians' promises, had felt that 'every kind of postponement' would be used to put off having the inquiry, but Asquith realised that the wiser approach was to get it over with.[92] He did prevaricate until the last minute on giving its terms of reference and Tim Healy complained 'we are to be bamboozled I fancy'.[93] No one trusted the intentions of the British.

As everyone suspected, the inquiry's scope was made deliberately narrow, other atrocities ruled out and evidence taken on a voluntary basis. Bowen-Colthurst was not recalled from England and other important witnesses were also purposely unavailable. Nevertheless, Hanna had wrested a great deal from a government possessing immense powers under wartime conditions. The personal cost was immeasurable. Once back home in Ireland, waiting for the inquiry to begin, knowing that all the horror would have to be re-lived, her health and mental state were severely strained. A short break with Margaret and her children in Bettystown, which they hoped might provide some respite before the rigours of the inquiry, had the effect of precipitating a minor collapse. It was a release from the unbearable tension, from the iron self-control that had to be clung onto when in public. Friends were upset to hear that she was in bed, suffering from neuralgia and headache.[94] To her family Hanna was more explicit, complaining of pain in her heart, which a worried Kathleen put down to 'muscular strain', begging her sister to consult a doctor even though, 'I know, old girl, that you don't care anything for life just now.'[95] From far away,

Gretta worried whether the family were 'being nice'.[96] She had in mind those members with whom Hanna was usually at loggerheads. On this appalling tragedy all had rallied round, although some had their own sadnesses with which to cope. That March, Margaret's husband had died unexpectedly, leaving her to struggle alone with four young children. The Culhane family had never accepted her, so her circumstances were more difficult than they should have been. War work offered her a way of maintaining the family, as she managed to get work as welfare superintendent in the National Shell factory in Dublin. Some family members were as solidly behind Hanna as they had always been. Aunt Kate, that loving godmother, was busy writing circular letters to all the family in Limerick, keeping everyone in touch with the latest twists in events, a task that was now beyond the arthritic Bessie.

The inquiry, chaired by Sir John Simon (who was, like Healy, a parliamentarian and a strong supporter of women's suffrage) opened in the Four Courts in Dublin on 23 August. Six days of hearing about madness, brutality and horror. The court was packed long before the commissioners took their seats and the public, eager to hear the evidence, found themselves unable to squeeze into the cramped space of Judge Ross's Court, the venue allocated to the Commission. Tim Healy, who headed the same legal team that had followed the court-martial on Hanna's behalf, made strong objections to the court, which he described as 'the most inconvenient in the whole building' and 'scarcely in keeping with the dignity of the inquiry'. Sir John Simon agreed it was 'uncomfortably crowded'. He hoped they would be able, later, to move into the Court of Appeal.[97] Inexplicably, the authorities had not anticipated this level of interest. Perhaps they hoped the smallness of the appointed chambers would help in minimising the impact of the hearing?

On each day of the inquiry Hanna was accompanied by her father David and her sister Mary. Dr Skeffington was there too, without legal representation. He was a Justice of the Peace in his own right, he wanted no one to stand between him and the truth behind his son's final hours. As the reports put it, he 'appeared on his own behalf'. Hanna brought Owen to court with her on the day that she took the witness stand. She wanted her son to hear the truth in his mother's words, and much of what she had to say concerned events that he too had been part of. The reporter from the *Freeman's Journal* described the seven year old as 'a bright little lad of ten', to the family's amusement.[98] Uncle Eugene, writing from London, ended one letter 'warmest love to the bright lad of 10'.[99] Muriel Matters understood the reporter's mistake, 'He is really very big for his age. It is only when one looks at the little legs and sandalled feet that one realises how young he is. I like those little legs.'[100]

Hanna gave her testimony on the third day. Tim Healy had just addressed the court in an emotional review of evidence that had gone on for three hours. His conclusion adroitly set the stage for her entrance. Quoting from a poem by Spenser was a masterly touch:

> Ah, ye mistook, ye should have snatched
> his wand and bound him fast.
> Without the rod reversed and backward
> mutters of dissevering power
> Ye cannot free the lady that sits here
> In stony silence, still and motionless.

Not free, but at long last able to speak of her ordeal. She told the world of the man she had been married to for 13 years, her 'school mate' she called him, a strong pacifist even in their school days, whom she last saw between 5.15 and 5.30 p.m. on the Tuesday evening of Easter Week. In clear tones she recalled the sequence of events during the days when she had attempted to find her husband:

> when he did not come home I began to feel rather uneasy, and I tried to find out what had happened him. The wildest rumours, as they seemed to me, reached me, but I refused to believe them, because I knew he was not involved, and I thought I would be notified. I heard that he was shot; that he had dropped in the street; that he was arrested, and so on. The first definite clue I got was on Friday morning from a man in the street. He put me on to another series of clues, and by degrees I followed these up with great difficulty to Mr Coade, and he told me he had seen my husband's body lying on the floor in the mortuary chapel in the barracks.

She described the raid on the house:

> I heard stirs about the house and on going to one of the windows I saw soldiers lining up as if surrounding the whole terrace, which is one of about seven or eight houses. I continued putting my boy to bed, and when it became clear to me that the soldiers were coming in I went down, with the intention of opening the door for them. In the meantime the little maid, who became scared, ran away to get out at the back. I went out at the back with my boy, knowing that soldiers were likely to be also at the back, and called the maid. When I had succeeded in getting the two in, I heard a volley fired. Almost immediately after I heard the smashing of glass.

As rifles with fixed bayonets were pointed at herself and Owen and they were ordered to put up their hands, her little boy gave a cry. She put her arms above him, and she believed she had said 'These are the defenders of women and children.' Her textbooks in German, French, Russian and other languages were taken away, sacks and other containers obtained from the neighbours for the purpose. One soldier had remarked that Skeffington must have been in correspondence with the Kaiser. A burst of laughter in the courtroom greeted that comment. As Hanna attempted to refer to a statement by the Prime Minister she was abruptly interrupted by Simon: they did not want to hear anything that involved political references. The tension lifted slightly when she informed the court that her husband always kept his study locked because he objected to it being dusted. The thought caused some amusement, abruptly quelled when she went on to say that Frank had had the key of the study with him on the day he left her. Whoever had opened the study door after her husband's death had somehow obtained that key, as the lock was not burst open. The distasteful image of a dead body being rifled for its possessions was in all minds. Before Hanna left the stand, she told also of her husband's signet ring, removed from his lifeless finger, which would never have been returned to her if it had not been for the intervention of Sir Francis Vane. Finally, she asked for the one thing she most needed to know, whether any medical man had seen the body of her husband immediately after his death. On that, the chairman said it would be attended to, and the court adjourned until the following day. She had made a powerful impression on all who listened to her steady recital of events.[101] Mr Powell, legal counsel for the military authorities, referred to her in his summing up as 'a very cultured lady'.[102] It was no consolation, but it was at least a belated recognition that the widow of Frank Sheehy Skeffington deserved more than the contemptible treatment that had followed his murder.

Two days later, Mary Kettle gave evidence of her fruitless quest to Portobello Barracks. In London, Kathleen was busy reading all the newspaper reports of the inquiry, 'hard to follow it all' she thought, as she praised her sister's performance. Mary's testimony was most 'characteristically given' in that decided manner typical of her.[103] She had provoked uneasy laughter in the court when she described Captain Bowen-Colthurst as 'a cold, collected type of Englishman' but, undaunted, she had continued to explain what she meant. He had 'a peculiar cruel look which goes with the unimaginative nature'. Simon, impatient with this attempt at psychologising, asked her to tell them what Bowen-Colthurst had actually done at this time, a rebuke which drew the haughty reply from Mary 'In view of the evidence at the court martial I thought it better to give you my impression.' She was obviously attempting to cast doubt on the 'insanity' verdict which had exempted the authorities from further responsibility, but Simon would not be drawn into these dangerous waters.[104]

The one other relative to give evidence was Dr Skeffington, anxious to make it very plain to everyone that his son had not supported the rebellion.

He told the court of Frank's visit to him before Easter, and of his uneasiness with the militaristic direction that affairs in Dublin were taking. As proof, he read out extracts from his son's letters detailing what he thought might happen in the coming months.[105] Frank was dead, but his reputation lived on and his father wanted his reputation as a pacifist to remain intact, a proud reminder of an honourable man. Innuendo would not be permitted to spoilt that.

Medical opinion was still not forthcoming. There was covert resistance at the highest levels. Tim Healy attempted to have Dr Balch, army medical officer in Portobello, produced in court. He had been the one who had examined the bodies after death, and he would have been in a position to tell them how many bullet wounds each body bore, and to provide other evidence which would help to establish the sanity or otherwise of Captain Bowen-Colthurst. But Dr Balch, they discovered, had been 'suddenly jerked out of Dublin' and was now in Sierra Leone.[106] Captain Colthurst's state of mind was outside the remit of the inquiry. Dr Balch did not give evidence. The information that Hanna had asked for so specifically was not to be given.

In spite of all the curbs placed on the inquiry it did manage to establish the main facts – Bowen-Colthurst's indiscriminate murder of a number of innocent civilians, his later unwarranted promotion, the dismissal of Sir Francis Vane, the raids on the Sheehy Skeffington household, the planting of evidence on Frank's dead body – and its conclusions were damning. Lieutenant Dobbin had been recalled from service in France to give evidence on the composition of the firing squad and to answer the question as to whether Frank had required a second round before, he died. Powell, on behalf of the military, tried to apportion responsibility to one demented officer and two inexperienced subalterns, their actions triggered by fear induced by the rebellion taking place in their midst. It did not convince. Healy wrote to his brother Maurice: 'Everyone is satisfied that we have done better than we had a right to expect. Bringing Lieutenant Dobbin back is a humiliation to the military. We have thrown new light on events … There will be little esteem for Martial law or for soldiers' decisions after the Skeffington disclosures.'[107]

Friends finally understood why Hanna had been so persistent and so uncompromising on the issue. Deborah Webb was glad it was over, admitting 'I understand better now why you felt it your duty to insist on its being held – at any cost to yourself. Just like you.'[108] From far-off India, Gretta wrote that her 'heart and whole being wept' as she read the details. Hanna's ordeal in court was dreadful, but she was right 'to use its ghastly horrors in the most public way as an object-lesson of the frightfulness of militarism'. Her friend's courage was 'drawing inexpressible love and sympathy and pride' to her from all over the world.[109] And what were Hanna's feelings as she considered the outcome of the inquiry? She was shocked from having witnessed the 'automatic and tireless efforts on the part of the entire official machinery, both military and political, to prevent the truth being made public' and she was angry that no-one in authority was removed from office as a result.[110] Her consolation was the knowledge that through the inquiry she had achieved a 'damning exposé of militarism' which would serve as a fitting tribute to the ideals which had inspired her husband and which would provide her with a means of keeping his name alive. The November issue of the *Citizen*, paying tribute to Hanna's 'indomitable, pluck, determination and "grit"' in making her husband's death 'a torch for the pioneers of liberty', believed her 'handling of a difficult, even formidable task, (gave) her a place in the nation's gallery of remarkable Irishwomen'.[111]

The costs of the inquiry (£512-1-0) were not awarded until September 1918. Even though fees for counsel totalled £348-12, Henry Lemass assured an anxious Hanna that he had never intended to 'add to her troubles' by claiming costs from her. He had, however, no scruples in accepting money from the government when it did appear.[112] It was not over-generous and neither had any urgency been shown in making the settlement. Hanna still wanted a breakdown of expenditure so that she could reassure herself that they were only accepting settlement of the actual costs incurred during the Inquiry. If she could have afforded to pay them herself, there is no doubt that she would have done so.

Physically and mentally worn-out, she was anxious for Owen's future. What would become of her son if he was to lose both his parents. Who would bring him up, and with what kind of beliefs would they bring him up? To allay some of her worries on that issue she made out a will, appointing Maurice Wilkins as co-executor with Kathleen and Mary. In response Maurice was 'touched and honoured' to be asked, although he wondered if he was fitted for the role, as he was 'not as strict in some points' as Hanna supposed. Her acute unhappiness had not led her to any abandonment of the principles she and her husband had based their lives upon and on which they had planned to bring up their son. Maurice had given up vegetarianism on health grounds eight months ago, and he was forced also to confess that he was 'not altogether a non-smoker nor invariable teetotaler'. He was, however, pleased to be able to say that he sympathised with Frank's views on organised religion, having no patience with sectarianism and 'narrowing cults'. Owen's future concerned him very much. He hoped the loss of such a father would not be so great on the purely material side as it would be in regard to moral and intellectual growth.[113] Hanna never attempted to become a substitute for

Frank; that was impossible, but she was determined, with regards to the most fundamental of their shared values, that Owen would be brought up as his father would have wished:

> In accordance with his father's express wishes I do not desire to have him brought up in any formal religious creed and I desire that steps should be taken by my executors so that during his school and college life he may receive only secular instruction. In general I rely on my executors in whom I have complete confidence to bring up my son as his father and I would have wished.[114]

Mary's strict adherence to the dogmas of Catholicism had led to many heated arguments while Frank was alive. Hanna, in drawing up her will, was confident that the tragedy of death had changed all that. No one, least of all her two sisters, would dare to flout these clearly expressed wishes. As an adult, Owen appreciated his mother's determination to allow her son the freedom to form his own opinions:

> One part of her principles, which she always applied, was that she believed in allowing people to be themselves. One of the things I am most grateful to her for is that, although she had her opinion; she never tried to force it on me.[115]

Family tragedy continued. Tom Kettle was devastated by the news of what had happened to his brother-in-law, 'the good comrade of many hopes'. Frank had remained 'an inextinguishable flame' even though they had chosen very different paths. His memorial tribute was eloquent and heart-felt: 'This brave and honourable man died to the rattle of musketry; his name will be recalled to the ruffle of drums.'[116] Tom, still wearing the uniform of the British army, had to suffer the pain of seeing his daughter and nephew, playing together, running away in fright at the sight of the khaki-clad man coming towards them. It was not long after the raid by Bowen-Colthurst, who had worn the same uniform.[117] The Easter Rising and the brutality of the British response ended Kettle's hopes of a peaceful solution to Ireland's struggle for independence. There was no further point in trying to persuade Irish men to enlist in the British army, so he volunteered himself for duty in France. On 9 September, at the Somme, Tom Kettle too heard that last rattle of musketry.

Three Sheehy sisters were all widowed in that one year of 1916. Louie Bennett, hardly knowing what to say, wrote of her shock at the news, 'truly your family is hard hit by fate'.[118] From Zurich, James Joyce read in the *Times* of the deaths of his old friends. On such an occasion even that master of the language could be nothing but conventional: 'I am grieved to learn that so many misfortunes have fallen on your family in these evil days.[119]

One of the ways by which Hanna eased the pain of Frank's loss was through negotiating to have his books re-published. If she could do nothing else, she could ensure that his words lived on. By August she was correcting the galley proofs of *In Dark and Evil Days*, his novel of the 1798 Rising, and trying (unsuccessfully) to interest publishers in producing a selection of Frank's journalism. Tom Kettle's last letter to his brother, written from the battlefield, had expressed a wish that his wife should write a memoir of him as a preface to his book on war. Mary now joined her sister in assuaging grief through work. *The Ways of War* was published in 1917, accompanied by his wife's long memoir of her husband, written, as she said, with 'the vision of love'.

Gretta, reading the copies of the *Citizen* posted out to her, wept because they were so deceptively normal to look at and to read, revealing nothing of all the 'loss and tragedy' that lay behind. Not only Frank's loss, but all those friends who had died in the past months or who were, like Constance Markievicz, suffering long periods of imprisonment as a consequence of their participation in the Rising. The heart of Dublin lay in smoking ruins, unbearable thought for those so far away. For a while, Hanna too, seemed to feel that if she was going to live in Ireland, it would have to be somewhere other than Dublin. She could no longer endure memories of the city. She made enquiries about her chances of a professorship in languages at Galway University, only to be told, politely, that a Galway graduate would almost certainly be awarded any such post.[120]

The outside world was informed that Mrs Sheehy Skeffington had fallen ill again, following the conclusion of the inquiry. Louie Bennett, like many others, was not surprised, 'especially as you have for so long held yourself in restraint and given yourself no natural outlet for grief'.[121] The reality was rather different. Now that she had achieved all she could through staying in Ireland, Hanna was carefully making plans to go abroad. John Byrne, Frank's old college friend, now settled in America, had been urging her to 'put her case before the American people'. He felt certain that if she did so, she would not go home empty-handed.[122] Her story that she was ill and had gone to the country to be nursed by a friend was an alibi, concocted to explain her absence from Dublin. The plan was meticulously conceived. She prepared letters, which were posted on her behalf by her friend, to support the fiction that she was resting quietly in the country. For some of her closest family, the reduction in communication was deeply worrying. Aunt Kate in particular was distraught, 'you have no idea how I feel at not hearing from you for past three weeks. What must be the cause? I am fearing that you are laid up or that you are gone from Dublin. I cannot hold out longer, I am in awful suspense. I write *(sic)* you on Wednesday last. It is so unlike you not to reply.'[123]

At the end of September Hanna and Owen slipped over quietly to Scotland to prepare for a surreptitious departure to America. In the names of 'Mrs O'Brien and son'; they spent two nights in the Imperial Hotel, Belfast, before getting the ferry, staying the following night in a Glasgow hotel.[124] Escaping the heavy surveillance that was a constant feature of her life at this time involved various disguises. At one stage in her travels she acted the part of an elderly invalid; at another, an unlikely sounding touring actress. She had confidence in her ability to adopt a convincing persona, believing that 'a woman has many helps to change her appearance, different styles of dress, of doing her hair etc. and she must avoid suggesting disguise'.[125] The old dressing-up games from her Belvedere Place days had helped her to lose inhibitions about playing 'make-believe'.

Margaret Skinnider, back in Glasgow after recovering from wounds incurred during the Rising, took care of them in her family home. It has been suggested that the genius of Michael Collins was behind this elaborate escape plan, but Collins had not yet been released from Frongoch internment camp.[126] Hanna was perfectly capable, using her own network of contacts, of devising this highly effective exit route. Writing in 1918 she said simply, 'How this was done, unfortunately, I may not yet say.'[127] These precautions might appear more appropriate in the pages of a spy novel, but, as it turned out, they proved vital. During her interview with Asquith she had intimated that she would go abroad as soon as she could, so the authorities in Dublin Castle were attempting to monitor her movements. Alice Schmitz, her landlady in Moynes Road, found herself under interrogation on several occasions while Hanna was supposedly recuperating in the country. Police demanded to see proof that all lodgers were registered. Despite being shown the correct forms they returned to demand a forwarding address for Mrs Sheehy Skeffington. Wartime conditions stipulated that boarders detailed their movements.[128] An irate Alice Schmitz, in a letter of complaint concerning police conduct, alleged that the police sergeant had also asked 'if Mrs Skeffington had any furniture and if she took her luggage with her'.[129]

Hanna suddenly reappeared. When she heard what had happened, and that her landlady had been told to tell the police as soon as Mrs Skeffington returned, she was furious. Her ability to swiftly gain publicity for this attempt at intimidation supports the notion that she was not particularly fragile at this time but was engaged in other, unspecified, activities. From the House of Commons her father sent her an ineffectual but well-meaning letter:

'I cannot do anything till tomorrow when the House meets, as I don't know where Dillon is now staying. I shall see Dillon early tomorrow and will write you afterwards. I am resolved to go home at end of week. It is killing to be here doing nothing.'[130] David wrote again, still waiting for the House to sit, pathetically adding that he had not seen her uncle 'though I wrote him to meet me here yesterday. He did not come yesterday or today.'[131] Not relying on her father for help, Hanna had succeeded in contacting Dillon at his Dublin home. As Dillon was not going to London he arranged for a colleague, T. P. O'Connor, to put a question on her behalf. O'Connor immediately sent Hanna a warm response, condemning the 'abominable treatment' to which she had been subjected and adding that he had often heard from Dillon 'of the courage and dignity with which you have met your dreadful bereavement'.[132] On 26 October, O'Connor's question was asked in the House of Commons:

> To ask the Chief Secretary to the Lord Lieutenant of Ireland, whether it is with his consent and sanction that Mrs Sheehy Skeffington has been subjected to police espionage and persecution since the murder of her husband; whether recently, when Mrs Skeffington was absent from home on a short holiday, her lodgings were visited by detectives, who cross-examined her landlady and threatened her with penalties ... and whether it is proposed to continue this system of persecution.[133]

In response to this publicity Charlotte Shaw wrote to express her sympathy, 'Saw paragraph in *Women's Dreadnought* about discomforts she was put to when she went away for a change of air.'[134] The reappearance had been a chance event. Her plans had suddenly altered. Owen had fallen ill with diphtheria while they were in Scotland and was now in an isolation hospital, where he would be for at least ten weeks. His mother was forbidden any visits because of the strict quarantine conditions, so she was forced into making a difficult decision:

> To further my chances of eventual success, and realising that I could be of no use to my boy while he was in the hospital, I returned to Dublin. I had recovered from my 'illness', and resumed my former occupation as a teacher. Thus I put the sleuths off the scent.[135]

And not only the sleuths. Aunt Kate, hearing from her nephew Jim McCoy that he had bumped into Hanna as she was walking to her evening class, wrote in pitiful terms:

> Why on earth did you not come in ... this evening and you having an hour and a half between your classes ... I ask you as only favour to grant me that happiness to come every evening that you are teaching to have something to refresh you. I beg

of you to grant me that favour. I will see it as a great compliment. If you refuse me I will feel it keenly.

My own dearest Hanna.[136]

And so, for the autumn of 1916, Hanna stayed in Ireland and tried to live an outwardly normal life. The poet Maeve Cavanagh, a Cumann na mBan and Citizen Army activist, whose socialist brother Ernest (who had been shot dead while standing on the steps of Liberty Hall at the start of the Rising) had contributed many cartoons to the *Citizen* as well as to labour journals, wrote a poem 'Francis Sheehy Skeffington: To His Wife', that was printed in the October issue of the *Citizen*:

Think not of him as dead, that thought
Would deeply wrong his victor soul,
Or that his last great fight was fought,
When he strode to Death's fiery goal.
Ah, far beyond, new beacons flared,
New battles waited where he fared.

Another stage, it. may be, too,
A higher in the soul's long climb,
When he our struggles still may view,
And we touch hands with him some time,
Whence his unconquerable will
Shall find some means to help us still.

For we who know his dreams, his worth,
Could never picture him at rest.
Oblivious to the woes of Earth,
Forgeful of his former zest,
Ah, no! Each cause he served shall know
Rich fruits of his life's after glow.

For Hallowe'en, grandfather Skeffington sent 'dear Owen' money for 'apples and nuts, cakes and sweets', but as he and Hanna did not meet, Owen's absence was not noticed.[137] Frank's suffrage play *The Prodigal Daughter* was staged in the Hardwicke Street Theatre on 16-19 November, along with a play by Maud Eden. The committee sponsoring the 'Sheehy Skeffington Memorial Programme' included Mary Hayden, George Bernard Shaw, Sir Francis Vane, George Russell and Michael Davitt, son of Frank's old hero. It was an affectionate tribute.[138]

Simon had made his report, but the government refused to publish it, despite many appeals from MPs sympathetic to Hanna. Dr J.B. was quick to write to the press, calling for its publication and emphasizing that the report had vindicated the reputation of his son, whose appalling treatment had been compounded by the 'terrorizing of his widow and infant son … facts so strange that Asquith said he didn't believe them.'[139] Hanna sent the report to prominent individuals – politicians, writers, all those who had been known to her or to Frank since the time of his hunger strike. Charlotte Shaw was as usual warm in her response. The newspapers had published full accounts of each day's proceedings, and Hanna took some consolation in that, but the principle of official publication was important to her and she would pursue principles to the bitter end. She wrote to the papers to point out that only Sir Francis Vane had been dismissed and Dublin Castle, despite everything that had been uncovered, had not investigated facts or punished those responsible.[140] If the government would not release the report, then she would use the evidence from the court martial and the inquiry to tell the world the truth. It was, in the end, the only way to keep sane. The need to publicise Frank's death had restored her fighting spirit and brought back the will to live. While biding her time in Ireland she had the certainty that, before long, she would be speaking to large audiences in America. By then she would be strong enough to admit publicly: 'Sometimes it is harder to live for a cause than to die for it. It would be a poor tribute to my husband if grief were to break my spirit. It shall not do so.'[141]

NOTES

1 Tariff for Waverly Hotel, Easter weekend 1916, Sheehy Skeffington MS (hereafter SS MS) 21,637.

2 Testimony of Dr J. B. Skeffington regarding his son's views in the days before the rising, given as part of his evidence to Simon Inquiry, in *Irish Times: Sinn Féin Rebellion Handbook* (Dublin, 1917), p. 222.

3 R. M. Fox, *Rebel Irishwomen* (Dublin, 1935), p. 76.

4 Included in her speeches and reproduced in Hanna Sheehy Skeffington, *British Militarism as I Have Known It* (New York, 1917), first edn, pp 2–4.

5 William O'Brien, introduction, in Desmond Ryan (ed.), *Labour and Easter Week 1916*, (Dublin, 1949), p. 20.

6 Ibid., p. 11. The members of the Civil Provisional Government were to be William O'Brien, Arthur Griffith, Alderman Tom Kelly, Councillor Seán T. O'Kelly and Mrs H. Sheehy Skeffington.

7 Hanna Sheehy Skeffington, 'Memories of the suffrage campaign in Ireland', in *The Vote*, 30 Aug. 1929.

8 Helen Little (ed.), *Revolutionary Woman: Kathleen Clarke, 1878-1972: An Autobiography* (Dublin, 1991), pp 222–3. p. 69.

9 Margaret Skinnider, *Doing My Bit for Ireland* (New York, 1917), pp 132–48.
10 Hanna Sheehy Skeffington, 'Unpublished memoirs', in Margaret Ward, *Hanna Sheehy Skeffington: Suffragette and Sinn Féiner: Her memoirs and Political Writings* (Dublin, 2017), pp 14–5.
11 Ibid., p. 14.
12 Eugene Sheehy, *May It Please the Court* (Dublin, 1951), pp 123–4. On her meeting with Father Eugene, see also Fox, *Rebel Irishwomen*, p. 74.
13 Mrs Eileen Murphy, née Eileen Walsh, Bureau of Military History, Witness Statement (hereafter BMH WS) 480, p. 7.
14 *Irish World*, 3 May 1924.
15 See Ruth Taillon, *When History Was Made: The Women of 1916* (Belfast, 1996).
16 Owen Sheehy Skeffington, 'Francis Sheehy Skeffington' in Owen Dudley Edwards and Fergus Pyle (eds), *1916 The Easter Rising* (London, 1968), p. 145.
17 For testimony of events leading up to the murder, see Hanna Sheehy Skeffington, *British Militarism*, pp 6–7; Hanna's statement to John Dillon, read out in the House of Commons during Dillon's speech, 11 May 1916, and evidence of Hanna to Simon Commission.
18 John Dillon, speech to the House of Commons, reprinted in Edwards and Pyle (eds), *1916 The Easter Rising*, pp 62–78.
19 *Irish Times*, *Rebellion Handbook*, pp 102–3.
20 Hanna Sheehy Skeffington, *British Militarism*, p. 7.
21 James Stephens, *The Insurrection in Dublin* (Dublin: Maunsel, 1916), p. 1.
22 Ibid., p. 51.
23 Ibid., p. 52.
24 Maeve McGarry, BMH WS 826, pp 7–8.
25 Hanna Sheehy Skeffington, 'Unpublished memoirs', in Ward, *Hanna Sheehy Skeffington*, pp 14–5.
26 Nancy Wyse Power, BMH WS 541, p. 26. Maire died on 19 July 1916.
27 Minnie H. Deale to Hanna Sheehy Skeffington, Thursday (1916), SS MS 41,178/23.
28 Mary Kettle, evidence to Simon Commission, *Rebellion Handbook*, p. 220.
29 Hanna Sheehy Skeffington, evidence reported in *Freeman's Journal*, 26 Aug. 1916.
30 Hanna Sheehy Skeffington to Dr J. B. Skeffington, SS MS 22,652.
31 Andrée Sheehy Skeffington, *Skeff: A Life of Owen Sheehy Skeffington* (Dublin, 1991), pp 16–17.
32 Hanna Sheehy Skeffington, evidence to Simon Commission, in *Freeman's Journal*, 26 Aug. 1916.
33 Reported in *Freeman's Journal*, 25 Aug. 1916.
34 Sir Francis Vane, *Agin the Governments: Memories and Adventures* (London, 1929), p. 270.
35 Ibid., p. 269.
36 Anna Vane to Hanna Sheehy Skeffington, 29 May 1916, SS MS 22,279.
37 Hanna Sheehy Skeffington, evidence to Simon Commission, *Freeman's Journal*, 26 Aug. 1916.
38 Nora Connolly O'Brien, *James Connolly: Portrait of a Rebel Father* (Dublin, 1935), p. 314.

39 Nora Connolly to Hanna Sheehy Skeffington, 12 May 1916, SS MS 33,605/2.

40 *Irish Times, Rebellion Handbook*, p. 224.

41 Hanna Sheehy Skeffington, *British Militarism*, p. 14; Evidence of Father O'Loughlin to Simon Commission, in *Freeman's Journal*, 25 Aug. 1916

42 Countess Markievicz, *Prison Letters of Countess Markievicz* (London, 1934, reprinted London, 1987), p. 51.

43 Hanna Sheehy Skeffington, *British Militarism*, p. 14.

44 John Dillon, in Dudley Edwards and Pyle (eds) *1916 The Easter Rising*, p. 77.

45 Court martial details as reported in *Freeman's Journal*, 7–8 June, 1916. Further details in *Irish Times, Rebellion Handbook*, pp 102–108.

46 See R. M. Fox, *Louie Bennett: Her Life and Times* (Dublin, 1958), pp 59–62 for an eye-witness account of proceedings.

47 Ibid., p. 60.

48 *Freeman's Journal*, 7 June 1916.

49 Ibid., 8 June 1916.

50 Hanna Sheehy Skeffington, *British Militarism*, p. 16.

51 *Irish Times, Rebellion Handbook*, p. 104.

52 Leah Levenson and Jerry Natterstad, *Hanna Sheehy Skeffington: Irish Feminist* (New York, 1983), p. 90.

53 *Freeman's Journal*, 8 June 1916.

54 Fox, *Louie Bennett*, p. 61.

55 Louie Bennett to Hanna Sheehy Skeffington, 3 Sept. 1916, SS MS 22,279.

56 T. M. Healy, *Letters and Leaders of My Day* (London, 1928), vol. 2, p. 563.

57 Undated Canadian newspaper clipping of death of Bowen-Colthurst, courtesy John Scully, Quebec. See also Tim Sheehan, *Execute Hostage*, (Cork, 1993). The most recent biography, more sympathetic to Bowen-Colthurst, is James W. Taylor, *Guilty but Insane, J. C. Bowen-Colthurst: Villain or Victim?* (Cork, 2016).

58 Margaret Sheehy O'Casey to Hanna Sheehy Skeffington, 28 Oct. 1926, SS MS 24,119.

59 Mrs Shanahan to Hanna Sheehy Skeffington, 12 May 1916, SS MS 22,279.

60 Names of those contributing to funds of National Aid Association became a daily feature in the press, see for example *Freeman's Journal*, 10 June 1916, giving details of amount required, names of contributors and details of temporary executive.

61 E. Donovan to Hanna Sheehy Skeffington, 16 May 1916, 3 Sept. 1916, 7 Sept. 1916, SS MS 22,279.

62 Inventory of household goods, 12 Mar. 1916. For example: 2 egg cups; 11 dinner plates, 10 best; 3 wine glasses; 6 saucepans; 3 enamel pie dishes; 4 candlesticks; 1 celery glass; 5 green dessert plates; 2 tea pots; 2 coffee pots, SS MS 21,637.

63 Andrée Sheehy Skeffington, *Skeff*, pp 17–19.

64 Louie Bennett, 'Frank Sheehy Skeffington as I knew him', in *Irish Press*, 1 May 1946.

65 *Irish Citizen*, July 1916.

66 Louie Bennett to Hanna Sheehy Skeffington, 11 Aug. 1916, SS MS 22,676.

67 Cissie Cahalan to Hanna Sheehy Skeffington, n. d., (Aug. 1916), SS MS 22,676.

68 Current Comment, 'Our future', in *Irish Citizen*, Sept. 1916.

69 *Irish Citizen*, Sept. 1916.
70 Levenson and Natterstad, *Hanna Sheehy Skeffington*, p. 94.
71 Hanna Sheehy Skeffington, *British Militarism*, p. 15.
72 Hanna Sheehy to Frank Skeffington (hereafter Hanna to Frank), 30 May 1901, SS MS 40,464/7.
73 Deborah Webb to Hanna Sheehy Skeffington, 28 June 1916, 3 July 1916, 18 Aug. 1916, SS MS 22,279.
74 Louie Bennett to Hanna Sheehy Skeffington, SS MS 41,177/13.
75 Gretta Cousins to Hanna Sheehy Skeffington, 17 Aug. 1916, SS MS 22,279.
76 Ibid., 12 Sept. 1916, SS MS 22,679.
77 Hanna Sheehy Skeffington, *British Militarism*, 1917 edn, p. 24 contains that sentence. Later editions omit that one sentence, continuing with the succeeding, 'The lesson of the Irish Rising…'.
78 Elfreda Baker to Hanna Sheehy Skeffington, 2 July 1916, courtesy of Andrée Sheehy Skeffington.
79 Hanna Sheehy Skeffington, testimony to Simon Commission, in *Freeman's Journal*, 26 Aug. 1916; Vane, *Agin the Governments*, p. 269. A half brick which formed part of the wall at Portobello Barracks (now Cathal Brugha Barracks) had embedded in it a bullet fired by the firing squad. This was given to Hanna in Dec. 1935, when she received a parcel containing a half brick with a .303 bullet embedded, accompanied by a letter explaining its context from F. McL. Scannell, who was given it by one of the builders forced by the soldiers in Portobello to repair the wall following the execution of the three men. Scannell explained:

> I tried through some of the 'Boys' to get in touch with you shortly after I got it but you were then endeavouring to reach America, and I could not do so. Although I knew you were the one with the greatest right to it I could not bring myself to offer such a ghastly memento and so rake up wounds which will never be forgotten.

In 1937 Hanna donated the brick to the National Museum of Ireland. See 'The Bullet in the Brick – the murder of Francis Sheehy Skeffington and the madness of Captain Bowen-Colthurst', from *The Cricket Bat that Died for Ireland – Objects from the Historical Collections of the National Museum of Ireland*, online, 1 June 2015 and see also Hanna's account in chapter 13.
80 Andrée Sheehy Skeffington, *Skeff*, p. 20.
81 Muriel Matters to Hanna Sheehy Skeffington, 27 June 1916, SS MS 22,279.
82 Hanna to Owen, 7 July 1916, SS MS 33,609/5.
83 Hanna Sheehy Skeffington, *British Militarism*, pp 19–20.
84 Owen Sheehy Skeffington, in Dudley Edwards and Pyle, *1916 The Easter Rising*, p. 147.
85 Hanna Sheehy Skeffington, *British Militarism*, pp 19–20.
86 Rebellion (Victims) Committee to Henry Lemass; 3 Nov. 1916; Henry Lemass to Committee, 4 Nov. 1916, SS MS 22,680.
87 For details, see Chapter 13.
88 Charles Oldham to Hanna Sheehy Skeffington, 15 Sept. 1916, SS MS 22,279.

89 E. Donovan to Hanna Sheehy Skeffington, receipt for terminating tenancy, 22 Sept. 1916, SS MS 22,279.
90 Fisher Unwin to Francis Sheehy Skeffington, 26 Sept. 1916, SS MS 22,279.
91 'Jillie' to Hanna Sheehy Skeffington, 15 Aug. 1916, SS MS 22,279.
92 Emmeline Pethick-Lawrence, 10 Aug. 1916, SS MS 22,279.
93 Tim Healy to Hanna Sheehy Skeffington, 18 Aug. 1916, SS MS 22,279.
94 Deborah Webb to Hanna Sheehy Skeffington, 18 Aug. 1916, SS MS 22,279.
95 Kathleen Cruise O'Brien to Hanna Sheehy Skeffington, 15 Aug. 1916, SS MS 22,279.
96 Gretta Cousins to Hanna Sheehy Skeffington, 7 July 1916, SS MS 22,279.
97 *Freeman's Journal*, 24 Aug. 1916.
98 Ibid., 26 Aug. 1916; mentioned in letter, Kathleen Cruise O'Brien to Hanna Sheehy Skeffington, 28 Aug. 1916, SS MS 22,279.
99 Eugene Sheehy to Hanna Sheehy Skeffington, n. d., SS MS 22,279.
100 Muriel Matters to Hanna Sheehy Skeffington, 1 Sept. 1916, SS MS 22,279.
101 *Freeman's Journal*, 26 Aug. 1916.
102 Ibid., 1 Sept. 1916.
103 Kathleen Cruise O'Brien to Hanna Sheehy Skeffington, 28 Aug. 1916, SS MS 22,279.
104 *Freeman's Journal*, 28 Aug. 1916.
105 *Irish Times Rebellion Handbook*, p. 222.
106 Ibid.
107 Healy, *Letters and Leaders*, p. 575.
108 Deborah Webb to Hanna Sheehy Skeffington, 1 Sept. 1916, SS MS 22,279.
109 Gretta Cousins, comments after court martial and anticipating inquiry, 7 July 1916, SS MS 22,279.
110 'Preface', in Sheehy Skeffington, *British Militarism*.
111 *Irish Citizen*, Nov. 1916.
112 Henry Lemass to Hanna Sheehy Skeffington, 14 Sept. 1916, SS MS 22,279.
113 Maurice Wilkins to Hanna Sheehy Skeffington, 7 Sept. 1916, SS MS 22,279.
114 Andrée Sheehy Skeffington, *Skeff*, p. 18.
115 Ibid., n. 17, p. 245.
116 T. M. Kettle, *The Ways of War* (London, 1917), pp 30–1.
117 Conor Cruise O'Brien, *States of Ireland* (St Albans, 1974), p. 98.
118 Louie Bennett to Hanna Sheehy Skeffington, 20 Sept. 1916, SS MS 22,279.
119 J. B. Lyons, *The Enigma of Tom Kettle: Irish Patriot, Essayist, Poet, British Soldier, 1880–1916* (Dublin, 1983), p. 303.
120 Revd Hynes, Sec. and Dean of Residence to Hanna Sheehy Skeffington, 17 Nov. 1916, SS MS 22,680.
121 Louie Bennett to Hanna Sheehy Skeffington, 3 Sept. 1916, SS MS 22,279,
122 J. F. Byrne, *Silent Years: An Autobiography* (New York, 1953), p. 139.
123 Kate Barry to Hanna Sheehy Skeffington, 2 Oct. 1916, SS MS 22,679.
124 Receipt from the Imperial Hotel Belfast, Sept. 29 and 30 1916 for Mrs O'Brien and son, room 21; receipt from St Enoch Station Hotel, Glasgow, 30 Sept. 1916, SS MS 41,207/5.

125 Hanna Sheehy Skeffington, RTE radio interview with Dr Dixon, 1945, partial transcript, SS MS 24,164.
126 Hayden Talbot, *Michael Collins' Own Story* (London, 1923), p. 95.
127 Hanna Sheehy Skeffington, *Impressions of Sinn Féin in America* (Dublin, 1919), pp 1–2.
128 Secretary to Chief Commissioner of Police, Dublin Castle to Hanna Sheehy Skeffington, 23 Oct. 1916, acknowledging receipt of her letter of complaint and explaining conduct of police who called, SS MS 22,679.
129 Alice Schmitz to Chief Commissioner of Police, n. d., SS MS 22,679.
130 David Sheehy to Hanna Sheehy Skeffington, n. d., SS MS 22,679.
131 Ibid.
132 T. P. O'Connor to Hanna Sheehy Skeffington, 20 Oct. 1916, SS MS 22,679.
133 Question put by T. P. O'Connor to House of Commons, 26 Oct. 1916, H. Doc. 99,3094.
134 Charlotte Shaw to Hanna Sheehy Skeffington, 5 Nov. 1916, SS MS 22,680.
135 Talbot, *Michael Collins*, p. 111.
136 Kate Barry to Hanna Sheehy Skeffington, 23 Oct. 1916, SS MS 22,679.
137 J. B. Skeffington to Owen, n. d., SS MS 22,679.
138 Flier for The Sheehy Skeffington Memorial Programme, National Library of Ireland.
139 Dr J. B. Skeffington, letter to *Irish News*, 26 Oct. 1916.
140 Letter to the *Irish News*, 22 Nov. 1916.
141 Hanna Sheehy Skeffington, *British Militarism*, p. 24.

NINE

CHALLENGING THE EMPIRE, 1917–18

Hanna tried orthodox methods first when making preliminary arrangements for her journey to America. A politician friend agreed to act as intermediary between herself and the authorities, bringing back the message that a passport (an innovation of war-time) could only be granted on condition that Mrs Sheehy Skeffington pledged herself, in writing, not to discuss Ireland, Great Britain, or the War while in the United States, even in a private conversation. The authorities must have anticipated the indignant response: 'I told my friend that I could accept no such conditions, but that I would pledge myself, while in the United States, "to tell the truth and nothing but the truth about Ireland, Great Britain and the War".' His cynical laughter, 'Truth in war time – impossible!', were words, she realised later, containing a profound truth.[1] Emmeline Pethick-Lawrence and other notable pacifists had been refused passports also, a restriction they, unwillingly, had to accept. The Irish, locked in confrontation with the British state, decided that evasion was both possible and necessary. It was essential to tell Irish-America of the situation in Ireland, and, normal channels proving impossible, many people decided upon subterfuge. Hanna dismissed passports as 'silly formalities', proud to say that in Ireland rebels had always, and would always, ignore any such restrictions on their movements.[2] After all, her father had been in that position over 40 years ago, and she was beginning to regard herself in a similar light to the Fenians of the past.

The preliminary task of writing to America to make arrangements for her tour, particularly posting documents to substantiate her case, was another task requiring ingenuity. The ever-vigilant censor ensured that nothing detrimental to the government could pass through. Her first attempts to bypass this scrutiny were not unsuccessful. She tried to get Irish political friends to smuggle some documents on her behalf but was told by William O'Brien of the United Irish League that 'owing to post office regulations and scrutiny of letters cannot send anything without being aware of contents'. Hanna hastily asked for everything to be returned to her. She was not prepared to reveal what she was trying to send abroad.[3] The more the authorities tried to block her, the more determined she became: 'the front door being barred to me, I took the side door, and took what used to be called "French" leave, but what we may now more properly call "Irish" leave, of the authorities'.[4] Once in America, she was scathing in her dismissal of the 'stupidity of the English policemen' she had succeeded in eluding.[5]

As Owen's health improved, the news that 'sonny' had recovered was wired to his mother. In late November 1916, back to Scotland she went. There she resumed her identity as Mrs Gribbin, an actual Scotswoman who had recently become an American citizen and whose family was happy to coach Hanna into learning the whole of their family history so that she could pass muster in any situation. Owen had become Eugene Gribbin, and, when Hanna went to fetch him from the hospital, she discovered she had a weak little boy, totally transformed in appearance and now speaking with a strong Scottish accent. He needed little coaching for his part.[6] The pair set sail for America, Owen's invalid status attracting a great deal of attention from the other passengers. Fortunately, this meant less attention for his mother, who slowly began to relax her guard, 'I encouraged him to chatter in the hearing of the British authorities, and his suddenly acquired Scottish burr was better for my purposes than a dozen passports!'[7] They arrived in New York just before Christmas, to a city festooned with Christmas lights, shops full of toys and no war-time rationing. The contrast with his seasick and not very pleasant crossing made Owen think he had come to fairyland. Margaret Skinnider, who had travelled earlier, was there to meet them.[8]

British intelligence caught up with them. When they realised where she had gone, said Hanna, 'the long arm of the British authorities was stretched out across the sea after me'.[9] The Americans were requested to detain the pair, so that they could be deported by the next boat, as offenders against the Defence of the Realm Act, but only steerage and 3rd-class passengers left the ship at Ellis Island, and they were able to disembark without difficulty at the Port of New York. Mrs Sheehy Skeffington was welcome in America. There was plenty of time to think about how she was going to get home again.

Irish Americans, an hospitable people, went out of their way to show kindness to the widow and son of an innocent martyr of Easter Week. Patriotic feelings had been stirred up by the tales of what had happened in the glorious fight for freedom 'back home', and newspapers were desperate for first-hand copy from participants in those historic events. It was an overwhelming experience for both mother and son, who found themselves, in Hanna's words:

> inundated in characteristic style by American newspaper men, photographs had been taken of us both (my boy and myself) until I dreaded the process as I would have dreaded a visit to a dentist. Even my little boy had been 'interviewed' by an enterprising young editor, eager for copy, while many newspaper women insisted on making what are called 'sob-stories' out of the case. The Americans, like the Germans and British, even perhaps to a greater degree, are incurably sentimental. They like rather blatant appeals to the emotions, and are very eager for 'thrills'.[10]

Photographs taken at this time reveal two very similar faces, solemnly facing the camera head-on: two people, transformed by sorrow into a single unit, the bond between mother and child powerful enough to enable them to survive future insecurities.

The Hotel Earle in Greenwich Village was the first place they stayed. Owen remembered fusing the electrical system at one hotel, after the inquisitive little boy had inspected its sockets. In the first weeks of their time in America he attended many of his mother's meetings, listening repeatedly to the story of how his father met his death. It must have greatly influenced his political thinking, as his future wife noted when writing her husband's biography.[11] Those events became almost routine to the small boy, familiar enough for him, on one occasion, to walk over to the table where Hanna was speaking and help himself to the glass of water meant for her. She loved to repeat that tale. It helped to re-awaken her sense of humour.[12] For Owen, who had lost his father, who had experienced armed raids on his home, who had suffered the loneliness of being desperately ill in a strange country without his mother, it was a time of bewilderment but also a time when the possibility of future happiness began to be glimpsed. America and its ways were novel to them both, and they were able to indulge in little treats that would have been impossible in Ireland – like relaxing after meetings by sneaking off to a drugstore for a midnight feast of ice-cream.

The first public meeting took place in the impressive surroundings of Carnegie Hall, on 6 January. It was chaired by Bainbridge Colby, an influential Irish-American politician. The 66 boxes of the hall were filled by journalists, judges, clergy, labour leaders, suffragists and prominent socialites. There was a strong Irish contingent, but the audience also included members of all the various radical groups that proliferated in that melting pot of a city. Hanna's lecture, entitled 'British Militarism as I Have Known It', was strengthened by the documents which she had succeeded in smuggling out in advance of her arrival:

> I confined myself entirely to *facts* without personal comment, and allowed the Americans to draw their own conclusions; I dealt not only with the story of my husband's murder but with the North King Street shootings, the death of the boy Coade, of Councillor Richard O'Carroll, the deportations and raids, and of the horrors that have become the platitudes and the every-day happenings in a country under military occupation.[13]

In the most heart-felt of terms she began by describing a man 'gentle and kindly even to his bitterest opponents … he had a marvellous, an inextinguishable good humour, a keen joy in life, great faith in humanity and a hope in the progress towards good.' She could not help becoming emotional when she spoke about Frank:

> My husband would have gone to his death with a smile on his lips, knowing that by his murder he had struck a heavier blow for his ideals than by any act of his life. His death will speak trumpet-tongued against the system that slew him.[14]

Press coverage, including the *New York Times*, was excellent. The *Gaelic American* praised her 'beautifully resonant and dispassionate voice' as she delivered 'the most moving and impressive lecture that has been heard in New York for a great number of years.'[15] She continued to be extensively reported for the next 18 months while carrying out an exhausting schedule, criss-crossing the country to speak at 250 meetings in 21 of the states. People found themselves turned away from packed halls, so popular were her lectures. She often dressed in black, a ruffle of white lace around her neck softening the draining harshness of the colour, but she was not one of the 'women in black' as the female relatives of the executed leaders were often described. Neither was she the dramatic vision in black weeds presented to the world by Maud Gonne (who now insisted on using her married name, MacBride). Hanna was thin and drawn, obviously in mourning for her loss, but she was her own woman with her own political agenda to communicate. Her lecture on the evils of British militarism formed the core of her addresses. What happened to Frank and to others would be broadcast as widely as possible. Occasionally, for different audiences, she spoke on the Ulster problem and on the labour movement in Ireland.

She kept in close touch with political developments in Ireland. At first, her speeches were confined to publicising what had happened during those terrible days in 1916, but gradually, as she settled into her role, her talks began to reflect the new direction being taken by Irish nationalists. She had always been an advocate of Irish independence and now, what had been an aspiration had been hardened by British brutality into a determination to work for immediate and total separation between the two islands. For her American audiences she stressed the urgency of Irish inclusion in future peace negotiations, making it a point never to refuse any invitation to address any society, 'from the most conservative and reactionary to the most advanced and democratic, because it was my objective to expose British hypocrisy to as wide a circle as possible'.[16]

The Friends of Irish Freedom, a front organisation launched by Clan na Gael early in 1916: 'to encourage and assist any movement that will tend to bring about the National Independence of Ireland', was sponsor for the majority of meetings.[17] Irish-American politics were a minefield for anyone coming in from the outside. Its leading organisation, Clan na Gael, controlled by the old Fenian, John Devoy (now over 70 and a veteran of many a battle against the British), had been hostile to Frank Skeffington during his tour of America. Pacifism was anathema to the old dynamiter, but Devoy was also an old friend of Father Eugene Sheehy, who would certainly have ensured that his niece was fully conversant with the niceties of the situation. Devoy, who made it his business to know everything, would have known how close the bond was between niece and Fenian priest. It might have helped to soften the old rebel who, unmarried, with a male assistant as companion, lived a life almost completely devoid of any female presence. Devoy's support for a figure like Hanna could never have been whole-hearted. Her feminism alone would have aroused his suspicions. When he appointed Seamus O'Sheel to help her meet influential politicians in Washington in 1918, he also had O'Sheel send him detailed reports on Hanna's every movement. That was the work of the inveterate conspirator, not the straightforward concern of a fatherly friend.[18]

Hanna managed to remain on good terms with the various factions, a remarkable feat when one considers the extent of the internal differences and ruthlessness of the Irish-American leadership. Liam Mellows, socialist-republican, friend of Connolly, an important figure in the regrouping of nationalist forces, was arrested in 1917 on conspiracy charges and left to rot in the Tombs Prison in New York after Devoy refused to allow Clan na Gael to put up bail and attempted to prevent anyone else doing so. He and his followers disagreed with Mellows' insistence on mobilising support for the Republic, proclaimed in 1916, preferring the less overtly political demand of Irish self-determination. Devoy ended up supporting the Treaty. What appeared as a mere difference in emphasis in 1917 later became a significant disagreement with tragic consequences. Hanna's prior briefings on the American scene and her discussions with kindred spirits once she arrived made her realise that Joe McGarrity, who controlled the Clan in the Philadelphia area, was a man she needed as an ally. McGarrity, much younger than Devoy, supported the stand taken by Liam Mellows. In another two years he would be instrumental in helping de Valera to defeat Devoy for leadership of the Irish-American movement. In mid-January 1917, a few weeks after her arrival in the States, while on the first leg of her tour in Stamford, Connecticut, Hanna wrote to McGarrity to ask if he would be willing to have her speak. She understood only too well that without his cooperation she would be unable to approach the Irish community in his area:

> Dear Mr McGarrity,
>
> Please let me know if you wish me to go to Philadelphia and when. I am speaking in Conn and Mass tomorrow up to Feb 16 and in Chicago on Feb 26 and in between the latter dates I should like to go on to Philadelphia. Two other societies (not Irish, but Labour and Peace) have already asked me to come and pressed for a date and I do not like leaving them unanswered. I should of course like to fit in these with other meetings and Cohalan told me several weeks ago that you had been inquiring whether I could go to Philadelphia.[19]

The confident and much less formal tone of her later correspondence indicates that by the end of her tour she was on social terms with McGarrity and his wife – 'Thanks for your and Mrs McGarrity's kind invitation'; 'I wish you and Mrs McGarrity and all the family a happy xmas and new year' – and felt sufficiently relaxed to be able to include news of Owen's welfare. Her letters no longer ended with the impersonal 'yours sincerely' but included the warmer greeting of 'best regards' or 'kind regards'.[20] The very fact that Hanna came back to America for three more lecture tours in the following decades is further evidence of her ease within that society. Her interests were broader than the Irish-American network, but she was careful not to alienate that essentially conservative Irish constituency.

Elizabeth Gurley Flynn, organiser for the International Workers of the World (IWW), was one who gave the Irish woman a warm welcome. James Connolly, when he had lived in America, had been a good friend of the 'rebel girl' who had inspired Joe Hill's song. Gurley, as she was known to friends, had warm memories of Connolly: a man who understood the symptoms of a woman's pregnancy; a man who knew how to soothe a baby with colic and who had no inhibitions about doing so during a political discussion. All the Irish radicals ended up at the front door of the small apartment in the South Bronx where the Irish Flynn family had grown up and where her mother, Annie, and her sister Kathie still lived. Annie and Kathie looked after Gurley's son Fred, who was a year younger than Owen. Mrs Flynn looked after Owen too, on occasion, providing welcome companionship in a family environment for a child whose experience of skyscrapers and meetings was beginning to pall.[21]

Sir Francis Vane, already full of admiration for Hanna's 'great energy' while she had 'worked every string' to get a Commission of Inquiry set up, now discovered that his friend was equally skilful in gaining access to influential politicians in America. Shortly after her arrival she succeeded in having a lengthy interview with former President Theodore Roosevelt. Roosevelt was so concerned by the story of murder and cover-up recounted to him that he immediately wrote to Vane, whom Hanna had assured him could verify as to the truth of this testimony. Significantly, Roosevelt did not send the letter through the usual channels, using diplomatic contacts instead. The American Ambassador in London did however consult the British government before handing over the letter to Sir Francis. Vane's reply was stopped by the military censor. British/American relations were at their most delicate in these weeks before America finally made up its mind to support Britain's fight against Germany. The facts of the Skeffington murder could have tilted the balance away from Britain. Finally, another copy of Vane's reply was forwarded to the British Ambassador in Washington, who then had it delivered to the ex-President. America's entry into the war was not prevented, but, according to Vane, this 'very curious piece of history' was an important factor in the process which led to the formation of the Irish Free State. Vane believed that Britain found it impossible to justify continuing its presence in that country with such high-level condemnation of the excesses of British militarism in Ireland.[22]

By the time of the New England tour it was obvious Hanna was travelling too much to make it feasible to keep Owen with her. Boston and 17 other towns were organising meetings on her behalf, and she was billed to speak also at Harvard and Columbia universities and at Wellesley women's college. She was that rare person, equally at home in an academic setting or addressing crowds in the largest hall a town or city possessed. Immediately afterwards she was to set off for the mid-west. Owen stayed behind with friends in Stamford, attending the local school and enjoying the snowy sports of a New England winter. It was part of his return to the life of the schoolboy, a time he remembered with great affection.[23] He forgot nothing of his upbringing and remained faithful to the principles instilled in him by his parents. While staying at the home of Judge Daniel Cohalan, leading figure in the Friends of Irish Freedom, it was assumed that Owen would join in the evening family rosary, a strong tradition amongst Irish Catholics. Although he was only eight years old he was quite capable of explaining to his disapproving hosts that this was impossible as he had been brought up 'a secularist'.[24]

Hanna soon realised the enormity of her undertaking: 'I was touring not a nation but a continent. San Francisco is in many respects as different from New York as Petrograd is from London, and no one can estimate the strength of Irish sentiment in the United States who has not included the west in his observations.'[25] As her tour progressed and events were responded to, she broadened out from an initial concentration upon her husband's murder. Frank's death was always her starting point, the reason why she was in America, but the brutalities suffered by the Irish people in the aftermath of the Rising became incorporated into a political message she delivered with increasing urgency once America entered the war in support of Britain. She dismissed the Home Rule settlement that had been mooted as the solution to the 'Irish question' before 1914:

> [Ireland] will continue to be but a pawn in the game, a land exploited for imperial ambitions, plunged into wars with which she has no interest or sympathy, a victim of secret diplomacy and entangling alliances, taxed for the upkeep of imperial armies and navies whose protection is problematical at best, an alien province misgoverned by absentees. This is the grim reality behind the glowing vision of colonial or other Home Rule.[26]

Invariably, at the conclusion of her speeches, her audience was asked to pledge themselves 'to press for Ireland's claim to be heard at the Peace Conference and her right to complete independence put before a jury of the nations'.[27] In the space of a few months she had become an outspoken separatist. Given the internal difficulties troubling Irish-American politics, it could also be argued that she had shown herself to be politically astute. The arguments she presented could be accepted by both factions; only supporters of the bankrupt policy of the parliamentarians of the Irish Party would be offended by her views. In the propaganda battle for American support waged so relentlessly between Irish and British, Hanna occupied a pivotal place. From huge auditorium to college-based women's club or trade union hall, her political appeal crossed boundaries that few others could reach. William B. Feakins, the agency that organised a later tour of America on her behalf, described in a publicity leaflet the reaction she had evoked in 1917-18: 'Everywhere that she went, audiences acclaimed her as a speaker of extraordinary acumen and discernment, well versed in international as well as Irish national affairs.'[28] Hyperbole, but thoroughly justified. The press described her as well educated, refined and a natural and eloquent speaker.[29] Those who were pro-British recognised her power and were less complimentary in their description of this 'dangerous person'.[30]

Although American intelligence had not considered the widow of the Irish pacifist editor to be a danger to national well-being on her entry into the country, the Department of Justice did begin to take an interest in her from April 1917 onwards, after America entered the war. In part this was prompted by a letter from a Mrs Kate Horrocks of St Louis, who wrote to Secretary Lansing on 12 April, objecting to the presence of 'this lady' in the country during war-time: 'The way I see it, she is working for German propaganda and thereby trying to influence the Irish Americans against enlisting for military service and creating a bad feeling against our ally England.' Mrs Horrock's letter and enclosed press cutting from the *St Louis Post-Dispatch* announcing a forthcoming visit by Mrs Sheehy Skeffington was promptly forwarded to the Bureau of Investigation, whose agents subsequently infiltrated a large number of her meetings.[31] All assumed that because her husband was deemed to have been 'executed during the recent Irish rebellion' she must be the widow of a rebel leader. Nevertheless, the eventual conclusion of the Department of Justice was that her lectures were 'extremely pro-Irish and anti-British but that they do not attack the United States'.

The Military Intelligence Section of the War Department was less temperate in its assessment of Hanna's subversive potential. In the eyes of Colonel Van Deman, she was the 'wife of an Irish traitor'. His explanation for her apparent lack of 'improper' views was that 'utterances which would tend to foment disloyalty in this country are made at informal gatherings and do not form part of the public lectures'. The reports from male and female agents attending a wide variety of the meetings addressed by Hanna all agreed on the undoubted quality of the person under investigation:

> The lady, who is highly educated, delivered a very interesting lecture showing why Ireland should be considered at the peace conference at the end of the war ... Her remarks could not be construed in anyway as anti-American or Anti-ally as she is quite well instructed as to her rights in speech from all appearances.[32]

Some were determined to make mountains out of no evidence at all, but, if anything, their evidence tended to enhance the view that Hanna was an ordinary person, eminently likeable and by no means harmful to national security:

> Mrs Burd observed an elderly man about 65 or 70 years of age, very tall and slender, apparently rather poor as his clothes were threadbare and he was not well groomed. This man presented Mrs Skeffington's son with some polished shells which he

> stated he had gathered on the beach near San Francisco. This occurred at the farewell dinner given Mrs Skeffington. Mrs Burd learned that this man had been quite an admirer of Mr Skeffington's and had sent her flowers on numerous occasions. On the night of the farewell dinner … Mrs Burd observed him hand some letters to Mrs Skeffington and heard him say to her that if she got into any trouble at any time in the United States she should use those letters and should communicate with Senator LaFollette and with Congresswoman Jeanette Rankin. He stated to Mrs Skeffington that these people – 'Are our friends.' Agent will endeavour to ascertain who the man mentioned by Mrs Burd is and what connection he may have with German affairs.[33]

America's entry into the war was a controversial decision that split political movements in the country just as much as the outbreak of war had done in Europe. It certainly gave rise to more internal dissension within Irish nationalist ranks. Some Irish-American democrats were vocal in their support of President Wilson and were rewarded for the stand they took. Bainbridge Colby, who had chaired Hanna's first meeting in New York, was appointed president of the government's shipping department. Hanna recognised the propaganda potential in American's involvement. Instead of 'British Militarism' her talks were now advertised under the title 'What Does Ireland Want?' The task of Irish propagandists was to convince the public that the freedom of Belgium and that of Ireland were essential parts of any peace settlement. The argument was very clear:

> When the fate of other small nations is being decided, the fate of Ireland too must be considered. Ireland from being a national problem is now international, and it is unlikely that America, entering this war as she states 'for the democratization of Europe', will jeopardise her own honour and the future peace of the world by closing her ears to the voice of Ireland pleading among the small nations for her independence. Hence it becomes important for America to know what Ireland wants so that there be no mistake about the final settlement … Their demand at the Peace Conference will be for complete and absolute independence. There can be no tinkering with a demand based on the principle of nationhood; anything that falls short of this is neither freedom nor true democracy.[34]

It was clever. Rather than condemning Wilson for bringing America into the war, she concentrated upon the benefits that this might bring to the Irish cause. For this reason, the secret service agents confessed that they could find nothing in her speeches that violated Federal Statutes. However, surveillance of her movements continued. If Hanna had not been regarded as an enemy of the British state before 1916, she was definitely seen in this light after that time. British reaction to her effectiveness included constant tailing by agents and sneers in the pro-British press on her naivety in being used as propaganda by sinister forces. In Buffalo on one occasion, close to the Canadian border, she was almost lured onto the wrong train by a group posing as her reception committee. Just in time, she discovered that the train was destined for the British controlled territory of Canada.[35] Had she ended there, she would have had no way of preventing her immediate deportation to England. She referred to this affair many times in various accounts of her American experiences. That she had been so nearly out-witted grated on her memory. The rest she shrugged off as one of the hazards of the times:

> I frequently found my luggage was tampered with, the contents of my desk ransacked, doubtless with the object of connecting me with some bogus 'plot' or other. As my propaganda courted publicity I was not embarrassed by these little attentions. We in Ireland are quite inured to them.[36]

Once America was at war on Britain's behalf, outspoken attacks by Irish nationalists upon its British ally were considered by many Americans as inappropriate. Hanna dismissed this airily as 'the usual war hysteria in a pretty virulent form when America first decided to go in'[37] but there were times when she was forced to maintain a diplomatic silence. At a lunch meeting in the mid-west, where the talk was on the 'patriotic' side, she refrained from making any comment. A vivacious woman sitting opposite, the president of the local ladies' club, did what good hostesses always do, and attempted to draw the outsider into the conversation. Asked for her opinion on how the war would end, Hanna replied dryly, 'I think it will end in peace'. Even this was controversial, the woman started 'as if stung by a serpent', exclaiming in tones of horror and consternation 'Oh, I had no idea you were a Pacifist!'[38] Voicing a hope that there might ever be peace again was close to treason. Hanna's deep love of Germany and the German language made some of the more ludicrous consequences of patriotism difficult to stomach. Harmless German words like sauerkraut and frankfurter were now changed to liberty cabbage and liberty sausage, while German measles was no longer a recognised illness. She mocked lightly, 'of course, one might still drink German beer under another name, and the flavour, I believe, is not impaired'.[39] At meetings she told her audience that she had been a teacher of the German language and when speaking to women's organisations was forthright in urging them not to support the war effort. Agent Needham reported that at a lunch given by women in San Antonio, Texas, she 'requested them not to donate supplies for the Red Cross, for the reason that the men had started the war, and now let the men finish it', while she advised the local women's suffrage league in San Antonio 'to cause strikes or anything else in their power to stop the present war.' Despite these reports, the Bureau of Investigation again concluded that nothing she said, 'could be construed to violate the Federal Statute.'[40]

Leah Levenson and Jerry Natterstad have criticised her for sacrificing 'accuracy for effect' in her American speeches. Examples cited are that Hanna predicted Germany would win the war; that she described Englishmen as 'hopeless cowards'; that she claimed conscription and another massacre were in store for Ireland in the near future and that 'the gaunt figure of famine' would soon be menacing the countryside.[41] Were these such exaggerated claims, made during 1916 and 1917, before America had entered the war and when it was by no means inevitable that Britain would be victorious? Hanna was a propagandist of the highest calibre, as her future position within Sinn Féin would indicate, but the ability to speak powerfully does not have to include speaking without regard for the truth. That charge deserves consideration. Placing Hanna's speeches in historical context not only exonerates her from the suggestion of fabrication of the facts, it also reveals her shrewd grasp of the issues preoccupying people back in Ireland.

The charge that Englishmen were cowards came, let us not forget, from a woman who had experienced prevarication, lies and refusal from the highest levels to admit responsibility for her husband's murder. Her resulting bad opinion of Englishmen was surely both understandable and pardonable. It was not an anti-British prejudice, but rather a condemnation of the British political establishment. On a personal level, she maintained friendships with many English people. No-one predicting the imposition of conscription in Ireland could possibly be accused of exaggeration. The threat was very real. Britain was desperate for more manpower to join the slaughter in the blood-soaked trenches of France. In the spring of 1917 the government edged one step closer to outright conscription in Ireland by barring employers from giving jobs to men aged between 16 and 62. As the Irish so rightly said, it was 'economic conscription', forcing men into the army because they had no other means of supporting themselves and their families. It was only the experience of a one-day strike on 23 April 1918, supported by the Catholic Church, the trade union movement and Sinn Féin, when hundreds of thousands of people across the country signed pledges to resist, that finally persuaded the British of the folly of attempting conscription. In addition, women trade unionists, feminists and Cumann na mBan together organised 'Lá na mBan', a women's day of protest, on Sunday 9 June, when thousands of women throughout Ireland signed pledges that they would not 'blackleg' by taking the job of any man if conscription was introduced. Members of the IWFL joined in this women's day, with the *Irish Citizen* giving extensive coverage to what it described as 'a glorious movement at once National, Religious, and Historic.'[42] The British government retaliated by arresting prominent Irish political figures, charging them with being party to a 'German Plot'. Seen in this light, Hanna's predictions of future unrest appear uncannily accurate.

Finally, what of the charge that she misled her audience by mentioning famine, that most potent of all horrors, to an audience composed of many of the descendants of those who had fled from the Great Hunger of the 1840s? Was that simply a cheap trick, to strike where her listeners were most vulnerable? Again, it demonstrates how close she was to public opinion within Ireland. The issues Hanna was most concerned about were issues that would be taken up by Sinn Féin once that organisation had reformed in late 1917 and decided upon its political programme. At the end of 1917 the *Irish Citizen* had reported a prediction by the President of the English Board of Agriculture to the effect that there would soon be severe food shortages. The *Citizen* feared that Ireland was 'being robbed of her products' so that England would not starve. During 1918 the imprisoned de Valera, President of Sinn Féin, concerned that high prices for food could be obtained by exporting produce to Britain, wrote to Cumann na mBan: 'We are anxious that the attention of the people should be directed to one food question only – that of retaining in Ireland sufficient food for the Irish people.'[43] Hanna was not talking about potato blight, but about the unequal economic relationship between Britain and Ireland and Ireland's role as provider of food for the British market, a role determined by market forces, to the disadvantage of the Irish poor. On this question, as on the other issues, she showed considerable foresight.

She was back in New York for the St Patrick's Day celebrations of 1917. She was there too for Easter Week, the first anniversary of her husband's death. She then travelled to St Louis before heading off for the west coast. It took a train journey lasting from Monday until the following Friday night to cover the 3,000 miles distance between east and west coasts; an exhausting schedule, not one that left much time for mourning or reflection. Neither did it leave any time for Owen. She did not want to leave her son back east while she was over on the other side of the country, and she worried about the effect the cold winter of New England was having on a child so recently recovered from serious illness. Friends told her of 'Boyland', a progressive school in Santa Barbara, California, run by a most unusual man, Prince (Prynce) Hopkins, a pacifist. The boys were taught to be cooperative and public-spirited. They had workshops in which they built furniture, small trains which they operated themselves, and they studied geography from a huge relief map of the world that was built on a lake. Their discipline came from self-motivation rather than corporal punishment. Hopkins maintained 'Example, not fear of the lash, is what builds character', and he offered to take Owen as a boarder. Arrangements were made for the boy to take the train, alone, across America, with only the Pullman car attendant to keep an eye on him. Hanna did not want her son to remain anywhere if he was not happy. She explained that if he did not like his new school she would come immediately and take him away. The promise was reassuring, but unnecessary. For Owen, his year at Boyland was 'paradise'; learning became a joy. In the warm climate of California, with its open spaces and free atmosphere, the boy blossomed. His happiness was an enormous relief to his mother.[44] Given the circumstances, it was the best arrangement she could have made. In later life Owen was thrilled to read in *American Testament* (a biography by American socialist Joseph Freeman) an account of a lecture given by Hopkins about the school. Freeman had thought it sounded 'like a dream', but Hopkins had to admit 'under present social conditions' such a school was only for the 'privileged few' who could afford it. Hanna's earnings from the tour and the support of her friends must have paid his school fees. Freeman's rollicking adventures in America and Europe brought back many memories for Owen, who urged his mother to read the book.[45]

The tour of America continued. She marvelled at the efficiency of a system which made travelling so easy, 'One may, by 'phone, from one's room in a New York hotel not only book reservations in the train, but may also dispatch one's trunk from one hotel to another across the Continent, and by means of a magic "baggage check" system find it waiting in one's room on arrival.'[46] While this was a startling contrast from her experience of the ramshackle, haphazard nature of European travel, her tour was a curious mixture of traditional Irish venues (complete with clerics, prominent citizens, shamrocks and yearnings for the 'old country') interspersed with socialist meetings and feminist gatherings. In all these diverse arenas Hanna was equally adept in dealing with different viewpoints and different ways of showing support for her cause. She also understood that some of the doors that had opened to her would not have been so welcoming if she had been there as representative of militant Irish womanhood rather than as sorrowing widow. The Ancient Order of Hibernians in San Antonio 'refused to have anything to do with this lady', agent Needham reported.[47] In remembering the animosity between the AOH and the suffragists at the height of the suffrage campaign it is likely that the 'lady' preferred not to be associated with them. She did, however, have contact with organisations sharing a similar conservative stance.

Hanna's first public meeting in San Francisco, on 14 June, was held in a hall owned by the Knights of Columb. Hundreds were turned away and every inch of standing room used to accommodate those who flocked to hear the widow of one of the 'martyrs' of Easter Week. American and Irish patriotism were much in evidence. The Star-Spangled Banner was sung, as was the Soldier's Song (soon to become the Irish national anthem). As the star of the evening she was billed to appear between recitations of 'Captain Molly' and 'Soldiers of Erin'. Her speech, on 'Military Autocracy and Conditions in Ireland' was greeted with repeated ovations as the crowd rose to its feet repeatedly, applauding her throughout her address. For more than an hour she relived the details of Frank's murder and the subsequent attempt to cover-up what had taken place in Portobello Barracks. She spoke also of the future and of her hopes for a 'United States of Europe' where each state would be free and independent, part of a great federation, modelled on the American example.[48] That reference would have flattered her audience, praised for their commitment to democracy. It was also a reflection of her great love of Europe and European culture. The speech was followed by 'Columbia, the Gem of the Ocean', presumably in honour of the venue. Some teeth gritting was necessary as she worked her way across the country, enduring other similar evenings.

These outspoken condemnations of British actions in Ireland created tensions within the Irish-American community. The California Civic League, after hearing her lecture on 14 June, withdrew its invitation for a luncheon reception. The organisers admitted that her remarks were true, but, as war allies of Britain, it would not be appropriate to provide her with further opportunities to air those views. She was unperturbed. Ten days later, speaking to a crowd of 8,000 (with another 1,000 unable to gain entry) in San Francisco's Dreamland Rink, she began her speech with zest, thanking the women of the Civic Centre who, by not permitting her to speak, had ensured the success of the meeting she was then addressing.[49] There were many other triumphant meetings on the west coast, with branches of her sponsors, Friends of Irish Freedom, being formed in the wake of several.

Portland, Oregon, was an important centre for west coast activists. A prominent radical there was Dr Marie Equi, of Italian-Irish background, suffragist and sympathiser with the International Workers of the World, a successful doctor and, in the words of her friend Elizabeth Gurley Flynn, with whom she had a long-standing relationship, 'stormy petrol of the Northwest', who entertained all the women speakers who passed through that City of Roses. Hanna and Kathleen O'Brennan, sister of Aine Ceannt, were two Irish women to be entertained by the doctor in the 'swanky Hotel Multnomah' where she had established her home, rejecting traditional domestic arrangements.[50] Other women included the socialist Anita Whitney and Margaret

Sanger, imprisoned in 1916 because of her advocacy of birth control. Gurley Flynn, whose life was very hard, said of the experience 'we all appreciated the unusual comfort'. In her view Marie Equi was one of the most feared and hated women in the north west because of her outspoken denunciation of politicians, industrialists and all those she considered to be exploiters of the poor. As a doctor who performed illegal abortions for many of Portland's leading citizens (as well as working class women) Equi believed she was immune from prosecution. In consequence her behaviour was often outrageous. Marie Equi hid nothing. She was openly lesbian and pursued even women who had always been heterosexual. As Margaret Sanger put it, the woman was 'so radical in her thinking that she was almost an outcast in Portland. Her reputation is or was lesbian but to me she was like a crushed flower which had braved the storms and winds of terror and needed tenderness and love.'[51] The Bureau of Investigation had a permanent watch on her and on all those associated with her. They finally had their revenge. One month after the First World War came to an end she was sentenced to three years under the Espionage Act, serving ten months in San Quentin Prison.[52] She and Hanna would meet again on Hanna's next tour of America and they continued an affectionate correspondence (on Equi's side, in sprawling purple ink) until the late 1930s.

Hanna made 'many enduring friendships' during her months in America, a country she would choose as her 'second home' if she had ever to live outside Ireland. One woman she remembered warmly and would remain in contact with was Jane Addams, lesbian, founder of Hull House in Chicago (a settlement house that united progressive middle-class women with those in great need), who was also a significant figure in the women's peace movement. Hanna was proud to be a member of the New York Heterodoxy Club, a notable gathering of nonconformists. Membership was open only to those who refused to accept the conventions of the day. Crystal Eastman was one such woman, 'an Amazon in a red shirt dress' was how Joseph Freeman remembered her. Elizabeth Gurley Flynn recalled the 'free and frank discussions' of women and their accomplishments. All were suffragists while some, in the eyes of Gurley Flynn, were 'quite extreme feminists'.[53] Within the Heterodoxy there existed 'both a strong stress on sisterhood and a nascent lesbian subculture'.[54] Emma Goldman was another revolutionary she encountered shortly after her arrival, a woman she recalled with great fondness: 'We as rebels spoke the same language, though sometimes with a different idiom' said Hanna, referring to Goldman's preference for anarchism rather than nationalism. Her description could well have applied to herself, as 'outwardly' neither looked like rebels. Emma looked 'like a busy *hausfrau* … peasant-like in build, sturdy and direct, her fine eye and brow revealing the leader.'[55] Both were impatient with those who clung to convention because they did not dare to be different.

Women who formed emotional – not necessarily sexual – relationships with other women, often as life-long partners (in New England they called them 'Boston marriages'), were a large part of Hanna's circle of friends from this time onwards. She was no longer a wife enjoying the warmth of a uniquely supportive marriage; she was now a mother on her own, with one young child to care for. While Hanna had no intention of sharing her home with another adult, at least on a permanent basis, she put up friends like Rose Jacob for long periods of time and she took in lodgers to supplement her income. She had the 'boon' of her sisters' invaluable support; she had her dear friend Meg Connery, Cahalan and others from the Franchise League. She was a woman with a talent for friendship and a lively curiosity in the world around her. She must have been lonely many times, missing Frank's lively conversation, but she never, except intentionally, had to be alone, even when she grew older. Emma Goldman urged Ethel Mannin to get in touch with Hanna when, during the 1920s, the writer visited Dublin for the first time. Emma had praised Hanna's 'fine spirit and her life-long devotion to the cause of justice and freedom'.[56] When Ethel met this paragon of revolutionary virtues she found a woman interested in the ideas of a younger generation, friendly and humorous, someone who hoped she would 'never grow elderly-minded', adding 'One needn't'. She warmed to her immediately.[57]

Alice Park was another important friend during this American sojourn. Older than Hanna, she was an experienced activist and supporter of many causes. Alice had been for many years a diligent disseminator of the various letters and items of information sent to her by Hanna in the hope that they would be reproduced in west coast papers, but it was more than a relationship based upon a common political cause. For example, in August 1916 Hanna received the marriage announcement of Alice's daughter Harriet.[58] Despite the fact that Hanna at that time was fighting the battle of her life to get an inquiry into Frank's murder, her friend Alice judged, surely correctly, that life had to go on and that Hanna would understand her desire to share her pleasure in her daughter's forthcoming wedding. Over the years, news of their children's progress in life was exchanged by the two women, along with mention of their own health and ailments and political news and latest campaigns. Palo Alto hosted several meetings on Hanna's behalf in 1917, enabling her to combine public duties with spending time with Owen in Boyland. When she left him, busily making a scale map of the world in the school grounds, she was again reassured that she had done the best she could for her son. As she wrote to Joe McGarrity, 'it was not good for him to be "on the loose" so much. He likes his school and is very happy there.'[59]

Alice Park was working for Congressman John Raker of California, chairman of the House Committee on Woman Suffrage, and because of this she joined Hanna in Washington at the end of 1917. Seamus O'Sheel, appointed by John Devoy to introduce Hanna to important politicians (and to report back on her every movement) gave a description of the American feminist, a triumph of political abuse, revealing as much about the author as it does of the subject:

> The latter is a suffragist, pacifist, vegetarian, prohibitionist, anti-tobacconist and professional writer and looks all those things; and she wears a peace badge legible at ten yards, which of course is a splendid card of introduction in Washington these days.[60]

That catalogue of all the causes a progressive woman of the time might espouse could apply equally to Hanna. Yet, with her understated yet feminine clothes, liking for hats, and eyes that twinkled disarmingly (but rarely in photos, where she lamented that she always 'looked grim'), Hanna did not appear anything like this terrifying stereotype of political correctness. The combination of Mrs Sheehy Skeffington and Mrs Park overwhelmed the hapless O'Sheel, who was a less than ideal choice as minder. He was out of work, anxious to use this opportunity of moving around the political circles of Washington as a means of securing some form of appointment for himself, and pathetically made use of the funds Devoy had put at his disposal: 'State of my health made luxury of Pullman car really necessary … cigars, necessary around Congress and newspaper men, cost $1.' The two women, 'being feminists, insisted on paying for their own meals', but O'Sheel claimed expenses because he 'generally tipped for all'.[61] The abstemious Devoy could not have been impressed. Nevertheless, O'Sheel's report, despite his personal vagaries, gives a valuable insight into Hanna's ability to play the political game at the highest level. He portrayed a woman who was self-confident and a formidable presence, well able to accomplish her own introductions, particularly as she had the constant presence of Alice Park, with her invaluable contacts. What became painfully apparent to O'Sheel was that Mrs Skeffington was not some poor widow from Ireland, grateful for any introduction into the Irish-American scene. She was a sophisticated intellectual, by now a seasoned veteran of American political life, who brushed aside O'Sheel's contacts as 'small fry' and 'old Tammanyites'.[62] Her self-confidence was evident on their first visit to Capitol Hill on 8 January 1918. As the British Ambassador walked past them, they discovered that he had been shut out of the crowded Diplomatic Gallery. O'Sheel reported that 'Mrs Skeffington decided to approach him right then… she chatted with Spring-Rice ten minutes and made appointment for the Embassy at 3 p.m.'

Washington was hectic; there had been a moratorium on discussing any issue except the war during the special War Congress, but that had come to an end and a backlog of legislation was up for discussion. Irish republicans were active, trying to gain a hearing with sympathetic politicians while arguments over America's involvement in the war continued to rage, and lobbyists came and went as key political appointments were made and the individuals wooed by a variety of opinion. Hanna discovered that Nora Connolly and Margaret Skinnider had been to see Jeannette Rankin of Montana, the first woman to be elected to Congress. She spent days trying in vain to get in touch with her friends.[63] For women in America, the suffrage question was as dominant as ever. Their pickets were being arrested outside Congress and women on hunger strike were force fed. The Woman's Party, led by Alice Paul and Lucy Burns (a militant breakaway from the Suffrage Association), was the women's organisation with which Hanna felt most in sympathy. Many of its members were Quaker, and it took an anti-war position. Hanna soon met up with Alice Paul and had lunch with prominent suffragists, all of whom were in Washington because the vote on the nineteenth amendment to the constitution was scheduled to take place on 10 January. The wording of the amendment was unambiguous: 'The right of citizens of the United States to vote shall not be denied or abridged by the United States or by any state on account of sex.' Its passing would be a tremendous victory for women everywhere and lobbying was intense.

The day before the vote, President Wilson informed Congressman Raker that he was in favour of the measure. Despite this support no one was able to foretell what the outcome would be. On the day of the vote congressmen came in from their sick beds, one from the death bed of his wife, who had been a staunch suffragist; another, from Tennessee, refused to leave to have a broken arm and shoulder set in case he would be prevented from returning. It was nail-biting stuff, and all the tallies that both sides kept could not predict the outcome. Hanna and Alice Park sat, along with many others, in the crowded galleries, waiting for the final count. The amendment passed by 274 to 136, exactly the two-thirds majority required.[64] Hanna's support for the Woman's Party was wholehearted: 'This wonderful victory would never have come about were it not for their plucky fight for democracy … It is these dauntless women who make one glad for women in these dark days – one feels that with them the future of the race is secure.[65]

Seamus O'Sheel crowded into the gallery to join them after the voting had ended and the bedlam was beginning to subside. He got his glasses broken in the crush. No one needed his presence. In the corridors outside Hanna spoke to Lucy Burns and the other jubilant leaders and then she and Alice Park went off to the telegram counter to compose a telegram to Ireland. O'Sheel later discovered that he had not been 'made privy' to the fact that the real purpose of this 'was to convey to Ireland, under cover of message about suffrage victory, the news that Mrs Skeffington was working in Washington'.[66] In Hanna's experience, the less that was known about her movements, the better. When members of the family wrote to her they were careful not to use her own name. Her father usually sent his letters to 'Mrs Mary Hanna'. Although he did sign them 'David Sheehy', the fact that the offending name of 'Sheehy' was not on the envelope might have been enough to delude the censor.[67] In sending her telegram from Congress, Hanna intended using a fictitious name and was furious when O'Sheel clumsily addressed her by name in the hearing of the man serving behind the telegram counter. She later had Alice Park send her message from another station. It was a stupid mistake from someone who should have understood about conspiratorial politics. Relations between the three were tense. As O'Sheel guided the women to suffrage headquarters, no doubt for a woman-only celebration, his description was bitter: 'Mrs P all the way expressing the conviction that I was taking them wrong, while she herself had no more sense of direction than a mole.'[68]

The next day O'Sheel was unquestionably snubbed. Hanna ignored the arrangements they had decided upon, informing the unfortunate man over the phone that she had decided to go to the House of Representatives with Mrs Park. She also made 'deprecatory remarks' concerning the quality of the congressmen he had managed to introduce her to. Hanna wanted much more than the tired old circuit of Irish-American males, most of whom would not have been sympathetic to her as a suffragist. That O'Sheel did not understand the intricacies of Washington politics is abundantly clear in his dismissal of Raker as a 'German-baiting, War-shouting idolater of Wilson'.[69] His attitude was influenced by the fact that Alice Park was working for Raker, but this was the man who, as Chair of the House Committee on Woman Suffrage, had played a crucial role in the proceedings of the previous day. He was obviously someone Hanna would have been keen on meeting. The battle of Irish and British women had not yet been won, and there might be important lessons from the American experience. Hanna also saw Senator La Follette and Congresswoman Jeannette Rankin without O'Sheel – he moaned 'it would have helped so much had she taken me with her' – but he was forced to report that La Follette was 'much impressed' by Mrs Skeffington.[70]

That day, 11 January (the day O'Sheel had hoped to 'really get her started') saw one of Hanna's greatest coups: her interview with President Wilson, a feat that had eluded all others who had come from Ireland to plead for support. It had been obtained through the intermediary of Bainbridge Colby, whose new appointment gave him easy access to the President. Hanna's decision to pursue the possibility of seeing the President had nothing to do with her own personal crusade. It came about as a result of a plea from women back home in Ireland. Some time previously she had been sent a message, one most certainly not 'passed by the censor', to say that the accompanying document was to be delivered personally into the President's hands. This was a petition, signed by Constance Markievicz; by Jennie Wyse Power and Louise Gavan-Duffy as two Cumann na mBan activists; by the academics Mary Hayden and Agnes O'Farrelly, and by other bereaved women: Kathleen Clarke, Nannie O'Rahilly, Aine Ceannt and Grace Gifford, putting forward the claim of Ireland for self-determination and appealing to President Wilson to include Ireland among the small nations for whose freedom America was fighting.[71] Nancy (always known as Nannie) O'Rahilly, daughter of a wealthy American family, her last child born after the death during the Rising of her husband, had travelled to America in 1917 in order to see her sisters. She might have been the person to have smuggled the petition amongst her luggage. The event had a double significance. It was also the first occasion when Hanna publicly identified with Sinn Féin, the organisation to which increasing numbers of men and women in Ireland were coming to believe could best represent nationalist hopes.

Hanna admitted feeling 'dismayed' at the prospect of delivering this in person to a President overwhelmed with work, but she was determined to 'work hard' to do it. The fact that the interview took place the day after the vote on women's suffrage, when Capitol Hill was still full of American suffragists, was a happy coincidence, contributing to her warm recollections of her time in Washington. She considered the place 'more democratic and kindlier than the Tory Clubroom of the British House of Commons. Most of all, it is an atmosphere more human and more courteous where women are concerned.' The President set her at ease with a 'cordial handshake and a pleasant smile'. By tradition, the content of the interview had to be kept private, but the fact that he had granted an interview to a 'declared Sinn

Féiner', as Hanna described herself, was widely commented on. That he was willing to receive a document unsubmitted to the British Censor and that he consented to discuss the future of Ireland was also, she hoped, of future significance. In Hanna's description of herself, she was more than simply an emissary for Cumann na mBan. She was not – and never would be – a member of that organisation. She felt herself to be representing her country and she took the responsibility very seriously, as 'the first Irish exile and the first Sinn Féiner to enter the White House and the first to wear there the badge of the Irish Republic, which I took care to pin in my coat before I went.'[72] Jubilantly, she sent John Devoy a copy of the petition:

> presented by me last Friday, January 11th, to President Wilson personally. I was presented by Mr Tumulty and had an interesting chat, though that was not for publication. The President was personally very courteous and acknowledged smilingly his Irish blood. I asked him to consider our claims as a small nation governed without consent. He took the petition and seemed interested ... Mr O'Sheel, who is here, tells me he sends you Washington notes and his note gives all details fully, but I want you also to know the above facts.
>
> It would be well, I think to run photos and special notes on the Irish women who signed petition – any of whose photos you have.
>
> HSS[73]

She was in confident mood, finding everyone 'very favourable', preparing to see numerous other politicians over the next fortnight. In her view, a big 'offensive' ought to be made on Congress. This was a woman who understood the political scene, who knew her own capabilities and who had no qualms in dismissing her ineffectual minder or in offering advice to an old Fenian conspirator.

Cumann na mBan, in their 1918 Convention, paid tribute to that achievement. Mrs Sheehy Skeffington was a woman 'to whom we owe a great deal, as her persistence and courage wore down the efforts of English diplomacy to prevent her reaching the President'. They added that she had also presented Wilson with a copy of the Proclamation of the Republic.[74]

During the terrible months of civil war in Ireland, Hanna re-wrote her account of that interview for *Éire*, the paper of the anti-Treaty faction, making some significant changes. The realisation that Ireland's failure to be included in the Peace Conference had, indirectly, been a factor in the series of events that culminated in civil war five years later, provoked an angry description of Wilson which contradicted the cosy image in the initial account:

> Before leaving I ventured to remind the President that he had Irish blood in his veins He rather gave himself away by replying quickly 'North of Ireland' thus showing the tinge of anti-Irish virus which characterized his dealings with the

> Irish in America and with the delegates later at Paris, when the inclusion of Ireland in the Peace Conference was being pressed.[75]

Wilson's failure to urge the Irish case for inclusion in 1919 had been an enormous disappointment. His refusal to support the American Commission on Irish Independence, noting that they had given the 'deepest offence' to the British, rendering it 'impossible' for him 'to serve them any longer', led to an American policy of non-intervention in the domestic affairs of Britain – a position Lloyd George greeted with much satisfaction.[76] By 1924 Hanna felt free to state openly what it would not have been politic to have said while there were still hopes that America would stand up to Britain.

She and Seamus O'Sheel had supper together on the evening of the interview. She had come to the conclusion that she could do without the services of Devoy's henchman in finding her way round Washington. He was an embarrassment, and, gently, she made it plain how much she disapproved of his efforts to make use of political contacts for his own betterment. Conscientiously, but possibly foolishly, O'Sheel reported: 'she subtly but pointedly indicated that she disapproved of one engaged in Irish work doing anything during the same day toward getting a job'.[77] The week of increasingly strained relations ended in a total rift. During the weekend Hanna did not contact O'Sheel in his 'obscure rooming-house'. At their last meeting she bluntly informed him she 'could get round town by herself'. She was off to see Alice Park, whom O'Sheel resented even more.[78]

She continued her work in the capital, meeting the influential, continuing to put forward Ireland's claims. She hoped that Jeanette Rankin could persuade the House of Representatives to support a resolution stating that Ireland was amongst the small nations for whose independence the USA was fighting. If successful, it would be a colossal victory for Irish nationalists. Small wonder that the British considered her dangerous to their interests. She was, in her own words, a 'Sinn Féiner'. Although much had still to be negotiated in defining the politics of the nationalist movement in the changed conditions following the Rising, she had thrown her weight behind the organisation. Her influence and prestige were considerable, as O'Sheel acknowledged. His chief regret was that he had not been seen enough in her company as he felt his position would have been much enhanced through being in the company 'of a recognised world-leader of the Irish'.

She remained on the east coast until April, basing herself in Washington but travelling to New York and other eastern cities. Continuing her work of interviewing senators and congressmen on the Irish question, she spoke at a meeting at George Washington University on 22 January and was a guest at numerous private events held in the homes of the well-connected. An Irish Mass Meeting was organised in Carnegie Hall, New York, on 18 February. The inevitable report from the Bureau's agent stated that the hall was 'fairly well filled' with several hundred people and a collection of about $300 taken. Amongst those sharing the platform with Hanna were Kathleen O'Brennan, Sydney Gifford and Liam Mellows. One newspaper report stated that 'Mrs Skeffington made an admirable speech.' The agent's summary of the event was succinct: 'The substance of most of the speeches was to the effect that Ireland must be absolutely free from England even if it meant the downfall of the British Empire.'[79]

In Philadelphia she met the powerful industrialist Henry Ford, another coup, as she reported to Devoy:

> I was delighted to find him in favour of an Irish Republic … I gave him our flag, which he put in his coat. We talked in his home for over two hours on Ireland and he asked me a lot about tillage and so forth. He is keen on Ireland's freedom and says that we'll surely get our independence, and that we'll never thrive until we do. The interview, of course, was private, but there could be no objection to your mentioning his views as he expressed them to T. P. without giving my name of course. He didn't give a cent to T. P. and said he had no use for his type, and that any help he'd give to Ireland would be to the people themselves, and to a free Republic. Wasn't that fine? You see we have more friends than we realise.[80]

It was satisfying to be considered in a more favourable light than men like T. P. O'Connor, veteran MP for the old enemy, the Irish Party.

She was back in New York in April 1918, this time to speak with Nora Connolly. Friends from Ireland provided much-needed relief from the drudgery of constant travel and speech making. Her last speech in Washington, intended to wind up the campaign, was attended by congressmen and senators and addressed by John Devoy, Liam Mellows, Padraic Colum, Dr Pat MacCartan and herself. She had pushed hard to have a big last event, writing a hard-hitting letter to Devoy when it looked like nothing would be organised:

> Had delayed my plans hoping to be here for it and to be able to take some cheering word home, but as there seems no prospect of its being called, and as things at home need all my attention, I have decided to leave at end of this month for Ireland. I am trying to have meeting arranged here before I go, and should be glad if you will have invitations sent for delegates from N.Y., and other cities, as we want a good gathering.[81]

Entwined American and Irish flags decorated the hall and a unanimous resolution in favour of Ireland's claim to independence was passed. In Hanna's opinion, it was 'a striking demonstration in the very capital of the United

States of America, to the strength of Ireland's demand'.[82] An upbeat moment on which to leave, heading back west to California and to Owen.

The first meeting on her return west was in support of Tom Mooney, a trade union activist of Irish background who was one of a group of five accused of having caused an explosion at an anti-labour 'Preparedness Parade' in July 1916. Ten people had been killed and Mooney had been sentenced to be hanged. His supporters were convinced that he was a victim of an attempt to discredit the IWW through a frame-up and frantic efforts were being made to secure a new trial. Hanna had been approached by Mooney's mother, a Mayo woman, after her first visit to San Francisco. She then attended the trial of his wife Rena and paid a prison visit to Tom, a 'sturdily-built man in the prime of life'.[83] The San Francisco meeting, organised by the Machinists Union Lodge and sponsored by the *Irish World* newspaper, had an advertising poster consisting of a photo of an exhausted-looking Hanna with the accompanying statement that the *Irish World* 'has prevailed on Mrs Skeffington to add her powerful voice to that of President Wilson to secure Justice for Tom Mooney and Warren K. Billings'.[84] It was further acknowledgement of the pivotal role she occupied as spokeswoman for Irish interests in America, but she was not the only speaker at the event. The platform speakers included Rena Mooney and taxi driver Israel Weinberg, both of whom had been acquitted of the Preparedness Day bombing, together with Mother Jones, the Cork-born labour organiser, and a very radical presence in the American labour movement.[85] The hostility that attended Hanna's subsequent meetings must have been due to this association, rather than as a reaction to her stance on opposing British policy in Ireland. After all, less than two years before, Joe Hill had been executed on another frame-up, because of his success as an IWW organiser. An influential Irish figure showing solidarity with socialist agitators was not a combination to be tolerated by the political establishment. She discovered that her meetings were now regarded with extreme disfavour. Opponents attempted to discredit her by implying that she was anti-American as well as anti-British. She was reputed to have refused to stand to 'The Star-Spangled Banner' while appearing on stage at the San Francisco Auditorium. Her response to that charge was humorous but categorical: 'Although I am not a musician myself, I know the difference between the American National Anthem and "God Save the Queen". I am always proud to stand up for the former, but never for the latter.'[86]

Attempts were now made to prevent her from speaking. All these efforts to oppose Hanna's public appearances began in the wake of the Mooney meeting. Although President Wilson did lend his voice to the call for release or a new trial, a new trial was denied. Mooney's sentence was eventually commuted to life imprisonment. Hanna was to visit him on two more occasions, in the 1920s and 1930s. By then he was 'prematurely aged', his mother dying before he finally won release in 1939.

At Sacramento on 22 April, the police were ordered to close the meeting if Mrs Skeffington spoke. The situation was tense as each side wondered how she would react. When the chairwoman presented her with a bouquet of roses Hanna expressed her thanks – and then turned to the audience to ask if they would like her to say a few words. Despite attempts to stop her, she began to speak of free speech, with the crowds shouting: 'go on' and: 'three cheers for Mrs Skeffington'.[87] The management of the Dreamland Rink, under pressure from the San Francisco office of the Department of Justice, cancelled a meeting billed for 25 April. Hanna's response was to march outside and announce from the steps of the building that the meeting would be held at the Knights of the Red Branch Hall. She and her supporters, who must have prepared for this eventuality, then walked through the streets to the new venue. Her opening statement signified how earnest was her determination to resist these attempts at neutralising her: 'I have not the slightest intention to allow myself to be muzzled.' If she was prevented from speaking she intended to refuse bail and to hunger strike, adding emotionally: 'The last meal has passed my lips, as far as this country is concerned … Dying for principle is in my family.' She dared the Federal District Attorney to arrest her.[88] The dramatics were highly effective. One man was so overwhelmed by this speech that he walked into a police station and tore up his draft card, declaring: 'I heard Mrs Skeffington speak last night and they'll never get me now in their army.' They sent him to jail.[89] The District Attorney, not knowing that the meeting had gone ahead until it was well underway, rushed to the Hall to put an end to the proceedings. Hanna had managed to speak for almost an hour before being interrupted by police and seven federal agents. She and the Reverend William Short (a 'rank socialist' in a Department of Justice report), who had chaired the meeting, held under the auspices of the People's Council, were then brought to the Southern Police Station for questioning. Tempers flared. An Associated Press dispatch reported that a police riot-call was used to disperse the crowd while a wagonload of officers had to scatter several gatherings of people to prevent them from rescuing the two detainees. Hanna's immediate reaction was again to declare that if arrested she would go on hunger strike. She had tremendous support from those who appreciated her determination. A telegram of protest was sent to the White House while the pair were in the police station:

> we citizens of San Francisco in mass meeting assembled protest against the arrest of Hanna Sheehy Skeffington and assert our sympathy with her in her appeal for the freedom of Ireland.[90]

The case against her was dismissed, but Short was released on bail of $10,000 while a case against him on charges of violating the Espionage Act was prepared for a grand jury hearing.[91]

Hanna wanted to go home to Ireland and there was certainly little point in her remaining – forcibly silenced – on America's west coast. However, while she was in California she learned that return to Ireland was not going to be straightforward. She was an illegal immigrant and the British government had taken the decision not to issue her with a passport. Without that document she and Owen could not get aboard a ship to Britain. Adopting any form of disguise was out of the question; she was too well known and under close surveillance. It would have to be a legal departure or nothing. The prospect of conscription in Ireland was now imminent and there were good reasons why the British did not want her return although, apparently, the British Ambassador in the United States requested that she be sent home as a 'dangerous agitator'.[92] Historian Elizabeth McKillen, analysing the lasting significance of Hanna's lecture tour, has concluded that she 'encouraged greater scrutiny of Wilson's foreign policies and undermined unquestioning loyalty to the war effort and to the agenda for the peace conference sought by his administration.' Given her standing with the American left, as well as within the women's movement, she quickly became 'an important voice in a broader American left that sought to commit the United States far more fully to an anti-imperialist agenda.'[93] On both sides of the Atlantic the authorities obviously wished Hanna was off the face of the earth. They shadowed her movements, made notes of her speeches and found that she could not be intimidated.

Back in New York, speaking at Madison Square Garden on the evening of 4 May, every word of her speech and every cheer from the audience was dutifully noted by the agent assigned to watch her, a fact of which she was well aware, 'I hope the Secret Service men are listening to me and have their pencils sharp.' She told her audience she felt she had spoken so often already in America that she would prefer to leave, to go home to keep Ireland free from conscription and safe for democracy. But she was prepared for a fight:

> And it seems to me if it is to be decided in this country that it is treason to the United States to talk against conscription in Ireland then I think the best place for any self-respecting man or woman is prison (wild applause). And my friends, if enough of you, as apparently you do, agree with that sentiment, there will not be prisons big enough to hold us Irish in this country (applause) … I say, if the continuance of the British Empire depends upon the life of a single Irish conscript,

> then I say, let the British Empire be wiped out ... I for one will lose no sleep at any time over the extinction of the British Empire (wild applause).

Frank was not forgotten. She told her audience how she had heard her husband at many meetings in Dublin administering the pledge to resist conscription, and it was on that account 'that he was done to death at the bidding of the Liberal Government (hisses)'. Her defiance and determination to resist were powerfully voiced:

> We Irish were never more attacked and maligned than we are at present; but, for my part, I am proud of Ireland today (applause). She is standing practically alone in her fight, and she is the only country in the world today that says that she will choose her quarrel and know what she is dying for if she is to die. You need not worry about the psychology of the Irish people. Everybody knows that the Irish love a fight; but everybody who respects the Irish race know that we like to choose our fight (applause) ... We are not going to be driven to that slaughter-pen in Flanders at the bidding of a government that is dripping red with the blood of our best countrymen (applause).

The end of her speech saw the meeting erupt in wild enthusiasm, as the Secret Service agent scrupulously reported:

> if conscription is defeated in Ireland, it will be defeated by the spirit of Sinn Féin (wild applause, waving of rebel flags and hats, stamping of feet, etc.) I want every one of you men and women to do your part now to see that the question of conscription will never be mentioned by a British statesman again.[94]

It had been billed as the 'Irish Peace Convention', the significant event she had been trying to persuade Devoy to call. She addressed the question of not participating in the war, but her argument was hardly that of the pacifist determined to have no part in any war and attempting to convince others that they should likewise reject violence as a tactic. Her argument revolved around Britain, a country she condemned as a 'discredited bankrupt' who never honoured bargains. There could be no trade-off in Home Rule and conscription with such a partner. She made it clear that there would be another fight in the future. Ireland would choose the hour and to that she gave her full support.

It was her last big occasion. Eventually, on 27 June 1918, she and her son were permitted to leave the United States, seen off from the docks by Liam Mellows. They had to 'strip to skin' and Hanna had to take down her hair before they boarded what she described as a virtual 'troop ship'. Nora Connolly and Margaret Skinnider travelled with them. Hanna had left Ireland as a widow devastated by personal tragedy. She would return home as a self-proclaimed Sinn Féiner, determined to be part of the struggle to rid Ireland of British rule.

NOTES

1 Hanna Sheehy Skeffington, *Impressions of Sinn Féin in America* (Dublin, 1919), p. 5.

2 Hanna Sheehy Skeffington, Radio interview with Dr Dixon, 1945, Sheehy Skeffington MS (hereafter SS MS) 24,164.

3 William O'Brien to Hanna Sheehy Skeffington, 23 Nov. 1916; 28 Nov. 1916, SS MS 22,680.

4 Hanna Sheehy Skeffington, *Impressions of Sinn Féin*, p. 6.

5 Interview in *Gaelic American* 23 Dec. 1916, quoted in Joanne Mooney Eichacker, *Irish Republican Women in America: Lecture Tours, 1916–1925* (Dublin, 2003), p. 63.

6 Andrée Sheehy Skeffington, *Skeff: A Life of Owen Sheehy Skeffington* (Dublin, 1991), pp 20–1.

7 Hayden Talbot, *Michael Collins' Own Story* (London, 1923), p. 111.

8 With thanks to Micheline Sheehy Skeffington for information on Hanna's arrival in America.

9 Hanna Sheehy Skeffington, *Impressions of Sinn Féin*, p. 6.

10 Ibid.

11 Andrée Sheehy Skeffington, *Skeff*, p. 21.

12 Andrée Sheehy Skeffington, personal interview with author, Mar. 1991.

13 Hanna Sheehy Skeffington, *Impressions of Sinn Féin*, p. 10.

14 Hanna Sheehy Skeffington, *British Militarism as I Have Known It* (New York, 1917), p. 21.

15 Quoted in Elizabeth McKillen, 'Reverse currents: Irish feminist and nationalist Hanna Sheehy Skeffington and U.S. anti-imperialism, 1916–24', in *Éire-Ireland*, 53:3&4, fall/winter 2018, p. 159.

16 Hanna Sheehy Skeffington, *British Militarism*, p. 13.

17 Seán Cronin, *The McGarrity Papers* (Tralee, 1972), p. 63.

18 See John Devoy Papers, MS 18,107, National Library of Ireland (hereafter NLI).

19 Hanna Sheehy Skeffington to Joe McGarrity, 18 Jan. 1917, McGarrity Papers, MS 17,638, NLI.

20 Hanna Sheehy Skeffington to Joe McGarrity, 5 Dec. 1917; 24 Dec. 1917, McGarrity Papers, MS 17,638, NLI.

21 Elizabeth Gurley Flynn, *The Rebel Girl: An Autobiography* (New York, 1973), p. 270.

22 Sir Francis Vane, *Agin the Governments: Memories and Adventures* (London, 1929), pp 273–8.

23 Andrée Sheehy-Skeffington, *Skeff*, p. 22.

24 As told by Owen Sheehy Skeffington to Owen Dudley Edwards. Recalled in conversation between Margaret Ward and Owen Dudley Edwards, Bath Spa University, Apr. 1997.

25 Hanna Sheehy Skeffington, *Impressions of Sinn Féin*, p. 19

26 Hanna Sheehy Skeffington, 'What does Ireland want?', article, n. d. (1917), Alice Park Collection, Hoover Institution Archives, Stanford, California.

27 Typescript report of 'Mrs Sheehy Skeffington's tour', Alice Park Collection, Hoover Institution Archives, Stanford, California.

28 Publicity leaflet, 1938, Alice Park Collection, Hoover Institution Archives, Stanford, California.

29 Mooney Eichacker, *Irish Republican Women*, p. 59.
30 Ibid., p. 58.
31 Hanna Sheehy Skeffington, File No: 9848 10204, Department of Justice, United States of America. A lengthy dossier, consisting of reports from Bureau of Investigation agents who infiltrated her meetings after the US entered the war, together with press cuttings and copies of pamphlets, is included in files of the Department of Justice as part of their investigations into potential pro-German sympathisers. It provides an invaluable account of her time in America. With thanks to Arthur Wheeler for first alerting me to this source.
32 Report of meeting in San Antonio, 15 Oct. 1917, US Department of Justice, file no. 9848 10204.
33 Report of meeting in San Francisco, 8 Oct. 1917, US Department of Justice, file no. 9848 10204.
34 Hanna Sheehy Skeffington, 'What does Ireland want?'.
35 Hanna Sheehy Skeffington, *Impressions of Sinn Féin*, p. 11.
36 Ibid., p. 12.
37 Ibid., p. 17.
38 Ibid.
39 Ibid., p. 18.
40 Reports of Agent Needham, 12 Oct. 1917 and 13 Jan. 1917, San Antonio. US Department of Justice, file no. 9848 10204.
41 Leah Levenson and Jerry Natterstad, *Hanna Sheehy Skeffington: Irish Feminist* (New York, 1983), p. 103.
42 *Irish Citizen*, July 1918.
43 Éamon de Valera to executive of Cumann na mBan, included in report read to Cumann na mBan Convention, Cumann na mBan Convention Report, 1918, C 633, NLI.
44 Andrée Sheehy Skeffington, *Skeff*, p. 22.
45 Owen Sheehy Skeffington to Hanna Sheehy Skeffington (hereafter Owen to Hanna), 12 July 1938, SS MS 40,483/3.
46 Hanna Sheehy Skeffington, 'The new Europe: A trip of scenes, sights and impressions', in *Sunday Independent*, 27 Oct. 1929, p. 5.
47 Report of Agent Needham, 8 Oct. 1917, San Antonio. US Department of Justice, file no. 9848 10204.
48 Mooney Eichacker, *Irish Republican Women*, p. 75; full programme of meeting, publicity leaflet, Alice Park Collection, Hoover Institution Archives, Stanford, California.
49 Mooney Eichacker, *Irish Republican Women*, p. 76–7.
50 Gurley Flynn, *Rebel Girl*, p. 197.
51 Rosalyn Baxandall, *Words on Fire: The Life and Writings of Elizabeth Gurley Flynn* (New Brunswick, 1987), p. 31.
52 Ibid., p. 240.
53 Gurley Flynn, *Rebel Girl*, pp 279–80.
54 Sheila Rowbotham, *Women in Movement: Feminism and Social Action* (London: Routledge, 1992), p. 235.

55 Hanna Sheehy Skeffington, 'Emma Goldman: Pioneer (1869–1940)', in *The Distributive Worker*, Aug. 1940.
56 Ethel Mannin, *Privileged Spectator* (London, 1939), p. 259.
57 Ibid., p. 258.
58 Alice Park to Hanna Sheehy Skeffington, 18 Aug. 1916, SS MS 22,279.
59 Hanna Sheehy Skeffington to Joe McGarrity, 5 Dec. 1917, McGarrity Papers, MS 17,638, NLI.
60 Seamus O'Sheel to John Devoy, 14 Jan. 1918, John Devoy Papers, MS 18,107, NLI.
61 Seamus O'Sheel, note on itemised list of expenses, in ibid.
62 Seamus O'Sheel to John Devoy, 11 Jan. 1918, ibid.
63 Ibid., 8 Jan. 1918, ibid.
64 Eleanor Flexner, *Century of Struggle: The Women's Rights Movement in the United States* (Harvard, 1975), pp 301–2.
65 Hanna Sheehy Skeffington, 'How suffrage stands in Ireland', in *Suffragist*, 30 Mar. 1918, Alice Park Collection, Hoover Institution Archives, Stanford, California.
66 Seamus O'Sheel to John Devoy, 10 Jan. 1918, John Devoy Papers, MS 18,107, NLI.
67 Levenson and Natterstad, *Hanna Sheehy Skeffington*, p. 104
68 Seamus O'Sheel, to John Devoy, 10 Jan. 1918, John Devoy Papers, MS 18,107, NLI.
69 Seamus O'Sheel, to John Devoy, 11 Jan. 1918, in ibid.
70 Ibid.
71 'Irish women's plea for national independence', in *New York American*, 14 Jan., 1918.
72 Hanna Sheehy Skeffington, *Impressions of Sinn Féin*, pp 27–9.
73 Hanna Sheehy Skeffington to John Devoy, n. d. (Jan. 1918), William O'Brien and Desmond Ryan (eds), *Devoy's Post Bag 1871–1925* (Dublin, 1948, reprinted Dublin, 1979), pp 519–20.
74 Cumann na mBan, Report of 1918 Convention, NLI.
75 *Éire*, 16 Feb. 1924.
76 Bernadette Whelan, 'Fighting for recognition', in *Century 1919* 13; see also Bernadette Whelan 'War and peace', in *Irish Times*, 21 Jan. 2019, p. 36.
77 Seamus O'Sheel, to John Devoy, 11 Jan. 1918, John Devoy Papers, MS 18,107, NLI.
78 Ibid., 14 Jan. 1918.
79 Report of Agent Simmons, at the request of Assistant to United States Attorney, Barnes, Washington DC, 13 Feb. 1918. US Department of Justice, file no. 9848-10204.
80 Hanna Sheehy Skeffington to John Devoy, 9 Mar. 1918, in *Devoy's Post Bag*, pp 524–5.
81 Ibid.
82 Hanna Sheehy Skeffington, *Impressions of Sinn Féin*, p. 30.
83 Hanna Sheehy Skeffington 'Tom Mooney: Three Visits', unpublished article, Sheehy Skeffington Papers, MS41,193/14.
84 Poster contained in Alice Park Collection, Hoover Institution Archives, Stanford, California.
85 Meeting advertisement, *Oakland Tribune*, 15 Apr. 1918; report of meeting in *San Francisco Chronicle* 17 Apr. 1918. With thanks to Micheline Sheehy Skeffington for showing me the research of Rosemary Feurer, Director of the Mother Jones Heritage Project, America.

86 Mooney Eichacker, *Irish Republican Women*, p. 84.
87 Ibid., p. 85.
88 Ibid., p. 86.
89 Ibid.
90 John F. Walters to the President, Palo Alto, 25 Apr. 1918, US Department of Justice, file no. 9848 10204.
91 Report and press cuttings submitted by Agent Swift, 26 Apr. 1918. US Department of Justice file no. 9848-10204.
92 Mooney Eichacker, *Irish Republican Women*, p. 87.
93 McKillen, 'Reverse currents', p. 171.
94 Report of speech delivered by Mrs Hanna Sheehy-Skeffington, Madison Square, 4 May 1918. Case File Number 9848-10204, Department of Justice, National Archives Record Group No 60, US National Archives, Washington DC.

TEN

A FEMINIST SINN FÉINER, 1918–21

Hanna had been out of Ireland for 18 months. It was a country 'changed utterly' in that time. The shock of the execution of 15 leaders of the Easter Rising had been traumatic, but it had not delivered the final blow to nationalist dreams. Sympathy for the defeated insurgents began to grow. At each requiem mass for the dead, the numbers paying their respects increased. Those who had escaped prison and internment camp worked hard to capitalise upon the grief of the moment. Many of those campaigners were the female relatives, left to sort out the shattered remains of their lives while struggling to provide continued resistance. By December 1916, when the untried internees were returned to Ireland, bonfires and torchlight processions were visible signs that the Irish people regarded them as heroes. By June 1917 all the prisoners (including Constance Markievicz, one of the last to gain freedom), had been released. Public opinion had been transformed. The work of political reorganisation began.

The press, at a loss as to how to describe the Rising, had dubbed it the 'Sinn Féin Rebellion'. Sinn Féin in 1916 was a small, hardly significant organisation, but the term was a convenient starting point for nationalist re-groupment. Behind the scenes negotiations ensured that when the Sinn Féin Convention of October 1917 took place, its policies bore little resemblance to the cautious nationalism of Arthur Griffith. Éamon de Valera, as senior surviving officer of the Rising, was elected president of the new style organisation. Determined lobbying by women grouped together as the 'League of Women Delegates' (many of whom had taken part in the Rising) ensured that women were promised equality and Kathleen Clarke, Doctor Kathleen

Lynn, Constance Markievicz and Grace Gifford were elected onto the executive. A concerted opposition to British rule in Ireland began. Young women, excited by tales of the activities of women during the Rising and outraged by the executions, flocked to join Cumann na mBan. Young men joined the Volunteers. Those who wanted to have a voice in deciding the future of the nation joined Sinn Féin. There was no question as to what Hanna would do if she succeeded in overcoming the British-imposed obstacles preventing her return home.

She was pleased with what she had achieved while away: 'I am so glad that I undertook the tour. It looked impossible at first, but I must say that it was successful beyond my dreams.'[1] Desmond Greaves, biographer of Liam Mellows, described her as a 'fearless, tireless and inspired propagandist'[2] while John Devoy, that most cantankerous of associates, considered her tour to have been of the utmost importance in mobilising previously uninvolved Irish-Americans:

> Mrs Skeffington has done more real good to the cause of Ireland during her short stay in America than all the Irish orators and writers who have undertaken to enlighten the American people for the past 25 years ... She has reached a class of American people who have never been reached before by a missionary from Ireland and has won them over. She has supplied our own people with unanswerable arguments which they can use with effect on their American neighbours.[3]

This ability to enflame passions was well recognised by the British. Hanna's passport gave her permission to go only to Liverpool. She was forbidden to travel to Ireland. Understandably, her reaction was defiant, 'I told them I was willing to chance their being able to keep me in England',[4] but the British state in war-time conditions possessed enormous power, as its officials took care to demonstrate when Hanna prepared to board the *RMS Metagama* in New York. She was not supposed to carry anything that would be considered unsuitable by the authorities and was required to sign a declaration to this effect: 'books in my possession are school books for my son and novels for perusal on journey'.[5] She had taken care to have the money raised in America sent to her bank account at home, rather than risk carrying it in her luggage.

After a 13-day journey they docked in Liverpool on 10 July 1918. Hanna remembered, 'the fun began for us four' as they were separated from the other passengers to be searched. The grey sea port of Liverpool, after the bright lights of New York, looked 'drabber than ever'. Owen said it was 'uncheerful'. When a military officer took him away to be searched Hanna whispered to him 'not to know anything if asked questions.' He could, she said 'be a clam on occasion.' Nora Connolly and Margaret Skinnider were given permission to proceed to Glasgow; Hanna was brought before a tribunal for interrogation. As she could not produce the (false) passport she had used to travel to America, she was told she was liable to six months imprisonment and therefore had to stay in Liverpool for the duration of the war. She was served with notice of this under the DORA regulations.[6] They had booked into the Bee Hotel; the same place Hanna had stayed (on the recommendation of Seán McDermott) when coming over to England to collect Frank after his American tour. It was no place for Owen who, fortunately, was deemed free to leave. On 16 July Kathleen arrived to take him back with her to Dublin.

The older generation could no longer offer support. Uncle Eugene had died on 17 July 1917, apparently speaking of his pride in Hanna to the last. Bessie, increasingly incapacitated by arthritis, died in January 1918.[7] Her death had taken them all by surprise and David was devastated by the loss of his wife. Aunt Kate, finally retired from Barry's Hotel and living in Glasnevin, was in mourning and 'longing' to have Hanna back home:

> I often feel very much at your dear mother not been there to welcome you and also your dear uncle Eugene. Your poor mother often said to me, that I should remain a few days with her when you should arrive home, in order to hear all your interesting news. It is indeed very sad to have her gone and poor Father Eugene who loved you with such a sincere love.[8]

We have no record of Hanna's feelings, but Kate Barry's letter reads as if it was in reply to one from her ('It is indeed very sad'). The fact that Hanna was careful to preserve family letters, despite constant travelling, reveals a great deal about how she must have been feeling. Adding to the gloom was the news that Dick Sheehy had been diagnosed as suffering from tuberculosis. He had sailed off to the West Indies, hoping for a cure. The family, anxious on his behalf, were 'in daily expectation' of a telegram to let them know he had landed safely.[9] As her friend Elfreda Baker commented, Hanna had had 'to suffer bereavement after bereavement … It must be difficult for you to be as bright as you need to be, for Owen's sake.'[10]

Once again, the sisters provided an emotional and practical network of support. Without it, the ability to live a life that insisted upon challenging every injustice would have been impossible. Kathleen wrote immediately to reassure her sister that Owen was fine, the two were 'great pals already'. She had taken the boy to see Aunt Kate and they wished she could get permission to join them, 'ventilation of the matter in the House ought to wring a permit from the government as the case hardly bears the light of day' was her opinion.[11] Everyone was grateful for the presence of Kathleen and her baby boy, Conor, born in November 1917, now happily providing the family with some entertainment and hope for the future.

David Sheehy's daughters, hoping for some rekindling of interest in life, had urged him to spend time with political colleagues in London. Hanna's presence provided further reason for his being there. She was told that her father was looking forward to meeting her. Politicians were not helpful. Her anti-war activities ensured that many doors in London remained closed. Dillon's opinion was that it was no use approaching the House of Commons, as 'Under the Defence of the Realm Act the government can do anything they like. People have no rights.'[12] Only with the radical, anti-war left, was she given a welcome. George Lansbury, socialist and old supporter of the IWFL, was warm in his greetings, 'glad she is back safe – sees boy has gone back, hopes pressure of public opinion will compel government to allow her to return to Ireland'.[13] But those who applauded her were not those who could determine her future and she remained adamant that her return to Ireland had to be without conditions. Equally, any kind of special pleading or asking for favours was not to be contemplated. Impatient, she decided to take matters into her own hands. Aided by willing friends, she did another disappearing trick: 'The government was so long in coming to a decision as to whether I was a fit and proper person to be allowed back to my own country that I thought it was better to leave without asking permission.'[14]

A detective was on permanent watch in the Bee Hotel and had first to be outwitted. Hanna settled her modest account of £6 and pretended to travel to London, to do battle on her own behalf.[15]In reality, a telegram to her father in the House of Commons was a ruse to deflect attention to the fact that she had contacted willing associates who had concocted a plan to have her smuggled home. Hanna spent the day evading surveillance by travelling in various trains around Manchester and was met that evening in Aintree by Irish women who produced a disguise of dungarees, sweater, peaked cap, brogues and muffler for her neck. Hanna was to be smuggled on board a steamer, a not uncommon event in the life of a sailor. Dungarees were a novelty to her, as she left the top of a tram she 'instinctively stood to catch up an imaginary skirt – such is habit – before climbing the steps.' She was led to a berth, 'draped in front with a towel & some seaman's underwear & I slipped in clothes & all, pulling the blanket over me'. When they landed at Kingsend Kathleen had sent a change of clothes for her, and she lay low for a few days before going to her sister's house. She decided to 'test the authorities' by applying at the local police station for her sugar ration card, determined not to remain 'on the run'.[16] Hardening her resolve was the fact that Hanna discovered Bowen-Colthurst had been released from Broadmoor while she was in America. She did not know where he was; she thought he was occupying a 'minor official post in Essex', but that was irrelevant.[17] The point was that he was free and she, his victim's widow, was being treated as a criminal by the government who had shielded him. James King MP, staunch ally for many years, was one of those most vocal in his abhorrence of this discrepancy. He sent Hanna a postcard from the House of Commons: 'Very distressed. Bowen-Colthurst allowed out of jail and you treated like this. As long as I have any strength I shall do my little bit to see you righted.'[18] He asked questions on her behalf. The government was immovable.

Dublin was not 'war darkened' like Liverpool, and more food was available: 'Jam was rather scarce & much adulterated, bread was coarse, but good, eggs, butter & meat were plentiful.'[19] It was wonderful to be home at last. The chairman of one of her last American meetings, aimed at raising funds for St Enda's, Patrick Pearse's former school, had stated Mrs Sheehy Skeffington hoped to secure a total of $40,000 during her speaking tour.[20] She had told Gretta how financially successful her tour of America had been, her friend writing her congratulations on her 'fine financial results'.[21] Hanna now contacted Michael Collins, a name new to her, to hand over money she had collected. The 'young and sprightly' Collins called over on his bike and 'talked intelligently on the situation in America, asking many shrewd questions.'[22] Collins, still mainly unknown within nationalist ranks, was slowly drawing together the political and administrative strands which became that intricate and complex web of information used so ruthlessly and effectively against the British. Hanna was not sure of her opinion of this man of action with a 'boisterous humour of the barracks type', 'recklessly brave, full of resource' but not 'without vanity and a desire for power.'[23] In the early stages of the War of Independence they appear to have worked together effectively. Hanna appreciated his efficiency and grasp of detail and, when involved in Sinn Féin, was prepared to ask his advice when preparing for executive meetings.[24] The British were not going to permit her defiance to continue unnoticed. As she made no attempt to hide, she was not difficult to trace. Stepping off the tram near the IWFL offices about a week after her return, Hanna found herself under arrest and taken off to the reeking hole of the Bridewell. This was a holding place for untried prisoners, wandering vagrants and, most of all, a place for drunks to sleep off the worst effects of drink, its stench of urine and vomit enough to turn the strongest stomach. The brother of IWFL member Mary Bourke-Dowling, seeing her walking between two detectives, realised the situation and immediately spread the word. The Chief Commissioner of Dublin Metropolitan Police, on being informed that he was holding a woman under the terms of the Defence of the Realm Act, was appalled when he discovered the identity of his prisoner. He wrote a strong letter of complaint to the Under-Secretary at Dublin Castle, pointing out that a woman who 'should be treated with special consideration' had been deposited in a place quite unsuitable for the purpose:

> Mrs Sheehy Skeffington, a delicate woman, was arrested and taken to the Bridewell at 5 pm on the 8th August last and was detained pending Home Office instructions until 6.30 pm 9th August. Her friends complained of the unsuitability of the accommodation, etc., and I feel sure that if anything had happened to her while in the Bridewell we should have had another 'Ashe affair'.[25]

Thomas Ashe had died the previous September, following a clumsy attempt at force feeding which had ended with his lung being punctured. Another martyr, and this time a female one, would have been catastrophic. The attitude of the majority, including many members of the police force, was steadily diverging from their British masters. The comparison with Ashe was not wide off the mark as Hanna had immediately informed her captors that she was refusing all food. Friends visiting her in the Bridewell unsuccessfully tried to dissuade her, fearing the effect on her heart. No one was told what was to happen. She was visited by the Lord Mayor, Lawrence O'Neill, who mistook the solicitor's office where their meeting took place for her cell, complaining how 'terrible' it was. A vigil was kept at the docks, a wise move, as the following day Hanna, accompanied by two wardresses and two detectives was put into a hired taxi and driven to the mail boat, en route for England.[26]She was able to slip the deportation order to a suffrage friend standing at the pier, amusing herself at this 'prick' of the bubble of officialdom. After that a 'melancholy', intensified by her fast, descended and she wondered how long it would be before she saw the lovely Irish coastline again.[27]

Ironically, on the very day she was apprehended in Dublin, Hanna had written to Constance Markievicz, then a prisoner in Holloway jail, along with Kathleen Clarke and Maud Gonne MacBride:

> Dear Madame
>
> I expect you have already heard I'm back in Dublin. I got your news from Mrs Power. I wish I could have seen you. At first I thought we would meet, but now that seems unlikely. I was sorry to hear you had had measles but trust you have now recovered and that you keep your health & spirits – the latter I'm fairly sure of always. I met many friends & admirers of yours out west. Kitty's divorce will I think be granted. On those matters westerners have wider ideas than the old world.

> I am well & so is the boy. My trip did me good in many ways & I was very glad of the experience, tho' of course I'm now glad to be at home once more. Give my regards to your companions – we follow your cases with great interest. I trust your sister is well & that you get pens & papers. I would like to hear from you and Mme Gonne, but I know you all have many correspondents & limited opportunities for writing. I hope we'll all meet again in happier times. Yours affectionately Hanna S Skeffington
>
> Is there anything I can send you or do for you? Please command. HSS[28]

The other three women had been there since May, victims of the 'German Plot' arrests when the government arbitrarily interned all those considered politically important. Hanna's letter was able to communicate that she had thought she might have been sent Holloway when she first arrived back in England; that the Americans supported the Irish cause and that independence (the veiled reference to 'Kitty's divorce') would be achieved. The women, kept apart from the 'ordinary' female prisoners on a separate landing, were housed in reasonable comfort but desperately bored. As they refused to give undertakings not to discuss political issues with visitors, they were unable to accept visits. Noticing another cell being prepared for occupancy Constance Markievicz realised who the likely occupant might be, remarking: 'Well, I hope it's Hanna Skeffington, for she'll tell us all about America.'[29] The addition of a fourth person into this cramped and increasingly strained little group was very welcome. Hanna and Constance had not seen each other since the Rising. Her appearance now was a great break in what Kathleen described as 'the monotony of our lives'.[30] The effects of the hunger strike had not yet taken its toll, so, as Hanna recalled, 'we talked and walked about all day together exchanging news'.[31] Constance was the woman Hanna felt closest to from that small group. Their experience of the Rising and shared grief over lost comrades was an important element in cementing friendship. Kathleen Clarke had grown irritated by her two companions and their little foibles. They might have rejected their privileged class background, but, as far as she was concerned, both retained sufficient mannerisms to provide an infinite catalogue of annoyances for a revolutionary Fenian like herself. Hanna was a breath of fresh air. She was of native Irish stock and her family, like Kathleen's, came from Limerick. Kathleen had the greatest of respect for her new companion: 'she was a very highly-gifted woman, and one of the straightest I ever met, and I had a great admiration for her'.[32]

The other women knew that this addition to their ranks would not be with them for long. Constance urged her to give up the hunger strike, reminding Hanna that they had all the appliances for forcible feeding in Holloway, having done this to many imprisoned suffragettes in the recent past. Hanna thought they would too, and dreaded the ordeal, having heard about it from many women, but she was determined to 'see the thing through.' The other three were unable to follow her example as they were Sinn Féin prisoners and the policy of the organisation, in the wake of Ashe, was against hunger striking. After two days Hanna was informed that she was released under the terms of the Cat and Mouse Act and allowed to go to the Gower Hotel near Euston, the venue which, over the years, had become a London base for various members of the Sheehy family.[33]

Recuperation from the effects of hunger strike was a familiar routine, but rationing restrictions made getting the right food more difficult. Eventually Dr Inglis, a former suffragist, procured a Milk Order for her. She had two weeks of freedom, under the terms of the Cat and Mouse Act, and her 'two friends' from Scotland came down to make plans for another smuggled journey home.[34] Letters of congratulations from family and friends flooded in. From Limerick, Kathleen wrote to say that Mary had been 'a great brick' as she scuttled from 'post to pillar and pillar to post' on her sister's behalf.[35] Mary was of course relieved, writing 'dearest old girl', while also giving blunt advice to her headstrong elder sister: 'to beg of you to remain quiet – now do listen to us and give us a chance this time'. Owen was 'splendid' and their father, greatly relieved, 'urges you to do as I say'.[36] Despite their very different political sympathies, the sisters never wavered in their support. Their brother Eugene, still in British Army uniform, was far removed from family concerns and David had not stayed long in London. He was back in Dublin again. It was Mary who had to make the necessary arrangements to ensure that a sum of £50 was paid into a London bank so that Hanna was able to live in comfort while forced to remain in England.

During this stay in London Hanna wrote a lengthy letter to Jennie Wyse Power, giving all the details she could on the three women in Holloway, who were unable to send out uncensored information on their own behalf. It was a thoughtful gesture and Jennie made it clear that it was greatly appreciated by their families and friends:

> letter containing news of Irish women in Holloway very welcome. When it had gone the Dublin rounds will send it to Mrs C's people in Limerick – now that you have made such a glorious win it seems to be quite feasible to win with her too. After all you suffered you were goodness itself to write such a long letter.[37]

Meg Connery who had called in to the Wyse Power home while Jennie was writing, added her own bubbly postscript, 'best love and wishes strong hope of seeing you soon. Free with us again.' Maud Gonne's son, Seán MacBride, also sent a letter of thanks for the 'very kind letter' he had received, giving news of his mother. She had told him that it was a 'great joy' to them all to see Mrs Skeffington and how glad they were that she was now free.[38]

All the old Franchise League members – Cissie Cahalan, Kathleen Keevey, Mary Bourke-Dowling, and many others – sent telegrams of congratulations. Patricia Lynch, very active in the London-Irish suffrage scene, sent a shy note as soon as she heard from Eva Gore-Booth that Hanna was at the Gower Hotel: 'I met you when you were in London before when you saw Miss S Pankhurst but I did not speak to you then as I did not like to intrude myself upon you. I am sorry you have had such an awful time.'[39]

As Hanna arranged to meet sympathetic MPs like James King and Philip Snowden, questions on her behalf were again asked and arguments raged over whether an Irish woman, convicted of no offence, whose young son was effectively orphaned through his mother being forbidden to join him, could now go home. Charlotte Despard 'bombarded' her brother Lord French, Lord Lieutenant of Ireland, as did Mary Kettle. Mary's irritation with her sister was understandable, as the situation had forced her to communicate with deeply hostile officials. Edward Shortt, who was now Chief Secretary to Lord French, the Lord Lieutenant, wrote from Dublin Castle:

> Your sister's refusal to give any sort of undertaking makes my position extremely difficult. If she came here would she promise to live with you and would you do what you can to keep her away from the Sinn Féin crowd? On those terms I might be able to do something to help you. The position is very difficult. I am afraid from what you say that you are imperfectly informed of your sister's US activities and associations. The latter were very dangerous ... I can assure you I would accept your sister's word if she would only give it as readily as I would accept your own.[40]

Hanna would have been livid if she had seen this at the time. She would never give her word to any such undertaking. Mary, unsympathetic to Sinn Féin because of her loyalty to her dead husband and his standing within the Irish Party, held different views from her sister. Yet surely Mary too, who had after all experienced the British state at its worst during the Portobello murder inquiry, felt insulted on her sister's behalf, seeing her referred to in tones which made her out to be little more than a delinquent, consorting with the worst types of subversive? The contrast between British officialdom and the mildest of public opinion, as expressed in the Irish Party organ, the *Freeman's Journal*, demonstrated the chasm that had opened between British and Irish:

> If British prestige cannot permit Mrs Sheehy Skeffington to live in her own country amongst her own people, then British prestige must be in a worse way

> than even its bitterest enemies imagined. The spectacle of Bowen-Colthurst walking the world as a free man while the widow of his victim is imprisoned under an administrative order, without any charge being preferred against her, is sufficient to revolt not merely the 'unreasonable Irish' but any man with a bias in favour of fair-play and even-handed justice.

Ireland had tolerated a great deal, but 'a second Sheehy Skeffington tragedy would be too much'. The leader writer warned that if anything happened, Ireland would be 'set ablaze' and the consequences from the American side would 'startle the Chief Secretary'.[41] Mrs Sheehy Skeffington could hardly have been more of an embarrassment to the government. Far better to send her back to Ireland where she would be less in the public eye than when stirring up adverse feeling in London. Permission was granted. Philip Snowden signed her passport. Her family's relief that the saga had finally come to an end was palpable. Mary urged her sister to 'only think of remaining quiet and getting well', relieved that the 'torture' was over.[42] By the end of the week, Hanna was back in Ireland, and she and Owen went off to Portmarnock, to spend a few quiet days with Meg and Con Connery. Wisely, no conditions had been imposed.

Old colleagues obviously expected her to return to action in the near future. On hearing of her release William O'Brien, Connolly's former associate in the Transport Union, had sent over 'bundles of papers dealing with Trades Congress'. In his opinion, 'I think you have beaten them and that very soon we will be welcoming you home again.'[43] John Dillon, however, in a letter marked 'confidential', urged her to stay clear of politics for the time being. She had no rights and he feared that if she was arrested again, she would not win release.[44] From Portmarnock, Hanna sent a searing reply, making it plain that she could not conceive of a life empty of commitment. In the heat of anger, she also revealed herself to be still grief-stricken at the loss of her husband, still ambivalent at the prospect of continuing the struggle without him:

> Yours marked 'confidential' received – you are, of course, aware that all my letters are read before reaching me & nothing of mine can be 'confidential' to the government. I was surprised & rather amused at your advice to 'avoid politics until some safer time, because next time Mr Shortt will let me die if I fall into his hands! Had I meant to give up public activities I would have given the guarantee Mr Shortt first desired & and so saved all concerned a good deal of trouble. It is not likely, having wrung the right to live in my own country so dearly, that I shall give up the right to do what I think fit in public matters unconditionally
>
> You must remember, my dear Mr Dillon, that I am over 40 years of age and convictions of a lifetime are dearer to me than life. Even if my arrest, as you suggest,

> leads to my death at the government's hands, I do not on that account intend to give up any of my activities & after all my last adventure might also be the last adventure of my assassins. If our militarists think they can dispose of me by letting me die in prison, it only shows how stupid they are. Life is not such an exhilirating [sic] adventure that I would not gladly relinquish it if called upon – as others before me[45]

It was an eruption of rage at anyone who dared to counsel caution. The British government had colluded in the murder of her husband and that government, with its acceptance of militarism, had forfeited all claims to authority. Inexorably, Hanna was finding herself in sympathy with the nationalists of Sinn Féin.

Dorothy Evans, former WSPU organiser in Belfast, had been over in Dublin, where she and Lilian Metge had given considerable support to a grateful Meg Connery organising deputations and interviews with the Dublin Castle authorities.[46] Dorothy was effusive in writing of her joy that Hanna was back in circulation: 'How we want that indomitable spirit that you still show.'[47] There were many who wanted to enlist that 'indomitable spirit' into their cause. Before her arrest the committee members who had kept the *Citizen* alive for almost two years had written of their relief that the visit to America had 'revived her strength', enabling her to return 'to her professional duties and to the editing of this paper with renewed energy.'[48] Now the executive of the IWFL wrote to congratulate her on her victory over the government, immediately making plans for a reception of welcome. Countless friends, both personal and political, wanted to see both Hanna and Owen. Elfreda Baker hoped they would spend a few restful days with her, 'sending a few eggs straight from the nest to help stomach in its present state'.[49] Less restfully, William O'Brien planned to bring Winifred Carney and Cathal O'Shannon to visit. Winifred was coming down from Belfast for the day and was most anxious to see Hanna. As she had stayed by the side of James Connolly in the GPO until the very end, surrendering with the men, there would have been much information to relay.[50] Feminists and socialists had good reason to believe that Hanna's loyalty would be with them.

The IWFL reception on 14 September was an intimate gathering, not a large public affair. Owen came with his mother, to be presented with a 'huge box of chocolates' while she received flowers in the League colours. Apart from the gaping absence of Frank, it could have been old suffrage times, as Hanna thanked her friends: 'it was worthwhile going to prison to realise the deep affection the members showed her and the gallant fight they made when she was deported'.[51] Where would she decide to direct her sought-after talents?

All the signs are that she was determined to operate from as wide a political platform as possible. She was not going to limit the struggle for freedom to one single issue. It went without saying that the citizen would be first on the list. It was more than a political priority; it was a precious link with Frank and the past. Maurice Wilkins was both astounded and pleased to receive a letter, enclosing the latest issue of the paper and requesting a 100-word article for the next issue. He assured Hanna that he always had copies sent to him and hoped that he could get an afternoon free from teaching so that he could help with proof-reading, a task 'sacred to me for Frank's sake'. He had suffered from the absence of his old friend, 'I don't suppose a day passes without my thinking of him … hope you will come to see us, and bring Owen … I am going to come to the Reception – I should like to hear you talk about everything.'[52] Cathal O'Shannon, then in England, was unable to get over in time for her welcoming reception as his passport was held up by the authorities. He would have represented the Socialist Party of Ireland; another link with Frank. He did agree to be included on the IWFL lecture list, choosing 'Women and the Workers' Republic' from the short list of possible titles he had been given. The IWFL programme of lectures had a number of interesting speakers booked for the coming season, including Dorothy Macardle, Charlotte Despard, and Nora Connolly, speaking of her experiences in America.[53]

Nationalists were of course also anxious to provide a welcome. Margaret Pearse was 'delighted she is back again with us in dear old Ireland'.[54] Rose Jacob, acting as intermediary on Hanna's behalf, arranged for a day on which Hanna could call to pay her respects to the family of Patrick Pearse, the man who, posthumously, was now considered to be first president of the Irish Republic.[55] From Cumann na mBan ranks, Louise Gavan Duffy wrote an admiring note, 'we knew that you would beat the British government but we weren't sure if they knew it too'.[56] The revivified Sinn Féin was winning plenty of recruits and Cumann na mBan was attracting a new generation of young woman, eager to play their part in the struggle for independence.

Ireland in 1918 was very different to the chaotic, demoralised country of two years ago. Unexpectedly, there was also something for women to celebrate. In February 1918 the Representation of the People Act was passed, and British and Irish women over 30 (with a property qualification) finally won the right to vote. In November, to the surprise of many, legislation would also be passed permitting women over 21 to stand for parliament. Hanna was sarcastic about this new 'sex barrier', commenting: 'It would be too revolutionary in a democratic government to allow the majority sex to vote on the same qualifications as the minority sex! Truly British statesmanship works in a mysterious and inscrutable way its wonders to perform.' She contrasted the Irish Republic which in 1916, had given 'full and free citizenship to all adults, men and women' with a British parliament only 'timidly opening its doors to British women of 30'.[57]

If she had not decided to join Sinn Féin before (despite her self-description as a 'Sinn Féiner') Hanna's experiences of British officialdom since her return made up her mind for her. In the changed circumstances of post-1919 Ireland, Sinn Féin was the dominant organisation. She felt it was 'in the foremost ranks of the fighting front.'[58] In September 1918 she applied for membership of the MacDonagh Sinn Féin Club in Ranelagh. The secretary immediately sent the new recruit an enthusiastic welcome: 'needless to say your application has been favourably considered as we consider an honour to our club to receive you as a member'.[59] By November, she was an elected member of the executive. Cumann na mBan were also attempting to enrol her within their ranks. While the executive of the latter asked her to speak at a meeting at the Mansion House, their membership secretary wrote to say that she had been nominated for membership and asked did she agree to let her name go forward?[60] On this, she did not. In her opinion, Cumann na mBan had not shaken off its 'auxiliary to the men' status. They were denied representation within Sinn Féin, even though they had requested this,[61] so although she remained on terms of warm friendship with many of their leading figures and would often lend her support to activities engaged in by the Cumann, she could not, on principle, join them.

More basic needs and responsibilities could not be ignored, despite the frenetic pace of those early days of her return. She and Owen had no home of their own. 2 Belvedere Place was still a VAD hostel. David Sheehy's address was now given as 30 Dartmouth Square, on the south side of the Grand Canal, together with his sons, Dick and Eugene.[62] Eugene was of course away from home, serving with the Army, and Dick was married with a young daughter, so this listing in *Thom's Dublin Directory* is puzzling. Perhaps, as a member of parliament, Sheehy preferred to give an address that did not belong to one of his daughters. David and Bessie had moved in with Margaret after they left Belvedere Place, but her circumstances were now very changed. David eventually moved in with Mary and Betty. Their home was to be his for the rest of his life. A lonely, rather crotchety figure in the armchair by the fireside, his routine never varied, punctuated by attendance at six masses a day.

After time spent living with various friends because Dublin had a scarcity of accommodation, Hanna found the ideal house. Nine-year-old Owen had gone back to Miss Tuckey's school in September and they did not want to live too far away from the part of Dublin both felt most at home in. While staying with Mary and Betty at their home in 3 Belgrave Park, Rathmines, she discovered that the lease of 7 Belgrave Road was free. It was a wide, quiet road, with spacious Victorian terrace houses on either side. The whole terrace had been built in 1863 as a speculative investment by the Plunkett family, who still owned much of the area.[63] Hanna's landlady was Countess Plunkett, mother of 1916 leader Joseph. She also owned other property, like Hardwicke Hall, used by Cumann na mBan. A tenancy agreement for five years was signed, at an annual rent of £60.[64] Hanna was a demanding tenant, insistent upon her rights and fully prepared to withhold rent if essential repairs were not carried out. She persuaded her new landlady to pay for an extensive programme of redecoration before moving in. Shortly afterwards, she and the Countess had a heated exchange of views regarding burst pipes and a collapsed ceiling during her first winter.[65] Despite the vehemence of the Countess's protests ('the interior repairs are to be done by the tenant otherwise I might as well make a present of the house at the rent we get for it'), one feels that Hanna won that battle.[66]

The refurbishment of the house began in mid-October and on 26 November 1918 they were able to move into the house that would be home for the rest of Hanna's life. With evident relief she sent a postcard to Alice Park: 'We have a home at last. I have a good garden with a lovely view.'[67] The reunion with her possessions went smoothly, apart from the loss of one bicycle which the packers swore had never come into the store. The house was perfect for their needs. The basement contained a kitchen and a dining room large enough to seat the various members of the Sheehy clan without difficulty. That became the part of the house used most. At street level, to the left of the front door, there was the drawing room, with Hanna's bedroom to the rear, overlooking a tree-lined garden at the back. Owen had a tiny bedroom on the return landing while the top floor contained a flat she hoped to rent out for a small amount of money. The drawing room, full of books and papers, contained some of her most precious mementoes: a portrait of Frank; a photo of Uncle Eugene looking 'shrewd, whimsical';[68] a print of Madox Ford's portrait of Millicent Fawcett and her husband Henry (an expression of husband and wife partnership of which she was particularly fond, despite disagreeing with Millicent Fawcett's political views); a photo of Sir Francis Vane, in full military uniform, which confused many visitors until they realised the personal significance of that particular soldier, now a close friend. In Grosvenor Place she had had a portrait of Christabel Pankhurst, but that had been removed when the WSPU announced it was supporting the British war effort and replaced by a portrait of Wolfe Tone. It was an eclectic mix of all that had most influenced her, all that she held most dear. There was the desk that Father Eugene had given so long ago, to encourage her schoolwork, some furniture from Belvedere Place, the bits and pieces from her married life. She had little of value, her idea of essential items in a household were the ideas and arguments spilling out from the papers surrounding her. Working in the garden gave her far more pleasure than any chores around the house. For that she employed a daily servant, someone who could do a bit of plain cooking and cleaning. If the money for wages was hard to find, she always managed it, determined not to waste hours in work she hated.[69]

Richard Fox, visiting Hanna in the 1930s, described a white death mask of Robert Emmet under a glass case perched upon her mantlepiece. She smiled as she recalled having to hide this in the months when the Black and Tans were on the rampage.[70] It had arrived in a parcel in 1908, at the time Frank was convalescing in Youghal. Hanna had written then how beautiful it was, but also how puzzled she was, not knowing who had sent it to them.[71] The death mask of the failed insurgent, taken by James Petine in 1803, was an incongruous possession. Was it possibly left to her by her uncle? It would have been in keeping with his principles. In 1930 she made a loan of it so that a copy could be made for the new civic museum. It was a valuable object. The Municipal Gallery of Modern Art, in arranging the details, insisted that the cost of its insurance be included in the corporation expenses.[72] Who, other than Hanna, could have possessed such a disparate and often conflicting collection of mementoes? Who else could have blended all these influences into a highly personal credo of beliefs?

Belgrave Road came to be known as 'rebel road'. It was apt. There was Hanna at number 7, her friends Kathleen Lynn and Madeleine ffrench-Mullen, both veterans of the Irish Citizen Army in number 9. Helena Molony sometimes stayed with them. Kathleen Lynn held her surgery on the ground floor. Robert Brennan, prominent Sinn Féiner and publicist for the cause, spent most of his time 'on the run', but he was officially listed as the tenant of number 10.[73] When Hanna was away, her friend Rose Jacob was happy to come up from Waterford to look after Owen and to mind the house. On one occasion, during the Civil War, Rose (with Hanna's permission), had lent a room to Sinn Féin's publicity department. When the house was raided by Free State detectives, Rose ended up in Mountjoy jail.[74] Later on, in the mid-1920s, Hanna's lodgers were Frank Gallagher, one of the most brilliant propagandists for the republican cause, and his wife Cecilia. Some moved into the area over the years, secure in the knowledge that, in those hard times of surviving an unsympathetic Free State, they would have the comfort of the company of like-minded individuals. In 1922 Sydney Gifford Czira, returning to Ireland from America with her young son, a new Hungarian name, but no husband, eventually ended up in number 10 Belgrave Road when it had been turned into flats.[75] It was a predominantly woman-centred existence, one dedicated to humanitarian service and political causes. In September 1918 Madeleine ffrench-Mullen and Kathleen Lynn were planning to open a small hospital for the treatment of infants suffering from syphilis, the numbers of which had risen because of the war and the increase in the numbers of soldiers.[76] They raised £500 to buy a site in Charlemont Street and, starting with two cots, the children's hospital of St Ultan's was opened in May 1919. Money was so scarce that friends were roped in to take shifts as cleaners.[77] Kathleen Lynn was also doctor to large numbers of republicans (possessing a no-nonsense belief in fresh air and cold water), part of a network of solidarity that sustained many over the years.

Hanna had a fierce loyalty to women who, like herself, were struggling to survive in difficult times. When Grace Gifford Plunkett, in some distress, showed her a cutting from a Philadelphia paper concerning a memorial statue to her husband Joseph to be erected in that city, she wrote a tactful letter to Joe McGarrity. The newspaper report had added that 'this would be the best form of memorial as the family of course did not need money'. Hanna explained in confidence that Grace had received a total of £200 from the National Aid Committee, which was 'exhausted'. The Gifford family, unsympathetic to the nationalist cause, had refused to help and neither did Grace receive help from the Plunketts, 'her people-in-law'. As Hanna's landlady was the Plunkett matriarch, Hanna knew only too well how rich that family was. It enraged her that they could ignore their son's widow, while having their nationalist credentials enhanced by the romantic tale of the candle-lit marriage in a Kilmainham Jail cell the night before Joseph's execution. Grace was an 'able artist' but could not live on that work 'as orders are few and precarious'. Hanna urged McGarrity's intervention:

> I feel sure I can leave the matter confidently in your hands and that you will take such steps as seem advisable to put the facts before this committee. I know that the Irish in America would not tolerate the thought that the widow of one of the executed leaders was suffering hardship while a marble memorial was being erected to him.[78]

For some women, their husbands killed in the most brutal of circumstances and left alone to bring up small children, the burden proved too great. That was possibly the case with Muriel MacDonagh, another of the remarkable Gifford sisters, whose drowning was caused by heart failure. Sadly, Maud Gonne explained that Muriel, in July 1917, 'swam out to sea towards Howth and never returned. She was such a lovely girl.'[79] Emotional and financial support were badly needed, and, in the absence of their families, the women helped each other as much as they could.

Oakley Road, where Áine, widow of Eamon Ceannt lived, just a few streets away from Belgrave Road, could also have been dubbed 'rebel road'. The MacDonaghs had lived in number 29, and Pearse's sister Brigid moved into that house when it became free. Cullenswood House in Oakley Road had housed Pearse's first school. Aine became a tower of strength to many in the years to come. Her son Ronan became a life-long friend of Owen's, despite the fact they held very different political views – the former strongly nationalistic, the latter determined to stay away from what he considered to be a bitter path to take. When the Irish White Cross was set up in 1920 to provide relief for those in need as a result of the political situation, Aine Ceannt was appointed secretary of the Children's Relief Association with responsibility for ensuring that those orphaned because of the war were cared for. Owen was one of around 1,000 children to receive a weekly grant from the White Cross funds. The amount never exceeded one pound a week, but it was a welcome addition to their small income.[80] To demonstrate that the White Cross grant was not being wasted, school reports had to be sent. Those who failed to do this found their allowances delayed. With Owen, there was nothing but praise for his excellent work. As late as 1926, his grant of an extra 5/– at Christmas was still being paid out.[81]

Dr J. B. Skeffington died in Belfast on 24 August 1919, leaving a bequest of £150 to Owen.[82] Whether he had continued to help with his grandson's upkeep before his death is impossible to determine. Visiting Hanna not long after Frank's death Rose Jacob noted in her diary that Dr Skeffington 'seems to be making himself very disagreeable to her & there may be danger of his trying to take Owen from her'.[83] Nevertheless, Hanna wrote a warm obituary, describing her father-in-law, improbably, as:

> a good friend of the *Irish Citizen* whose chequered career he continued to follow with interest and affection even after the murder of his son had deprived it of its editor. He was opposed to militarism (as one whose heart was broken by its ravages) and was keenly interested in educational problems and in the advancement of women. His brilliant son's untimely and terrible death was a blow from which he never recovered.[84]

The following July, out of the blue, she received a letter from F. V. Quinn, a cousin of Dr Skeffington and, with his widow, executor of the will. It was written in extremely conciliatory terms: 'I never had the pleasure of meeting my cousin Francis, and his tragic and untimely end I shall always deplore'. Dr J. B. had left £20 in his will, 'towards completion of a monument' to Frank in Glasnevin. That December Hanna received a cheque of £18 (less £2 duty). The cousin added: 'I think your ideas re wording on the stone are correct and would be suitable and pleasing to all'. Other family news was that Cousin Bella was now in the Mater Hospital in Belfast and would never be fully well again; she would like Hanna to visit and to have some family portraits 'in the event of anything occurring to her.'[85] Bella would be visited by both Hanna and Owen in the years to follow.

Hanna had secured evening class teaching as soon as she returned to Ireland, but the pay was small. Her cheque from the Technical Education Committee for January/February 1919 totalled £16.[86] Other amounts of money were earned from journalism and from occasional fees for lectures. As she was in such great demand as a lecturer, unable to fulfil all the requests she received, her expenses and a small fee were invariably offered as inducement. In September 1920 she was appointed French teacher at the Technical Institute in Dun Laoghaire at a salary rate of four shillings an hour, plus part-timer's bonus of one shilling and four pence. With the time taken to travel there and back, her Tuesday evenings had little time for anything else. She must have been hard up to have accepted this addition into her overcrowded schedule. Visits to Britain, if not booked for holiday periods, had to be squeezed into the days between classes. The boat-train from Dublin to London was arduous enough, doubly so when the brief interval before the return left no time for recovery.

The armistice on 11 November 1918 brought the Great War to an end. The British government called a general election for the following month. There was barely time to unpack the furniture before Hanna was frantically busy, ensuring that now women had the right to vote and to stand for election, they would make their mark. Would she be a candidate? There seemed to be considerable confusion on which women, if any, would be selected as candidates. Sinn Féin had been a proscribed organisation since July, large numbers of its leaders were in jail, and the ordinary routine of political organisation was fraught with difficulties. In insisting upon a democratic solution to Ireland's future the British were attempting to ensure that the dice was weighted to secure the result they favoured. In the confusion of deciding upon candidates, the people being considered were not always consulted. Maud

Gonne, recently released from Holloway, read an announcement by Cumann na mBan that Constance Markievicz had been selected as a candidate. She wrote immediately in puzzlement to Hanna: 'Where is it for? I don't think she knows. She certainly didn't up to the time of my release and yesterday her sister said she did not know where it was for or anything about it.'[87] Would Hanna have consented to allow her own name to go forward? There were plenty amongst her friends who assumed her candidature would be automatic. Gretta Cousins had been full of curiosity as to how America might have changed her friend ('want to know intimate things about you … what kind of clothes you are wearing, whether you have caught the American accent, do your hair in same way') and she was desperately homesick to have the opportunity of returning from India so that she could help Hanna to be elected, 'whether you choose to sit in parliament or not'.[88] Rose Jacob assumed that there would be several female candidates, Hanna included:

> I suppose the three women in jail will be put up too, though I see no sign of it at present – I hope the Dublin women at least are stirring themselves to get women candidates selected – women in most other parts of the country are too scattered to be able to do much, but the Dublin women ought to be able to insist on enough to get a start made anyhow. It seems to me the important thing for Irish suffragists to be doing at present. I hope they won't try to run women as independent candidates … That would be hopeless everywhere, I should think, and would give the impression that they didn't care about national issues.
>
> With love [89]

There seems to have been no question that Sinn Féin were happy to put Hanna forward, the question is, would they would select her for a winnable seat? On 22 November, the Seán Connolly Sinn Féin Club wrote to say that she had been unanimously selected to contest the Harbour Division. They hoped she would attend a meeting the following day to go into the necessary details.[90] The constituency covered the docks and the red light area of Dublin and would be won easily by Sinn Féin, despite the popularity of Alfie Byrne, the Irish Party incumbent. Hanna's response is unrecorded. The following week, Stephen O'Mara, Sinn Féin Director of Elections, received a wire from HQ which stated:

> Unanimous opinion Mrs Skeffington can do best propaganda work in Ireland fighting North Antrim. Make her stand. Sure wire reply immediately. Donnelly waiting.

In response to queries from Hanna, O'Mara was forced to admit 'of course it is hopeless, but they want an answer. Please wire direct.'[91] The conclusion must be that Hanna refused to accept this token gesture of equality. She was not interested in quixotic gestures, and there was no possible way that the women's cause would be advanced through her standing for a 'hopeless' seat. This attitude was recognised and shared by Aine Ceannt, prominent in the republican women's pressure group, the League of Women Delegates (now called by its Gaelic name, Cumann na d'Teachtaire), who assured Hanna that she had not been put forward for the Rathmines constituency because it was a 'hopeless' area. She was, however, getting the executive of Sinn Féin to pledge that Hanna would be put forward elsewhere.[92] She was unsuccessful.

Meg Connery was outspoken in her frustration that the feminist movement continued to be marginalised. In agreeing to speak on behalf of Winifred Carney, the only other female candidate, standing for an unwinnable constituency in Belfast, Meg admitted to having been influenced by the news that Sinn Féin was putting forward Hanna in Dublin. On hearing that this had not happened, she was furious. What angered her further was the fact that Sinn Féin had also asked Meg to take charge of Constance Markievicz's election campaign, obviously based on the assumption that feminists would unquestioningly look after the interests of other women:

> The very nerve of Sinn Féin sets my teeth on edge. The one woman they have thrown as a sop to the women of the country has her interest neglected and what is one to say of Cumann na mBan -surely it is their special duty to concentrate on election of their own president! Why should work be left to the chance care of 'outsiders' as they are so fond of calling us. They are too busy running after the men – the camp followers![93]

Some, in slightly less heated fashion, shared those sentiments. Moirin Chavasse, arranging to off-load a 'bilingual' cat belonging to ex-Inghinidhe member Ella Young onto Owen, remarked that she and Ella had been very disappointed to learn that Hanna was not a candidate: 'It was a great shame that you were not offered a safe seat and I hope greatly that you will get one of those that have to be vacant again. It is astonishing how behind the times and timid over new ideas people are outside Dublin:[94]

Other women suffered their own disappointments. Kathleen Clarke, still in Holloway, a loyal member of Sinn Féin, also expressed her sense of disappointment that she had not been chosen as a candidate. She wanted to stand for office in Limerick, to continue the struggle for which her husband had sacrificed his life but found that internal machinations had ensured a male candidate was put forward in her place.[95] Her opportunity would come, eventually, in 1921, at the election to the Second Dáil. In 1918, the two women chosen had both been 'out' in the Rising. In the end, that appeared to be the determining criterion. After the election Eva Gore-Booth, as a life-long suffragist, asked her sister why Hanna had not been included in the ranks of Sinn Féin MPs. Constance was still in Holloway and unaware of all the internal controversies of the election period. Her reply was defensive as she defended her organisation from feminist criticism:

> Hanna S. could have been an MP *if she had wanted to.* A seat was offered her. She is not altogether an SF I think, and *I know* prefers to work from the Women's platform.[96]

As a senior member of Sinn Féin, Hanna fulfilled numerous requests to speak on behalf of a variety of candidates. However, it was obvious that her heart was set on ensuring that there would be an election victory for women as well as for Sinn Féin. Feminists from the Franchise League and members of Cumann na mBan were both campaigning on behalf of the Countess, but it was not a joint campaign. Hanna made this plain in an outspoken note to Nancy Wyse Power (the former Aine de Paor, 'Irish language correspondent' of the *Citizen*), who was coordinating Cumann na mBan's efforts:

> It's the worst managed constituency in Dublin – every other constituency has had more frequent meetings (many nightly) and has been better canvassed. The committee can't play 'dog in the manger' so, finding them hopeless in cooperation we decided as I told you a week ago, to have our own meetings in future. All first week only one set of meetings (Wednesday) and so far today we had offer of Mrs Connery who wanted to speak for Madame. There are four meeting places we have taken two. Committee can take them and take ours by having different hour. As a woman's organisation we feel we have a duty in this matter and think it is a disgrace to the women's organisation if Madame Markievicz is let down by an inefficient committee.[97]

In a letter to Hanna, Constance Markievicz had included a bubbly election address to the women of the IWFL: 'One reason I'd love to win is that we could make St Patrick's a rallying ground for women and a splendid centre for constructive work by women',[98] but the day of polling was highly symbolic of the extent to which feminism alone could not be a unifying force. Ireland's leading feminists had very different causes once it came to decisions on where their vote would go. The *Citizen* commented: 'It speaks well for the broadmindedness of the new women voters that women of all parties – Unionist, Irish Party and Sinn Féin – joined heartily to honour Mrs Haslam and Suffrage' as the various suffrage societies held a joint demonstration of celebration.[99] Anna Haslam, a first-time voter at the age of 89, cast her vote for the unionist candidate, Maurice Dockrell, who was a member of the IWSLGA. Mary Kettle remained loyal to the tradition of her husband

and father by voting for the Irish Party.[100] Members of the Franchise League supported the cause of Irish independence, and they were wholehearted in their support for Constance Markievicz, who duly became the first woman to be elected to the British Parliament. The Labour Party had wanted to put Louie Bennett forward as candidate, but she declined. In the end, Labour decided to stand aside and let Sinn Féin sweep the boards.

Newspapers reported that women voters were up early to vote and the *Citizen*, with sarcasm, noted that the election 'passed quietly' and 'babies were washed and husbands fed on Election day just as they are on Washing Day or at spring cleaning ... Babies were wheeled along to the booths and policemen looked after them while mothers voted – sometimes even fathers condescended to the task.'[101] Hanna scrawled a note to Alice Park: 'All goes well – we got the Countess in, the only woman.'[102] The *Irish Citizen* was triumphant as it headlined 'Bravo, Dublin!':

> Dublin leads in feminism and deserves congratulations as the only place that elected a woman candidate during the recent General Election ... And so Ireland again leads the way, and while Britain wallows in reaction and turns her back on woman M.P.s, Ireland proudly writes Progress on her banner to show the world how much in advance she is of those who would rule her.[103]

Sinn Féin obviously felt, despite the tensions of the campaign, that it could count on the support of the League. Harry Boland asked them to place their rooms in Westmoreland Street at the disposal of the Sinn Féin executive because it was intended to announce the results of the election on a screen 'and think your premises are very central and would suit the occasion'.[104] Hanna was still busy speaking in a great number of constituencies. When Pembroke celebrated its victory by organising a public meeting and torchlit procession, they begged her to speak for them: 'in view of the fact that the women voters were the most important factor in our polling district notwithstanding that they have not yet been addressed by any women speaker. In returning thanks to them we know of no one whose words would be more appreciated.'[105]

David Sheehy and his colleagues in the Irish Party suffered a humiliating defeat as the electorate swung behind this radical new voice in Irish life. Seventy-three Sinn Féiners won seats. They had already announced, if elected, they would defy the authority of the British House of Commons and set up their own national assembly. The Irish Parliament, Dáil Éireann, came into being on 21 January 1919, a symbol of nationhood that challenged British control over Ireland. Few of the new MPs could be there as they were still in jail. Hanna, knowing what conditions in Holloway were like, was concerned for the well-being of Constance Markievicz and Kathleen Clarke, both still imprisoned. She and other members of the Franchise League attempted to organise a campaign on their behalf but were quickly left in no doubt that they had gone beyond the boundaries of what was permitted in terms of solidarity. The women were first and foremost nationalists, not women prisoners. It was therefore inappropriate to draw attention to their sex as a means of applying pressure for their release:

> Surely you do not think Cumann na mBan wants any incentive to agitate for release of Madame – Madame's own letter which I enclose, shows she wishes at all events consultation before she is detached from other prisoners in any effort to obtain her release. This I know for a long time and after my crossing with Mrs Clarke I realised fully that neither of them wished any special efforts made on their behalf as women. And resented keenly any special reference to them apart from the men. Whether we think this judgement is right or not, at all events we have got to abide by it.[106]

It was not easy for someone used to the relative freedom of a small women's group to accept the discipline required in a large political organisation. Hanna's dual membership and occasionally conflicting loyalties made for an uneasy relationship. She was also critical of the limited radical potential of Dáil Éireann, which in its desire to prove to the world that the Irish could be constructive and constitutional if given their own parliamentary machinery, had taken over the ceremonial trappings of the British system. In her capacity as editor of the *Irish Citizen* she congratulated the Dáil for its progressive action in appointing Constance Markievicz as Minister for Labour, while regretting that it had not 'cast off the whole system of British cabinet making and British parliamentary methods, a system that has strangled true democracy and is responsible for the present moribund condition of the doddering "Mother of Parliaments"'. She preferred the system adopted by 'progressive small nations' of the Scandinavian countries.[107] As Arthur Mitchell points out in his assessment of the revolutionary nature of the Dáil, some within Sinn Féin shared her views, but she was one of the most vocal.[108] Having the *Citizen* as a platform was a distinct advantage when minority views were being expressed. Of personal and political significance is the fact that those views belonged to the daughter of someone whose father had been a member of the British House of Commons for 32 years. She understood the parliamentary system and its limitations.

The need for more effective women speakers was acute. Hanna, frenetically busy though she was, could not be everywhere. Cumann na d'Teachtaire decided to ask her to organise classes for speakers as soon as possible. They also agreed to write to the executive of Sinn Féin, suggesting a list of women who could be put forward for the double seats that some male candidates now represented, one of which they would be required to vacate. The name Mrs Sheehy Skeffington was top of their list.[109]

Hanna remained on close terms with William O'Brien and other associates of the labour movement, a delegation of which was preparing to attend an International Labour Conference in Lausanne in January 1919. They wanted her to be one of the group, appreciating her command of languages and familiarity with the European mind. Since the execution of Connolly, Irish Labour was struggling hard to regain its position within the nationalist movement. A strong presence at Lausanne would demonstrate that it had a role to play on the international stage in the task of establishing the right of Ireland to be treated as a separate nation. The British authorities also were aware of Hanna's value as a propagandist. The Passport Office 'regretted' that she could not be issued with a passport.[110] Thwarted in their plans, before setting sail the Irish trade unionists were able to arrange for Hanna's presence at a Russian solidarity meeting in London's Albert Hall on 9 February. They were anxious to have an Irish speaker at that gathering of socialists and progressives. Belfast suffragist Elizabeth Priestly McCracken wrote to say how delighted she had been with the 'splendid reception' given to Hanna by the audience, although disappointed that the *Dreadnought* newspaper had not covered her speech.[111] Irish feminists also voted for Hanna as one of four delegates to the Congress of the Women's International League for Peace (shortly to be renamed the Women's International League for Peace and Freedom), being held in Zurich. Louie Bennett was able to go, and so were Lilian Wills and a Miss Rowlette from Sligo. The 25 members of the British delegation had no difficulties in attending. Once again, however, Hanna was refused a passport.[112]

As 1919 continued, the Irish Republican Army (as the Volunteers were now known) and the British forces began to engage in direct conflict. IRA raids on barracks for weapons and ammunition led to reprisals and to further republican attacks on police and army. What became known as the War of Independence had begun. Although the 'German Plot' prisoners were finally released in March 1919, the majority would not be free for long. Hanna continued as a diligent member of Sinn Féin. She was a member of the 'Scoil Eanna Committee' set up to ensure that there would be funds to maintain the school established by Patrick Pearse. That appealed to the teacher within her, just as it did to her republican principles. When Harry Boland (who had helped to organise de Valera's escape from jail), was sent to America to prepare the way for the Sinn Féin President's forthcoming tour, she became Boland's replacement on the Sinn Féin Standing Committee, a directorate of individuals elected from its executive *(ard-choile)*. On 6 May she was appointed Organising Secretary, responsible for ensuring that the local branches of Sinn Féin were running efficiently.[113] Michael Collins complained that the policy appeared 'to squeeze out anyone who is tainted with strong fighting ideas'. He disliked what he called 'a Standing Committee of malcontents' who were much too 'political and theoretical' and not militant enough for that soldier.[114] While de Valera was there, Collins felt himself to be marginalised within Sinn Féin'; that would soon change. From a feminist perspective, there were elements of Collins' personality Hanna disliked: 'He rather liked to shock and had the usual soldier's contempt of civilians, particularly of women, though these often risked their lives to help him.' In her opinion the Republic he visualised would have been 'a middle-class replica of an English state (certainly not ancient Gaelic Ireland) for he knew no other.'[115] Once the President was out of the way, the physical war against the British intensified. The first reports from the Organising Secretary show little trace of Hanna's influence. However, by 1921, the lengthy *Instructions to Sinn Féin Cumainn regarding Programme of Work 1921–22* bears her unmistakeable hallmark, as distinctive as a fingerprint:

> NOTE: An impression exists in some districts that membership of Cumainn is confined to men. This is a mistake and every effort should be made to secure that women shall not only be on the roll of members but take an active share in the work of Cumainn and the Sinn Féin movement generally.[116]

Hanna's most effective contribution to this bitterly fought war was her skill in publicising the republican message – an essential task as the Irish sought to isolate Britain amongst world opinion. The soldiers of the IRA engaged the enemy in the traditional way as their politicians and propagandists struggled to convey the reality of life for a people living in a country overrun by heavily armed troops, bristling with machine guns, military lorries and armoured cars. It was an exhausting schedule. As Hanna's political appeal crossed so many boundaries she had a particularly busy timetable. The Franchise League continued to organise its weekly programme of meetings. Sinn Féin, Cumann na mBan and the Transport Union all wanted her presence. So too did the various Irish solidarity movements across the water. For 1919, it was Limerick in January (organised by a former pupil from Eccles Street, Kitty Murphy, now married to Michael O'Callaghan), followed by Waterford, Cork, Dundalk and Galway. In February, the Socialist Party of Ireland sent her a membership form and an accompanying request for her to lecture for them in April. She was in London in February, followed in March by visits to both Glasgow and Liverpool. Margaret Skinnider, her old Glasgow friend, had invited Owen over as well, but he stayed at home. Hanna's memories of what could happen during travel to Britain meant that he had to be content with the gift of a cake from Margaret instead. She was glad 'sonny boy' liked it and hoped he was not made ill from eating too much.[117] The United Irish Societies of London wanted Mrs Sheehy Skeffington for 21 March, to speak at a mass meeting calling for the release of all Irish political prisoners and self-determination for Ireland. Several places hoped she could join them for St Patrick's Day events – and the requests kept pouring in. For the third anniversary of Frank's death she was in Carrick-on-Suir, speaking at a Cumann na mBan event. Rose Jacob, arranging to meet Hanna in Waterford, had immediately recognised the significance of the date: 'I'm glad they hit on that day for you, to keep you busy.'[118] The IWFL erected a flag in his honour outside their office, which stayed up throughout the Saturday and Sunday before police removed it on the Sunday night.[119] Time had not faded the memory.

Hanna appears to have been in a particularly combative mood throughout her first year back in Ireland. There were so many tensions, so many demands on her time, so many difficult memories to live through. Not surprisingly, she sometimes boiled over and unfortunate officialdom was a likely victim. The Dublin Tramways Company wrote an abject apology following her complaint about the behaviour of a conductor, 'regret the unpleasantness and inconvenience, hope she won't have occasion to complain again'.[120] She battled successfully with the censor over her pamphlet *Impressions of Sinn Féin in America*, after the exasperated printer finally suggested that Hanna should deal with the censor herself because he had made no headway on that front.[121] Royalties of £6-3-9 were paid out in 1920, a fairly substantial sum for a small pamphlet. By then her first pamphlet, *British Imperialism as I Have Known It*, had been reprinted three times.

In the meantime, the IWFL struggled to continue with activities which, while forming part of the general opposition to the British presence would, it was hoped, also bring a distinctively feminist voice into the political sphere. Hanna and Meg Connery worked with Maud Gonne MacBride and her associates (and with Cumann na mBan) on campaigns in support of various prisoners, bombarding the authorities for information on each occasion under-age children were arrested. They used the central location of the IWFL offices to great effect on several occasions, protesting the arrest of friends who had been speaking at socialist meetings in Beresford Place and countering a British 'peace day' with a large white flag on which they had painted black letters declaring 'Peace Morya!' They managed to be a small irritant in the heart of the city. Hanna's international links were often of great use. She, Meg Connery and Mary Bourke-Dowling (who had joined Cumann na mBan) were invited by Lawrence O'Neill, the Lord Mayor, to a reception in the Mansion House, organised to welcome Irish-American delegates who were there to investigate conditions of life for people in Ireland. Jane Addams, the American feminist, was amongst the party. There were many occasions when memorials for peace and for the release of prisoners were addressed to international delegations. The names of Hanna Sheehy Skeffington and Maud Gonne MacBride were always prominent. Constance Markievicz would sign her name when she could, but for much of the time she was in prison. Meg Connery tended to work more closely with the labour people, Hanna with Sinn Féin. Together, they were a conduit for various differing interests. Gretta Cousins phrased it well in a letter written in November 1919: 'Must write to Meg – what a dear she is and what a specially hard path you two are treading as non-militarist non-masculine ardent nationalists.'[122]

By September 1919 Dáil Éireann had been declared a dangerous association, its ministers were on the run and forced to conduct business underground. All nationalist organisations were outlawed in October. With the coming of 1920 came martial law, curfews, further arrests, night raids and the constant fear of reprisals from the terrifying forces brought in by the British to subdue the population – the Black and Tans and the Auxiliaries – battle-hardened men who revelled in a total lack of discipline, knowing that their superiors would do nothing to deprive them of their enjoyment of their sadistic terror tactics. Hanna tried to describe the reality of life at home during one of her countless speeches to a British audience. Speaking in Bermondsey she declared that the Black and Tans were 'war-wrecks, men with shattered nerves … drugged with drink', sent 'to create terror' in Ireland. She wanted to emphasise the consequences if the British people did not fight to have that army of occupation withdrawn from Ireland and the legitimate government of the Irish people recognised; the conflict would end only with the extermination of the Irish people.[123] The British Directorate of Intelligence kept a close watch on such meetings, its agents dismissive of the 'propaganda' put forward: 'Mrs Sheehy Skeffington gave her usual account of appalling outrages alleged to have been committed by the servants of the Government.'[124] The tone might have been different if they had visited Ireland. Amongst her papers is a draft of a letter to a newspaper in which she refers to the 'detestable outrage by Black and Tans in cutting off the hair of Republican girls by way of "reprisals"'.[125] She also compiled a lengthy

'Statement of atrocities on women in Ireland', which included items on the terrorism of women relatives of Sinn Féin members; the 'wanton terrorism of young mothers'; the murder of children; arrests of women and cases of sexual assault perpetrated against women, although she added 'cases of this kind very difficult to verify as victims shamed and terrified.' The evidence was compiled from press reports, information gathered by IWFL members, the Dáil propaganda bureau and her own observations.[126]

As the conflict intensified it took courage to maintain one's political commitments. On 10 August 1919 she defied the police to speak at a meeting in Kilbeggan, County Westmeath. The meeting had not been banned, nevertheless the local district inspector announced that if Mrs Sheehy Skeffington spoke the proceedings would be broken up by police and military. Sixty soldiers were drafted into a town containing a population of only a few hundred. Sinn Féin decided against holding the meeting but later in the evening attempted to defy the police by assembling at the market square. Hanna stood up on a makeshift platform supported by barrels and began to speak of America and the help that the League of Nations could give to Ireland. Twenty armed policemen rushed towards her and demolished the platform. Hanna and McGuinness, the Sinn Féin organiser, were flung to the ground. As she recounted the incident in a long letter to historian Alice Stopford-Green, the police 'swung carbines like hockey sticks' and she was struck twice from behind, on the shoulder and ear and then on the side of her head. McGuinness was arrested but escaped in the crowd while she was saved from arrest by the crowd pushing her into an open door where a priest was standing. She suffered concussion and 'septic poisoning' from her wounds. The press censor suppressed all mention of the attack on the grounds 'it would be likely to cause disaffection towards the police force and to create sedition'.[127] However, the underground republican journal, the *Irish Bulletin*, wrote about the incident and plenty of friends heard all about it. From Cork Jail Constance Markievicz wrote to her sister Eva: 'Mrs Skeffington has been awfully knocked about. She interfered with the police who continued to hammer an unconscious man with clubbed rifles and she was clubbed over the head. She lost a lot of blood and will have to keep quiet for a bit.'[128] Censorship meant that only the briefest of comments could be permitted in the *Citizen*. The editor announced she had been 'incapacitated for several weeks' after being struck by the butt end of police carbines. She hoped readers would forgive any editorial shortcomings.[129] It was enough information for Gretta: 'my blood boiled to hear you had been bashed on the head after that meeting. Please God you are better now.'[130]

For a time, Belgrave Road was not a safe place to stay. The Christmas of 1919 saw her 'on the run'. Writing a card to Owen, Rose Jacob commented 'what a horrid way to spend xmas. It is too bad. I wonder how long it will last.'[131] Kathleen Keevey, faithful worker for the IWFL (she had sold 500 copies of their paper at a meeting in late 1918) was very ill (the flu pandemic hitting hard) and worrying frantically for Hanna's welfare. In panic, Cissie Cahalan scrawled a hasty note to ask Hanna to pay a visit if at all possible: 'Just come from seeing poor Keevey. Greatly afraid she will not last long. She told me to ask you not to sleep in your own house. She is fretting about you. I told her you were as safe at home as anywhere else. Someone must have been talking to her of current events.'[132] Fortunately, unlike thousands of others, Keevey recovered.

Before falling ill, Keevey had written to urge Hanna to agree to allow her name to go forward in the forthcoming local government elections, 'I think you ought to go on as any other women's name mentioned tonight didn't seem to go down.'[133] The local government elections of January 1920 opened up a new range of possibilities for those who wanted a voice in planning for the needs of their community. There was still resistance to putting women forward but the fact that so many men were in jail, while others rejected the political path in favour of a military role within the IRA, gave a small number of women the opportunity to stand. The IWFL organised a 'model election' at their Tuesday evening meeting so that the Proportional Representation Society of Ireland could instruct members on the intricacies of proportional representation, particularly the importance of the transfer in getting minority groups elected.[134] Multi-candidate constituencies offered a much better hope of women being elected and most of the women who stood were elected. Altogether, 42 women were returned. Five women were elected to Dublin Corporation: Hanna, Jennie Wyse Power, Kathleen Clarke, Margaret McGarry and Anne Ashton. The IWFL claimed Mrs McGarry as a member (she had been on their executive in 1912-3), along with Hanna and Jennie Wyse Power. Rathmines was also good for women. There, six out of 21 councillors were female, amongst them Kathleen Lynn, Madeleine ffrench-Mullen, Mary Kettle and Aine Ceannt. A number of republican women became Poor Law Guardians and, in June, more women successfully contested the district council elections.[135] Constance Markievicz repaid those who had worked for her Dáil election by braving arrest through appearing on public platforms on their behalf:

> I spoke five times for various women in the elections and had some very narrow shaves. At one place I spoke for Joan, and they sent an army, just about an hour too late. At another, I wildly and blindly charged through a squad of armed police, sent

> there to arrest me, and the crowd swallowed me up and got me away. The children did the trick for me.[136]

This is the only documented occasion when she referred to Hanna by the old family name of 'Joan', an indication of how close the two women had now become.

Hanna had asked Louie Bennett before Christmas 1919 if she would take over the editorship of the *Citizen*, leaving Hanna 'just a corner of it'. Louie had said no, but after Hanna's election to Dublin Corporation, realising the additional workload this would create, she relented, but wanted to stipulate a number of conditions:

> How far would you tie me down on policy, or would you just trust me not to go against your principles? Would the IWFL, especially Miss Keevey and Miss Cahalan, still support and work for the paper (this is an important point) – could you hand it over free of debts?[137]

They had a meeting to discuss this, but Hanna remained as an editor. Louie was hopeful of being able to establish a good working relationship: 'You can pull me up whenever you like and I somehow do not fear serious disagreements with you. If it's left to the two of us we can compromise without trouble, I am sure, but there is always danger in numbers, don't you think?'[138] They were printing 2,000 copies an issue. In the circumstances and considering the numerous other demands on their time, this was a respectable figure. It had only printed 3,000 at the height of the suffrage campaign. In May 1919 the page size had finally increased from four to eight, but the difference now was that they were only publishing monthly. In March 1920 this became bi-monthly and finally quarterly. The next edition of the *Citizen* was sharp in its assessment of the election results: 'We do not think 5 in 80 members of Dublin City Council or 42 women throughout Ireland a "fair proportion of women" – which the *Irish Independent* declares.' Sinn Féin, 'the party of the majority', was commended for its 'good example' while all other parties were condemned for their tardiness in promoting women.[139]

An attempt to disqualify Hanna as councillor on the grounds of her employment as a part-time teacher in city technical schools was speedily defeated through the efforts of sympathetic legal advisors.[140] From around the world messages of congratulations poured in. Close friends from times past appreciated the significance of this. Mary Bourke-Dowling was sensitive in her reaction:

> Of course it was always a certainty. I am sure you value it all the more because it is a tribute to your husband as well as to you. I keep thinking how pleased he would be. Dublin has done its duty for *once*. I hope Mrs Kettle is in too.[141]

News of the elections was broadcast throughout the dispersed Irish community. From Chicopee, Massachusetts, Marietta Grady wrote of her delight at reading the result, 'First thing that met my eye Sunday coming home from church was your picture front page of *Boston America*.'[142] Sir Francis Vane hoped that the republican takeover of so many former British institutions would prove that 'government cannot be carried on without the concurrence of the people except by alien force'.[143] This was the challenge: to demonstrate Irish commitment to self-government through the complete transference of all institutions from British to Irish control. There was, in addition, the possibility that real changes to peoples' lives could be made by those now presenting themselves for service in council chambers around the country.

The duties of a councillor began as soon as the votes were counted. Hanna was informed by the Town Clerk's office that the Cleansing Committee was due to meet at 12 noon on 18 January 1920. She was also a member of the Technical Education Committee and the chair of the Public Libraries Committee. She quickly began to undertake the necessary research to help her effectiveness in her new public role. The unequal position of female local government employees was one of the first areas on which she focused attention. All the town councils were written to and asked for the numbers of women they employed as clerical workers, what their pay scales were and whether or not they were eligible for promotion.[144] This enforced scrutiny of employment practices had results. Hanna later received letters from women thanking her for having improved their access to different jobs. She was appointed corporation representative for Cheeveston Convalescent Home, where working conditions of staff were again an important issue. After she was appointed to the Finance and General Purposes Committee in 1921 she became involved in promoting the 'Orion' system of building corporation houses, the first completed set of buildings being officially opened in Clontarf in July.[145] As Kathleen Clarke said, 'Meetings were held every day, nearly every hour, all having the one purpose, doing the work of the Corporation and upholding the Republic.' This was despite attempts at intimidation, including a raid by the Black and Tans during one meeting of the council. They grabbed hold of the roll-book and called the names of members. No one answered but anyone whose face betrayed the slightest flicker was pounced upon and arrested.[146] The public visibility of elected officials made them easy targets for the enemy. Some were shot in cold blood by the Tans, amongst them Michael O'Callaghan, a former Mayor of Limerick, who was killed in front of his wife Kitty. As a widowed woman, she became a public figure, Kate O'Callaghan, when elected to the Second Dáil. She was an outspoken advocate of women's interests during the difficult days of debate over the Treaty.

Hanna felt strongly that, despite the pressures upon them, republicans had a duty to participate in local government. In 1925, battling against the Cumann na nGaedheal government, she continued to insist upon the need for 'fearless and independent critics … such a group, even in a minority, can achieve much and can form a strong bulwark against further onslaughts upon democratic control'. In itemising the achievements of that first republican council, she was pleased to recall that they had raised workers' wages, planned for a pension scheme, appointed a Food and Drugs Inspector to inspect the quality of milk in the city and set out a scheme for child welfare so that children of school age would have regular health checks.[147] All these plans, which women like Kathleen Lynn knew from her experience as a doctor were essential reforms for the inhabitants of the capital, were to be rejected once the Free State was a reality. Then, fiscal responsibility and economic orthodoxy were the priorities and social responsibilities set aside. But now, for a short time, the radical republicans worked hard to organise for a different society. Sinn Féin, in further defiance of the British, established their own system of justice. If a woman had a case heard by the court, then a woman was appointed to serve as judge. Hanna joined many women in taking part in these underground courts, where again those with views on social justice and a fair society attempted to put them into practice. Her area was South City Dublin. They met sometimes in York Street working men's club, sometimes in Hatch Street Hall, where Court Laundry had its business. Tenant/landlord disputes, petty theft, minor assaults and marriage disputes were the most common cases, and agreement often reached by consensus. Hanna remembered hearing 'lorries of tans flashing by in the street outside' as they met, but they were never given away to the authorities.[148] By June 1920 the Dáil had set up a whole system of civil and criminal courts and lawyers bowed to the inevitable and took their cases to them.

In July 1920 Hanna and Owen, together with Mary and Betty, took a summer holiday in the Isle of Man. She wrote to friends of feeling much better for the rest. Then the relentless round of meetings began all over again. Rose Jacob wondered if she was ever at home these days. Complicated arrangements for picking up Owen and collecting him had often to be made. Miss Tuckey gave up the Rathgar school in 1919 and after that time Owen attended a variety of experimental schools before ending up in Sandford Park.

House raids were a constant hazard. Those on the run looked for shelter from sympathetic colleagues and friends. The penalties for harbouring those on the wanted list ranged from imprisonment to having one's house burned down. That happened to the Dalys in Limerick – Kathleen Clarke's family home. The military and Black and Tans left the house a smashed and empty shell after taking out the entire contents to be burnt. Kathleen's mother, 80-year-old aunt and three sisters were left homeless, unwilling to seek shelter with anyone in case they brought trouble onto those who helped them.[149] As the population closed ranks against the British intruders even old women could be considered subversive. There was, indeed, much that they did to help, from hiding IRA volunteers to secreting outlawed copies of the *Irish Bulletin*, the propaganda broadsheet that was doing so much to let the world know about the atrocities perpetrated by the British. So damaging was the paper to British interests that they instituted a full-scale hunt for printing press and workers, who were constantly on the move, always one step ahead. The raid upon Hanna's home in October was simply a fact of life. It did not have the added dimension of terror that people experienced on the occasions when the Black and Tans were involved:

> At one o'clock in the morning, the residence of Mrs Sheehy Skeffington TC, 7 Belgrave Road, was entered by military accompanied by two officers of the district military police. They remained two hours, and searched even the nursery, the garden, and the pockets of Mrs Skeffington's dressing gown. Match boxes were also inspected. They appeared most anxious to discover addresses only one of which they found – that of Mrs Skeffington's charwoman. They removed copies of the *Irish Bulletin*, some American literature, and some manuscript. The officers were courteous and expressed dislike for their task.[150]

The *Citizen* was not the thorn in the flesh of the authorities in the manner of the overtly propagandist *Bulletin*. However, even a report of the success of the general strike of 13 April 1920, aimed at forcing the government into making concessions on prisoners' conditions, which praised 'the common people of Ireland [who] have never failed in their whole-hearted support of the cause of freedom' was sufficient challenge.[151] The *Citizen* would not be allowed to continue indefinitely. Louie Bennett had hopes of turning the paper into a journal for the Irish Women Workers' Union. Her political views caused considerable friction between herself and Hanna and the hoped-for harmony soon disappeared. Louie became more insistent on the need to make fundamental changes. She could 'understand the many objections your former readers may have to our particular line of stuff, but as I clearly explained to you changes will have to be made if I am to increase sales'.[152]

News from Denmark House, headquarters of the Irish Women Workers' Union, dominated the paper for most of 1920, although Hanna was still named as editor. She was reluctant to relinquish control of something that had been so great a part of her life but must have recognised that she did not have the time to devote to the work. Kathleen Keevey and Cissie Cahalan were tireless in their efforts on the administrative side, but here too Louie had complaints on their going 'beyond her resources' in having new circulars printed. It was agreed that the summer issue would appear without any further changes while it was decided what could be done to secure new readership. Fundamentally, the labour woman wanted to ensure that the political orientation of the paper was far removed from nationalism - 'we must do something about the Irish Heading' - was one comment.[153] She also had less scruples about ignoring some of the editorial principles that had characterised the *Citizen* since Frank had put his distinctive style on the paper. Carrying an article that urged people to smoke Irish rather than Imperial tobacco would help to save jobs in the Irish industry and was not, she argued, the same as carrying advertisements encouraging people to smoke.[154] A lively correspondence had followed Meg Connery's spirited response to an article extolling the virtues of looking after the home, – 'Smiling or frowning homes'[155] – but some former members of the IWFL were unenthusiastic about seeing the paper continue. The normally supportive Deborah Webb was blunt in her objections. She would not take out a subscription. It would be better to promote women's causes by writing to papers with large circulations instead of trying to keep up a paper through such difficult times: 'There are so many claims on our sympathy and purse.'[156] Debt was increasing. Ernest Manico, printer of the *Citizen*, sent a polite note for the attention of the treasurer, indicating that their bill was over £60 and 'still mounting.'[157] None of these setbacks weakened Hanna's sense of the importance of the paper and her absolute conviction that its continued existence was essential for women. It had not become an outlet for women workers 'because we feel we ought to be the organ of all women, not of the few.'

In the September 1920 edition she made an emotional plea to women's loyalties:

> Since 1912, that is for eight long and difficult years half the time being consumed in a world war, the *Irish Citizen* has championed the cause of women's emancipation ... In Ireland at the present crisis, we are in a state of war, and all the conditions prevailing in other countries during the late European War now apply at home. Just as then the woman's movement merged into the national movement, temporarily at least, and women became patriots rather than feminists, and heroes' wives

> or widows, rather than human beings, so now in Ireland the national struggle overshadows all else … Meanwhile we can but mark time. There can be no woman's paper without a woman's movement, without earnest and serious-minded women readers and thinkers – these in Ireland have dwindled perceptively of late, partly owing to the cause above mentioned, and partly because since a measure, however limited, of suffrage has been granted, women are forging out their own destiny in practical fields of endeavour … We still believe that we have a mission and a message for Irishwomen as a purely feminist paper and emboldened in that belief we shall carry on. It will be for our readers and supporters to help us by an increase of their support so that when time and conditions permit, we may return to our former strength.[158]

We do not know if her strength of purpose could have prevailed since, not long after, the Black and Tans raided the printers and the *Irish Citizen* did not appear again. Hanna's notes contain a draft statement, handwritten in red ink, explaining what had happened:

> Owing to a raid by Crown forces upon our printer our entire copy for quarterly issue (December) has been seized and taken away. We are consequently reluctantly compelled temporarily to suspend publication but hope to resume when circumstances permit. Yours faithfully (*HSS – crossed out*), Editor[159]

When Manico's was asked later that month when the *Citizen* was likely to appear next, they could give 'no definite information'.[160] Ernest Manico wrote to Cissie Cahalan in July 1921, complaining that as she had ignored two previous requests for settlement of their account he would be putting the matter into the hands of 'Messrs. Stubbs' for collection. Annoyed, Cahalan scribbled a note to Hanna at the bottom of the letter, 'Isn't he a nice old Shylock. I'm thinking of writing & telling him to do his best shall I. I have nearly £5.0.0 & grudge to give it to him.'[161]

Irish republicans worked hard on convincing their allies of the importance of keeping up pressure on the government. For this, Hanna's former suffrage ties came in useful. American feminism gave considerable support to Ireland at this time. Hanna sent a telegram to leaders of the women who were picketing the White House on Ireland's behalf: 'Will the newly enfranchised American women show their love of freedom and justice by asking their government to prove its good faith to the democracies of the world by stopping the murder of Mayor MacSwiney?' In response, the women sent a delegation to talk to Secretary of State Colby, as well as sending pickets to a number of other sites, including the New York docks.[162] Jane Addams became a member of the American Commission on Conditions in Ireland during 1920-1, hearing from witnesses regarding atrocities committed during the

War of Independence, one of the few sources to provide evidence of crimes committed against women.[163] In October 1920 ten members of the Women's International League for Peace and Freedom, headed by Helena Swanwick and Ellen Wilkinson, concluded that the British were governing only 'by force and fraud'.[164] In early December Hanna spoke in London at a meeting organised by the Fellowship of Reconciliation, seconding Fred Pethick-Lawrence, who had proposed the following resolution. The Fellowship:

> records its horror at the policy of coercion and reprisals at present being pursued by government in Ireland and calls upon the government to make this possible by the immediate withdrawal from Ireland of the armed forces of the crown and the leaving to a free people the determination of their own destiny.[165]

Each such statement was significant, building up an inexorable pressure for some kind of truce to bring an end to the cycle of violence. The energetic work in encouraging recruitment into the different Irish solidarity organisations was having some result. The Americans had formed a Committee for Relief in Ireland and were sending over thousands of pounds in aid. The outcome of this was the formation of the Irish White Cross to organise the distribution of those funds. Hanna was appointed to its executive committee, together with six other women, including her sister Mary, Maud Gonne MacBride and Kathleen Clarke. Would there ever be a limit to their workload?[166]

Her Christmas list for 1920, scrawled on the back of an envelope, revealed unconscious emotional priorities: perfume for Mary, a brooch for Meg Connery, a necklace for Kathleen and a card for Margaret. She couldn't decide what to get for the 'boy' (Owen), whose name, with Mary's, headed the piece of paper. Her nephews and nieces – Garry, Patricia, Frank and Peggy Culhane, Betty Kettle, Conor Cruise O'Brien and Dick's daughter Frances – were marked down to receive the usual small gifts of sweets, plasticine, calendar and diary, etc. Only then was her father's name included.[167] Around this time Margaret who, to outward appearances seemed the one Sheehy daughter to have accepted the conventions of the day, astonished her family by falling in love with a Michael Casey, a young man (and a poet) who also happened to be a godson of hers. When Margaret became pregnant the families of both sides persuaded them to marry and emigrate to Canada, thereby easing their considerable embarrassment.[168] They took only Garry, the oldest of the Culhane children with them. The other three remained in Dublin, looked after by the highly disapproving Culhanes. Their son Ronan O'Casey was born in Montreal in August 1922.

1920 was a bad year, and it ended in utter chaos. Whole towns were being sacked and burnt by the British forces in reprisal for the IRA shooting of police and military. Martial law covered much of the country and pressure for the British to open up negotiations with Sinn Féin increased. Their response was to introduce the Government of Ireland Act, which partitioned the country and provided for two separate parliaments – one in the north and one in the south – both under the control of Westminster. Elections to the two parliaments were called for May 1921. Sinn Féin decided to contest the southern elections, while ignoring the provisions of the Act by treating the venture as nothing more than an election to a Second Dáil. This time five more women were elected: Kathleen Clarke, Margaret Pearse, Kate O'Callaghan, Ada English and Mary MacSwiney. Hanna did not stand.

In June 1921 Hanna and Meg Connery (representing the IWFL) and Helen Chenevix and Miss Whitty (the Women's International League) united as the Irish Women's Deputation to the Dominion Premiers. They went to London with the intention of persuading the Premiers who had assembled in London for an Imperial Conference to visit Ireland in order to see for themselves the atrocities that had been described in the report of the White Cross. They had already ensured the political position of the League was clearly understood when they provided a strong condemnation of government policy to the American Commission: 'the responsibility for the bloodshed and violence in Ireland rests upon the British Government, which refuses to allow Ireland the indefeasible right of all nations to freedom, out-laws her duly elected Parliament, and persistently attempts to rule the people by force'.[169] Sinn Féin, as a proscribed organisation, was unable to send anyone in an official capacity, so the women's initiative was an ingenious contriving. They were described by one newspaper as 'unofficial ambassadors of the Irish Republic.'[170]

Not all the delegates were republican, but all agreed in their denunciation of the actions of the British forces in Ireland. Hanna explained to the media: 'We gather from some of their entourage that they seem to have had plenty of opportunity of hearing the anti-Sinn Féin side of the case. We thought the women's side of the case would have appealed to them particularly because it is now stated that large concentration camps are to be got ready for the women as well as the men as the result of the intended drive by the Government.' It was a deliberate move to revive memories of the British tactics during the Boer War, but General Smuts, Prime Minister of South Africa, responded that there would be 'no advantage gained by reception of the deputation'. He added: 'Dominion Premiers will no doubt, when an opportunity presents itself, tender such advice to H. M.'s Government as they think fit, and in view of this I do not propose to meet any association connected with the present political affairs in Ireland to discuss the matter.'[171]

Perhaps it was a delegation of women he objected to, as he did then visit Ireland, meeting de Valera and suggesting Dominion status for Ireland as a compromise solution. The Prime Minister of New Zealand met with them and the Women's International League (the name of the British section of the Women's International League for Peace and Freedom), organised an 'At Home' so that members could hear at first hand from members of the deputation.[172] Sir John Simon, who had chaired the inquiry into the murder of Frank, wrote to Meg to apologise for being too busy to meet, but he asked for a memorandum on their findings, and suggested that they also contact the Peace with Ireland Council, near Westminster, with which he kept in touch.[173]

The British Labour Party had organised a fact-finding expedition to Ireland, condemning the horrors they discovered and calling for immediate British withdrawal. Joe Devlin MP, one of the few surviving members of the Irish Party, was Hanna's link with officialdom. They had had their disagreements, but he had been a suffrage supporter and was only too happy to meet them and to host a tea in Westminster.[174] She used her contacts to the best of her ability, and the women stressed the humanitarian cost of the war to anyone who would listen. Hanna was one of a number of people to help Emmeline Pethick-Lawrence, increasingly concerned about reports of Black and Tan atrocities, make a clandestine visit to Ireland in order to gather evidence. Pethick-Lawrence had collected a number of sworn statements from victims, including a woman threatened with rape, whose house was burnt and wrecked after she reported the matter, and a married woman forcibly raped, whose husband had fought on the British side in the Boer War and who now demanded reparation.[175] Evelyn Sharp, editor of *Votes for Women* and a former WSPU militant who had joined the Women's International League, later apologised for not meeting Hanna at this time – she had had a breakdown and was in the country, part of her condition caused by the 'cumulative shame of being an Englishwoman with Ireland in its present condition.'[176] It was increasingly evident that the war of attrition could not go on. There had to be negotiations. General Macready arrived at the Mansion House on 8 July to negotiate terms with Sinn Féin. On 11 July, a truce was called.

NOTES

1 *Irish Citizen*, Mar. 1918, reprinted article from the *San Francisco Leader*.

2 C. Desmond, Greaves, *Liam Mellows and the Irish Revolution* (London, 1971), p. 120.

3 *Gaelic American*, 3 Mar. 1917, quoted in Joanne Mooney Eichacker, *Irish Republican Women in America: Lecture Tours, 1916–1925* (Dublin, 2003), pp 90–1.

4 Hayden Talbot, *Michael Collins' Own Story* (London, 1923), p. 112.
5 Hanna Sheehy Skeffington, affidavit, 24 June 1918, Sheehy Skeffington MS (hereafter SS MS) 24,102.
6 Hanna Sheehy Skeffington, 'My trip home again', July-Aug. 1918, unpublished memoirs, in Margaret Ward, *Hanna Sheehy Skeffington: Suffragette and Sinn Féiner, Her Memoirs and Political Writings* (Dublin, 2017), p. 19.
7 Leah Levenson and Jerry H. Natterstad, *Hanna Sheehy Skeffington: Irish Feminist* (Syracuse, 1986), p. 108.
8 Kate Barry to Hanna Sheehy Skeffington, 16 July 1918, SS MS 24,102.
9 Kathleen Cruise O'Brien to Hanna Sheehy Skeffington, 18 July 1918, SS MS 24,102.
10 Elfreda Baker to Hanna Sheehy Skeffington, 3 Jan. 1919, SS MS 24,109.
11 Kathleen Cruise O'Brien to Hanna Sheehy Skeffington, 18 July 1918, SS MS 24,102.
12 John Dillon to Hanna Sheehy Skeffington, 17 July 1918, SS MS 24,102.
13 George Lansbury to Hanna Sheehy Skeffington, 18 July 1918, SS MS 24,102.
14 *Interview with Mrs Sheehy Skeffington*, n. d., (1918). Interview given to Dublin press, suppressed by English censor in Ireland, published as short pamphlet, IR 94109 P30, National Library of Ireland (hereafter NLI).
15 Bee Hotel bill, 10 July 1918, SS MS 24,102.
16 Hanna Sheehy Skeffington, 'My trip home again, 18–20'.
17 Talbot, *Michael Collins*, p. 113.
18 James King to Hanna Sheehy Skeffington, 17 Aug. 1918, SS MS 24,103.
19 Hanna Sheehy Skeffington, 'My trip home again', p. 22.
20 Report of meeting in United States Playhouse, 19 June 1918, Bureau of Investigation, US Department of Justice, National Archives, Washington DC.
21 Gretta Cousins to Hanna Sheehy Skeffington, 22 June 1918, SS MS 24,102,
22 Hanna Sheehy Skeffington, 'My trip home again', p. 20.
23 Ibid., pp 22–3.
24 Hanna Sheehy Skeffington to Michael Collins, n. d., (1919), SS MS 22,686.
25 Chief Commissioner Dublin Metropolitan Police, to Under Secretary, Dublin Castle, 3-9-18, C0904/169, Public Record Office, London.
26 *Irish Citizen*, Aug. 1918.
27 Hanna Sheehy Skeffington, 'My trip home again', pp 23–4.
28 Hanna Sheehy Skeffington to Constance Markievicz, 8 Aug. 1918, SS MS 41,178/23. The letter reached Markievicz, as the envelope had 'passed' written on it by the prison censor. Hanna must have asked for it to be returned to her, or she took it with her on release from Holloway; a wise decision as little of Markievicz's correspondence (other than that saved by Eva Gore-Booth) remains.
29 Countess Markievicz, *Prison Letters of Countess Markievicz* (London, 1934, reprinted London, 1987), p. 99.
30 Helen Little (ed.), *Revolutionary Woman: Kathleen Clarke, 1878-1972: An Autobiography* (Dublin, 1991), pp 222–3, p. 161.
31 Hanna Sheehy Skeffington, notes on Constance Markievicz, SS MS 24,189.
32 Little, *Revolutionary Woman*, p. 161.

33 She calls the hotel 'Tower' in her memoirs (or the typist could not read her sprawling handwriting), but the hotel bills, letters and telegrams to her are addressed to the Gower Hotel, where she and the family always stayed.
34 Hanna Sheehy Skeffington, 'My trip home again', pp 25–6.
35 Kathleen Cruise O'Brien to Hanna Sheehy Skeffington, 13 Aug. 1918, SS MS 24,103.
36 Mary Kettle to Hanna Sheehy Skeffington, n. d., SS MS 24,103.
37 Jennie Wyse Power to Hanna Sheehy Skeffington, 15 Aug. 1918, SS MS 24,103.
38 Seán MacBride to Hanna Sheehy Skeffington, 22 Aug. 1918, SS MS 24,103.
39 Patricia Lynch to Hanna Sheehy Skeffington, 16 Aug. 1918, SS MS 24,103.
40 Edward Shortt to Mary Kettle, 13 Aug. 1918, SS MS 24,103.
41 *Freeman's Journal*, 10 Aug. 1918.
42 Mary Kettle to Hanna Sheehy Skeffington, n. d., SS MS 24,104.
43 William O'Brien to Hanna Sheehy Skeffington, 16 Aug. 1918, SS MS 24,103.
44 John Dillon to Hanna Sheehy Skeffington, 17 July 1918. SS MS 24,102.
45 Hanna Sheehy Skeffington to John Dillon, 24 Aug. 1918, SS MS 24,103.
46 *Irish Citizen*, Aug. 1918.
47 Dorothy Evans to Hanna Sheehy Skeffington, n. d., SS MS 24,104.
48 *Irish Citizen*, Aug. 1918.
49 Elfreda Baker to Hanna Sheehy Skeffington, 19 Aug. 1918, SS MS 24,103.
50 William O'Brien to Hanna Sheehy Skeffington, 20 Aug. 1918, SS MS 24,103.
51 *Irish Citizen*, Sept. 1918.
52 Maurice Wilkins to Hanna Sheehy Skeffington, 11 Sept. 1918, SS MS 24,104.
53 Cathal O'Shannon to Hanna Sheehy Skeffington, 24 Sept. 1918, SS MS 24,104.
54 Margaret Pearse to Hanna Sheehy Skeffington, 21-8-19 18, SS MS 24,103.
55 Ibid.
56 Louise Gavan Duffy to Hanna Sheehy Skeffington, 22 Aug. 1918, SS MS 24,103.
57 'How suffrage stands in Ireland', in *Suffragist*, 30 Mar. 1918. This was an American journal, linked to the National Woman's Party.
58 Hanna Sheehy Skeffington, '1918-Treaty', in Ward, *Hanna Sheehy Skeffington*, p. 27.
59 M. Kennedy, Secretary, MacDonagh Sinn Féin Club, to Hanna Sheehy Skeffington, 12 Sept. 1918, SS MS 24,104.
60 Cumann na mBan, 9 Aug. 1918, SS MS 24,103.
61 See minutes of League of Women Delegates (Cumann na dTeachtaire), 20 Sept. 1917, SS MS 21,194.
62 *Thom's Dublin Directory* for 1918 and 1919.
63 Information from owner of 7 Belgrave Road, visited by author in 1995.
64 Hanna to Mary Kettle, Thursday, Thomas Kettle papers LA34/59, University College Dublin Archives (hereafter UCDA).
65 Prim Bros. to Hanna Sheehy Skeffington, 4 Oct. 1918, SS MS 24,105.
66 Countess Plunkett to Hanna Sheehy Skeffington, 14 Jan. 1919, SS MS 24,109.
67 HSS to Alice Park, 23 Jan. 1919, Alice Park Collection, Hoover Institution Archives, Stanford, California.
68 R. M. Fox, *Rebel Irishwomen* (Dublin, 1935), p. 73.
69 Information on Belgrave Road: Sheehy Skeffington family members and owner in 1995.

70 Fox, *Rebel Irishwomen*, p. 81.
71 Hanna Sheehy to Frank Skeffington (hereafter Hanna to Frank), 28 June 1908, SS MS 40,466/1.
72 Municipal Gallery of Modern Art to Hanna Sheehy Skeffington, 5 June 1930, SS MS 24,120.
73 *Thom's Dublin Directory*, 1919, 1920.
74 Daisy Lawrenson Swanton, *Emerging from the Shadow* (Dublin, 1994), p. 92.
75 *Irish World*, 9 July 1932, address of 'John Brennan' listed in public tribute to Maud Gonne MacBride.
76 Committee for Protection of Ireland from Venereal Disease, Secretary, Madeleine ffrench Mullen, 27 Aug. 1918, SS MS 22,682.
77 Women's Commemoration and Celebration Committee, *Ten Dublin Women* (Dublin, 1991), p. 64.
78 Hanna Sheehy Skeffington to Joe McGarrity, 1 May 1919, McGarrity Papers MS 17,638, NLI.
79 Maud Gonne MacBride to Ethel Mannin, n. d., Mannin Papers MS 17,875, NLI.
80 Information on Owen's White Cross grant, Andrée Sheehy-Skeffington, personal interview, Mar. 1992. For further information on the White Cross, see Aine Ceannt, *Irish White Cross 1920–1947* (Dublin, n. d.).
81 Irish White Cross, 4 Dec. 1926, SS MS 24,119.
82 Andrée Sheehy Skeffington, *Skeff: A Life of Owen Sheehy Skeffington* (Dublin, 1991), p. 20.
83 Leeann Lane, *Rosamond Jacob: Third Person Singular* (Dublin, 2010), p. 141.
84 *Irish Citizen*, Sept. 1919.
85 F. V. Quinn, Dungannon, to Hanna Sheehy Skeffington, 27 July 1920 and 6 Dec. 1920, SS MS 41,178/23. Hanna's papers include reference to repairs on the monument.
86 Technical Education Committee to Hanna Sheehy Skeffington, 3 Mar. 1919, SS MS 22,687.
87 Maud Gonne MacBride to Hanna Sheehy Skeffington, 9 Nov. 1918, SS MS 22,684.
88 Gretta Cousins to Hanna Sheehy Skeffington, 29 Oct. 1918, SS MS 22,682.
89 Rose Jacob to Hanna Sheehy Skeffington, n. d., SS MS 24,108.
90 J. Lawless, Director of Elections, Seán Connolly Sinn Féin Club, 22 Nov. 1918, SS MS 24,106.
91 Walsh, Sinn Féin headquarters, 27 Nov. 1918; O'Mara to Hanna Sheehy Skeffington, 27 Nov. 1918, SS MS 22,684.
92 Aine Ceannt to Hanna Sheehy Skeffington, n. d., SS MS 24,108.
93 Meg Connery to Hanna Sheehy Skeffington, 1918, SS MS 22,684.
94 Moirin Chavasse to Hanna Sheehy Skeffington, n. d., SS MS 22,685.
95 Clarke, *Revolutionary Woman*, p. 164.
96 Constance Markievicz to Eva Gore-Booth, 30 Jan. 1919, in *Prison Letters*, p. 192.
97 Hanna Sheehy Skeffington to Nancy Wyse Power, 1919, SS MS 22,697.
98 Constance Markievicz to Hanna Sheehy Skeffington, 12 Dec. 1918, SS MS 22,696, printed in *Irish Citizen*, Jan. 1919.
99 *Irish Citizen*, Jan. 1919.
100 Ibid., Dec. 1918.

101 Ibid., Jan. 1919.
102 Hanna Sheehy Skeffington to Alice Park, 23 Jan. 1919, Alice Park Collection, Hoover Institution Archives, Stanford, California.
103 *Irish Citizen*, Jan. 1919.
104 Harry Boland to Irish Women's Franchise League, 23 Dec. 1918, SS MS 24,107.
105 Patrick O'Donnell, Sinn Féin, Rathfarnham to Hanna Sheehy Skeffington, 29 Dec. 1918, SS MS 24,107.
106 Jennie Wyse Power to Hanna Sheehy Skeffington, 1 Mar. 1919, SS MS 22,689.
107 *Irish Citizen*, May 1919.
108 Arthur Mitchell, *Revolutionary Government in Ireland* (Dublin, 1995), p. 46.
109 Cumann na dTeachtaire, minutes of 30 Jan. 1919, SS MS 21,194.
110 William O'Brien to Hanna Sheehy Skeffington, 24 Jan. 1919; passport office 27 Jan. 1919, SS MS 22,686.
111 Elizabeth Priestly McCracken to Hanna Sheehy Skeffington, 20 Feb. 1919, SS MS 22,686.
112 Visa application by Hanna Sheehy Skeffington, correspondence with Louie Bennett, 2 May 1919, SS MS 22,688.
113 Sinn Féin to Hanna Sheehy Skeffington, 8 May 1919, SS MS 22,688; see also report of Hon. Sec Seán T. O'Kelly and Hanna Sheehy Skeffington to Sinn Féin Ard Fheis, 16 Oct. 1919, pamphlet, P 2383, NLI.
114 T. Ryle Dwyer, *Éamon de Valera* (Dublin, 1980), p. 30.
115 Hanna Sheehy Skeffington, 'My trip home again, p. 23.
116 Sinn Féin: Instructions to Sinn Féin Cumainn regarding programme of work 1921–22, pamphlet P 2272, NLI.
117 Margaret Skinnider to Hanna Sheehy Skeffington, 24 Feb. 1919, SS MS 22,686.
118 Rose Jacob to Hanna Sheehy Skeffington, 25 Apr. 1919, SS MS 22,687.
119 *Irish Citizen*, May 1919.
120 Dublin Tramways Company to Hanna Sheehy Skeffington, 29 May 1919, SS MS 22,688.
121 Davis Publishing Company to Hanna Sheehy Skeffington, 10 Jan. 1919 and 31 Jan. 1919; SS MS 22,686; Davis Publishing Company 21 July 1920 on royalty payment, SS MS 22,691.
122 Gretta Cousins to Hanna Sheehy Skeffington, 4 Nov. 1919, SS MS 22,688.
123 Levenson and Natterstad, *Hanna Sheehy Skeffington*, p. 135.
124 Intelligence report, cabinet minutes 24 Feb. 1921, Cab 24/120, PRO, London, with thanks to Liz Curtis for the reference.
125 Hanna Sheehy Skeffington, one-page fragment, 'Dear Sir…n. d., SS MS 24,134.
126 'Statement of atrocities on women in Ireland, made and signed by Mrs Hanna Sheehy Skeffington', n. d. (1920), in Ward, *Hanna Sheehy Skeffington*, pp 182–6.
127 Hanna Sheehy Skeffington to Alice Stopford Green, 16 Sept. 1919, Stopford Green Papers, MS 10,919, NLI.
128 *Irish Bulletin*, 12 Aug. 1919; Constance Markievicz to Eva Gore-Booth, 14 Aug. 1919, in *Prison Letters*, p. 237.
129 *Irish Citizen*, Sept. 1919.
130 Gretta Cousins to Hanna Sheehy Skeffington, 4 Nov. 1919, SS MS 22,688.

131 Rose Jacob, 23 Dec. 1919, SS MS 22,688.
132 Cissie Cahalan to Hanna Sheehy Skeffington, n. d., SS MS 22,697.
133 Kathleen Keevey to Hanna Sheehy Skeffington, 19 Nov. 1919, SS MS 22,688.
134 *Irish Citizen*, IWFL annual report, Mar./Apr. 1920.
135 Electoral results, *Freeman's Journal*, 14, 16, 18 June 1920; *Thom's Directory* 1922.
136 Constance Markievicz, 'on the run', n. d., in *Prison Letters*, p. 216.
137 Louie Bennett to Hanna Sheehy Skeffington, 18 Jan. 1920, SS MS 41,177/13.
138 Ibid., 5 Mar. 1920, SS MS 22,690.
139 *Irish Citizen*, Feb. 1920.
140 J. Donovan to Hanna Sheehy Skeffington, 2 Mar. 1920, SS MS 22,690.
141 M. Bourke-Dowling to Hanna Sheehy Skeffington, Jan. 1920, SS MS 22,690.
142 M. Grady to Hanna Sheehy Skeffington, 20 Jan. 1920, SS MS 22,690.
143 Sir Francis Vane to Hanna Sheehy Skeffington, 1 Oct. 1920, SS MS 22,652.
144 Correspondence to Hanna from Town Clerk, City Hall, Belfast and Town Hall, Limerick, in response to her queries on women employees, contained in SS MS 22,690.
145 Ryan Manufacturing Company, invitation to opening to Hanna Sheehy Skeffington, 7 July 1920, SS MS 22,691.
146 Clarke, *Revolutionary Woman*, p. 171.
147 *Irish World*, 4 July 1925.
148 Hanna Sheehy Skeffington, '1918-Treaty', in Ward, *Hanna Sheehy Skeffington*, p. 27.
149 Clarke, *Revolutionary Woman*, p. 186.
150 *Irish Independent*, 6 Oct. 1920.
151 *Irish Citizen*, Apr./May 1920.
152 Louie Bennett to Hanna Sheehy Skeffington, 1 July 1920, SS MS 22,691.
153 Ibid., 16 July 1920.
154 Ibid., 5 Mar. 1920, SS MS 22,690.
155 *Irish Citizen*, July/Aug. 1920.
156 Deborah Webb to Hanna Sheehy Skeffington, 9 June 1920, SS MS 22,691.
157 Ernest Manico to *Irish Citizen*, 13 Jan. 1920, SS MS 41,178/23.2
158 *Irish Citizen*, Sept./Dec. 1920.
159 Note written on *Irish Citizen* notepaper, 1 Dec. 1920, SS MS 41,178/23.
160 Letter to Hanna Sheehy Skeffington, asking for information on future publication, 21 Dec. 1920, SS MS 22,696.
161 Ernest Manico, 'The Temple Press to Miss Cahalan', in *Irish Citizen*, Educational Committee, 7 July 1921, SS MS 33,606/7.
162 Elizabeth McKillen, 'Reverse currents: Irish feminist and nationalist Hanna Sheehy Skeffington and U.S. anti-imperialism, 1916–24', in *Éire-Ireland*, 53: 3&4, fall/winter 2018, p. 174.
163 *The American Commission on Conditions in Ireland: Interim Report* (Chicago, 1921).
164 Information included in evidence given by Ellen Wilkinson, as representative of British Branch, Women's International League, to American Commission, 21 Dec. 1920, p. 620.
165 Report of meeting contained in letter from Paul Gliddon, sec. Fellowship of Reconciliation, to Hanna Sheehy Skeffington, 22 Dec. 1920, SS MS 22,696.
166 See Ceannt, *The Irish White Cross*.

167 SS MS 22,696.

168 Ronan O'Casey, telephone conversation with author, Sept. 1996.

169 Statement by the Irishwomen's International League, *American Commission on Conditions in Ireland*, Appendix B.

170 *The Bulletin*, 30 June 1921.

171 *Irish Independent* 27 June 1921.

172 Invitation from Catherine Marshall on behalf of the Women's International League, for an 'At home' 4–6 p. m. Monday 20 June, at 70 Overstrand Mansions, Battersea, to meet the members of the Irish Deputation to the Colonial Premiers, SS MS 33,606/4.

173 Sir John Simon to Meg Connery, 21 June 1921, SS MS 33,606/4.

174 Joe Devlin to Hanna Sheehy Skeffington 20 June 1921, SS MS 33,606/4.

175 Emmeline Pethick-Lawrence, *My Part in a Changing World* (London, 1938), pp 341–2.

176 Evelyn Sharp to Hanna Sheehy Skeffington, n. d. SS MS 33,606/4. Sharp had a long affair with Henry Nevinson, suffragist and socialist, who was a campaigning journalist and friend of the Sheehy Skeffingtons. They married shortly after the death of Nevinson's wife in 1933. An indication of the close ties between Irish and British radicals is the fact that when the homes of Hanna, Dr Kathleen Lynn, Kathleen Clarke and Mrs Coffey were raided on 7 Oct. 1920, the authorities found Nevinson in one house, see Greaves, *Liam Mellows*, p. 220.

ELEVEN

REPUBLICAN ENVOY, 1921–5

The British had released most of the leaders, it being impossible to negotiate without their presence, and General Macready promised that the 'better educated' would be let out soon. Hanna was not impressed. 'Miserable snob' was her response.[1] Constance Markievicz was one of those still in jail and Hanna was concerned that the sole woman in government, a person the British had often victimised, would be still in prison long after the others were released. Eva Gore-Booth was also concerned for her sister, and the two women discussed how they could intercede on her behalf. Hanna, mindful of past disagreements, realised that the campaign would have to be conducted with discretion: 'when our League tried that before, you know, we were snubbed by C. herself and told to stop! … I know she hates being treated as a woman so it ought to be as "Lab. Min."' Sydney Gifford Czira, pretending to be a typist in response to Constance's demand to be able to write a will (chosen presumably because she was unknown to the authorities, having recently returned from six years in America) reported back from Mountjoy that Constance was 'excited to get out and very eager about it.'[2] In another warm letter to Eva ('Of course I should love to call you "Eva" rather than "Miss" and am glad of the privilege') Hanna repeated her conviction, 'had she been a man, she would be out, but then she herself so hotly resents that imputation that it impedes our doing anything *qua* woman'. She had gone to de Valera and Griffith to find out if they had mentioned Constance to the British, to be told that all the prisoners should be released soon, if negotiations continued, and, she added to Eva: 'if they don't – well *nous recommencerons*!'[3]

Constance was released shortly afterwards, ecstatic in her freedom, 'It is so heavenly to be out again and to be able to shut and open doors ... Life is so wonderful. One just wanders round and enjoys it.' She had not yet adjusted to the fact that she was supposed to be a minister in a government, 'It is so funny, suddenly, to be a Government and supposed to be respectable! One has to laugh.'[4]

In the period of the truce, although busy organising Sinn Féin branches into properly functioning political groups, Hanna had grave reservations for the future. Peace alone was not enough, not after all the years of bloodshed and sacrifice. She could not share in the euphoria of the crowds cheering in the streets outside. Could discussions with the British provide a solution to all the problems Ireland had to deal with? De Valera had gone over to London to talk to Lloyd George. The only women accompanying him were typists and secretaries, which she supposed 'breaks the monotony' of the all-male presence, but which did not inspire her with faith in the democratic process. She wished Constance could have been included in these meetings, a woman whose integrity she respected. She was full of foreboding:

> there are many who would regard Peace short of Independence as a defeat – and in spite of my desire for Peace, I am one of these. It's a very difficult matter and one of responsibility either way. Of course, if the country votes Peace on a plebiscite there is nothing to be done but accept for the time being. And a lot depends on how the leaders put it. Democracy to many is only a name and people in masses do as they are told.[5]

Formal talks between the British and the Irish began in October 1921. On 6 December, after two months of intense negotiations, the Irish plenipotentiaries were worn out and outmanoeuvred. Arthur Griffith, Michael Collins and the other members of the team, under the threat of 'immediate and terrible war', signed the Articles of Agreement to an Anglo-Irish Treaty. There was to be no Irish Republic. Instead, Ireland was to have dominion status within the British Commonwealth. The British had used every resource at their disposal to ensure that the imperial connection would be maintained. Griffith had been persuaded into signing an undertaking agreeing to the north opting out of the arrangement, on the understanding that the unionists would take part in a Boundary Commission to settle the territory of what was to be 'Northern Ireland'. The Irish believed that the Boundary Commission would report that a separate self-governing entity was unworkable and impossible. The British, giving separate assurances to the unionists, knew that would not happen. The reality of partition was, through this sleight-of-hand, left to another day. But who was prepared to trust the assurances of the British Government? Hanna thought the whole situation was a 'queer jumble' which needed explaining. In a brief letter to Alice Park ('so that you know where I am') she treated the proposed solution with cynicism. It was a 'bad compromise' which she predicted would lead to 'some decades of reaction under a temporary false prosperity, reinforced by our native militarism'. Her fears were reinforced by seeing who was most vociferous in their support for the settlement: 'There is a regular stampede for it of all the moderates, and the 'safe' people with stakes in the country, of the press, and the clerics.'[6]

On 14 December Dáil Éireann began its debate. By 6 January 1922 a decision could be postponed no longer. A vote had to be taken. Amidst scenes of deep emotion and acrimonious exchanges the Treaty was ratified, with 64 votes in favour and 57 against. Éamon de Valera resigned as President of the Dáil, to be replaced by Arthur Griffith. Adding to the confusion, a provisional government, composed of the pro-Treaty TDs, under the chairmanship of Michael Collins, was now set up. Its task was to organise for the withdrawal of British forces while what was now known as the 'Irish Free State' came into existence.

R. M. Fox, collecting opinions for journalistic pieces, interviewed prominent people from both sides. It was his first meeting with Mrs Sheehy Skeffington, an experience he found disturbing, 'from no one did I get such a clear impression of implacability, of irreconcilable opposition to anything less than complete national independence.' He was puzzled. How could a woman who did not look like a fanatic, whose eyes had a twinkle, whose sense of humour was obvious, and whose soft voice 'conveyed the impression of a pleasant cultivated woman who was not likely to push matters to extremes' be 'so flintlike and unyielding?'[7] Hanna had made her feelings plain from the beginning. During the weeks while Dáil Éireann had continued its debate in the buildings used by University College Dublin, some of the younger members of Cumann na mBan, fearing the worst, decided to intervene. They knew that they had a reliable ally in 'Mrs Skeff'. Maire Comerford explained that they 'got a wild idea … that we would expose what was going on, by getting the Union Jack and putting it up over the debate in UCD'. To achieve this, they stole notepaper from the Sinn Féin office and, with Hanna's permission, typed a letter on the typewriter in the Franchise League office (conveniently located a short walk away from their target), then delivered the note round to the smart shops in Grafton Street, asking for the loan of their Union Jacks. The plot was discovered by the wife of W. T. Cosgrave while out buying herself a new dress in Switzers. It was also discovered that the demand had been typed on a machine known to be owned by Mrs Skeffington. Maire remembered her friend's steadfastness with admiration: 'she was great, they

IRISH REBELLION, MAY, 1916.

FRANCIS SHEEHY-SKEFFINGTON,

Arrested on Easter Monday, 1916, and Shot without trial at Portobello Barracks, April 26th.

21. Frank Sheehy Skeffington Memorial card, 1916.
Image courtesy of the NLI.

22. From left: Meg Connery, Mary Sheehy Kettle, Kathleen Sheehy O'Brien, Hanna Sheehy Skeffington, arriving for the court martial at Richmond Barracks, May 1916. Image courtesy of Library of Congress, Prints and Photographs Division (LC-B2-3962-9).

23. Hanna and Owen in New York, December 1916. Image courtesy of Library of Congress, Prints and Photographs Division (LC-B2-4085-15).

24. Maud Gonne in front of Women's Prisoners' Defence League banner. Image courtesy of the MacBride family.

25. Poster advertising Hanna as speaker for the Tom Mooney campaign, San Francisco, 1918. Image courtesy of the NLI.

26. The Sinn Féin Standing Committee, 21 February 1922. Hanna on extreme right front row. Also in front row: Kathleen Clarke and Dr Kathleen Lynn. Jennie Wyse Power is standing left in second row. Image courtesy of the NLI.

27. Irish Women's Mission to America, 1922. Front row, left to right: Linda Kearns, Hanna and Kathleen Boland. Image courtesy of the NLI.

28. Rosamond Jacob. Image courtesy of the NLI.

29. Owen Sheehy Skeffington in cricket clothes. Image courtesy of the NLI.

30. Mary Thygeson, American suffragist and friend, alongside Alice Park, and Hanna, outside Hotel de Nice, Paris, June 1926, attending the International Women's Suffrage Congress. Image courtesy of the NLI.

31. Hanna on far left with delegates from France, Germany, America, Canada and Belgium in Dresden, September 1929. **Image courtesy of the NLI.**

DROGHEDA'S EX-INTERNEES GREET MRS SHEEHY-SKEFFINGTON

An Ocean Liner of the Future. This interesting model by Norman Bel Geddes, an American engineer, will probably be the design of ocean liners of the future.

CIVIC RECEPTION TO MRS. SHEEHY-SKEFFINGTON by the Mayor and Corporation of Drogheda. (L. to R.) Ald. J. Dowd (Mayor), Mrs. Skeffington, Miss E. Coyle (Pres. Cum. na mBan) and members of the Corporation.

A view of the Square, Dundalk, during the Release Welcome Meeting to Mrs. Skeffington.

32. Coverage of Drogheda meeting of welcome, 1933, *Irish Press*, 22 February 1933. Image courtesy of the NLI.

33. Hanna in New York City on her last visit to America, 1938. Image courtesy of the NLI.

34. Dr Marie Equi, 1938. Image courtesy of the NLI.

35. Andrée Sheehy Skeffington. Image courtesy of the Sheehy Skeffington family.

36. Owen and Andrée Sheehy Skeffington, *c.*1968 at a rose show. Image courtesy of the Sheehy Skeffington family.

never got passed her. I remember that in particular. You know she'd never let you down. She was a wonderful woman.'[8]

There are a number of reasons why Hanna felt so strongly on the issue. They are rooted both in her personal tragedy and in her longstanding and deeply felt political opinions. She had encountered the duplicity of the British government at first hand while she struggled to discover the truth behind her husband's murder. That experience had left her with a deep distrust for its reassurances of honest intent. Dividing the country into two self-governing entities would create what she described as a 'crazy patchwork frontier'.[9] The Skeffington relatives in Belfast and County Down, with whom she and Owen were still in contact, would no longer be living in the same country as themselves. How could Irish people agree to this separation of kin? From every perspective the Treaty provisions were deeply flawed. Hanna's efforts in the months before the issue was finally put to the electorate were two-fold: to demand the right of all women to a voice on the issue and, when that was denied, to use this disenfranchisement as an indication of its undemocratic and fraudulent nature. She was convinced the majority of women were opposed to the Treaty, and in consequence 'there is great bitterness against us all just now'.[10] Most politicised women did appear to reject the Treaty, but there were some who welcomed it as Michael Collins did, as a stepping-stone to freedom. Within the Cumann na mBan executive Jennie Wyse Power was the woman they most regretted losing. She was also the person who tried hardest not to turn away from her old colleagues. The six women members of the Second Dáil all spoke strongly in the debate. Mrs Pearse's heart-felt response, based upon what she thought her sons Patrick and Willie would have decided, contrasted with Constance Markievicz's protest that the Treaty was designed to uphold the capitalists' interests in Ireland. And yet, was there a great difference between the arguments put forward by each woman? Despite their varying abilities as orators and thinkers (not all were as articulate or as long-winded in expressing their feelings as the formidable Mary MacSwiney), they looked forward to an Ireland where its citizens, male and female, would be free to contribute to society.[11] That hope underpinned each of their contributions. On 5 February, Cumann na mBan became the first organisation publicly to reject the Treaty. Members at its convention voted against by 419 votes to 63. Confronted with this evidence, those who supported the Treaty were beginning to find women a convenient scapegoat with which to categorise hard-line opinion.

The issue had still to be put to the electorate and the ramifications surrounding this proved to be as contentious as the Treaty itself. Who would be eligible to vote? The 1918 act passed by Westminster enabling women over

30 years of age to vote was still in force. This meant that women under 30 remained disenfranchised and the electoral registers were so completely out of date that most young men would not be able to vote. For many feminists, the denial of the vote to so many women was in itself sufficient reason to distrust the intentions of those who had taken over as government ministers. Hanna found it impossible to believe that Irishwomen would accept such a settlement under these terms. Marie Johnson, wife of labour leader Thomas Johnson and a former member of the short-lived Belfast branch of the IWFL, was one of the suffragists who took part in a deputation to the Dáil, witnessing Hanna's determination to 'let the leaders Griffith and Dev realise that there were women of intelligence in the country, (as) she with others formed a deputation and asked for an interview with each stressing the need for the consideration of women's views on the situation'. The outcome was unsatisfactory: 'Griffith was ungracious to the last degree, almost brutally so … Dev more suave, more inclined to placate, seized the chance to agree.'[12] Rose Jacob, that invaluable observer, described the internal politicking that went on before the delegation was agreed. Cumann na mBan had wanted to have their deputation 'all alone', with Constance Markievicz involved in heated argument with Meg Connery: 'C.na mb. feels that the IWFL disgraced itself in the past by asking votes from England – that made good ground-work for getting annoyed, as Mrs C. distinctly did.' In the end, the delegation consisted of a number of women's groups, with Rose Jacob included as a representative of the Women's International League. De Valera she described as civil but not helpful, while at the fraught interview with Griffith, 'the C. na mb. people & he getting cross & Hanna always amiable.'[13]

The partition of the country would be institutionalised; the British monarchy would still have a role in the Irish constitution, and any hoped-for transformation of Irish society under old Gaelic ideals of communality would be nothing more than a discarded utopian dream. It was a repetition of the old scenario of the Home Rule era: a proposal devised by men, now to be voted upon by an electorate dominated by men. For feminists, women's issues were firmly back on the agenda as the old suffragist methods were revived. Lobbies were organised, the IWFL sent letters to all TDs and, finally, women succeeded in having a motion on the issue introduced in the Dáil, handing out leaflets to deputies as they arrived to take part in the debate:

> 'Justice for Irish Women'
>
> The will of the people. Are Irishwomen under 30 people?
>
> British law says no. The Republican Proclamation says yes! What does Dáil Éireann say? A general election is at hand. The will of the whole Irish nation must

> be consulted on this issue. We demand government by consent. Women must vote in this election on the same terms as men.[14]

For a brief time, Hanna's spirits lifted: 'the fight for this absorbed all my energies and it seemed like old suffragette times again'. It is very likely that she was the guiding force behind Kate O'Callaghan's attempt to have the issue debated in the Dáil. This was, after all, the same 'Kitty Murphy' who had been her pupil at Eccles Street, and to whose branch of Cumann na mBan in Limerick she had willingly spoken during the War of Independence. Hanna was well-versed in the niceties of drawing up parliamentary legislation. She had experience of suffrage campaigning and the lobbying on the school meals issue to draw upon. Now, with the cooperation of her old pupil and friend, she was frantically busy in preparing this stand on behalf of the women of Ireland. The debate on the extension of the franchise to women between the ages of 21 and 30 finally took place on 2 March. In introducing her motion Kate O'Callaghan declared: 'I have the cause very much at heart. I was in a Suffrage Society ten years ago. It is not a measure or cause I am espousing today for Party purposes.' She based her plea upon the promise contained in the Proclamation of Easter Week. It was an eloquent appeal from a woman who had cradled her husband's body as he lay dying in their hallway, shot by the Black and Tans:

> I cannot believe that there is in this Parliament of the Irish Republic a single Deputy but holds with me that we ought now to remedy this injustice to a section of Irishwomen. During these last years of war and terror, these women in their twenties took their share in the dangers. They have purchased their right to the franchise and they have purchased their right to a say in this all-important question before the country. Without their votes or their voice, nobody can say that the will of the whole people of Ireland will have been ascertained.[15]

The bitterness that had been fomenting over the past two months was all too evident in the contributions to the debate. From the Provisional Government side came accusations that those who supported the women were attempting to 'torpedo' the Treaty. There was no admission that the principle of democracy should take precedence over some supposed threat by the British that the elections had to take place without unnecessary delay. Those who so abruptly dismissed that motion, although aware that it was being called for by women from outside as well as from inside the Dáil, had little sense of the depth of feeling the issue aroused. Constance Markievicz pleaded for justice to be done 'to these young women and young girls who took a man's part in the Terror', but supporters of the Free State regarded the issue as nothing more than a plot by their opponents. Jennie Wyse Power, despite her feminist sympathies, had refused to join the deputation to Griffith, on the ground only the Free State had the authority to change the franchise, and that had yet to be voted into power. She accused the feminists of inconsistency.[16] For his part, Griffith was brutal in his explanation of the rejection of the deputation:

> When this deputation of the various Societies was sent to me, knowing that they were sent – or most of them – not in enthusiasm for Woman Suffrage but in enthusiasm to destroy the Treaty, I told these ladies exactly what the position was. They were there representing certain bodies that wanted to queer the pitch of the Treaty. I told them then what I tell you now – that you are not going to queer the pitch of the Treaty. You are not going to get off on that false issue. You are not going to go out and pretend that we, on one side, are against Woman's Suffrage and that they on the other side, are for it.[17]

His premature death five months later lends credence to the explanation that ill-health was a contributing factor in this intemperate attack upon suffragists. However, Griffith realised that the younger generation, if permitted to vote, undoubtedly would have 'torpedoed' the Treaty, so lower blood pressure would not have altered his determination to resist. He was forced to promise that women would be given equal voting rights under the provisions of the constitution of the Free State (when that 'comes along') but he continued to maintain that the attitude of the campaigners was 'insincere'. The number of votes cast on each side reflected attitudes towards the Treaty. The motion was defeated by 47 to 38. 'For the present we are beaten', admitted Hanna. But she had not yet given up the fight. In a lengthy letter to the American journal *The Freeman*, she drew out the implications for the electorate on voting with an out-of-date register. It was not merely a feminist concern as working-class voters and young men would also be affected by the consequences:

> the antediluvian property-franchise, with all its anomalies and rottenness, its plural votings and university electorate … (which would) naturally be to the advantage of the vested interests, for the propertied classes, the people that boast of 'stakes in the country!', are all in favour of the Free State. These will all vote at the election.

In contrast, those who had done most to bring about the present offer of terms of peace would be cut off from voting because of their past activities, as members of the IRA would have had to risk 'being tracked down, imprisoned and perhaps put to death' if they had gone to the trouble of getting their name put on the parliamentary register during the past two years. Along with expert opinion on the anti-Treaty side, Hanna firmly believed that one name in six on the old register was wrong and that it would be possible to amend the register in three months rather than the eight months claimed by Griffith. But even if it took longer, it should be done, it was a question of democracy. She echoed the argument of Constance Markievicz as she praised the role played by women during the recent war:

> The young women between 21 and 30 number one-seventh of the total electorate. It is upon these women that much of the brunt of the Terror fell: upon their morale depended, in effect, that of the entire Republican army. Many of them played a very active part in fighting for freedom, many suffered imprisonment, torture, deportation for their principles. being under 30 did not exclude them from court-martials and convict cells, but now excludes them from voting in the coming election.

She argued it would be 'statesmanship' to defer the election, which would be of far more significance than voting the usual 'Tweedledum and Tweedledee of politicians' as it concerned 'the future destiny and status of the nation.' She was not impressed by the promise of adult suffrage at the election after the next. It was 'a case of "Jam yesterday, jam tomorrow, but never jam today." We may not vote for the Free State or the Republic, but we may vote later when others have voted us into the Free State.'[18]

Despite such entreaties, the election was held on 16 June. A pre-election pact between de Valera and Collins fell apart at the last moment and the pro-Treaty side won a majority, ignoring protests that the contest was weighted in their favour because the constitution of the Free State was only published on the morning of the elections, allowing no time for serious reflection. With the inevitability of Greek tragedy, the opposing sides continued to mobilise their forces, establish their power bases and prepare for imminent confrontation. There was nothing anyone could do to prevent the inevitable. The Free Staters insisted on their right to keep order and demanded the surrender of all weapons before talks could begin. This was unacceptable to the IRA headquarters, encamped at the side of the Liffey, in the imposing edifice of the Four Courts. Liam Mellows, who combined the roles of IRA general and Dáil deputy, continued to walk to the Dáil from his base in the Four Courts but the escalation of hostilities continued. The Four Courts were surrounded by those members of the IRA who accepted the Treaty and who, under Michael Collins, had organised themselves into the army of the Free State. On 28 June 1922, following pressure from the British government to get rid of this threat to authority – and with the loan of British weaponry – the shelling of the Four Courts began.

The citizens of Dublin, waking to the sounds of heavy artillery, responded in many different ways. Most prayed for peace; some reported for mobilisation at various republican outposts (including Constance Markievicz and Margaret Skinnider), and a few women responded to the plea of Lawrence O'Neill, the Lord Mayor, to help him in a final attempt to negotiate peace. The 'irregulars' had hoped that their base in the Four Courts could emulate the stand taken by their heroes in the GPO, but this was not a re-run of 1916. The women were too late to prevent the enforced surrender of the Four Courts garrison but, as that bedraggled group were marched off to prison cells, the need to prevent further such scenes galvanised the peace delegation into anxious activity. On 2 July, an enlarged group of women met at the Mansion House. Hanna was there, together with her close friends Meg Connery and Rose Jacob. Also present were Maud Gonne MacBride, Charlotte Despard (who had recently moved from London to Dublin), Agnes O'Farrelly and, from the labour movement, Louie Bennett, Marie Johnson and Mary O'Connor. Louie Bennett and Hanna were amongst the group who contacted the anti-Treaty side, to try to persuade the IRA to hold their fire until after the new Dáil met. Because of the danger of moving around the streets they were taken in an ambulance loaned by the Mayor's office. Hanna knew many of those involved and her group left the pleading to her:

> We went into some sort of dark room, with sacks all around it ... I sat on a sack of flour or something. We couldn't see any of the Republicans, but eventually someone – a General-somebody-or-other, but I could never remember since who he was – had a long talk with Mrs Sheehy Skeffington. They said they were into it now, and there was no way out but to fight it out.[19]

With the surrender of the Four Courts, resistance centred upon outposts on the east side of O'Connell Street. Places which had been familiar haunts of the Sheehy clan only a decade previously were now packed with armed men, assisted by women from Cumann na mBan. Barry's Hotel, initially a place for the anti-Treaty IRA to congregate in during the weeks before the fighting began, was now a republican headquarters, commanded by Oscar Traynor. It was to Barry's that Nora Connolly reported for active service when she heard the shelling begin.[20] The building was one of a series of hotels held by the anti-Treaty side as the fighting spread to the north part of the city and desperate men tunnelled their way through walls in an attempt to establish an impregnable ring of resistance to the Free State forces. Constance Markievicz was active too, acting as sniper throughout those days, going 'on the run' afterwards. On 5 July fighting in Dublin came to an end with the death of Cathal Brugha, who had refused to surrender his position at the Hammam Hotel. At the request of his widow Caitlín, republican women formed the guard of honour at his lying-in-state and they fired the salute at his funeral. Hanna joined the crowds who filed past his coffin, gazing at the 'still proud face as he lay in his uniform in the modest mortuary chapel attached to the Mater Hospital'.[21] Under the wise guidance of Lawrence O'Neill, Dublin Corporation continued to meet, although, in the circumstances of war, its influence was more moral than real. Hanna proposed a motion that prisoners taken in action should be treated as prisoners-of-war. Jennie Wyse Power, who was not a diehard pro-Treaty supporter, seconded the motion.[22] The welfare of the prisoners was an issue which Hanna would raise again within the Corporation.

Sixty people were dead, hundreds wounded, and yet more of Dublin lay in ruins. The fighting moved to the countryside as the better equipped Free Staters continued their inexorable push south, driving their opponents into the hills and to inevitable defeat. The prison population rose to an estimated 20,000. There was an urgent need for fundraising, not only for the prisoners but also for countless dependents left destitute as the Civil War continued. As relatives clustered helplessly around the great doors of Mountjoy prison, their little parcels of clean clothes and food refused at the jail gate, the need for an organisation to look after the interests of the prisoners was painfully apparent. Maud Gonne MacBride's son Seán was one of those captured after the fall of the Four Courts. She and Sarah Mellows, the mother of Liam, began to talk as they stood with the rest of the crowd. The idea for the Women's Prisoners' Defence League (WPDL) was born. The only qualification for membership was to have a relative in jail and to pay a subscription of one half-penny a week. That group of women organised vigils, pooled information on the whereabouts of prisoners, protested on the streets against acts of coercion introduced by an increasingly dictatorial government and, for years to come, held a proud record of an unbroken series of meetings every Sunday at 'ruins corner' on O'Connell Street. It was generally acknowledged that without their vigilant presence the conditions of the prisoners would have been much worse.

The ordeal of public speaking for most women, particularly those grieving through the loss of their loved ones, was impossible to contemplate. For many, coming up from the country to find out what had happened to their men, simply being in Dublin was a new experience. Most women who spoke in public on behalf of the League did not have a relative in jail, but they spoke on behalf of those who needed a voice and in so doing they formed something that went beyond being a prisoners' support group.[23] The WPDL was an organisation of central importance in the lives of many women who stood in defiant opposition to the Free State government. Their meetings were banned and broken up, and they were often in danger of imprisonment, but they had given themselves a focal point for meeting each other, for sharing their hopes and their fears. Hanna had described how the impact of the European war and the national struggle in Ireland had led to women becoming 'patriots rather than feminists, and heroes' wives or widows, rather than human being'[24] and Meg Connery had talked of the 'importance and necessity of maintaining an independent feminist group to watch women's special interests and keep up a standard for women'. At that time of 'violent upheaval' women needed to 'hold together and stand by one another'.[25] She was referring to the Black and Tan period and to the role that could be played by the IWFL. Times had changed and the IWFL no longer existed, but this new League went a long way towards providing some means of enabling women to be 'human beings'- particularly those who would otherwise, as Meg said, have their 'needs overlooked'. As Leeann Lane has described so powerfully, 'the domestic sphere was increasingly, in this context, indistinguishable from the public sphere'. With the development of the WPDL:

> Public vigil in honour of family members brought women of the WPDL and other female activists subversively into the visible public domain. Their discernible presence, acting as the fulcrum of republican street theatre, served to underwrite the uncontained nature of the threat to the authority of the Free State.[26]

As a prominent Sinn Féin member, Hanna was in demand as a speaker at protest meetings. In late October she was a speaker in Derry ('another new county for me'), jauntily reassuring Owen she would not be arrested 'only Dev is threatened, so I'm safe & so are all others, we are told. *Tant Mieux! Alors*!' At the end of October, she was the sole speaker at three meetings in Belfast, 'I've no voice left ... no trouble though we had 80 police and an armoured car at one', taking time also to pay a visit to Owen's aunt Bella.[27] Joe Devlin sent her a warm letter, enclosing a subscription towards a fund for the release of the Belfast prisoners, with assurances that he was very sympathetic to the plight of the internees. He had wanted to join her on the platform, regretting his request was not accepted by the organiser of the meeting. These were changed times – Devlin remained a powerful political figure, but one marginalised from political life given his isolation in Westminster and Unionist dominance of the new post-partition state of Northern Ireland. Now that votes for women was no longer an issue, he and Hanna were able to have a cordial relationship. He regretted she had left Belfast before he could meet with her as he had wanted to drive her to Bangor to see a home for working women he had started: 'I hope the next time you are in Belfast, whatever your mission may be, you will let me know because I am particularly anxious you should see this place.'[28]

Owen was at Father Sweetman's school, Mount St Benedict, in Gorey, along with Ronan Ceannt. He had been suffering from a number of throat infections, and it was partly for his health and partly for his general well-being that he had been dispatched there, together with his friend Ronan. Hanna and Aine, concerned mothers both, were, as Hanna said, 'frightfully busy' and, although Owen's absence left a 'large gap', she insisted, 'I want no return with that throat still sore.'[29] From Burnley, Lancashire, she wrote to him of one particularly hectic period:

> I got home all right on Friday & was in middle of my tea (tho' not having a bath in it as this might suggest) when Alex Lynn arrived in a taxi for me to go to conference in Suffolk Street. I went there & then & was asked to go to London next morning so I had an awful rush scrambling some I. World stuff, packing, etc. Then to Lon. & from there after lobbying to here, arriving last night.
>
> I'm very glad you are staying over – you ought to stay till Halloween now ... by then I hope you will be quite well again & that I'll be fairly settled down, if ever!
>
> your fond mother Hanna S.[30]

Later that autumn Owen began Sandford Park school, in Ranelagh, which was just being established. It had only 50 pupils and was non-denominational. He excelled at both sports and academic subjects and was exceptionally happy in that environment, becoming head boy in his last year. He was a notable personality, a sense of fun combined with strong principles. Rose Jacob had been staying with Hanna, using Owen's bed in his absence, ('she's company and helps to fill the large gap your absence makes').[31] She would stay on in Belgrave Road, having been asked by Hanna to take care of Owen while she went to America that November.

Eamon de Valera sent Hanna, together with Linda Kearns (who had been in the Hammam Hotel outpost before the final surrender of the Dublin IRA) and Kathleen Boland, the sister of Harry Boland, who had been captured and shot dead by Free State troops in July, as the 'Irish Women's Mission', sponsored by the American Committee of Irish Republican Soldiers and Prisoners' Dependents Fund, with a brief to raise funds for the relief of the families of the prisoners and for the prisoners as well. It was a big undertaking.[32] From the familiar environment of the Bee Hotel in Liverpool Hanna sent Owen a brief postcard, telling him that she was leaving for Montreal, travelling on the *Antonia*.[33] Now that the war with Britain was over, she felt free to travel to Canada, to see for herself that her sister Margaret was happy in the life she had made and to admire baby Ronan, her new nephew. When asked by the *Montreal Star* for comments on the political situation she was carefully muted in her response. She had come over on a 'private visit'. However, it was reported, 'as she believes in the republican form of government, Mrs Skeffington does not think the outlook for peace in Ireland bright'.[34]

Hanna enjoyed the experience of being back in America, parts of which had become so familiar to her. On arriving at the Park Avenue hotel in New York she was delighted to be greeted by the porter: '"Hello! Mrs Skeffington, glad you're back" – after 4 years as if I had only gone for the weekend!', as she described the scene to Owen.[35] She would be away from home for seven months, a long time to leave her son, who was now 13. Rose Jacob had commented that Hanna was always out 'except at meals' and Owen was often on his own, waiting for his mother to come home. She hinted at Hanna's lack of maternal qualities, and in her diary recorded the difficulties she was experiencing as she tried to make up for Hanna's absence, particularly getting homework done in time and getting out on time in the morning.[36] Despite everything, Rose enjoyed Owen's company and he clearly enjoyed hers. Hanna told her that Owen was 'gone' about her, although he 'seldom & slowly … gets really fond of a person'.[37] Did Hanna rely too heavily on others for the care of her son? Possibly, particularly in those frenetic years when republicans mobilised all their resources in a desperate attempt to realise the Republic envisaged by the Easter Proclamation. One wonders what alternative she had. Her correspondence with Owen reveals her as an extraordinarily busy woman, but one who never forgot that she had a dearly loved son at home. Despite the distance between them, through frequent postcards and the occasional letter, she managed to convey something of her experiences of the tour, combined with maternal concern for his welfare: 'Your letter was very full & good – 90% I'd give you for it, because it gave me all the news … lots of people are asking for you … we are kept very busy & find crowded audiences everywhere, all Republicans. I am glad Rose is up & that you are going on so well. I'll have to bring you a fountain pen as a diving prize. Aunt Margaret will come to NY to see me before I leave. With love, old boy, Mama.'[38] 'Meetings every day … keep up your first place & don't sit up too late.'[39] She could be stern when he failed to correspond often enough, as a telegram indicated: 'Continue writing. Mama.'[40] She could also, however, be cavalier in her correspondence with a young son missing her presence: 'sorry to be away so long but expect to be jailed on my return so it doesn't matter much! much love, Mama'.[41] Her sister Kathleen took in Owen for some of the time and in late summer, before he went back to school, he stayed with Meg and Con Connery.

Irish Americans were as split over the question of acceptance of the Treaty as the Irish at home were, but their greater distance from events meant that some found it difficult to understand the intense bitterness of those who had lived through the disillusionment of the past months. John Byrne felt that Hanna was a different woman from the person he had last encountered as she was leaving America in 1918. He could not understand why circumstances should have led to this, but his testimony provides us with a picture of a woman whose antipathy towards the Free State was as deeply felt as was her anger against the British establishment:

> For hours I talked to her ... and I remember saying to her, 'I hadn't even begun to realise how terrible the state of affairs is over there till you came; and now that you are here I can sense an actual exudation of hatred for certain people from every pore in your body.' And she admitted freely that in sensing this I was quite correct.[42]

Byrne must have been singularly unimaginative not to have understood. It was impossible for someone who had lost a husband as a result of deliberate brutality on the part of a British army officer to accept that those who were an important part of the Irish political establishment were advocating the same methods they had once denounced. Hanna hated the way John Devoy, now a vociferous supporter of the Free State, had turned upon former allies, 'He has clamoured for the blood of all (Mellows included) and in some cases his blood lust has been sated.'[43] The murder of Liam Mellows was a bitter blow. As Hanna would have heard the news of his execution at around the date she arrived in America and had her encounter with Byrne, his omission of that fact slants the evidence considerably. In all the bloodshed and violence that was the Civil War, some acts stood out in terms of their brutality and capacity to inflict upon political life a sore that festered for decades to come. The execution without trial of the 'four martyrs' as they became known, was one of the most notorious. Liam Mellows, Joe McKelvey, Dick Barrett and Rory O'Connor, deliberately chosen as representing the four provinces of Ireland, all captured after the fall of the Four Courts, were taken out and shot by the Free State on 8 December 1922 (the Feast of the Immaculate Conception, an important date in the Roman Catholic calendar), as retaliation for the IRA shooting of two members of the Dáil. Thomas Johnson, leader of the Labour Party, almost the sole voice of opposition in a Dáil composed solely of those who supported the Treaty, voiced his horror at the news:

> most foul, bloody and unnatural. The four men in Mountjoy have been in your charge for five months. You were charged with the care of those men; that was your duty as guardians of the law. You could have charged them with an offence.

> You held them as a defence, and your duty was to care for them. You thought it well not to try them, and not to bring them to the Courts, and then, because a man is assassinated who is held in honour, the Government of this country – the Government of Saorstat Éireann, announces apparently with pride that they have taken out four men, who were in their charge as prisoner, and as a reprisal for that assassination murdered them.[44]

It was a dirty deed, and, as Johnson predicted, it destroyed in many minds the association of the Government with the idea of the rule of law. The bitterness created by that act was incalculable, especially for those who had numbered the men among their friends and who recognised in Mellows the one man capable of continuing to uphold the socialist ideals of James Connolly. Dublin Corporation had insisted that the men were prisoners-of-war, entitled to the treatment accorded to that status. Hanna could not forgive.

The 3 women travelled to 25 states during their tour. In various photos taken during this time the two younger women seem relatively carefree as they pose for publicity shots. There are fewer photos of Hanna, or perhaps she did not bother to keep them, given her dislike of how she looked in photos. She appears more anxious and is considerably less polished in appearance than her companions, despite the obvious quality of her blouse and jacket. She enjoyed clothes, but her stocky little figure thwarted any attempt to wear them with flair. They visited Marie Equi while in Oregon and obviously made an impression: 'What became of Kathleen Boland and Linda? Liked 'em. I was so overcome on seeing you all at the Portland Hotel that I was of an incoherency. No, I don't talk all of the time, darlen.'[45] Their respectability in later years surprised her: 'So all the girls are married! babies too. Can't imagine Linda being in a married state. Kathleen B's sister was here, came to see me, but always accompanied by a bodyguard. My money ok but, I am contagious!'[46]

As a 'women's mission' their appeal was in terms of the human cost of the war and the need for Irish Americans to be generous in their support of those who were suffering. They did not want to antagonise possible contributors. Joe McGarrity had taken the anti-Treaty side and a letter to him from Hanna, enclosing a further appeal from de Valera, provides a clear picture of the type of appeal being made:

> We find it absolutely necessary to appeal for a hundred thousand dollars. There are still in the jails of Ireland 18,000 republican prisoners of whom nearly 2,000 are women. The Free State makes no allowance to the families of these republican prisoners and internees whose dependents rely almost entirely on the help they receive from the US. The necessaries of life must be provided for about 50,000 dependents ...

> The Free State by forbidding collections in Ireland, by raiding and looting our Dublin offices, by continued arrests of our helpers, hope to reduce to starvation the wives, children and aged parents of our prisoners and so weaken the morale of the prisoners and reduce them to submission. This danger must be averted. We appeal to our race in the US to guarantee the necessary funds to enable our committee at home to carry on. Let no child of a republican prisoner go hungry while we can prevent it.[47]

Hanna was invited to speak to the State Legislature in Minneapolis in February 1923. While illness prevented her from speaking in Sacramento on 1 March, her two companions addressed the audience and were outspoken in their condemnation of those who signed the Treaty as 'traitors to their country … [who] should have been arrested and tried for treason by the supporters of the republican movement'.[48] Was this aggressive approach a response to the views of the audience, or a reflection of young speakers who had suffered bereavement and trauma, substituting for a more astute companion? Hanna, with vastly more experience, was more subtle in her public statements. In a letter to the New York paper, the *Nation*, she defended the anti-Treaty republicans, explaining the reasons for their return to armed conflict:

> The Constitution gives 'southern Ireland' but the status of a slave state. We have no control over our parliament, our judiciary or even over the spending of our money. Our judges are appointed by the King's governor-general. The parliament is called and dismissed by the King … it is British injustice, caused by greed and self-interest that is to blame for what some people like to call 'Republican violence'.[49]

Unlike her companions she was careful not to put the blame on Collins and Griffith and the other signatories of the Treaty. Her objection was not that they had been coerced under threats by the British into signing, but that the majority of the Irish people had not been permitted to vote on the issue. If they had been given that opportunity, she was convinced that they would have stood up to the British bullies. It was a point of view she continued to hold as, in 1926, she explained to the Congress of the Women's International League for Peace and Freedom:

> We hoped that the method of referendum might be employed in order to ascertain what form of government Ireland would desire. The settlement of the Treaty is one imposed on the Irish people – not given as of their choice but given as an alternative to 'Immediate and Terrible War'. The Irish people have not had the opportunity of settling freely for themselves what form of Government is wanted.[50]

On 6 March there were 3,000 people in the audience to hear the women speak in the San Francisco Civic Auditorium. It was emphasised that Irish women were dedicated to Irish liberty and would accept nothing short of the Irish Republic. A meeting on 22 April 1923, organised by the Irish Republican Councils of Boston, commemorated the 'seventh anniversary of the Irish Republic' and the committee gave Hanna $1,000.[51] A farewell reception was held in Brooklyn, New York, at the Academy of Music on 29 April and at a mass meeting in Philadelphia on 6 May Hanna told the audience that Americans had contributed a total of $120,000. She spoke at a final meeting in Washington before returning to Ireland. Altogether, $123,000 had been raïsed by the women's tour.[52] Back home in Ireland, the Civil War was drawing to a close. On 24 May 1923 de Valera conceded defeat and Frank Aiken, the new IRA Chief-of-Staff, called on his troops to dump arms. The fighting was over, but political resistance continued. Hanna returned to play her part in the next stage of the republican attempt to defeat the forces of the Free State.

At the beginning of 1923 de Valera had announced plans for reorganising Sinn Féin. Once the military struggle ended, attention turned to the work of rebuilding the political machinery. Many welcomed the opportunity to continue resistance by non-violent means. A short programme of 'immediate work' was issued by the Sinn Féin Reorganising Committee. As with other Sinn Féin documents, it bears the hallmark of Hanna Sheehy Skeffington's influence in some of its instructions to branches. A fund for prisoners' dependents was to be instituted, the release of prisoners and a national amnesty was to be demanded, public meetings on prisoners' behalf were to be held and local councils pressurised to declare their support. Finally, branches were exhorted that: 'Special stress should be laid on the imprisonment of women and the treatment of women prisoners.'[53] This was certainly achieved in the coverage of *Éire*, the paper of the anti-Treaty forces, which began publication on 20 January 1923. Edited for a time from the safety of Scotland by Constance Markievicz, it devoted much space to conditions within prison and to the struggles of women prisoners. Dorothy Macardle, a prisoner herself, was a prolific correspondent.

Free State troops had raided 7 Belgrave Road while Hanna was in America. Frank's Remington typewriter was amongst the property confiscated, to her intense annoyance. The task of retrieving her belongings (including cutlery) on her return proved difficult, and there was an obvious edge of vindictiveness in the uncooperative response she encountered. The Colonel in charge of Island Bridge Barracks informed her that it was 'not deemed advisable' by the authorities to let her have her property A lengthy correspondence developed, which she described in caustic tones, mocking the contrived use of the Irish language in official letters, 'at least the Staters must begin and end in Gaelic'. So far, her efforts had been to no avail, 'My typewriter, like our prisoners, seems on each occasion to be located in a different barracks … I seem to be collecting autographs of various colonels and adjutants, but so far with no tangible result. My Remington is still in the hands of the enemy.'[54] That biting sense of humour was an effective weapon, both on the rostrum and on the printed page. Austin Ford, editor of the *Irish World*, the long-standing and highly respected Irish-American journal, recognised her ability as propagandist. She had written pieces for the paper over the years, now in July 1923 he wrote to offer her a position as 'special correspondent and news reporter', authorising her to send cable messages for important items.[55] She began contributing lengthy articles, never less than half a page and sometimes of greater length, informing American readers of the events of the past week in Ireland. She was paid on average $15 per week, an amount which formed a large part of her income for the next few years.

When Devoy used the pages of his *Gaelic American* to launch a bitter attack against her, Hanna was able to retaliate by using her column to maximum effect. Informing the readers that Devoy had denounced her relatives 'living and dead, including a few especially invented for the occasion' she declared that it was a tribute to her work to be valued 'for to be attacked by John Devoy is praise indeed'.[56] Constance Markievicz and Nora Connolly both wrote in defence of their friend. Accusations on the lines that the Sheehy Skeffingtons used the opportunity provided by the 1913 Lockout to proselytize the children of the Dublin working class by having them sent to homes in Protestant England, were nothing more than 'a vulgar effort to bespatter with mud his clever widow and damage the great work that she is doing for the Irish Republic.' Constance was furious that such 'scurrilous and lying articles' should be printed about Frank Skeffington, a man 'so straight, so kindly and so human … that even those who differed with him politically were glad of his friendship'.[57] To besmirch her husband's name was an unforgiveable act in Hanna's eyes; the fact that some of her political opponents had no compunction in doing so helps to explain the continuing bitterness.

The money from the *Irish World* was a lifeline because in June all those who had taken the anti-Treaty position found themselves axed from the list of examiners appointed under the Intermediate Board. It meant the loss of £100 a year for the task of setting and marking exam papers, a sum Hanna could ill-afford to lose. She sent an angry letter of protest to the Board, accusing them of devising a new set of penal laws, this time for republicans rather than Catholics:

> If my republican views unfit me for a purely educational post which I have filled in previous years were these views not fully known in April? Why has this ban

> been imposed?… honester and simpler for the Free State authorities to make a general rule 'no Republican need reply' – like penal prohibitions of the eighteenth century.[58]

All those working in any public capacity had to take an Oath of Allegiance to the Free State, an impossible undertaking for republicans, who now found themselves barred from many avenues of employment. For the government, this had the additional benefit of providing it with the means of rewarding supporters with jobs. The next ten years were a time of great hardship for the vanquished. Along with thousands of others, Hanna was unable to work as a teacher.

Those who opposed the Treaty continued in their attempts to prevent the regime from gaining legitimacy on the international stage. In their eyes, de Valera was still the President of the Republic and the Second Dáil still the legitimate source of authority. In September 1923 Hanna was sent on an important mission by de Valera, her ability with languages and her familiarity with the European world a great asset to the republican cause. The Free State had applied to join the League of Nations as a newly independent state and William Cosgrave, head of government since the deaths of Griffith and Collins, travelled to Paris to present his case. To counter this move Hanna composed a lengthy eight-point circular in French which was distributed to all the delegates to the Assembly of the League of Nations. Partition; the duress placed upon signatories to the Treaty; the existence of 16,000 prisoners in the Free State and the suspension of trial by jury; the inability of the Free State, due to its subordinate status, to enter into direct relations with any other government without the permission of Britain, were some of the issues itemised by her.[59] The attempt was unsuccessful. On 10 September the League of Nations admitted the Irish Free State to membership of its ranks.

It was a miserable time. There was little consolation to be had from the Sheehy family. Dick had not been cured of tuberculosis, and in October 1923 he died of the disease. He had been teaching law in Galway, leaving behind a wife, Catherine, and daughter Frances. Family rumour condemned Hanna for missing the funeral because of political commitments.[60] If so, it is a measure of the intensity of the political struggle. Hundreds of prisoners were still in internment camps and prisons, kept without trial and with no knowledge when they would be released. Winter was looming; no one wanted to endure the hardships of another prison winter, and so hunger strike, the last resort of all, was decided upon. It began on 14 October – involving women as well as men – and went on for 41 days. On 20 November Constance Markievicz was arrested while she and Hanna were collecting signatures on a petition calling for the release of the prisoners. While Constance was being held in Pearse Street police station, Hanna and Maud Gonne MacBride tried to leave food and warm clothing. They discovered their friend had joined in the hunger strike. She was 55 years old. Maud had won her own release from prison by a lengthy hunger strike in April. She and Hanna knew only too well what a difficult experience that was. The WPDL continued their defiant campaign, their placards 'Freedom or the Grave' a regular sight around the streets of Dublin. Charlotte Despard, reflecting on the year's events in her diary, felt they had been 'protesting the whole time':

> meetings on O'Connell Street, Sundays, in spite of machine guns have gone on regularly. We have had processions, poster-parades, vigils at prison doors, letters to the papers, home and foreign. Possibly if we had held our tongues things would have been worse than they are. We know the agitation has kept up the courage of our boys and girls in prison.[61]

Suddenly, on 23 November, following the deaths of two hunger strikers, the protest was called off. It was obvious to all that the Free State government had no intention of capitulating to their demands.

In these circumstances, meeting up with the rest of the Sheehy family would have been very difficult. Eugene, no longer a soldier in the British Army, had returned to the law chambers. He would end his career as a circuit judge, having benefited from the establishment of a state he had done nothing to help bring about, while his sister and her companions continued to struggle to support themselves and to speak out on behalf of those who remained on the margins of society. Despite this, Eugene's affection for his sister remained, as did his undoubted pride in her intellectual qualities. He had the wit to realise that if things had worked out differently, it might have been Hanna in high office.[62]Hanna did still see her sisters. Her diary entry for 6 January 1924 stated: 'dine at Mary's – little xmas'. The women kept the custom of celebrating Women's Christmas, the one day in Ireland when men undertook the household chores, leaving their womenfolk free to socialise amongst themselves. It was a custom most associated with Kerry and Cork, reflecting the Sheehy family heritage and the feminist convictions of the Sheehy women - lacking menfolk but valuing female companionship.[63]

The deliberate removal of republicans from public spheres continued. Hanna suspected that Dublin Corporation, of which she was still an active member, would be dismissed by a government that disliked its political leanings. She was right. On 15 May 1924, at a meeting of delegates from all the County Councils, she succeeded in having standing orders suspended so that she could propose the following motion: 'that this General Council of County

Councils is of the opinion that the time has come to release unconditionally all prisoners tested and untried'. The motion was lost by nine votes to ten.[64] Less than a week later, on 20 May, the government dissolved the Corporation, appointing three commissioners to run the essential services required by the citizens of Dublin. One of the appointees was Jennie Wyse Power. Lawrence O'Neill, in his capacity as Mayor, immediately called together all the members of the Corporation, but there was nothing that could be done.

Once the prisoners had called off the hunger strike, the Free State, in its own interests, opened the prison gates. It preferred not to have the likelihood of mass influenza rampaging through a weakened prison population. In late December thousands of people, including all the women prisoners, were released. On the day after her release Constance Markievicz was given an enthusiastic reception when she spoke at the weekly WPDL meeting in O'Connell Street. Although thin and pale, she was, Hanna thought, 'as undaunted as ever' as she described her experiences in jail and outlined plans to continue the struggle in support of the large numbers of remaining prisoners.[65] That autumn, Meg Connery, in London with the support of the British Labour Party to lobby on behalf of the prisoners, provided 'a most friendly and sympathetic' George Bernard Shaw with a list of those imprisoned and had an evening with Eva Gore-Booth and Esther Roper, both of whom sent their love to Hanna, Constance and to Madame MacBride. Owen was ill but Meg was delighted to learn from Hanna that he had won a gold medal at school.[66]

Two days before Christmas, Hanna was down at the old Sinn Féin offices in Harcourt Street, where the women's committee had set up a reception centre to look after the prisoners. Their condition was symptomatic of the defeated republican cause. She saw 40 men leaving the little canteen after being provided with a meal and clean clothes from the 'devoted women' who tended them with loving care. None had hats or caps, many were without even collar or tie. All they had were little gifts for those at home, made in jail 'out of all sorts of odds and ends'. They were men from the west, heading off far too early to the station, but, they assured Hanna, 'they'd feel they were on their way home and nearer home in the station just to be looking at the train!'[67] Mindful of the donations that had been made to the Women's Peace Mission on behalf of the prisoners, she made sure to let her American readership know of the good use being made of those funds. Despite the releases, many remained in jail and, as political opposition to the Free State had not abated with the ceasefire, there was the imminent prospect of arrests starting up again. The defeated republicans were faced with unemployment and the danger of utter demoralisation if organisations like the Political Prisoners Committee were not able to make some contribution to their welfare. The prisoners, and the memories of those 77 men executed by their former comrades, provided an emotive focus for continued opposition. Hanna's personal sense of loss was clearly reflected in her journalism. In describing the 'Book of Cells' (poignant punning title for a small prison samizdat initiated by Liam Mellows and Rory O'Connor), her language was unusually emotional. Examining those separate pages, each written in laborious capitals with a fine etching pen, she felt that 'they come to us who honour and mourn them as the letter of a loved friend that reaches one after the writer is no more'. The little journal contained a hasty farewell, written by Mellows to his 'dear comrades' only half an hour before he faced the firing squad. It was a deeply pathetic reminder, not only of all those who had been lost in the past two years of horror, but also of those who had gone before:

> I wish your readers could but see these pages as they lie scattered on my desk – the neat penmanship, delicate and precise, every line a true labour of love, the worn pages lovingly scanned and thumbed by the prisoners till the edges are wearing thin, yellowing already and with the faint prison odour – that mixture of dry rot and fetid air, that compound mustiness of jail still clinging to them. Yet how great and free the spirit of man – they carry us away to the primeval Canadian forest, and while we read we slip past the bolts and bars and breathe the pure air of the snowbound heights.

The journal cover reproduced the door and part of the interior of one of the Mountjoy cells, familiar to the suffragette jailbird also: 'Who dare not recognise every nail as an old familiar friend – have not most of this generation, male and female, graduated in Mountjoy?' was her defiantly rhetorical cry.[68]

While de Valera and many of the most prominent of the republicans remained in jail it was left largely to the women to keep things going in their absence through speaking at political meetings, particularly when contesting by-elections. Hanna tried to maintain a positive tone in her articles, telling readers of Sinn Féin's 'marvellous recuperative powers, rooted in the soil of Ireland like shamrock'.[69] The phrase jars, its mysticism out of character. The sentiment bears the stamp of Maud Gonne, a passionate believer in the symbolism of the trinity of the shamrock: the people, the land, the spirit of life. Perhaps Hanna repeated a phrase she heard during a reunion dinner of a group calling themselves 'the Optimists', brought together through the 'happy inspiration' of Maud Gonne MacBride. Many were prominent artists and writers; most had spent some time in prison because of their support for the republican cause. It was a glittering array of talent. There was Arthur

Darley, violinist; Jack Yeats, artist brother of the poet; Francis Stuart, writer and husband of Iseult Gonne; Dorothy Macardle; Ella Young; Rose Jacob; the artists Estella Solomons and Cecil Salkeld; Grace Gifford Plunkett, and others.[70] Regular meetings of the 'Optimists' continued for some time. It was a help to know that despite all the bloodshed there remained people with heart and commitment and vision.

Maud Gonne MacBride and Charlotte Despard had set up house together in Roebuck, a spacious mansion on the outskirts of south Dublin. Over the years Roebuck would be many things – convalescent home, safe house, meeting place, employment centre. To the government, Roebuck House and its aged inhabitants were a thorn in the flesh, but to many others Roebuck was a beacon of resistance, a place where there was always a welcome for those who risked all in the continued fight for the Republic. On Sunday afternoons some would go back to Roebuck immediately after the 'ruins corner' meeting. Constance Markievicz, one of the few car owners, was generous in providing lifts, saving the elderly residents of Roebuck the tiring ordeal of the tram journey home. Charlotte Despard's car was notorious for its unreliability. Other friends would arrive later in the afternoon, ready for Maud's scones and lively conversation. Mrs Despard's eightieth birthday, on 15 June 1924, saw 'a crowd to tea and plenty of fun and good fellowship'.[71] On 3 August, the day before the August bank holiday, the crowds gathered as usual for their meeting, despite heavy rain. Maud and Hanna were two of the speakers. The diarist added, with pleasure, that 'the crowd did not move'. More than one hundred friends went back to Roebuck that afternoon. A fiddler played while they had their tea in relays.[72] Although Hanna was a fairly frequent contributor to the Sunday meetings, she was nowhere near as regular in her appearances as Constance Markievicz or Helena Molony, two of the names that crop up continually in the Despard diaries. If she was not campaigning for Sinn Féin, Sundays were reserved for family lunches and games with her sisters and their children. On Sunday afternoons they often went for rambles with the 'Pilgrims', a group that included the Connerys, Cissie Cahalan and other old friends. However, in the busy year of 1924, only five Pilgrim gatherings were listed, political meetings dominating. Hanna cancelled a rare treat of a theatre visit when Owen was sick, her calendar marking each occasion he was ill. On the first Sunday of April she and Mary MacSwiney were in Limerick, where a by-election was pending. In mid-May she was the main speaker at after-mass meetings in Enniscorthy and in Carrick-on-Suir, while in June she was back in Limerick, this time with Constance Markievicz, Linda Kearns, Seán T. O'Kelly and Robert Brennan, campaigning hard for the republicans. The Free

State candidate won, but with a majority cut by 19,000.[73] Following the Sinn Féin Ard Fheis in November she spoke in Letterkenny, Mallow and Cork.[74]

The rest of the prisoners were released in July 1924. It was a huge relief. At last the Civil War could be put behind and plans made for the future. As people crowded into the Suffolk Street headquarters of Sinn Féin, friends clasping hands with friends they feared never to see again, bridging 'the chasm of the weary months – across the very shadow of the scaffold', Hanna looked around the room and watched faces shed years as 'everyone felt young again'.[75] Some might begin to make a new start; for others, including herself, that would be much more difficult. In September, returning from London, she discovered that she had been travelling on the same boat as members of the Bowen-Colthurst family, who were returning to Ireland. The fact that the government had not prevented this from happening brought barely suppressed memories back to the surface. Her hatred remained intact:

> It will be remembered that this 'planted stock' owned castles in County Cork which were burnt by Republicans during the war. Now peace is restored and even the murderer himself may return to the land which rang with his misdeeds. For there is peace for the murderer of Irishmen under the Free State, which wages ruthless war only upon the enemies of England.[76]

Adding to the anger was the news that the bodies of Erskine Childers and other republicans executed during the Civil War were being exhumed from Beggars Bush barracks and secretly reinterred. Still more memories flooded back:

> The Free State fears if the bodies were handed over the Irish people would flock in their thousands to give them full honours. I well recall how the British in Portobello disinterred my husband's body from the hole in the yard where it lay in a sack on condition I should not be informed and that my father-in-law would promise not to allow any 'demonstration'. These reinternments are right to fear the dead.[77]

Other actions by the government were equally objectionable in a different way. The Free State had had enough of troublesome women. In the words of P. S. O'Hegarty in his vitriolic book, *The Victory of Sinn Fein*, published in 1924, women were: 'unlovely, destructive-minded, arid begetters of violence, both physical violence and mental violence'. O'Hegarty's conclusion was shared by each member of Cosgrave's cabinet: 'We know that with women in political power there would be no more peace.'[78] There was a desire for 'normality' after the years of upheaval and removing women from the public sphere seemed one way of starting the process. There was, of course, a more ideological impetus behind all of this. Research by historians has uncovered no evidence that this hostility towards women was shared by the majority of the population. It was all about the assertion of governmental authority and in this, women were easy targets.[79]

Feminists uninvolved with republican politics attempted to maintain some presence in public life. A Haslam Memorial Committee was set up in 1924, to consider how to honour the work of Anna and Thomas Haslam (a bench dedicated to them both would be placed in Stephen's Green). Sarah Cecilia Harrison was the secretary of the committee. She wrote to Hanna at this time, asking for permission to send a portrait of Frank she had painted to an exhibition in connection with the Tailteann Games, 'not so much for art sake, as to show the manner of men who gave their lives for Ireland'.[80] Despite Hanna's radical reputation, old friends of different persuasion stayed in touch. Mary Hayden, who had regarded the Rising with horror, in arranging to visit Hanna along with her 'little aunt', commented: 'she enjoys your company although she informs me she feels very sorry for your spiritual welfare and often prays for you and the boy … I hope my saying this won't turn you against her.'[81] Mary would soon be politically active again, protesting against government policies that discriminated against women. The contribution made by women to the success of the republican courts during the War of Independence counted for nothing as Kevin O'Higgins, Minister for Justice, decided to do away with women's right to be judged by their peers. Feminists gathered forces and managed to have the 1924 Juries Act modified to allow women, if they wished, to opt out of jury service. This would not be enough for O'Higgins. In 1927 there would be another move to remove women from juries altogether.

Mary Kettle was emerging as a formidable feminist leader, still active in local government, her opposition to the Free State based not on republicanism but on its anti-woman ethos. As chair of Rathmines Council, she was the only woman to hold such a position in the whole country. Gretta Cousins believed that Mary, rather than Hanna, could give the lead to women in the changed circumstances of the Irish Free State:

> Nothing in Ireland impressed me so much as its emergence as a Catholic country and that great bulk of Catholic women now in the ring of power must be led by Catholic women and it is up to her or someone like her to do it.[82]

Hanna, as a member of Sinn Féin, was not in a position to make common cause with the average woman, despite her importance as a powerful propagandist. She could back her sister 'for steadiness and perseverance', but Gretta, on a brief visit to Ireland in the summer of 1925, saw clearly that political identification with republicanism made Hanna unsuitable as a unifying figure for

Irish womanhood in the climate of post-Civil War Ireland. It is most unlikely that Hanna was giving any serious thought to the possibility of revivifying feminism as a political movement, despite Gretta's urgings. In a situation where, as she believed, half the population had been coerced into a 'Free' state that was proving to be anything but free, concentration upon women's issues alone was inappropriate in her view, although she would continue to fight for the rights of her sex whenever the occasion arose. For her, at that time, Sinn Féin was the only choice. The Irish Labour Party, under Thomas Johnson, bore no resemblance to the vigorous socialist organisation that had existed in the Connolly years. The backlash against women was overwhelming but she felt the priority was to rebuild radical republicanism as an effective force. If this succeeded, and the republic was achieved, the Irish state would be reconstituted. It would no longer be anti-woman and anti-working class, favouring the rich and the well-connected. That was the theory at least. How this would be achieved while Sinn Féin insisted upon abstaining from the political processes remained an unanswerable conundrum.

How much at home was Hanna within Sinn Féin? She was a useful member, especially for public meetings, but did that make membership a satisfying experience? There were many people who felt it was a difficult relationship, particularly as time wore on. Hanna was not a doctrinaire republican like Mary MacSwiney, who would tolerate no deviation from the pure idealism encapsulated by her brother's *Principles of Freedom*. As the heated discussions between the Irish Women's Franchise League and Inghinidhe na hÉireann 20 years earlier had demonstrated, women like Constance Markievicz felt little conflict in placing national considerations before women's needs. That had never been Hanna Sheehy Skeffington's position and even within Sinn Féin she remained what she had always been – an outspoken feminist. She had no qualms in bemoaning the lack of women members within the organisation and she was forthright in regretting the continued refusal of Sinn Féin to admit Cumann na mBan, the republican women's organisation, as of right to its conventions.[83] Most of all, there was the inherent contradiction at the heart of Irish republicanism: the uneasy relationship between its military and political wings. As a political thinker of some sophistication, Hanna was manifestly uncomfortable associating with those who continued to regard themselves as soldiers rather than politicians. This she revealed, rather indiscreetly (but perhaps writing for an American audience encouraged candour?) in her appreciation of Cardinal Mannix, Archbishop of Melbourne, a champion of the republican cause, who was accorded an enormously popular civic reception while visiting Dublin:

> To hear him develop his theme is a rare pleasure in these days when it is the habit, rather the pose, of the military type of speaker to begin by announcing with a swagger, that he is 'no orator' but a plain, blunt man of action, the implication being that oratory is something second rate, not to compare with knocking your man out or blowing him up.

Wistfully, she added, 'when a real orator appears the pleasure is all the greater because it is now so rare'.[84] She struggled hard to find constructive work in which she could engage. Speaking for Sinn Féin around the country was all very well, but the electorate was clearly uninterested in giving a mandate to those who refused to work within the institutions of the state. As a former suffragist, Hanna always believed in using one's vote effectively, and abstentionism began to seem unsatisfactory as a tactic. Some progress was made in July 1925 when a few republicans were elected to Dublin County Council. Amongst the successful candidates were herself, Constance Markievicz, Kathleen Lynn and several male members of Sinn Féin. Hanna was delighted at the result, while regretting the fact that more had not stood for election because of their fear of harassment. She was stern in her rebuke:

> This is to be regretted, for on local public bodies a number of fearless and independent critics of the present regime is much needed, and such a group, even in a minority, can achieve much and can form a strong bulwark against further onslaughts upon democratic control that are even now being planned.[85]

Those that accuse her of simply opposing the government during this period should reconsider their charge. Her willingness to act in local government is evidence that she wanted to play a constructive part in developing a political alternative. There were many schemes of social welfare she hoped the Council would be able to institute, despite the opposition of a monetarist government resistant to any expansionist programme. During Gretta's visit to Ireland the pair had some intense conversations as they discussed current events. Gretta was prophetic in her assessment of her friend's position:

> You have my entire sympathy in the difficult path you have chosen as a party woman. I foresee a point at which you will be faced with a choice between feminism and Party as we were in the Home Rule Party days.[86]

She could not have made such a remark if Hanna had not provided her with some insight into the internal difficulties she was experiencing. Much later, Cathal O'Shannon, a colleague from the days of the Socialist Party of Ireland, wrote that in his view, in her later membership of Sinn Féin, 'neither she nor Sinn Féin could have been very happy about it'.[87] Her reconsideration of her position within Sinn Féin led her to refuse a nomination to its executive at the start of 1925.[88] She did remain a member and, that July, when Austin Stack was given responsibility for local government within the organisation, he immediately wrote to ask if she would act on the committee with him.[89] She must have reconsidered her decision not to continue on the executive because, at the start of 1926, she was elected a member of a new, enlarged executive body of 30 members. She also continued to speak for Sinn Féin throughout the country. It was, however, no longer the most interesting of her political allegiances.

Her desire to work with women was partly fulfilled through her continued involvement with the Women's Prisoners' Defence League, while her sympathy with the cause of labour on an international scale led to her becoming an executive member of the Irish section of the Workers' International Relief Organisation, dedicated to working for the 'Irish victims of British imperialism and capitalism'. On this she, Charlotte Despard, Maud Gonne MacBride, Margaret Skinnider and other republican women were joined by Jim Larkin and members of the Dublin Trades Council.[90] This was short-lived, a casualty of internal divisions in the labour movement. Hanna's duties as a councillor continued, enabling her to use her position on the Technical Instruction Committee to put forward names of unemployed members of Cumann na mBan as temporary workers during election time. Eithne Coyle, in charge of Cumann na mBan's Economic Department, had a long list of unemployed members who were often suffering great hardship, many with families unsympathetic to their daughter's politics. She was grateful for any help in alleviating their poverty.[91] The residents of Roebuck had started their own small-scale industries to give work to a few. Charlotte Despard had launched 'Roebuck Jam', which was to drain her financial resources over the years as she attempted to make this a profitable concern. Maud had a workshop making ornaments from shells. Hanna admired them greatly, 'things of beauty from the Irish sea, as ravishing as any from France' she felt.[92] These, and other artefacts, were sold diligently at every republican sale of work and fair, and people made special efforts to buy their gifts from such sources, but it was little more than a gesture in the face of desperate need, as all were aware. Travelling around the west of the country while on a speaking tour for Sinn Féin, Hanna saw the results of an exceptionally wet spring. The harvest had been badly affected while fluke was rampant amongst the sheep. The situation was giving rise to a great deal of concern, and others on the political left travelled west to see for themselves. She condemned the exaggerated claims of famine that were made, but she also condemned those who minimised the extent of distress. Both sides, in her view, were 'acting not in the interests of the Irish people, but of their own vested interests'.[93] There would be no solution until a republican government functioned once again. She was getting impatient with the futility of remaining on the margins of political life while the victorious continued to profit from their monopoly on political and economic power. In another year's time she would make an ill-fated decision out of a desperate attempt to regain some semblance of political relevance.

NOTES

1 Hanna Sheehy Skeffington to Eva Gore-Booth, 17 July 1921, Eva Gore-Booth Papers, MS 21,816, National Library of Ireland (hereafter NLI).

2 Ibid., n. d., 1921.

3 Ibid., 17 July 1921.

4 Constance Markievicz, *The Prison Letters of Countess Markievicz* (London, 1934, reprinted London, 1987), p. 300.

5 Hanna Sheehy Skeffington to Eva Gore-Booth, 17 July 1921, Eva Gore-Booth Papers, MS 21,816, NLI.

6 Hanna Sheehy Skeffington to Alice Park, 25 Feb. 1922, Alice Park Collection, Hoover Institution Archives, Stanford, California.

7 R. M. Fox, *Rebel Irishwomen* (Dublin, 1935), p. 73.

8 Maire Comerford, personal interview with author, Jan. 1975.

9 Hanna Sheehy Skeffington, speech to International Women's League for Peace and Freedom, July 1926, Alice Park Collection, Hoover Institution Archives, Stanford, California

10 Hanna Sheehy Skeffington to Alice Park, 25 Feb. 1922, Alice Park Collection, Hoover Institution Archives, Stanford, California.

11 See speeches of women TDs in Margaret Ward (ed.), *In Their Own Voice: Women and Irish Nationalism* (Dublin, 1995), pp 111–18.

12 Marie Johnson memoirs, Sheehy Skeffington MS (hereafter SS MS) 21,194/1.

13 Leeann Lane, *Rosamond Jacob: Third Person Singular* (Dublin, 2010), pp 151–2.

14 Included in Hanna Sheehy Skeffington to Alice Park, 25 Feb. 1922, Alice Park Collection, Hoover Institution Archives, Stanford, California.

15 See debate on franchise, Ward, *In Their Own Voice*, pp 119–22.

16 Marie O'Neill, *From Parnell to de Valera: A Biography of Jennie Wyse Power* (Dublin, 1991), p. 138.

17 Dáil Éireann, *Official Report 1921–1922*, pp 202–3, National Archives of Ireland.

18 *The Freeman*, 10 May 1922.

19 R. M. Fox, *Louie Bennett: Her Life and Times* (Dublin, n. d., [1958]), pp 77–8.

20 Uinseánn MacEoin (ed.), *Survivors* (Dublin, 1980), pp 211–12.

21 *Irish World*, 2 Aug. 1924.

22 Marie O'Neill, *From Parnell to de Valera*, p. 142.

23 For more on the WPDL, see Margaret Ward, *Maud Gonne: A Life* (London, 1990), Chapters 8 and 9.
24 'Do you want the Irish citizen?', in *Irish Citizen*, Sept.–Dec. 1920.
25 Meg Connery, introducing annual report of Irish Women's Franchise League (hereafter IWFL), in *Irish Citizen*, Mar.–Apr., 1920.
26 Lane, *Rosamond Jacob*, pp 210–11.
27 Hanna Sheehy Skeffington to Owen Sheehy Skeffington (hereafter Hanna to Owen), 17 Oct. 1922; 30 Oct. 1922, SS MS 40,484/1.
28 Joe Devlin to Hanna Sheehy Skeffington, n. d. SS MS 33,606/10.
29 Hanna to Owen, 22 Oct. 1922, SS MS 40,484/1.
30 Ibid., n. d. (1922). Alex Lynn was a lawyer who defended many political prisoners. Sinn Féin had their offices in Suffolk Street.
31 Ibid.
32 Joanne Mooney Eichacker, *Irish Republican Women in America: Lecture Tours, 1916–1925* (Dublin, 2003), pp 168–80.
33 Hanna to Owen, n. d., SS MS 40,484/1.
34 *Montreal Star*, n. d., courtesy of John Scully, Quebec.
35 Hanna to Owen, 1 Nov. n.d., SS MS 40,484/9.
36 Lane, *Rosamond Jacob*, p. 143.
37 Ibid., p. 142.
38 Hanna to Owen, 24 Oct. 1922, SS MS 40,484/1.
39 Hanna to Owen, Nov. 1922, the Ten Eyck Hotel, Albany, NY, SS MS 40,484/1.
40 Hanna to Owen, 24 May 1923, addressed to 44 Leinster Road, home of sister Kathleen, SS MS 40,484/1.
41 Hanna to Owen, 29 Jan. n.d., SS MS 40,484/9.
42 J. F. Byrne, *Silent Years: An Autobiography* (New York, 1953), pp 140–1.
43 *Irish World*, 26 Jan. 1924.
44 Thomas Johnson, Debate on Mountjoy Executions, *Dáil Éireann, Third Dáil*, vol. 2, no. 3, 8 Dec. 1922.
45 Marie Equi to Hanna Sheehy Skeffington, 1 Apr. 1938, SS MS 41,177/16.
46 Ibid., 19 Feb. 1932.
47 Hanna Sheehy Skeffington to Joe McGarritty, 18 June 1923, McGarritty Collection, MS 17,638, NLI, Dublin.
48 Mooney Eichacker, *Irish Republican Women*, p. 175.
49 Quoted in *Éire*, 11 Aug. 1923.
50 Hanna Sheehy Skeffington, speech to International Women's League for Peace and Freedom, July 1926, Alice Park Collection, Hoover Institution Archives, Stanford, California.
51 *Éire*, 26 May 1923.
52 Mooney Eichacker, *Irish Republican Women*, p. 179.
53 Sinn Féin reorganising committee, programme of immediate work for Cumainn, n. d., 2-page pamphlet, P 2260, NLI, Dublin.
54 *Irish World*, 16 Feb. 1924. In Aug. 1924 Hanna did receive £31-1-0 as compensation for property taken in raids. The money order had to be cashed within a month. Hanna and Owen were in France so Rose Jacob, who was still in Belgrave Road, went to see

Kathleen, anxious that the order would be cashed in time. Rose Jacob to Hanna Sheehy Skeffington, 19 Aug. 1924, SS MS 41,177/27.

55 Austin Ford to Hanna Sheehy Skeffington, 12 July 1923, SS MS 24,091.

56 *Irish World*, 26 Jan. 1924.

57 Ibid., 3 May 1924.

58 Hanna Sheehy Skeffington, 29 June 1923, draft of letter to editor, in *Irish Independent*, SS MS 24,091.

59 Hanna Sheehy Skeffington, 'Protest to Geneva', addressed to the delegates to the League of Nations and to members of Sixth Commission now considering question, published in *Éire, the Irish Nation*, 15 Sept. 1923. Circular letter in French from Hanna Sheehy Skeffington to delegates to the Assembly of the League of Nations, Desmond Fitzgerald Papers, University College Dublin Archives (hereafter UCDA). With thanks to James Kirwan for the reference.

60 Leah Levenson and Jerry Natterstad, *Hanna Sheehy Skeffington: Irish Feminist* (New York, 1983), p. 148.

61 Charlotte Despard, note in front of 1924 diary, D 24791/8, PRONI.

62 Eugene Sheehy, *May It Please the Court* (Dublin, 1951), p. 147.

63 Hanna Sheehy Skeffington diary, 1924, SS MS 41,183/3.

64 Minutes of County Councils General Council, 15 Parnell Square, 15 May 1924, SS MS 24,091. Hanna, representing Dublin Borough, was the only female delegate.

65 *Irish World*, 19 Jan. 1924.

66 Meg Connery to Hanna Sheehy Skeffington, 15 Oct. 1924 and 16 Oct. 1924, SS MS 41,177/10.

67 Ibid.

68 *Irish World*, 10 May 1924.

69 Ibid., 18 Mar. 1924.

70 Ibid.

71 Charlotte Despard diary, 15 June 1924, D 24791/8 PRONI.

72 Ibid., 3 Aug. 1924.

73 Hanna Sheehy Skeffington, weekly column in *Irish World*, Apr.-June 1924.

74 Hanna Sheehy Skeffington diary, 1924, SS MS 41,183/3.

75 *Irish World*, 9 Aug. 1924.

76 Ibid., 27 Sept. 1924.

77 Ibid., 4 Oct. 1924.

78 P. S. O'Hegarty, *The Victory of Sinn Féin* (Dublin, 1924), pp 104–5.

79 See for example Maryann Valiulis, 'Power, gender and identity in the Irish Free State', in *Journal of Women's History*, winter/spring 1995, pp 117–36.

80 Sarah Harrison to Hanna Sheehy Skeffington, 7 May 1924, SS MS 41,178/24.

81 Mary Hayden to Hanna Sheehy Skeffington 23 May 1924, SS MS 41,178/24.

82 Gretta Cousins to Hanna Sheehy Skeffington, 23 Aug. 1925, SS MS 24,117.

83 *Irish World*, report on Sinn Féin Ard Fheis, 25 Nov. 1924.

84 Ibid., 14 Nov. 1925.

85 Ibid., 4 July 1925.

86 Gretta Cousins to Hanna Sheehy Skeffington, 23 Aug. 1925, SS MS 24,117.

87 Cathal O'Shannon, in *Irish Times*, 23 Apr. 1946.

88 Austin Stack to Hanna Sheehy Skeffington, 6 Jan. 1925, SS MS 24,116.

89 Ibid., 23 July 1925, SS MS 24,093.

90 Executive committee, Workers International Relief (Irish Section), 8 Apr. 1925, SS MS 24,117.

91 Eithne Coyle to Hanna Sheehy Skeffington, 31 May 1925, SS MS 24,092.

92 *Irish World*, 22 Jan. 1927.

93 Ibid., 28 Mar. 1925.

TWELVE

THE STRUGGLE CONTINUES, 1925–32

Frank Gallagher, adroit propagandist for the republican cause, shared a page of the *Irish World* with Hanna. A dedicated journalist (unfairly described as the 'Goebbels of the republican movement')[1] his contributions always arrived on time, as an aggrieved Austin Ford cabled when Hanna's column was, yet again, late. Gallagher and his wife Cecilia were now the tenants of her small top-floor flat, their monthly rent of £6 a small but welcome addition to Hanna's yearly income of £200 (half of which was derived from journalism). The Gallaghers were also useful animal sitters when Hanna and Owen were off on holiday. In a series of chatty letters Cecilia kept her landlady informed of the animals' welfare: the cats were hungry monsters, the rabbit continually escaped from its hutch and they were, as always, plagued by Kathleen Lynn's dog, Shuler, who was in regular pursuit of the rabbit.[2] The state of constant warfare between Shuler and Owen's dog, Pete, extended to the owners, who were fierce defenders of their own pets and well able to hurl insults about 'mongrels' and 'bullies' while remaining, in every other respect, the best of friends. Pete's ability to escape onto the road and his consequent scratching of the front door when locked out, led to the sensible arrangement of a brass plate being screwed onto the bottom. It stopped complaints from Countess Plunkett, who objected to the sorry state of her door. Such was the reputation of the inhabitants of number seven that it was rumoured that the plate had been put there to protect the door from the depredations of Black and Tan boots.

As the horror and upheaval of the war years began to fade, the household arrangements settled down into something akin to normality. It was, despite the lack of a father, in many ways the happy, chaotic household that all children should experience. Owen was now 16, an independent thinker, a young man admired by his schoolmates for his honesty and integrity of purpose. To his mother's bafflement, he loved sport, particularly cricket. He and his friend and close neighbour, Spencer Hackett, would practice their cricket on an ideally wide and quiet surface – Belgrave Road – despite universal disapproval from neighbours.[3] He had the Sheehy look, his mother's blue eyes and shortness of sight. But in his individualist adherence to a gospel of pacifism and radicalism, he was his father's son. The republican cause was not his, although many of his mother's friends were his as well. They had helped to care for him when Hanna was away from home and, as he grew up, the friendships persisted. Rose Jacob had always treated him as a potential adult, encouraging his interest in photography and sharing a love of animals. Holidays with his mother, aunts, cousins and friends were opportunities to share in laughter, lively conversation and in the pleasures of the outdoor life.

The summer of 1925 was the first time in many years (apart from the brief respite of the summer of the Truce) when republicans felt free to relax. It was time to recoup one's energies, time to put some colour in one's wardrobe. Lilian Metge, on holiday in England, promised to bring back some shoes, warning Hanna that she would have to 'take her chance' on the colours as choice was limited to red and white or green and white.[4] New clothes were a treat, given her limited budget, and therefore worthy of comment 'got a new dress and hat, blue and white, nice…'[5] There were many who encouraged Hanna to take her life a little easier. Her sister Margaret, who had witnessed Hanna driving herself to exhaustion during the brief visit to Montreal, urged her 'give your mind and body a rest from the Republic. It's no use overdoing things and I know how you do spend yourself.[6] The 'Pilgrims', walkers and talkers around Ireland, continued to meet up.[7] Cissie Cahalan was amongst the group to join Hanna on a walking holiday around Glengarriff, County Cork. Rose Jacob, on holiday with Dorothy Macardle who was engrossed in writing her monumental history of the Republic, was impatient to see them. An enthusiastic climber, she complained that Dorothy 'gets tired if you take her up a mountain'. The demands of the author were such that Rose, forever in the service of others, had been able to do little but act as 'cook, washer up, secretary etc'[8] Meg Connery, admitting her nerves were 'overtired' wrote to tell Hanna how much she was missing her. Seeing how fit Cahalan looked on her return, Meg added wistfully, 'I should have enjoyed being with the crowd down there.'[9] Owen spent some time with his mother before continuing a cycling tour to the Aran Islands, staying there to improve his Irish. Even those short weeks in August were not purely holiday. Sinn Féin sent a car to meet Hanna at Cork and at Waterford, so that she could get to meetings arranged to coincide with her presence.[10] She also found, in the middle of the month, that she had to return briefly to Dublin to attend a council meeting. Friends protested that it was a 'shame', but duty took precedence.

Hanna had been an enthusiastic and broad-minded theatregoer throughout her adult life and, now that Owen was old enough, she had begun to enjoy nights out with her son. They fell into the habit of discussing what they had seen over a late-night cup of cocoa in the Broadway Soda Fountain in O'Connell Street. One of the more enlightened moves of the Free State government was the awarding, in 1925, of a modest grant of £850 to the Abbey Theatre, unremarkable in these days of government sponsorship of the arts, unheard of in a country struggling to define itself despite grudging acceptance and downright hostility. The suspicion was that the government, desperate for allies, had resorted to buying its friends. Any play put on by the Abbey in such an atmosphere would be subject to scrutiny.[11] The first two of Seán O'Casey's Dublin plays – *The Shadow of a Gunman* and *Juno and the Paycock* – had already shaken up audiences. The former, dealing with the Black and Tan period, was staged while the Civil War was being fought outside the theatre. The Irish were being forced to look at themselves in a way that was not heroic, in plays that centred upon the struggle of tenement dwellers to survive in the midst of turmoil. Hanna considered those plays to be 'not without power, with a grim and sinister humour of their own', but now she felt that O'Casey's cynicism fitted the mood of the Abbey directorate. She sensed 'a new audience, sleek and smug in after dinner mood', who indulged in 'ribald laughter at the sallies of tenement drolleries'. O'Casey, in her view an 'eternal grouch' who saw everything through warped vision, fitted in with these changed times.[12] Over *The Plough and the Stars*, the third of Seán O'Casey's Dublin plays, Hanna and her son were in total disagreement. Owen felt the play was an accurate representation of the 'lumpen proletariat' and the way in which they behave in time of war and revolution 'with all the pettiness, meanness and pathetic attitudes of their lot and their condition'. He found it an 'admirable and moving' picture of the way in which society conditioned men and women.[13] Not only did his mother disagree, she ensured that the playwright, the country and prosperity were made fully aware of how intensely she disliked this play:

> Not a single character has a gleam of nobility or idealism; the men are all poltroons, drunkards, slackers or criminals, inspired by no motives save that of vanity, greed or empty boastfulness, while the women are backbiting harridans, half-witted

> consumptives, neurotics or prostitutes … the moral of the piece appeared to be the foolishness of it all.[14]

There were those who maintained that the most offensive aspects of the play concerned the role of the prostitute Rosie Redmond and the implication that those who fought in the Easter Rising were drunkards who consorted with such women. Hanna was not concerned with narrow-minded morality. For her, it was a question of politics, of the victors of the Civil War trampling over the ideals of the defeated. She provided the most sustained and eloquent of all the critiques of the play.

Joseph Holloway, an inveterate theatregoer and tenacious scribbler, knew O'Casey. He had attended the dress rehearsal of *The Plough and the Stars* (finding it 'not nearly as interesting and gripping' as *Juno*), and he knew that the play was bound to cause offence in certain quarters. Dublin, he said, was 'agog' and there was 'electricity in the air' by the time of the opening night on 8 February. W. B. Yeats, one of the three directors of the Abbey (and now a member of the Free State Senate), had dined with members of the cabinet earlier in the evening. They were in the audience, epitomising all that Hanna disliked about the direction being taken by the Abbey. The ordinary populace too was keen to see the play. Before the doors opened the queue to the pit entrance had extended past old Abbey Street, but barely a quarter of them were able to get in. Hugh Kennedy, now Lord Chief Justice and his wife were amongst the establishment figures in that first-night audience. Dublin was a small place. This was the same Kennedy who had rejected Skeffington and Joyce's contributions to the *St Stephen's* magazine. After the play, Holloway stood on the pavement outside, the street packed on either side with motor cars, noticing four real 'Rosie Redmonds' being hastily dispersed by a policeman.[15] Who could believe the fiction that Dublin had no prostitutes when they plied their trade openly in many parts of the city? Politics and morality were so intertwined in O'Casey's portrayal of the impact of the Rising on the Dublin tenement dwellers that deciding who had been offended by what was difficult. Holloway witnessed Kennedy declaring the play 'abominable'. Kevin O'Higgins owned he did not like it either. For many, the character of Rosie Redmond, and her familiarity with men supposedly about to engage in the 1916 Rising was uncomfortable, while the affront caused by the introduction of a tricolour into a public house was the last straw. It was desecration. The implication that their heroes might have enjoyed a drink touched a raw nerve for those suffering the grimness of defeat. Word spread.

Women in Cumann na mBan were determined to make their point. Despite the fact hisses and jeers had greeted the actors on the succeeding nights, the concerted opposition planned for the Thursday evening was different. It was organised in some secrecy by women who were resolved, as they saw it, to stand up for the ideals of those who had given their lives for the Republic. They were more than willing to disrupt the proceedings, but they needed someone capable of standing up and making a speech while chaos surrounded her. Hanna was the obvious choice. Eithne Coyle, an executive member of Cumann na mBan, asked her to join them. When the doorman saw Eithne, who had achieved considerable notoriety for holding up trains at gunpoint during the War of Independence, he immediately said: 'don't let that one in, she's an old Cumann na mBan woman'. Apparently, however, when he saw Hanna Sheehy Skeffington standing firmly alongside, he did not persist. As Eithne remembered the scene, 'she was big and stout and I was like a little fairy beside her, he didn't want to tackle it.'[16] Hanna's reputation was also large. Who would want to be accused of having manhandled or mistreated such a woman, and someone who, disconcertingly, looked rather like everyone's favourite aunt?

The usual catcalls echoed around the auditorium during the first act. During the interval, Joseph Holloway overheard Dan Breen, a famous IRA gunman who was now an independent member of the Dáil, comment that 'Mrs Pearse, Mrs Tom Clarke, Mrs Sheehy Skeffington and others were in the theatre to vindicate the manhood of 1916.' Holloway looked forward to the next act. When the curtain opened on Rosie Redmond in the pub, pandemonium ensued. Some of the women managed to get onto the stage, to be thrown off with a certain amount of brutality by the actors. From the back of the balcony all agreed that Mrs Skeffington 'kept holding forth' while others were speaking in the pit.[17] She did not take part in any of the action, her protest was a verbal one. As the demonstrators were driven out of the theatre, Hanna's voice could still be heard:

> We are now leaving the hall under police protection (cheers and jeers). I am one of the widows of Easter Week. It is no wonder that you do not remember the men of Easter Week, because none of you fought on either side. The play is going to London soon to be advertised there because it belies Ireland. We have no quarrel with the players – we realise that they at least have to earn their bread. But I say that if they were men they would refuse to play in some of the parts. All you need do now is sing 'God Save the King'.[18]

The following night a detective-lined theatre included the 'G' men, a group detested for their past surveillance of those the British had considered subversive. Now they were employed by their former enemies, to ensure that there would be no further disruption. That Monday, the first of Hanna's letters appeared in the *Irish Independent*, explaining why the demonstration had been staged. It had nothing to do with the 'moral aspect of the play':

> It was on national grounds solely, voicing a passionate indignation against the outrage of a drama staged in a supposedly national theatre, which held up to derision and obloquy the men and women of Easter Week.
>
> It is the realism that would paint not only the wart on Cromwell's nose, but would add carbuncles and running sores in a reaction against idealisation. In no country save in Ireland could a State-subsidised theatre presume on popular patience to the extent of making a mockery and a byword of a revolutionary movement on which the present structure claims to stand.[19]

As someone who had been going to the Abbey for over 20 years, and who had enjoyed plays such as *Cathleen ni Houlihan* which had 'helped make Easter Week' she hated the fact that the Abbey, 'in its subsidised, sleek old age, jeers at its former enthusiasms'.

O'Casey replied. He could see nothing wrong in showing life as it really was, 'the National tocsin of alarm was sounded because some of the tinsel of sham was shaken from the body of truth'. He could see 'nothing derogatory' in the fact that 'Some of the men of Easter Week liked a bottle of stout.' He had seen the Tricolour in many places, not only in public houses, but painted on a lavatory wall and flying from some of the worst slums in Dublin. Nora Clitheroe was more representative of the women of Ireland than those who protested. As O'Casey continued, his tone became more personal and more abusive:

> The heavy-hearted expression by Mrs Sheehy Skeffington about 'the Ireland that remembers with tear-dimmed eyes all that Easter Week stands for,' makes me sick. Some of the men cannot get even a job. Mrs Skeffington is certainly not dumb, but she appears to be both blind and deaf to all the things that are happening around her. Is the Ireland that is pouring to the picture-houses, to the dancehalls, to the football matches, remembering with tear-dimmed eyes all that Easter Week stands for. Tears may be in the eyes of the navvies working on the Shannon scheme, but they are not for Ireland. When Mrs Skeffington roars herself into the position of a dramatic critic, we cannot take her seriously: she is singing on a high note wildly beyond the range of her political voice and can be given only the charity of our silence.[20]

They were worthy adversaries in their mastery of the art of abuse. It was a correspondence of intellectual heavyweights, dragging in literary and political references to support their respective arguments. Hanna's second letter refuted any suggestion that she was unaware of the ordinary people and their struggle for existence. She was also highly indignant that O'Casey felt he could define what Irish women felt:

> May I suggest that when Mr O'Casey proceeds to lecture us on 'the true morality of every woman' he is somewhat beyond his depth. Nora Clithero is no more 'typical of Irish womanhood' than her futile, snivelling husband is of Irish manhood. The women of Easter Week, as we know them, are typified in the mother of Padraic Pearse, that valiant woman who gave both her sons for freedom.[21]

The dreadful irony was the fact that, had her husband not been concerned to prevent the looting depicted by O'Casey, he would, in all probability, have been alive and in the theatre alongside her. The playwright had used looting as a device to demonstrate how far removed from those who planned the Rising were the destitute members of the Dublin working class. Frank Skeffington's concern to prevent the idealism that had inspired the Rising from being lessened by charges of theft had put him in the path of Bowen-Colthurst. She did not make any specific reference to her personal tragedy, but Hanna truly was a 'widow of Easter Week', and her outrage needs to be understood in that context. It is argued by many that the riots 'illustrated the intolerant mindset which existed among even socially progressive republicans',[22] but in the context of the times, and particularly for Hanna, *The Plough and the Stars* was a negation of her husband's final act:

> A play that deals with Easter Week and what led up to it, that finds in Pearse's words … a theme merely for the drunken jibe of 'dope', in which every character connected with the Citizen Army is a coward, a slacker, or worse, that omits no detail of squalid slumdom, the looting, the squabbling, the disease and degeneracy, yet that omits any revelation of the glory and the inspiration of Easter Week, is a Hamlet shown without the Prince of Denmark.

The emotional heart of her objection is clear in the final paragraph. She had too much pride and dislike of personal revelation to mention her husband, but Frank was surely in her mind:

> That Mr O'Casey is blind to it does not necessarily prove that it is non-existent, but merely that his vision is defective. That the ideals for which these men died have not been achieved does not lessen their glory nor make their sacrifices vain. 'For they shall be remembered forever' by the people if not by the Abbey directorate.[23]

Later, she pithily re-worked that line from *Cathleen ni Houlihan* in referring to the Abbey directorate: 'The police shall protect them forever.'[24]

Frank Ryan, a young graduate of University College Dublin, an IRA member and republican journalist, had instigated the Cumann na mBan-led protest. He now suggested that the Universities Republican Club host a debate on the play. Hanna agreed, and the challenge was issued. On Monday 1 March crowds packed into the Mills Hall to hear the debate between the two. Both had speakers lined up in support. On Hanna's side there was Eileen McCarvill, a lecturer in English at University College Dublin and Maud Gonne MacBride, target for O'Casey's worst vitriol, one whose voice was 'querulous, from whom came many words that were bitter, and but few kind'.[25] The debate, chaired by Arthur Clery, old college friend of the Sheehy Skeffingtons and supporter of the IWFL, was closely followed by partisans of each side. From all accounts, and not only from Joseph Holloway, who shared her dislike for the play, Hanna came out well from the debate. Holloway described a woman it would have been difficult to dislike:

> Mrs Skeffington spoke mostly about the right to disapprove as well as approve in theatres and was totally opposed to the police being brought in, and spoke most interestingly in soft, low, carrying tones. She is an easy, agreeable speaker and says what she wants to say clearly and well.[26]

O'Casey felt no personal animosity towards this opponent, whom he later acknowledged as 'a very clever and a very upright woman'. He had challenged his detractors on other occasions, but no one before had risen to the challenge. She had courage and integrity. It was not an even match. Hanna was an experienced public speaker, O'Casey was not. His eye problem had worsened, and his sight was so bad he could not read his notes. Confronted with an unfriendly audience, he broke down before he had said more than a few words. Lyle Donaghy stepped into the breach, but he too quickly subsided and sat down. Eventually O'Casey recovered enough to stand up again, his speech drifting into 'a sort of Salvationist address at a street corner', as Holloway put it. Other supporters from each side then jumped up to have their say. Hanna contributed the final summing up in a 'very subtle speech, full of sly thoughts and humour'.[27] Her style was not rhetorical 'sunburstry'; she exercised her powers in too cool and calm a manner for that. Cathal O'Shannon, who listened to her speaking countless times, said she was 'always analytical, never dull, never boring, never empty'. Her speech was 'smooth, equable, excellently ordered and modulated', a product of her intellect and powers of reasoning.[28] It was small wonder that she should have been the person to confront O'Casey and, in so doing, drawing upon herself undeserved censure. Would she have had a different view on the important question of state-support for the arts if the government had not been that of the hated Cumann na hGaedheal?

As the debate concluded Hanna felt that the general sense of the meeting was with the protestors and against the Abbey. Even O'Casey's defenders had attacked the subsidy and the 'unfree and venal press'.[29] Holloway felt it had been conducted 'in the most peaceful way and in the best of good humour.

Each taking or receiving hard hits in their turn.' At the conclusion of the evening, Hanna went over to shake hands with O'Casey. She is reported to have said that she had been reading his account of the Irish Citizen Army and wanted to thank him for his moving tribute to Frank, whom he had called the 'first martyr to Irish Socialism':

> the soul of revolt against man's inhumanity to man. And in this blazing pyre of national differences his beautiful nature, as far as this world is concerned, was consumed, leaving behind a hallowed and inspiring memory of the perfect love that casteth out fear, against which there can be no law.[30]

It might have happened in this way, for Hanna to demonstrate that she felt no personal ill-will,[31] but she did not go over because those words were some revelation to her. She had first read them in 1919, while reviewing O'Casey's pamphlet for the *Irish Citizen* and had made it plain then, while the tribute was 'touching', it was not one with which she was in total agreement. She was aware that O'Casey had used his praise for Frank as a means of attacking Connolly for his participation in the Rising. Skeffington was described as the 'living antithesis of the Easter Insurrection', but his widow steadfastly refused to make any distinction between the two men:

> What matter which is the Socialist or National hero: both died as they lived for their ideals ... One to Peace and one to Freedom and neither looked for fame or laurels, in death or in life.[32]

While she thanked O'Casey for his words on Frank, her toughness of intellect was not distorted by emotion. Neither did kind words weaken her resolve to continue her opposition to the play. Connolly had died for the Workers' Republic. She still supported his dream. When the play returned to the Abbey in May, she, Maud Gonne MacBride and Charlotte Despard were at the head of a group of women holding placards of protest who stood in front of the theatre's entrances.[33] Historian Diarmaid Ferriter's assessment of this controversy is that O'Casey depicted with accuracy the 'complicated and difficult reality' of the Irish rebellion, challenging 'the heroic narrative' in order to condemn the revolution for its failure to improve the living conditions of the Dublin working class.[34] Her argument was different – she insisted that she had witnessed the idealism which O'Casey sought to deny.

Todd Andrews, one of the students involved in hosting the debate, had his first meeting with Hanna while making preparations for the event. Not a person who gave praise lightly, his summary of the woman he knew was extravagant in its enthusiasm: 'I have never met anyone, woman or man, who combined to the same degree clarity of mind and singleness of purpose. She was also a person of great courtesy and showed much kindness to me:[35] On many occasions Hanna was the lynchpin in connecting groups and individuals who otherwise would have found cooperation difficult. Although there was overlap in the interests of the Women's Prisoners' Defence League and the Cumann na mBan-organised Political Prisoners' Committee, they were very different organisations and it required a person with an unassailable reputation to ensure that joint ventures respected the identity of each. Invariably, that person was Mrs Skeffington. On 25 February 1926 she presided over a crowded meeting at the Rotunda, a joint meeting of the WPDL and the Political Prisoners Committee protesting against the condition of prisoners in British, Free State and Northern jails and calling for their unconditional release.[36] It was a gesture only, a morale-boosting exercise. No-one in power was about to take any notice. Nothing would change while republicans remained on the fringes of political life.

Within Sinn Féin, pressure to enter the mainstream while remaining true to the principle of opposition to the Treaty was mounting. Hanna's decision to remain on the executive reflected an undercurrent of opinion that a change of direction had to be agreed. De Valera was the driving force in this. On 9 March 1926 a special Ard Fheis was called by Sinn Féin to consider his motion that once the Oath of Allegiance was removed 'it becomes a question not of principle but of policy whether or not republican representatives enter the Dáil'. Abstention from all institutions of the Free State would no longer be republican policy. As de Valera put it: 'the left as well as the right arms, the constitutional as well as the military should be tried'. The military arm had been inactive since the ceasefire ending the Civil War; it was time to attempt to wield the other arm. Once the 'obnoxious oath' was removed, republicans would be free to enter the Dáil in order to dismantle the Treaty settlement. It was a strategy that had the full support of Hanna, who felt that at last a solution to the political stalemate was close at hand. In recounting the gist of what had happened at the Ard Fheis she echoed the physical force analogy: 'Personally I hold this view. It is no 'recognition' of a building to enter it with a bomb in order to blow it to pieces.'[37] By the narrowest of majorities – 223 to 218 – the motion was defeated. The organisation was split down the middle. Amongst the women to support de Valera were Hanna, Margaret Pearse, Constance Markievicz and Kathleen Clarke. Against any change in policy were Kathleen Lynn, Mary MacSwiney and Maire Comerford. Hanna's fear of any repetition of the bitter splits in the past was evident in her fervent reassurance that this division would make no difference to the movement or to individual friendships, 'each respects the sincerity and integrity of the other, and while remaining close friends "agree to differ"'.[38] Charlotte Despard was distressed by the outcome, 'I am giving up Sinn Féin. I feel that it is hopeless and dead.'[39] She began to revive her plans for a new Irish socialist party under the leadership of James Connolly's son Roddy. She hoped to interest Hanna in the venture, inviting her to speak at meetings of the Connolly Club, a socialist debating society. On 28 March she noted with pleasure that 'Mrs Sheehy Skeffington gave a fine lecture on Education in Russia. Good debate. Roddy and Fox gave their experiences'.[40]

Events in the republican camp moved quickly. The preliminary planning had been undertaken behind the scenes before Sinn Féin met. De Valera had not wanted to reform Sinn Féin. He wanted a new political organisation with no past history, suitable to a new age, to put to the electorate.[41] The possibilities were infinite. On 17 May Constance Markievicz presided over the launch of a new political party – Fianna Fáil ('Soldiers of Destiny'). It offered, Hanna believed, the possibility of developing 'a progressive constructive programme broadly based on national lines'. She agreed that those elected would take part in an Irish elected assembly, but only, she insisted, 'once they are not required to violate their principles by an enforced act of perjury'.[42] She described the oath-taking ceremony as a mockery in a cubby hole, by people who prostituted themselves.[43] Opposition to the oath was a fundamental principle that could not be fudged in any way.

Hanna's participation in local government was one indication that she disliked the moral high ground of abstentionism which had achieved little more than to condemn those who took that path to impotent fulminations against the status quo. It was becoming an outmoded tactic. People were getting on with their everyday lives and purist rhetoric had little appeal. Meanwhile, of course, the government was free to stamp the character of the new state as deeply conservative and almost wholly male. There would be no place for women in public life if this trend continued. For feminists who had fought for women's right to enter the public sphere, a policy of continued abstentionism was difficult to accept. Hanna's reasoning was not necessarily that of Eamon de Valera, but it was recognition that a political organisation capable of confronting the hated functionaries of the Free State might provide a way out of the impasse.

As the new party began to organise, it was careful to incorporate as wide a cross-section as possible in its first executive. It would give no hostages to fortune by failing to include women in leading positions. Constance Markievicz, Margaret Pearse, Kathleen Clarke, Dorothy Macardle, Linda Kearns and Hanna herself were the women voted onto the first executive.

It was the only time Fianna Fáil would have so many women as visible and highly prominent supporters. However, decisions on policy were made by a small group of associates close to de Valera. No women held officer positions on the executive. Even Markievicz remained without specific responsibilities, despite her years of experience. Hanna was too independently minded to be one of the select few. Once, speaking of politicians with whom she worked – 'somewhat uneasily' as Desmond Ryan put it – she laughed, 'They suspect me. I should suspect myself if they didn't!'[44] As a Fianna Fáil member, she continued speaking at after-Mass meetings, and she was drawn into the work of helping to administer applications for relief coming from destitute republicans. She was also a key member of anti-Armistice Day protests, representing Fianna Fáil on an 'Anti-Imperialist Vigilance Association' as well as attending meetings of a 'Poppy Day' committee, the purpose of which was to challenge the pro-British habit of wearing poppies in memory of those who had died fighting during the First World War.[45] Skirmishes around poppy wearing and union jack flying were a regular feature of each November, particularly in Dublin, as republican and unionists clashed over the issue. Mary Kettle stubbornly insisted on her right to wear a poppy, regardless of what her sister might argue. Within the family Hanna might have tried hard to keep silent. That poppy was, after all, in memory of her brother-in-law, Tom Kettle.

Her membership of Fianna Fáil had not curtailed association with either Cumann na mBan or the WPDL. Two Cumann na mBan members – Brigid O'Mullane and Sheila Humphries – were serving two-month prison sentences for their part in trying to influence juries not to convict republicans. Their release on a sunny morning in June was an occasion for celebration. Charlotte Despard and Maud Gonne MacBride, in Despard's little car, picked up Hanna on their way in from Roebuck. Clutching bouquets of flowers, a 'joyful little crowd' of Cumann na mBan and WPDL members assembled outside the gates of Mountjoy.[46] Constance Markievicz was there too, even though she had had to resign her presidency of Cumann na mBan in order to join Fianna Fáil. Welcoming the prisoners home was a symbolic gesture to demonstrate that the recent political developments would not prevent republican women from continuing to support each other. They made a strong plea for the life of a woman condemned to hang within the week for the crime of infanticide. Sheila and Brigid had encountered the poor unfortunate while they were in jail. Prison warders shared their view that she was in no state to be held accountable for her action. Hanna commented, 'Once again even jail authorities recognise that it is only "politicals" who will get prison wrongs righted, prison grievances redressed.'[47]

It was a busy summer. Owen was hoping to study French in university if he passed the necessary exams in a year's time. Hanna had to go to a conference in Paris in June, and he came along. He stayed in France after his mother returned to Ireland. Lola Lloyd, an old American friend from the Women's International League, in a letter to Hanna full of feminist news, added that her daughter Jessie had caught sight of Owen in the Louvre in August.[48] Owen, who had met so many of her friends from his time in America, was something of a favourite. Former suffragist Florence Murphy Baker, living in France and Spain while she developed textbooks for language teaching, met him in Paris a few years later, enthusing, 'He is so alive, so full of interest and so intelligent.'[49]

Hanna's conference was an International Women's Suffrage Congress, attended by representatives from forty nations. There were two delegations from Ireland: one from the north, one from the south. She was not a part of either, 'getting my authority from an international body, the International Women's League, which recognises no frontier'. She found the congress to be right wing and non-revolutionary and, to her great annoyance, accepting of partition as an accomplished fact.[50] She was pleased to see Alice Paul and the non-conformist American feminists she had so much in common with. She also enjoyed interviewing the Egyptian feminist, Hoda Shaarawi, comparing the Irish and Egyptian experiences of people under the yoke of British imperialism.[51] Other than that, she did not think the congress had done much to forward the cause of women. Sight-seeing was fun. Katherine Blake wrote fondly from Interlaken, 'have thought of you many times since we parted and your many kindnesses to me – sending enlargement of picture I took of you upon Montmartre'.[52] She paid her first visit to James Joyce, now living in Paris, meeting his family and enjoying dinner in his favourite restaurant, where they talked of the past, remembering 'Dublin and Dubliners'.[53] On hearing this, her sister Margaret wrote wistfully: 'Meeting Joyce was interesting. I wish he'd send me *Ulysses* I want to read it – Mary always appealed to the Joyce's … demure madonna face got them every time.'[54] Hanna also visited Sylvia Beach in her bookshop Shakespeare and Company, the intention being to present the woman who had become the Paris publisher of *Ulysses* with some copies of the Skeffington and Joyce pamphlet. Joyce's contribution, *The Day of the Rabblement*, his first published writing, was a collector's dream. According to Eugene Sheehy, Beach insisted on paying Hanna a 'substantial sum' for each of the copies she brought.[55] Hanna retained a number of the pamphlets, which she later tried to sell in 1937, at another time of financial hardship. She must have bought some copies of *Ulysses*, as she gifted a copy of the book to Rathmines Public library that year.[56] A few years later Owen, on his mother's urging, also visited Joyce, who gave him the task of checking the statues on O'Connell Street for him. This Owen dutifully did, subsequently reporting back. Joyce did not reply and the two did not meet again.[57]

That July a most important feminist event took place in Dublin. The Women's International League for Peace and Freedom had chosen Ireland as venue for its congress. It was a significant event for the Irish government as well as for women, with 150 delegates representing twenty countries crowding into the buildings of University College Dublin. Helena Swanwick, one of the English delegates, thought Cosgrave's government 'fairly established' but added that 'one could sense more than a mere parliamentary opposition to it'.[58] One did not have to be particularly perceptive to sense this. William Cosgrave attended the opening session and so did Éamon de Valera, the first occasion the two political leaders had sat in the same room. As the opposing groups glared at each other, Louie Bennett, chairing the first session, announced 'the President.' The proceedings were in danger of disintegrating before they had begun. To enormous relief, the small figure of Jane Addams, in her capacity as President of the League, appeared on the platform.[59] Republican women recognised the opportunity presented to them. Hanna wrote that 'At last, informed and representative women from outside were enabled to penetrate our gloom. Journalists, doctors, teachers, world leaders among women, saw Ireland for themselves.'[60] She was determined to have her say at this Congress. The occasion was too important to be left to women like Louie Bennett, pacifists who would not speak out against the Free State government in the way republicans wished. The WILPF had in the past debated the issue of using force to achieve social justice. At the 1919 Congress in Zurich, a resolution on support for peaceful methods of effecting change had passed by only one vote, and the issue continued to be perceived differently by delegates from countries suffering under colonial rule and in places where socialists were coming under attack by the right.[61] As Congress had long ago come out firmly in support of Ireland's right to self-determination there was much to be gained by a concerted intervention into the proceedings at Dublin. This was clearly recognised by Hanna, despite the fact that the printed programme of public proceedings for the five-day event listed no speakers from Ireland, apart from Louie Bennett, in her capacity as President of the Irish Section. Louie was also to chair a public meeting in the Mansion House, on the topic 'Next Steps Towards World Peace', at which the speakers included Jane Addams and Helena Swanwick.[62] There were considerable personal and political tensions within the Irish section, some feeling that Louie Bennett was too domineering, others disliking the increased numbers of republican women on the committee.

Swanwick maintained that in Dublin the republicans, some of whom had previously belonged to, or still did belong to, the International League, remained outside the conference because 'they had taken part in the Civil War and were, even at that time, involved in relations with revolutionary Republicans'.[63] Hanna was not an outsider at this event: a republican, yes, but she remained a woman committed to the feminist cause. The first session of the Congress dealt with the subject of Imperialism (Economic and Colonial) and the speakers were Mr E. F. Wise from England, Dorothy Detzer from America and M. Delaisi, from France. There was an addition of 'and others' in the programme, which must have provided Hanna with an opportunity to speak as she presented a paper on Irish political and economic affairs, apologising that 'confusion regarding procedure' meant that she had no written report. Off the cuff, she delivered a devastating and uncompromising indictment of Free State policies:

> Ireland is, as you are doubtless aware, the worst example in the world today of a victim of imperialistic capitalism or of economic imperialism. Personally, I find it, as other speakers have found it, very difficult to disentangle imperialism from militarism. We must consider both together.

She went on to examine the economic exploitation of Irish agriculture by Britain and the malign effects of free trade in wiping out native Irish industries and preventing the development of mineral resources. Famine, emigration, the continued declining birth rate, the Treaty and the consequent pernicious effects of partition were all included in a crisply delivered denunciation of the evils wrought upon the world by the British Empire.[64] Swanwick, well versed in the political nuances of the Irish situation, watched the bewildered delegates attempt to understand the difference between the 'rebels' and the members of the Irish section who also wanted Irish freedom, but who rejected the republican path.[65] In part, the Congress was an opportunity for both groups to attempt to win over delegates to their way of thinking. Not all were swayed by the republicans. Helena Swanwick was an old friend of Charlotte Despard from the days of the Women's Freedom League in London. As a suffragist and staunch pacifist, she and Hanna had come into contact on many occasions and had often disagreed with each other. However, this did not prevent Swanwick from appreciating Mrs Sheehy Skeffington's qualities as 'a woman of the greatest ability and force of character'.[66] One of the strongest sources of disagreement concerned the use of force. As a pacifist,

Helena Swanwick could not support those who 'maintained the necessity for catastrophic revolution' at home while uniting in opposition to international wars.[67] Hanna, of course, felt no such dilemma. The weak were entitled to rise against their oppressor. International wars were fought by the powerful in pursuit of their own self-interest. Her views were not supported by the *International Suffrage News*, which regretted the 'intense nationalist propaganda' as a 'misuse of what should be purely international and pacifist.'[68]

Delegates at the Congress were inundated with information and besieged by deputations representing prisoners, working women, the unemployed and the sick. The Irish Women Workers' Union, the Political Prisoners Committee and many other groups were given time to address the Congress. One whole day was allotted to the 'Republican Hostesses Committee' (Maud Gonne MacBride and friends in another guise), who organised an excursion to inspect the archaeological riches of the Boyne Valley. There was more than mere sight-seeing involved. Each woman was presented with a 'souvenir booklet' full of quotations from the nationalist canon of Tone, Pearse, MacSwiney etc., coupled with the more socially radical views of James Connolly and Frank Sheehy Skeffington. Hanna enjoyed the outing immensely, judging it the 'happiest and most successful day' of the whole conference.[69] R. M. Fox attended important sessions of the Congress. His wife, the novelist Patricia Lynch, was a former suffragist and friend of Sylvia Pankhurst. Their sympathies were with the republicans. Fox felt that 'pacifist women from Britain poured out a gospel of peaceful submission to the Empire – a travesty of honest pacifism as understood by the Skeffingtons'. Trying to be fair, he felt that they had crossed over to Dublin without having any understanding what 'Empire' meant there.[70] Such ignorance Hanna was determined to expel. That she was not a pacifist is evident in the manner of her intervention. Louie Bennett continued to argue for passive resistance and non-violence and was active in presenting a report on the minority problems of Ireland which argued for the complete disarmament of the Free State Army, the British Army in occupation in the north, and the IRA. With a very different objective in mind Hanna concentrated on persuading delegates to condemn the existence of the Free State and the continued presence of Britain within Ireland. One of the commissions set up by Congress was given a brief to consider 'colonial and economic imperialism'. A preamble from this commission declared its conviction that 'economic competition and rivalry between states is the chief cause of war'. Significantly, the statement continued: 'We hold that a lasting peace is only possible under an order of society which excludes every kind of imperialism, colonial and economic.'[71] Hanna was pleased with what had been achieved. As she observed caustically, a 'self-evident axiom' had been agreed: 'that uprisings by natives against foreign governments should not be classed as "Rebellious", a proposition that Britain for one has never yet accepted in her relations with her oppressed nationalities.'[72] Her most important contribution to the Congress, two days after her intervention at the session on imperialism, encapsulated the worst fears of all those who hoped that the republican agenda would not be allowed to intrude into the main proceedings. Jane Addams had paid Frank Sheehy Skeffington the compliment of including some of his writing in her speech at the Mansion House meeting on the Monday evening. She had met Frank while he was in America in 1915 and had enormous respect for the man she described as 'a great Irish pacifist known to pacifists all the world over'. Afterwards, Hanna was called upon to speak on behalf of Irish women. As she began, she endorsed her husband's appeal to have 'the age-long fight against injustice clothe itself in new forms suited to a new age', but she went further, making a passionate plea for peace and freedom, quoting the powerful words of Pearse: 'Ireland unfree can never be at peace.' Fox declared, 'The audience rose to her for she spoke as one inspired.'[73] Rose Jacob wrote in her diary 'a roar of applause broke out for all the world as if it was de Valera, and went on and on and on (with cries of up the Republic) till Louie got quite annoyed with the enthusiasm …'[74] Hanna's own conclusion was, 'Some who came, believing that Ireland was free and had freely accepted the Treaty, went away wiser.' However, and significantly, the official report of the congress omitted any mention of the enthusiastic reception she had received, failing also to include her references to the Irish experience of 'foreign violence and militarism'.[75]

Her membership of Fianna Fáil continued, but not for much longer. Given the composition of its early membership, heavily reliant upon former members of the IRA and close intimates of de Valera, it was not only a male-dominant organisation but also an organisation with a masculine ethos forged over years of struggle. De Valera made no effort to encourage women's participation. Todd Andrews, although a devoted supporter of 'Dev', felt so strongly about his leader's cavalier treatment of his devoted secretaries that he once bluntly told his chief that he felt he did not give women sufficient recognition for their dedication. He recalled that Hanna had 'no great liking for Dev; in her estimation he was anti-feminist'. On that, Andrews agreed whole-heartedly, a view reinforced by complaints from his girlfriend Mary Coyle, a staunch member of Cumann na mBan, who declared that her organisation disliked the man's 'sexism'.[76] Nevertheless, the party seemed to offer an alternative from the stark choices of resumption of armed warfare or perpetual political irrelevance. A constructive programme for regeneration of the economy needed to be developed, and many felt that Fianna Fáil had the talent to do that. As the radical republican leader Peadar O'Donnell admitted, years after the event, Fianna Fáil was 'a burst of political realism'.[77] Hanna's membership, uncharacteristic and short-lived though it was, indicated an openness on her part to considering various political options. At a huge open-air rally in September, with crowds clambering on the statues and lamp posts around O'Connell Street in their efforts to catch sight of de Valera, she put her hope in the man with whom, instinctively, she knew she had little in common:

> One could see the listening faces lightening up with the old hope, with a wistfulness and a yearning; and many of those faces looked pinched and wan, for in every crowd gathered in Dublin's streets today there are hungry men and women, workers and homeless, yet clinging to a grim hope that things may yet mend and that their dreams of better days are not entirely vain.[78]

The bitterness between republicans and government forces intensified. As resistance to the Free State continued, repressive measures grew worse. A steady trickle of arrests rounded up the most outspoken of republican protestors. In response, women continued their indefatigable efforts to support those in jail, with the usual round of meetings, poster parades, jail demonstrations and chalking of slogans on walls and hoardings. 'George Gilmore no criminal' was to be seen everywhere, as Gilmore sat naked in a prison cell, refusing to accept criminal status by wearing prison clothes. Hanna was secretary of a 'National Emergency Fund' established to help dependents of those arrested. People found it difficult to believe that the state had no responsibility to care for those left without an income on the arrest of their breadwinner, and she spent much time explaining the situation for the benefit of her American readership, urging donations to be sent over. Her greatest flow of invective was aimed at Kevin O'Higgins, Minister for Justice. Women as well as republicans had cause to detest the measures he introduced. The juries convicting republicans were juries from which women had been excluded by government decree. Hanna, listening to that debate, had felt the attitude of the Dáil to be deeply hostile: 'The whole tenor of the debate revealed the low standing … of women … a contempt that was scarcely concealed pervading the discussion.'[79] There was, O'Higgins argued, 'not the necessity of putting this unpleasant duty on the women section of the country's citizenship'. When pressed, he resorted to such lame excuses as the 'difficulties' involved in the lack of 'bathroom facilities' which made it preferable to rely upon all-male juries in the newly constituted Irish system of justice.[80]

There were forceful and widespread protests from women's groups. A protest meeting in February 1927 saw the Irish Women Workers' Union, the National Council of Women in Ireland, the Women's Cooperative Guild, the Irishwomen's Citizen's and Local Government Association, the Irish branch of the International Women's League for Peace and Freedom and the Irish Women's Equality League all united in condemnation of the government. Hanna wrote a trenchant letter to the *Voice of Labour*, challenging O'Higgins' claim that few women had showed any interest in serving on juries. He had not told the whole truth. As women who presented themselves for jury service were told to 'stand aside', the question to be answered should have been how many had presented themselves for service:

> for over three years practically no woman has been chosen by the State to serve on criminal cases, women being ordered en masse (as Catholics used to be in John Mitchell's day) to 'stand aside' when they answered their names in court. Mr O'Higgins was asked during the debate (and by a deputation of women who interviewed him) to produce figures showing how many women answered their names when called for service. He replied that no such figures were available, knowing full well already that it is the court practice not to allow women to serve … There is no record available, in fact, no note being taken of the number of women challenged by either State or prisoners, and Mr O'Higgins' statement, therefore, is based on a deliberate misrepresentation.[81]

Rose Jacob wrote to the *Irish Times*, giving her view that the proposed measure was 'a manifestation of the fear of women that lies so deep in the average masculine mind.'[82] Hanna put her feminist contacts to good use, working for the hastily-formed Women's Equality League in a concerted attempt to amend the proposed bill. She liaised with Professor William Magennis in the Senate, providing references to the situation in America, England and Belfast for use in debate, which he used to good, if ultimately futile, effect: 'It sets at naught the experience of other countries. There are over twenty States in the American Union in which women serve on juries, and judges have frequently pronounced encomiums on the value of their services.'[83] The measures taken by the Free State not only exacerbated the antipathy already felt by many women activists, it provoked some women who had supported the Treaty into changing sides. Jennie Wyse Power, now a senator, had broken away from the Cumann na nGaedheal Party in 1925 and thereafter sat as an independent. She could no longer tolerate government policy on a number of issues. Speaking in the Senate on the Juries bill, she regretted the fact that 'the civic spirit that is developing in women will be arrested' if the Bill became law.[84] But it did, despite protests. There was no effective parliamentary opposition to prevent it. Now, when juries convicted republicans and sent them to jail, Hanna insisted on pointing out that these were all-male institutions. In her eyes, anti-feminism and anti-republicanism were even more synonymous than before.

In April 1927 Hanna attended the trial of Peadar O'Donnell, editor of *An Phoblacht*, a new republican journal which reflected the views of the IRA leadership. Despite her Fianna Fáil membership, she was in broad agreement with the views of the paper. She enjoyed O'Donnell's journalism and often repeated his arguments in her *Irish World* column, continually emphasising the militancy of the tone of *An Phoblacht*. O'Donnell was being tried for his role in encouraging the small farmers to refuse payment of land annuities to the government. The land had been taken from them by the British, now a campaign was being mounted to end the system whereby farmers paid annuities to compensate the government for having returned land ownership to them. Sitting in court, Hanna felt she could have been back in the days of the Land War, remembering when her Uncle Eugene, Parnell, Davitt and many others were in court because of their support for the no rent agitation. She was clearly impressed by O'Donnell, an IRA fighter, journalist and author of fine stories about his people in County Donegal:

> he stood there, his face pale, his features clear-cut, his black hair, greying at the temples, his shrewd grey-blue eyes, now lit with kindly humour, now ablaze with passion as he told of the sufferings of his people in Tirconnail. His speech, after the dreary platitudes of the state prosecutor and the hair-splitting quibbles of the judge, made a strong impression.[85]

In the June 1927 elections Fianna Fáil did well, polling only three seats less than Cumann na nGaedheal. When de Valera led his deputies to the door of the Dáil, claiming the right to take their seats without the oath, they were refused entry. As long as republicans abstained, the government had little opposition with which to contend. It tried to manoeuvre the situation to keep the republicans out. Hanna explained the situation, 'The oath has been the government's strongest asset; and it is clung to now by the present Junta because they realise that it alone keeps them in power.'[86] She rejected with indignation any suggestion that the Fianna Fáil deputies, having made their formal protest, would then take the oath in order to break it. The plan was that a nationwide campaign against the oath would begin, forcing a referendum on the issue. That strategy had her support. However, what she had dismissed as scurrilous rumours put out by government sources soon proved to be true. The search 'for a means of circumventing the oath' had begun.[87] It soon became a matter of urgency.

On 10 July Kevin O'Higgins was assassinated by unknown republicans. Conor Cruise O'Brien remembered the day vividly. The ten-year-old boy was returning from a Sunday spin in a motor car, an exciting event because it was his first ever drive, when the car containing himself, his aunt Hanna and a friend of hers was stopped at a roadblock. The police sergeant, recognising Hanna, smiled and said 'Ye'll be delighted to hear Ma'am – Kevin's been shot!' Hanna did not smile. Her nephew said, 'she was not disposed to be amused either by murder or by policemen'.[88] She felt no regret over O'Higgins, whom she considered 'Mussolini in miniature, ruthless, unrelenting, arid, reactionary and self-righteous'. Her harshness was directed at the man's personality as much as his politics. She felt Michael Collins had had kindly personal traits, allowing estranged colleagues to mourn his death, despite everything. O'Higgins had none.[89] The government, reeling in shock, redoubled its repressive measures, rounding up prominent activists with no attempt at legality. Emergency legislation was rushed through to justify whatever actions it took. A Public Safety bill empowered the government to declare unlawful any organisation it wished and made provision for 'Special Courts' with the power to impose the death penalty.

Five days after O'Higgins, another death occurred. Constance Markievicz, who had looked old and ill in photos of the newly elected Fianna Fáil deputies, was rushed to hospital with acute appendicitis. She remained there for a number of days, struggling for life, rejecting any suggestion she should be moved to the comfort of a private ward. Kathleen Lynn, her doctor, was in constant attendance and many of her closest friends kept vigil in a room set aside for them by the hospital authorities. When they realised that Constance was not going to survive, Hanna, Dorothy Macardle and Esther Roper decided to telegram Casimir Markievicz in Warsaw.[90] He arrived in time to be with his wife. Her death, at the age of 59, was a shock to many. Eva Gore-Booth had died of cancer the year before, and Esther Roper, her partner, was distraught by the additional loss of Constance, her last link with Eva. She and Hanna became close over the next years: Esther, lonely, urging Hanna to spend the night at her London home whenever she was passing through, and Hanna, sensitive to the desolation of bereavement, occasionally doing so, forsaking her usual haunt of the Minerva Club.

The body of Constance Markievicz lay in state in the Rotunda, the government having refused permission for the use of the City Hall or any other building it controlled. With great sadness her friends stood there for hours, watching the crowds as they filed into a room lovingly decorated with wild flowers and leaves by women from Cumann na mBan. They touched the wood of the coffin as if it was a relic, pressing kisses on the glass covering her face. This was a tale of two funerals, with both sides wanting to honour their dead, hoping to attract the greatest crowds. In the end, there was no contest. Officialdom attended Kevin O'Higgins and the people flocked to pay tribute to their 'Madame'. The O'Higgins funeral was an overwhelmingly male event, while the coffin of Constance Markievicz was followed by hosts of her former comrades, street traders of Dublin, factory workers, and her constituents, the poorest of the poor. As one of the crowd commented to Hanna, 'Madame was a friend of the woman with the shawl.' The funeral oration was given by Eamon de Valera in a tribute that captured the heart of a unique woman while managing to ignore her more revolutionary side:

> Madame Markievicz is gone from us. Madame, the friend of the toiler, the lover of the poor. Ease and station she put aside and took the hard way of service with the weak and downtrodden ... We knew the friendliness, the great woman's heart of her, the great Irish soul of her, and we know the loss we have suffered is not to be repaired.[91]

Hanna, reflecting the differences between those in power and those who struggled to give voice to the powerless, concluded with the thought that, in the end, terror and coercion could not prevent the assassination of those whom the people hated:

> The love and loyalty of one's own people are a better armour than all the machine guns ever made; a securer protection than all the treason and safety acts ever devised. Having this shield, Constance Markievicz needed no further weapon; without it, the vice-president of the Free State's Executive Council perished.[92]

She, whom Constance had respected greatly, was appointed executor of her estate, liaising with her daughter Maeve de Markievicz and the Dublin Book Agency in the disposal of Markievicz's books.[93] Over the years Hanna did much to keep alive the memory of Constance Markievicz, whom she sometimes referred to as 'Ireland's Joan of Arc'. She wrote innumerable articles on her memories of their work together, some of which Esther Roper included in her edited collection of the *Prison Letters*, prompted to do this after listening to Hanna on the radio - 'wishing you were writing the introduction to the letters. You are much better than I am so full of life and vivid colour – you made Con live again for me.'[94] Meg Connery, back at her family home in Westport, had been informed by Tom Powell, Fianna Fáil TD for Galway, that Hanna would be the Fianna Fáil candidate to replace Markievicz, which she thought 'would be a happy choice ... You would have the best chance of winning the seat; and it should be given to a woman.'[95] Would she have been the candidate chosen? Was it a mistake for Hanna to sever her connection with the party? Or had her experience as a party member led her to conclude that there was little to be gained by remaining?

Along with the Public Safety bill the government had rushed through an Electoral Amendment bill. In future, candidates would forfeit their seats if they did not take the oath by a specified time. It was a blatant attempt to prevent their rivals from ever gaining power. That day, 11 August, de Valera, realising that otherwise he would face permanent exclusion, led 42 members of Fianna Fáil into the Dáil. Kathleen Clarke, with many misgivings, followed his example, although finding it a very hard decision to take.[96] The oath that had been the cause of so much bloodshed was now described as 'merely an empty political formula.' Hanna did not see it in this light. She had resigned from the executive of Fianna Fáil in May (and from her positions on their Prisoners and Publicity Committees), disagreeing with decisions being taken, one of them concerning a reversal of a decision regarding Patrick Belton.[97] It is difficult to ascertain internal party politics, but in July Belton ignored official policy by taking the Oath of Allegiance, thereby entering the Dáil. At the time Hanna continued to affirm her belief in the party but now she felt it impossible to remain a member of the organisation. From her holiday in France she wrote a terse letter of resignation:

France Aug 16

Dear Mr de Valera,

The detailed accounts in the home press, just to hand, of the recent step taken by your party, indicate so complete reversal of policy on the part of the Executive of Fianna Fail that it is impossible for me to remain any longer a member of that body or of the organisation. I beg, therefore, to tender my resignation and shall be obliged if you will communicate same to Executive at its next meeting.

Sincerely,
Hanna Sheehy Skeffington[98]

It was an immediate and unequivocal response. The issue of the oath provided a convenient opt-out, a question of principle she could focus upon. It was of enormous symbolic significance, to be sure, but for Hanna Sheehy Skeffington, feminist and republican, it seems to have been a relief to have this peg on which to hang her resignation. There were many friends who agreed with her decision. Meg very quickly wrote in support: 'Well, I for one am thoroughly fed up with Dev and his Jesuitical conscience. I never thought he would swallow the Oath of Allegiance'[99] and by early September, now knowing Hanna's views on the issue, was pleased to add: 'I was glad to find we are of one mind re the F. F. mess.'[100] From America, Florence Murphy Baker hoped that her decision in going against this powerful strand in Irish politics would not 'constrict the family purse', but she and many of Hanna's feminist friends gave her their support:

> I need not tell you how glad I was to hear you had resigned from de Valera's party and were not going to help him play politics anymore. I had noticed that your articles had not been appearing any more in the Irish World after my return and concluded that as a result of that step this work had been discontinued. I saw Alice Park a week ago and she confirmed this suspicion.[101]

Hanna's articles in the *Irish World* had become less frequent and much less prominent, although she continued to send in copy, hoping for publication. Those who appeared in print were Frank Gallagher and Robert Brennan, both loyal followers of de Valera. The *Irish World* was a vociferous supporter of Fianna Fáil. Within the party ranks the differences between the radicals and the staunch followers of de Valera were becoming apparent. Once she broke with de Valera, Hanna was unforgiving in her antipathy. Some were more conflicted in resigning their membership. Dorothy Macardle did not leave Fianna Fáil until 29 August, doing so 'very reluctantly' while appreciating the motives behind the change of policy. She remained on friendly terms with de Valera.[102] When a second election was called for October, Sinn Féin, having done so badly in June, did not stand. With her mantle of constitutionalism abandoned, Hanna was free to agree publicly with the attitude expressed in *An Phoblacht*. All accepted that it was the immediate duty of republican voters to drive the government out, and so Fianna Fáil had to be supported. But that was not the only goal: there was still hope of a future revolution. Hanna summarised the attitude as 'Vote against Cosgrave and keep your powder dry!'[103] Cosgrave's gamble in calling a snap election did not pay off, the two major parties winning seats at the expense of the smaller. One particular cause for regret amongst women generally was that the female candidates failed to be re-elected. The backlash against women in the public sphere was having results. The only woman left in the Dáil was a Cumann na nGaedheal member, Margaret Collins O'Driscoll, sister of Michael Collins.

While his mother was increasingly being drawn towards the left-republican position, Owen was about to become a student in the most pro-British institution in Ireland. He did well in his final year at school, winning a junior exhibition and an entrance prize in French. In October 1927 he entered Trinity College Dublin, to study French and English. The university was a bastion of British imperial values; its staff and students had rallied to defend the college against the rebels in 1916, so the choice was a surprising one for a Sheehy Skeffington. It was also a challenge to the authority of the Roman Catholic church, which Hanna relished, writing to Owen, 'Your being in TCD is regarded as a horror, which word has gone round to the 'Sec of a Minister' forsooth, that Betty may follow…'[104] Owen proved to be as independent as his parents had been, continuing the argument on behalf of women students, rejecting the unionist ethos of the college and excelling as a debater. It was a struggle to pay the fees, despite his scholarships and Owen's own efforts to earn money through giving 'grinds' to struggling students, so it was a relief when he won a Foundation Scholarship at the end of his second year. Hanna was immensely proud, addressing his envelopes to 'O. S. Skeffington Esq. Sch. TCD'[105] He was now entitled to free food and accommodation and so moved into college rooms, returning home most Sundays for a family lunch.

On Christmas Day 1927 Francis Cruise O'Brien died suddenly from a heart attack, collapsing while giving his son Conor a present of a bow and arrow. Abruptly, shockingly, Kathleen joined her sisters in widowhood. There was tension between them at first, as Mary showed her disapproval of Kathleen's decision, respecting the agnosticism of her husband, not to call a priest. Conor was greatly distressed by his mother retiring to her room 'roaring crying' after Mary, 'in high dudgeon' had left the house. He remembered the appearance that evening of Hanna and Owen, coming to bring Conor and his mother back to Belgrave Road, as a 'mercy mission'. They gave their support to Kathleen, just as Hanna and Frank had previously supported her in her long battle to marry Cruise O'Brien. Owen put on a magic-lantern show to entertain his traumatised cousin and when, three days later, Owen quietly contradicted his mother by insisting that Conor could have a light to read in bed, his grateful young cousin concluded: 'I now knew that I had a protector, and that he was the strongest personality in the family.' Owen was also responsible for ensuring that Conor attended Sandford Park rather than a Catholic school, which was another issue on which Mary was attempting to exert pressure on her sister. She had formidable adversaries: 'Mary was quite a strong character on her own, but she stood a bit in awe of Hanna. And she was altogether outgunned when Hanna and Owen acted in concert, as on this occasion.'[106]

Despite these tensions, the three women continued to spend Sundays together, usually at Kathleen's, where the cousins Betty, Owen and Conor would join their mothers. The youngsters found it hard to get a word in as arguments on the issue of the moment raged and forceful opinions were expressed. All agreed on questions of feminism, but there was little common ground when it came to Irish political affairs. The Sheehy sisters met up with their brother Eugene less frequently. In writing to her cricket-mad son Hanna revealed her opinion regarding her brother's politics: 'Glad England was smashed by Australia if its only cricket – Eugene was actually on England's side – he is a lost soul!'[107] Carmel, his wife, was uncomfortable in the presence of the intellectual, unconformist Sheehy women, feeling that they despised her conventional values and lifestyle. Christmas was the one occasion when all would get together and then the old family word games would be played, at a level of sophistication that precluded participation by children. It did away with the need for stilted conversation. Eugene's son David, too young to be anything except an excited member of the audience, felt that watching the grown-ups play charades was better than being at the theatre. He remembered his mother's horror in seeing Hanna coming down the stairs dressed up in her clothes and her fury at the end of the evening, seeing the devastation of her bedroom with clothes and hats strewn around. The Sheehys would not have dreamed of asking permission.[108] Kathleen missed 'the Sheehy clan' feeling when Hanna was in Canada during the Christmas of 1937, 'It wasn't the real thing at all … still Sheehy is Sheehy!'[109]

As Owen needed to spend time in France, Hanna arranged for him to spend the summer of 1928 with the Denis family in Amiens. Her encouragement regarding Owen's studies reflected her experiences in Paris, almost thirty years before: 'Glad you are progressing at the French – try to get the three hours in plus lesson – I'd like you to get a few Lycée lessons when college opens.'[110] Her old friend Germaine Fontaine, to whom she had confessed so long ago her desire for a daughter, was now married and the mother of three sons and a daughter. Andrée, her 18-year-old daughter, would become Hanna's much-loved daughter-in-law.[111]

Gretta Cousins visited Ireland in late 1928, taking the opportunity to give lectures on 'India Today' to audiences in Dublin and Belfast. She had become a supporter of the Indian independence movement and tried to persuade Hanna to travel to India as an Irish representative of the independence movement. The Delhi Intelligence Bureau, monitoring Gretta's mail, noted that Hanna was 'a lady of known extremist tendencies.'[112] While Hanna did not go to India, she did lend her support to Irish solidarity movements. An Irish section of the League Against Imperialism had been formed in 1928, its main focus to organise solidarity with 'the Indian masses in their struggle against British imperialism.' The staff of *An Phoblacht* were founders and leading members. In September 1930 she joined a speaker's platform chaired by Seán MacBride, along with Peadar O'Donnell, Frank Ryan, Helena Molony and others,[113] and also supported Charlotte Despard and Maud Gonne MacBride in their later involvement with the Indian-Irish Independence League.

Hanna spent a busy week in London in late July 1928; so busy that she confessed to 'mental indigestion' as a result. She had at last a publisher for a re-print of Frank's biography of Davitt, 'but it's the devil's own job trying to land them!'; met up with Nora Connolly O'Brien, both women being treated by Mr Diamond (editor of the *Catholic Herald*) to a 'great lunch' at the Savoy Hotel and presented with a beautiful bouquet of flowers ('I'd have preferred the "dough" myself') and spoke at two meetings, one on Ireland and one at the Women's Freedom League, on the moves to introduce censorship of publications in Ireland. A detective called at the Freedom League office to inquire where she was staying and for how long, which amused her greatly, 'Perhaps he's going to send me a bunch of flowers!' While all this was mostly business, she enjoyed lunch with George Bernard Shaw and his wife Charlotte as well as the excitement of a visit to the courtroom where there was a hearing on whether Radclyffe Halls's lesbian novel *Well of Loneliness*, first published on 27 July, should be tried for obscenity:

> Am lunching with Mr and Mrs GBS today – a treat I believe Americans would give anything for! She is very decent & he wants to talk all about Ireland. I am much more a prophet (or prophetess) outside my own country, which is the natural way of prophets since time began! I got into an important court case yesterday, packed to the doors (over banned book 'Well of Loneliness') by saying 'Irish Press' simply! Got seat at press table! All literary world was there – Hugh Walpole, the authoress Storm Jameson … It was very thrilling. More anon.[114]

Shaw lent his support to Radclyffe Hall, so either he or her friends in the Freedom League must have provided the information that sent Hanna rushing to the court room. She also began to read Shaw's *Intelligent Woman's Guide to Socialism* ('it's great on governments, the church etc.'), recommending the book to Owen.

With her son away, Hanna took the opportunity to catch up with old friends and family, providing snapshots of her activities in a series of long and chatty letters to Owen that mixed the mundane with the more political in her typically lively prose: 'Pete and I both miss you – I guess Pete quite a lot as he looks up and down looking for you.' – 'had quite a party last night to tea … Conor pinched loganberries when he thought no one was looking'; 'Aunt K. got permanent wave. Conor has new dog and "skinny" little kitten has been stolen! He certainly gets though a goodly number of pets!'; holidaying with Cahalan and Rose Jacob in Kilkee, ('made progress with swimming so feeling very fit. Got 16 bathes while away'); visiting Mary Bourke-Dowling in Termonfeckin (who suggested she not bring 'Poor Pete' on account of his 'rambling propensities'); dinner at the Connery's ('it was great'); going to the Abbey for *An Phoblacht* to see a one-act play by Kathleen O'Brennan on Irish-American theatre; visiting Maud Gonne MacBride, who needed her language skills when she had a German visitor hoping to start a student exchange system ('brushed up my German').[115] Owen's time away was also enlivened by letters full of jokes from his aunt Kathleen. Kathleen and Mary had both succumbed to what Kathleen described as 'the germ of Bobbitis' by having their hair cut short. The others did not follow their example as Betty Kettle 'sorrowfully surveys a free world from behind her bush of ringlets', lent 'moral support in her lonely vigil' by a stubborn Hanna, who retained her bun of hair, despite insisting on women's right to defy convention.[116]

What most exercised Hanna that summer was the prospect of an 'Evil Literature measure' which would establish 'a rigid censorship over books in the Free State'. A 'Committee on Evil Literature' had been established by Kevin O'Higgins with a remit to investigate how censorship powers could be extended. Hanna had just experienced censorship in London and with Fianna Fáil 'pressing for it for all it's worth!' she added she and Rose 'had decided that we would not vote for Fianna Fáil the next time - will probably not vote at all.'[117] Censorship of films was also being instituted, and the Women's International League, with many pacifists in its membership, decided to lobby to have war films included within the Act. Hanna was involved in this. Former suffragist Lucy Kingston, meeting Montgomery, the Film Censor, along with Mrs Stephens and Hanna, noted that it was 'a most interesting interview, helped out by his loquacity and niceness and by Mrs S.S.'s wit.'[118] She returned to London later that year, speaking at another meeting at the Women's Freedom League on the proposed censorship bill and its effect on women in Ireland. She had hoped for 'constructive legislation' in an independent Irish state, but instead they had 'this fussy, negative kind of legislation' to contend with. The Minister for Justice was to decide 'what is good and what is bad' and they would not be allowed to use their free will. Advertisements dealing with birth control or venereal diseases would also be banned, meaning that some of the best newspapers, because they contained advertisements dealing with such subjects, would come under the ban. Addressing an audience of feminists, she was clear in her message:

> it seems we are always to be legislated for by the other sex. This is one of my main grievances: that we should be legislated for by men who in their prudish way think that women should not be allowed to serve on juries because it is not nice (Laughter). For the same reason women stenographers have been removed from the Court, although they are usually far more skilful than men ... Such legislation is fostered or suggested by the monastic, celibate type, to whom women are not

> only dangerous and explosive, but also a rather indecent quantity (Laughter). They linger on the shortness of women's hair or her skirts, and seem to regard such things as just a little immoral (Laughter).[119]

In the summer of 1929 she joined the staff of *An Phoblacht*, now edited by Frank Ryan. Peadar O'Donnell had moved *An Phoblacht* towards Marxism during his time as editor, a political approach supported by Hanna. Ryan's politics were much more 'traditional Pearsean rhetoric.'[120] Frank Edwards told a good story that revealed the political differences between Ryan as editor and Hanna, assistant editor. Ryan, about to rush off somewhere, would leave instructions that a blank space in a column be filled with a quotation from Pearse, to be told by his strong-minded colleague: 'I will not, I have a far more appropriate one here from James Connolly.'[121] Rose Jacob recalling how the pair 'disagreed and enjoyed and laughed at each other', said Ryan called her 'Skeffy', 'but that, from him, was only a sign of respect.'[122] Hanna wrote in humorous tone to Owen of her activities, but there was no hiding the fact that these were dangerous times:

> I barely escaped being sent to Clare again this week. I think they thought if I got beaten up, 'twould be good publicity, till editor said 'who would write it up? in that case I said 'twould be better for me to leave a dying statement before I went. As, however, there was other work to be done here, I hadn't to go after all.[123]

Free State repression worsened in the aftermath of the O'Higgins murder. Seán MacBride was one of the suspects arrested under the new legislation. For those who remained in opposition to the state, the years up to 1932 were punctuated by new laws, raids, arrests, imprisonment. Some wondered if Cumann na nGaedheal was trying to provoke a new Civil War, so draconian were its actions and so intolerant its attitudes. The home of the elderly Mrs Pearse was one of those visited frequently by the CID, and over Easter 1929 the home and shop of Jennie Wyse Power were raided twice by detectives looking for a woman in her employment. An elderly woman was sentenced to two months imprisonment after two old revolvers were found in her home. Hanna commented angrily, 'The intensive war now going on illustrates even more clearly than in the case of the men how provocative the campaign of persecution is and how utterly futile from an ordinary police point of view.' No one believed the lie that all those women were criminals to be 'hounded down' and 'stamped out' as the government maintained.[124]

In autumn 1929 Hanna and Rose were delegates to the Sixth Congress of the Women's International League for Peace and Freedom, held in Prague, capital of the old Bohemia and of the new Republic of Czechoslovakia.

Hanna was still scrabbling for money, dependent solely on journalism and lecturing, often not earning enough to reach the tax threshold. She occasionally, through friendly contacts, had some exam work, but the teaching profession remained closed to those who would not take the oath. Rose was making even less money by her writing and often had to resort to teaching crafts to make ends meet. In 1920, using the pseudonym of 'F. Winthrop' she had published a novel, *Callaghan*, set in the Ireland of 1914, which tackled in uncompromising form the question of religion, suffrage, revolution and relationships between the sexes. She was not to write another novel until 1938.[125] Hanna was able to write articles on her travels for the *Irish Independent* and, as the League paid most of her expenses she could, for once, relax and enjoy a reasonable amount of comfort.[126] She also wrote in more propagandist vein for *An Phoblacht*, lamenting that Ireland was now 'off the map', confused with Britain, the struggle for national independence limited to knowledge of the past heroics of Terence MacSwiney and Roger Casement, whose personal sacrifices had made headlines around the world.[127] She spent four weeks travelling through Germany, Austria and Czechoslovakia, pleased to have an invitation to stay in a Czech household. A holiday came first, staying in a friend's house outside Vienna. She and Owen wrote frequently to each other, warm, witty letters full of gossip: 'I've got the map of Europe added to my passport now. I'd like to go to Buda Pesth if poss. That would add three new countries to my list, making 16 in all.' She loved the view of the Alps and decided that she preferred Austria to France, remembering to warn Owen not to mention that to his French hosts. He had returned with eagerness to the warm welcome of the Denis family, enjoying a normal family life for a second summer. Hanna was pleased that her son was so well integrated, 'glad to hear you do your bit in the house too. I wish someone would teach you to sew & mend.' In family games with the Sheehy's '"O. and A." now replaces in family slang the "me & Owen" of former times.' Far from feeling displaced by her son's growing friendship with Andrée Denis, she wrote with genuine warmth, 'I am delighted A. is coming to us at xmas. Tell her any accent is preferable to the Haw-Haw British.'[128]

Congress was a hectic event; each minute of the day being crammed with activity. Hanna and Rose shared a drawing room for their brief moments of relaxation. It was all 'very charming and stimulating' she declared.[129] A highlight was the speech of the Indian delegate, who made 'an impassioned and telling indictment of British Imperialism that starves and exploits suffering India'. Some of the British delegates, said Hanna with some relish, 'hung their heads in shame at her story', but she had nothing but praise for the intervention of Ellen Wilkinson, the radical British Labour Party MP, who denounced British Imperialism in a 'refreshing un-English candour'. On 1 September she joined delegates from France, Germany, America, Belgium and Canada in Dresden, to speak at a public meeting on the theme of 'A World Without War'. She began by explaining Ireland's position, as a partitioned colony on whom an enforced treaty was imposed, before going on to outline the republican goal of an independent nation, part of a European commonwealth. In her eyes this was 'a peace of freedom, compatible with the ideals of Peace and Freedom of the Women's International League'.[130] Louie Bennett, unable to travel to Prague as her mother was seriously ill, remained concerned by the gulf between the 'really pacifist group' and those who considered 'the use of force essential to achieve a social revolution, or to achieve national freedom.' She was sure a split in the Irish organisation was inevitable.[131]

To help in securing convictions a Juries Protection Act was introduced, allowing for a majority of nine out of twelve for conviction and providing complete anonymity for jurors. Now charges of 'seditious libel' were levelled at those who argued against the law and Maud Gonne MacBride was one of the first charged with that offence. When her case came to court, in November 1929, Hanna was in court, representing *An Phoblacht*. The police made immediate objections to the 'republican press representative' in the courtroom. Other representatives of the press were allowed to remain but the judge, having scrutinised the various pages of *An Phoblacht* handed up to him by a police inspector, ruled that its articles were calculated to intimidate jurors. Hanna was ordered to leave the court. According to Maud Gonne MacBride her response was to comment, 'in her clear, musical voice, "The freedom of the press!"' as she rose to leave.[132] In spite of everything, the verdict was an acquittal by the jury and the defendant received a tremendous ovation from her massed women friends as she came out of the courthouse. When Hanna became assistant editor, she was often solely responsible for the paper as Ryan was a target for continual arrest. On one occasion, shots were fired into the two small rooms in Exchequer Street that served as the paper's offices. No one was injured, but it was an indication that taking up the pen in defence of the republican cause was not an easy option. Rose Jacob frequently helped with production before Hanna joined the staff. She was living in a flat at the office of the Gaelic League, with a big cat, 'the sleeping Thomas' in the basement. Frank promptly dubbed the animal 'the stinking Thomas', without Rose taking offence.[133] In hasty notes to Hanna she sounded almost girlishly pleased about Frank managing to put in an appearance at a ceílí, and full of enthusiasm for a party she was about to give. Rose's secret love affair with

Ryan began in 1928, continuing for a number of years, to the disapproval of Dorothy Macardle, with whom she was then sharing a flat.[134]

In July 1930 Frank Ryan, returning from a trip to America 'by underground route' as he was refused a passport, reported to Hanna as they worked together in the *An Phoblacht* office that he believed the *Irish World* was 'hopeless', suggesting that they both went back to America in Easter 1931 for a 'lightening tour'.[135] In the same month she found herself 'suddenly and unaccountably' removed from the register for superintendent of exams. She suspected either the Catholic church or Denis Coffey, President of UCD, as retaliation for Owen's attendance at Trinity.[136] She wrote to all the major towns in Ireland, offering her services as a lecturer, but many replied regretting that her proposed topics were not suitable. These were not good times for radical dissidents to spread their views, even if they confined their talks to historical and literary themes. In America, Florence Murphy Baker approached various Speakers' Bureaux on her behalf, trying to interest them in organising a lecture tour. The Open Forum Speakers Bureau in Boston paid about $50 a lecture 'which is not very exciting but would help anyway'. The Feakins Bureau had no openings until the winter of 1931 and did not hold out much hope as Hanna, obviously trying not to put off a conservative audience, suggested cultural and travel topics rather than the political issues which were really her strong point.[137] Her willingness to consider marketing herself was an indication of how desperate her financial situation had become. Florence urged her to sell herself better: 'it would be well to send newspaper cuttings or letters from any big-wigs telling of your talks in the US in the past and particularly emphasising your ability as a speaker'.[138] She would, eventually, pursue these suggestions, but in the meantime, another avenue, not lucrative but of great interest, had opened.

In a world of mounting fascism, the Soviet Union stood out as a beacon of hope. In one country at least, the working class had seemed to come into its inheritance. Increasingly, the threat of the 'communist menace' was used by church and state authorities to dampen down revolutionary fervour. Against that, it became the duty of progressives everywhere to defend the Soviet Union from its detractors. In Ireland, as in many other countries, a 'Friends of Soviet Russia' (FOSR) was started as a means of promoting the soviet system and of explaining the reality of life in Russia. It was a tiny group but immensely enthusiastic and full of excitement about the prospect of travelling to see the revolution for themselves. R. M. Fox said his trip to Russia 'was by far the most interesting experience I have had'.[139] Helena Molony, whom Hanna always referred to as 'Emer' (her old Inghinidhe na hÉireann name), had also travelled to the Soviet Union. 'Russian farewell parties' were organised for those about to embark on tours, popular with those who formed a tiny bohemian, counter-cultural challenge to the prevailing orthodoxy. Helena brought a pot of caviar to Hanna's party and Hanna amused herself trying to describe the delicacy to Owen: 'Caviare is an acquired taste and I haven't yet acquired it! It's like shoe polish only not as sweet. Just a polish that has been left in some decayed fish.'[140] Despite her financial problems, 'can only pay small bills' and the knowledge that her rent from her lodgers would be her only income, not even bureaucratic forms could dent her good spirits:

> Filling in forms – one query is how often and for what you were in jail & I felt chippy, but it applies, alas, only to Russia! Governments seem to love all this. I think they ought to adopt as anthem 'wrap the red tape round me, boy!' Another joke I have patented is taking the 'Rush' out of Russia – ha-ha![141]

She hoped to be able to publish articles and possibly a book after the Russian trip. Kathleen O'Brennan encouraged her to think about a book on Russian women and promised to put in a word for her when attending a book conference.[142] From London her old friend Henry Nevinson, hoping she would come and visit after her trip, suggested possible newspapers to place articles as well as advising her to undertake a lecture trip to America rather than the 'badly paid' circuit of lectures in England.[143] She must have written to many friends, hoping for advice and support. The only anxiety she displayed before setting off concerned a little attaché case of a tea basket with full equipment for two given to her by Mary as a gift for her journey – a generous gesture, given Mary's cynicism about the venture which she articulated in her poem marking the occasion.[144] Hanna was delighted with her 'lovely' present which would be greatly appreciated by 'comrades', but disconcerted to be told by 'Emer' 'it knocks me down as "bourgeois" ... she says I'll have to explain it as a loan only from a rich friend!' As the poem indicates, Maud Gonne MacBride had given one to Charlotte Despard, also a member of the delegation.[145]

The six Irish delegates, together with fifteen British communists, had a send-off meeting in Essex Hall in London before sailing to Russia on 8 August 1930. Kathleen Price of the Nurses' Union and secretary of FOSR, had made it plain to the delegates that they were not guests of the Soviet Republic, but were there as guests of the Central Council of Trade Unions in Russia. The distinction was important: 'people say if the government invites you, it just shows you what it likes. It is not the government but the trade unions, giving the hospitality.'[146] Hanna and Sheila Bowen Dowling of the

Irish Women Workers' Union shared a cabin, with Charlotte Despard and Mrs Crawford next door. Their cabins, to Hanna's surprise, were 'very elaborate', with beds not bunks, and electric reading lamps. Images of Lenin, Marx and Engels were prominent on the ship, so the artist Harry Kernoff, one of the Irish delegates, presented a drawing of James Connolly, based on his wood cut of Connolly in Irish Citizen Army uniform in front of Liberty Hall, a photo of which Hanna had with her. She reported, 'The crew are charmed. There is no English revolutionary martyr, so that adds a thrill!'[147] Irish and British had some interesting political discussions, the Irish being intent on countering what they considered to be the misinformed attitudes of the British comrades. The exchange of views was so successful that, as Charlotte Despard scribbled in her diary: 'Mrs Sheehy Skeffington's stock of Irish revolutionary mementoes was almost exhausted.'[148] The four-and-a-half-day boat journey from London to Leningrad went some way to acclimatising them to a different way of life. The Soviet ship had 'brown bread and red pamphlets' and Hanna found the different food and different political views a source of great fascination. They were fed well, if unusually. Breakfast was cold meat, boiled egg and coffee in a glass, lunch was meat and cheese, vermicelli, cutlet and peas and Russian tea. Friday's breakfast, to her surprise, was cheese and sardines. The 'Hammer and Sickle' was everywhere. Discipline on board was strict, with the ship being run, she thought, as an autocracy, yet she felt it 'worked well'. The ideal of the 'dictatorship of the proletariat' was present in every detail, the workers were not wage slaves like in the west, so would have been insulted if they had been tipped.[149]

As Hanna busily jotted down her first impressions, admitting that her preconceived notions had 'got a shake', she decided (a radical decision for someone used to the wet Irish weather) that she would leave her umbrella behind. She felt it was 'bourgeois'. That term and 'counter-revolutionary' were the hardest words that could be used. For a 53-year-old Irish woman to worry that possession of an umbrella would make her appear bourgeois reveals someone anxious not to offend her host society, a person without pretensions, flexible in her attitude towards life's inessentials. She was a modern woman, who saw no reason why she should conform to the expectations surrounding middle age. And, as a modern woman, she liked what she saw when she arrived. There was no 'tyranny of fashion and clothes', a freedom which could be liberatory 'if you regard these as a fuss and a bore', although, as a hat lover, she did not go so far as to welcome the prospect of the ubiquitous headscarf. She felt scornful of 'bourgeois tourists', obviously feeling that she and her party had escaped that ignominious description, and she was delighted by the general liberation of women from the 'pots and pans', her particular dislike in life. That phrase of Lenin's – 'the tyranny of the pots and pans' – was one she would use incessantly, even in her last writing of all. She admired the freeing of children from parental bondage as well as from the bondage of the church. It was how she had tried to bring up her own son, to be free from the burden of imposed views. Was she quoting a guide when she jotted down 'churches a bad habit like drink or dope' or would she have expressed that sentiment in that American-sounding manner? She wondered about the effect of 'no Sundays' on Irish life, without indicating what she herself thought of the abolition of a day of rest. The only reservation she expressed concerned the 'adoration of the machine' which was evident everywhere as the soviet system developed its ambitious Five-Year Plans for a mass programme of development designed to challenge the capitalist west. This was, she hoped, simply 'a phase in the liberation movement'.

Russia, the first proletarian nation, worked hard to show its best side to its allies. They in turn were anxious to show revolutionary solidarity, to the extent, maybe, of failing to probe issues that they would undoubtedly have investigated further if they had been in a capitalist country. On purgings, Hanna noted that there were 'only a quarter million' and prisons were places of sequestration, not punishment, where prisoners were permitted holidays and the use of a radio. Was this really what she was told? Mrs Despard had pursued the matter of prisons and had finally, after delay, been told of offenders being 'trained for citizenship', with 'island penal settlements' reserved for 'incurable' offenders.[150] No one was able to see prison life for themselves, so they had to take their information on trust. Stalinist excesses had not yet begun, but even when they did, they remained hidden from many. The name of Trotsky could still be mentioned at this time. Hanna was aware of his contribution to the revolution, noting on several occasions in her jottings his desire to see the revolution spread to other countries.

After Leningrad they spent six days in Moscow, touring factories, craft centres, childcare centres, communal restaurants and rehabilitation centres for petty criminals. Then it was a long trek to Baku on the Caspian Sea, before returning via Poland. She summed up her overall impression as 'making the world better for the workers, letting them into their heritage'. In a speech to the Rotary Club in November 1930 she described roads being paved for the first time, of workers being housed in large houses, divided up so that everyone had somewhere to live, of good plain meals to be had in cooperative restaurants, of free welfare schemes and no unemployment. The people looked fit and vigorous with 'an indifference to time that is quite Irish'. She had enjoyed being away from the consumerism of the west. The first newspaper she had read after five weeks had a competition about an aspidistra. So irrelevant was it, after the life and death struggle to move human existence onto a new plane, it was 'like waking up into a nightmare.'[151]

Delegates returned to Ireland full of zeal, anxious to spread the word. Irish Friends of Soviet Russia organised a series of weekly meetings where those who had seen the soviet system at work gave talks on their experiences, reassuring the Irish public on tricky issues, like religious freedom. Helena Molony assured her audience that she had had no problem in attending Mass while in Russia. Hanna's contribution to the series was, naturally, on women. A Women's International Week was launched on March 8, International Women's Day, its purpose to 'draw attention to the enslaved conditions of women in all parts of the capitalist world and to encourage women of those countries to take an active part in the struggle for freedom'. She spoke enthusiastically on the benefits to both sexes of the communist system:

> Equal pay for equal work in Russia, without regard to sex, had done away with jealousy between the sexes. The woman worker was no longer used by the boss to break strikes. She was no longer absolutely dependent on the man to be breadwinner and this independence freed her from fear and made her, as she was intended to be, the true comrade of man.[152]

This was a period of international congresses, of links being made between organisations fighting empires around the globe. Many IRA members attended League Against Imperialism congresses and travelled to meetings of the Comintern in revolutionary Russia. The huge public meeting organised by the League Against Imperialism in Dublin in November 1930 had a list of speakers that Seán MacBride felt could have formed a 'Republican Who's Who': Peadar O'Donnell, Helena Molony, Éamon de Valera, Hanna Sheehy Skeffington, Seán T. O'Kelly, Frank Ryan. Eithne Coyle said, in appreciation of Hanna's approachability, 'Give her two minutes and she would come and speak anywhere for you.'[153] Occasionally, reading the newspapers of the time and seeing just how often her name does crop up, one wonders at the energy and the commitment of the woman and at her ability to cross so many different political boundaries. For her, speaking along with IRA members at College Green, working for the Women's International League of Peace and Freedom, or applauding women's achievements in athletics, aviation and swimming in articles for the British feminist paper *The Vote*, were entirely natural and complementary activities. All were part of the struggle for human emancipation – as she understood it at least.

There was more travel at Easter, fulfilling a speaking engagement at a St Patrick's Day dinner hosted by the Irish community in Paris. Sir Francis Vane, now living in Brittany, sent a letter regretting that illness prevented him from attending. Recalling Easter Week and Portobello, he hoped he might be remembered 'if only because he had done his best to right a hideous wrong'. As private as ever about her emotions, Hanna did not refer to Frank by name when reading out the letter, saying only that it recalled 'a tragic memory of Easter Week'.[154]

Owen was selected to represent Trinity College and the Free State at a student conference on international affairs and peace in New York in the summer of 1931. He and his mother always made great efforts to maintain close contact with Margaret and the family in Canada, so while he was in America he took the opportunity to phone them for a long, relatively cheap chat. He had also entertained his cousin, Garry Culhane, in his college rooms when the latter was in Ireland the previous winter. That trip, and the need to study for finals on his return, meant that he missed a family holiday that summer. Hanna, Mary and Kathleen, together with Betty and Conor, spent August together in Normandy. Goodness knows how they managed to afford it; perhaps it was the small bonus of the sale of the Joyce-Skeffington pamphlets? She sounded in excellent form as she scrawled a postcard to Garry, telling him they were enjoying 'life à la France', with the Denis family in a nearby villa and hoping some of his family could get down to New York to see Owen before he left.[155]

In September, Saor Éire, a new radical group, appeared. It was one of the few organisations she was not part of during these years of hectic opposition. The programme of Saor Éire offered much but its method of coming into existence militated against recruiting from outside the most orthodox of republican ranks. It was, as Conor Foley has described, a front for the IRA, organised from the top down with delegates appointed by local commanding officers.[156] The two members of Cumann na mBan active in the organisation, Eithne Coyle and Sheila Humphries, had strong personal links with IRA members.

Hanna's work with *An Phoblacht* was increasingly time-consuming. Ryan was in jail almost continually between June and September and she had the task of ensuring that a nervous printer continued to produce the paper, despite the intimidatory presence of detectives. Owen was now teaching in Paris for a year, having graduated with first class honours. She was glad that he was away from the repression, describing her daily life:

> proclaimed meetings, baton charges and the rest. I think Phoblacht will be seized whatever is in it. I put up some proposals as a counter-offensive, but don't know

> whether they will be accepted. – Not much news as I only see the family on Sundays as a rule … All around and about me is being raided for 'sedition', but so far I have escaped. Anything Russian is pounced on. The church is rampant just now all over the place…[157]

In October the government inserted article 2A into the Constitution. A state of martial law now existed, with military tribunals replacing courts, twelve organisations proscribed, police raids all over the country and the total suppression of *An Phoblacht*. That December Ryan was again arrested while he was about to enter its office, beaten for resisting arrest and charged with seditious libel. Other republicans were already in Arbour Hill prison, suffering the most appalling conditions, naked and freezing in windowless cells because of their refusal to wear prison uniform. Hanna was left on her own to bring out the paper. This she did with great commitment until March 1932. Her 'counter-offensive' proposal must have been *Republican File*, the riposte to the banning of *An Phoblacht*. It carried clippings from other (unbanned) newspapers, cleverly juxtaposed with suitable headings to make political statements. Its first issue came out on 28 November 1931. She sent Owen copies of the paper, which he thought 'a very good stunt', pleased with his mother's success in defying censorship.[158]

The First National Aid Association set up a new committee to collect funds for the dependents of the prisoners. The usual names were all there: headed by Maud Gonne MacBride, with Hanna Sheehy Skeffington and Charlotte Despard as treasurers and many prominent republicans, male and female, as committee members. In their appeal for Irish-Americans to give assistance they emphasised the high reputation of the leaders: 'The names of those in charge of the association are, of themselves, full and sufficient guarantee that all moneys received will be devoted solely to the relief of those in need.'[159] By the end of February, $1,563.92 had been donated. It was not a large amount by the standards of the past. The *Irish World* talked about Irish-American organisations standing together in the face of this onslaught. The reality was that Ireland was now ruled by a native Irish government and many Irish Americans did not understand what was happening to all the high hopes of the past.

The same women who were appealing for donations were also frantically busy organising public opposition to the government. The WPDL were banned, evicted from their offices and unable to rent anywhere else. They resorted to afternoon tea at Woolworth's and Bewley's, where visiting journalists were able to sit at adjoining tables and conduct their interviews. They refused to stop their weekly meetings, despite the ban, so they invented a new organisation – the People's Rights Association. On its first outing Helena

Molony, to great applause, quoted Shakespeare's 'a Rose by any other name would smell as sweet'.[160] An American visitor to Ireland, writing of her travels and impressions, was impressed by the women's public visibility: 'Madame MacBride, Madame Despard and Mrs Skeffington and others are deserving of great respect and credit for keeping up Sunday protests in spite of wind and weather and other and greater discouragements. I am told they have not missed holding a weekly Sunday meeting since 1922.'[161] The government felt that they had subversion on the run, if not totally defeated. The ring-leaders of the IRA and Cumann na mBan were in jail, socialism discredited through the joint efforts of church and state, leaving only the interminable protests of the 'Mothers' to harry ministers whenever they appeared in public. The women were a great irritant, prompting Fitzgerald-Kenny, the new Minister for Justice, to burst out: 'We are going to put people like these in prison, and if they persist, and if it is necessary, we are going to execute them:[162] It was a government losing touch with reality, so confident of having decimated the opposition that they thought they could call a quick general election and secure themselves in power indefinitely. They were wrong.

Republicans responded immediately to the news of an election. A special edition of *An Phoblacht*, edited by Peadar O'Donnell, was printed. O'Donnell made up the headline himself – 'Put Cosgrave Out'. Cumann na nGaedheal had been in power for ten years. The economy was in deep recession, numbers of unemployed were rising, they had cut public service pay and old age pensions, instituted censorship of publications, attacked the rights of women, and the list went on. In other words, it was a government deeply unpopular with many sections of society. The IRA and other groups prepared to support the only other party capable of winning – Fianna Fáil.

On 8 February the Eighth Dáil met. Eamon de Valera was now head of a Fianna Fáil government. The Oath of Allegiance was abolished, the prisoners were released, the Public Safety Act suspended. The WPDL announced it was disbanding, its existence no longer necessary. It was the first time in ten years that no political prisoners languished in a Free State cell. Huge, ecstatic crowds applauded the prisoners as they appeared in College Green, with special cheers greeting Frank Ryan as he climbed onto the platform of speakers. His speech emphasised his sense of gratitude: 'There was also one woman in particular of whom he wished to make special mention, and that was Mrs Sheehy Skeffington who had kept his department going while he was away.'[163] Hanna followed the lead of the other speakers in paying an unqualified tribute to the contribution of Cumann na mBan, recalling Armistice Day, when she had last spoken at College Green:

> when a few women of the movement organised an anti-Imperialist demonstration and faced the batons of the police and sticks of the C.I.D. Some of the women – members of Cumann na mBan – afterwards faced the Tribunal and helped by their splendid and defiant attitude in no small way to break down that infamous machine:[164]

Once Fianna Fáil was in office and republicans no longer had to devote their efforts to keeping the movement together through years of repression, a new freedom to be openly critical of policies emerged. Once again, there were arguments and debates on the way forward and the extent to which the new government should be supported. For Hanna, many of the thoughts she had had to suppress, in the interests of unity, were now articulated in her unmistakeable prose. An unequivocal feminism that had no hesitation in challenging prevailing orthodoxies was first item on the agenda.

NOTES

1 Graham Walker, 'The Irish Dr Goebbels: Frank Gallagher and Irish republican propaganda', in *Journal of Contemporary History*, 27, 1992, pp 149–65.

2 Cecilia Gallagher to Hanna Sheehy Skeffington, 22 Aug. 1925; 24 Aug. 1925, Sheehy Skeffington MS (hereafter SS MS) 24,117.

3 Andrée Sheehy Skeffington, personal interview, Mar. 1991.

4 Lilian Metge to Hanna Sheehy Skeffington, 20 July 1925, SS MS 24,093.

5 Hanna Sheehy Skeffington to Owen Sheehy Skeffington (hereafter Hanna to Owen), 17 July 1928, SS MS 40,484/3.

6 Margaret Sheehy O'Casey to Hanna Sheehy Skeffington, 8 Aug. 1925, SS MS 24,117.

7 Andrée Sheehy Skeffington, 'A coterie of lively suffragists', in *Writers, Raconteurs and Notable Feminists* (Dublin, 1993), p. 44.

8 Rose Jacob to Hanna Sheehy Skeffington, 18 Aug. 1925, SS MS 24,094.

9 Meg Connery to Hanna Sheehy Skeffington, 22 Aug. 1925, SS MS 24,094.

10 Eamon Donnelly to Hanna Sheehy Skeffington, 19 Aug. 1925, SS MS 24,094.

11 See Lauren Arrington, *W. B. Yeats, the Abbey Theatre, Censorship and the Irish State: Adding the Half-Pence to the Pence* (Oxford, 2010) for a scholarly examination that concludes the suspicion was correct.

12 Hanna Sheehy Skeffington, in *Irish World*, 13 Mar. 1926.

13 Andrée Sheehy Skeffington, *Skeff: A Life of Owen Sheehy Skeffington* (Dublin, 1991), p. 30.

14 *Irish World*, 13 Mar. 1926.

15 Joseph Holloway, in Robert Hogan and Michael O'Neill (eds), *Joseph Holloway's Abbey Theatre: A Selection from His Unpublished Journal Impressions of a Dublin Playgoer*, (Carbondale, 1967), pp 251–2.

16 Eithne Coyle O'Donnell, personal interview with author, June 1975.

17 Holloway, *Abbey Theatre*, p. 254.
18 Donal Dorcey 'The great occasions', in Seán McCann (ed.), *The World of Seán O'Casey* (London, 1966), p. 65.
19 Quoted in Holloway, *Abbey Theatre*, pp 255–6.
20 Ibid., pp 257–260.
21 Ibid., pp 260–263.
22 Fearghal McGarry, *Frank Ryan* (Dundalk, 2002), p. 14.
23 Holloway, *Abbey Theatre*, pp 261–3.
24 *Irish World*, 13 Mar. 1926.
25 Seán O'Casey, *Inishfallen, Fare the Well* (London, 1949, reprinted, London, 1972), pp 178–9.
26 Holloway, *Abbey Theatre*, p. 266.
27 Ibid.
28 Cathal O'Shannon, in *Irish Times*, 23 Apr. 1946.
29 *Irish World*, 27 Mar. 1926.
30 Seán O'Casey, *The Story of the Irish Citizen Army* (Dublin, 1919), p. 64.
31 Gary O'Connor, *Seán O'Casey: A Life* (New York, 1988), pp 203–4.
32 *Irish Citizen*, Sept. 1919 (writing under the name of 'Joan').
33 Holloway, *Abbey Theatre*, p. 268.
34 Diarmaid Ferriter, *A Nation and Not A Rabble: The Irish Revolution 1913–1923* (London, 2015), p. 27.
35 C. S. Andrews, *Man of No Property* (Dublin, 1979), p. 55.
36 *Irish World*, 20 Mar. 1926.
37 Ibid., 3 Apr. 1926.
38 Ibid.
39 Charlotte Despard, 1926 Diary, 11 Mar. 1926, D24791/9, Public Record Office Northern Ireland (hereafter PRONI).
40 Ibid., 28 Mar. 1926.
41 Richard Dunphy, *The Making of Fianna Fáil Power in Ireland 1923–48* (Dublin, 1995), p. 71.
42 *Irish World*, 15 May 1926.
43 Ibid., 16 July 1927.
44 Desmond Ryan, 'Hanna Sheehy Skeffington', in Bakery Trades Journal, Apr.-June 1946.
45 Seán Lemass to Hanna Sheehy Skeffington, 26-10-26, SS MS 24,095
46 Charlotte Despard 1926 Diary, 19 June 1926; *Irish World*, 10 July 1926.
47 *Irish World*, 10 July 1926.
48 Lola Lloyd to Hanna Sheehy Skeffington, 28 Sept. 1926, SS MS 24,119.
49 Florence Murphy Baker to Hanna Sheehy Skeffington, 7 Mar. 1932, writing from Madrid, SS MS 41,177/1.
50 *Irish World*, 26 June 1926.
51 Ibid., 3 July 1926.
52 Katherine Blake to Hanna Sheehy Skeffington, 20 Aug. 1926, SS MS 24,119.
53 Andrée Sheehy Skeffington, 'The hatter and the crank: Reflections and speculation on the Joyce-Frank Sheehy Skeffington relationship', in *Irish Times*, 5 Feb. 1982.

In this article Andrée dates the meeting to 1930, but Margaret's response to her sister makes it plain that the meeting took place in 1926.

54 Margaret Sheehy O'Casey, 9 Aug. 1926, SS MS 24,119.

55 Eugene Sheehy, *May it Please the Court* (Dublin, 1951), p. 35.

56 SS MS 33,606/13.

57 Andrée Sheehy Skeffington, 'The hatter and the crank', 5 Feb. 1982. This meeting probably came about as a result of Hanna's letter to Owen, suggesting that he drop in to see Sylvia Beach as a way of getting to meet Joyce. Hanna to Owen, 9 Nov. 1931, SS MS 40,484/6. In Andrée Sheehy Skeffington, *Skeff*, the meeting is dated early Dec. 1931, and brought about by Thomas McGreevy bringing Owen a message that Joyce wanted to see him, p. 62. In Aug. 1934 Hanna wrote to Owen who was in France with the Denis family, to enquire 'Did you look up Joyce?' Hanna to Owen, Aug. 1934, SS MS 40,484/7, but there is no record of other meetings.

58 Helena Swanwick, *I Have Been Young* (London, 1935), p. 450.

59 R. M. Fox, *Louie Bennett: Her Life and Times* (Dublin, 1958), p. 89.

60 *Irish World*, 7 Aug. 1926.

61 Gertrude Bussey and Margaret Tims, *Pioneers for Peace: Women's International League for Peace and Freedom 1915–65* (London, 1965), p. 39.

62 Women's International Congress, programme of meetings open to the public, Saturday 10 July to Wednesday 14 July 1926, SS MS 41,202/5. Hanna must have typed up her address as copies of her script are in MS 41,202/4. Members of the Irish Section of the Women's International League at this time were Louie Bennett (chair) and Committee: Hanna Sheehy Skeffington, Meg Connery, Rose Jacob, Charlotte Despard, Helen Chenevix, Susan Manning, Mrs Richardson, Mrs Mortishead, Miss E. Mills, Mrs Stevens, SS MS 41,202/2.

63 Swanwick, *I Have Been Young*, p. 450.

64 Typed report of speech, July 1926, Alice Park Collection, Hoover Institution Archives, Stanford, California.

65 Swanwick, *I Have Been Young*, p. 451.

66 Ibid., p. 450.

67 Ibid., p. 451.

68 Rosemary Cullen Owens, *Louie Bennett* (Cork, 2001), p. 57.

69 *Irish World*, 7 Aug. 1926.

70 R. M. Fox, *Rebel Irishwomen* (Dublin, 1935), p. 81.

71 Gertrude Bussey and Margaret Tims, *Pioneers for Peace*, pp 53–7.

72 *Irish World*, 7 Aug. 1926.

73 Fox, *Rebel Irishwomen*, p. 81.

74 Cullen Owens, *Louie Bennett*, p. 57.

75 Ibid.

76 Andrews, *Man of No Property*, p. 55.

77 Richard English, *Radicals and the Republic: Socialist Republicanism in the Irish Free State 1925–1937* (Oxford, 1994), p. 63.

78 *Irish World*, 7 Aug. 1926.

79 Ibid., 19 March 1927.

80 Maryann Valiulis, 'Defining their role in the new state: Irishwomen's protest against the Juries Act of 1927', in *Canadian Journal of Irish Studies*, 18:1, July 1992, pp 43–60.
81 Hanna Sheehy Skeffington, 'Sex equality: A reply to Victor Hall', in *Voice of Labour*, 12 Mar. 1927.
82 *Irish Times*, 16 Feb. 1927.
83 Hanna Sheehy Skeffington to Professor Magennis, 3 Mar. 1927, SS MS 41,170/55; Professor Magennis in Senate debate, 22 Mar. 1927.
84 Marie O'Neill, *From Parnell to De Valera*, pp 158–62
85 *Irish World*, 7 May 1927.
86 Ibid., 2 Apr. 1927.
87 Dunphy, *The Making of Fianna Fáil*, p. 131.
88 Conor Cruise O'Brien, 'Passion and Cunning: An essay on the politics of W. B. Yeats', in A. Norman Jeffares and K. G. W. Cross (eds), *In Excited Reverie: A Centenary Tribute to W. B. Yeats, 1865–1939* (London, 1965), p. 248.
89 *Irish World*, 16 July 1927.
90 Gifford Lewis, *Eva Gore-Booth and Esther Roper* (London, 1988), p. 178.
91 Anne Haverty, *Constance Markievicz* (London, 1988), p. 229.
92 *Irish World*, 6 Aug. 1927.
93 Maeve de Markievicz to Hanna Sheehy Skeffington, 6 July 1928, giving her permission to dispose of her books and papers and to keep what she wanted 'as a gift from me,' She added 'don't bother about the pictures at the dealers – I have plenty without them so do what you like about them', SS MS 33,606/7.
94 Esther Roper to Hanna Sheehy Skeffington, post card, n. d. around 1933, SS MS 33,606/22.
95 Meg Connery to Hanna Sheehy Skeffington, 2 Aug. 1926, SS MS 41,177/10.
96 Helen Little (ed.), *Revolutionary Woman: Kathleen Clarke, 1878–1972: An Autobiography* (Dublin, 1991), pp 222–3. p. 211.
97 Hanna Sheehy Skeffington, draft letter, SS MS 33,609/2.
98 Hanna Sheehy Skeffington to Éamon de Valera, 16 Aug. 1927, P/176/27, Archives of the Fianna Fáil Party, University College Dublin Archives (hereafter UCDA). With thanks to Barry Walker for the reference.
99 Meg Connery to Hanna Sheehy Skeffington, 19 Aug. 1926, SS MS 41,177/10.
100 Meg Connery to Hanna Sheehy Skeffington, 6 Sept. 1926, SS MS 41,177/10
101 Florence Murphy Baker to Hanna Sheehy Skeffington, 10 Dec. 1927, SS MS 41,177/1.
102 Dorothy Macardle to Éamon de Valera, 29 Aug. 1927, Fianna Fail Archives.
103 *Irish World*, 24 Sept. 1927.
104 Hanna to Owen, 21 July 1930, SS MS 40,484/3.
105 Hanna to Owen, 22 June 1929, SS MS 40,484/3.
106 Conor Cruise O'Brien, 'Two deaths in Rathmines, in *The Atlantic Monthly*, 283:6, pp 44–9.
107 Hanna to Owen, Aug. 1934, SS MS 40,484/7.
108 Judge David Sheehy, interview with author, Apr. 1996.
109 Kathleen Cruise O'Brien to Hanna, 30 Dec. 1937, SS MS 41,176/5.
110 Hanna to Owen, July/Aug. 1927, SS MS 40,484/3.
111 Andrée Sheehy Skeffington, *Skeff*, Chapter 3.

112 Kate O'Malley, *Ireland, India And Empire: Indo-Irish Radical Connections, 1919–64* (Manchester, 2008), p. 59. With thanks to Bill Rolston for bringing this to my attention.
113 Ibid., pp 38–9.
114 Hanna to Owen, 27 Aug. 1928, SS MS 40,484/3.
115 Hanna to Owen, 9 July 1928; 22 July 1928; 27 Aug. 1928, SS MS 40,484/4.
116 Kathleen Cruise O'Brien to Owen, 16 Aug. 1928, SS MS 40, 490/1.
117 Hanna to Owen, 27 Aug. 1928 SS MS 40,484/3; letter from Marion Bourke-Dowling to Hanna, 6 July 1928, SS MS 33,606/17.
118 Daisy Lawrenson Swanton, *Emerging from The Shadow, the Lives of Sarah Anne Lawrenson and Lucy Olive Kingston, Based on Personal Diaries 1883–1969* (Dublin, 1994), p. 110.
119 'A woman's view of censorship: "Ridiculous and impossible"', in *Irish Times*, 23 Nov. 1928.
120 McGarry, *Frank Ryan*, p. 22.
121 UinSeánn Mac Eoin (ed.), *Survivors* (Dublin, 1980), p. 11.
122 Rose Jacob, 'Waterford Lady's recollections of Mrs Sheehy Skeffington', in *Waterford News*, 3 May 1946.
123 Hanna to Owen, 29 July 1929, SS MS 40,484/4.
124 *Irish World*, 4 May 1929.
125 Damian Doyle, 'Rosamond Jacob (1888–1960)' in Mary Cullen and Maria Luddy (eds), *Female Activists Irish Women and Change 1900–1960* (Dublin, 2001), pp 169–192.
126 Hanna Sheehy Skeffington, 'The new Europe: A trip of scenes, sights and impression', in *Sunday Independent*, 27 Oct. 1929, p. 5.
127 Hanna Sheehy Skeffington, 'Ireland off the map', in *An Phoblacht*, 28 Sept. 1929.
128 Hanna to Owen, 29 July 1929, SS MS 40,484/4.
129 Leah Levenson and Jerry Natterstad, *Hanna Sheehy Skeffington: Irish Feminist* (New York, 1983), p. 156.
130 *An Phoblacht*, 28 Sept. 1929.
131 Cullen Owens, *Louie Bennett*, p. 60.
132 *Irish World*, 4 May 1929.
133 Nora Harkin, personal interview, Apr. 1996.
134 Leeane Lane, *Rosamond Jacob: Third Person Singular* (Dublin, 2010), p. 118.
135 Hanna to Owen, 26 July 1930, SS MS 40,484/5.
136 Hanna to Owen, 21 July 1930, SS MS 40,484/5.
137 Florence Murphy Baker to Hanna Sheehy Skeffington, 11 July 1930, SS MS 24,120.
138 Florence Murphy Baker to Hanna Sheehy Skeffington, 21 July 1930, SS MS 24,120.
139 R.M. Fox to Hanna Sheehy Skeffington, 3 Aug. 1930, SS MS 41,178/68.
140 Hanna to Owen, 26 July 1930, SS MS 40,484/5.
141 Hanna to Owen, 21 July 1930, SS MS 40,484/5.
142 Kathleen O'Brennan to Hanna Sheehy Skeffington, 10 July 1930, SS MS 41,178/68.
143 Henry Nevinson to Hanna Sheehy Skeffington, 23 July 1930, SS MS 41,178/68.
144 Poem by Mary Kettle 'To Joan', 23 July 1930, regarding the Russian trip, SS MS 41,178/68.

> Oh, Joan, she is off to the Soviet State!
> Father did pine, but not so Sister Kate,

'I wish it were Poland, tis quieter there,'
Said David, but the Rush out of Russia was our lady's care.
'Splendid,' said Conor, 'I wish I were going,'
'Crumps,' exclaimed Betty, 'I'd rather do sewing.'
'The sea & the Soviet, Red Russians,' said Mary,
'Of these, if you're wise, you ought to be chary.'
Owen had gone for three months off to France
And thought only of *… and Youth and Romance!
So 'tis settled. She's off to the far distant places,
Where they have no use for silks, perfumes or laces.
We hear they'll have meals, if there's any time,
For regular repasts they don't care a dime.
So, 'to make some provision it sure would be wise,'
Said Madame McBride – on her there's no flies! –
And to Mrs Despard, the 80 years young,
Whose deeds and whose ventures sure ought to be sung,
She made presentation, both timely and fair,
To make herself tea, any time, anywhere.
'Well done,' then said Mary, and I won't be lacking
To show that our sister has also some backing.
To Madame McBride many thanks for the tip,
To Joan just a warning.
No slip twixt the cup and the lip.
M.S.K.
*(The task of filling up the blanks I'd rather leave to you!)

145 Hanna to Owen, 26 July 1930, SS MS 40,484/5.
146 Kathleen Price to Hanna Sheehy Skeffington, 9 June 1930, SS MS 41,178/68.
147 Hanna to Owen 8 Aug. 1930, SS MS 40,484/5. For details on Harry Kernoff and Russia, see Elaine Sisson, 'Designing modernism: Harry Kernoff, Russia and post-independence Ireland', in *Éire-Ireland*, 52:3/4, 2017, pp 31–56.
148 Margaret Mulvihill, *Charlotte Despard* (London, 1989), p. 170.
149 Notes on 'Russia as I see it', SS MS 24,163.
150 Andro Linklater, *An Unhusbanded Life: Charlotte Despard, Suffragette, Socialist and Sinn Féiner* (London, 1980), p. 237.
151 Draft of speech, SS MS 24,163.
152 *Workers' Voice*, 21 Mar. 1931.
153 Mac Eoin, *Survivors*, p. 158.
154 *Irish World*, 18 Apr. 1931.
155 Hanna Sheehy Skeffington to Garry Culhane, postcard, 3 Aug. 1931, in possession of Roisin Sheehy-Culhane.
156 Conor Foley, *Legion of the Rearguard: The IRA and the Modern Irish State* (London, 1992), p. 94.
157 Hanna to Owen, 13 Sept. 1931, SS MS 40,484/6.
158 Andreé Sheehy Skeffington, *Skeff*, p. 66.

159 *Irish World*, 16 Jan. 1932.

160 Maud Gonne MacBride, 'How we beat the terrorist proclamations', in *An Phoblacht*, 12 Nov. 1932.

161 Mrs McWhorter, *Irish World*, 11 Oct. 1930.

162 *Republican File*, 13 Feb. 1931; for more details see my *Unmanageable Revolutionaries: Women and Irish Nationalism* (London, 1983), chapter 6.

163 *An Phoblacht*, 19 Mar. 1932.

164 Levenson and Natterstad, *Hanna Sheehy Skeffington*, p. 161.

THIRTEEN

FEMINISM, REPUBLICANISM, COMMUNISM, 1932–7

In April 1932 Margaret Pearse, mother of Patrick and Willie, died. She had given her sons so that the Irish nation could be born and, for the next 16 years, had devoted her life to bearing witness to their sacrifice. That selfless spirit of denial was an idealisation of the role that some wished all Irish mothers would emulate: not to think of themselves as individuals, only as mothers of the nation. It was a personal tragedy for Mrs Pearse, still grieving for her boys shortly before her death, unable to face the emotion of seeing their graves at Arbour Hill after the newly-elected Fianna Fáil government had succeeded in gaining public access to the burial ground of the 1916 leaders, yet the sorrows of her life were obscured by the heroic myth.[1] In 1916 the women who had made sacrifices for the Republic were lauded for their courage. 1932 was a very different era. The argument now was that independence was won and women's contribution was no longer necessary. They should be content to return to the home and the hearth. Mrs Pearse's death provided the ideal opportunity for the role of the self-sacrificing mother to be praised, while emphasising that such sacrifices were no longer required. Éamon de Valera once again provided the graveside eulogy:

> But for the fame of her sons the noble woman at whose grave we are gathered would, perhaps never have been heard of outside the narrow circle of her personal friends. Her modesty would have kept her out of the public eye.[2]

It was what he wished for all Irish mothers: to produce good nationalist sons while staying out of the public arena themselves, unless exceptional circumstances required them to fulfil the work begun by their children.

Women were not to have an agenda of their own, being merely 'a living vessel through which the dead may speak'.[3] It was a picture that could not be left unchallenged. That July, Hanna wrote a scorching rebuttal of de Valera's portrayal of Constance Markievicz, arguing that, in praising her life, he had represented her as a philanthropist, and not as a revolutionary. In her eyes it was characteristic of the man who had refused to allow women to enter his 'rebel fortress':

> This fact sufficiently illustrates the radically conflicting viewpoints of Connolly and de Valera – both consistent, both divergent – towards women and towards class distinctions and revolution as distinguished from revolution and constitutionalism. To the one, woman was an equal, a comrade; to the other, a sheltered being, withdrawn to the domestic hearth, shrinking from public life. Each viewpoint has its exponents, but none will deny the self-evident fact that Constance Markievicz, Ireland's Joan of Arc, belongs to the former category. As typical of resurgent Ireland's revolutionary womanhood, she has her place in history and all ... will salute her as one of Ireland's revolutionary leaders.[4]

The vehemence of her response reflected a realisation that a new age had been ushered in with the victory of Fianna Fáil and women were going to have to consider the implications. Two years previously, she had written a sober assessment of the scant progress made by women in Ireland since independence:

> Women in Ireland still suffer from the effects of the revolution that missed and of the subsequent reaction. What was given at first with gladness has been gradually filched away. Equality has ceased to be accorded to us, save on paper.

Apart from Sinn Féin, irrelevant because of its abstentionist policy, all the political parties shared an anti-feminist bias. She claimed that Seán Lemass of Fianna Fáil had remarked that he would like to see female suffrage repealed. As women should vote with their menfolk, their vote was an unnecessary duplicate. De Valera, while 'not anti-feminist in theory' wanted to save women from the 'care and stress of the political arena'. She felt sure that the two big parties had a 'gentleman's agreement' to limit women candidates being nominated. They were so oblivious to the 'woman factor' in elections, it was if women had never voted or been involved in the political round. Just as the leprechaun had to be held firmly if he was to lead one to the crock of gold, so too would women have to keep their eyes on the politicians, because 'if you take your eyes off him for a moment he slips away and his golden treasure with him'. After all women had been through in the fight for citizenship, Hanna was determined to ensure that they had their share of that hidden fortune.[5]

Other women were also reassessing their position. *An Phoblacht* carried a lengthy article by Nora Connolly O'Brien, analysing the part played by women in the revolutionary struggle. She criticised women for having 'relinquished their right to share in the dangers of peace' and warned of the consequences if women did not become involved in the ongoing struggle for a socialist republic:

> Progressive and revolutionary women have no voice in the council of the revolutionary movement The men and women of the revolutionary movement would do well to take heed of the warning of James Connolly that a continuance of this policy will cause the race to lose 'its capacity to withstand the assaults from without and the demoralisation from within'.

Her conclusion was that men and women must insist that 'men and women in Ireland have equal rights and duties'.[6] Increasingly, the precedent set by the Proclamation of 1916 would be raised by those struggling to prevent the implementation of policies which deliberately sought to redefine rights and duties as gendered concepts. Women who had been active in movements since the early suffrage days could only view with horror the prospect of their rights being redefined into the right to remain within the home and their duties whittled down into some notion of their domestic responsibilities. However, the inexorable process of removing them from the public sphere, which had started with the 1924 Juries Act, continued with renewed zeal under de Valera, who did indeed wish to, as Hanna had said, 'save women' from politics. Gloomily, she summarised the new state of affairs in a letter to Esther Roper:

> What a time we live in! Here we are rapidly becoming a Catholic statelet under Rome's grip – censorship and the like, with a very narrow provincial outlook, plus a self-satisfied smugness. Result of a failure in revolution really. I have no belief in de Valera. Well meaning, of course, better than Cosgrave, but essentially conservative and church-bound, anti-feminist, bourgeois and the rest. A sort of professor-type, like Wilson and enamoured of phrases and abstractions.[7]

Despite these pressures to limit women's public visibility, a ceremony to emphasise the achievements of one woman was staged on 31 May 1932, in the comfortable surroundings of the Gresham Hotel. Over 100 feminists came together to present Mary Kettle with a municipal robe and hat - cherry-coloured, fur-trimmed, poplin-lined and embroidered by the women of the

Dun Emer Guild, with the inscription that the robe was presented to Mrs Kettle 'as a tribute for her unfailing loyalty and devotion to women'. It was a notable occasion, presided over with warmth and humour by Professor Mary Hayden, who recalled her own childhood when only two ideal paths were open to women: that of a religious life or a family life, both ending with a holy death. Although much remained to be achieved, she believed matters had improved for women in Ireland and the gift of the robe to a woman who had been a consistent feminist throughout her life was a symbol of those changes.

Cissie Cahalan, Helena Molony, Lucy Kingston and Rose Jacob were amongst the other speakers to pay tribute. It was a truly heterogeneous gathering, ranging from former members of the Irish Citizen Army, the Irish Women's Franchise League, non-militant suffragists, the Women's Prisoners' Defence League, Senator Jennie Wyse Power, Sarah Cecilia Harrison, Kate O'Callaghan, and women who had been involved in political affairs at the start of the century but who were now married and preoccupied with family life. Only present-day members of Cumann na mBan were absent. Hanna and Kathleen, the proud sisters, were in the audience.[8] Gretta Cousins' comment that Mary, rather than her better-known sister, had the power to form the nucleus of a new woman's organisation, makes sense when one sees the wide appeal of Mary and the potential she possessed for crossing political divisions. It was also an indication of how far to the left-republican position the oldest Sheehy sister had moved.

The deterioration in women's status would be a constant source of contention during the 1930s. So too would be the continued anomaly of the border, isolating six northern counties from the rest of Ireland. The unionist government, anxious to prevent destabilisation of its authority, issued exclusion orders to many prominent republicans, forbidding them from entering the six-county area. In 1924 de Valera was sentenced to one month's imprisonment after speaking at an election meeting in Derry. Hanna was served with her order in 1926 while visiting Frank's elderly aunt Bella. In July 1932 Joseph Devlin wrote to the northern Home Secretary, Dawson Bates, seeking permission for Hanna to visit Portrush. The reason for the visit is unclear, but probably in connection with another of Devlin's schemes for the welfare of young women, and on that occasion, permission was granted, on condition that Mrs Skeffington 'applies for and gives an understanding not to indulge in any political activities in Northern Ireland'. Devlin was asked to inform the authorities of the date of her trip so that the police could be informed.[9] There was no possibility of Hanna ever conforming to such restrictions, and no evidence that she ever went to Portrush.

In January 1933 she was invited to speak on behalf of republican prisoners at a meeting in the border town of Newry. Two members of Belfast Cumann na mBan had been given jail sentences that month after protesting against a visit by the Prince of Wales. Hanna decided to defy the ban and, on 15 January, travelled up from Dublin by bus. However, she went to Armagh (where the women were in jail) rather than Newry. Her reasoning appeared to be, since the Armagh meeting was not banned, she would successfully defy the order without incurring any penalty. At her trial District-Inspector Cook admitted that they had expected her at another place and she had not turned up. The formal notice, served to her under the Special Powers Act, stated that she had 'entered the County of Armagh and thereby failed to comply with an order served on her 4 April 1926 prohibiting her from entering said county of Armagh.'[10] She was therefore justified in retorting, with extravagant rhetoric: 'There was a meeting in Armagh and it was not banned … Only I was banned. It is the country of the banned.'[11] She refused to accept the right of the unionists to bar her and she obviously realised that there might be unwelcome consequences arising out of her defiance, but she was not eager for another prison experience. Her correspondence shows quite clearly that she had not settled her affairs at home in anticipation of any such eventuality.

On arriving in Armagh Jail immediately after arrest she scribbled a quick note to Mary, wanting to reassure her family that she was fine, it was 'much like 1912 times'. She had had a 'headache bout' before leaving home but was 'quite well now'. The adrenaline was surging, she was excited, not yet ready to settle down into the numbing boredom of prison life, her mind full of a dozen domestic details that had to be attended to: would Mary tell Annie the maid to carry on as usual and ask her lodger to pay the maid each Saturday out of her rent money; she would write to Owen and for Annie to readdress his letter to Paris; she would write to Conor too; the messages flowed on:

> Please ask Annie to lock my room while I'm away. She generally does. And ask her please to make up a parcel of things and post them in – change of linen, stockings, comb and brush, black sweater and black dress … tell news when I see you all. That turkey dinner will now be a Lenten one after all! – and please don't worry for I needn't tell you I'm not doing so! Joan.[12]

Her father had died on 17 December. The reference to the lack of a 'turkey dinner' must have meant that the family, out of respect, had decided to postpone their Christmas dinner until January. Now it would be Lent before they would be able to gather together. The estrangement between father and daughter had modified in his final years. Two years earlier the Sheehy siblings had decided to create some variety in David's life by alternating where he would eat. Eugene, now the only son, had the honour of Sunday dinner; Hanna's turn was Thursday evenings.[13] In hoping to alleviate their father's loneliness this way, they had all rallied round, despite their differences. Now, in the wake of bereavement, the Sheehy family came together in Hanna's support, intimations of mortality strengthening old ties of affection. Most unusually of all, Eugene, now circuit judge in Monaghan (a county adjoining Armagh but the other side of the hated border), decided to take the train to visit his sister. The Royal Ulster Constabulary in Armagh police barracks were 'courteous', he reported, but quite at a loss on how to deal with this respectable figure who had come in asking to visit his imprisoned sister. Patience exhausted after being passed from one official to another, Eugene resorted to the old-boy network. He phoned none other than Babington, the British Attorney-General, an old friend at the Irish Bar and on the golf links. Within ten minutes Eugene was in the jail and with his sister, explaining to the 'astonished' prison governor that 'the criminal of one generation became the judge and lawmaker of the next', such were the vagaries of Irish politics.[14] Hanna would not have seen it with the same eyes as her brother. 'Topsy-turvy' might be how 'the game' was played but, so far, the game had been played exclusively by men who had left no space for radical Irish women. Eugene's reminiscences talk fondly of Babington as 'a kindly Irish gentleman', while giving the impression that everyone he encountered was pleasant and well meaning. No mention was made of his actual meeting with his sister. Might her comments have provided too jarring a note for such geniality?

Other members of the family were outspoken on her behalf. Her letter to Owen, ending 'love, your fond mother' had been wholly concerned with the politics of the situation. She was hastening to write to him on that Saturday night in case regulations changed and she was unable to get out letters. MPs Devlin and Collins had both visited her and she believed that all agreed that her case 'has served to emphasise the anomalies of the whole situation & it is a good object-lesson just now. A new order has been issued I hear making several other things formerly innocuous now illegal. Taking lessons out of Cosgrave's book.'[15] In response, Owen, still in Paris, wrote an article for the French newspaper *L'Eveil des Peuples*; an indignant and proud declaration of support for his mother, whom he described as a journalist and lecturer, well known both in England and in the United States, who, having had:

> the temerity to have gone to Ulster, birthplace of my father, in order to protest against arbitrary and tyrannical imprisonment of northern republicans, she has been found guilty of having set foot in Ulster and uniquely, for that offence, sentenced

> to one month's imprisonment. Her presence, it is claimed, would turn the spirit of the people against the government and therefore she found herself in Armagh jail. Must I add that the English press has remained strangely silent about this dictatorial act? The English love to talk about Ulster loyalty but not on the foundation on which this is based. A government which finds it necessary to resort to such measures obviously does not feel very sure about '*l'appui*' of its 'loyal' people.[16]

Friends said that Owen adored his mother. His first published writing reveals that affection very clearly. Mary Kettle, in characteristic form, reminded everyone that 50,000 Irishmen had died fighting so that small nations could be free. If her sister could not travel freely around Ireland, then their sacrifice had been in vain.[17]

After 15 days' detention, Hanna appeared in court. Henry Collins, who had visited her in his capacity as Nationalist Party MP for Newry and South Down, was also a solicitor. He sat beside her, assuring the judge that she did not need his professional services. Hanna then proceeded to interrogate the police as they attempted to give evidence. As she did not deny the charge the case did not take long. She was required to give an undertaking to be of good behaviour for a year and fined £50. She had committed no criminal act and strongly rejected the insult in a powerful denunciation of partition:

> Obviously the charge is fully proved. I make no denial. I am not an alien in Armagh or any part of the 32 counties. I recognise no partition. I recognise that it is not a crime to be in my own country. I would be ashamed of my own race. I would be ashamed of my own murdered husband if I admitted that I was an alien in Armagh, Down, Derry, or any of the 32 counties. I believe that the time will come when partition will be as dead as Queen Anne. I believe that the action of the authorities in holding me up will lead to the death knell of partition.[18]

The Boundary Commission (established in 1924 under Article 12 of the Treaty to determine the boundaries between Northern Ireland and the rest of Ireland) had been a complete fiasco. All the hints from the British that the border would not last were exposed as false reassurances to hasten the signing of the Treaty. For those living in border areas, cut off from family and friends, coerced into becoming citizens of a state they hated and suffering the discriminatory regime of the unionist government, partition was a nightmare. After the trial, Collins sent Dawson Bates, as Minister for Home Affairs, a strong letter of protest, reiterating the sense of outrage felt by local people over the court's decision:

> As the public representative of the people of Newry and South Down, I desire to enter my protest against the Order … excluding from this district the widow of the late Mr Sheehy Skeffington, who was a native of this county.

> Mrs Sheehy Skeffington, MA, is a lady whose culture, high-standing, educational and intellectual attainments make her welcome in any part of the civilised world where these things are valued.[19]

As Collins said, 75 per cent of the population of the Newry area were nationalists and resented the action of the unionist government. Hanna's speech from the dock may appear hyperbolic, but she was right to acknowledge that her case had highlighted the inequity of partition. Dundalk Urban Council and Dublin Corporation also passed motions condemning her imprisonment.[20] Such protests were not confined to nationalist councils in Ireland. Hanna's reputation was international and support for her case came from many leading figures. From America, the International Committee for Political Prisoners sent a strong letter of protest to Lord Craigavon, Prime Minister of Northern Ireland. They had 'learned with amazement' of the trial of Mrs Sheehy Skeffington for crossing the border to 'her own home county', thus preventing her from speaking at a meeting concerned with imprisoned republican sympathisers. It was an infringement of political rights recognised 'throughout the civilised world … Such a prosecution of a woman so well known internationally, and particularly in the United States, passes grave reflection on the good sense of your government'.[21] Included within a list of over 50 names were Roger Baldwin, Clarence Barrow, Waldo Frank, Professor Felix Frankfurther, Sinclair Lewis, Judge Julian Mack, Professor Robert Morss Lovett and Norman Thomas.

The experience completed Hanna's sampling of British and Irish jails. It was obvious that the prison authorities were deeply embarrassed by her presence. When she threatened hunger strike a visiting magistrate came to the prison to sign the order permitting her to wear her own clothes and, said Hanna with some satisfaction, 'no one said another word about "suitable tasks"'. When writing an account of her time in Armagh, to a readership well-versed in prison life, she added dryly:

> If ever you are in jail – as well you may, reader of *AN PHOBLACHT*, whatever else your jailers may take away from you, do not let them deprive you of your sense of humour. For you will be sure to need it in jail more than anywhere else. I was always glad to have kept mine – in Armagh, in Mountjoy, in Holloway and in various bridewells, barracks and police stations.

Surprisingly, she admitted finding Armagh 'the humanist jail' she had known, benefitting from various reforms regarding prison uniform, with enlightened regulations permitting association and conversation between prisoners. She hoped that such reforms would be copied in the south of Ireland where the penal system had not changed with the times. Women in Armagh no longer wore the 'silly caps' insisted on at Mountjoy, 'most of the prisoners had bobbed hair, I noticed, so do fashions spread'. Her anger at the authorities for imprisoning her did not prevent her from being fair when it came to assessing the manner in which they ran the prison. However, although it had been 15 years since she had last served time, in some essentials, nothing had changed:

> Now there are salt cellars of brown pottery instead of the unhygienic wooden containers of old, but the horn spoon that serves for entire table cutlery survives even the Great War. Its characteristic is that when you are stirring your tea there lingers a flavour of cabbage soup and vice versa.

She was kept apart from the other prisoners, exercising alone for an hour and a half each afternoon, only a wardress for company. They decided to place her in the more spacious surroundings of the condemned cell, the last inmate of which had been a woman found guilty of infanticide (who later had her sentence remitted). As this was built to accommodate two wardresses to look after the condemned prisoner, it was roomy, with a fire grate and windows that opened outwards: 'One could, with the aid of table and stool, a rickety structure, see the skyline and the silhouette of Patrick's old cathedral.'[22]

Winifred Carney sent her a letter from Belfast, quietly ironic and acerbically critical of labour politics and Fianna Fáil:

> It was not my intention to write to you at all while on your delightful visit north, as under the circumstances one would expect that you were swamped with every kind of attention - my way is generally to look after the most neglected yet if everyone was to make that assumption, you would find your presence as coldly accepted as the north is supposed to be … I hope you are comfortable & not suffering in any way; these days are so cold sometimes.

She apologised her letter was not written as she intended - it was a disconnected mixture of the personal and the political, including her disappointment with labour leader William O'Brien – 'Everything has become subservient to his consuming desire for a political career in the Dáil' – and her belief that the *Irish Press* emphasis on 'Faith', which was 'rather much … for a general newspaper' was probably due to 'fear of communism'. However, her admiration for Hanna and her family was very clear: 'Mrs Kettle … I noticed a change in her style of hair dressing I hope it doesn't alter her looks. I thought her so beautiful that evening at your house and that she had not modernised her style of hair dress made her distinctive I thought.'[23]

The authorities tried to minimise the potential propaganda value of Hanna's incarceration. When she heard that she was to be released a day early, she smelt a rat and demanded permission to write to her people informing them of the change. Her letter to the governor went on to make it plain that she would not be a party to any arrangement that they might make:

> I do not know whether you were joking when you spoke of a police escort, not to [the] border but to my own home! If this is serious, I would most strongly object to police from here accompanying me, a released prisoner, out of this our own territory to a place where they have no authority or right to be. I should have to take strong exception to such action. I can see to my own arrangements by car or otherwise. Once I am on the other side of six county border that is my own affair. Will you please convey this to the police and let me know as soon as possible if Wednesday is the day?[24]

They were right to try to lessen the impact of her release from jail. Her letter was written on a Sunday and they released her the following day, despite her protest that Thursday was the date posted on her cell door. When the governor intimated that the early release was a reward for 'good conduct', an outraged Hanna gave an interview to the *Irish Press* to insist that she had 'never been a model prisoner in any prison' and had refused to wear prison clothes or to do prison work.[25]

Despite the governor's intrigues, the homecoming turned out to be a triumphal tour. She spent the Monday night and Tuesday at the home of a Mrs Maguire, captain of Dundalk Cumann na mBan, resting and allowing time for preparations to be made for her welcome. Eithne Coyle, President of Cumann na mBan and resplendent in full military uniform, had come up from Dublin to act as her escort, greeting her with a most unmilitary hug. The first event was a reception in the town centre. A long procession conducted her to the Market Square where the Town Clerk read an illuminated address on behalf of the Urban Council. In reply to messages of welcome Hanna stated modestly that she realised the tribute being paid to her was really a symbol of 'republican resistance to tyranny'. A cavalcade of 20 cars escorted her to her next stop, the town of Drogheda. On the way, past numerous small villages, she saw cheering crowds waving tricolours as they stood by the roadside. Drogheda too gave her a civic reception, the Mayor leading members of his corporation, all dressed in ceremonial robes. There was a torchlit procession, bands, a guard of honour and a vast banner festooning the Mayoralty Buildings, inscribed with the words 'Drogheda ex-internees greet Mrs Sheehy Skeffington'. In his speech the Mayor declared that the people of Drogheda, in common with the rest of Ireland, wished to protest in the strongest possible manner against her arrest and imprisonment: 'It was a deplorable state of affairs when an Irish citizen could be arrested for no other crime than that of travelling to Armagh to address a meeting.' In reply, she said she owed a debt of gratitude not only to the people of Drogheda for their welcome, but also to the Northern Junta, whose action in imprisoning her helped to expose the abomination of the Boundary'.[26]

Then it was on to Dublin. Despite the cold and a slight scattering of snow, the crowds gathered at Tolka Bridge to wait for her. She arrived at 8.40 p.m. and a procession of three bands, followed by contingents from the IRA, Cumann na mBan, Fianna Éireann and Fianna Fáil Clubs, unemployed workers and members of the Newsvendors' and General Workers' Union headed a torchlit procession that escorted her car, by now also full of flowers from admirers, to a vast crowd waiting in the cold at the familiar setting of College Green. Included on the platform were Maud Gonne MacBride, Charlotte Despard and Mary Kettle (surely only for her sister would the latter have agreed to share a platform with republicans). So many had crowded into College Green that the car had difficulty in making its way forward. Her small figure, clutching a handbag, was an incongruous figure on the platform. It was a republican-organised event, an opportunity to criticise the record of the Fianna Fáil government. Peadar O'Donnell seized the moment to urge support for the socialist Jim Gralton, about to be deported by the government and 'a fouler outrage than the arrest and deportation of Mrs Skeffington.' Seán MacBride challenged the government to declare a republic and prove their republican credentials. For her part, Hanna stuck to the original point of the rally:

> The Six Counties were a prison to Republicans and even the Twenty-Six Counties were a prison within the British Empire. They had got to break down the border and cut the last link that bound them to the British Empire. They were not going to be content with a trumpery dominion status, even for the whole of the 32 counties.[27]

As a deportee, she had sympathy with the plight of Jim Gralton and, a few days later, chaired a public meeting, supported by the Revolutionary Workers' Groups, on behalf of the 'Keep Gralton Here' campaign. Gralton, a self-declared atheist and communist, was a difficult subject to mobilise support around in the hysterical climate of the period. Irish fascists were starting to organise, and the Catholic Church was active in encouraging anti-communist activity.[28] They were unable to prevent Gralton's deportation. After some time on the run he was arrested and, in August, put on board ship for America.

On 21 March, in a more intimate setting than the public podium, the old stalwarts of the IWFL held a supper party for their president, presided over by Meg Connery. She applauded Hanna for having 'started a fire that will end the hateful partition of Ireland' and, expressing her own political allegiances, went on to praise the commitment of revolutionary socialists, 'The women of Ireland have been humiliated and insulted because they stood for the Republic, but the Revolutionary Workers' movement will win, because it has the best of its women behind it.'[29] Meg was close to the Revolutionary Workers' Group (soon to become the Communist Party of Ireland) along with Charlotte Despard, Helena Molony and, partly, Hanna herself. She and Rose Jacob had travelled to Russia the year after Hanna. Other women at the meal included Maud Gonne MacBride, Cissie Cahalan, Grace Gifford Plunkett, Linda Kearns and all sorts of people who were not famous but who wanted to pay their respects. It was a stridently nationalist occasion, on each table a red menu card, the front emblazoned with: 'We love them yet, we can't forget the felons of our Land' and a verse from Tom Kettle's parody of Rudyard Kipling: 'Ulster is ours, not yours/Is ours to have and hold' inscribed on the inside. They must have had fun concocting the menu: Consommé Armagh, Celery Holloway, Limerick Ham, Salad Partition, Tipsy Cake Mountjoy and Meringues Franchise League were some of the dishes consumed.[30] The contrast with the orthodox formality with which Mary Kettle was presented with her ceremonial robes is striking. Gretta Cousins, 17 years in India and an important figure in the Indian Women's Movement, had recently received a one-year sentence for preaching 'Home Rule' for India. The supper party sent greetings to their old friend, now in Bombay Jail. Twenty years after their suffrage experiences, Gretta and Hanna had again risked imprisonment for principle. It was a measure of their lasting commitment to the causes of feminism and democracy.

Three days after that pleasant social evening, Connolly House, headquarters of the Revolutionary Workers' Group, was besieged by a crowd of right-wing fanatics. They remained there for three days, in a turmoil of religious hate and fundamentalist fanaticism, before setting fire to the building. They then marched to Eccles Street, where Charlotte Despard had recently bought a house, part of which she loaned to the Irish Workers' College. Seán MacBride, now one of the most prominent of IRA leaders, was ensuring that the IRA stuck to an orthodox republican path, fearing that a more left-wing turn would lose them support to Fianna Fáil. Despard, a veteran of the left, wanted to be free to give her support to a more radical group. She had handed over Roebuck House to Gonne MacBride and, at the age of almost 90, moved on.[31] These were not good times for new ventures. Meg Connery and Hanna both came to her defence, braving mob rule to do so. As the crowds sang hymns and shouted, 'Down with Russia', Hanna was struck over the eye. 'For faith & fatherland' she said sarcastically. Not slogans she could have sympathy with.[32] The police did not busy themselves to prevent what the communists described angrily as 'the scandalous scene of an angry mob attacking two women'.[33] Hanna advised the elderly idealist to move to Belfast. It was the one place in Ireland where she felt a non-sectarian workers' movement could become a possibility.

Hanna had returned to her work with *An Phoblacht*, but not for long. She and Frank Ryan were finding it difficult to maintain their editorial independence while an internal power struggle in the IRA dictated the policies of the paper. Moss Twomey, chief-of-staff at this time, complained that Ryan would not print what he was ordered to, using his partial deafness as an excuse to continue writing what he wanted. That tactic had a limited life. Ryan resigned the editorship in February and Hanna followed in April, writing to Twomey: 'Now we seem to get cut-&-dry commands instead of an openly & freely discussed policy. We seem to be at a cross-road at present & while I see the need of caution & independence, it would be lamentable if your organisation were moving to the right.'[34] As she was not a member of the IRA she was not subject to military discipline, and so there was no bad feeling about her departure. Donal O'Donoghue (future husband of Cumann na mBan leader Sheila Humphries), the new editor, paid her warm tribute when announcing her resignation:

> Through all the later stages of the Cosgrave Junta, with its intense coercion and periods of almost daily raids on the offices of *An Phoblacht* she carried on her duties calmly, under nearly impossible journalistic conditions.[35]

Ryan, O'Donnell and Gilmore were amongst the radicals who resigned from the IRA in order to launch the Republican Congress. It was another short-lived attempt to unite republican socialists around the demand for a Workers' Republic and it soon split into two factions: one headed by Roddy Connolly and Nora Connolly O'Brien and the other by O'Donnell. Nora attempted to interest Hanna in becoming a member, but she was not involved with either group.[36]

Hanna tried to secure some paid work with the *Irish Press*. Many of her old friends were working on the paper, but her former friendship with its editor, Frank Gallagher, did not work in her favour. The past relationship between tenant and landlady must have soured during the Fianna Fáil oath-taking controversy and she complained to friends of Gallagher's attitude towards her. Her friend Florence Murphy Baker voicing her disappointment, advised Hanna to quit,[37] but she was made second review editor, which at least enabled her to indulge her love of theatre and film. Money was very scarce, as many of her letters to Owen indicate: 'money v. low, waiting on everything but will have £40 soon'; 'haven't got paid by civil service yet so fairly low but can cover yours & mine travel just'.[38]

Hanna was in court again in 1934, this time in a libel action against the New Catholic Press, publishers of the Irish *Catholic Herald*, the editor of which had stated that she was a hypocrite 'posing as a republican' because she enjoyed a pension from the British government, who had also paid for the education of her son. In an affidavit Hanna made it plain why she was taking the action:

> My sole source of income is my work as lecturer and journalist and my economic position has been no secret to the Irish people resident in Great Britain. In addition to these professional activities. I have for many years held the honourable position of Irish National Propagandist, not only at home, but likewise in Great Britain and in the USA.[39]

It was, she contended, a gross libel on her as a private individual and in relation to her professional and political activities. The case was reported sympathetically in all the major British and Irish papers. They understood her position, as she explained in an interview with the *Manchester Evening Chronicle*. If the *Catholic Herald* article was unchallenged, she would find it 'very difficult, if not impossible, to place any article in Irish and American newspapers'.[40] Her entire livelihood was at stake, as well as her reputation. The High Court action was heard in June. Sir Francis Vane, whom she had hoped would give evidence for her, had died shortly before. But the Lord Mayor of Dublin, Alfie Byrne, spoke on her behalf, as did Muriel Matters (now Mrs Muriel Porter), who had accompanied her during the meeting with Asquith in July 1916. She confirmed that Hanna's account of that meeting and her rejection of an offer of compensation was correct. It was a cruel act of fate, to have to go to court to prove that she had refused compensation for the murder of her husband, reliving those times yet again. As the headline of the *Evening Herald* put it, 'Libel Action Recalls Grim Drama of Easter Week'. The libel had also insinuated that Hanna was a communist and so the defence, in trying to prove that what was said was fair comment, concentrated upon her political views. During her time on the witness stand her replies were testy as she criticised the manner of questioning of her interrogator, but she made no attempt to minimise the extent of her radicalism. Honesty and integrity were vitally important qualities and she never disguised unpalatable truths:

> Cecil Lavery – 'Do you object to being described as an unadulterated republican?'
>
> Hanna Sheehy Skeffington – 'I do not know what you mean by this unadulterated republican. I think it is very sloppy English. She was, she said, a republican, not a member of the Communist Party. She did not describe herself as a communist, 'although she had a good deal of sympathy with their educational and social ideas'.[41]

The judge and jury awarded her £750 damages for libel. However, as Diamond, the paper's editor, had died in February, the paper was declared insolvent and she was unable to claim the costs to which she was entitled. Her correspondence with her lawyer reveals how welcome that money would have been.[42] Maurice Healy, nephew of Hanna's lawyer Tim Healy (and a college contemporary of Eugene and Dick Sheehy), was a well-respected solicitor, practicing in England, who offered to help. When Eugene contacted Healy on his sister's behalf, he received a warm reply recalling their student days: 'Shall be delighted to see your sister Mrs Sheehy Skeffington. I don't suppose the little man agreed with me on a single subject but I loved and admired him and I think he liked me and your sister always tolerated my intolerance.'[43] Maurice had a 'very low opinion of Diamond' and agreed with Eugene Sheehy that his widow might be engaging in a game of bluff regarding the assets of her late husband. In March 1935 he extended a warm invitation to Hanna and Owen (who were passing through London, en route to Owen's wedding in France), to meet him for lunch in a small Italian restaurant near Soho so that they could discuss the case further: 'it would give me a great deal of pleasure', adding 'I do not forget that I have enjoyed a good deal of Sheehy hospitality in my day'.[44] It was obviously no bluff on Mrs Diamond's part, as no money was forthcoming, despite Healy's expert advice.

Hanna's lecture tour of America finally took place in the last months of 1934. The Open Forum Speakers Bureau agreed to act as her agents, aiming their publicity to as wide an audience as possible. Her topics for lectures were: 'Dublin memories grave and gay'; 'Irish writers of today'; 'The new Ireland'; 'Women in public life'; 'From Leningrad to Baku'.[45] She went first to Canada, lecturing in Quebec and Montreal. She had received briefings on the position of women in the different states, noting that women did not have the vote in provincial elections and could not become lawyers in Quebec.[46] Hanna enjoyed Montreal, which she had described to Andrée as 'a lovely city and though owned by the British, it is v. French, even in its denying votes to women!'[47] Before travelling down to New England she stayed with her sister Margaret and her family. It was her nephew Ronan's first meeting with his aunt. A somewhat neglected child of parents who continued to be engrossed with each other, he was surprised and pleased to be talked to by Aunt Hanna, given interesting books to read and rewarded by a tiny amount of money when he had demonstrated that he had read and understood the book she had given him. A small, grey-haired, bustling woman, who called him her 'dotie child' and made him feel, for the first time, that he did have a family.[48] She ended her tour in New York, pleased to see that the Heterodoxy Club remained active. She could still boast to her friends that she was a member of a club which demanded as qualification for entry the stepping outside of current conventions. She was very well qualified. On 11 January she sailed for home in the *SS Andania.* It was a less ambitious tour than her previous ones, but some money was raised as a result.

Her ten-year-old nephew David, Eugene's son, was intrigued to be telephoned by his Aunt Hanna and invited to accompany her to the RTE studio. As he remembered, he went to her shabby old house where she made him a tea of boiled egg and bread before they travelled together to the old RTE sound studios in Henry Street. He didn't listen to what his aunt was saying but he enjoyed the thrill of the control room.[49] That was the delightful aspect of Hanna, an uncompromising republican who had no scruple in buying her nephew Conor one of Rudyard Kipling's books, because she freely acknowledged that the arch-imperialist was also a fine writer for children. She was an aunt who understood that a visit to a radio studio in the 1930s was an event that would stay in the memory of a young boy, a treat she wanted him to have. She had no regrets that her political life prevented a fuller development of her teaching career – she would never have had it any other way – but her zest for life appealed to the young. Over the years she gave countless lectures in a series of talks organised by the public libraries to provide children with stimulating information on a wide variety of topics. Her subjects ranged from a history of Dublin and its parks, zoo, picture galleries and museum, to 'Boy heroes and girl heroines of Ireland' and 'Makers of Irish history'.[50] She was a popular speaker, top of a bill and always asked back for another talk. She was fun to be with, the type of woman who, when air travel became accessible, insisted on finding out what it was like to fly. Once prices became 'well, reasonably reasonable, I took the plunge, or rather the flight,' flying from Dublin to Shannon and back, marvelling at the landscape that unfolded beneath her.[51]

Owen returned to Dublin in 1933, to take up a post as lecturer in French in Trinity College. He was 24, a young man with very decided views of his own. He immediately became active in numerous left-wing causes, particularly anti-fascism, having seen its ugly reality while travelling in Europe. He supported the Republican Congress (in so far as it was fighting Irish fascism) and helped to form a short-lived Secular Society which struggled to voice its belief in complete freedom of thought – until the opposition proved too great. All this, said Andrée, pleased Hanna a great deal. His mother, she felt, 'would have been not only surprised but rather ashamed if her son had taken a purely academic path and turned away from political and social problems'.[52] Hanna paid no attention to fears that he might be jeopardising his college tenure. Such timidity of spirit was not the way to live. She was delighted to learn that Owen and Andrée had decided to marry, commenting to Owen: 'She'll make you more human, you lack that quality (or seem to) sometimes, boy. Too tied up and afraid of showing a heart except to Pete or the cats. (I suppose to them because they can't give you away).' Andrée she had liked 'from the first day & better every time since', her 'demureness' hiding an 'adventurous spirit' and she thought she and her prospective daughter-in-law would 'pull all right' together.[53] Hanna was soon describing herself, affectionately, as '*ta belle-mère*', the French for mother-in-law, a title used also by Andrée.

Owen, impatient, wanted a Christmas wedding, but Hanna felt that was 'a funny sort of time' and tried to persuade them of Easter or June, giving them time to save some money. Owen would have the £150 legacy from his grandfather, Dr J. B. Skeffington and £50 when she hopefully collected her legal compensation from the *Catholic Herald* case, but that was all.[54] And, of course, the £50, in the wake of Diamond's demise, was never to materialise. There must have been some compromise because the wedding eventually took place in Amiens on 23 March 1935. Apart from the bridegroom, his mother was the only Irish person present. His friend Spencer Hackett was to have been best man but did not turn up, confessing later that he had had no money for travel. The young couple honeymooned in Italy, taking advantage of a reduced ticket offered to newly weds by the Mussolini government, the only condition being to go as far as Rome to have their travel cards stamped. They were able to compare Italian and German fascism, an experience Owen would bring back to political life in Ireland.[55]

James Wellwood, a college friend of Owen's (and who was that year Auditor of 'the Hist', the prestigious College Historical Society), sent a long letter to Hanna, in response to one from her sent immediately after the wedding. His reply reveals a great deal about the inner Hanna, who for once, due to the emotion of the occasion, wrote about her own feelings. She was upset by her son's lack of support from friends at such a momentous occasion in his life – and she confessed that she had felt 'lonely' on the day. She was also 'disheartened' by the fact that during the ceremony Andrée had had to promise to obey 'her lord and master'. Wellwood wrote warmly and consolingly, with a maturity unusual in one so young: 'surely the word, to women of intelligence, has always been 'an empty formula'? – I don't anticipate very much trouble between our two friends on that score! Yes! I am sure you felt lonely, but, though it is conventional to say it, you have gained a daughter, and as you say, a charming one – I am looking forward to meeting her very much. I also look forward to discussing with yourself the future of Ireland some day soon.' Although he had no money, he would have taken a plane to Paris to be there as best man: 'I was annoyed to hear that not one of Owen's Irish friends was present at his wedding – I hope there is an adequate explanation of Spenser Hackett's absence, for the sake of "ould Ireland".'[56] Was a lack of funds also an explanation for the absence of aunts and cousins?

Hanna broke her homeward journey in London, staying at the Minerva Club, the Women's Freedom League's social centre in Brunswick Square. More than 30 members attended a Saturday evening dinner of welcome to their 'old friend' and to hear of her recent visit to America. She was in good form, happy and optimistic as she started her talk saying that when she went to another country she 'always looked out for the forward part of the women's movement'. She was 'eager to note women's successes and to report on successes at home'. A woman had been appointed to a Chair in Law in Dublin and her 'distinguished countrywoman, Professor Mary Hayden' would soon be receiving a high honorary degree. They were the only examples she cited of women's triumphs in Ireland (in those days there were few enough to boast of), before she went on to tell her audience about the progress being made by women in Canada and America. She did not want to give a false impression: 'Women's position indeed was as difficult in the States as in other parts of the world. But women were alive to these difficulties, and that was the thing that mattered.'[57] Hanna's continued association with British feminists, particularly with the Women's Freedom League, proved to be a necessary outlet, almost a safety valve, allowing for freer expression of feminist views without the complications of the Irish situation. In her writings and in her speeches in England, when women were the topic, she was relaxed, witty, well-read and well-informed. The polemics characteristic of her Irish speeches were notably absent. Surrounded by well-wishers, her short stay was an oasis of woman-centred endeavour. The League was looking forward to a visit from their first president, Charlotte Despard, in June, when they would be celebrating her 91st birthday.

While Hanna was away, a new round of IRA arrests took place in Ireland. The church had again denounced the republicans and when the IRA intervened on the side of striking bus and tram workers, deflating tyres of strike-breaking lorries and attacking guards, the honeymoon with de Valera was at an end. Maud Gonne MacBride wrote her friend a lengthy letter, filling her in on all she had missed:

> Hanna dearest,
>
> I would love to talk with you and will try and get a lift out to your place to tea soon for I cannot walk so far. I agree with a lot you say, especially as regards women in the present movement. It is largely by our own fault, we ought to have a movement of our own. If you realise the intrigues that had been going on and these underhand attempts to identify the IRA with the Communist Party, the destruction of Connolly House would be understandable.
>
> The present burlesque came on me as a great surprise. I was totally unprepared for it. The first I knew was a midnight raid, for Seán, who luckily had not got home and only returned after and … I have not seen him since … is it the visible sign of some new unholy alliance? It doesn't much matter, as it will inevitably lead to one…
>
> The WPDL fed all prisoners in the Bridewell very successfully – the only help we got from any organisation was £2 from the Political Prisoners Committee as we are bankrupt – but the prisoners were looked after, as usual 'The Mothers' were on the spot. At the Bridewell at 8 o'clock in the morning for breakfast!
>
> In haste with best love
>
> Hope you enjoyed your time in France and that the young ones are very happy.[58]

Cumann na mBan's Republican Political Prisoners' Committee also wrote, to ask her to act on a new independent committee as there were over 100 republicans in jail and fund-raising was again a priority.[59] The IRA was declared illegal by a Fianna Fáil determined to be tough on its former allies. *An Phoblacht* was suppressed. The bad times were back, as Gonne MacBride had feared, and these were bad times also for women.

During her suffrage days, Hanna's argument for rejecting the basis on which Irish society was constituted had been that man-made laws excluded women. The fact that Ireland had not been free to pass its own laws was not the only issue, because Irishmen proved to be as reluctant as Englishmen when it came to giving pledges to extend the franchise to women. However, once women won the vote and Ireland gained its (limited) independence, political women in Ireland had a choice: either to maintain a feminist agenda of prioritising women's interests, or to fight on a broader political platform. For Hanna, in the years of Cumann na nGaedheal rule, the defeat of the government was the primary task, although women's issues (particularly the bar on jury service) were raised on different occasions by many women. With the triumph of Fianna Fáil and the relaxation of the political atmosphere, the focus, to some extent, returned to women's needs. Comments from Maud Gonne MacBride's letter would indicate that Hanna had been critical of the lack of any direction from the existing republican women ('I agree with a lot you say, especially as regards women in the present movement') and, it would seem, there were some who were thinking once again of 'a movement of our own'.

In Ireland a law had been passed in 1932 preventing the hiring of married women as teachers and it soon extended to the whole of the civil service. It was another example of how unfree women really were. Owen and Andrée had moved into Belgrave Road while they searched for a flat they could afford. The fact that Andrée, because of her married status, was barred from the type of professional work her qualifications as a Sorbonne graduate would otherwise have enabled her to undertake, incensed her mother-in-law. In 1934 the Criminal Law Amendment Act banned the importation of contraceptives. Hanna's gesture in giving the newly-weds a copy of Marie Stopes' *Married Love* was both the act of a concerned mother and a small private act of political defiance.[60]

In 1935, confronting the most serious threat yet faced by women, concerning their rights within the work place, many different groups and individuals came together. The controversy concerned the Conditions of Employment bill, ostensibly introduced by Seán Lemass as Minister for Employment to improve working conditions for all workers, which contained a notorious 'Section 16' giving the minister various powers to curtail the numbers of women working in any branch of industry. At a time of rising unemployment, this move was not opposed by male trade unionists, and women struggled to convince the public of the basic injustice of the bill. While most kept their arguments directed solely upon the single issue, Hanna insisted upon using it as a platform to berate the Fianna Fáil party for a whole range of reactionary attitudes. Her independence of thought and ability to sustain an argument, regardless of opposition, were again much in evidence. She wrote to the *Irish Press*, pointing out that as women in the County Dublin area were now in a numerical majority, they could register an effective protest against the bill by declining to vote for the Fianna Fáil candidate in the next election. As far as she was concerned, the bill 'out-Hitler's Hitler' and, if such arbitrary power was not checked, it could end with women driven to the lowest paid drudgery. She did not leave her argument there. She was writing in the paper that was the voice of Fianna Fáil and she wanted to make it plain to the party that she had broken with it for ever:

> Hitherto I have always voted Fianna Fáil, not because I always approved of its policy, but as a choice between bad and indifferent. In future I shall no longer support Fianna Fáil in any way and shall abstain from voting, unless there is a

> third party, or a genuinely Independent candidate that I can vote for. I know many Republicans who for many reasons will do likewise.[61]

Frank Gallagher was provoked into carrying, in the same issue, an editorial against this argument, possibly to minimise the influence her letter might have. His argument did not convince Hanna, who dismissed the plea that women received doles, pensions and unemployment relief as 'small mercies'. Her feminism, she said, was based on James Connolly's, on the right of equal pay for equal work and equal opportunities for all citizens. In contrast, she believed Lemass, the Minister for Employment, was bringing about fascism.[62] This was not an argument accepted by everyone. Dorothy Macardle had followed Hanna's lead in resigning from Fianna Fáil in 1926, but she refused to follow her on this occasion:

> If we were a free people, women's struggle could take the form of bargaining with the parliamentary vote – the only effective way of influencing Governments, as a rule. But we are not free, a struggle of even greater importance than our feminist movement is still unfinished; the struggle for Irish independence is not yet won.[63]

In her eyes, only Fianna Fáil could achieve full independence. She wished 'good fighters like Madame Gonne MacBride and Mrs Sheehy Skeffington' agreed with her. It was a significant difference of opinion, but had Hanna cast aside all other considerations to fight for her sex, or was her hostility towards Fianna Fáil in part based upon its recent crack-down on republicans? It is difficult to separate one cause from the other, so intertwined had they become in her life. There is evidence, as she had demonstrated in her arguments with Sinn Féin and Cumann na mBan during the 1918 elections, that the feminist cause would come first. Her desire to ensure the election of Constance Markievicz had led her to cooperate with elements she felt were less than whole-hearted in their commitment to Markievicz. She had not made public her criticisms of the inadequate election campaign because a show of unity by nationalists had been essential at that time. Her public declaration now, in 1935, that she would in future choose an independent political line appears to have allowed her a psychological freedom to speak out in a manner reminiscent of her suffrage days. Dorothy Macardle soon had second thoughts over her vow to support Fianna Fáil no matter what. It must have been an agonising dilemma. Her book, *The Irish Republic*, when published in 1937 was, she asserted in the frontispiece, 'inspired by Éamon de Valera', who also wrote its preface. Owen Sheehy Skeffington was one of the people included on her list to receive a complimentary copy from Gollancz, her publishers. She too was a prominent figure on the protest platform when mass campaigning against the bill began.

A large public meeting in the Mansion House succeeded in mobilising a wide cross-section of support in opposition to the bill. Louie Bennett, as secretary of the Irish Women Workers' Union, proposed a resolution protesting against the infringement of the principle of equality of rights entailed by the threat to limit women's employment. She was clear that the motive behind this 'was not concern for the welfare of the workers'. Dorothy Macardle seconded this resolution. She carefully steered clear of any party-political reference, maintaining that this was 'part of a necessary world-wide campaign for women's independence'. Speakers from the professions, including a high proportion of academics, described the deterioration in women's position in all sections of the teaching profession and in the civil service. Professor Mary Hayden, representing the National Council of Women in Ireland (formed in 1924 in the wake of the first Juries bill, to 'promote cooperation among women all over Ireland interested in social welfare') moved a resolution calling for the provision of public works of national utility as a means of alleviating male unemployment. Hanna seconded this resolution in a contribution that was hard-hitting and outspoken in its acknowledgment of the unpalatable reality of prostitution:

> Mr Lemass's attitude was that of a fascist dictator. There was much talk about religion at present, but it was immoral to let young women be driven out of jobs perhaps when they had old and infirm dependents. There was a terrible alternative such unfortunate women might take, and it would be at the door of Mr Lemass and other politicians if women were driven to take that alternative. Men who would displace women under such circumstances were nothing short of blacklegs. Women should go further now and point out to Mr Lemass that many of his so-called factories were really sweat-shops.[64]

She was now almost 60, the freedom afforded by age and the experience of a lifetime of political meetings behind her enabling her to say just what she pleased, regardless of the susceptibilities of her audience. 'Spirit, courage and character' was how her friend Anna Kelly (who, as Anna Fitzsimons had been a Sinn Féin worker for the *Irish Bulletin* at the time of the First Dáil and, later, a republican on the anti-Treaty side), summarised her qualities.[65] Another felt that, as a public speaker 'she was in a class by herself … in irony, humour, quickness of wit and sharp, penetrating thrust a real delight'.[66] The Conditions of Employment bill passed into law. Irish women who read the news and saw what was happening in Europe braced themselves for more. What was happening to them was being duplicated elsewhere: a backlash against the 'modern woman' and a return to conservative social values fostered by an alliance between the Catholic Church and fast-spreading fascism.

Hanna's close relationship with her son did not prevent a whole-hearted welcome from being extended to his wife. At weekends when Owen played cricket the two women enjoyed occasional walks together. Both were lovers of gardens. Hanna adored orange lilies, despite their political connotations. 'We can't just leave them to the Orangemen,' she would say. Cuttings of her lilies were to flourish in her son's garden and the three of them, in letters, referred frequently to plants and trees in gardens at home and encountered on holiday. She was pleased to bring her new daughter-in-law to meetings and to republican sales of work, showing her off to her friends, but careful not to impose her own views on the young woman. Andrée was grateful for Hanna's sensitivity and, in retrospect, amazed that someone of her calibre could have been so understanding: 'she didn't try to enrol me or to bully me or dominate me in any way, for anything, and I thought after that it was really good of her, though she had such a strong personality, to withdraw, for a daughter-in-law who obviously had not the same background or ideas.'[67] Hanna, a lover of hats and clothes, did try to persuade the ascetic Andrée to become more fashionable. Her Christmas list for 1934 had, in the following order, 'hat –Andrée; doctor gown – Owen', before listing the usual gifts of plant, scarf, brooch etc. to family and friends.[68] In 1935 Owen would be awarded a Ph.D. for his thesis on Jules Romaine, his proud mother obviously anticipating this success. The warmth of her affections was shown too by her action in giving Andrée the cherished desk from Uncle Eugene. It would be, she hoped, for Andrée's daughter in the years to come. Hanna wished for generations of new, strong, Sheehy Skeffington women. The closeness of their relationship was evident a year after the wedding when Owen, radiantly happy ('yes we are an old married couple by now'), on holiday with Andrée in Macreddin village in the Wicklow hills, wrote to his mother, thanking her for her card and promise of flowering plant, urging her to join them. Pete was with them ('Pete has been fairly good though he misbehaved in the sun porch yesterday and had a wild tear after rabbits'), so she wouldn't have the 'complication' of getting the dog looked after. They felt she would enjoy hearing the birds sing as the sun went down, and they would welcome her presence.[69]

Owen's own politics continued to evolve. He was working closely with individuals like Seán Murray, General Secretary of the Communist Party of Ireland, although far more critical of Dublin's working class, as he commented after one rowdy anti-fascist meeting: 'This rabble doesn't deserve to be saved from capitalism! No one really hurt, but what a Christian crowd! Bricks, bottles, and the Bible…'[70] While Owen did not consider himself a communist, he had great affection for Murray: 'Seán was in good form and seemed to enjoy the opportunity of addressing a bourgeois audience' was his comment after one party. Murray was also the third guest at a 'select dinner party' when the newly-weds invited Owen's TCD friend Grattan Freyer and his French fiancée Madeleine Giraudeau to dinner. It was, by Dublin standards, a grand occasion, organised by Andrée, with omelette, leg of mutton, brussel sprouts, baked potatoes and jam roll, accompanied by two bottles of claret and a bottle of white wine. Owen went into such detail, when reporting on the event to his mother, because of what occurred when he telephoned to place his order of wine, offering to pay cash on delivery, to be told by the merchant: '"For your father's son everything is perfectly all right" – I didn't point out that Dada wouldn't have touched their filthy stuff!'[71] Frank was never forgotten.

For a while both Owen and Andrée would be members of the Irish Labour Party. Andrée said that Hanna 'defended her fanatical opinions – laughingly – but you could feel that she favoured the fanatical approach rather than the mild approach'.[72] Support for Spanish republicans was a cause to which both son and mother gave their full support. Both Sheehy Skeffingtons were prominent in reports of meetings in aid of the Irish Friends of the Spanish Republic. In February 1936 the Spanish people elected a republican government, composed of socialists and a minority of communists and anarchists. In France too, a combination of socialists and radicals were elected. These victories completely bucked the trend of growing fascist support and progressives everywhere felt that maybe the tide could be turned. When, a few months later, General Franco led a fascist revolt against the Spanish government and a Civil War between left and right began, help for the Spanish republicans became the leading international cause. In Ireland, republicans like Frank Ryan, disillusioned by the lack of support for the ideals of the Republican Congress, volunteered their services for the International Brigade. The Irish volunteers became the 'Connolly column', many dying on the Spanish battlefields. An 'Irish Friends of the Spanish Republic' launched an appeal for medical aid. Hanna chaired a Women's Aid Committee. At first, they appealed for money to help Basque women and children left homeless because of the ferocious air bombardment of Basque towns.[73] Later, they turned to helping the volunteers returning from Spain, providing them with a small amount of money to help them settle back home. In February 1937 *The Worker* (a short-lived publication of the Communist Party) reported that Mrs Sheehy Skeffington 'earnestly appeals to all the readers of the *Worker* to pour in donations of parcels and money for the men of the Irish section.'[74] Owen teased his mother: 'I used to like (your) style very much: "Now come on All you Lousers, Subscribe to me fund. Its for Spain … HSS" – Fetching prose I used to think.'[75]

Nora Harkin, a young woman involved in her first political campaign, recognised the importance of Hanna's presence. Supporting anti-clerical Spanish republicans was not a popular cause in Ireland, and few public meetings could be held without disruption. With Hanna's involvement, Nora felt there was a 'solidity' that reassured the more inexperienced members that nothing would go wrong.[76] Nora and her friends, young people in their twenties, were in great contrast to the woman who reminded them (much as she would have detested the comparison) of the small, plump figure of Queen Victoria. (Her nephew Conor, also seeing that resemblance to the monarch, added that he thought Hanna would have preferred Krupskaya, the wife of Lenin, as a comparison.)[77] But Hanna had a twinkle in her eyes, a dry sense of humour, and a disarming sense of the ridiculous. Nora believed that nothing could frighten her: 'she supported all the good things, she supported boys that went to Spain, she chaired meetings, had meetings in her own house, she never spared herself'. No worthy cause was dismissed or simply supported the easy way, by a small donation, the conscience-saving resort of so many. She would speak on anti-vivisection platforms, help to organise efforts to prevent the sale of worn-out donkeys and horses, hating cruelty and injustice from whatever the quarter. Support for the Spanish republicans was the kind of cause Hanna would have become involved with anyway, but her efforts intensified when it became clear that Frank Ryan had been taken prisoner. A 'Free Frank Ryan' campaign went on for many years, without success. A letter he sent from prison in 1940 sent greetings to many old friends, 'in particular to Mrs Sheehy Skeffington',[78] but he was to die a lonely death in Dresden in 1944, a pawn in the political game.

As war on an international scale looked increasingly likely, Hanna went to some lengths to revive interest in her dead husband and in his resolute opposition to militarism. Her account of his death, 'An Irish Pacifist', was published in a collection of pacifist writings in 1935[79] and her pamphlet *British Militarism as I Have Known It* was republished in 1936, its fourth printing. It was well reviewed, its subject matter striking a chord for many who realised that they were, once again, living under the shadow of impending war. A reviewer for *The New English Weekly*, mentioning that Skeffington's widow had been Irish delegate at the World Peace Congress in Brussels, recalled 'the sanity of such a pacifist as Francis Sheehy Skeffington, whose gentle spirit was tempered with that fine courage which leads ever to the championship of unpopular causes'.[80]

In March 1936 Hanna wrote a 'stocktaking' assessment of the current position of Irish women. It was timely, although not encouraging. Starting from the high ideals of the Proclamation women in Ireland had declined in status, while British women had slowly advanced. In terms of women in public office there were three women in the Dáil, three in the Senate and three in Dublin Corporation - obviously a 'mystic number', she jested. There were hardly half a dozen women on public boards and there still had been no female mayor. Women had been elected as justices in the Sinn Féin courts during the War of Independence, but these were swept away with the setting up of the Free State and the re-establishment of the conventional court system. Ireland now had no female justices, and women were deprived of the right to sit on juries. The few women police that existed had no uniforms and lacked the power to effect arrests. This contrasted with Britain, where there was a regular corps of women police under their own officers. In dealing with offences against women and girls, Irish women were at the mercy of men. The only bright spot in her eyes was the National University, where women had formal equality of status and where some women were professors. Trinity College was different. As she knew well from Owen's accounts of its antiquated practices, women were still barred from its premises after 6 p.m. and the 'quaint caption' of 'Public (Men only)' still applied to announcements of public lectures. She deeply regretted the fact that women who were mothers were unable to teach. Only in the university system could married women teach: 'There is still room for mothers at the top of the educational tree!' she said, with sardonic humour. The ban on married women workers in the Civil Service was enforced much more strictly than in England and widows remained barred from returning to their former jobs. As she concluded, 'marriage is not popular in the Free State', a country which, unusually, had a higher percentage of males in the population because more women emigrated in response to the dullness of rural life and their lack of opportunities. There was, she said 'at least one village in the West which is a sort of male Cranford, where practically the entire population consists of bachelors housekeeping for themselves'.[81] She did not exaggerate, although she put it more vividly than the state bureaucrats who were beginning to realise that the Irish nation was in danger of disappearing if these demographic trends continued. One remedy to this situation of postponed marriage and excessive female emigration could have been to make prospects at home more appealing. The alternative scenario of emphasising Catholic social and religious values smacked of brainwashing, with authoritarian discipline to ensure compliance. It was not the solution favoured by feminists, but it was the solution dear to the heart of church and state in Ireland.

Hanna was not a committee member of the National Council of Women in Ireland, the majority of whom had been non-militant suffragists 20 years previously, but many were old friends: Mary Hayden, Jennie Wyse Power, Violet Crichton and Lucy Kingston in particular. When an international peace campaign was organised in Brussels in September 1936, the Council nominated Hanna and their Vice-President, Miss E.S. Montgomery, a northerner, as delegates for the League.[82] Lord Robert Cecil, who had been a champion for women's suffrage in the British parliament, was President of the League, which was a heavy-weight organisation, dominated by Britain and France, attracting five thousand delegates representing more than 600 national movements and 20 international organisations to its congress. They gathered together to launch an International Peace Campaign with the intention of mobilising support for the League of Nations and educating public opinion on the urgency of 'collective security and peaceful cooperation amongst the peoples of the world.'[83] Italy and Germany were not represented. The 'Irish Free-State' was listed, which could not have pleased Hanna. Louie Bennett wrote to her, suggesting that she proposed de Valera as mediator for the Spanish crisis while admitting that she did not think Hanna would agree to that. Why was she chosen as delegate, give the long-standing experience of the National Council executive members? Her familiarity with Europe, ease with languages and links with the international women's movement must have made her an obvious choice. She wrote immediately to Florence Underwood at the Women's Freedom League, to notify her friends that she would be travelling to Brussels. Florence, lamenting 'What a terrible state Europe is in at the present time!' informed her that at least four British women would be attending, and that Charlotte Despard hoped also to go.[84] Margery Corbett Ashby, President of the Women's Freedom League, became a member of the Executive Committee of the International Peace Campaign, but, despite the fervent hopes of delegates, the League of Nations was unable to prevent Europe moving further towards war. The Peace Campaign was heavily male, with only two women out of eleven speakers at the closing session. Although female participants issued their separate 'Call to Women', there is no evidence, from examination of the papers she preserved from Brussels, that Hanna contributed to the proceedings.

April 1937 was the 21st anniversary of the murder of Frank and, in a macabre coincidence, Hanna found herself presented with a 'a broken half brick, with a ricocheted bullet embedded in it sideways, part of the wall against which three men were shot on the morning of April 26, 1916.' The person who handed this to her explained what had happened after the bricklayers ordered by Captain Bowen-Colthurst had cleared up and left the barracks. One noticed that a 'small half-brick, with a tell-tale bullet embedded in it, had fallen, unknown to him, into his tool basket.' The terrified man, meeting a civil servant on the premises, implored him to take away the brick. It was from the lower part of the wall, the bullet aimed at Frank as he lay on the ground, not yet dead. Hanna was now given this distressing memento by someone who 'vouches for its authenticity.' The National Museum of Ireland was beginning to develop a '1916 Museum' and republicans were donating articles. It might have been what prompted the person holding the brick to give it to Hanna, who would in time donate it to the museum.[85] Reminders of those terrible days kept coming. She received a letter from Canada, informing her that Bowen-Colthurst was running in a provincial general election. The sender, R.B. Matier, wanted copies of her *British Imperialism* pamphlet sent urgently as part of a campaign 'to spoil any chance that he may have'[86] and from London she received a similar request from the London Irish Republican Unity Committee, wanting to expose the 'monstrous outrage' of his standing for election by sending messages to the Canadian electorate.[87] She would have been gratified to know that he received only 13 votes, the lowest of all candidates, but she must also have felt as though her heart had broken yet again, knowing that her husband's murderer was free to stand for his crack-pot views while all she had was a brick with a bullet.

In the wake of the defeat on the Conditions of Employment bill, a Joint Committee of Women's Societies and Social Workers (chaired by Mary Kettle) was formed to scrutinise all future legislation and to make known women's views. At the same time, the National Council of Women in Ireland announced that it was forming a Standing Committee on Legislation Affecting Women. Its chair was Louie Bennett. Hanna was a committee member. There was going to be further erosion of women's status and Irish women were preparing for a determined battle against any such changes. De Valera had scrapped the Senate in May 1936 – mainly because its overwhelmingly conservative and pro-British nature meant that it was unlikely to accept the new constitution he was about to unveil to the public – but his action also deprived women of the voices of Jennie Wyse Power and Kathleen Clarke, both of whom had been powerful opponents of the Conditions of Employment bill when it was debated in the Senate. Beginning on 1 July 1936, the Joint Committee began to write to de Valera, asking for a meeting to discuss 'matters affecting the constitutional and economic position of women'. Finally, after two refusals, de Valera met the women on 29 January 1937. There were several items on the agenda: a quota of women in any new second chamber to be set up; restoration of jury service to women; the establishment of a women's police force; the Conditions of Employment Act and women's position in the civil service. Nothing positive came out of the meeting.[88]

That May, de Valera published his draft constitution, appalling those who had hoped that lobbying would have helped to improve the position of women. The most contentious clauses were the following:

> Article 41.2.1 and 2.2:
> In particular, the State recognises that by her life within the home, woman gives to the State a support without which the common good cannot be achieved.
>
> The State shall, therefore, endeavour to ensure that mothers shall not be obliged by economic necessity to engage in labour to the neglect of their duties in the home.
>
> Article 45.4.2:
> The State shall endeavour to ensure that the inadequate strength of women and the tender age of children shall not be abused, and that women and children shall not be forced by economic necessity to enter avocations unsuited to their sex, age or strength.

This paternalistic nonsense was opposed by the women's organisations and they immediately launched a campaign to have the offending clauses deleted. Many wanted a simple return to the Proclamation of 1916, but that would have had other political implications and it would certainly have been resisted by those less sympathetic to republicanism. The most vocal group of women were those in the Women Graduates' Association, of which Hanna had been a member since its inception. The three women professors – Mary Hayden, Agnes O'Farrelly and Mary Macken – were involved, together with Hanna and Mary Kettle. Other distinguished scholars were involved in the association, but its numbers were small. A total membership of 67 in 1930 was in reality less than half of the women who graduated that academic year.[89] Their demand was for the deletion of Articles 40, 41 and 45 and the retention of Section 3 of the 1922 Constitution, which ensured the equality of all citizens 'without distinction of sex'.

The women got together immediately, to begin organising their campaign. Anna Kelly wrote to Hanna: 'I suppose you will be at this Graduates' meeting of protest against Constitution. If so, I do hope they will not break up and disperse after passing a few resolutions. Invite to it non-graduates such as women labour leaders and so forth, and get going on a campaign.' She had read a searing critique of the proposed constitution's impact on women by journalist Gertrude Gaffney of the *Irish Independent*, but wondered 'how much of it was dictated by sheer anti-Government policy' as she had 'never found much sympathy heretofore for women from the political party which the Independent supports.'[90] Kelly's suspicions reflected the division within Irish political life that had begun with the Treaty, and could have explained the *Independent's* willingness to give women a platform, but sincerity and righteous indignation blazed from Gaffney's article – she was after all, a journalist operating in a very male environment:

> The death knell of the working woman is sounded in the new constitution which Mr de Valeria is shortly to put before the country ... Mr de Valera has always been a reactionary where women are concerned. He dislikes and distrust us as a sex, and his aim ever since he came into office has been to put us in what he considers is our place, and to keep us there.'[91]

The women graduates had agreed to organise a deputation to the Dáil and to begin a letter writing campaign. They soon agreed to extend this 'Emergency Committee' to include non-graduates, members of other women's organisations as well as women affiliated to no particular group. Replying to the Gaffney article provided an ideal first opportunity for publicity and Hanna replied in a long letter which reflected both her feminist and her republican allegiances:

> Women generally are under a debt of gratitude to Miss Gertrude Gaffney for her able and courageous exposé of the defects in the Draft Constitution, certain clauses of which deprive them alike of equal status and equal opportunities hitherto accorded. No casuistry can explain away the fact that the 1916 Proclamation with its explicit guarantee (without limitations of any kind) of equal citizenship, with all that it implies, in a free Republic, is being scrapped for a Fascist model, where women are relegated to permanent inferiority, their avocations and choice of calling limited because, apparently, of an implied permanent invalidism as the weaker sex ... Having been his colleague for many years on National Executives and committees of various kinds, I can testify to this: His ideal is the strictly domestic type of woman who eschews "politics" as male concerns ... other members of his cabinet and present entourage are similarly tainted, one Minister having often declared to me and others that he was opposed to votes for women, holding the 1916 gesture of emancipation a bad mistake ... This decline is, after all, but the inevitable result of the loss of our best in 1916 and 1922–3, the power falling into the hands of lesser men who no longer really care for the ideals inspiring Easter Week ... It is up to women of all parties to wake up and demand the complete restoration of the clauses of the 1916 Proclamation and Clause III of the Constitution which confirms the principle of equal pay and equal opportunities.

Mary Kettle had a letter published in the *Independent* on the same day, writing in her capacity as Chairman of the Joint Committee of Women's Societies:

> Women) will soon realise that if these articles become law no woman who works – be it in trade, factory or profession – will have any security whatever. The only protection women need, and the only protection women ask, is equality under

> the Constitution, of rights and opportunities. If President de Valera dislikes the phraseology of Article 3 of the Free State Constitution, let him fall back on the classic simplicity of the language in the Proclamation of the Republic ... That is unequivocal and will satisfy all women.[92]

The Sheehy sisters were in fine campaigning form. Hanna wrote to the women who had been part of the Second Dáil, to enlist their support in the campaign. Kathleen Clarke regretted not being able to participate in their forthcoming Mansion House meeting in June, but she would be 'with you in spirit though, applauding your efforts.' Her letter of support, as well as that of Kate O'Callaghan, also unable to travel to Dublin, but 'anxious to know' how the meeting went, were read out at that final meeting before voting. They were also reproduced in *Prison Bars*, a small newsheet edited by Maud Gonne MacBride which covered issues of importance to the Women's Prisoners' Defence League. The July issue was devoted to the Constitution, with statements from Kathleen Clarke, Kate O'Callaghan, Hanna and Maud herself.

Although many women who had been politically active over the decades were vehemently against the proposed clauses relating to women (Kathleen Lynn noted in her diary that 'women are rizz and rightly'),[93] not everyone agreed with the feminist case. Jennie Wyse Power, even though she had not followed de Valera's side during the Treaty crisis, was firm in her belief that the attacks on him were unwarranted and that some of the opposition was motivated by party politics. In an otherwise warm letter thanking Hanna for taking the trouble to find out the birthplace of Anna Haslam, she made it plain she would not support the campaign:

> About the new constitution I believe there is ambiguity in the section regarding the status of women. I regret however the tone of some of the speeches made by women on the subject. Believing that the statements referring to de V as a re-actionary and an anti feminist to be untrue. I wrote to the 'Irish Press' stating that my experience of him during my years of co-operation with him in national work was different. However my letter has not been published.
>
> I consider Miss Gaffney's letters were entirely political on behalf of the Independent. When we were deprived of jury service & other set backs – the Independent sang dumb.[94]

The historian Helena Concannon, a sitting Fianna Fáil TD for the National University (she did not contest the 1937 election), had been a contemporary of Hanna's at university, also studying languages and travelling abroad to further her studies. As a graduate, a former professor at University College Galway and author of well-received books on the part played by Irish women in history, she could have been a significant figure in the women's campaign against the constitution. Her reply to Hanna however, although meant kindly, was explicit in its rejection of the women's arguments. She felt Hanna's letter was written: 'under the stress of emotions engendered by your fear that that certain articles in the Constitution might tend to inflict lasting injury in the cause for which you and Frank (RIP) made such tremendous sacrifices … Isn't underlying it the assumption that I interpret the Articles in the same way as yourself. Since I do not the question of resigning from my party does not even present itself to me.' It was difficult not to acknowledge their long association, but nothing would change her mind: 'I know you voted for me as a woman, and I am very proud of the fact that your vote for me came from Armagh jail. Miss O'Farrelly, too, voted for me as a woman – to my party I owe an allegiance which I could not think of breaking.'[95]

Deputation after deputation met the leaders of the three main political parties and tried to persuade the three women members of the Dáil to support their sex. Margaret Pearse did not speak in the debate. Brigid Redmond for Fine Gael did agree to press for the re-insertion of 'without distinction of sex', putting forward an amendment that failed to win support. The Joint Committee of Women's Societies, the Standing Committee on Legislation Affecting Women and the Women Graduates' Association all put their case. De Valera, under heavy pressure, agreed to re-insert 'without distinction of sex' in Article 16, dealing with the right to vote, and he amended Article 45, broadening its scope to include men: 'The State shall ensure that the strength and health of workers, men and women, and the tender age of children shall not be abused and that citizens shall not be forced by economic necessity to enter avocations unsuited to their sex, age or strength.' It could, however, still be used to discriminate against women, particularly as he refused to alter in any way the fundamental principle that, in his Ireland, women's primary place was in the home.[96]

The Irish Women Workers' Union, satisfied by these amendments, withdrew from the campaign, although Helen Chenevix later wrote to Hanna to say that they had wished to speak at the June Mansion House meeting, but unfortunately had sent to the wrong address their request to Miss Hogan, the secretary for the campaign. While Chenevix was conciliatory: 'There seems to be always a point at which a certain difference arises between the Labour Woman and the pure Feminist, but in this case I don't think the difference is very great, and I hope it can be faced on both sides with good will',[97] Louie Bennett made it plain that amendments to articles 9, 16 and 45 had 'removed the really serious menace' and the union would be working with the Labour movement to advance the principles of equal pay and equal opportunities.'[98]

The *Irish Times* gave sympathetic coverage to the women's campaign, but it was a paper little read outside Dublin, and mainly confined to the professional classes. The *Irish Independent* was viewed with suspicion by many nationalists and the *Irish Press*, strongly in support of Fianna Fáil, reported on the feminist campaign while printing articles in favour of the proposed constitution, including one with the headline: 'Rights of women in the Constitution: Principles which it is the duty of Catholics to accept', which mentioned the 'strange views' of those who objected.[99]

On 14 June the draft constitution passed the Dáil by 62 to 48 votes. That was no surprise, seeing that Fianna Fáil had a majority of the seats. A plebiscite on the issue was due to be held on 1 July, the day of the general election, and the campaigners now threw their energies into trying to convince women voters to vote against. The Emergency Committee of the National University Women Graduates' Association's meeting in the Mansion House on 21 June, presided over by Professor Mary Macken, had a speakers' platform dominated by the old guard: Mary Hayden, Dr Kathleen Lynn, Mary Kettle, Sheila Bowen Dowling, Geraldine Plunkett-Dillon (sister of James Plunkett), Agnes (née Ryan) McCullough (of pre-Rising Belfast Cumann na mBan and wife of Dennis McCullough), Eileen Davitt (daughter of Michael Davitt, who had been so revered by Frank), and Hanna Sheehy Skeffington.[100] One member of the younger generation who was in the audience was Andrée Sheehy Skeffington, who admired her mother-in-law's ability as a public speaker: 'She had a power in her appeal, her voice carried well and she had a lot of wit. She was able to dig at the right spots. Her wit was really very effective.'[101] The audience was composed of women possessing a wide variety of political allegiances, a few of whom expressed their disagreement by calls of 'no' during part of Kathleen Lynn's speech: 'there would have been no Easter Week but for women'. Some of the speakers uttered little more than platitudes, but Mary Kettle and Hanna focused strongly on the implications of the constitution for women. Mary argued: 'Who looks after child welfare and orphans; who cares for the blind, the destitute and the aged? If you took women out of all these activities whom would you have left?' and Hanna, the final speaker, aware of the many shades of opinion she was addressing, struck a resolutely feminist note that steered clear of party politics. She proposed yet again the formation of a Woman's Party with branches throughout the country, to safeguard the interests of women in every sphere of activity. She wished they would not vote for the Constitution: 'By doing so they would be menacing the livelihood of their daughters, and putting a very serious barrier in the way of the progress of women in this country. It was quite all right to vote against the Constitution and they could, of course, aside from that, vote for any party they wished.'[102] Her decades of public speaking enabled her to connect with many different audiences. This approach was very different from the impassioned article she contributed to *Prison Bars:*

> There is no woman in Mr de Valera's Cabinet and but two in his Party. No woman appears to have been consulted by him. He and his Party are up against the entire body of organised women … Many supporters of Mr de Valera have bombarded him and his party … Never before have women been so united as now when they are faced with Fascist proposals endangering their livelihood, cutting away their rights as human beings. The outcome will probably be the formation of a Woman's Party; meanwhile a special emergency committee has been set up and a fighting fund inaugurated.
>
> Mr de Valera is thoroughly angry and full of declarations that his words do not mean what they seem. He says he only means to honour mothers in the home and that there is now no need to emphasise equality, as we have it! When pressed upon the "inadequate strength" reference he says it means women should not be miners or navvies. Mr de Valera shows a mawkish distrust of women which has always coloured his outlook; his was the only command in Easter Week where the help of women … was refused … Connolly, in his Citizen Army, would have welcomed women as soldiers were they so minded, and he saw to it long before that those that were, had military training …
>
> De Valera has refused to alter, except that he has restored "without distinction of sex" for voting purposes. He has refused to restore 1916 Equal Rights and Equal Opportunities for Women.[103]

As a last resort the women embarked on a mass mailing campaign, sending postcards urging a 'no' vote. Their opponents sneered that those who organised the campaign had 'a poor national record' and the Emergency Committee issued a lengthy rebuttal of this charge, profiling the women on their platform, 'to give the lie to any insinuation that the women on the platform had failed to give any account of themselves in the arduous days of 1916 and subsequent years.' Many of the women also had 'a distinguished record of public service in civil and social affairs.' While the women's statement was probably written collectively, their final retort sounds very like the prose style and dark humour so often shown by Hanna. In referring to de Valera's statement 'that women are eligible for every post in Ireland, even for the Presidency', they were reminded of the statement made after Catholic emancipation in 1829 – that Catholics 'became eligible for everything with the certainty that they got nothing.'[104] Mary MacSwiney, having being briefed by Mary Kettle after the Mansion House meeting, reckoned: 'On the whole they are not getting such a big majority for their constitution.'[105] It was a fair assessment. According to Andrée, it was Hanna's idea to reproduce a cartoon from the *Dublin Opinion*, showing Queen Maeve and Grainne O'Malley standing over de Valera in bed, with the caption 'Hey Big Boy, about the articles in the Constitution'.[106] It appealed to her sense of humour. Although the Constitution was ratified by 685,105 to 526,945 votes, this was hardly a massive mandate; there was also a high abstention rate and 116,196 spoiled votes. There was also a majority vote against the constitution in Dublin, Dublin County, Cork County West, Sligo and Wicklow. Fianna Fáil and Fine Gael both lost seats in an election which saw a modest resurgence of the Labour Party. Women had failed to prevent the constitution becoming law, but it would be untrue to say that they had had no impact.

During the campaign Hanna wrote to friends from her suffrage days, to let them know of the 'offensive clauses' in the forthcoming constitution. Alice Paul wrote from Washington on behalf of the National Woman's Party: 'We will give publicity to your letter and to the whole situation in our official paper. Don't know whether there is anything else we can do, but I will consider. My warmest greetings.'[107] Muriel Matters wrote a furious response: 'There is evidently going to be a determined move to inhibit women. So we are to be put under male governance once more'. She wondered if the pressure came from 'the R.C Hierarchy, vested economic (trade union) interests and how much to agelong damned male arrogance and impudence.' Regarding the hypocrisy of nothing being done to remove men from pubs in order to prevent them from squandering the family income, she suggested 'A pub crawl for negligent husbands' should be a slogan for the next election, regretting it was not possible 'for sophisticated old witches like you and me', to return to 'a golden age when our world and we were very very young.'[108] Matters was right, it was more than dispiriting for those who had been stalwarts in the fight for the vote and for national freedom to have now to organise a fresh mobilisation against the collective forces of male power.

It might be thought that political campaigning consumed all of Hanna's life at this period, but she had many preoccupations; one of course was that of ensuring she had an income. She still had to earn a living and was inventive in some of the directions her energies took her. She and Linda Kearns recorded two twenty-minute radio programmes – discussions on *Women Voter Problems* and *For and Against Women Police* - which were broadcast by Radio Athlone in late May and early June 1937. NUI asked her to act as superintendent of a matriculation exam in Athlone, entailing a total of six day's work plus travel and subsistence. Scribbled calculations by her on the bottom of the letter led to conclude that she could clear £13, a substantial enough amount. That took her out of the action for a week during the women's campaign.[109] Aine

Ceannt, writing about the Widows and Orphans Pensions bill going through the Dáil in May (extending pensions to all 'necessitous widows'; those over 55 in age rather than the existing 60; and allowing for pensions to be paid even to those whose husbands had not contributed towards national insurance), urged Hanna to accept if she was eligible: 'It is Irish money no matter who handles it', but the income threshold was so low there was no chance of her ever collecting a state pension.[110] And from May through to September of that year M. J. MacManus, book editor for the *Irish Press*, and a source of great personal support to her, attempted to help Hanna sell more copies of *The Day of the Rabblement*, using his contacts in the book trade. She had at least twelve copies she wished to sell, but he advised her to offer only six, as 'the value of the modern 1st edition has gone down'. MacManus hoped by suggesting two guineas for a copy she might get £10, but after several months of effort no offers had been received.[111]

The final Mansion House meeting had mandated women to bring together a 'provisional committee', the purpose of which was to form a new organisation of women. Mary Hayden's name was at the head, Mary Kettle was next, Hanna was listed as one of two honorary treasurers. This nucleus of women, by November, had become the Women's Social and Political League, soon to be renamed the Women's Social and Progressive League, in the hope of appealing to those outside of the usual groups.[112] It was the long hoped-for women's party, of some consolation to those who despaired of having any role in this patriarchy, now called 'Éire' instead of 'Free State', and with the Catholic Church given constitutional recognition as the dominant ideological force. Dorothy Macardle had informed de Valera that opposition to the constitution was 'a tragic dilemma for those who have been loyal and ardent workers in the national cause'.[113] Now she too turned towards the new League, as a 'humiliating necessity' if women were ever to improve upon their dismal showing in public life. Meg Connery sent 5/- towards 'the fighting fund of the woman's party', delighted that there appeared to be a feminist resurgence: 'Its high time there was a woman's party to protect what small liberties women still have left! – Isn't de Valera outrageous? The women of this generation are so torpid it will take a de Valera to rouse them!'[114] Former Cumann na mBan member Nora O'Keefe, now living in Dublin with Margaret Skinnider, wrote with interest: 'We had been saying only the other night before, that a good live women's organisation was much needed, and would be about the only thing that would arouse an enthusiasm just now.' She enclosed £1, 'being a 50-50 contribution from us. We hope to do better next month.'[115] Hanna received other contributions from women welcoming the prospect of a new women's organisation and no doubt her colleagues also received similar funds from their contacts. The bruising experience of the campaign to prevent primacy being given to women's place in the home had re-energised a generation, even if it had not succeeded in attracting those younger women who would be most affected. That protest – the 'discursive construction within the constitution that all women, whatever their marital status, and whether they were mothers or not, were enmeshed in traditional families' – would be 'the last high-profile feminist campaign until the revival of feminism in Ireland in the 1970s.'[116]

Although Hanna was listed in the first committee of the organisation, she was not greatly involved in its first months of existence. Owen, who had been unable to shake off the effects of recurring bouts of bronchitis, was discovered to be suffering from tuberculosis. Mary MacSwiney wrote to say how sorry she was 'Hope you are not fretting too much about it … We shall not forget to pray for him',[117] but Hanna was utterly distraught, remembering only too clearly that her brother Dick had died of the same disease.

NOTES

1 *Irish World*, 2 Apr. 1932.

2 Maryann Valiulis, 'Neither feminist nor flapper: The ecclesiastical construction of the ideal Irish woman', in Mary O'Dowd and Sabine Wichert (eds), *Chattel, Servant or Citizen* (Belfast, 1995), p. 169.

3 Ibid., p. 170.

4 *An Phoblacht*, 16 July 1932.

5 Hanna Sheehy Skeffington, 'Irishwomen's place in the sun', in *The Vote*, 15 Aug. 1930.

6 Nora Connolly O'Brien, 'Women in Ireland: Their part in the revolutionary struggle', in *An Phoblacht*, 25 June 1932.

7 Hanna Sheehy Skeffington to Esther Roper, n. d., Sheehy Skeffington MS (hereafter SS MS) 24,134.

8 *Irish World*, 9 July 1932.

9 J. O'Neill, Private secretary to Sir Dawson Bates, to Joseph Devlin MP, 30 July 1932, SS MS 33, 606/22.

10 Notice served on Hanna Sheehy Skeffington that she would be charged under the Civil Authorities (Special Powers) Act (Northern Ireland) 1922, at Armagh Courthouse on 24 Jan. 1933 at 11.30 am. SS MS 40,484/6.

11 Press cutting, n. d., Tom Kettle Papers, University College Dublin archives (hereafter UCDA).

12 Hanna Sheehy Skeffington to Mary Kettle, 15 Jan. 1933, SS MS 24,121.

13 Hanna Sheehy Skeffington to Owen Sheehy Skeffington (hereafter Hanna to Owen), giving family news, 9 Nov. 1931, SS MS 40,484/6.

14 Eugene Sheehy, *May It Please the Court* (Dublin, 1951), pp 146–7.

15 Hanna to Owen, Armagh Jail, Sat. night, 21 Jan. 1933, SS MS 40,484/31.

16 Owen Sheehy Skeffington, 'The problem of Ulster', in *L'Eveil des Peuples*, 5 Mar. 1933, SS MS 24,169.

17 Florence Underwood, Secretary, Women's Freedom League, in a letter to *Manchester Guardian*, 30 Jan. 1933.

18 *An Phoblacht*, 28 Jan. 1933.

19 Press cutting, n. d., Tom Kettle Papers, UCDA.

20 Ibid.

21 Ibid.

22 Hanna Sheehy Skeffington, 'Behind the bars', in *An Phoblacht*, 18 Mar. 1933.

23 Winifred Carney to Hanna Sheehy Skeffington, 2 Feb. 1933, SS MS 33,606/22.

24 Hanna Sheehy Skeffington to Mr Lyon, 19 Feb. 1933, SS MS 24,121.

25 *Irish Press*, 22 Feb. 1933.

26 *Irish Independent*, 22 Feb. 1933.

27 *Irish Press*, 22 Feb. 1933.

28 Conor Foley, *Legion of the Rearguard: The IRA and the Modern Irish State* (London, 1992), p. 122.

29 *An Phoblacht*, 1 Apr. 1933.

30 Menu card, dated 21 Mar. 1933, SS MS 24,170.

31 Margaret Mulvihill, *Charlotte Despard* (London, 1989), pp 179–80.

32 Leah Levenson and Jerry Natterstad, *Hanna Sheehy Skeffington: Irish Feminist* (New York, 1983), p. 166.

33 Obituary of Hanna Sheehy Skeffington, in *Workers' Review*, May 1946.

34 Fearghal McGarry, *Frank Ryan* (Dundalk, 2002), p. 32.

35 *An Phoblacht*, 9 Apr. 1933.

36 Andrée Sheehy Skeffington, *Skeff: A Life of Owen Sheehy Skeffington* (Dublin, 1991), p. 250, n.4.

37 Florence Murphy Baker, New York City, to Hanna Sheehy Skeffington, 3 Mar. 1935, SS MS 24,122.

38 Hanna to Owen, letters dated 1 Aug. 1934; 24 Aug. 1934, SS MS 40,484/7.

39 Hanna Sheehy Skeffington, *Irish Independent*, 10 Feb. 1934.

40 *Manchester Evening Chronicle*, 9 Feb. 1934.

41 *Irish Times*, 12 June 1934.

42 Hanna Sheehy Skeffington to McGonagle, 7 Mar. 1939, SS MS 24,126.

43 Maurice Healy to Eugene Sheehy, 6 Mar. 1935, SS MS 24,122. Eugene must have passed the letter onto Hanna, as it is included in her correspondence.

44 Maurice Healy to Hanna Sheehy Skeffington, 13 Mar. 1935, SS MS 41,178/88.

45 Publicity material, Alice Park Collection, Hoover Institution Archives, Stanford, California.

46 Letter from correspondent in Toronto, 29 Sept. 1934, SS MS 24121.

47 Hanna Sheehy Skeffington to Andrée Denis, July 1933, SS MS 41,176/22.

48 Ronan O'Casey, phone conversation with author, Sept. 1996.

49 Judge David Sheehy, personal interview with author, Apr. 1996.

50 Rathmines Children's Library, winter programme of talks, 1930–1, Alice Park Collection, Hoover Institution Archives, Stanford, California.

51 *Irish Press*, 25 Oct. 1940.
52 Sheehy Skeffington, *Skeff*, p. 72
53 Hanna to Owen, Aug. 1934, SS MS 40,484/7.
54 Ibid.
55 Sheehy Skeffington, *Skeff*, p. 74.
56 James Wellwood to Hanna Sheehy Skeffington, 27 Mar. 1935, SS MS 41,178/88.
57 'Mrs Sheehy Skeffington at the Minerva Club', in *Women's Freedom League Bulletin*, 5 Apr. 1935.
58 Maud Gonne MacBride to Hanna Sheehy Skeffington, 3 Apr. 1935, SS MS 24,122.
59 Cumann na mBan to Hanna Sheehy Skeffington, n. d., SS MS 24,122.
60 Andrée Sheehy Skeffington, personal interview with author, Nov. 1993. First published 1918, *Married Love* was reprinted many times, selling one million copies in Britain by 1939.
61 *Irish Press*, 14 June 1935.
62 Handwritten draft, SS MS 24,134.
63 *Irish Press*, 15 June 1935.
64 *Republican Congress*, 30 Nov. 1935.
65 Anna Kelly, 'Hanna Sheehy Skeffington: an appreciation', in *Irish Press*, 27 Apr. 1946.
66 Cathal O'Shannon, 'Hanna Sheehy Skeffington', in *Irish Times*, 23 Apr. 1946.
67 Ibid.
68 SS MS 24,177.
69 Owen Sheehy Skeffington to Hanna Sheehy Skeffington (hereafter Owen to Hanna), 21 Mar. 1936 and 23 Mar. 1936, SS MS 40,483/1.
70 Owen to Hanna, 7 Apr. 1936 SS MS 40,483/1.
71 Owen to Hanna, 18 Mar. 1937, SS MS 40,483/2.
72 Andrée Sheehy Skeffington, interview, 1977, Brian Harrison Suffrage Collection, Fawcett Library, London.
73 Circular, Irish Friends of the Spanish Republic, Women's Aid Committee, SS MS 24,178.
74 *The Worker*, 20 Feb. 1937.
75 Owen to Hanna, 22 Dec. 1937, SS MS 40,483/2.
76 Nora Harkin, personal interview with author, Oct., 1992.
77 Conor Cruise O'Brien, 'Passion and cunning: An essay on the politics of W. B. Yeats', in A. Norman Jeffares and K. G. W. Cross (eds), *In Excited Reverie: A Centenary Tribute to W. B. Yeats*, 1865–1939 (London, 1939), p. 207.
78 Seán Cronin, *Frank Ryan: The Search for the Republic* (Dublin, 1980), p. 155.
79 Hanna Sheehy Skeffington, 'An Irish pacifist', in Julian Bell (ed.), *We Did Not Fight* (London, 1935), pp 339–53.
80 *The New English Weekly*, 31 Dec. 1936.
81 Hanna Sheehy Skeffington, 'Women in the Free State: A stocktaking', in *The New English Weekly*, 19 Mar. 1936.
82 Lucy Kingston to Hanna Sheehy Skeffington, 24 Aug. 1936. Full list of committee members: President – Mary Hayden; Acting Vice-President Miss E.S. Montgomery; Vice-Presidents Senator Wyse Power, Mrs Crichton, Professor Elizabeth O'Sullivan; Hon. Sec. Miss Kingston; Hon. Press Sec. Miss Mellone, SS MS 41,203/1.

83 Congress information, agenda, circular letters to delegates are contained in SS MS 41,203/1.
84 Florence Underwood to Hanna Sheehy Skeffington, 21 Aug. 1936, SS MS 41,203/1.
85 Hanna Sheehy Skeffington, 'A Brick that Holds a Bullet', in *Irish Press*, 30 Apr. 1937.
86 R. B. Matier to Hanna Sheehy Skeffington, 28 Apr. 1937 and 4 June 1937 giving election result, SS MS 41,178/97.
87 London, 30 May 1937, on behalf of the London Irish Unity Committee, SS MS 41,178/97.
88 Maria Luddy, *Hanna Sheehy Skeffington* (Dundalk, 1995), p. 42
89 Maria Luddy, 'A "sinister and retrogressive" proposal: Irish women's opposition to the 1937 draft Constitution', in *Transactions of the Royal Historical Society* (2005) 15, pp 175–95.
90 Anna Kelly to Hanna Sheehy Skeffington, 8 May 1937, SS MS 41,178/88.
91 G. G. 'The death knell of the working woman', in *Irish Independent*, 7 May 1937.
92 Catriona Beaumont, 'Irish women and the politics of equality in the 1930s', in *Phoebe*, 3:1, spring 1991, p. 28.
93 Quoted in Maria Luddy, 'A 'sinister and retrogressive' proposal, p. 180.
94 Jennie Wyse Power to Hanna Sheehy Skeffington, 15 May 1937, SS MS 41,178/99.
95 Helena Concannon to Hanna Sheehy Skeffington, 25 May 1937, SS MS 41,178/97.
96 Beaumont, 'Irish women and the politics of equality', pp 26–32.
97 Helen Chenevix to Hanna Sheehy Skeffington, 1 July 1937, SS MS 41,178/99.
98 Letter from Louie Bennett, in *Irish Press*, 22 June 1937.
99 *Irish Press*, 14 May 1937.
100 *Irish Times*, 22 June 1937; *Irish Press*, 25 June 1937.
101 Andrée Sheehy Skeffington, interview, 1977, Brian Harrison Suffrage Collection, Fawcett Library, London.
102 *Irish Press*, 22 June 1937.
103 *Prison Bars*, July 1937.
104 Emergency Committee of the National University Women's Graduates' Association, statement in response to criticisms, in *Irish Press*, 25 June 1937.
105 Mary MacSwiney to Hanna Sheehy Skeffington, 5 July 1937, SS MS 41,178/99.
106 Andrée Sheehy Skeffington, personal interview with author, Mar. 1991.
107 Alice Paul to Hanna Sheehy Skeffington, 14 June 1937, SS MS 41,178/99.
108 Muriel Matters Porter to Hanna Sheehy Skeffington, 21 May 1937, SS MS 41,176/5.
109 NUI to Hanna Sheehy Skeffington, 3 June 1937, SS MS 41,178/97.
110 Aine Ceannt to Hanna Sheehy Skeffington, 11 May 1937, SS MS 41,178/97.
111 Letters from M. J. MacManus to Hanna Sheehy Skeffington, 1 Apr. 1937; 15 May 1937; 4 Sept. 1937, SS MS 41,178/97.
112 Beaumont, 'Irish women and the politics of equality', pp 28–9.
113 Maria Luddy, *Hanna Sheehy Skeffington*, p. 46.
114 Meg Connery to Hanna Sheehy Skeffington, 8 June 1937 (from Gorey, Co Wexford – Meg was out of Dublin during the campaign), SS MS 41,177/10.
115 Nora O'Keefe to Hanna Sheehy Skeffington, 3 June 1937, SS MS 41,178/99. With thanks to Mary McAuliffe for identifying which 'Nora' had written the letter.
116 Maria Luddy, 'A sinister and retrogressive proposal', p. 194.
117 Mary MacSwiney to Hanna Sheehy Skeffington, 5 July 1937, SS MS 41,178/99.

FOURTEEN

'THE SEEDS BENEATH THE SNOW', 1937–46

The republican sisterhood, those women who had woven a closely-knit extended family out of the sorrows of bereavement, swung into action when Owen's illness was diagnosed. Hanna was away (most likely in Athlone, working as matric examiner) so he had to write himself to tell her, breaking the news as gently as he could:

> Dearest mother,
>
> I've seen a *médecin sérieus* all right. News not too good I'm afraid: one lung definitely affected and in one spot only, the other (left) is ok; a year off work at least. There you have it all at best & worst. A bit of a blow all right. Micks has just been in with Dr L. & broken it to us, so I'm writing you at once ... Your only boy is a bit of an ass to go & get this damn thing, but he has no intention of being depressed about it so why should others? I know you'll take it well, but I know also that it will be a nasty shock.[1]

He and his wife, only two years married, had little money and no hope of affording the kind of specialist care that tuberculosis demanded. With Owen unable to teach they faced an uncertain future. Dr Kathleen Lynn had been the first to insist that Owen consult a specialist and she continued to provide valuable medical advice. Aine Ceannt, still employed by the White Cross's Children's Society, persuaded the organisation to pay the costs of travelling to Switzerland. T. B. Rudmose-Brown, ('Ruddy' to Owen) Professor of Romance Languages at Trinity, was also anxious to do all he could to help. He managed to persuade the board of Trinity that Andrée's degree from the

Sorbonne qualified her to act as substitute teacher for her husband. Hanna had commented that the only sector in teaching where the marriage bar did not apply was in higher education, yet she could never have imagined what a blessing that was to prove for her family. It emphasised – if emphasis was necessary – the dire consequences of discriminatory legislation, condemning families to destitution if the male breadwinner fell ill.

Owen was sent to Davos, to the best sanitorium they could find, a search helped by their friend Madeleine Giradeau. He and Andrée travelled together, breaking the journey by staying with the Denis family in Amiens. Shortly afterwards, Hanna went out alone to Switzerland, to reassure herself that her son was in good hands. Andrée was back in Dublin and she wrote reassuringly, 'no need to worry my dear'; Owen was 'well and cheerful' despite having a cold and was 'charmed' by all the xmas presents she had brought out to him, in the knowledge that he would still be there in another three months. The woman running Hanna's *pension* was German, bringing back girlhood memories and she enjoyed listening to the local dialect.[2] She wrote a postcard to Kathleen from Baden, sounding a more positive note than his real state of health warranted:

> All going on well here. Owen is over his cold. He is still in bed ... They say they are surprised at his good and swift recuperative powers. He looks well, sleeps and eats well and cough is less. Weather glorious – I've been doing tremendous walks and my heart shows no reaction whatever so it must be ok. There is pleasant company here. I leave London Sunday 17-10 – home.[3]

In London, staying as usual at the Minerva Club, she gave a talk, chaired by the novelist Kate O'Brien, on 'Irish Women Writers'. It was so well attended many failed to gain admittance to the standing-room only hall. With the warm support of old friends like Emmeline Pethick-Lawrence she provided her audience with what they agreed was a 'real treat', describing Irish women poets, novelists, dramatists, scholars and historians. 'Compared with the volume of output by English women writers', she said, 'that of Irish women was but a streamlet to a flood, still it was not negligible, for the Irish brook had a music, a liveliness of its own.' She praised Nora Connolly O'Brien, whose *Portrait of a Rebel Father* she considered to be the outstanding book of the year. She mentioned the historical work of Mary Hayden and dramatists such as Dorothy Macardle, Margaret O'Leary and Maura Mallory. Many were, of course, her friends; writers and political activists combined, now coming to the peak of their powers. Hanna's speaking voice, often described as melodic in its soft Irish tones, was an effective medium for literary recitation. When she read the poetry of Eva Gore-Booth, Lady Gregory, Maeve

Cavanagh and Alice Milligan ('propagandists and rebels of the first order'), the emotional impact was tangible:

> those who were merely English experienced a sudden catch in the throat as the music of our language with its sweet Irish undertone of wistful dreams and accent was lilted to our ears.[4]

Of Kate O'Brien, whom she described as the 'Irish Galsworthy', a novelist 'in the foremost rank', she added, in tones that indicated that this might be the greatest commendation of all, that 'she also has the distinction of having had one of her books banned in Ireland'. Lesbian heroines and critiques of the stifling lives lived by middle-class Irish women were not well received by the Censorship of Publications Board, despite critical and popular acclaim. *Mary Lavelle*, published in 1936, had a lesbian heroine. *The Land of Spices*, her best-known work, appeared five years later. It was banned because of its reference to homosexuality. Hanna was an avid reader, as the scope of this talk revealed, relishing books featuring strong female characters.

With Owen settled in his sanitorium, Andrée accepted an invitation to come and camp out in the sitting room of Belgrave Road. As there was a lodger in Owen's old bedroom, a small clearing at one end of the busy sitting room was the only space that could be created.[5] Hanna was back in London in July, as one of a large gathering in Caxton Hall celebrating the 93rd birthday of Charlotte Despard.[6] That November she embarked on a lengthy tour of America. Andrée believed that she was convinced Owen was going to die, and she couldn't face staying at home, waiting for that day. Leaving her daughter-in-law in charge of house, lodgers, cat and Pete the dog, and with the task of taking over Owen's teaching, off she went, to Montréal and the comfort of Margaret and family. There she had a family Christmas in the midst of her sister's hectic, slightly bohemian circle. The William Feakins Agency, not the Open Forum Speakers Bureau, were her agents this time, organising a very effective publicity campaign. Henry Nevinson had advised her that they were the best lecture agents. One thousand copies of a circular, headed by a photograph, detailed the lectures on offer, accompanied by an effusive commendation: 'Mrs Hanna Sheehy Skeffington, Leader of Feminists, Delegate to Peace Congresses, Former Judge in Irish Courts, Editor, Author, Critic.' A lengthy press release provided a glowing testimonial, listing her vast range of achievements:

> Mrs Skeffington is undoubtedly one of the most colourful and distinguished women in the Irish Free State. Not content to attain renown in one field alone, she has been influential in the literary, political, pacifist and feminist movements of her native land … Everywhere that she went, audiences acclaimed her as a speaker of extraordinary

> acumen and discernment, well versed in international as well as Irish national affairs. Progressive and sincere, Mrs Skeffington will be welcomed by audiences aware that she deserves a high rating in the long list of women of accomplishment.[7]

A lecture on Russia was not listed. In the anti-communist atmosphere of the times it would not have been a selling point. One lecture had the ambiguous title of *The European Scene: Lights and Shadows*, which would have given her free rein, depending on how she gauged the sympathies of her audience. Otherwise, the topics were *Irish Writers; Rebel Irishwomen; Irish Folklore; Woman's Place in the Old World*, and one called *Dublin Memories: Extracts from Work in Progress*, which concentrated upon the excitement of the suffrage years. This was the first instalment of the memoirs so many kept urging her to write. Conversational and vivid, it provided a snapshot view of past times. She kept her outline for the lecture on *Women in the Old World*. The following notes, although sketchy, give some insight into her assessment of women's position in the final years before the outbreak of war. We can faintly glimpse how powerful an address this would have been, when expanded and presented by this seasoned polemicist:

> Like waves – highest in 1929-34 – now receding somewhat, but some gains.
> *(the position of women in various countries analysed separately)*
> The 'tyranny of pots and pans' – fascism
> Women – cannon fodder or relaxation
> Ireland's new Constitution reactionary – 3 clauses – inadequate
> strength…
> Women scapegoat of unemployment
> Dismissals on marriage – teachers
> In US and Soviet Union women seem freest but world still largely a man's world.
> Man needs woman's help today more than ever – even if he doesn't know it.
> Peace 'mother' on battlefield.
> Producers of cannon fodder should have something to say about it.[8]

Marie Equi, saddened by the news of Owen – 'Years ago I thought he might have a lung tendency. Don't you remember I advised California for him … life deals us blows thru our children … Dublin is not the place for Owen, too damp' – was scathing in what she perceived as Hanna's lack of radicalism: 'you have been doing a helluva lot of talking, but you have become a bit abstract in your titles and academic subjects – where is your old time militancy Hanna?'[9] The old comrades did not meet – Portland for lectures was 'dead' the doctor reckoned - but they had a long telephone conversation: 'your voice sounded happier than the days of old. More elasticity and flexibility. The years have softened your grief, of this I am assured.'[10] Hanna's letters to Owen included reminders of his childhood experiences in America, as he had written from his sanitorium to say 'I'm looking forward very much to your (our!) trip to America',[11] pleased to be reminded of those times, 'Yes I remember well that log hotel at the Grand Canyon…'[12]

Hanna was in New York when news reached her of the death of her sister Kathleen, who died very suddenly in February 1938, following a stroke. Conor, running home from college on nearing the news, to find a mother who never regained consciousness, had terrible memories of his father's collapse. The family blamed overwork. Hanna had been very proud of her sister's publication of her Gregg-Irish book in 1929, 'a big effort' which she believed would add to her prestige. Kathleen had been under the care of Dr Lynn and, shortly before her death, had written to Hanna in her usual bouncy tone, sending newspapers and complaining that, with the diet she had been put on, 'You'll have to look for me with a microscope when you come back.' Preoccupied with her job as teacher and superintendent of Irish, she added that Mary was 'working like the devil with that League. She has the Drawing Room in the Mansion House for tonight's meeting.'[13] She had always been 'Kay' while Hanna was always 'dearest Joan'. She was the sister on whom Hanna relied for news and her loss was a huge shock. Florence Murphy Baker and other friends in New York rallied round, but Hanna was relieved to get away and be on the road again, telling Andrée, 'I have lots to do and that's the best pain killer there is … while I'd like to go home right away, I dread that too, with dear K. missing. But its hardest just now for all at home, especially Mary and Conor … Owen will feel his aunt's death acutely as they had so many ties & memories & he was like her son.'[14] Owen, grieving, recovering from an operation on his lung that had taken place the day before Kathleen's death, wrote immediately to his mother about the 'horrible news about poor Aunt Kathy … I know this will be a terrible shock to you as it was to me; and as it must have been to all at home'. While Owen understood Mary's regret that they had not managed to persuade Kathleen to rest more, he counselled against feelings of guilt, reassuring his mother: 'She hated resting & she loved her work, every minute of it; there had been talk of her retiring, but I feel glad she didn't.' He believed continuing with her tour was the best thing Hanna could do, given the circumstances. By the time she would have arrived back in Ireland Mary would be over the initial shock, and it would be a shame to miss California and seeing her friend Alice Park:

> K. was my favourite aunt and of course things at home will never be quite the same again – the best thing you can do is to get into the thick of the hectic American whirl – and be glad you have it. All best love; and try not to feel too bad.[15]

Hanna stayed with Alice Park for a time and her tour was covered by the *Daily Palo Alto Times*, where the reporter appreciated her Dublin accent and Irish wit as well as her 'deadly seriousness about the causes she represents'. She spoke in Eagles Hall, San Francisco, on 'Ireland, the British Empire and World Peace', and a lecture on Irish affairs, with a sub-title referencing the new constitution -'Is it a straight-jacket painted green?'- made her political views very plain.[16] Press coverage was muted, but those who interviewed Hanna warmed to her strong personality. Dorothy Thomas, for the *Independent Woman*, was gushingly descriptive: 'Mrs Skeffington has direct, fearless blue eyes. She is grey-haired, motherly and soft-spoken. But you know she will fight for her convictions as a mother will fight for her young.' That was probably not an analogy appreciated by Hanna, who had started off the interview by exclaiming 'You'd think a woman was born with a home on her back – like a snail – just because she's a woman', as she explained the inequities of the new Irish constitution to her interviewer.[17] Publicising the constitution was one of her major preoccupations during the tour. De Valera was still a hero in Irish-America and she, increasingly his opponent on every major political issue, was determined to use this opportunity to speak out on behalf of Irish women, breaking the convention that Irish public figures refrained from such direct talk when abroad. She was exceptionally outspoken. There was 'an insidious but strong tendency of the present regime towards fascism', exemplified in the power possessed by the President under the new constitution, as well as in its various clauses. The woman described by Dorothy Thomas as a 'mild-mannered militant' explained how women were being forced out of the labour force, even though the reality was that their economic contribution was often vital:

> Men may not much regard feminine logic, but it does seem that the gentlemen are putting the cart before the horse when they prevent a married woman from holding a job before they give her husband sufficient economic security to support the home himself. And as for the 'different physical capabilities', Irish women have for centuries been considered – and still are considered – robust enough to do the hardest work in the fields.[18]

She believed work to be too important a part of life 'to be regulated according to sex … (Women) have a right to choose what work they will do. There is a psychological as well as an economic necessity for every human being to find some work within his *(sic)* capabilities.' In this insistence she was unquestionably a woman of the modern age, even if the times in which she lived were steadily regressing in their attitudes towards women.

While in San Francisco she took time to visit Tom Mooney, still unjustly imprisoned in San Quentin, before heading off to Altadena and Mrs Kate Crane Gartz, yet another of the remarkable women she had met during her lifetime of activism. Kate Crane Gartz, sister to Chicago socialist and activist Frances Crane Lillie, was the heiress to Crane Plumbing and her house in Pasadena was a centre for political and cultural activism, her salons attended by intellectuals such as Upton Sinclair, Max Eastman and Albert Einstein.[19] On the west coast, interest in Hanna's visit centred on the question of Ireland's attitude if war broke out. Her view was that 'Ireland will fight on England's side in the next war – she'll have to – but England trims and wangles so much that only God knows which side that will be.'[20] This was not as wrongheaded a conclusion as it might appear on hindsight. De Valera was in the process of concluding a new Anglo-Irish Treaty, amending the external relations between Britain and Ireland. According to Malcolm MacDonald, the Dominions Secretary, de Valera acknowledged that 'The wish of his countrymen in any war would be to remain neutral … But he thought it very likely that the Irish Free State would be drawn in on our side.'[21] Hanna's comments were a reflection of the *realpolitik* of the times.

When she returned to New York in early April 1938 Florence Murphy Baker wrote to invite her to a 'little supper', as the Irish feminist writer Nora Hoult was with her and was anxious to meet Hanna.[22] Hoult, who 'employed the popular novel for feminine protest',[23] had walked away from her marriage to writer Oliver Stonor when she realised that she was expected to do the domestic chores. Her first novel, *Time Gentleman! Time!* published in 1930, concerned a woman's marriage to an alcoholic. She would eventually write 20 novels and produce 4 short story collections, receiving much critical acclaim. We do not know if the meeting took place, but, if it did, the two women would have had much in common, not least in their understanding of the power of literature. Hanna returned to Montreal before sailing back to Ireland. The return visit to Montreal was probably unplanned, a response to news of the death of Kathleen and a need to see Margaret so that the sisters could come together and share their grief. For Ronan, who knew little about the family his mother had left behind, it was the first time he had heard of this aunt. It was Hanna, despite all the demands on her time, who had written the letters keeping the scattered family in touch.

She was home in May. Andrée, relieved of her responsibilities, travelled over to Switzerland to be with Owen, now finally making progress. Alpine flowers were appearing with the melting of the snow and she wrote regularly to Hanna, enclosing samples of the flowers, wrapped and labelled in German.

She was touched to find them, after Hanna's death, stored carefully amongst her hoard of papers.[24] Cahalan had been lodging with Kathleen at the time of her death because her husband, John Burns, had died in 1936, after only four years of marriage. She now received support from Hanna, who settled her in Belgrave Road. It was back to dreary reality, with a pile of summer exam scripts to mark. In July Owen congratulated her on only having 80 more papers to get through, but in August she then had a huge pile to work through in her role as examiner in French for the civil service. It was more drudgery – £2 for setting the paper and one shilling and three pence for each script marked. 409 scripts netted her a total of £25.11.3s. At approximately £1,200 in modern currency values, this was a substantial addition to her income, albeit time-consuming.[25]

On 23 August Owen finally left the sanitorium, spending a few days in Paris and London as he made his way home to Ireland, to stay in Belgrave Road with his mother. Andrée was given permission from Trinity to continue teaching his classes for the next two terms. Owen was full of gratitude: 'TCD treated me very handsomely. Roddy has always been a good scout, but the Provost was particularly kind.'[26] Belgrave Road was too small for them all and Owen's health required a place away from Dublin's polluting air. Yet again, Aine Ceannt's contacts helped them out. Through some of her republican women friends they were able to rent a small cottage, Hazlebrook, standing in the grounds of a large estate that had once been owned by a Lord Chancellor of Ireland. It was appropriate, given the long struggle waged by the mother of the new tenant, that this estate in Terenure should have been transformed into a school for female gardeners. Surrounded by cows, fields and market gardeners, Owen and Andrée began an enthusiastic foray into the joys of gardening. Following old traditions, they established their own Friday 'At Homes' and settled happily into Dublin life once more.

The family had another shock that August. Margaret's young husband Michael, on a fishing trip to Cape Cod, had died of a heart attack. Margaret had not been with her husband because, perennially hard up, she had not been able to afford the expense.[27] Garry Culhane, her son, wrote to explain that the dislodgement of a blood clot to the brain had killed Michael. He had stopped drinking, resuming when on holiday, and the 'excitement' had fatal consequences.[28] Garry sounded matter of fact, but his mother's letters to Hanna were full of heartbreak at her loss. She felt she could not bear to remain in Canada without him and so she and Ronan, Michael's child, returned to Ireland. Past scandals ensured that some quarters of the family gave them a cool welcome. Ronan, uprooted from everything he knew, was grateful for the warmth extended by Hanna's side. Her inexhaustible interest in the young, and her desire to broaden their outlook in life, led to 'dotie' being taken to Roebuck, to have tea with Maud Gonne MacBride. Ronan remembered his aunt telling him that he would meet one of the most important women in Ireland. He was terrified by what he thought of as 'an angel of death', an immensely tall figure dressed in black, long, boney hands pouring out the tea. As the two friends chatted to each other, the teenaged boy sat in mesmerised silence.[29]

By 1938 the Nazi threat of war was overshadowing other political issues. A Dublin Anti-War Committee – a coalition of communists and republicans – was formed, the Sheehy Skeffington name prominent amongst committee members. She could always be relied upon, even imposed upon, when the need was urgent. As German troops prepared to march into the Sudetenland, Seán Murray, organiser for the committee, booked a meeting in the Hatch Street Hall, confident that his colleague would agree with his hasty decision:

> Big meeting next Tuesday … booked in your name and in virtue of this honour something will be expected from you, namely, to preside at the meeting! I look to you to do this for certain as I think it will be a gathering of solidly useful people … Then there is no knowing, by the time we may be in the cauldron of war or on the very edge of the precipice, if we can be nearer than we are at the present. Hence the importance of this meeting. Ring me, or wire, or write, but above all be with us.[30]

It could not have been easy, to have to summon up, yet again, the energy to protest against the imminent catastrophe of a war that would engulf the world. Memories of Frank and of his determination to resist militarism at all costs were uppermost in Hanna's mind during these months. Fenner Brockway, who had been a conscientious objector in the First World War, wrote to thank her for her 'little note reminding me of our war-time stand – you and the memory of your husband will always be an inspiration'.[31] He hoped the copy of *New Leader*, sent 'in plain wrapper' would get through. The intensifying censorship posed a challenge.

Few of the comforts of middle age were there to provide some buttress from the harshness of the outside world. Death and illness had decimated the Sheehy clan, making it, in Hanna's eyes, more important than ever to care for those who needed support. When young Ronan decided he wanted to become an actor and planned to act in a play of George Bernard Shaw's, his aunt was happy to use her vast network of friendship on her nephew's behalf. Shaw's permission was needed, so Shaw was written to. Back came a postcard from the great man: 'for your sake your nephew has my permission'.[32] Increasingly, Owen, the oldest cousin, was assuming a paternal role regarding the welfare of the younger cousins. He could be stern and often clashed with Conor, who he was trying to coach for language exams, chiding his mother, 'I think it's a mistake to think of Conor as going always through "a phase". That's been said of him since he was 7, he's nearly 21 now.'[33] However, when Conor, to the astonishment of his family, announced his engagement to Christine Foster, Owen was staunch in his support: 'It seems a bit hard on him to get no congratulations! I know she's a Northerner and a Prod, but Conor's father did not exactly get the glad hand for marrying a Catholic. I think its fine – a very nice girl and intelligent, so what the hell!'[34] Owen knew his family history well, 'Conor is certainly, or has been, pretty fickle, but I could think of an aunt of two of mine.'[35] Despite her criticisms of her nephew, his aunt Hanna could also be relied on for support, no matter how apparently outlandish the request. In 1937 she had lent Conor her copy of Emma Goldman's *Anarchism and Other Essays*. When he announced that he was going to start a 'new revolutionary weekly' in Trinity College she had given him Goldman's address, enabling her self-assured nephew to write to her with an audacious request for a 'favour':

> A letter, or brief article from you would set a fine note for our first number. Anything on anarchism, marriage (in this College women are not admitted after six o'clock nor are they permitted to pollute the male dining hall with their presence), on your recent stay in Spain, or simply a letter on the foundation of such a revolutionary magazine, would be accepted most gratefully. Or if you prefer, something which other magazines are afraid to print. You see we are committed to no policy except one of attack on established tradition and working towards individual liberty. I am very sorry this will be a 'thank you job' but like most revolutionaries we have no capital.

Conor's carefully crafted postscript must have been designed to provoke a reaction from the veteran anarchist: 'P.S. Our rooms here in College are decorated with two of the anti-fascist posters which you gave my aunt – the one with "*Au viva nuestros*..." and the ad. for Tierra y Libertad. They have caused a good deal of discussion.' He calculated correctly and received a generous reply: 'I was glad, indeed, to hear from someone related to my dear friend Mrs. Sheehy Skeffington, for whom I have a great admiration.' While Goldman regretted her work on behalf of the Spanish cause left no time to write, she added her own thoughts on the out-moded traditions of Trinity College:

> It was astounding to me to hear that such hoary traditions in regard to women are still prevailing in your College. Well, there must be something organically wrong with the male members if they cannot endure the presence of the opposite sex in their midst! Even Spain, where the status of women is still 50 years behind

> that in the Scandinavian countries, the United States and England, is beginning to show a different attitude than that which was held prior to the Revolution of July 19th, 1936.
>
> I am preparing some articles for publication, among which will be one on the struggle of Spanish women for the emancipation and enlightenment of their sex, I will be glad to send you a copy when it is ready.
>
> Please keep in touch with me and let me see your paper when it appears. I am so glad you have posters of TIERRA Y LIBERTAD. If I was sure that new posters and photographs would reach you, I would be glad to mail you some, but knowing of the severe censorship prevailing there, I do not like to risk sending them.[36]

Bolton Street Technical College had written to welcome Hanna back on the staff as a part-time teacher of German, and she had similar work at the Marino Institute, but by the following February her second-year German class in Marino had been cancelled, 'owing to continuing low attendance'.[37] The German language was not the most popular option on the eve of the Second World War. The need for extra income was pressing enough for her to apply to the Dublin Theatre Company for a place on their Sunday 'Question Time'. The attraction was the prize of one guinea and payment for any questions submitted that were later used on the programme.[38] She still had outstanding legal expenses to pay following the débâcle of the outcome of her libel case. Seán MacBride, now a barrister, advised her to settle the bill. Mr McGonagle was 'a decent fellow' who was not over-charging. She must have been in a state of acute anxiety over the issue because Seán went to the lengths of drafting a letter to the solicitor on her behalf, explaining her financial difficulties.[39] Hanna eventually accepted this advice and sent McGonagle an instalment of £5, with an accompanying apology for the delay. Her tone was rueful: 'I appreciate how decent you have been about this unfortunate piece of litigation – it seems to have been specially unfortunate for you and I.'[40] So many women were suffering severe financial hardship in their old age, despite the sacrifices they had made for the Irish cause. It was galling to see well-dressed and well-fed politicians profiting from those past sacrifices. When Hanna and Rose Jacob intervened on behalf of Sarah Mellows, trying unsuccessfully to ensure that she received a pension from the state, Rose commented with bitterness: 'If de Valera had any decent regard for Mellows' memory, he'd pay Mrs Mellows £100 a year out of his own ample money.'[41]

W. B. Yeats died in January 1939. He had been denounced by republicans for his record as a Free State Senator, yet when news of his death came to Hanna, she chose her words with care. Conor, having lunch with his aunt, was fascinated, waiting to hear what she would eventually come out with:

I was genuinely moved, a little pompous, discussing a great literary event with my aunt, a well-read woman who loved poetry.

Her large, blue eyes became increasingly blank, almost to the polar expression they took on in controversy. Then she relaxed a little: I was young and meant no harm. She almost audibly did not say several things that occurred to her. She wished, I know, to say something kind; she could not say anything she did not believe to be true. After a pause she spoke:

'Yes,' she said, 'he was a Link with the Past.'

I had been speaking of the poet; she was thinking of the politician.[42]

Conor was from a different generation, born a year after the Rising, too young to remember controversies like *The Plough and the Stars* and the opposing sides taken by poet and aunt. However, not all the younger generation regretted that those elderly campaigners had remained so single-minded in attitude. Single-mindedness did not have to mean narrow-mindedness, certainly not for Hanna. Emma Goldman had urged the writer Ethel Mannin to make contact with Hanna when she visited Dublin, and Mannin found her to be a kindred spirit, a rarity in her interest in the ideas of a younger generation. She was 'ready to listen at all time, her mind open to new ideas'.[43] Mannin had had a brief affair with Yeats, shortly before meeting Reginald Reynolds, the man who would become her husband. In the summer of 1939, she brought Reginald to Ireland for a holiday. He was entranced to meet what he called the 'Grand Old Girls' with whom his wife had become so friendly. Hanna he found to be a 'great character', her disarmingly conventional exterior at total odds with her unconventional views:

> She would sit so demurely, balancing a teacup like any suburban lady and looking like somebody's respectable great-aunt, and even her soft, purring brogue seemed to contradict the words she uttered, for she was a militant Irish Republican, an ardent feminist and a natural anarchist. Once a gap in the conversation let in a phrase of Hanna's from the other side of the room, 'I didn't really approve of what he was doing – but he was breaking the law, which I always take to be a good thing.' The tone and the voice suggested a polite comment on a game of croquet.[44]

Her unconventionality extended beyond politics. Once, at a family gathering at Eugene's, Ronan had announced innocently, to a deathly hush, that his cousin Conor had a homosexual friend in Trinity. It was left to Hanna to break the silence with the interested query: 'do you know what a homosexual is, Ronan?' His awkward reply: 'yes, Mum used to keep one in the attic' (a reference to a homosexual lodger in Montreal), led to Hanna bursting out laughing and, ever afterwards, repeating this as her favourite 'Ronan story'.[45]

She was in Paris in August 1939, reporting home that everyone there was hoping negotiations for peace would continue. Paris was 'full of soldiers and uniforms' and Parisians and foreigners alike were being advised to leave but she was defiant: 'I take it the big lines will always be open, even with delay ... *Au fond* I don't see any reason to quit just yet.' If she had to leave, she would stay a few days in London before coming home.[46] When Britain and France declared war on Germany on 3 September 1939, de Valera's success in regaining the 'Treaty ports' meant that Ireland was no longer tied to following British foreign policy. De Valera announced his intention of ensuring that 'Éire' remained neutral in the war. Hanna was sceptical, believing that he would be more than willing to trade neutrality for the Six Counties, if the British could persuade the unionist government to agree to such a deal. Only the intransigence of the unionists, particularly Craigavon, their Prime Minister, prevented a deal being struck – at least, this was how she read the situation. To the astonishment of many of her republican friends she took to raising her cup of tea for a toast, murmuring: 'Thank God for Craigavon.'[47]

Feminist activities had not been abandoned, despite the war. The Women's Social and Progressive League remained in existence, chaired by Hanna, with Mary Kettle, Mary Hayden and Mary Macken of the old generation amongst the committee members. There were new faces, mainly unmarried, younger women, but such recruits to the cause were few in an age when marriage meant hearth and home and where the workplace was proving hostile to women's presence. Only those who remembered their youthful dreams of woman as citizen, and the fight that had been necessary for that to become reality, retained the confidence to give voice to women's claims. Those who volunteered to give talks in the League's rooms at their Thursday evening meetings were the same old names: Hanna Sheehy Skeffington, Rose Jacob, Maud Gonne MacBride, Roisin Walsh (Dublin City Librarian, long-standing republican and organiser of many of Hanna's lectures within Dublin libraries) and former suffragist Lucy Kingston. One younger woman was Andrée, cajoled into speaking on 'Frenchwomen of Today', but her presence was largely a tribute to her friendship with her mother-in-law.[48] While Hanna was in America Meg Connery had given a talk to the group on the history of women's fight since 1918. It was not a happy experience as she clashed with Mary Kettle, old wounds re-opening:

> began by 1918 and women defeating Irish Party in favour of republicanism, whose policy was equal citizenship for women thanks to the 1916 Leader's Proclamation. I went on then to the Treaty Party attitude to women and the F. Fáil party policy towards women – and the need for women to organise politically to use the vote

to protect our interests now. Apparently the audience agreed with me, but judge my surprise when in the discussion Mrs Kettle got up and accused me of 'attacking the Irish Party' – though I only devoted my opening remarks to them – and went on to say she actively endorsed the Irish Party policy towards the women's claim ... I decided for the sake of a 'United Front' to hold my peace – Mrs K. has not grown politically one inch since 1912 ... I'll stick it till you return anyway, but I'm not enjoying myself at these meetings.[49]

Leeann Lane, referring to Rose Jacob, believed 'such female-centred organisations as the WSPL were much more than vehicles to secure political change. These organisations fulfilled a strong social need for Jacob, her social interaction and an outlet in a public space that was very limited for single women.'[50] However Rose did not appear particularly enthusiastic about the group, as one cryptic note to Hanna indicated: 'can't go to the WSPL tonight anyway, even if there wasn't another place I ought to go to:[51] She missed the meeting addressed by Meg as she had a bad cold.[52] If long-standing activists of their calibre were less than keen, and new members were hard to attract, it is not surprising that it failed to make much inroad into the political landscape.

The 1938 general election had not been particularly successful for the League, despite their circulation of 'An Open Letter to Women Voters' detailing the numerous ways by which women were being discriminated against. Women were urged 'DO NOT VOTE for any candidate, however plausible pre-election promises may be, unless you are satisfied that he or she will defend your interests and guarantee your equal right of citizenship.'[53] Only three women were returned to the Dáil, widows of former members and destined to be known collectively as 'the Silent Sisters' because of their failure to contribute to debates. On the other hand, there was cheering news in the election, in June 1939, of Kathleen Clarke as first woman Mayor of Dublin. Nobody was more surprised than the mayor herself but, typically, she felt it appropriate that the widow of the first signatory to the Proclamation should be so honoured. Her time in office coincided with a revival of IRA militarism, in the form of a bombing campaign in England. The military men had taken over from the left-wingers within the organisation. Kathleen's response to the repressive legislation introduced by Fianna Fáil to combat the republicans was one shared by Hanna: 'while thoroughly out of patience with it (the bombing campaign), but knowing the purity of their motives, my sympathy went out in full measure for those involved and their dependents'.[54] Hundreds were interned, including a few members of Cumann na mBan, but meetings in support of the prisoners were banned. Maud Gonne MacBride, now bed-ridden, could do no more than write furious letters to the papers, but the papers too were subject to heavy censorship. It was the lowest point republicanism had reached since the defeat of the Civil War. It had no political presence at all.

Propaganda about the rape of nuns in Catholic Belgium at the start of the First World War paled into insignificance beside the monstrosities perpetrated by the Nazis. The full horrors of the gas chambers had not yet been revealed, but the persecution of Jews, communists and socialists in Germany was known about. Hanna's wide range of contacts had been writing for several years of scenes of anti-semitism they had witnessed while on holiday or travelling around Europe. Owen too had experienced the ugliness of fascism. The fate of the Denis family, isolated in German-occupied Amiens, was a source of enormous anxiety during those dreadful years. The country Hanna was so fond of, whose language she spoke almost as fluently as her own, was an international pariah once again, while her own country maintained a neutrality that implicitly favoured the British and used the opportunity of war-time censorship and repression to hound the IRA out of existence. De Valera did not flinch from using the death penalty when necessary, hiring the English hangman for the job, the ultimate obscenity.

Ireland was not at war but struggling to survive the period known to the Irish as 'The Emergency'. Its population suffered many of the consequences of war, particularly shortages of food and fuel, while lacking the benefits of being on a war footing in terms of government rationing to ensure some equality of access to resources. In Ireland, those with money bought and hoarded, those without suffered. Malnutrition and disease caused by dirty food were real issues that affected many and some young women decided that, although the world of work was barred to them, the role of consumer could be turned into one of actively campaigning for government intervention to ensure that the production and distribution of food benefited all members of society. At Andrée Sheehy Skeffington's suggestion a petition to the government was drawn up, calling for fair prices, a system of rationing and measures to encourage farmers to produce more food. After a great deal of effort Andrée, her friend Hilda Tweedy (whose husband Robert was a good friend of Owen's) and three other young women managed to persuade a total of 640 women to sign. They succeeded in attracting favourable publicity and Louie Bennett, who had been asked to sign the petition, suggested that they try to form an organisation to continue the work. She lent them the Irish Women Workers' Union hall, her sister Susan Manning lent her support and 40 curious women turned up to the advertised meeting. On 12 May 1942, with a total membership of twelve, the Irish Housewives Association was formed. A new generation of activists began their public careers.[55]

Before the launch of the organisation, Andrée and Hilda had told Hanna of their plans. As Andrée recalled, the older woman was very pleased and asked them what they were calling the group. When she heard the name, she remained silent for a moment, her fingers drumming a rhythm on the table as she struggled to find words which were not too harsh. Finally came the famous comment: 'You are not married to the house you know.'[56] Andrée rightly took this as a reproach. Hanna did not approve of women reinforcing public perception of their role in the home but, wanting to support any new venture, she tried hard to suppress her objections. She could not bear the name 'housewife', and, in fact, the name gave a misleading impression of the kind of woman who joined. The committee members were mostly Labour Party supporters, anxious to make links with working-class women in an effort to improve the quality of their lives.

Given the dismal atmosphere, the decision by the Women's Social and Progressive League to field candidates in the 1943 elections was a courageous attempt to reaffirm the feminist belief that political activity had to continue if there was ever to be a civilised society in the future. There were plenty who thought they were crazy to make the attempt. Young David Sheehy remembered his father arguing fiercely with Hanna. In Eugene's view it was a senseless gesture and they would achieve nothing but the loss of their deposits. David also remembered Hanna arguing back at her brother, more than capable of holding her corner.[57] In the end, four women stood as independents: two in Tipperary, one in Galway and one in South Dublin. Hanna was the candidate for Dublin, back in the constituency she had represented as a councillor almost 20 years previously. Women were standing in both city and country, a good enough spread, they felt, to form the nucleus of a Women's Party. Their programme stressed the need for greater representation of women, their slogans called for 'Equal Pay for Equal Work' and 'Equal Opportunities for Women' and they argued with eloquence that 'there can be no true democracy when the voice of half the community is silent in parliament.'[58]

Hanna hoped that South Dublin, a seven-seat constituency with a large working-class population, would favour her. There were 19 candidates chasing those seats. Owen had been voted out of the Labour Party, a victim of internal intrigue, so had no conflict of loyalties to prevent him from throwing his energies into the task of organising the printing of leaflets and the chore of canvassing. There was not enough money to match the efforts of their rivals, and they found themselves appalled by the cost of electioneering, reckoning that £1,000 (which they did not possess) was now required when £300 had been ample in the past. Times were changing. The *Irish Times* applauded Hanna as 'transparently honest in all her views and actions', an 'uncompromising politician', who was 'one of the most colourful candidates' in the election. Her election platform differed to some extent from the other women as she insisted upon stressing the fact that she was a republican as well as a feminist. Her ideal was still the republic for which James Connolly had given his life and she included his slogan, 'The woman worker is the slave of a slave' in her manifesto. All the best impulses in Irish political life were hers; her programme was inclusive, not exclusive, deserving of greater support than it received:

> There can be no true democracy where there is not complete economic and political freedom for the entire nation, both men and women. How can there be effective administration where the political machine is entirely controlled by one sex only … Nationally I stand for the complete independence of Ireland and for the abolition of partition which has dismembered our country. My attitude towards Ireland's right to unfettered nationhood is unchanged and unchangeable … Under the 1916 Proclamation Irish women were given equal citizenship, equal rights and equal opportunities, and subsequent constitutions have filched these, or smothered them in mere 'empty formula'.[59]

The obstacles confronting those independent women were too great. They lacked the resources of the other political organisations; they suffered a press boycott and the preoccupations of the times were not conducive to promotion of the feminist cause. Hanna's teaching responsibilities, with classes continuing until 5pm in some cases, meant that her time for personal canvassing was limited, as she apologised in a letter to the press.[60] One young volunteer in the campaign, Rosaleen Mills, remembered that they held a bicycle parade in the city centre, displaying placards declaring the demands of Hanna's campaign as they had no money to hire a hall. She also recalled, late in the campaign, word was spread that Hanna was a lapsed Catholic, 'so that put paid to her chances'.[61] As Hanna put it, 'Our experiment, a bold enough challenge to masculine monopoly, failed. We were all beaten.'[62] Out of a quota of 6,641, she received only 917 first-preference votes. James Larkin junior got in for the Labour Party. Dublin South had not rejected all radical candidates; that knowledge must have been hurtful. She was unable to conceal her anger at those 'smug' women who declared that they had no interest in politics. Such comments infuriated the doorstep canvassers. However, despite her disappointment, she managed to sound a philosophical note when writing of her experiences for *The Bell*, a radical journal edited by Peadar O'Donnell. Starting with the rhetorical question and answer 'Is the Dáil a fit place for Women? The answer of the electorate would appear to be No', she concluded by refusing to give up hope. There had been a point to it all – at least women's demands had, for a short time, been visible in the streets of the capital:

> It took a while before the slogans 'Equal Pay' and 'A Square Deal for Women' on Dublin's hoardings were superseded by the device of 'Bisurated magnesia.' When next an election comes the seed sown should be ready to germinate – the seed beneath the snow as Silone calls it, speaking of those seeds of new growths that lie for a while submerged, but living.[63]

She was exhausted by the effort. It was June, summertime, and she went off to recuperate in the Wicklow hills. It was her last big campaign, fitting that it should be one in which her unique combination of political allegiances could be articulated with so much conviction. Fitting too that her son should have been so involved in fighting for the same cause. The following year, her zest for life undiminished, she worried about Andrée, just out of hospital, urging her to 'rest and just <u>look</u> at the countryside', adding, 'isn't it grand that none of us have any responsibilities for election work – though I have promised to speak for Miss Bennett!' Irrepressibly, she ended her letter 'I'm getting a great thrill out of my electric light and hope later to give you an electric pie.'[64]

She had been shocked to learn, in August 1944, of the death of Dorothy Evans, former organiser of the WSPU in Belfast. She was only 55, a woman with whom Hanna had retained a friendship since those turbulent years before the First World War. As secretary of the British feminist 'Six Point Group', Dorothy Evan's life had been devoted to furthering women's interests and she continued to be a frequent visitor to Ireland. On behalf of the Women's Social and Progressive League Hanna wrote a warm eulogy, the final words of which could soon be written of herself: 'What a gap she leaves, cut off in her prime; a victim to her abounding energy which overtaxed a frame weakened by earlier prison hardships. May her great work survive and thrive – that would be her best monument.'[65] Hanna was still a familiar figure on the Rathmines Road, heading off to her classes, her papers bundled into one of her numerous bags, doing duty as briefcase. Despite the cancellation of German lessons, she still taught in two technical schools, journeying across the city to Marino on the north side. Her family tried to persuade her to give up some of her commitments but, with no pension to fall back upon, she had no option but to continue doing what she could, for as long as she could, arguing 'I have to earn enough to live on.'[66] She found it difficult to admit to weakness, dreading the prospect of ever becoming dependent, but her health was beginning to deteriorate. She fretted about the things she still hoped to do. Friends urged her to complete her memoirs. She had contacted the Talbot Press in 1933, sounding them out as a possible publisher, but there was nothing they could do until they saw a manuscript, promising 'we shall give your Memoirs our very careful consideration, if you care to submit them to us.'[67] Desmond Ryan, a chronicler of the Irish revolution himself, hoped that she would be able to complete her memoirs. She told him that she had finished a third, yet she had not gone beyond the suffrage years and there was so much that remained to be told.[68] She intended to write 14 chapters, but only managed to reach the establishment of Dáil Éireann and the start of her work for Sinn Féin. Her last two chapters, written in a huge scrawl while she was bed-ridden, were in note form only and not given to Nora, the woman who had typed up her early chapters. She also planned to reprint her account of Frank's murder as well as write his biography and republish his *Life of Davitt*, which she considered his 'chief work'.

Desmond Greaves, national secretary of the Connolly Association in London, wrote to her in February 1945 with a warm invitation to speak at their annual Wolfe Tone commemoration in June: 'We make a point at all our big meetings of permitting different shades of opinion to have their say and you would be entirely at liberty to say whatever you thought fit.' Dorothy Macardle had been the speaker the previous year. Hanna scrawled a note at the bottom of the letter: 'couldn't poss. acc. out of pl. in pres. conds.' She felt that any discussion of Tone, that greatest of republican revolutionaries, whose creed was to break the connection with the source of all our ills, could only be an 'abridged' version at such an event. With a world war being fought it was too difficult a time to enter into a meaningful discussion of the political views of Tone and Connolly.[69]

Alice Park was selling her papers to the Hoover Institution on War, Revolution and Peace, urging Hanna to do the same. The librarian of the Hoover Library wrote to her, hoping 'you will have the library in mind in disposing of material on the history of Ireland since 1914.'[70] She did, eventually, begin to sort out copies of the *Citizen* and other literature to send to the Hoover, but gave no indication that she intended to send her personal papers there.[71] Florence Murphy Baker had written to urge her to contact the historian Mary Beard, who was organising a Women's Archives Centre in America, 'you must have a great deal of interesting material',[72] but Hanna was still intent on using it for her own writings and she had her eye on the future, hoping that one day a feminist historian would do justice to the struggle of Irish women. She was sure only a woman would acknowledge how important that struggle had been. One of the reasons for her difficulty in completing substantial pieces of writing was the fact that she was constantly churning out small pieces of journalism. The *Irish Digest* was waiting for her article on 'unusual occupations' and wanted her to submit ideas for another series of six articles.[73] The *Irish Workers' Weekly* said they could offer her one guinea for an article on the need for more social workers,[74] but as she could not resist opportunities to comment on current affairs she also wrote articles like one for the October 1945 *Workers' Review* (produced by a far left group in Glasgow which must have had a tiny circulation), discussing British women MPs, the numbers of which had increased from 14 to 24 as a result of the recent election that had put a post-war Labour government into office. She had praise for the achievements of a number of the Labour women and urged the party to extend the principles of democracy to women by implementing the woman's programme. Her comments on the failure of suffragists to win election provide some clues to her own past relationships with various political organisations:

> it is curious though quite comprehensible and regrettable that no 'votes for women' stalwarts got into the House of Commons. Partly, of course, because they did not make good Party members, parties being scared of them, partly because (see our own history) rebels do not make parliamentarians.[75]

By the time Ethel Mannin came to visit her in January 1946 she had lost her brief optimism that the Labour Party would be capable of fulfilling any radical programme. Both women agreed the party had lost its socialist inspiration, Hanna adding, 'It's the old story of power corrupting.' She believed de Valera to be utterly corrupted by power and confided she was 'more and more' inclined towards Ethel's anarchist point of view.[76]

The popular novelist and former Cumann na mBan member Annie M. P. Smithson paid a visit to her and Rose Jacob at Hanna's home in April, before what would be one of Hanna's last outings, to the fourth 1916-1921 Annual Commemoration Dinner on 26 April, held in Clery's new restaurant. Hundreds were there, many of whom were close friends: Kathleen Clarke, Kathleen Lynn, Eithne Coyle, Nora Connolly O'Brien, Brigid O'Mullane. It was a big event, a gathering of republicans who came from many different organisations. Some had been part of the old 'Mothers' organisation, although their inspiration, Maud Gonne MacBride, was too frail to attend. In the following month Hanna's health deteriorated. Andrée said that the signs of her extreme fatigue were 'only too obvious' but she refused to leave her home and move in with them. She valued her independence too much to curb either her own or theirs. Besides, they now had a child and she felt sure that the new parents had enough to do without her presence. Her grandson, born on 17 May, was named Francis Eugène, after his Irish grandfather and, also, his French grandfather, although the name was also a tribute to Uncle

Eugene. She wrote proudly to Alice Park, 'the babe is bonny, more French, I think, than Irish, as sons favour mothers. Interesting to watch, just four months old today!'[77] With a sense of shock at how time had passed she realised that her youthful Frank would have aged also, 'Strange to think of F. S. S. as a grandfather, if he lived now.'[78] Her heart, she explained, 'went on strike ... not weak, but jerky and overstrained, then liver out of order'. Her blood pressure rose, and she was put on dosages of calomel, digitalis and coramtine. She also had to follow a rigid diet. Dr Lynn ordered bed rest and no work, not even typing. Thankfully she was permitted to read and write in bed, otherwise she would never have consented to the regime. The Department of Education wrote of their regret at being deprived 'of your valued and valuable assistance in the correction of the papers this year', hoping this would be a temporary affair and sending wishes for her 'speedy and complete recovery'.[79] After four months she felt she was 'past the worst' and was able to bring out the typewriter again. She promptly began to catch up on her correspondence. It was easier to confide her fears in old friends who were far away. To Alice Park she admitted that she would hate to be an invalid or dependent. Death would be preferable. On the other hand, striking a more positive note, she reflected that George Bernard Shaw was in his ninetieth year and 'still going strong'. She scrawled a heartfelt postscript at the bottom of a letter to Alice, 'I hope you keep well and fit – you are a beacon to me!'[80] Her American friends were in constant touch, anxious to help despite the distance. Kate Crane Gartz sent 'pounds of precious tea' a most welcome gift at that time of scarcity. She also sent her newspapers from America, discussing current affairs, hoping 'total disarmament and stopping war will be on the international agenda now.'[81] Elizabeth Gurley Flynn, not realising how ill she was, wrote from Paris where she was attending a meeting of women from left-wing organisations. She wanted Hanna to join them, as Irish representative. Apparently, the original invitation failed to reach Hanna, who was not unduly surprised, 'We live in censored times.'[82] Her old friend from the turbulent years of suffrage and Cumann na mBan controversies, Elizabeth Bloxham, in hospital in Gorey, wrote a lively letter of support. She had been in hospital for almost a year, 'I find we have had wonderfully similar experiences.' She was glad her niece and nephew didn't treat her as an 'elderly aunt' ... which is one of the things which women like you and me do not desire even if our bodies fail to keep as young and spritely as our minds.'[83]

The war had finally come to an end while Hanna was ill. A new era was on the threshold but the signs for the future were anything but optimistic. While it was 'great to have an end to the carnage, the censor and all that', the 'common people' were still suffering and the potential for more destruction negated hopes of a permanent peace. She felt apprehensive for the future, 'The horror of the Atomic bomb is just ghastly and there is a scramble for it for the next War.' Babies were being born in great numbers, but it was difficult to rejoice when the kind of world they would inherit remained unknown, 'I guess Nature's filling up gaps, but one wonders for what?' she asked.[84] With little hope of the 'very tame' Labour government in Britain she remained what she had always been, a convinced revolutionary, but one who had lost her confidence in the future.

The articles continued to flow. In one of her last pieces she joked about the excessively musical character so often given to Heaven. She much preferred books to music and hoped that in the other world there would be libraries as well as orchestras. With 'that flash of wit she could bring into the most serious discussion', said Desmond Ryan, enjoying her flight of fancy, she added, 'after all, we are told that there are many mansions'.[85] In November she was pleased to be interviewed about her life for an RTE radio series (it paid £4) but news of her ill-health must have been widespread. Dr Dixon, the interviewer, began by asking her about her health. Her answer acknowledged that she was unwell, but she was still able to joke, 'on ticket-of-leave in my doctor's friendly if firm hand. She calls me her "impatient".'[86] It was a notable interview and she received letters of congratulations on her performance from many friends. Budge Mulcahy Clissmann, who had met her husband Helmut Clissmann when he came to Ireland to organise an exchange programme for students (Hanna had been translator for his meeting at Roebuck House) was in Europe during the war. She had been a pivotal figure in helping the imprisoned Frank Ryan and one of the few to attend his lonely funeral. She had managed to hear and enjoy Hanna's broadcast while in Copenhagen.[87] A McCoy cousin wrote to say her clear voice had a 'marked resemblance to Mary's ... you carved a life and a world which was so interesting';[88] while old friend Mary Macken was 'thrilled to hear your voice - I was moved to tears.'[89]

She had lost 35 pounds in weight but felt she could afford to do so. What troubled her was that she found walking a difficulty and climbing stairs impossible. She was going deaf in her left ear, which was 'a bother' in teaching. It was unbelievable that she could attend to her classes but, stubbornly, she kept on a limited number, still insisting that she had to earn her livelihood. It was a worry to her friends, who wondered what they could do to help without making her feel that she was the object of charity. Louie Bennett, so often the person who had helped in a crisis, wrote a sensitive letter to Hanna in March 1946, thanking her for comments on an article she was submitting to the

Irish Press, and inquiring if she was 'really better again now.' She wondered: 'Can you face up to the position of surrendering your teaching and devoting yourself to writing – an occupation which would release you from physical fatigue and leave you free to rest when you felt like it.'[90] Tactfully, a testimonial was organised, Bennett doing much of the soliciting. A first instalment of £100 was presented to her at Christmas, with another to follow at Easter. It was, they declared, 'a small token of our respect and admiration for your long, brave, and self-sacrificing service to the cause of justice and freedom.'[91]

The Irish Housewives were planning to bring out a journal. Generously, Hanna agreed to write an article for the first issue. In characteristic style she made it quite plain that she had never considered herself as a 'housewife'. Her words were pithy, robust, radical. No one reading them could possibly imagine that they came from the pen of a 68-year-old woman who would be dead by the time they were published:

> I dislike the word described in dictionaries as 'female domestic manager' or, alternatively, 'a small case for articles for female work.' The Irish *Bean a Tighe* (woman of the house, or Herself) and the French ménagère are better, they at least fit the idea. I believe wife is still described in legal documents as of 'no occupation' just as an unmarried woman has to be called a spinster even if she's an architect or Chief Executive and never saw a spinning wheel unless in a museum. These clumsy man-made words remind us how little free we really are, so 'housewife' is accepted more or less meekly by most women as we accept men's names in marriage and live in their inconveniently constructed houses. There is no masculine form of the word – houseman, the nearest, being a superior servant. Well, let it pass.

She admitted that it had been those kinds of thoughts which had 'overwhelmed' her when 'a band of energetic and determined women' had first started the Housewives Association. Now, having seen what their campaigning had achieved in ending the black market, in obtaining price controls and other measures that improved the lives of so many, she gave her thanks 'to the valiant band … shamelessly benefiting by their labours'. It was a public and wholehearted apology for her previous hostility, but she still made sure that the feminist message came through:

> The example of the Housewives has shown that women too must organise, must educate themselves in citizenship, must become vocal, if need be, clamorous. The Association needs more members, additional subscribers, investigators, workers, politically-minded women – much work remains to be done in '46. Go to it, housewives![92]

By March even Hanna knew she could no longer pretend that she was capable of earning a living. Her diary for 1946 reveals how often she had to stay in bed: Sunday 20 January - 'bitter black cold, stayed in bed all day'; 10 February - 'chez moi tea. Bed. Fall'; Friday 1 March – 'Classes large again & rowdy – flu absence over!'; Wednesday 6 March - 'bed'. She was unable to attend WSPL meetings, crossing out all those dates. The last entries of all consisted of a crossed-out League meeting for 2 May and a reminder that it was baby Francis' first birthday on 17 May.[93] In April Käthe Oldham, having just learned 'with deepest regret' that she was not well, sent a 'little nosegay … hoping it will gladden your heart to see these pretty messengers of spring.'[94] She had only three weeks left.

As her health grew worse Owen went to stay with his mother; their last days of a close and loving relationship. Her movements were limited, but she could still write. She wrote a letter to the *Irish Press*, published on 4 March, commenting on an interview given by William O'Brien regarding the murders of Frank and Councillor Richard O'Carroll, making the point that both had been victims of Bowen-Colthurst.[95] A national school teachers' strike had begun in Dublin, a protest against appalling rates of pay. Her last letter to the *Irish Press* expressed her strong support for the teachers, 65 percent of the INTO membership was female, and women were hardest hit by the proposed changes. She reminded readers: 'The teachers have always played a brave part in every national struggle – Pearse, McDonough, Thomas Ash and how many others…'[96] Owen tried to comfort his mother, upset at not having completed her memoirs or written her life of Frank, by arranging to have the pamphlet on his father's death reprinted. This was done, but she did not survive to see it. It was left to Owen to attend to the pamphlet's distribution. He made sure, as his mother would have wished, that her friends received copies. The Alice Park Collection contains one, with the inscription: 'May '46, To Mrs Gartz, a good friend to my mother. Owen Sheehy Skeffington.'

Although in considerable pain and beginning to long for the release of death, Hanna remained her indomitable self. She had once said to her son: 'I want you to remember, Owen, that I am an unrepentant pagan. If I die, as I must someday, it is you who will have all the trouble from the Christians: not only the Catholics but the Prods, when you carry out my instructions.'[97] When her sisters Mary and Margaret tried to persuade Owen to let a priest call to the house he refused. As far as he was concerned it would be a betrayal of his mother's life. Margaret's son Frank Culhane, a priest, wrote from Switzerland to tell his aunt that 'All were praying for her. As she is so ill.'[98] A priest did come to the door, some suspected sent by Eugene's highly Catholic wife, but Owen stood his ground. Hanna was adamant on the issue, urgently telling her son that he was to ignore her if she suddenly started asking for a priest. It would only be, she assured him, because her mind was 'weakened'. It would not be what she really wanted. She need not have worried. She remained lucid to the end, her great strength of mind undiminished by pain.[99] At her death, with Owen standing by her side, she suddenly looked up and murmured, 'Frank'. He was, said Andrée, 'glad to have given her this ultimate happy illusion'.[100]

She died at 7 a.m. on Easter Saturday, 20 April 1946. It was almost exactly 30 years to the day since the great adventure of the Easter Rising, an event of fundamental importance to the formation of the Irish state, the consequences of which had left Hanna to carry the burden of an inexpressible and unassuageable sorrow throughout those 30 years.

Maud Gonne MacBride, bedridden and dependent on friends for visits, was devastated by grief on hearing of the death. Isolated from the company she had enjoyed for so long, she had only the solace of letter-writing to ease her pain. She broke the news to Ethel Mannin:

> Our dear, dear friend Hanna is gone – she was almost the dearest friend I had and the woman I admired most on earth. Her loss to Ireland is terrible and Dublin won't be the same place without her ... can't think of anything else since heard last night of her death.[101]

Her subsequent letters to Ethel nearly always contained a comment on how much she still missed Hanna. To Brigid O'Mullane, who had worked with both women in the Women's Prisoners' Defence League, Maud was honest enough to admit that she and Hanna had had different views at times, although nothing ever affected their friendship:

> Hanna's death is a great blow to me, I loved her very much and for half a century she was perhaps the one with whom I was most closely associated in work and though we sometimes thought differently it never made the slightest difference in our friendship. I think she was the ablest of all the fearless women who worked for Ireland's freedom and she is a great loss to Ireland.[102]

Hanna was buried in Glasnevin cemetery, in the same grave where Frank's body had been reinterred beside his mother. It was not a religious service. She could, if she had wished, been given the public tribute of a final resting place in the Republican Plot, where so many of her friends lay, and where so many more would eventually end. Her contribution to Irish life puts her in the ranks of the patriots, but Frank had the final claim to her. It was a small funeral, attended by no more than 30 old friends, suffragists, republicans, assorted radicals.[103]

Obituaries about Hanna appeared in all the Irish papers and in many feminist and socialist journals. Most were written by friends who went to some lengths to capture her warm-hearted nature as well as to pay tribute to her many talents. Desmond Ryan recalled her as a 'gracious, unbending, humorous personality who loved a garden and a book as much as she loved a battle in any good cause at all'.[104] For the *Irish Press*, M. J. MacManus contrasted the private woman with the public figure: 'In private she was gentle and unassuming, but a brilliant conversationalist, with a wide variety of interests. She seemed to have met everybody who had taken part in progressive and democratic movements during the past 40 years and she was on terms of close friendship with men like Henry Nevinson and Bernard Shaw.'[105] The *Evening Herald*, also agreeing on her 'attractive personality' mentioned her 'full life' and interest in the arts, theatre, politics, social welfare, feminism ('above all') and her career as a teacher. In public she was: 'An able, and indeed a brilliant speaker … distinguished for her grasp of public affairs and her outspoken style of expressing her views. Many did not agree with Mrs Sheehy Skeffington, but none denied her capabilities or her sincerity.'[106] In the *Irish Times* Cathal O'Shannon considered her to be 'the ablest of the women' in Irish public life over the past 40 years: 'and in some respects she had a place of her own even among those of her political class and calibre in America and Great Britain. That distinction impressed many who observed her at gatherings of leading women from different countries.' In trying to describe her politics, he confessed that he could not give a satisfactory answer, although he had worked with her since 1912. What he could say was that she was a feminist: 'First and foremost, and above all, and maybe last as well as first'.[107]

The *Workers' Review* concentrated upon her support for the struggle of the working class and her defiance of the Blueshirts. She was 'a truly great woman' and in her 'the cause of Irish freedom had no better champion … With her passing Ireland has lost a really outstanding woman, and the working class a genuine friend.'[108] From Britain, Ethel Mannin wrote an obituary for the anarchist journal *Freedom*, claiming Hanna as a 'revolutionary libertarian'.[109] Marion Reeves, stalwart of the Minerva Club, wrote a short but warm note for the *Women's Bulletin*, recalling Hanna's 'ready wit, her great ability as a speaker, and her warm personal affection for her English friends – however divergent their political outlook – (which) made her popular and welcome in any gathering.' The women's movement everywhere 'is the poorer for her passing'.[110] So many different organisations felt justified in claiming Hanna Sheehy Skeffington as one of their own. They were right to do so, because her causes were many and she continued to fight for them all, often at the same time, because she saw no separation between them. While all stressed the warmth of her personality and her love of life, the most heartfelt of all appreciations came from Anna Kelly, who took the opportunity to devote an entire page of the *Irish Press* to her memories of Hanna, complete with photo of her beloved 'Skeffy' that showed her with a twinkle in her eye, displaying her sense of humour in a manner rare in photographs. She paid full tribute to Hanna's intellect: 'sharp as a sword, and it was the only sword she believed in', but it was the everyday woman she concentrated upon, describing her love of clothes and hats, her delight in gardens and flowers, how she would: 'go off by herself with her modest shilling and sit in the back seats of the theatre. She would meet her sisters … to go to the pictures as happy as larks. She was no high-boiled highbrow.' Anna remembered too how Frank, dead for 30 years, had never died in her mind: 'She would bring his name into conversation as if they had been together but a moment before.' As a republican, she acknowledged the importance of the Sheehy Skeffingtons in influencing the organisers of the Rising to include women's suffrage within the Proclamation of the Irish Republic. It was their enduring contribution to Irish life and she urged Irish women to crown that monument 'by carrying on the work she began, but did not live to finish'.[111] It was recognition that, had she lived, Hanna Sheehy Skeffington would have gone on organising, speaking, writing and fighting for the principles she had always upheld.

Owen guarded his mother's integrity jealously. In that he was as uncompromising as she had been. The Rory O'Connor branch of Fianna Fáil sent a letter of condolence. He received it on the morning that news came of the inquest on Seán McCaughey, who had died on hunger and thirst strike while protesting the deplorable conditions in which republican prisoners were being held. At the inquest Seán MacBride, through merciless cross-examination, had been able to bring out into the open the reality of those dreadful conditions, forcing the prison doctor to admit he would not treat a dog in the way those men were being treated. In those circumstances, Hanna Sheehy Skeffington, a life-long campaigner for prisoners' rights, would not have appreciated any message from Fianna Fáil and her son was scrupulous in carrying out what he believed would have been her wish:

> I can accept no official sympathy from Fianna Fáil, nor would my mother have wanted me to she had nothing but contempt for the party which so assiduously carried on the British tradition in its treatment of soldiers and so consistently betrayed the ideals for which it was founded … As for Rory O'Connor, I can imagine what he would have thought of this latest murder by the pitiless official machine … I cannot accept the condolence of any official branch of Fianna Fáil and I am returning your letter.

Just to make sure his objections were seen by the man who mattered the most, he sent a copy of the letter to Éamon de Valera, with a note saying: 'for information.'[112]

Owen wrote a lengthy letter to the *New Leader*, paper of the Independent Labour Party in Britain, correcting some inaccuracies in Ethel Mannin's obituary of his mother. While it was a 'sensitive' article, and he accepted Mannin knew his mother well, he felt there was a 'faulty emphasis' on occasion. Referring to Asquith's attempt to persuade her to accept compensation for Frank's murder and her subsequent *Catholic Herald* libel case, he informed readers she had been £100 out of pocket as a result and had 'no pension whatsoever'. It was a loving portrait, as well as a corrective of various details:

> Hanna S.S. did think of herself as a pacifist, though she 'knew she was not a hundred-per-center. She used to say: 'There is nothing to be said for war, though there is a lot to be said for well-directed assassination!' In actual fact she would struggle to save a fly from a spider's web, or a mouse from a cat…
>
> The 'Irish Times' obituary was in fact quite correct in saying that after her trip to Russia in 1929 she 'pronounced the Soviet experiment an exciting and exhilarating one'. It was not until the Moscow trials that she became suspicious and critical of Stalin's policy.
>
> There must be some mistake about this 'public memorial service' for her. She died, as she said to me shortly before her death, 'an unrepentant pagan'. There could be no question of such a service. I suspect a misprint!
>
> The British papers which to the end she read with pleasure were: 'The New Leader', 'War Commentary' (now 'Freedom'), 'Forward', and the 'Women's Bulletin'. With none was she in full agreement, but they offer a good synthesis of what she thought good and hopeful in Britain today.[113]

Despite Owen's dismissal of the prospect of a memorial service, Hanna's friends did want some memorial to her. Louie Bennett wrote to Owen, to say how much she liked his proposal for a memorial, noting that such a suggestion was coming also 'from other quarters'. As she added, 'it should surely be possible to get the *Life of Davitt* published this year in the ordinary way', some scheme must have been proposed.[114] Sally Ryan, who had been a contributor to the fund for Hanna the year previously, wrote to say she hoped the funds Owen had in hand could form the start of a bigger scheme, suggesting there could be a prize or scholarship for girls, as well as the re-publication of Frank's book on Davitt, which could be accompanied by a memoir from Owen.[115] From London, Emmeline Pethick-Lawrence, remembering how 'very young' Owen was when she met him, wrote of the 'measureless admiration' she and her husband had 'for our dear friend - your mother – and also for your father. It was impossible to separate them in thought or to forget the great tragedy which your father met with such a grand spirit.'

They wished him to spend their 'little gift that expressed in some small way the love and admiration which we all felt for your mother in any way that you deem appropriate to her wishes.'[116] Perhaps the scholarship was initiated? A more public memorial does not exist.

How can we assess the achievements and the legacy left by Hanna Sheehy Skeffington? She was undoubtedly one of the leading intellectuals within the Irish nationalist movement of the time. The failure of the male leadership in 1918 to ensure her inclusion as a member of the First Dáil deprived the emerging nation of a voice guaranteed to make a radical and vital contribution. As an Irish feminist, she regarded the vested interests of religion, capitalism, male power and British influence a pernicious alliance holding back the creation of an egalitarian society based upon principles of respect for all individuals. Feminist demands for equality of status and the right to determine one's choices in life were demands she supported. As a woman who lived in a society divided by sectarian tensions, with governments on both sides of the border hostile to radical ideas and with the combined power of church and state stifling the potential of the female half of the population, her ability to retain the conviction that the revolutionary path was the only road to take is noteworthy.

When Hanna Sheehy Skeffington lay dying there was much she had no sympathy for in the world she was about to leave. But what she disagreed with were those aspects of life that everyone should want to see abolished: weapons of war, injustice, inequality, poverty. The loss of her husband almost destroyed her, but her determination to confront evil and to expose the horrors of militarism gave her a reason to carry on. She became an important part of the nationalist movement, not juxtaposing the women's cause to the nationalist as though they were rivals, instead seeking ways of ensuring that women's right to freedom was embedded within the fight for national freedom. She became a figure of global status, finding herself in sympathy with feminists around the world, united in their determination to challenge the imperial power of Britain, while counting British feminists amongst her closest friends. If she had been willing to compromise, she would have had a much easier life: a highly paid teaching post or a place in government. If she had done so, however, her distinctive voice, the feminist conscience of so many causes, could have been stifled. She campaigned until the end for a society based upon feminist and egalitarian principles, believing she had helped to sow 'the seed beneath the snow', which was waiting for the right conditions to germinate and flourish. Nearly 80 years have passed since she wrote those words. Eventually, the harvest that Hanna Sheehy Skeffington worked for will bear fruit.

NOTES

1 Owen Sheehy Skeffington to Hanna Sheehy Skeffington (hereafter Owen to Hanna), 25 June 1937, 2 p.m., Sheehy Skeffington MS (hereafter SS MS) 40,483/2.

2 Hanna Sheehy Skeffington to Andrée, Davos, 14 Oct. 1937, SS MS 41,176/22.

3 Hanna Sheehy Skeffington to Kathleen Cruise O'Brien, 17 Oct. 1937, SS MS 24,125.

4 *Women's Freedom League Bulletin*, 19 Mar. 1937.

5 Andrée Sheehy Skeffington, personal interview with author, Nov. 1993.

6 *Irish Press*, 16 July 1937.

7 Press release and advertising circular, Alice Park Collection, Hoover Institution Archives, Stanford, California.

8 HSS, notes for lecture tour of USA, 1938, SS MS 24,177.

9 Mari Equi to Hanna Sheehy Skeffington, 24 Mar. 1938, SS MS 41,177/16.

10 Ibid., n. d.

11 Owen to Hanna 25 June 1937, SS MS40,483/2.

12 Owen to Hanna, 26 Jan. 1938, SS MS 40,483/3.

13 Kathleen Cruise O'Brien to Hanna Sheehy Skeffington, 10 Feb. 1938, SS MS 41,178/5.

14 Hanna to Andrée, Chicago, 28 Feb. 1938, SS MS 41,176/22.

15 Owen to Hanna, 23 Feb. 1938, SS MS 40,483/3.

16 *Daily Palo Alto Times*, 31 Mar. 1938.

17 *Independent Woman*, Mar. 1938.

18 Ibid.

19 Kate Crane Gartz, *The Parlor Provocateur or From Salon to Soap Box* (California, 2017).

20 *Daily Palo Alto Times*, 31 Mar. 1938.

21 J. J. Lee, *Ireland 1912–1985: Politics and Society* (Cambridge, 1989), p. 213.

22 Florence Murphy Baker to Hanna Sheehy Skeffington, 4 Apr. 1938, SS MS 41,177/1.

23 Heather Ingman quoted in Sinead Gleeson, 'A long gaze back at Nora Hoult on her 117th birthday', in *Irish Times*, 10 Sept. 2015.

24 Andrée Sheehy Skeffington, *Skeff: A Life of Owen Sheehy Skeffington* (Dublin, 1991), p. 89.

25 Owen to Hanna 5 July 1938 and 15 Aug. 1938, SS MS 40,483/3.

26 Owen to Hanna, 24 Mar. 1939, SS MS 40,483/4.

27 Margaret Sheehy Casey to Hanna Sheehy Skeffington, 4 Sept. 1938, SS MS 24,125.

28 Garry Culhane to Hanna Sheehy Skeffington, 19 Sept. 1938, SS MS 24,125.

29 Ronan O'Casey, phone conversation with author, Sept. 1996.

30 Seán Murray to Hanna Sheehy Skeffington, 24 Sept. 1938, SS MS 24,125. Speakers included Hanna, Alex Lynn, Roddy Connolly, Seán Murray and Frank Edwards.

31 Fenner Brockway to Hanna Sheehy Skeffington, 30 Dec. 1938, SS MS 24,125.

32 Ronan O'Casey, information supplied in phone conversation with author, Sept. 1996. Hanna gave him the card as a keepsake. To his regret, he lost it.

33 Owen to Hanna, 12 July 1938, SS MS 40,483/3.

34 Ibid., 8 Aug. 1938. Christine's parents, from Presbyterian backgrounds, were also Gaelic League members and strong Irish republicans.

35 Owen to Hanna, 15 Aug. 1938, SS MS 40,483/3.

36 https://irishanarchisthistory.wordpress.com/2018/02/25/conor-cruise-obrien-hanna-sheehy-skeffington-and-emma-goldman-1937, accessed 19 Jan. 2019.
37 Marino Institute, 7 Feb. 1939, SS MS 24,126.
38 Hanna Sheehy Skeffington to Dublin Theatre Company, 18 Oct. 1938, SS MS 24,125.
39 Seán MacBride to Hanna Sheehy Skeffington, 24 Jan. 1939, SS MS 24,126.
40 Hanna Sheehy Skeffington to Mr McGonagle, 7 Mar. 1939, SS MS 24,126.
41 Rose Jacob to Hanna Sheehy Skeffington, n. d., SS MS 24,140.
42 Conor Cruise O'Brien, 'Passion and cunning: An essay on the politics of W. B. Yeats', in A. Norman Jeffares and K. G. W. Cross (eds), *In Excited Reverie: A Centenary Tribute to W. B. Yeats, 1865–1939* (London, 1939), pp 207–8.
43 Ethel Mannin, *Privileged Spectator* (London, 1939), p. 258.
44 Reginold Reynolds, *My Life and Crimes* (London, 1956), pp 158–9. With thanks to John Newsinger for the reference.
45 Ronan O'Casey, phone conversation, Sept. 1996.
46 Hanna Sheehy Skeffington to Owen Sheehy Skeffington (hereafter Hanna to Owen), 30 Aug. 1939, Paris, SS MS 40,484/8.
47 Reynolds, *My Life and Crimes*, p. 168.
48 Women's Social and Progressive League, programme for 1939–40, Alice Park Collection, Hoover Institution Archives, Stanford, California.
49 Meg Connery to Hanna Sheehy Skeffington, 4 Feb. 1938, SS MS 41,177/10.
50 Leeann Lane, *Rosamond Jacob: Third Person Singular* (Dublin, 2010), p. 256.
51 Rose Jacob to Hanna Sheehy Skeffington, n. d., SS MS 24,140.
52 Ibid., 9 Feb. 1938, SS MS 41,177/27.
53 Open Letter to Women Voters of Ireland, Women's Social and Progressive League, 1938, National Library of Ireland (hereafter NLI).
54 Helen Little (ed.), *Revolutionary Woman: Kathleen Clarke, 1878–1972: An Autobiography* (Dublin, 1991), pp 222–3.
55 Hilda Tweedy, *A Link in the Chain: The Story of the Irish Housewives' Association, 1942–1992* (Dublin, 1992), pp 11–15.
56 Andrée Sheehy Skeffington, personal interview with author, Nov. 1993.
57 David Sheehy, personal interview with author, Apr. 1996.
58 Hanna Sheehy Skeffington, 'Women in politics', in *The Bell*, 7:2, 1943, p. 143, quoting from the Women's Social and Progressive League election literature.
59 Hanna Sheehy Skeffington, Electoral address, SS MS 41,201/12.
60 Hanna Sheehy Skeffington, *Evening News*, 16 June 1943.
61 Rosemary Cullen Owens, *A Social History of Women in Ireland 1870–1970* (Dublin, 2005), p. 282 and n. 14, p. 364.
62 Hanna Sheehy Skeffington, 'Women in politics', p. 144.
63 Ibid., p. 148.
64 Hanna Sheehy Skeffington to Andrée Sheehy Skeffington, 15 May 1944, SS MS 41,176/22.
65 The Six Point Group, *Dorothy Evans and the Six Point Group*, 1945, The Fawcett Library. With thanks to Catriona Beaumont for the reference.
66 Hanna Sheehy Skeffington to Alice Park, 17–12–45, Alice Park Collection, Hoover Institution Archives, Stanford, California.

67 H. L. Doak, editor, the Talbot Press, to Hanna Sheehy Skeffington, 12 Dec. 1933, SS MS 33,606/22.
68 Desmond Ryan, 'Hanna Sheehy Skeffington', in *Bakery Trades Journal*, Apr.-June 1946, p. 15.
69 Desmond Greaves to Hanna Sheehy Skeffington, 19 Feb. 1945, SS MS33,607/21. Hanna's scrawled, much abbreviated comments underneath are unusual, and look as though she was developing her thoughts before finally writing her reply.
70 Librarian, Hoover Library to Hanna Sheehy Skeffington, 19 Sept. 1945, SS MS 33,6-7/21.
71 Ryan, 'Hanna Sheehy Skeffington', p. 15.
72 Florence Murphy Baker to Hanna Sheehy Skeffington, 30 Nov. 1935, SS MS 41,177/1.
73 *Irish Digest* to Hanna Sheehy Skeffington, 8 June 1945, SS MS 33,607/21. Hanna had four suggestions for a series: Great Irish Women; Books that Make History; Irish Women Poets; Beauty Spots. In pencil she wrote on the letter 'no response'.
74 *Irish Workers' Weekly* to Hanna Sheehy Skeffington, 12 Apr. 1945, SS MS 33,607/21.
75 Hanna Sheehy Skeffington, 'Women M. P.s in Britain', in *Workers' Review*, Oct. 1945, p. 6.
76 Ethel Mannin, 'Again the government: A memoir of Hanna Sheehy Skeffington', in *Freedom*, London, n. d., (1946), Alice Park Collection, Hoover Institution Archives, Stanford, California.
77 Hanna Sheehy Skeffington to Alice Park, 17 Sept. 1945, Alice Park Collection, Hoover Institution Archives, Stanford, California.
78 Ibid., 17 Dec. 1945.
79 Miceál Breatnac to Hanna Sheehy Skeffington, 31 May 1945, SS MS 33,607/21.
80 Hanna Sheehy Skeffington to Alice Park, 17 Dec. 1945, Alice Park Collection, Hoover Institution Archives, Stanford, California.
81 Kate Crane Gartz to Hanna Sheehy Skeffington, 8 Sept. 1945, SS MS 33,607/21.
82 Ibid.
83 Elizabeth Bloxham to Hanna Sheehy Skeffington, 27 Aug. 1945, SS MS 33,607/21. Bloxham, although forced to retire from work, moved to Dublin and lived until 1962.
84 Hanna Sheehy Skeffington to Alice Park, 17 Sept. 1945, Alice Park Collection, Hoover Institution Archives, Stanford, California.
85 Desmond Ryan, 'Hanna Sheehy Skeffington', p.15.
86 RTE radio, incomplete transcript of radio interview with Dr Dixon, SS MS 24,164.
87 Budge (Elizabeth) Clissmann to Hanna Sheehy Skeffington, 16 Nov. 1945, SS MS 33,607/21.
88 D. McCoy to Hanna Sheehy Skeffington, n. d., SS MS 33,607/21.
89 Mary Macken to Hanna Sheehy Skeffington, 15 Nov. 1945, SS MS 33,607/21.
90 Louie Bennett to Hanna Sheehy Skeffington, 31 Mar. 1946, SS MS 41,177/13.
91 SS MS 33,607/21. Those who signed were: Lilian Metge, Louie Bennett, Helen Chenevix, Rosamond Jacob, Mary Quinn, Sally Ryan, Helena Molony.
92 Hanna Sheehy Skeffington, 'Random reflections on housewives: Their ways and works', in *The Irish Housewife*, 1:1, 1946, pp 20–2.
93 Hanna Sheehy Skeffington 1946 Diary, SS MS 41,183/5.
94 Käthe Oldham to Hanna Sheehy Skeffington, 1 Apr. 1946, SS MS41,178/106.

95 Hanna Sheehy Skeffington, 'Tragic coincidence of 1916', in *Irish Press*, 4 Mar. 1946.
96 Hanna Sheehy Skeffington, 'Women teacher's case', in *Irish Press*, 6 Mar. 1946.
97 Andrée Sheehy Skeffington, *Skeff*, p. 124.
98 Frank Culhane to Hanna Sheehy Skeffington, 8 Apr. 1946, writing from Switzerland, where he was recovering from TB, SS MS 41,178/106.
99 Andrée Sheehy Skeffington, personal interview with author, 1993.
100 Andrée Sheehy Skeffington, *Skeff*, p. 124.
101 Maud Gonne MacBride to Ethel Mannin, 21 Apr. 1946, Mannin Papers, MS 17,875, NLI, Dublin.
102 Maud Gonne MacBride to Brigid O'Mullane, n. d., O'Mullane Papers, MS 22,988, NLI, Dublin.
103 The headstone reads:

> Sacred to the memory of Mrs Rose Skeffington born Magorrian in Ballykinlar County Down, died at Ranelagh Dublin 6th Apr. 1909 and Francis Sheehy Skeffington her son murdered in Portobello Barracks Apr. 26th 1916 and his wife Hanna Sheehy Skeffington feminist republican socialist. Born May 1878/Died April 1946 and their son Owen Lancelot Sheehy Skeffington born May 19th 1909 died June 7th 1970 who like them sought truth/taught reason & knew compassion.

104 Desmond Ryan, 'Hanna Sheehy Skeffington', p.15.
105 *Irish Press*, 22 Apr. 1946.
106 *Evening Herald*, 20 Apr. 1946.
107 *Irish Times*, 23 Apr. 1946.
108 *Workers' Review*, May 1946.
109 *Freedom*, cutting, n. d. (1946), Alice Park Collection, Hoover Institution Archives, Stanford, California.
110 *Women's Bulletin*, 10 May 1946.
111 *Irish Press*, 27 Apr. 1946.
112 Owen Sheehy Skeffington, 18 May 1946, Sheehy Skeffington File 1517, de Valera Papers, Franciscan Library, Killiney, County Dublin. With thanks to Medb Ruane for the reference.
113 Owen Sheehy Skeffington to the editor, *New Leader*, 23 May 1946, SS MS 41,182/1.
114 Louie Bennett to Owen Sheehy Skeffington, 17 Aug. 1946, SS MS 41,182/.
115 Sally Ryan to Owen Sheehy Skeffington, 12 Aug. 1946, SS MS 41,182/1.
116 Lady Pethick-Lawrence of Peaslake to Owen Sheehy-Skeffington, 17 Aug. 1946, SS MS 41,182/1.

Bibliography

PRIMARY SOURCES

National Library of Ireland
John Devoy Papers
Eva Gore-Booth Papers
Joseph Holloway Papers
Ethel Mannin Papers
Joe McGarrity Papers
Brigid O'Mullane Papers
Sheehy Skeffington Papers
Alice Stopford-Green Papers

University College, Dublin, Archives
Desmond Fitzgerald Papers
Tom Kettle Papers
National University Women Graduates' Association Archives

National Archives of Ireland
Bureau of Military History Witness Statements
Dublin Street Census 1901
Dublin Street Census 1911
General Prisons Board, Dublin Castle, Suffragette Boxes 1, 2, 3
Thom's Directory

Fianna Fáil Archives
1926: Correspondence from Hanna Sheehy Skeffington and Dorothy Macardle

Franciscan Library, Killiney, County Dublin
De Valera Papers: Sheehy Skeffington File

Official Publications
Private Sessions of the Second Dáil
Debate on the Treaty between Great Britain and Ireland
Dáil Debates 1922–3

Public Record Office Northern Ireland
Charlotte Despard Diaries

Public Record Office London
Cabinet Papers 1921

Fawcett Library, London
Tape recordings of Irish suffragists and friends: Brian Harrison, 1977

Hoover Institution Archives, Stanford, California
Alice Park Collection, Box Number 19

US National Archives, Washington DC
Bureau of Investigation, Department of Justice, case file number 9848-10204
National Archives Record Group Number 60

Annual Reports
Irish Women's Suffrage and Local Government Association, 1902–10
Irish Women's Franchise League, 1909–20
Cumann na mBan, Convention Reports, 1918, 1921
Reports of Officers and Directors, Sinn Féin Ard Fheis, 1919
Instructions to Sinn Féin Cumainn Regarding Programme of Work, 1921–2
Sinn Féin Reorganising Committee: Programme of Immediate Work for Cumainn, n.d., (1923)

Newspapers
An Phoblacht
Bean na hÉireann
Cork Free Press
Daily Express
Éire: The Irish Nation
Evening Herald
Freeman's Journal
Irish Bulletin
Irish Citizen
Irish Independent
Irish Press
Irish Times
Irish Worker
Irish World
Prison Bars

Republican Congress
Republican File
Sinn Féin
United Irishwomen
The Vote
Votes for Women
Women's Freedom League Bulletin
The Worker

Journals
The Bell
Englishwomen's Review
The Irish Housewife
The Irish Review
The Irish Nation
Workers' Voice

Interviews
Maire Comerford
Eithne Coyle O'Donnell
Nora Harkin
Ronan O'Casey
Judge David Sheehy
Andrée Sheehy Skeffington

Major writings and speeches of Hanna Sheehy Skeffington cited in text
Ward, Margaret (ed.) *Hanna Sheehy Skeffington, Suffragette and Sinn Féiner: Her Memoirs and Political Writings* (Dublin: UCD Press, 2017)

Contemporary Accounts
Andrews, C. S. *Man of No Property* (Dublin: Mercier Press, 1979)
Byrne, J. F. *Silent Years: An Autobiography* (New York: Farrar, Straus and Young, 1953)
Ceannt, Aine *The Irish White Cross, 1920–1947* (Dublin: Sign of the Three Candles, n.d.)
Clarke, Kathleen *Revolutionary Woman: Kathleen Clarke 1878–1972: An Autobiography* Helen Little (ed.) (Dublin: O'Brien Press, 1991)
Colum, Mary *Life and the Dream* (Dublin: Dolmen Press, 1947)
Cousins, James H. and Margaret E. *We Two Together* (Madras: Ganesh, 1950)
Curran, C. P. *Under the Receding Wave* (Dublin: Gill and Macmillan, 1970)
Czira, Sydney Gifford ('John Brennan') *The Years Flew By* (Dublin: Gifford Craven, 1974)
Deuchar, Maud L. *The Sheehy Skeffington Case* (London: The National Labour Press Ltd, 1916)
Devoy, John *Recollections of an Irish Rebel* (New York: Charles P. Young, 1929)
Fitzgerald, W. G. (ed.) *The Voice of Ireland* (Dublin: Virtue and Co., 1924)
Flynn, Elizabeth Gurley *The Rebel Girl: An Autobiography* (New York: International Publishers, 1973)

Fox, R. M. *Rebel Irishwomen* (Dublin: Talbot Press, 1935)
Ibid. *Green Banners: The Story of the Irish Struggle* (London: Secker and Warburg, 1938)
Ibid. *Louie Bennett: Her Life and Times* (Dublin: Talbot Press, n.d., [1958])
Healy, T. M. *Letters and Leaders of My Day Vol. 2* (London: Thornton Butterworth, 1928)
Holloway, Joseph *Joseph Holloway's Abbey Theatre: A Selection from His Unpublished Journal Impressions of a Dublin Playgoer* Robert Hogan and Michael O'Neill (eds), (Carbondale: Southern Illinois University Press, 1967)
Irish Times, *Sinn Féin Rebellion Handbook: Easter 1916* (Dublin: *Irish Times*, 1917)
Joyce, Stanislaus *My Brother's Keeper* (London: Faber, 1958)
Kearns, Linda *In Times of Peril* (Dublin: Talbot Press, 1922)
Kettle, T. M. *The Ways of War* (London: Constable and Co., 1917)
MacBride, Maud Gonne 'How we beat the terrorist proclamations', *An Phoblacht*, 12 November, 1932.
Ibid., 'Must we fight again for Ireland's honour', *An Phoblacht*, 9 December 1933.
Macken, Mary 'Yeats, John O'Leary and the Contemporary Club', *Studies*, vol. xxviii, 1939, pp 136–42
Ibid. 'Women in the university and the college: A struggle within a struggle', in Michael Tierney (ed.), *A Struggle with Fortune: A Miscellany for the Centenary of the Catholic University of Ireland* (Dublin: Browne and Nolan, 1954), pp 142–65
Mannin, Ethel *Privileged Spectator* (London: Hutchinson, 1939)
Markievicz, Countess *Women, Ideals and the Nation* (Dublin: Inghinidhe na hÉireann, 1909)
Ibid. *The Prison Letters of Countess Markievicz* (London: Longmans Green & Co., 1934; reprinted Virago, 1987)
Meenan, James (ed.) *Centenary History of the Literary & Historical Society of University College, Dublin, 1855–1955* (Tralee: Kerryman Press, 1957)
O'Brien, William *Forth the Banners Go* (Dublin: Three Candles, 1969)
O'Brien, William and Desmond Ryan (eds) *Devoy's Post Bag 1871–1928* (Dublin: Academy Press, 1979, [1948])
O'Casey, Seán *The Story of the Irish Citizen Army* (Dublin: Maunsel, 1919)
Ibid. *Inishfallen Fare Thee Well* (London: Macmillan, 1949; reprinted Pan, 1972)
O'Hegarty, P. S. *The Victory of Sinn Féin* (Dublin: Talbot Press, 1924)
Pankhurst, Sylvia *The Suffragette Movement* (London: Longman's, 1931; reprinted Virago, 1977)
Pethick-Lawrence, Emmeline *My Part in a Changing World* (London: Victor Gollancz, 1938)
Reynolds, Reginald *My Life and Crimes* (London: Jarrolds, 1956)
Sheehy, Eugene *May It Please the Court* (Dublin: C. J. Fallon, 1951)
Sheehy Skeffington, Andrée *Skeff: A Life of Owen Sheehy Skeffington* (Dublin: Lilliput Press, 1991)
Sheehy Skeffington, Francis *Michael Davitt: Revolutionary Agitator and Labour Leader* (London: Fisher Unwin, 1908)
Ibid. *The Prodigal Daughter* (Dublin: 1915)
Ibid. *In Dark and Evil Days* (Dublin: James Duffy, 1936)
Sheehy Skeffington, Francis and James Joyce *Two Essays* (Dublin: Gerrard Brothers, 1901)

Sheehy Skeffington, Owen 'Francis Sheehy Skeffington', in Owen Dudley Edwards and Fergus Pyle (eds), *1916: The Easter Rising* (London: MacGibbon and Kee, 1968) pp 135–48
Skinnider, Margaret *Doing My Bit for Ireland* (New York: Century, 1917)
Stephens, James *The Insurrection in Dublin* (Dublin: Maunsel, 1916)
Swanton, Daisy Lawrenson *Emerging from the Shadow* (Dublin: Attic Press,1994)
Swanwick, Helena *I Have Been Young* (London: Victor Gollancz, 1935)
Talbot, Hayden *Michael Collins' Own Story* (London: Hutchinson, 1923)
Tiernan, Sonja (ed.) *The Political Writings of Eva Gore-Booth* (Manchester: Manchester University Press, 2015)
Vane, Sir Francis Fletcher *Again the Governments: Memories and Adventures* (London: Sampson-Low, Marston, n.d. [1929])
Wyse Power, Jenny, 'The political influence of women in modern Ireland', in William G. Fitzgerald (ed.), *The Voice of Ireland* (Dublin: Virtue and Co., 1924)
Young, Ella *Flowering Dusk* (London: Dobson, 1945)

SELECT SECONDARY SOURCES

Akenson, Donald Harman *Conor Cruise O'Brien* (Montreal: McGill Queen's University Press, 1994)
Alberti, Johanna *Beyond Suffrage: Feminists in War and Peace 1914–1928* (London: Macmillan, 1989)
Arrington, Lauren *Revolutionary Lives: Constance and Casimir Markievicz* (Princeton: Princeton University Press, 2016)
Beale, Jenny *Women in Ireland: Voices of Change* (London: Macmillan, 1986)
Beaumont, Catriona 'Irish women and the politics of equality in the 1930s' *Phoebe*, vol. 3, no. 1, 1991
Ibid. 'After the vote: Women, citizenship and the campaign for gender equality in the Irish Free State (1922–43)', in Louise Ryan and Margaret Ward (eds), *Irish Women and the Vote: Becoming Citizens* (Dublin: Irish Academic Press, 2007, reprinted 2018) pp 231–49
Bussey, Gertrude and Margaret Tims *Pioneers for Peace: Women's International League for Peace and Freedom 1915–1965* (London: Allen and Unwin, 1965)
Coogan, Tim Pat *The IRA* (London: Fontana, 1971)
Côté, Jane *Fanny and Anna Parnell: Ireland's Patriot Sisters* (Dublin: Gill and Macmillan, 1991)
Coulter, Carol *The Hidden Tradition: Feminism, Women and Nationalism in Ireland* (Cork: Cork University Press, 1993)
Cronin, Seán *The McGarrity Papers* (Tralee: Anvill Books, 1972)
Ibid. *Frank Ryan: The Search for the Republic* (Dublin: Repsol, 1980)
Cullen, Mary *Girls Don't Do Honours: Irish Women in Education in the 19th and 20th Centuries* (Dublin: Women's Education Bureau, 1987)

Cullen Owens Rosemary *Smashing Times: A History of the Irish Women's Suffrage Movement, 1889–1922* (Dublin: Attic Press, 1984)

Ibid. *Did Your Granny Have A Hammer?* (Dublin: Attic Press, 1985)

Ibid. 'Women and pacifism in Ireland 1915–1932', in M. Valiulis and M. O'Dowd (eds), *Women & Irish History* (Dublin: Wolfhound Press, 1997), pp 220–38

Ibid. *Louie Bennett* (Cork: Cork University Press, 2001)

Ibid. *A Social History of Women in Ireland 1870–1970* (Dublin: Gill & Macmillan, 2006)

Curtis, Liz *The Cause of Ireland: From the United Irishmen to Partition* (Belfast: Beyond the Pale, 1994)

Dinnage, Rosemary *Annie Besant* (Harmondsworth: Penguin, 1986)

Doyle, Damian 'Rosamond Jacob (1888–1960)', in Mary Cullen and Maria Luddy (eds), *Female Activists Irish Women and Change 1900–1960* (Dublin: The Woodfield Press, 2001), pp 169–92

Dunphy, Richard *The Making of Fianna Fáil Power in Ireland, 1923–1948* (Oxford: Clarendon Press, 1995)

Dwyer, T. Ryle *Eamon de Valera* (Dublin: Gill and Macmillan, 1980)

Edwards, Owen Dudley and Fergus Pyle (eds) *1916: The Easter Rising* (London: MacGibbon and Kee, 1968)

Ellman, Richard *James Joyce* (Oxford: Oxford University Press, 1982)

English, Richard *Radicals and the Republic: Socialist Republicanism in the Irish Free State 1925–1937* (Oxford: Clarendon Press, 1994)

Faderman, Lillian *Surpassing the Love of Men* (London: Junction Books, 1980)

Fairhall, James *James Joyce and the Question of History* (Cambridge: Cambridge University Press, 1993)

Fallon, Charlotte 'Civil War hunger strikes: Women and men', *Éire-Ireland* vol. 22, no. 3, 1987

Ibid. *Soul of Fire: A Biography of Mary MacSwiney* (Cork: Mercier, 1986)

Ferriter, Diarmaid *A Nation and Not A Rabble: The Irish Revolution 1913–1923* (London: Profile Books, 2013)

Flexner, Eleanor *Century of Struggle: The Women's Rights Movement in the United States* (Harvard: Belknap Press, 1975)

Foley, Conor *Legion of the Rearguard: The IRA and the Modern Irish State* (London: Pluto, 1992)

Foster, R. F. *Vivid Faces: The Revolutionary Generation in Ireland 1890–1923* (London: Allen Lane, 2014)

Greaves, C. Desmond *Liam Mellows and the Irish Revolution* (London: Lawrence & Wishart, 1971)

Ibid. *The Life and Times of James Connolly* (London: Lawrence & Wishart, 1972)

Harford, Judith 'The admission of women to the National University of Ireland', *Education Research and Perspectives*, vol. 35 no. 2, 2006, pp 44–54

Haverty, Anne *Constance Markievicz: An Independent Life* (London: Pandora, 1988)

Hayes, Alan (ed.) *Hilda Tweedy and the Irish Housewives Association: Links in the Chain* (Dublin: Arlen House, 2012)

Hearne, Dana 'The Irish Citizen 1914–1916: Nationalism, feminism and militarism', *Canadian Journal of Irish Studies* vol. 18, no. 1, 1992, pp 1–14

Heilbrun, Carolyn G. *Writing A Woman's Life* (New York: Ballantine Books, 1988)

Henke, Suzette and Elaine Unkeless *Women in Joyce* (Hertfordshire: Harvester, 1982)

Hill, Myrtle and Vivienne Pollock *Image and Experience: Photographs of Irishwomen 1880–1920* (Belfast: Blackstaff Press, 1993)

Hutchins, Patricia *James Joyce's Dublin* (London: Grey Walls Press, 1950)

Innes, C. L. *Women and Nation in Irish Literature and Society 1880–1935* (Hertfordshire: Harvester, 1993)

Jackson, Margaret *The Real Facts of Life: Feminism and the Politics of Sexuality c1850–1940* (London: Taylor & Francis, 1994)

Jeffares, A. Norman and K. G. W. Cross (eds) *In Excited Reverie: A Centenary Tribute to W B Yeats, 1865–1939* (London: Macmillan, 1965)

Knirck, Jason *Women of the Dáil* (Dublin: Irish Academic Press, 2006)

Lane, Leeann *Rosamond Jacob: Third Person Singular* (Dublin: UCD Press, 2010)

Lee, J. J. *Ireland 1912–1985: Politics and Society* (Cambridge: Cambridge University Press, 1989)

Levenson, Leah *With Wooden Sword: A Portrait of Francis Sheehy Skeffington, Militant Pacifist* (Dublin: Gill and Macmillan, 1983)

Levenson, Leah and Jerry Natterstad *Hanna Sheehy Skeffington: Irish Feminist* (New York: Syracuse University Press, 1983)

Lewis, Gifford *Eva Gore-Booth and Esther Roper: A Biography* (London: Pandora, 1988)

Liddington, Jill *The Long Road to Greenham: Feminism and Anti-Militarism In Britain Since 1920* (London: Virago, 1989)

Liddington, Jill and Elizabeth Crawford '"Women do not count, neither shall they be counted": Suffrage, citizenship and the battle for the 1911 census', *History Workshop Journal* vol. 71, no. 1:1, March 2011, pp 98–127

Linklater, Andro *An Unhusbanded Life: Charlotte Despard, Suffragette, Socialist and Sinn Féiner* (London: Hutchinson, 1980)

Litton, Helen *The Irish Civil War* (Dublin: Wolfhound, 1995)

Luddy, Maria and Cliona Murphy (eds) *Women Surviving: Studies in Irish Women's History in the 19th and 20th Centuries* (Dublin: Poolbeg, 1989)

Luddy, Maria *Hanna Sheehy Skeffington* (Dundalk: Dundalgan Press, 1995)

Ibid. 'A "sinister and retrogressive" proposal: Irish women's opposition to the 1937 draft constitution', *Transactions of the Royal Historical Society* 15 (2005), pp 175–95

Lyons, J. B. *The Enigma of Tom Kettle: Irish Patriot, Essayist, Poet, British Soldier, 1880–1916* (Dublin: Glendale Press, 1983)

McAuliffe, Mary 'Women voted early and in large numbers: Irish women's activism and the 1918 General Election, in *The Kerry Magazine*, 2018, pp 29–32

Macardle, Dorothy *The Irish Republic* (London: Victor Gollancz 1937; reprinted 1965)

McCann, Sean (ed.) *The World of Seán O'Casey* (London: Four Square Books, 1966)

McCoole, Sinead, *Easter Widows* (London: Doubleday Ireland, 2014)

MacCurtain, Margaret and Donncha O Corráin (eds) *Women in Irish Society: The Historical Dimension* (Dublin: Arlen House, 1978)

MacCurtain, Margaret 'Women of Eccles Street', *The Lanthorn*, yearbook of the Dominican College, Eccles Street, Centenary Year 1982

McDiarmid, Lucy *At Home in the Revolution: What Women Said and Did in 1916* (Dublin: Royal Irish Academy, 2015)

MacEoin, Uinseann (ed.) *Survivors* (Dublin: Argenta Publications, 1980)

McHugh, Roger 'Thomas Kettle and Francis Sheehy Skeffington', in Conor Cruise O'Brien (ed.), *The Shaping of Modern Ireland* (London: Routledge and Kegan Paul, 1960) pp 124–39

Ibid. (ed.) *Dublin 1916* (Dublin: Arlington Books, 1966)

McGarry, Fearghal *Frank Ryan* (Dundalk: Dundalgan Press, 2002)

McInerney, Michael *Peader O'Donnell: Irish Social Rebel* (Dublin: The O'Brien Press, 1974)

McKillen, Beth 'Irish feminism and national separatism, 1914–1923', *Éire-Ireland*, vol. xviii, no. 3, 1982 pp 52–67; vol. xviii, no. 4,1982, pp 72–90

McKillen, Elizabeth 'Reverse currents: Irish feminist and nationalist Hanna Sheehy Skeffington and US anti-imperialism, 1916–24', *Éire-Ireland*, vol. 53, nos 3 & 4, Fall/Winter 2018, pp 148–85

MacLochlainn, Alf and Andrée Sheehy Skeffington *Writers, Raconteurs and Notable Feminists* (Dublin: National Library of Ireland Society, 1993)

Mitchell, Arthur *Labour in Irish Politics 1890–1930* (Dublin: Irish Academic Press, 1974)

Ibid. *Revolutionary Government in Ireland: Dáil Éireann 1919–22* (Dublin: Gill and Macmillan, 1995)

Mooney Eichacker, Joanne *Irish Republican Womanhood: Lecture Tours, 1916–1925* (Dublin: Irish Academic Press, 2003)

Moriarty, Thérèse 'No vote, no information', *Irish Times*, 3 April 1981, p. 12

Mulvihill, Margaret *Charlotte Despard: A Biography* (London: Pandora, 1989)

Munro, Keith *Through the Eyes of Margaret Cousins Irish & Indian Suffragette* (Derry: Hive Studios, 2018)

Murphy, Cliona *The Women's Suffrage Movement and Irish Society in the Early Twentieth Century* (Hertfordshire: Harvester, 1989)

Murphy, William 'Suffragettes and the transformation of political imprisonment in Ireland, 1912–1914', in Louise Ryan and Margaret Ward (eds), *Irish Women and the Vote: Becoming Citizens* (Dublin: Irish Academic Press, 2007, reprinted 2018), pp 114–35

Ibid. *Political Imprisonment & the Irish, 1912–1921* (Oxford: Oxford University Press, 2014)

Ibid. '"Voteless alas": Suffragist protest and the census of Ireland in 1911', in Diarmaid Ferriter and Susannah Riordan (eds), *Years of Turbulence: The Irish Revolution and its Aftermath* (Dublin: UCD Press, 2015), pp 25–43

Nic Chongail, Ríona 'Gaelic Ireland and the female dream: Agnes O'Farrelly's cultural nationalism', in Sarah O'Connor and Christopher C. Shepard (eds), *Ireland: Dissenting Voices?* (Cambridge Scholars Publishing, 2009), pp 51–66

Norman, Diana *Terrible Beauty: A Life of Constance Markievicz* (London: Hodder & Stoughton, 1987)

O'Brien, Conor Cruise (ed.) *The Shaping of Modern Ireland* (London: Routledge and Kegan Paul, 1960)

Ibid. *States of Ireland* (St Albans: Panther Books, 1974)

Ibid. *Ancestral Voices: Religion and Nationalism in Ireland* (Dublin: Poolbeg, 1994)

O'Brien, Nora Connolly *Portrait of a Rebel Father* (Dublin: Talbot Press, 1935; reprinted 1975)

O'Connor, Garry *Seán O'Casey: A Life* (New York: Atheneum, 1988)

O'Céirín, Kit and Cyril *Women of Ireland: A Biographic Dictionary* (Galway: Irish Books & Media, 1996)

O'Dowd, Mary and Sabine Wichert (eds) *Chattel, Servant or Citizen: Women's Status in Church, State and Society* (Belfast: Institute of Irish Studies, 1995)

O'Malley, Kate *Ireland, India and Empire: Indo-Irish Radical Connections, 1919–64* (Manchester: Manchester University Press, 2008)

O'Neill, Marie *From Parnell to De Valera: A Biography of Jennie Wyse Power 1858–1941* (Dublin: Blackwater, 1991)

O'Toole, Fintan 'The life and times of Conor Cruise O'Brien, part one, in *Magill*, April 1986

Ouditt, Sharon *Fighting Forces, Writing Women: Identity and Ideology in the First World War* (London: Routledge, 1994)

Pašeta, Senia *Irish Nationalist Women 1900–1918* (Cambridge: Cambridge University Press, 2013)

Quinlan, Carmel *Genteel Revolutionaries, Anna and Thomas Haslam and the Irish Women's Movement* (Cork: Cork University Press, 2002)

Quinn, James and James McGuire (eds) *Dictionary of Irish Biography* (Cambridge University Press & Royal Irish Academy) on-line edition

Raughter, Rosemary 'The suffragettes and the chief secretary: An "amusing scene" on greystones pier', in *Greystones Archeological and Historical Society*, 2018, accessed on-line www.countywicklowheritage.org

Regan, Nell *Helena Molony: A Radical Life, 1883–1967* (Dublin: Arlen House, 2017)

Reynolds, Paige 'Staging suffrage: The events of 1913 Dublin Suffrage Week', in Louise Rowbotham, Sheila *Women in Movement: Feminism and Social Action* (London: Routledge, 1992)

Ryan, Louise and Margaret Ward (eds) *Irish Women and the Vote: Becoming Citizens* (Dublin: Irish Academic Press, 2007, reprinted 2018), pp 60–74

Ryan, Louise 'Women without votes: The political strategies of the Irish suffrage movement', *Irish Political Studies* no. 9, 1994, pp 119–39

Ibid. *Winning the Vote for Women: The Irish Citizen Newspaper and the Suffrage Movement in Ireland* (Dublin: Four Courts Press, 2018)

Scott, Bonnie Kime *Joyce and Feminism* (Hertfordshire: Harvester, 1984)

Sheehan, Tim *Execute Hostage (*Dripsey Press: Cork, 1993)

Sisson, Elaine 'Designing modernism: Harry Kernoff, Russia and post-independence Ireland', *Éire-Ireland* vol. 52, nos 3/4, 2017

Smith, Brid 'Cissy Cahalan: A tribute', in *Labour History News* no. 8, Autumn 1992, pp 14–17

Smith-Rosenberg, Carroll 'The female world of love and ritual: Relations between women in nineteenth-century America', *Signs*, vol. 1. no. 1, Autumn 1975, pp 1–29

Society of Jesus, Fathers of the *A Page of Irish History: Story of University College, Dublin, 1883–1909* (Dublin: Talbot Press, 1930)

Steiner-Scott, Elizabeth '"To bounce a boot off her now & then…": Domestic violence in post-famine Ireland', in Maryann Gialanella Valiulis & Mary O'Dowd (eds), *Women & Irish History* (Dublin: Wolfhound Press, 1997) pp 125–43

Taillon, Ruth *When History Was Made: The Women of 1916* (Belfast: Beyond the Pale, 1996)

Taylor, James W. *Guilty but Insane, J. C. Bowen-Colthurst: Villain or Victim?* (Cork: Mercier Press, 2016)

Tiernan, Sonja *Eva Gore-Booth: An Image of Such Politics* (Manchester, Manchester University Press, 2010)

Tweedy, Hilda *A Link in the Chain: The Story of the Irish Housewives' Association, 1942–1992* (Dublin: Attic Press, 1992)

Valiulis, Maryann 'Defining their role in the new state: Irishwomen's protest against the Juries Act of 1927', *Canadian Journal of Irish Studies*, vol. 18, no. 1, July 1992, pp 43–60

Ibid. 'Power, gender and identity in the Irish Free State', *Journal of Women's History* vol. 6 no. 4; vol. 7, no. 1, 1995 pp 117–36

Ibid. 'Neither feminist nor flapper: The ecclesiastical construction of the ideal Irish woman', in Mary O'Dowd and Sabine Wichert (eds), *Chattel, Servant or Citizen: Women's Status in Church, State and Society* (Belfast: Institute of Irish Studies, 1995)

Van Voris, Jacqueline, *Constance de Markievicz in the Cause of Ireland* (Amherst: University of Massachusetts Press, 1967)

Walker, Graham 'The Irish Dr Goebbels: Frank Gallagher and Irish Republican propaganda', *Journal of Contemporary History*, vol. 27, 1992 pp 149–65

'War and Peace', *Irish Times*, 21 January 2019, pp 35–6

Ward, Margaret *Unmanageable Revolutionaries: Women and Irish Nationalism* (London: Pluto, 1983)

Ibid. *Maud Gonne: A Life* (London: Pandora, 1990)

Ibid. (ed.) *In Their Own Voice: Women and Irish Nationalism* (Dublin: Attic Press, 1995)

Ibid. 'Nationalism, pacifism, internationalism: Louie Bennett, Hanna Sheehy Skeffingon and the problems of "defining feminism"', in A. Bradley and M. G. Valiulis (eds), *Gender and Sexuality in Modern Ireland* (Amherst: University of Massachusetts Press, 1997) pp 60–84

Watkins, Sarah-Beth *Ireland's Suffragettes* (Dublin: The History Press, 2014)

Whelan, Bernadette 'Fighting for recognition', *Century 1919*, no. 13

Women's Commemoration and Celebration Committee *Ten Dublin Women* (Dublin: Women's Commemoration and Celebration Committee, 1991)

Index